P9-DIF-879

RACE RELATIONS
AND AMERICAN LAW

RACE RELATIONS
and AMERICAN LAW

By JACK GREENBERG

NEW YORK AND LONDON

COLUMBIA UNIVERSITY PRESS

COPYRIGHT © 1959 COLUMBIA UNIVERSITY PRESS
ISBN 231–02313–8
Library of Congress Catalog Card Number: 59-11179
PRINTED IN THE UNITED STATES OF AMERICA
10 9 8 7 6 5

For Sema

PREFACE

The basic law dealing with race relations in the United States is fairly well settled, and most of the factors bearing on social responsiveness to legal requirements can now be identified. While almost daily new statutes are passed and new cases are decided, few of these present unique problems. Of course, the meaning of "deliberate speed" has hardly been established with exactitude; legal dispute will probably also continue over, for example, the Civil Rights Act of 1957, electoral apportionment, new segregation tactics in interstate travel, affirmative integration by quotas, miscegenation, discrimination in the military reserves, FHA and Title I federally aided housing, and so forth. These sectors of indecision can be multiplied, but in all situations we can identify the relevant, fundamental principles and often make informed predictions. Therefore, while these pages were of necessity closed to new developments some months before publication, I believe that I have described and discussed race relations and American law essentially as they exist today and in a manner that will remain useful in the future. The addition of new material was terminated in April, 1959, although the more important occurrences reported by July, 1959, have been worked into the text or notes, and the most recent significant legislation is set forth in Appendix E.

I owe a great deal to the many who helped me in this work. First, my labors were greatly lightened by a grant from the Fund for the Republic, which was administered by the Columbia University Council for Research in the Social Sciences. My good friend Jack B. Weinstein, who generously agreed to supervise the administration of this grant for the Council, cooperated also by reading the entire manuscript and by making available the results of various questionnaires which he circulated concerning the actual application of legal rules about race. Will Maslow, whose counsel assisted me in launching this project, also read the entire manuscript, as did Charles W. Quick.

Others who helpfully responded to requests for advice concerning particular chapters included: for chapter I, "The Capacity of Law to Affect Race Relations," Harold Fleming, Robert Johnson, and Walter Metzger; for the state action portion of chapter II and for chapter VI, "Earning a Living," Louis Pollak; for the portion of chapter VI treating the President's Committee on Government Employment Policy, Ross Clinchy; for the portion treating the President's Committee on Government Contracts, Jacob Seidenberg; for the section on FEPCs, Henry Spitz. June Shagaloff lent to me her valuable collection of materials concerning racial school problems in the North and also read that portion, which helped me greatly with chapter VII, "Education." Frances Levinson, Madison Jones, and George and Eunice Grier read chapter VIII, "Housing and Real Property." James C. Evans gave me essential information for and read chapter XI, "The Armed Forces."

It is not, however, stereotype to say that none of these persons or institutions, nor any other person or group with which I have been connected, is responsible for what the book says. Indeed, I would be astonished if there were total agreement among us. Moreover, as any lawyer knows, the generalizations of a text are hardly a substitute for specific legal advice in particular cases.

For research assistance I was able to enlist three seniors at Columbia Law School. My chief reliance was on Sanford Katz. I was also helped by Sidney Silverman and Aaron Bernstein.

My wife Sema, to whom the book is dedicated, typed the greatest part of the manuscript through many drafts, all together thousands of pages, while tending our children—Josiah, David, Ezra, and Sarah—the first two of whom were old enough to complain often about my absence during the evenings and weekends I was at work on this study.

Finally, after the manuscript was assembled, it profited greatly from the excellent, painstaking editorial work of Columbia University Press, particularly of Barbara Melissa Voorhis. Nelda Cassuto prepared a most comprehensive and useful index for the volume.

JACK GREENBERG

New York City
July, 1959

CONTENTS

CONTENTS

RACE RELATIONS
AND AMERICAN LAW

CHAPTER I

THE CAPACITY OF LAW TO
AFFECT RACE RELATIONS

The ideal of human equality was proclaimed early in the development of Western civilization by Alexander the Great. His prayer at Opis for *homonoia* (a union of hearts between Greek and barbarian) was perhaps the first public declaration of this wish. It interests us particularly because it may also have been the first recorded of what we would now call legal pronouncements on race relations. Alexander was an emperor. But he was more than that: for some he was a deity; for others he must have been the embodiment of a social aspiration and an ethic. W. W. Tarn wrote of him:

Above all, Alexander inspired Zeno's vision of a world in which all men should be members one of another, citizens of one State without distinction of race or institutions, subject only to and in harmony with the Common law immanent in the Universe, and united in one social life not by compulsion but only by their own willing consent, or (as he put it) by Love. . . . there is certainly a line of descent from his [Alexander's] prayer at Opis, through the Stoics and one portion of the Christian ideal, to that brotherhood of all men which was proclaimed, though only proclaimed, in the French Revolution.[1]

The same ideal is found in our own Declaration of Independence ("We hold these truths to be self-evident, that all men are created equal . . .") and in that legal linchpin of equality, the Fourteenth Amendment ("equal protection of the laws"). But today the power of the state, the voice of religion, and the expressions of society on race relations are not embodied in any single man or institution. Yet in a sense they remain strands of one thread: we cannot consider law and

[1] I TARN, ALEXANDER THE GREAT 147–148 (1951); see also 2 TARN at 417, 423.

race relations, especially the potential of law to affect those relations, without knowing the strength and direction of other forces. Therefore, while the primary focus of this study is the American law of race relations, we shall try to see that law in its matrix.[2]

From this vantage point we may perceive the questions: Can the law alter race relations? Can it create or end discrimination and prejudice? Have the thousands of laws and lawsuits cited in the following pages been able to cause or prevent social change? If so, to what degree? Or are the only effective agents the hearts and minds of men, influenced, perhaps, in a slow, evolutionary manner by social forces and education? In other words, was William Graham Sumner right when he said that "stateways cannot change folkways"?

Race relations apart, law unquestionably is often an appropriate and effective mode of regulating behavior. Statutes forbid murder and false advertising, adultery and larceny, and assert thousands of other rules which society enforces through the machinery of state. Moreover, as Dean Roscoe Pound has pointed out, laws may not only set standards but may also help to create habits of conformity to them. Although we know that legal canons generally are always being violated to some degree, we know too that they are usually being obeyed. There has never been much support for a regime without law. The debate has almost always been over whether a proposed law is good, desirable, enforceable, or otherwise proper, not over whether there should be laws. Moreover, alleged choice that is required between law and education as a means of persuading men to change their practices and attitudes usually is not meaningful. Law itself educates and lawsuits, especially if well publicized—as they often are in the field of race relations—convey at least as much information about fundamental rights as most civics courses or religious sermons. As for race relations in particular, the thesis of this book is that law often can change race relations, that sometimes it has been indispensable to changing them, and that it has in fact changed them, even spectacularly. Indeed, it might be said that in many places law has been the greatest single factor inducing racial change. But law alone, like other social forces, and like laws affecting other institutions, may not be able to alter these relations

[2] The principal documentation of this chapter is the rest of this volume; it would be redundant to cite here all the sources and discussion of future pages. The index and table of cases will lead to more detailed discussions of particular points. General materials bearing on this chapter are discussed in the Bibliographical Note.

beyond a certain point, and in some situations it cannot make much difference.

The limitations have certain real foundations. Law has, first of all, bounds of effective action set by other influences. As Georg Jellinek has written, "There are social forces independent of the state which are essential guarantees of compliance with legal norms." [3] In general, however, law not only works along with social forces, but may also transform them. In particular, legal rules affecting jobs, housing, education, and so forth, when combined with antidiscrimination precepts, may make for a greater difference in race relations than could those precepts alone. For example, if employment is slack, an FEPC law could mean much more when combined with legislation which stimulates full employment. Second, law has intrinsic limitations which are determined by the way the legal system operates, especially by rules of procedure, which, although ostensibly designed to achieve efficiency, also may be used to make legal action inefficient. Recognizing these intrinsic curbs is different from holding the diffuse sentiment that race relations is not a matter for legal treatment, that a greater degree of equality must await, for example, education or economic evolution. For in view of what law has demonstrated it can do, acknowledging its insufficiency in some circumstances helps better to define the area of its competence, as well as the area in which social change can better be sought by other means.

The sociology of Sumner was one of the influences which helped to shape a view of the law as a wholly passive instrument. The great protagonists of the common law, Holmes and Cardozo, who contributed heavily to creating an image of the law widely held today, tended to complement Sumner and others who viewed law as an expression of underlying forces in society. Holmes's "the life of the law has not been logic: it has been experience" and Cardozo's analysis of legal rules as the harmonization of precedent, historical development, customs, and morals are generally accepted.[4] But as common law advocates Holmes and Cardozo were concerned chiefly with how law is born; they were less concerned with the changes it wrought or failed

[3] ALLGEMEINE STAATSLEHRE 333-336 (3d ed. 1914) (reprinted and translated in 2 SIMPSON & STONE, LAW AND SOCIETY 1559-1560 [1949]). On the general subject of law's effectiveness see also SIMPSON & STONE, ch. IV.

[4] See HOLMES, THE COMMON LAW 1 (1881); CARDOZO, THE NATURE OF THE JUDICIAL PROCESS 30, 64-66 (1921). See also Holmes, Law and Social Reform, in LERNER, THE MIND AND FAITH OF JUSTICE HOLMES 399 (1943).

to achieve. Those persuaded by their thinking agreed that society gives rise to law, as undoubtedly it does, often without then considering law's effect on society. In fact, we must consider both. A new canon, though it speaks for a dominant coalition of forces, does not always resolve conflicts. When a legal rule comes into being there frequently remain (or even are generated) forces pulling away from the standard. Some may conform to the rule, others may eventually have to yield or perhaps the law itself may be altered. One question which the following pages explore is: In race relations what difference does law make for those who do not concur in the dominant opinion?

In answering this question it is necessary, on the one hand, to distinguish between law's effect on conduct and its impact on prejudice. A white employer may by law be compelled to hire Negroes, or a restaurateur to serve them; yet each may continue to feel prejudiced against the "race." Schools may be desegregated despite widespread sentiment against the change. This indicates the difference. On the other hand, the effects of law on conduct and on prejudice are not wholly separable. People often tend to agree with the law, or at least to abide by it, and the habits law induces may in various ways dissipate biased attitudes. Conversely, violent prejudice may in some places actually avert social change if the public means of enforcement are insufficient; and if change does occur, deep antipathy obviously can affect its course or success.

RACE RELATIONS CHANGES WROUGHT BY LAW

Few legal doctrines in the United States have been as widely observed as both those requiring and those forbidding racial distinctions. Thus, even well before the *School* decisions, patterns of race relations followed patterns of the law countless times in various human activities all over the nation toward the obliteration of racial distinctions. After outlawry of the White Primary in 1944, Southern Negro voting registration rose in a short time from a few hundred thousand to well over a million, and it continues to go up. The teachers' salary cases equalized Negro and white teachers' salaries throughout the Southern states. The *Sweatt* and *McLaurin* decisions were crucial to the admission of thousands of Negroes to institutions of higher learning. Suits for nondiscriminatory interstate rail and bus accommodations reversed segregation on carriers. The *School Segregation* litigation was indispensable in desegregating hundreds of school districts. Few social changes have been as thorough and striking as school desegregation after the Supreme Court decisions of May 17, 1954, in the District of Columbia, Louisville, St. Louis, Wilmington, Delaware, virtually the entire states of Missouri, Oklahoma, West Virginia, large parts of Kentucky, Maryland, Texas, and elsewhere. Law has also reversed educational segregation in Arizona, Illinois, Kansas, New Jersey, New Mexico, New York, Ohio, and other non-Southern areas, where outright, purposeful segregation has been forbidden and, occasionally, *de facto* segregation caused by housing patterns alleviated.

Public recreation has been opened to Negroes in scores of cases by court decree. Local bus and trolley lines throughout the South have desegregated in large numbers since a 1957 Supreme Court decision. Following the Supreme Court's holding that a long-forgotten District of Columbia civil rights law was still effective, the District underwent a rapid transition which in a short time revamped it—so far as racial practices in public accommodations were concerned—from a city resembling Atlanta to one like New York. Fair Employment Practice Commissions have proven their capacity to increase minority employment. By governmental edict the armed forces were rapidly transformed from America's largest segregated institution to its largest nonsegregated one.

From another angle, often the only barrier to nonsegregation has been laws requiring separation. Hundreds of occurrences in the South attest that this is true. A classic instance is Berea College, which, in 1908, was forced by Kentucky's segregation law to eject Negro students. When this law was devitalized in 1950, Berea and scores of Southern private institutions of higher learning were able to, and did voluntarily, admit Negroes. In another area, after legal enforcement of restrictive covenants was outlawed by the Supreme Court, Negro housing in many communities spread through sections from which it had previously been barred. In *The Strange Career of Jim Crow*, C. Vann Woodward has demonstrated the great extent to which social patterns of segregation were created by laws, and not the other way around.

THE VOICES OF LAW

In the transitions from legal approval of racial distinctions to their condemnation by the law legal rules have been expressed in various ways. There have been judgments against specific defendants who almost always complied when their duty became clear. Less common but better publicized have been the few instances in which public force has been overt, *i.e.*, applied by contempt procedures, or, in the lone instance of Little Rock, by federal military force. But most pervasive and least marked has been legislation (in the word's broadest sense) with no immediate threat of enforcement. There is, of course, legislation in the form of statutes, ordinances, executive orders, administrative edicts, and so forth, but in addition, the principle declared in a lawsuit is legislative in nature for nonparties: it affects them as does a statute and is directly enforceable in approximately the same way— by further litigation.

A striking feature of school desegregation is the great amount of it accomplished without individual court decrees but simply as a result of the legislative nature of the 1954 precedents. Most of the 400,000 Southern Negro children now in integrated school situations (where biracial classes are permitted though not necessarily attended by all) have not arrived there via specific judgment. The District of Columbia, Topeka, Kansas, and two small towns in Delaware, which desegregated shortly after May 17, 1954, were the defendants in the original *School Cases* and under obligation to change (though all moved to comply before there was an actual decree). But Baltimore, Louisville, St. Louis, practically all of Missouri and West Virginia, large parts of Kentucky, Maryland, Oklahoma, and scattered districts in a few other states gave up segregation without judicial compulsion after the 1954 decisions. Some communities in Arizona, Kansas, New Mexico, and other non-Southern states undertook the transition even before May 17, 1954, to comply with state law, usually without direct court orders. It would be misleading, however, to ignore the possibility that anticipation of court action may have spurred them to act. Between May, 1954, and early 1957, some sixty suits involving lower and higher education were filed in Southern states, with about eighteen resulting in judgments or agreements to desegregate. Suit was pending in Baltimore and in at least some of the counties of the other desegregating states when they switched; additional petitions had been filed, auguring court action if they were denied. Many jurisdictions had already undergone litigation to open their higher educational facilities, public recreation, and other such places to Negroes a few years prior to 1954, and they knew that the resources to bring suit were available.

The response to the *School* opinions was not unusual. After the *Re-*

strictive Covenant Cases few Negroes who bought homes in formerly forbidden neighborhoods were involved in suit over the right to move there. While no survey has been taken on why the various desegregated Democratic primaries were opened to Negroes after the primary cases, undoubtedly only a minority of the many county or local organizations actually were the subject of suit, in view of the fact that there were sufficient cases to emphasize the law's requirement. There is probably not a Southern state with desegregated higher education where there was no court test or the beginnings of one to fight segregation at that level. Yet of the formerly all-white Southern public higher schools which now admit Negroes, most do not seem actually to have been in court over racial problems, although in Louisiana, where a substantial number of Negroes attend formerly white schools, there has been legal struggle every inch of the way. Only a few railroads were involved in proceedings to desegregate Pullman facilities, and only one was a party to the case which ordered an end to segregation in dining cars. Most of the desegregation which took place in Pullmans and diners thereafter did not occur under direct order. (The legality of segregated coach travel was ended, however, by an omnibus suit against most of the South's major carriers joined as defendants. But after losing, none appealed.) Most Southern transit companies which abandoned local bus and trolley segregation were not sued.

The actual legal contests, however, doubtlessly encouraged consent by nonparties. And sometimes the case and the general rule have worked in this combination: a defendant, who would willingly yield, has awaited suit, or has asked (often privately) to be sued, so that the decree might be used as a shield against opposition to desegregation.

Compliance without the prod of directly enforceable decrees points up a strong strain of lawabidingness. For some it may indicate agreement (or lack of strong disagreement) with desegregation; for others it does not necessarily mean that their prosegregation feeling has disappeared or that law has transformed biased attitudes. In a number of newly desegregated communities the change has not been popular. Still, enough citizens uphold it to make the rule a reality.

In certain places, however, law as legislation often has failed to change even conduct. Sometimes vigorous courtroom effort has been required; and then specific judgments have been ignored or evaded. A hard core of states has hardly altered at all. Why is it that some places have responded to the rule of law, while in others it has been disregarded? An over-all formula answer would be difficult, probably impossible, to state. But in the many situations considered hereafter we shall note a number of forces working as both agents for and agents against the law.

THE CHANGING SOUTH IN A CHANGING WORLD

It is beyond the scope of this study to do more than acknowledge some of the profound forces that are transforming the South and re-modeling its racial attitudes. Yet we must take notice of them, for, although they do not decide concrete cases or trigger specific changes, they create an essential predisposition in that direction. The 1896 in which the *Plessy v. Ferguson* decision was handed down was a decidedly different milieu from the 1954 of the *School Segregation Cases,* and there is no doubt that the eras in which the cases were decided more than the formal logic involved in the controversies made the difference in the results. Among the general factors at work in mid-twentieth century are the industrialization of the South, with the concomitant need for social stability and an ample, able labor corps, many of whom must be Negroes; urbanization, which engenders an atmosphere of anonymity and thus security in which civil rights can flourish as they cannot in rural areas; the homogenization of the South and the rest of the nation, which is being effected by national television and radio networks, newspaper wire services, nationally distributed popular magazines, rapid air transportation, great new highway networks, migration to both Northern and Southern cities from Southern farms, and the southward movement of Northern managerial personnel; universal military training in nonsegregated armed forces; increased education; the antisegregation stand of virtually every major religious denomination; the need of the United States to support civil rights in order to gain and hold allies in a world where most of the population is colored; the growing economic and political strength of Negroes; and the changing image of the Negro in the eyes of the white majority and indeed in his own eyes. We have focused here on the South where the racial issue has traditionally been viewed as most acute, but these considerations, or most of them, apply in the North as well.

Public opinion polls have consistently shown a more liberal attitude on racial questions among the better educated, among city dwellers, among younger persons, and in the North. A study of attitudes toward desegregation between 1942 and 1956 by Hyman and Sheatsley shows that the number of white persons in the South who approve school integration grew during that period from 2 to 14 percent. Each of these indicators seems to augur growing receptivity to the anti-discrimination rules which the courts are handing down and the legislatures are enacting and growing pressure for such standards to be proclaimed.

Yet, even with this trend, changes will not occur by themselves. Other factors have a lot to do with how, when and, indeed, whether these general forces operate on the racial situation. The forces neither work evenly throughout the nation, nor do they affect a uniform scene. There is greater industrialization taking place in North Carolina than there is in Mississippi; the opening of a large factory in the former influences a different situation than it does in the latter. Moreover, prejudice and susceptibility to incitement vary not only according to geographical area but with the institution affected. Change in some situations (*e.g.,* travel) is more agreeable to many than change in others (*e.g.,* intermarriage). Then there is the matter of *who* is in authority. A Faubus or a Kasper may provoke results quite different from those induced by such leaders as former Governor McKeldin of Maryland or Governor Chandler of Kentucky. We must also consider whether state or federal law applies and which courts have jurisdiction (some state courts have issued decisions clearly contradicting federal law). Moreover, the affected persons and institutions differ in their response to change: Negroes may take advantage of a rule of law in their favor or remain apathetic, depending on local leadership, legal assistance, and the general militancy of the community; an affected institution, such as higher education, may be able to absorb qualified Negro applicants, as exemplified by many formerly white universities, or, like housing, it may be so inelastic that change is very slow.

INDEPENDENCE OF THE LAWGIVER AND HIS AUTHORITY
IN THE FEDERAL SYSTEM

Another series of important questions related to changing patterns of race relations deals with the lawgiver himself. Who makes the decision? How independent is he? How far can he extend his power under the limitations of America's dual, federal-state form of government?

Some authorities asked to change legal rules about race relations are close to the local community and dependent upon its favor. These include city councils, local judges, and state legislatures. Others are remote and thus more independent. They include the federal judiciary, the Interstate Commerce Commission, the President, the armed forces, the Veterans Administration, and so forth. Some of these may answer to a nation-wide constituency in which antisegregation forces are dominant. Authority inaccessible to local popular will can more readily be forthright in implementing desegregation, but where integration is popular or politically rewarding those responsive to the grass roots will lean that way too. The federal judiciary, whose life tenure and guaranty against diminution of salary is secured by the Constitution, has, perhaps, the widest jurisdiction of the independent lawmakers. As long ago as 1895 James Bryce suggested that the independence of the federal courts is this nation's best assurance of impartial, constitutional law enforcement,[5] and that is just as true today.

There are individual differences among federal judges, however, and each one may possibly embody, at least to some degree, the attitude of the community in which he developed and may perhaps respond in some measure to intangible local influences. Nevertheless, it is notable that most federal judges in the Southern states have been prompt to strike down evasion. A few who have been tolerant of it have generally been reversed. State judges, on the other hand, usually are elected at relatively short intervals and are involved in state politics. It is not surprising that in contrast to the federal judiciary's treatment of racial issues some state courts have openly flouted not only the spirit but also the letter of the Supreme Court's decisions on civil rights.

A recent, striking example of the difference between state and federal courts in the handling of these matters is shown in the University of Florida case. After more than five years of what can only be called evasion by the Florida courts, the Supreme Court suggested that the plaintiff shift to a federal forum. There, relief was obtained promptly. Similarly, a lower Alabama state court recently refused to desegregate the Birmingham police force on the clearly incorrect ground that the Federal Constitution forbade the suit as one against the state; the Alabama Supreme Court affirmed, holding

[5] 1 BRYCE, THE AMERICAN COMMONWEALTH 271 *et seq.* (3d ed. 1909).

that under state law the personnel board may not be enjoined. After the case was re-filed in federal court, the defendants abandoned their segregation policy. In Little Rock, near the outset of the school conflict, a state judge enjoined the desegregation plan which the federal judiciary had approved. The federal court enjoined enforcement of that injunction. Although Federal District Judge Lemley in effect restored the state court ruling before the next school year opened (1958), the upper federal courts reversed his decision.

Sometimes, though, it is not the political sources of the authority (*i.e.*, state or federal) which determine independence. Rather, it may be the degree of urbanization. It has been observed that school boards in large cities, elected or appointed, where the members hardly know the citizenry, can act more independently than those in small towns where board members and citizens are often in daily contact.

The independence of the federal judiciary raises the question of which discrimination is amenable to federal rules. By and large, it is the big institutions that are federally controllable (though often for different legal reasons): those owned by the state (schools, colleges, parks, public housing); or those so large and important that the state helps to empower or support them (labor unions, urban renewal projects, government contractors); those so great or monopolistic that the state requires them to serve all (local carriers, inns, public utilities); and those which constitute an important part of interstate commerce (trains, planes, buses, and their terminals).

Of course, federal law outlaws state legal rules requiring private undertakings (even small ones) to discriminate. But this does not prevent management from making distinctions (which raises the issue of whether it is subject to federal rules). Consequently, in effect, important activities are beyond the reach of national jurisprudence: privately owned public accommodations, a great deal of private employment, private housing, and day-to-day personal relations are among the most significant. Generally, unless state or local civil rights law or common law apply—as they do to some extent in more than a score of non-Southern states—these sectors remain immune from legal requirements against discrimination.

OPPOSITION

Assuming that the appropriate antidiscrimination public force is invoked, against exactly what must it operate? Alongside lawabidingness we must juxtapose for Southern communities what John Hope Franklin calls the tradition of the "militant South," which he has suggested is still important in race relations today and which W. J. Cash has observed to be one of the most salient Southern traits.[6] This readiness to fight unwanted authority is greater to the extent that prejudice is more deeply felt. It increases in intensity to reach a peak in the centers of the Old Confederacy; yet even there it is weakened in so far as the Southern economic and demographic revolution has diluted the old patterns.

A long-standing explanation of the degree of white resistance to desegregation still offered is the Negro-white population ratio. One scholar who has examined carefully the effect of this proportion on racial attitudes affirms what he calls "the familiar point that compliance with the Supreme Court decision is related to the ratio the Negro population is to the white population and that the degree of compliance reflects racial attitudes." [7]

But others question whether clear inferences can automatically be drawn from mere percentages. One writer in *With All Deliberate Speed* says:

it would be easy to conclude that compliance came easiest where Negro numbers were smallest. But this theory cannot be pressed too far. Though each border state as a whole shows a relatively small Negro population, each has within it communities where Negro numbers are as high as in some typically southern communities. And it was in some of those communities that desegregation was accomplished with little friction and no serious problems.

He cites Baltimore with 39 percent, Wilmington with 29 percent, and Louisville with 26 percent.[8]

The impression that percentages are crucial to desegregation may have arisen because large Negro concentrations occur in areas where the slave tradition was strong. The assumption then arose that the two invariably went hand in hand. In fact, we must not forget that Negro numbers may tend to evoke a pro-civil rights climate by contributing to colored economic and political strength. Actually, a complex of

[6] FRANKLIN, THE MILITANT SOUTH at x (1956); see also CASH, THE MIND OF THE SOUTH, 123-130, 301-312, 354-356, 411-413 (Anchor ed. 1941).

[7] Stephan, *Population Ratios, Racial Attitudes, and Desegregation*, 26 J. NEGRO EDUCATION 22, 27 (1957).

[8] Lasch, *Along the Border*, in WITH ALL DELIBERATE SPEED 60 (Shoemaker ed. 1957).

factors must be considered, of which population ratio is only one. Among these is the fact that high-ratio rural areas, which are chiefly Deep-Southern, exercise disproportionate power in the state legislature and often prohibit Negro voting. In the border states, on the other hand, the high-ratio areas of changeover have been urban where liberal forces are more effective and Negroes do vote.

Some kinds of desegregation attract hostility more readily than others. Gunnar Myrdal has pointed out that white resistance to various types of desegregation decreases in the following order: most unwelcome is intermarriage; next most unwelcome is the abolition of discrimination in personal relations (dancing, bathing, eating, drinking together, etc.); third, elimination of discrimination in public facilities (schools, churches, means of conveyance); fourth, eradication of political disfranchisement; fifth, abolition of discrimination in the courts, by the police, and by other public servants; and sixth, removal of discrimination in securing land, credit, jobs, and so forth. (The Negro ranking in favor of desegregation is almost the reverse, *i.e.*, Negroes are most interested in securing jobs, least desirous of intermarriage.) [9] Actually, Myrdal's hierarchy of resistance may not hold true in all situations. In a plentiful job market, for example, there will be less insistence on employment bias than when jobs are hard to find.

Intransigence is more effective to the extent that it is better organized. But some activities are inherently not suited to becoming focal points of opposition. Interstate travel is an example. On an interstate journey a passenger who would segregate has no necessary relationship to any other traveler; all are temporary companions. Indeed, for all that anyone knows, some may come from parts of the country where integration is a matter of course. Nobody really knows anyone else or how he feels. Local police do not accompany the trains. Perhaps for reasons such as these travelers have been known to violate any number of conventions, not only racial ones. This has helped to contribute to a relatively easy breakdown of segregation on trains, though some problems still remain. In railroad stations, however, where the same legal rule operates, segregation has yielded less. Local police have easy access to these places, and, especially in smaller towns, people in the station may know one another.

While interstate buses are in many respects comparable to trains

---

[9] MYRDAL, AN AMERICAN DILEMMA 60–61 (1944).

they partake more of a local flavor, picking up more passengers in isolated rural areas and stopping at stations which are local enterprises. Often the driver is known personally by those along his route. Consequently, desegregation on interstate buses has not been as widespread as on trains.

Another example is the armed forces. The authority of the services is so nearly absolute that there was no real chance of anyone's successfully challenging orders to integrate. Yet, there might have been obstruction, or grudging compliance, very little of which appeared. The fact that service units are made up of persons from all sections of the nation, that they have shifting personnel and are not rooted (but only temporarily stationed) in communities in which segregation is the way of life, undoubtedly aided change.

But most activities—education, recreation, housing—are far more localized. Any given desegregation, however, may be easier in a city because of the anonymity of metropolitan life, which creates dissociation among even neighbors. City dwellers have much in common with travelers. This has made it more difficult to muster lawless mobs or hostile movements in urban areas, and is one reason why most mob opposition to school desegregation has probably been rural, or, where urban, seems to have consisted substantially of outsiders. In Baltimore, Nashville, Little Rock, and Washington, many of the rioters appear to have been from out of town. Nevertheless, there seems to be no sure way of predicting when an outsider, or an insider, will succeed in fanning prosegregation feelings to open opposition.

At this juncture we should observe how defiance works. If, in the manner of some legal realists, we were to match the outcome of litigation against community violence, we would find that it is doubtful whether forceful opposition has any effect on the courts—indeed, the evidence points the other way. In Little Rock, Hoxie, Clinton, Nashville, Clay, and Sturgis, where there had been rioting, lawsuits ended by favoring the Negro applicants. Suits by dissident white groups in Baltimore and Washington, coupled with demonstrations there, failed. Apparently only in the University of Alabama and the Milford, Delaware, cases did the lawsuits go against the plaintiffs, but even in those cases the courts asserted that violence had no bearing on whether there could be enjoyment of the asserted rights and that other factors created the ruling against them. Opposition most often now combats lawabidingness not by overtly overriding the law but by exploiting inherent qualities of our political-legal system. Government officials may be deterred from following the course set by the law through fear of political reprisals; therefore, cases must be brought by plaintiffs represented by lawyers; opposition tries to deter both the plaintiffs and the lawyers; even after suit is brought there are extensive opportunities for procedural maneuver which can long delay decision.

Where violence is employed, however, it may deter the exercise of rights. It is no light matter to send one's child to school through a hostile mob. But violence can also create such morale in the Negro community as to achieve the opposite effect.

Opposition, however, latent or overt, does not mean that a legal rule will be thwarted. Much depends on whether officials are insistent on compliance. After the Supreme Court ruled that Maryland public parks and beaches had to be desegregated, the transition was easy and thorough, despite the fact that the trial judge had written that the sexual connotations of swimming would stir antagonism. Desegregation of some Florida swimming facilities, however, provoked disturbances and resulted in their being closed. One important difference between the cases was that Maryland's governor would tolerate no interference with the law, while the path Florida's authorities have followed to lawabidingness has been to oppose the desegregation rather than the violators. This points up the fact mentioned earlier that the manner of enforcement may determine the success of the change.

TECHNIQUES OF ENFORCEMENT

Civil rights laws may be enforced in essentially three different ways, which represent the manner of most other law enforcement: criminal prosecution, private civil suit for damages or injunction by an aggrieved person, and administrative or injunctive implementation by public officials. Experience has shown the inherent shortcomings of criminal laws in the matter of civil rights. Trial has to be by jury, which may very likely be as prejudiced as the defendant; proof must be beyond a reasonable doubt; the statutes must be specific enough to meet the constitutional requirement that a defendant have notice of the alleged offense, leaving room for flexible, evasive conduct outside the letter of the law; the burden is on the minority group member to persuade the prosecutor or grand jury to act, and they, at the same time, are preoccupied with the more traditional crimes against the person or property. Prosecutions have been few, convicitions even fewer.

In civil suits for damages proof need be only by a preponderance of the evidence. But these cases involve jury trial too, as well as the expense of engaging counsel, whose fee is unlikely to be recompensed by the amount of damages awarded, even if they are won. Private suit for injunction avoids the jury aspect of a damage action but is otherwise the same as civil suits for damages. In both of these cases, as in criminal prosecutions, however, the burden of going forward is on the minority group. And all of the above approaches cannot correct a situation in which minority group members do not try to use a facility or refrain from becoming involved in a situation both because they do not want to be rebuffed and because they must use their energies where they have greatest chance of success.

An administrative agency, or an attorney general or other official with comparable powers, can be more effective than private suitors or criminal prosecutors. Proof, as in civil suits, need not be shown beyond a reasonable doubt, but is satisfied merely by a preponderance of evidence. Statutes may be sufficiently general to allow novel attempts at evasion or subterfuge to be caught. The expense of investigation and proceeding is borne by the government. There is no jury; on the contrary, an administrative body will become expert at discerning bias and its findings will be upheld if supported by evidence. Moreover, an administrative agency may be authorized to seek out the discrimination which members of a minority avoid, or to take complaints from civil rights organizations, although, of course, proceeding upon individual complaint remains an important mode of operation.

An administrative approach offers opportunity to employ law in unusual ways. Conciliation and mediation are often used in labor disputes and are a common feature of FEPC activity. FEPCs also conduct educational campaigns. It seems, however, that no appreciable gains have been achieved in bettering race relations by conciliation groups which do not also have ultimate enforcement powers.

More important than theoretical procedure, however, is the actual vigor of enforcement. Administrative approaches will be unproductive where they are weak, while a criminal statute, well enforced, may produce results. Even where juries will not convict, a forceful policy of pressing criminal or civil suits can result in law enforcement, for the expense of defending an antidiscrimination suit runs from several hundred to several thousand dollars, and there is always the risk of conviction. A prosecutor's forthrightness will, however, be determined in large part by political considerations. The expense factor cuts two ways, of course, in the bringing of civil suits, but civil rights organizations may help to absorb these costs for plaintiffs and otherwise spur enforcement. Where a government agency itself is the defendant, as in a school segregation suit, the fact that public funds are spent in defense of segregation eliminates expense as a deterrent for defendants. Here, injunctive suits or administrative implementation by the federal government would seem to be the most efficient way to proceed, although private injunctive suits supported by private agencies have been productive in securing civil rights; indeed this has been the chief method of enforcement until now.

A number of leading authorities agree that a clear and unequivocal statement of policy, firm enforcement, willingness to deal with violators by employing appropriate sanctions, refusal to compromise principle, and an appeal to the community on a moral and religious level help to smooth a changeover in racial patterns. Involvement of community relations agencies, clear communication between the affected groups, and police work by officers schooled in intergroup relations all contribue to successful transition. To cite these factors, however, and to attribute success or failure to them tells only part of the story. What makes a community capable of such implementation? What of enforcement in a community with virtually none of these aids? Fundamental elements—political alignments, economic patterns, urbanization, leadership, and so forth—some of which are discussed elsewhere in this chapter, contribute to disposing the community one way or the other.

THE LAW'S INEFFICIENCY

So far we have not given much attention to the extent to which methods provided by the law can be used to prevent realization of substantive rights which it declares. Cases often can be bogged down by administrative remedies, discovery proceedings, motions, continuances, appeals, stays of execution, rehearings, and innumerable dilatory devices. These constitute the law's delay. While some may be needed for a fair decision on the merits of a case, others are purposefully used for hindrance. As William Seagle has pointed out in his *Law—The Science of Inefficiency*, law in a democratic state has

deliberately been made inefficient; for while we have developed a
legal system to implement society's rules, by force if necessary, we
also often object to the exercise of that power which, as Seagle writes,

can be curbed only by making the law inefficient. . . . Humanity has con-
stantly drawn back from legal efficiency as from the brink of an abyss.
When threatened by efficient law enforcement, it has loudly demanded
Twelve Tables, codes, bills of rights, declarations of the rights of man, and
full-fledged written constitutions—all for the purpose of protecting the
weak against the strong, and the individual against the state.[10]

Another means of achieving that inefficiency is to place a host of
procedural hurdles between complaint and judgment. Seagle notes
that procedure is in large part determined by those interests most often
involved in lawsuits, writing that litigants who may be plaintiffs today
but defendants tomorrow cannot wholeheartedly support procedural
reform and that there is a direct correlation between the complexity of
procedure and the importance of what is at stake.[11]

A number of rules can slow the law's application to race relations.
Of primary importance, no suit can be commenced without a plaintiff,
as we have previously remarked. And the order in which plaintiffs appear and the relief they seek may bear no relationship to systematic
legal development. To some extent a civil rights association can select
among the cases it chooses to support in an effort to build precedent
step by step. But if this factor were entirely controllable, it seems
likely that after the graduate and professional school cases were
decided by the Supreme Court, civil rights lawyers would have brought
college cases before proceeding to what became the *School Segregation
Cases*. The fact is that after the *Sweatt* and *McLaurin* decisions (indeed, while they were pending), complaints continued to mount about
Negro elementary and high schools, while at the higher level, where
conditions were no better, there were for a time no great efforts to
seek legal redress.

Sometimes, notwithstanding the existence of an equalitarian rule of
law, no plaintiff may appear to claim its benefits. Social factors often
discourage some persons from participating in lawsuits. Outright
intimidation and legal harassment may keep others out of court. Even
in the North, potential plaintiffs may take the path of least resistance
and fill their needs where they can be assured of no rebuff or embar-

---

[10] Seagle, Law—The Science of Inefficiency 9–10 (1952).   [11] *Id.* at 67.

rassment. Negroes are not likely to apply for whites-only jobs, or they will make few attempts to use accommodations which bar them. This is why antidiscrimination commissions seek the power to start cases on their own initiative. Civil rights organizations have thus been important in educating minorities concerning their rights and in supporting legal action to secure them.

In addition, discrimination must be proved. In the early days of civil rights law this was relatively easy, since the statutes often discriminated by their very terms, and since, where discrimination was effected by custom or practice, the administrators were not ashamed to admit it. Today in the North few who discriminate will concede it; they will try to attribute the rebuff to some nonracial factor. Restrictive covenants now do not expressly bar Negroes; they speak in Aesopian terms about compatability of neighbors and give discretion to, for example, boards of directors to bar sales to "undesirables" for any reason they choose. The first report on the administration of New York City's fair housing law emphasizes these evasive tactics. Although the chairman announced a significant degree of compliance, he also said that "there appeared to be a trend away from open discrimination . . . . there was no expressed opposition to the law, and . . . most of those charged with discrimination denied it." [12]

In more and more Southern racial cases it is becoming necessary to prove every inconsequential fact as well as the main one, discrimination. For example, nowadays there rarely is a flat rule excluding Negroes from juries in biased courts. Indeed, sometimes a token few are deliberately chosen to confound the defendant. Then they may later be peremptorily challenged by the prosecutor. Some pupil assignment laws designed to avert or minimize school desegregation have refrained from mentioning race but speak of health factors, mental adjustment, and a host of vague standards which can cover up a racial selection. The Tallahassee bus ordinance treats of weight and balance as bases upon which the drivers are to assign seats. Perhaps we can devise a formula to describe the situation: As rules against discrimination become more clear, proof of discrimination becomes more difficult.

A striking example of evasion involves a South Carolina law which barred members of the NAACP from state employment. When this was attacked in the courts by school teachers, in *Bryan v. Austin* (1957), and it became obvious that the statute could not be sustained, it was

[12] N.Y. Times, July 21, 1958, p. 23

repealed. The case, therefore, was declared moot. In place of the first statute a law was substituted which merely required that state employees list the organizations to which they belong. The state may have believed that local school boards would fire known NAACP members without giving a reason connected with membership in the association. Proof of discrimination would be difficult in such instances, and besides, the legislators may have thought that the mere existence of the new statute would deter individuals from joining the association.

There are also the delays of appeal and further appeal, fresh problems presented by fresh legislation, administrative hearings, and innumerable devices not yet even tried out. The key to the effectiveness of these tactics is the stay of execution. Few informed persons seriously believe that the substantive arguments offered by segregationists during these protracted proceedings are a legal bar to desegregation. Yet if stays of execution can be freely obtained, time can be bought almost indefinitely while litigation goes on. There has been some indication that the courts may begin to stop granting stays. Already in a few cases judgments to admit plaintiffs to schools have been placed in effect, leaving defendants to spin out their theories while desegregation is a reality. Preliminary injunctions or temporary restraining orders, summary dismissals of appeals as frivolous, and assessment of damages for unwarranted appeals are other devices which may cut litigation short.

Finally, a decree against one school district or park is enforceable against it alone. If others will not comply voluntarily, they must be sued separately, permitting the use of the same delaying tactics all over again.

The antidiscrimination commissions of some Northern jurisdictions which enforce civil rights laws exemplify the best means of overcoming the problems of legal inefficiency. Most of them may commence proceedings on their own, and they are equipped to ferret out the proof and to implement broad, flexible standards, substantive and procedural, asserting the initiative and absorbing the cost and trouble which would ordinarily be the plaintiff's burden. Their findings, like those of other administrative bodies, are sustained if supported by evidence. Most important, a policy of vigorous enforcement by such a commission, or indeed by any enforcement official, may have an educational effect and help to dissolve so-called "apathy." On the federal level, the proposed Part III of the Civil Rights Act of 1957, which was not enacted but became part of the Civil Rights Bill of 1958 (affording the government administrative and injunctive modes of securing civil rights), could, if firmly applied, pitch implementation at its most effective level.

THE MINORITY COMMUNITY

Among other factors contributing to the enforcement of desegregation may be determinants in the Negro community itself. In a legal system in which court orders can be obtained only at the suit of an aggrieved plaintiff or on complaint to the government, most change has come about through Negroes' initiative. To the extent that law operates other than through the judiciary, basically it still has been the Negro who has regulated the pace by lobbying, petitioning, and pressuring.

Negro political power is perhaps the most important factor within the minority group helping to set the viewpoint of those who implement the law: governors, mayors, local judges, police, school boards, administrators, and the public generally. For example, it appears that sentencing in the criminal courts often tends to be fairer where there is a substantial Negro vote. The attitude of executive authorities and the police determines whether agitators will succeed in stemming desegregation. The mood of administrators such as school authorities may decide the spirit and course of racial change.

However, urban Negro political organizations—the strongest Negroes have—are up against the fact that rural segregationists who dominate some state governments can use that power as a lever to incite city opposition to desegregation. In Virginia, for example, Norfolk probably would have taken steps toward desegregation if not for massive resistance on the state level; perhaps Richmond, too, would have moved in that direction but for the same reason. Shortly after the *School* decisions Greensboro would have commenced to change over, but was stopped by the state. Miami and Atlanta, to take only two more examples, would probably show a good deal of desegregation in various activities but for restraint from the state level. The disproportionate power of rural counties is a national political issue, and not one in race relations alone. As urban areas grow more powerful and tend to incorporate some country sections, the imbalance will probably be somewhat lessened. The situation may also change if the 1957 Civil Rights Act is able to increase rural Negro votes. But both alleviatives will probably come only over the long run.

Once more, it should not be forgotten that political power is important for civil rights in the North too. In Northern communities Negro political power has helped to get civil rights laws enacted and to pitch the vigor of their enforcement.

THE NEGRO LAWYER

Another factor related to legal change—and one generally ignored —is the Negro lawyer. The position of leadership which De Tocqueville ascribed to American lawyers generally is probably even more true of the Negro lawyer in his relationship to the Negro community. Not until Howard University in the thirties began graduating numbers of Negro lawyers trained in civil rights did the race relations picture begin to change (of course, other circumstances were involved, and there long have been some Negro lawyers in the South educated at Northern schools; but the role of the Howard law alumni has been crucial in civil rights cases). The Howard graduates have in recent years been joined by those from Southern state law schools desegregated under the law. In Arkansas, Maryland, North Carolina, Texas, and elsewhere Negroes who have attended state schools now appear in civil rights cases. The Negro lawyer handles 99 percent of the Southern antidiscrimination litigation, and most of it in the North; he plays an important role in legislative campaigns; and he provides community leadership. The Southern white attorney who will handle a desegregation case is almost unique. Yet many large Negro centers and even some important cities in the South still have no Negro lawyer or but a few. Some Negro attorneys, like some white ones, are not well trained; some prefer to devote all their time to earning a living. The economic resources of the Negroes in a locale may decide whether there is to be a Negro lawyer there or not, for unless there is enough legal business in a place to support a lawyer he cannot very well settle there.

LEADERSHIP AND COMMUNITY ORGANIZATION

In some places Negro insurance executives, bankers, doctors, teachers, and other business and professional persons with education, status, and leisure also provide guidance, both where there are Negro lawyers and where there are none. But unpredictably, persons of other stations in life—housewives, government workers, laborers, farmers—may have the ability and perhaps the "personal magic" to guide a change. The Reverend Martin Luther King of Montgomery, among the most striking personalities of the new stewardship, symbolizes and has stimulated the spread of church leadership, although the Negro churches themselves have long been important meeting places for the NAACP and other civic groups.

Group activity is the medium through which the most effective civil rights leadership works. The United States, as Arthur Schlesinger, Sr., has pointed out, is a nation of joiners and Americans work for social change through groups. Litigation on questions of public importance is often group-supported, lobbying is almost invariably an organized activity, and groups aid in policing and law enforcement. There are the NAACP, the Urban League, the Southern Regional Council, the American Civil Liberties Union, and various lay religious associations, as well as civic, labor, fraternal, and church groups generally, all working against discrimination. Sometimes a grouping may arise spontaneously as in the case of the Montgomery boycott, out of which grew the now permanent Montgomery Improvement Association. The MIA, in turn, has given rise to the Southern Christian Leadership Conference. The many Southern state laws and other devices to outlaw the NAACP indicate recognition of its effectiveness.

Group activity has been particularly efficacious in local transportation changeovers because a disproportionately high number of local bus riders are colored, and alternatives to public transportation can be arranged readily. Under this pressure bus lines in a score of cities complied when the Supreme Court held local travel segregation unconstitutional. The Montgomery boycott did not achieve its aim, however, until after the courts had outlawed the Montgomery regulations. The Montgomery bus company and others elsewhere were able to use the legal ruling as a shield against local segregationists.

Some institutions, particularly universities, not only provide leadership or organization but sometimes help to influence attitudes in favor of civil rights. Atlanta University is a major liberal force in that city. The fact that Knoxville College and the University of Tennessee are located in Knoxville is said to have contributed to the easy move away from transportation segregation there. The site of the University of Arkansas, Fayetteville, is said to be the community fairest in the administration of justice in that state. At times, of course, liberal sentiment in some university towns may be outweighed by other forces. Prosegregationists have worked to suppress campus freedom, so that many Southern faculty members have been or can easily be persuaded to leave for Northern campuses.

THE MINORITY'S RESPONSIVENESS TO AVAILABLE RIGHTS

An antidiscrimination rule of law and community forces favorable to its enforcement do not settle the extent to which a minority will become integrated into the community. The quickness of Negroes to respond to available rights also helps to decide whether those rights will play a real role in life relationships or remain abstract rules. Not only must cases be filed at the behest of plaintiffs, or legislation pushed in the assemblies, but once suits are won or laws enacted, the rights they confer must be exercised; otherwise they mean nothing. There are school districts where the board has agreed to cease segregating but few or no Negroes have applied for transfer. In some communities carriers have abolished Jim Crow seating, yet most Negroes continue to sit in the rear. There are no restrictions on voting in many Southern counties, but Negro registration is well under that for whites. In some Northern places where public accommodations laws are obeyed, there is little Negro patronage.

A long history of segregation and discrimination directly limits the number of Negroes who can exercise the new freedoms. Of those who have had inferior high school and college educations, not many can qualify for new graduate school opportunities. Those who have never been trained cannot accept new openings in engineering and other specialties. Those without adequate incomes cannot take advantage of a law like New York City's which forbids racial restriction in private housing. The better "white" restaurants in cities may be inconveniently located to Negro housing and proportionately more Negroes may be unable to pay their prices. But in some instances (e.g., voting, travel, and public recreation) the barrier is hardly so clear-cut and external, so some have called this failure to respond "apathy." The term, however, is misleading unless it is understood to incorporate reference to generations of segregation and thus enforced lack of aspiration of all sorts. And obviously it is not necessarily apathetic to retreat or stand pat, as some do, under fire or threat of economic or physical reprisal. The local transportation example underlines the importance of the minority's response. Here a shift can be made fairly easily, and it is the younger Negro passengers, on whom the time-worn patterns have been less firmly pressed, who are more likely to sit in front in the once-"white" section, while old-timers usually continue to occupy Jim Crow seats. As time goes on, of course, those taking advantage of the new opportunities appear to be multiplying. In Baltimore, where any child may attend virtually any school, Negro registration in formerly white schools has grown from 4,601 in 1955 to 14,826 in 1957, although 80 percent of the colored children still attend all-colored schools. "Apathy" is decreasing there while housing segregation is becoming the main cause of all-colored schools.

THE ELASTICITY OF THE INSTITUTION TO BE CHANGED

Given a legal rule, assuming obedience and the minority's responsiveness, still other factors must be counted in figuring whether law can change race relations. How elastic is the institution on which law is operating? A rule ending Jim Crow higher learning is limited in realization if colleges are overcrowded. To step back one level, the extent to which the college rule is realized will reflect the capacity of high schools to prepare once-segregated Negro pupils for higher education. Removing bias from hiring signifies little in a depression or a tight job market. But during prosperity, as antibias rules open apprenticeship training and technical education, qualified applicants can begin to fill openings and can commence to accumulate seniority. Ending exclusion from housing does not count for much if there are few homes or apartments available; it can mean more with plentiful housing. Abolishing distinctions in the armed forces when the number of personnel decreases and the need for skill increases may not have much significance for desegregation; it cannot equip Negroes for enlistment or retention in the same ratio as whites nor give them the background training to qualify for higher positions. At an earlier time when the armed forces were larger and there were relatively fewer skilled posts, Negroes entered and advanced more easily. In each case the rule means less if the institution to be changed does not have sufficient play in its joints to shift readily from a biracial to a nonracial system.

LAW AND PREJUDICE

The quotation concerning Alexander at the outset of this chapter referred to unity "not by compulsion but only by . . . willing consent or . . . Love." Yet one outgrowth of Alexander's prayer has been its expression in legal rules which by definition imply the possibility of resort to compulsion. A related manifestation is the demand for equal treatment on the part of disadvantaged minorities. Few would deny, however, that the most agreeable condition would be that in which unity is achieved by willing consent. In this state racial prejudices would not exist. We may inquire what role law can play in working toward such an order.

Up to this point we have discussed largely the law's effect on conduct. But what of the attitudes underlying that conduct? Can law change them? Studies of desegregated situations, including the armed forces units, housing projects, and employment situations, indicate that change required by law *has* lessened prejudice.[13] One of the closest students of the psychology of prejudice, Gordon Allport,[14] explains why there should be such a reaction. Improved conditions which come with lessened discrimination help to raise minority levels to permit equal status contacts. Such contacts permit familiarization and improved communication between majority and minority group members. Knowledge and familiarity, studies show, abate prejudice. Moreover, outward nondiscriminatory action, which the law compels, "has an eventual effect upon inner habits of thought and feeling."

But apart from the change in attitude caused by the change in situation, does the mere existence of law affect prejudice? Allport says of this: "Laws in line with one's conscience are likely to be obeyed; when not obeyed they still establish an ethical norm that holds before the individual an image of what his conduct should be." [15] Enforcement, particularly a well-publicized lawsuit, at the very least makes the existence of such norms known.

However, the ability of law to affect prejudice depends in part on

[13] See MANDELBAUM, SOLDIER GROUPS AND NEGRO SOLDIERS (1952); NICHOLS, BREAKTHROUGH ON THE COLOR FRONT (1954); DEUTSCH & COLLINS, INTERRACIAL HOUSING 34 *et seq.* (1951); WILNER, WALKLEY & COOK, HUMAN RELATIONS IN INTERRACIAL HOUSING 5, 127 (1955); FLEISCHMAN & RORTY, WE OPEN THE GATES (1958); Davis, *Negro Employment: A Progress Report,* Fortune, July, 1952, pp. 102, 158; SEIDENBERG, NEGROES IN THE WORK GROUP 45 (N.Y. State School of Industrial & Labor Relations Research Bull. No. 6, 1950).

[14] See generally ALLPORT, THE NATURE OF PREJUDICE ch. 29 (1954); SAENGER, THE SOCIAL PSYCHOLOGY OF PREJUDICE ch. 15 (1953).

[15] These views of Allport parallel remarkably those of the ancient Greeks, who viewed legislation as more than just a means of defining and securing rights. "Even the truly good," writes J. Walter Jones, in his study of Greek law, "though they did not need the laws, might find support for a life of virtue in them" (LAW AND LEGAL THEORY OF THE GREEKS 12 [1956]). Law also helped to teach virtue to the others. In the LAWS, Plato viewed law and education in a reciprocal relationship, in which law has an educative force, by means of which it rules, and is also a standard, to the obedience of which people should otherwise be educated.

its cause, which is not yet entirely clear, but is complex, and may vary from person to person. A perceptive English author, studying the color problem throughout the world has hypothesized:

Surely it is nearer the truth to think of the feeling as primarily one of fear, taking many different forms. There are fears of all kinds, some of them well-grounded in a thoughtful prognosis of what is likely to happen, others irrational because based on something which has not been faced. There is the vague and simple fear of something strange and unknown, there is the very intelligible fear of unemployment, and the fear of being outvoted by people whose way of life is quite different. There are fears for the future and memories of fear in the past, fears given an extra edge by the class conflict, by a sense of guilt, by sex and conscience, and by the fact that a hard line of separation has been drawn. Fear may also act as a catalytic agent, changing the nature of factors previously not actively malignant, such as the association in metaphor of the ideas of white and black with good and evil. And there is a great significance in numbers. Where the dominant are in the minority they are surely more frightened. . . . But it would be easy to push the question of numbers too far.[16]

Allport, too, tenders a number of explanations of prejudice, holding that no one alone is valid, but that multiple causation is at work. He discusses a "historical emphasis" which finds the roots of anti-Negro prejudice in slavery, carpetbagging, and Reconstruction; an economic explanation which argues that class differences (exploiter-exploited relationship) is the foundation; a sociocultural approach which stresses urban insecurity giving rise to snob appeal; a situational emphasis which simply postulates that "a child grows up surrounded by immediate influences and very soon reflects them all"; a psychodynamic hypothesis based on factors supposedly rooted in man's nature (instinctive combativeness; need to find scapegoats; character structure of individual persons); and an emphasis on earned reputation.[17]

It probably would be unrealistic to expect—assuming some validity for at least some of these explanations—that mere legal change can counteract all the diverse proprejudice forces at work in the race relations picture. Moreover, even where law desegregates schools or housing, for example, prejudice may very well be nourished from other sources, such as employment or public accommodations, where the law has not yet worked or where for lack of elasticity or responsiveness its rule has not been realized.

Armed forces desegregation provides a good example of the relationship between law, discrimination, prejudice, and social change.

---

[16] MASON, AN ESSAY ON RACIAL TENSION 80 (1954).
[17] ALLPORT, op. cit. supra note 14, ch. 17.

Here, legal control is theoretically as great as can be obtained in a democracy. The directives have been well observed; an integrated military establishment is a reality. Prejudice has diminished. But some prejudice and discrimination survive. Complaints continue to crop up, caused partly by the covert bias of some officers and enlisted men. While the services usually try to investigate and correct these situations, the proof problem alone hinders the completion of a perfect job. Probably, also, in many cases of injustice no complaints are made. Furthermore, integration in the armed forces alone can hardly be expected to dissolve the lifetime prejudices from diverse sources and of diverse natures of every serviceman who has them during short tours of duty, especially when so much of nonmilitary life is tainted by prejudice. But the limitation should not obscure the fact that the directives have changed relationships and attitudes in the armed forces. To the extent that law and other antidiscrimination influences operate in other areas (schools, housing, jobs) armed forces integration, both in act and in attitude, will become more complete.

Some have questioned, however, whether the application of law does not exacerbate prejudices and thereby do more harm than good to the cause of interracial amity. Herbert Wechsler, for example, has asked:

Who will be bold enough to say whether the judgment in the segregation cases will be judged fifty years from now to have advanced the cause of brotherhood or to have illustrated Bagehot's dictum that the "courage which strengthens an enemy, and which so loses, not only the present battle, but many after battles, is a heavy curse to men and nations." [18]

In making such an appraisal we must consider not only the places where existing prejudices have been aggravated but also those in which desegregation has proceeded smoothly—including large portions of the border area and some spots beyond it—where, if Allport's evaluation is correct, prejudices probably are on the wane. Moreover, we must throw into the balance the first real steps toward genuine separate-but-equal treatment that the Deep South has taken, taken only under the threat of desegregation, and the eventual meaning of this improvement for those of minority status. Since the question is one of alternatives, there must be weighed also what would have been the minority reaction to an adverse decision in the *School Cases*. Would

[18] Wechsler, *Reflections on the Conference*, 3 COLUMBIA LAW ALUMNI BULL. No. 2, p. 2 (1958); see also NATIONAL COMMUNITY RELATIONS ADVISORY COUNCIL, THE USES OF LAW FOR THE ADVANCEMENT OF COMMUNITY RELATIONS 23 (1955) (discussion of "boomerang" effects).

not the frustration engendered have found social expression, especially
in the border areas where greatest progress has been made, with results more harmful than those caused by segregationist outrage? These
considerations seem to indicate more a positive than a negative reply.
But probably more fundamental, a question which asks whether segregationists would be less outraged if Negroes did not press their demands
as insistently as they do is hypothetical in the extreme. For the pressure of the demand and the many outlets it finds—in the courts,
through boycotts, political action, even occasionally in demands for
violence—shows that Negroes will not be stilled despite the hostility
of the opposition.

READINESS

Often the question is asked whether a particular institution or community is "ready" for desegregation or for action to obtain it. "Readiness" may refer, of course, either to a moral or to a physical condition. Taken in the first sense, the views held of right and wrong usually
provide the conclusive answer. Those who believe in the rightness of
desegregation will not concede the morality of standing still; those who
adhere to the status quo will not admit the propriety of desegregation.
In the second sense, "readiness" refers to a proposition of fact, to
whether desegregation may be expected actually to occur and develop.
(An intermediate group might be those who morally approve action
to secure change when it seems certain that change will in fact ensue.)
Viewed in the second sense, the foregoing discussion may shed some
light on the question of whether a particular social arrangement is
"ready."

In any case, it is difficult, in the abstract, to say in precisely what circumstances a particular situation in a particular community is ready
for legal efforts seeking racial change. A rule of thumb might be:
When the Negro community or the government with the support of
that community decides to commence and sustain a legal effort for desegregation of an institution, it is ready. That institution in that area
would probably then capitulate in the not-too-distant future. A move
by the minority group is itself an index of readiness. The success of
the effort will, of course, be proportionate to the vigor and the pressure of other prointegration influences. But the demand and supporting action are per se evidence of Negro community organization,
awareness, and responsiveness. They probably indicate concomitant

Negro political activity and show that there are Negro lawyers, supported by Negro business and professional men, other leaders, and the minority community generally. This, in turn, is most likely a reflection of economic and social development of the larger community, which means that there will be at least some concurring whites. But the extent and thoroughness of racial change will also depend on such other elements as the general responsiveness of the Negro community to the available rights and the elasticity of the institution to be changed. Even these two factors, however, may be at least somewhat responsive to the law. Legal action can be an education for the entire community and an encouragement to exercise rights. And it is now generally acknowledged that government can stretch housing, schools, jobs, and other institutions to create more room for all.

CHAPTER II

A LEGAL OVERVIEW

A study of law and race relations could be designed in several different ways. There might be a historical presentation, or a geographical one. Perhaps more plausible than these would be an analysis of the relevant legal doctrines as they cut across social institutions—such doctrines as equal protection of the laws, those of the Federal Civil Rights Acts, the common law, state civil rights statutes, and so forth—which might be called a "horizontal" legal analysis. Still another approach could, by the same token, be called "vertical," that is, a division of the work according to the main categories of social activity in which civil rights problems arise—housing, earning a living, public accommodations, the armed forces, voting, and so on. The last is the angle of attack which actually has been adopted, and for two reasons in particular. (1) It is customary among lawyers who practice civil rights law, as well as among laymen who undertake a legal treatment of racial issues, to view law and race relations in this way; for what they face are "housing problems," "public accommodations cases," or other social situations, and what they must look for are all the rights and remedies applicable to these situations, whether derived from constitutional, statutory, administrative, or common law. (2) If we are trying not only to describe the rules but also their impact within the social matrix, a division by social institutions is more helpful in organizing the pertinent experience.

Nevertheless, this approach, like the others, has its shortcomings; there will be gaps and overlaps in it. An effort was made in chapter I to overcome one of the deficiencies by dealing comprehensively with the capacity of the law to affect race relations. Other insufficiencies may, of course, be surmounted by cross referencing and indexing. Some important features of the leading issues can, however, best be treated only through separate, "horizontal" discussion. These are the development and meaning of the equal protection and due process guaranties in race relations; the state action concept of the Fourteenth Amendment; and the chief methods of enforcement and means of delay which the law affords. The development and meaning of the equal protection–due process themes will be treated in the first section of this chapter, the other matters in the sections that follow. Thereafter we shall enter into the "vertical" analysis.

FROM SEPARATE-BUT-EQUAL
TO THE COLLAPSE OF PLESSY

By 1938 the situation was this: *Plessy v. Ferguson* (1896) [1] had entrenched in federal jurisprudence the concept of separate-but-equal. The Supreme Court in *Gong Lum v. Rice* (1927) [2] had indicated that that doctrine applied to education in holding that Mississippi could properly classify an Oriental girl with Negroes for purposes of assigning her to school. But in fact, in schooling as well as in other areas, while separation was observed, equality almost never was. In a number of other important sectors of race relations, however, separate-but-equal as a legal doctrine seemed to have no application. In jury discrimination cases no allowable substitute was proclaimed for selecting panels without regard to race. Moreover, *Strauder v. West Virginia* (1880),[3] while confined to the jury issue, contained some of that early egalitarian language which constituted the material out of which the 1954 *School Segregation Cases* doctrine was constructed:

The very fact that colored people are singled out and expressly denied by a statute all right to participate in the administration of the law, as jurors, because of their color, though they are citizens and may be in other respects fully qualified, is practically a brand upon them, affixed by the law; an assertion of their inferiority, and a stimulant to that race prejudice which is an impediment to securing to individuals of the race that equal justice which the law aims to secure to all others.[4]

So far as housing was concerned, racial zoning ordinances were outlawed in *Buchanan v. Warley* (1917) [5] as an unreasonable classifica-

---

[1] 163 U.S. 537 (1896). The ensuing section is hardly a complete exposition of due process–equal protection, but the discussion, it is hoped, describes generally the development of limitations on government against making racial classifications and what the state's power is in that regard today.
[2] 275 U.S. 78 (1927).   [3] 100 U.S. 303 (1880).
[4] *Id.* at 308.   [5] 245 U.S. 60 (1917).

tion and hence a denial of due process. A fundamental principle was declared in this case too, cited by the United States Supreme Court as recently as the Little Rock conflict: popular opposition or violence is no ground upon which the courts may deny constitutional rights. The Court said:

It is urged that this proposed segregation will promote the public peace by preventing race conflicts. Desirable as this is, and important as is the preservation of the public peace, this aim cannot be accomplished by laws or ordinances which deny rights created or protected by the Federal Constitution.[6]

State laws barring Negroes from primary elections were held unconstitutional in *Nixon v. Herndon* (1927),[7] as were such party executive rules authorized by statute in *Nixon v. Condon* (1932).[8] In the first *Nixon* case we find a statement of Justice Holmes which has remained basic:

States may do a good deal of classifying that it is difficult to believe rational, but there are limits, and it is too clear for extended argument that color cannot be made the basis of a statutory classification affecting the right set up in this case.[9]

Moreover, arbitrary discrimination against a class (class in the sense of owners of laundries in wooden buildings, to take an example) constituted of Chinese subjects had been condemned in *Yick Wo v. Hopkins* (1886) in this language:

Though the law itself be fair on its face and impartial in appearance, yet, if it is applied and administered by public authority with an evil eye and an unequal hand, so as practically to make unjust and illegal discriminations between persons in similar circumstances, material to their rights, the denial of equal justice is still within the prohibition of the Constitution.[10]

Yick Wo held unconstitutional the statute which permitted, or in the circumstances of that case, invited, a racially biased result.

Racial cases aside, from an early date the general test of classifications to determine whether they comply with the Fourteenth Amendment's equal protection clause is that they be reasonable, that is, based on real or substantial differences pertinent to valid legislative objec-

---

[6] *Id.* at 81. Quoted in Cooper v. Aaron, 358 U.S. 1, 16 (1958).
[7] 273 U.S. 536 (1927).   [8] 286 U.S. 73 (1932).   [9] 273 U.S. at 541.
[10] 118 U.S. 356, 373-374 (1886).

tives.[11] Due process has imposed a similar standard.[12] In each doctrine
the argument that racial classifications do not meet these criteria has
been latent.

Besides the separate-but-equal doctrine, another major legal bulwark
of segregation was the state action concept of the *Civil Rights Cases*
(1883),[13] the idea that the Fourteenth Amendment applies to governmental but not to private conduct. The jurisprudence of state action
is discussed more fully in the next section, but we should note here
that *Corrigan v. Buckley* (1926) [14] implied the validity of racial restrictive covenants on real property, presumably because although enforceable by court injunction they were "private" agreements. And
Grovey v. Townsend (1935) [15] upheld a Texas whites-only primary
because, allegedly, government was not sufficiently involved in the
exclusion, which had been adopted by the party convention without
express state sanction.

Since 1938, however, the constitutional antidiscrimination concepts
have proliferated until we now have the doctrine of the *School Cases,*
and there is no doubt that state-imposed racial discrimination is invalid. We shall trace briefly here the transition from the elementary
structure of *Strauder–Buchanan–Nixon–Yick Wo* to the edifice of the
School Segregation Cases. The development was not based entirely on
chance; there was a planned legal program. And although this is no
place to describe them in detail, the far-reaching social changes which
coincided with and created a climate conducive to new legal and social
relationships cannot be ignored.

About 1930 an effort was begun by the American Fund for Public
Service, established by Charles Garland, to foster, in conjunction with

---

[11] See Barbier v. Connolly, 113 U.S. 27, 31–32 (1885); Minneapolis & St. Louis
Ry. v. Beckwith, 129 U.S. 26, 29 (1889); Moore v. Missouri, 159 U.S. 673 (1895);
Quaker City Cab Co. v. Pennsylvania, 277 U.S. 389 (1928); Truax v. Raich, 239
U.S. 33 (1915); Skinner v. Oklahoma, 316 U.S. 535 (1942). For a general discus-
sion of equal protection classification see THE CONSTITUTION OF THE UNITED STATES
OF AMERICA 1141 *et seq.* (Corwin ed. 1953).

[12] See the following Fifth Amendment due process cases: Steward Machine Co.
v. Davis, 301 U.S. 548, 584–585 (1937); Currin v. Wallace, 306 U.S. 1, 14 (1939);
Sunshine Anthracite Coal Co. v. Adkins, 310 U.S. 381, 401 (1940); Detroit Bank
v. United States, 317 U.S. 329, 337–338 (1943). Nebbia v. New York, 291 U.S.
502, 525 (1933), sets forth the general Fourteenth Amendment due process test:
"that the law shall not be unreasonable, arbitrary or capricious, and that the means
selected shall have a real and substantial relation to the object sought to be
attained." A recent exposition by the Supreme Court appears in Williamson v.
Lee Optical of Okla., 348 U.S. 483 (1955); and see cases cited *id.* at 488.

[13] 109 U.S. 3 (1883).   [14] 271 U.S. 323 (1926).   [15] 295 U.S. 45 (1935).

the National Association for the Advancement of Colored People, doctrine favorable to civil rights.[16] Some of the cases discussed above were supported by the NAACP, but neither that organization nor any other had made a coherent effort to develop a well-articulated body of precedent in this field. By the early thirties, however, it had become apparent that a coordinated drive might achieve even greater success. The genesis of such an endeavor by the Garland Fund and the NAACP is summarized in the 1934 *Annual Report* of the association:

On November 5 the American Fund for Public Service forwarded to the N.A.A.C.P. check for $10,000, to be used exclusively for a campaign of legal action and public education against unequal apportionment of public funds for education and discrimination in public transportation. Expenditures in these efforts and direction of the campaign was vested in a joint committee representing the American Fund for Public Service and the N.A.A.C.P., composed of the following members: Morris L. Ernst, Lewis S. Gannett, James Weldon Johnson, James Marshall, Arthur B. Spingarn, Roger N. Baldwin.

It will be remembered from previous annual reports that the American Fund for Public Service, more generally known as the Garland Fund, had voted a much larger appropriation to the N.A.A.C.P. for a comprehensive campaign against the major disabilities from which Negroes suffer in American life—legal, political and economic. Shrinkage in the assets of the Garland Fund, due to the depression, resulted in drastic reduction of funds available. Mr. Nathan R. Margold, now Solicitor in the Department of the Interior, was retained and he made as a basis for his campaign a comprehensive study of the legal aspects and background of these various disabilities.

At a conference in New York City on October 26, 1934, between the joint committee and Mr. Charles H. Houston, Mr. Houston was retained to direct this campaign, serving on part-time in conjunction with his duties as vice-dean of the school of law of Howard University through June 30, 1935, and on full time commencing July 1.

Because of the importance of the matter and the wide extent of the problem, it has been agreed that the major emphasis shall be placed upon educational inequalities. It should be made clear that the campaign is a carefully planned one to secure decisions, rulings and public opinion on the broad principle instead of being devoted to merely miscellaneous cases.[17]

Before Margold was appointed the Garland Fund had had a memorandum prepared which proposed an initial attack on the civil rights

[16] The papers of the American Fund for Public Service are in the New York Public Library.
[17] 1934 NAACP ANNUAL REPORT 22.

issue.[18] He quoted the following portion of the memorandum in his study.

It is proposed that taxpayers' suits be brought to force *equal* if separate accommodations for Negroes as well as whites. The minimum cost of such taxpayers' suits, including attorney's fees, travelling expenses, printing of briefs and other legal documents, would average $2,000 per suit. It is suggested that seven (7) suits in the worst states, as follows, be instituted: South Carolina, Georgia, Mississippi, Louisiana, Florida, Alabama, Arkansas. . . .

Such taxpayers' suits, it is believed, will (*a*) make the cost of a dual school system so prohibitive as to speed the abolishment of segregated schools; (*b*) serve as examples and give courage to Negroes to bring similar actions; (*c*) cases will likely be appealed by city authorities, thus causing higher court decisions to cover wider territory; (*d*) focus as nothing else will public attention north and south upon the vicious discrimination in the apportionment of public schools funds so far as Negroes are concerned, in certain of these states.

Margold himself, however, would have preferred an all-out attack on segregation itself—based upon *Yick Wo*—which he believed would gain not only the improvements suggested by the memorandum, but probably more. His report urged:

It would be a great mistake to fritter away our limited funds on sporadic attempts to force the making of equal divisions of school funds in the few instances where such attempts might be expected to succeed. At the most, we could do no more than eliminate a very minor part of the discrimination during the year our suits are commenced. We should not be establishing any new principles, nor bringing any sort of pressure to bear which can reasonably be expected to retain the slightest force beyond that exerted by the specific judgment or order that we might obtain. And we should be leaving wholly untouched the very essence of the existing evils.

On the other hand if we boldly challenge the constitutional validity of segregation if and when accompanied irremediably by discrimination, we can strike directly at the most prolific sources of discrimination.

We can transform into an authoritative adjudication the principle of law, now only theoretically inferable from *Yick Wo v. Hopkins*, that segregation coupled with discrimination resulting from administrative action permitted but not required by state statute, is just as much a denial

[18] The quoted excerpts from the preliminary study and Margold's report are taken from that report, which is in the files of the NAACP Legal Defense and Educational Fund. Annual Reports of the NAACP during the period under discussion also contain references to the efforts to develop a legal strategy.

For related history see Vose, *NAACP Strategy in the Covenant Cases*, 1955 W. RES. L. REV. 101 (1955). Note, *Private-Attorneys-General-Group Action in the Fight for Civil Liberties*, 58 YALE L.J. 574 (1949); NAACP v. Patty, 159 F. Supp. 503, 507, 511 (E.D. Va. 1958).

of equal protection of the laws as is segregation coupled with discrimination required by express statutory enactment. And the threat of using the adjudication as a means of destroying segregation itself, would always exert a very real and powerful force at least to compel enormous improvement in the Negro schools through voluntary official action.

In fact, the aspect of elementary and high school education segregation which Margold proposed to assail was not approached seriously by participants in the campaign he helped to map out until about 1950. Under Charles H. Houston's guidance the actual casework was launched in the 1930s with suits against graduate and professional schools. The reasoning behind this tack appears to have been that inequality in higher education could be proved with ease. There were virtually no public Negro graduate and professional schools in the South, and judges would readily understand the shortcomings of separate legal education, which some of the cases concerned. Since it would be financially impossible to furnish true equality—both tangible and intangible—desegregation would be the only practicable way to fulfill the constitutional obligation of equal protection. Small numbers of mature students were involved, undercutting opposing arguments based on violence and widespread social revolution. Finally, Negro leadership would be augmented whether there was desegregation or enriched separate schools.

While schools were the primary interest in this undertaking, cases involving restrictive covenants, public accommodations, interstate travel, recreation, the rights of criminal defendants, voting, and other activities were also brought or defended as part of a coordinated effort to create civil rights precedents in the courts. Most of these legal actions were conducted under the aegis of Houston or his successor, Thurgood Marshall, who took charge of the NAACP's legal work in 1938. The Garland Fund contributions ultimately amounted to only $20,700, so the association alone almost wholly supported the court program until the incorporation in 1939 of the NAACP Legal Defense and Educational Fund, which still aids and directs litigation in the civil rights field. At least fifty-five cases decided by the United States Supreme Court in the race relations area have been suits presented by lawyers connected with the NAACP or the Legal Defense Fund. Among these [19] have been the leading decisions of *Lane v. Wilson*

---

[19] A list of cases presented to the United States Supreme Court by the NAACP and the NAACP Legal Defense and Educational Fund, including the cases enumerated in the text with their full citations, appears in appendix B.

(1939) and *Smith v. Allwright* (1944), involving voting; *Shelley v. Kraemer* (1948) and *Barrows v. Jackson* (1953), involving restrictive covenants; *Missouri ex rel. Gaines v. Canada* (1938), *Sweatt v. Painter* (1950), *McLaurin v. Oklahoma State Regents* (1950), and *Brown v. Board of Education* (1954 and 1955) (the last comprising the *School Segregation Cases*, four suits decided under this single title), all involving education; *Morgan v. Commonwealth of Virginia* (1946) and *Gayle v. Browder* (1956), involving interstate and intrastate travel, respectively; *Mayor and City Council of Baltimore v. Dawson* (1955), involving recreation; *Chambers v. Florida* (1940) and *Fikes v. Alabama* (1957), involving coerced confessions; *Shepherd v. Florida* (1951) and *Hill v. Texas* (1942), involving discrimination in the selection of jurors; and *NAACP v. Alabama* (1958), involving the right to associate freely to promote civil rights.

There were also numerous other suits supported by the association and the Legal Defense Fund in various lower courts,[20] and other groups aided in similar suits.[21] Moreover, a large number of *amicus curiae* briefs were filed by other sympathetic associations.[22] Of even greater significance were the *amicus* briefs and arguments of the United States Department of Justice in support of the Negro plaintiffs in a number of the cases cited above, including the *School Segregation Cases*. In addition, some significant civil rights decisions were achieved which had not been organizationally underwritten. All of these court actions

[20] For cases in the Fourth Circuit see NAACP v. Patty, *supra* note 18, at 528 n. 10.

[21] Henderson v. United States, 339 U.S. 816 (1950), was financed by the Alpha Phi Alpha fraternity.

[22] The following organizations filed *amicus* briefs in discrimination cases before the Supreme Court from 1938 up to and including the *School Cases:* American Association for the United Nations, American Civil Liberties Union, American Federation of Labor, American Federation of Teachers, American Indian Citizens League of California, American Jewish Committee, American Jewish Congress, American Unitarian Association, American Veterans Committee, Civil Liberties Department of Grand Lodge of Elks I.B.P.O.E.W., Civil Rights Defense Union of Northern California, Congress of Industrial Organizations, Executive Committee of General Council of Congregational Christian Churches of the United States, Human Rights Commission of Protestant Council of the City of New York, Japanese-American Citizens League, National Bar Association, National Lawyers Guild, Non-Sectarian Anti-Nazi League To Champion Human Rights, Workers Defense League.

In 1949 Rule 42 of REV. R. U.S. SUP. CT. sharply curtailed the number of *amicus* briefs by requiring consent of both sides or the Court's permission before they may be filed.

are discussed in subsequent chapters according to the subject matter they represent.

It would be highly misleading to imply that all of the suits which were part of what might be called the NAACP program were planned with precision. How and when plaintiffs sought relief and the often unpredictable course of litigation were frequently as influential as any blueprint in determining the sequence of cases, the precise issues they posed, and their outcome. But we cannot elaborate on this here, for it would take perhaps a volume the size of this one to tell the whole story of the litigation program.

Actually, as it turned out, the greatest significance of the Margold and related studies preceding the lawsuits, which were to a large extent conducted pragmatically, was that their scholarly, thorough, and thoughtful approach underscored the need for a program which would employ the highest skills, build precedent, and treat each case in a context of jurisprudential development, not as an isolated private lawsuit. This was combined with a realistic view of how great a next step the courts could be expected to take, the lawyers being always mindful that courts may be persuaded to move ahead or to hesitate not only by the letter of the law but by awareness of social factors often unmentioned in opinions.

Perhaps the keynotes of the civil rights jurisprudence of 1938–1954 and indeed of today were sounded by the language of two cases involving the rights of Japanese-Americans. *Hirabayashi v. United States* (1943), while upholding a curfew on Americans of Japanese descent on grounds of urgent military need, stated:

Distinctions between citizens solely because of their ancestry are by their very nature odious to a free people whose institutions are founded upon the doctrine of equality.[23]

Korematsu v. United States (1944), which validated transfers of members of this same group to wartime relocation camps, asserted that

all legal restrictions which curtail the civil rights of a single racial group are immediately suspect. That is not to say that all such restrictions are unconstitutional. It is to say that courts must subject them to the most rigid scrutiny. Pressing public necessity may sometimes justify the existence of such restrictions; racial antagonism never can.[24]

[23] 320 U.S. 81, 100 (1943).   [24] 323 U.S. 214, 216 (1944).

Such a critical scrutiny of racially restrictive laws was quite unlike the normal presumption of constitutionality afforded general economic regulation.

The legal citadels of racial discrimination were undermined from many angles under this view. *Missouri ex rel. Gaines v. Canada* (1938) [25] rejected an out-of-state law school (there was no Negro law school in Missouri) as a substitute for legal education at the white state university. Under those circumstances desegregation might have been the only answer, but the plaintiff disappeared and no one pressed for that resolution of the case. Subsequently the state erected a colored law school. But meanwhile a reaffirmation of the *Gaines* opinion in *Sipuel v. Oklahoma State Regents* (1948) [26] required that a Negro student be afforded immediate equality in legal training without waiting for a law school to be built. Then in 1950 the separate-but-equal equation in education was reconstituted in *Sweatt v. Painter* [27] and *McLaurin v. Oklahoma State Regents* [28] to mean that instead of separate-but-substantially-equal (which is the most it had ever really meant) there must be a careful balance of *all* aspects of education, including such intangibles as reputation of faculty, experience of administration, position and influence of alumni, standing in the community, traditions, prestige, and opportunity to engage in exchange of views and contacts with members of the dominant white group, an appraisal which would make segregation of any state school impossible. Moreover, in *McLaurin* it was held that once a Negro has been admitted to a white school he may not be segregated, for this impairs and inhibits his ability to study, to engage in discussions and exchange views with other students, and, in general to learn his profession. In that situation at least, segregation per se was proclaimed unconstitutional. McLaurin was studying education and reference in the opinion to his calling was also suggestive about the future of lower school education:

Those who will come under his guidance and influence must be directly affected by the education he receives. Their own education and development will necessarily suffer to the extent that his training is unequal to that of his classmates. State-imposed restrictions which produce such inequalities cannot be sustained.[29]

[25] 305 U.S. 337 (1938).   [26] 332 U.S. 631 (1948).   [27] 339 U.S. 629 (1950).
[28] 339 U.S. 637 (1950).   [29] *Id.* at 641.

This invited argument that segregation of the pupils themselves "produce[s] such inequalities."

Lack of sympathy with segregation was expressed in another way in a series of cases involving the Constitution's commerce clause and the Interstate Commerce Act. Under the former, state travel segregation laws were outlawed because enforcement of the different racial rules of each state in the course of an interstate journey was deemed to be an undue burden on interstate carriers (*Morgan v. Virginia*, 1946).[30] Yet a Michigan antidiscrimination law which had been enforced against discrimination on a carrier to Canada was upheld (*Bob-Lo Excursion Co. v. Michigan*, 1948),[31] even though it too was inharmonious with the laws of some other states. In a suit raising similar commerce clause issues, *Railway Mail Association v. Corsi* (1945), Mr. Justice Frankfurter spoke of antidiscrimination laws as statutes which seek to achieve "cherished aims of American feeling." [32]

Under the Interstate Commerce Act, whose equality provisions require treatment like that secured by the Constitution's equal protection clause, it was held that Negroes might not be denied seats in Pullman or dining cars.[33] The roads had pleaded that it would be financially ruinous to furnish separate-but-equal space; but the fact that the racial class might not supply enough traffic to warrant identical segregated equipment was held insufficient reason to deny any single Negro the accommodations he could buy if he were white. In one of the Commerce Act cases, *Henderson v. United States* (1950), Mr. Justice Burton expressed an antipathy for segregation that apparently covered more than travel. He criticized "the curtains, partitions and signs [which] emphasize the artificiality of a difference in treatment which serves only to call attention to a racial classification of passengers." [34]

On another front, earlier views of state action were liberalized to include activities claimed to be private.[35] *Grovey v. Townsend* [36] was overruled by *Smith v. Allwright* (1944) [37] and the Texas Democratic party convention's White Primary rule held to be an integral part of governmental elections—hence invalid. Restrictive covenants were

---

[30] 328 U.S. 373 (1946).   [31] 333 U.S. 28 (1948).   [32] 326 U.S. 88, 98 (1945).
[33] Mitchell v. United States, 313 U.S. 80 (1941); Henderson v. United States, 339 U.S. 816 (1950).
[34] 339 U.S. at 825.
[35] A fuller discussion of this development appears at pp. 46–61 *infra*.
[36] *Supra* note 15.   [37] 321 U.S. 649 (1944).

held unenforceable in *Shelley v. Kraemer* (1948),[38] despite the earlier contrary precedent, *Corrigan v. Buckley*.[39] Discrimination by federally certified railroad labor unions was held invalid under the Railway Labor Act in *Steele v. Louisville & Nashville R.R. Co.* (1944) [40] in the light of the court's suggestion, which reflected the traditional course of avoiding constitutional decision where possible, that were it to rule otherwise on the statutory question there would be a constitutional issue of whether the union's deeds were state action.

In a variety of cases, some of which were mentioned above, the Supreme Court displayed a keenness to ferret out "sophisticated as well as simple-minded modes of discrimination," while in another generation it might have looked the other way. The quotation is from *Lane v. Wilson* (1939) [41] which invalidated a variant of the electoral grandfather clause that permitted registration during a twelve-day period *only* of Negroes otherwise excluded by that clause. In other voting suits the federal judiciary struck down tactics designed to keep Negroes from voting, which under the guise of rules allegedly free from racial bias, were in truth devices to discriminate.[42] In jury discrimination cases it was also asserted that the courts must be vigilant to discern bias.[43]

In *Barrows v. Jackson* (1953) [44] a white restrictive covenantor was sued for damages because he sold to a Negro. Although an award of damages would not have disturbed the Negro's possession, which plaintiff argued was the only right that the *Restrictive Covenant Cases* [45] purported to secure, the Court permitted the white man to assert as his own the defense which the Negro could have used if the action had been one to oust him—a not unprecedented but an unusual kind of transference, indicating the disfavor with which the Court viewed racial discrimination.

Indeed, by the time of the *School Segregation Cases* counsel for the Negro school children could appropriately assert in their brief that:

[38] 334 U.S. 1 (1948).   [39] *Supra* note 14.   [40] 323 U.S. 192 (1944).
[41] 307 U.S. 268, 275 (1939).
[42] See pp. 143–145 *infra* and especially Terry v. Adams, 345 U.S. 461 (1953) ("private" preprimary election held part of electoral process), and Davis v. Schnell, 81 F. Supp. 872 (S.D. Ala. 1949), *aff'd*, 336 U.S. 933 (1939) (requirement that voters "understand and explain" any article of Constitution).
[43] See pp. 323–328 *infra* and particularly Avery v. Georgia, 345 U.S. 559 (1953) (names of Negroes in jury box on yellow tickets, names of whites on white tickets; although no evidence of discrimination in selecting jurors, conviction reversed).
[44] 346 U.S. 249 (1953).   [45] Shelley v. Kraemer, *supra* note 38.

Every member of the present Court has from time to time subscribed to this view of race as an irrational premise for government action.[46]

Given this clear, steady, strong development, of which the above cases are merely the high points, the outcome of the *School Cases* could hardly have been astonishing.[47] The opinions in these cases treat segregation under the equal protection and the due process clauses as follows. Of equal protection:

In the field of public education the doctrine of "separate but equal" has no place. Separate educational facilities are inherently unequal.[48]

Of due process:

Liberty under law extends to the full range of conduct which the individual is free to pursue, and it cannot be restricted except for a proper governmental objective. Segregation in public education is not reasonably related to any proper governmental objective, and thus it imposes on Negro children of the District of Columbia a burden that constitutes an arbitrary deprivation of their liberty in violation of the Due Process Clause.[49]

Despite their solid foundation in the law, however, there have been assertions that the *School Segregation* decisions were based on the testimony and writings of social scientists and were not legal decisions in the regular sense of that term. This argument has been made because the Supreme Court held:

To separate [Negro children] from others of similar age and qualifications solely because of their race generates a feeling of inferiority as to their status in the community that may affect their hearts and minds in a way unlikely ever to be undone.[50]

It cited findings to the same effect of the Kansas and Delaware courts, which tried two of the *School* suits, and in a footnote enumerated a number of social scientific writings dealing with segregation. Social scientists did testify in the cases concerning segregation's harm, and social scientific writings were cited and discussed in the briefs. The

---

[44] Brief for Appellants in Nos. 1, 2, and 4 and for Respondents in No. 10 on Reargument, in U.S. Sup. Ct., Oct. 1953 Term, p. 23. The brief cited, in addition to cases discussed above, Mr. Justice Jackson in Edwards v. California, 314 U.S. 160, 180, 185 (1941) (race described as "constitutionally an irrelevance"), and Mr. Justice Douglas dissenting in South v. Peters, 339 U.S. 276, 278 (1950) (discriminations based upon race, creed, or color are "beyond the pale").

[47] See Leflar, *"Law of the Land,"* in WITH ALL DELIBERATE SPEED 1 (Shoemaker ed. 1957).

[48] 347 U.S. 483, 495 (1954).   [49] 347 U.S. 497, 499–500 (1954).

[50] 347 U.S. at 494.

question is, though, what role these presentations played in the final result.

The use of social science evidence in litigation is now, although not commonplace, well established.[51] Yet the review of the course of decision at least since the *Gaines* case should make clear that the *School* decisions were based on a firm footing of legal precedent, and not on this single aspect of the record. Social, economic, and moral pressures also contributed to the result.

The finding in the Court's opinion that segregation causes psychological harm to Negro pupils was not a finding of fact in the traditional sense, as that a traffic light was red at the scene of an accident or that a signature was appended to a document. The finding was what may be called a "legislative" one, such as courts always must make in assessing general social or economic conditions as a basis of constitutional or common law decision. This appraisal of what the Court did is fortified by the fact that the District of Columbia school case, decided along with the others, struck down segregation in the District with no testimony at all in its record because the suit was decided on the legal pleadings alone.

If the findings of psychological harm had been of the traditional fact-finding sort, it would conceivably be possible in some future school segregation suit to present evidence that some particular child was not being psychologically affected by segregation, and thereby to uphold segregation as to him. But this obviously is impossible. The Court, in the decision providing for implementation of its May 17 ruling, has held that "all provisions of federal, state, or local law requiring or permitting such discrimination must yield to this [the *School Cases*'] principle." [52] In *Cooper v. Aaron*, the Little Rock case, the Court held, without once mentioning psychological harm, that "the right of a student not to be segregated on racial grounds . . . is indeed so fundamental and pervasive that it is embraced in the concept of due process of law." [53]

---

[51] On the social scientists' testimony in the *School Cases* and social science evidence generally, see Greenberg, *Social Scientists Take the Stand—A Review and Appraisal of Their Testimony in Litigation*, 54 MICH. L. REV. 953 (1956); for a view of the social science testimony in these cases, and issues raised by the participation of social scientists in litigation generally, which favors "receptivity seasoned with critical judgment," see Cahn, *Jurisprudence*, in 1954 ANNUAL SURVEY OF AMERICAN LAW, 30 N.Y.U.L. REV. 150 (1955); Cahn, *Jurisprudence*, in 1955 ANNUAL SURVEY OF AMERICAN LAW, 31 N.Y.U.L. REV. 182 (1956).

[52] 349 U.S. 294, 298 (1955).   [53] 358 U.S. 1, 19 (1958).

But although it is clear that the legal result did not flow directly from social science, it must be recognized that the research of social scientists of recent decades has helped to create the general recognition of segregation's harm and the sense of injustice concerning its application. The testimony in the cases, summarizing, emphasizing, and particularizing this general knowledge in terms of the plaintiffs and schools involved, illuminated this aspect of the issues, and may have been informative for one or more of the justices, whose interests had not led them earlier to such information. Actual presentation of testimony, subject to cross examination and rebuttal, put it before the judges in a particularly trustworthy manner; it was fortified by the fact that the defendants' experts did not seriously challenge the validity of the conclusions of the plaintiffs' experts.

"How to inform the judicial mind, as you know, is one of the most complicated problems," [54] said Mr. Justice Frankfurter from the bench during argument of the *School* suits. The social science materials provided some of the information needed to make the decision, though the Court, or some of its members, may have already known these things. It would have been unfortunate, however, if, as some state, the decision had been a "social scientific" one in the sense that it rested solely or chiefly on the expert witnesses' testimony in those suits or on adoption of the tenets of a particular school of sociology or social psychology. For, as Edmond Cahn has pointed out, "Recognizing as we do how sagacious Mr. Justice Holmes was to insist that the Constitution be not tied to the wheels of any economic system whatsoever, we ought to keep it similarly uncommitted in relation to the other social sciences." [55] The *School Segregation Cases* did not effect such a commitment, though social science in general over the years, and more narrowly the social scientists in the particular suits, were among the numerous factors contributing to the final outcome.

Plessy v. Ferguson could not have any vitality left after the *School* decisions, notwithstanding the legalistic argument later made that *Plessy* was an intrastate travel case and these were school cases in which *Plessy's* applicability was disavowed by the Court—although the rationale of *Plessy* was clearly condemned by the *School* opinions. In fact, not long thereafter, in the intrastate bus case growing out of the

[54] Transcript of Argument, Briggs v. Elliott, No. 102, in U.S. Sup. Ct., Oct. 1952 Term, p. 59. The Justice added: "It is better to have witnesses but I did not know that we could not read the works of competent writers." *Ibid.*

[55] Cahn, *Jurisprudence,* 30 N.Y.U.L. REV. 150, at 166 (1955).

situation which gave rise to the Montgomery bus boycott,[56] a federal district court ruled that *Plessy* was no longer valid and the Supreme Court affirmed this judgment without opinion. Barring some abberations, unimportant to note here, the invalidity of state-imposed discrimination now has been proclaimed wherever it has been called into question—in public recreation, public housing, voting, transportation, the administration of criminal justice, employment, and other areas. Some of these decisions, of course, antedate the *School* decision.

The big contemporary questions are of a different sort. They include: What is state action? How are the rights upheld to be implemented? Inevitably more time is being consumed with proof and procedure, as evaders, unable to win on the merits, try to prevail on the proof or by tactics of litigation. And, most consequential, the legislatures, federal, state, and municipal, are growing in importance as forums for fashioning new rights and new means of implementing those already established.

STATE ACTION

The Fourteenth Amendment (and the Fifth and Fifteenth too) restrains government, not individuals or private entities. But even at the beginning, Justice Bradley, who in the *Civil Rights Cases* of 1883 was a principal spokesman for confining the application of the amendment, did not insist that the only forbidden acts were affirmative, official ones by state officers; rather, he used the term "sanctioned in some way by the state." [57] Taken literally, this phrase could reach almost every "private" act, but, of course, it has not. In the *Civil Rights Cases* themselves the United States was held powerless to prosecute proprietors of public accommodations who excluded Negroes, even though this exercise of private property rights was in fact (although not in Bradley's eyes) "sanctioned in some way by the state." Without state recognition of their proprietorship the owners could not have properly commanded the premises.[58]

[56] Browder v. Gayle, 142 F. Supp. 707 (M.D. Ala. 1956), *aff'd*, 352 U.S. 903 (1956) ("we think that Plessy v. Ferguson has been impliedly, though not explicitly, overruled," 142 F. Supp. at 717).
[57] 109 U.S. 3, 17 (1883).
[58] Karl Renner observed long ago that relationships created by private law can have just as widespread social effect as those established by what is called public law, THE INSTITUTIONS OF PRIVATE LAW AND THEIR SOCIAL FUNCTIONS (1949 ed.); and this concept underlies BERLE & MEANS, THE MODERN CORPORATION AND

The limitation to some sort of governmental deed often has provoked the issue of whether an act is governmental or private, and as antidiscrimination pressures and state participation in all sorts of affairs mount, the problem comes to court ever more frequently. Some try to show that allegedly private actions really are in a constitutional sense the doing of government; others assert that enterprises like schools or parks turned "private" to evade antisegregation rulings are no longer closely enough state-connected to come under constitutional control; this may be said to pose the question of whether sometimes state nonaction comes under the amendment.

Interestingly, other federal systems have faced the same questions, although not as often and not in as acute form. A leading text on comparative federalism states that

in general, bills of rights have been conceived as protecting freedom against government and not against other individuals or groups within the society. . . . Nevertheless some . . . attempts have been made to include in formal statements of rights certain proscriptions against private action.

And it adds:

It would seem to be especially important that a federal system, embodying as it does divergent groups, make clear provision for federal authority to ensure protection of the individual against private action.[59]

Article 19 of the constitution of India (the so-called "seven freedoms") provides that "all citizens shall have the right" to freedom of speech, assembly, association, and so forth. Article 31(1) states that "no person shall be deprived of his property save by authority of law." An authoritative commentator on the Indian constitution, after citing the *Civil Rights Cases*, writes that

in the same strain . . . our Supreme Court held that the rights guaranteed by Articles 19(1) and 31(1) of our [Indian] Constitution are available only against state action. Violation of such rights by individuals is not within the purview of these articles.[60]

PRIVATE PROPERTY (1932); and see note 66 *infra*. *Cf.* Justice Jackson's discussion of public law and private law in Garner v. Teamsters C. & H. Union, 346 U.S. 485, 492–501 (1953).

[59] STUDIES IN FEDERALISM 601 (Bowie & Friedrich eds. 1954) (a comparative study of federalism in Australia, Canada, West Germany, Switzerland, and the United States). See also Holcombe, *The Coercion of States in a Federal System* 137, 150, in FEDERALISM MATURE AND EMERGENT (MacMahon ed. 1955).

[60] 1 BASU, COMMENTARY ON THE CONSTITUTION OF INDIA 70 (3d ed. 1955). See Shamdasani v. Central Bank of India, Ltd., [1952] 39 All India Rep. 59 (Sup. Ct.); University of Madras v. Shantha Bai, [1954] 41 All India Rep. 67 (Madras)

But the experience of other federal systems sheds little light on the problem; it only underscores its universality.

While it is too early in terms of constitutional development to state definitively the full extent of the "state action" concept under the Fourteenth Amendment, it may be helpful to chart the major tendencies and clusters of authority. The cases have been catalogued in enough places [61] to preclude another full treatment here, but they will receive some general discussion in this section, as well as presentation with regard to particular activities elsewhere in this volume.[62] First, however, it seems more important to treat of general ideas.

The Fourteenth Amendment has been concerned with preventing the *state* from interfering with *private* liberty; in this the amendment seeks the same ideal as did the early political philosophy of the English liberals (from Bentham through James and John Stuart Mill and T. H. Green), and has developed in somewhat parallel fashion. English liberals at first held that the highest degree of liberty would be achieved if government kept hands completely off individual conduct. Later— John Mill personally underwent the transition in belief—they concluded that restricting the state alone was not enough and that in some situations government should restrict private action in the interest of greater freedom. Ultimately, T. H. Green virtually equated state inaction with intervention, holding that in a given case government's failure to limit private freedom to some extent could mean subjecting others to the constraint of powerful private forces which might stifle liberty as effectively as might government.[63] The state

(restriction on admission of women held reasonable; state-aided university as distinguished from a state-maintained university not a "state"; reviews most of the American cases.)

[61] See HALE, FREEDOM THROUGH LAW 366–382 (1952); HART & WECHSLER, THE FEDERAL COURTS AND THE FEDERAL SYSTEM 810 *et seq.* (1953); *State Action: A Study of Requirements Under the Fourteenth Amendment*, 1 R.R.L.R. 613 (1956), and bibliography therein; MILLER, RACIAL DISCRIMINATION AND PRIVATE EDUCATION ch. IV (1957); Comment, *The Impact of* Shelley v. Kraemer, *on the State Action Concept*, 44 CALIF. L. REV. 718 (1956); Horowitz, *The Misleading Search for "State Action" Under the Fourteenth Amendment*, 30 So. CAL. L. REV. 208 (1957). Note, *The Disintegration of a Concept—State Action Under the Fourteenth and Fifteenth Amendments*, 96 U. PA. L. REV. 402 (1948); Watt & Orlikoff, *The Coming Vindication of Mr. Justice Harlan*, 44 ILL. L. REV. 13 (1949).

[62] The state action question is treated as it relates to specific activities in the following pages: 85–100 (public accommodations); 129–130 (interstate travel); 143–145 (elections); 183–184 (earning a living); 240–243, 267–269 (education); 279–304 (housing and real property); 316–323 (criminal law).

[63] On English liberalism see generally Ruggiero, *Liberalism*, in 9 ENCYC. SOC. SCI. 435 (1933); SABINE, A HISTORY OF POLITICAL THEORY chs. 31, 32 (1950);

action concept of the Fourteenth and other state action amendments has been undergoing a similar evolution. Judicial decision has been bringing an increasing number of nominally private acts under their regulation. As the later liberals saw that political control of private conduct often is essential to freedom, so courts today have found that what some call "private" should really be construed as public and answerable to the constitution. Of course, the jurisprudential evolution is part of a much broader political and social development in which government, for the purpose of achieving greater welfare for all, has participated more fully in a host of activities once considered the exclusive domain of private persons.

It is obvious that what may be called "law" or "state action" in some instances may not be so characterized in others. John Chipman Gray [64] has observed that we might

call the by-laws of a corporation the statutes of the State, because the State, if it saw fit, could prevent their being passed by the stockholders, and because it will open its courts to enforce the observance of them by the members of the corporation.

But this he rejects, for if it were true

we should have to call every general rule issued by a person whom the State permits to issue it, and which it will regard in its courts, a statute of the State.

In this case the following conclusion, which Gray regards as absurd, would result:

A master has a right to tell a servant to bring him the mustard. Should she refuse, he has a right to dismiss her, and the State will protect him in this right; and, therefore, on the theory we are considering, the order to bring the mustard is a command of the State. Even Austin, I think would shrink from such a conclusion.[65]

Gray was not trying to chart the scope of the Fourteenth Amendment, and therefore did not make a distinction between law considered in terms of defining the amendment's ambit and law in general. When we have the amendment in mind, however, there may well be a differ-

---

GREEN, LECTURES ON THE PRINCIPLES OF POLITICAL OBLIGATION (1941 ed.), esp. ch. M ("The Right of the State To Promote Morality"); JOHN S. MILL, AUTO-BIOGRAPHY (Harvard Classics ed. 1909), esp. 148 *et seq.*, in which Mill discusses evolution of his views.

[64] THE NATURE AND SOURCES OF THE LAW 156 (2d ed. 1927).

[65] *Id.* at 156, 157.

ence between an order to bring the mustard and, for example, the by-laws of a corporation. Indeed, A. A. Berle, one of a number of legal thinkers who has questioned a strict definition of state action for constitutional purposes, feels that all is not well with a formalistic, fixed interpretation when it comes to important corporate enterprises.

We are now, in fact, beginning to converge on a doctrine which may well push right over the line when the next case comes up. This doctrine is that where a corporation has power to affect a great many lives (differing from the little enterprise which can be balanced out by the market) it should be subject to the same restraints under the Constitution that apply to an agency of the Federal or state government. In that case, the Bill of Rights and the Fourteenth and Fifteenth Amendments would apply. At the moment this is one jump ahead of current law. Yet it seems probable that this will be the next phase—just as we already have the constitutional doctrine that under the Fifth or Fourteenth Amendment you may not by private contract prohibit a Negro from buying land.[66]

We may recall, too, that the first Justice Harlan, in the *Civil Rights Cases*, questioned the majority's classification, which held that certain private businesses of public importance were nonstate for purposes of the amendment. He would have included business entities smaller than those contemplated by Berle:

In every material sense applicable to the practical enforcement of the Fourteenth Amendment, railroad corporations, keepers of inns, and managers of places of public amusement are agents or instrumentalities of the State, because they are charged with duties to the public, and are amenable, in respect of their duties and functions, to governmental regulation.[67]

For Elias Clark state action is involved in the creation and administration of private trusts, and he would look at the whole picture

---

[66] ECONOMIC POWER AND THE FREE SOCIETY 17–18 (Fund for The Republic pamphlet, 1957). In *The Changing Role of the Corporation and its Counsel*, 10 THE RECORD 266, 275 (1955), Berle writes: "I do not know of any statute which forbids a great oil company from announcing as a policy that gasoline shall not be sold to Negroes at the gas stations it controls—though the control is more often by contract than by direct ownership. Yet I surmise that any sane house counsel would tell any board of directors ill-advised enough to attempt such a policy that they could not make it go down. If, at long last, the Supreme Court did not apply the rule of *Shelley v. Kraemer*, then it would find some other rule."
See also Friedmann, *Corporate Power, Government by Private Groups, and the Law*, 57 COLUM. L. REV. 155, 176 (1957) ("the corporate organizations of business and labor have long ceased to be private phenomena"). See *id.* at 177 ("'government' or 'law-making' by private groups is today an irreversible fact"); Howe, *Political Theory and the Nature of Liberty* (Foreword), 67 HARV. L. REV. 91 (1953).
[67] 109 U.S. at 58.

rather than dispose of the issue on the basis of formal categories.[68] He is uncertain about the bounds of state action in trust cases, believing, for example, that notwithstanding extensive, indispensable state contacts, trusts to help minorities, like scholarships for Negroes, should not be felled by an arbitrary rule which flatly holds that private trusts are "state" and incapable of favoring a race.

Arthur S. Miller, considering whether genuinely private schools (not those set up to evade desegregation) come within the scope of the Fourteenth Amendment, acknowledges their contacts with the state but then turns to what he views as policy considerations: many of the virtues of private education inhere in lack of all but tenuous state control; to extend the state action concept to private schools would "open" a legal "Pandora's box." [69]

Whether one agrees or disagrees with these writers with respect to private trusts, private schools, or private corporations, discussion obviously is now removed from the question of whether there is state action to what kind of state action, how much, in connection with what, and what difference it makes for society. We may note, however, that a decision articulating and concatenating such considerations would not necessarily "open a Pandora's box;" rather, it would, probably, invite careful consideration and perhaps difficult balancing.

There has, in fact, been no contemporary cut-off of the doctrine's growth potential. In the area of race relations at least, the Supreme Court in the cases it has reviewed has not found in any recent Fourteenth Amendment case that there was *no* state action.

What has been held state action by the cases so far is generalized in *American Communications Association v. Douds* (1950), in which Chief Justice Vinson wrote: "when authority derives in part from Government's thumb on the scales, the exercise of that power by private persons becomes closely akin, in some respects, to its exercise by Government itself." [70] Vinson did not conclude in this case that unions were government agencies, but his metaphor is a key to understanding the state-private issue. In those ambiguous cases where action is neither clearly all "private" nor all "state" the decisions generally seem to reflect how heavily the "governmental thumb" has weighed.

Marsh v. Alabama (1946) [71] perhaps most clearly recognizes the

[68] *Charitable Trusts, the Fourteenth Amendment, and the Will of Stephen Girard*, 66 YALE L.J. 979 (1957).
[69] MILLER, RACIAL DISCRIMINATION AND PRIVATE EDUCATION 95 (1957).
[70] 339 U.S. 382, 401 (1950).   [71] 326 U.S. 501 (1946).

thumb of government in nominally private affairs. It held that the Fourteenth Amendment controlled a company town (Chickasaw, Alabama) whose private ownership right to bar unwelcome Jehovah's Witnesses as trespassers was vindicated by state criminal prosecution. The Witnesses' freedom of press and religion was upheld against this "state action." Qualitatively, as a matter of state "private" property law, the company's property right was like that of any private owner. Quantitatively, that right was greater—so great that its constitutional nature was changed. Although one lower court has rejected the claim that the *Marsh* rule governs Levittown, Pennsylvania, which has refused to sell homes to Negroes [72] and which in its single ownership (at its inception) and size was like Chickasaw, *Marsh* could warrant rulings that large areas (measured geographically and perhaps otherwise) under the control of a single owner (or perhaps a few) are juridically like the town in *Marsh*. If so, might not the size of the area progressively diminish in subsequent suits? How far? Perhaps the uncertainty over the extent of its reach is what has caused sparing application of that precedent.

At any rate, other cases have been based upon a more substantial government-private nexus. State-required discrimination imposed by public officials has, of course, presented no question (*e.g.*, the *School Cases*).[73] A proposed limitation of this category of state action to the performance of governmental functions has been rejected,[74] as has been one excluding action in a "fiduciary" capacity.[75] Governmental ad-

---

[72] Johnson v. Levitt & Sons, 131 F. Supp. 114, 117 (E.D. Pa. 1955) ("too far-fetched to require discussion").

[73] The state may speak through its legislature, *e.g.*, Brown v. Board of Educ., 347 U.S. 483 (1954); executive, *e.g.*, Sterling v. Constantin, 287 U.S. 378 (1932); judiciary, *e.g.*, Shelley v. Kraemer, 334 U.S. 1 (1948); administrative officers, *e.g.*, Lonesome v. Maxwell, 220 F.2d 386 (4th Cir. 1955), *aff'd per curiam sub nom.* Mayor, etc., of Baltimore v. Dawson, 350 U.S. 877 (1955); municipalities, *e.g.*, Buchanan v. Warley, 245 U.S. 60 (1917); see generally 1 R.R.L.R. 613 *supra* note 61. There is state action even when state officers violate state law. Screws v. United States, 325 U.S. 91 (1945); Williams v. United States, 341 U.S. 97 (1951) (private detective with quasi-police position acts under color of law); see Valle v. Stengel, 176 F.2d 697 (3d Cir. 1949) (exclusion of Negroes from private swimming pool with aid of police chief); *but compare* Barney v. New York, 193 U.S. 430 (1904), *with* Home Tel. & Tel. Co. v. City of Los Angeles, 227 U.S. 278, 294 (1913); see HART & WECHSLER, *op. cit. supra* note 61, at 832, 833. Private persons who conspire or act with state officers are within the concept (see p. 320 *infra*). Sometimes state inaction may be included within the concept, Catlette v. United States, 132 F.2d 902 (4th Cir. 1943); Lynch v. United States, 189 F.2d 476 (5th Cir. 1951). See Truax v. Corrigan, 257 U.S. 312 (1921).

[74] City of St. Petersburg v. Alsup, 238 F.2d 830 (5th Cir. 1956), *cert. denied*, 353 U.S. 922 (1957); see also cases cited pp. 94-95 *infra*.

[75] Pennsylvania v. Board of Directors of City Trusts of Philadelphia, 353 U.S. 230 (1957) (court below had used the "fiduciary" justification).

ministration of private property is within the rule,[76] as is private administration of public property [77] by, for example, leaseholders. Private persons who discriminate because they are required to by state law are also performing "state action." [78] Of course, where a lease is made for the express purpose of avoiding desegregation of schools, it invites condemnation as an ingenuous mode of attempting to evade constitutional duties, but also constitutes, in the words of *Cooper v. Aaron:*

> State support of segregated schools through any arrangement, management, funds, or property [which] cannot be squared with the Amendment's command that no State shall deny to any person within its jurisdiction the equal protection of the laws.[79]

In some situations, however, part but not all of the funds involved is governmental and some but not all of the control is governmental. The ultimate governmental basis of "private" action in the sense that the exercise of private property rights reflects relationships declared and enforced by the state is also involved in these cases. *Dorsey v. Stuyvesant Town* [80] (a New York Court of Appeals case) held that at least some substantial state aid and control—condemnation of a widespread area, tax abatement, rent and profit limitations—do not transform a "private" housing venture into a public one for constitutional purposes. That ruling's vitality may, however, be doubted in approaching a similar, important series of questions in the housing field. Federal and state governments afford even more massive aid to Title I urban renewal projects than New York gave to Stuyvesant Town; considerable and often indispensable federal help and control are involved in FHA-insured housing. Questions are pending in the

[76] *Ibid.; cf.* Parker v. University of Del., 31 Del. Ch. 391, 75 A.2d 225 (1950) (university considered a state agency notwithstanding substantial private grants which it administered).

[77] See, *e.g.,* Tate v. Department of Conservation & Dev., 133 F. Supp. 53 (E.D. Va. 1955), *aff'd per curiam,* 231 F.2d 615 (4th Cir. 1956), *cert. denied,* 352 U.S. 838 (1956); Kerr v. Enoch Pratt Free Library, 149 F.2d 212 (4th Cir. 1945), *cert. denied,* 326 U.S. 721 (1945). A "salvage" theory has been suggested by dictum in Derrington v. Plummer, 240 F.2d 922, 925 (5th Cir. 1956), *cert. denied,* 353 U.S. 924 (1957) (lunchroom in courthouse may not discriminate, but government may lease out property otherwise useless to it and lessee may discriminate without constitutional restraint); see also cases cited pp. 94–95 *infra.*

[78] Browder v. Gayle, 142 F. Supp. 707 (E.D. Ala. 1956), *aff'd per curiam,* 352 U.S. 903 (1956); Flemming v. South Carolina Elect. & Gas Co., 224 F.2d 752 (5th Cir. 1955), *app. dism.,* 351 U.S. 901 (1956) (both local bus cases).

[79] 358 U.S. 1, 19 (1958).

[80] 299 N.Y. 512, 87 N.E.2d 541 (1949), *cert. denied,* 339 U.S. 981 (1950). See also Mitchell v. Boys Club of Metropolitan Police, 157 F. Supp. 101 (D.D.C. 1957) (insufficient governmental involvement).

courts about these programs: Can government be restrained from giving these benefits to owners who discriminate? Can they, after profiting from public aid, continue to show bias? Thus far there has been no final answer, although the most recent lower court holding views FHA as subject to the Fifth Amendment's due process clause.[81]

Another form of governmental aid and regulation beyond those of conventional property right enforcement and financial assistance is that of licensing. Probably most economic activities are now licensed in one or more ways, and in a sense licenses may be considered indispensable to a licensee, for without them he cannot function. Some licenses, however, may be viewed as conferring more power than others, in the sense of granting exclusive or enhanced power to function. Transportation companies, public utilities, labor unions, liquor sellers, and others enjoy this kind of privilege.[82] To date, so far as race relations are concerned, only the labor union has been the subject of meaningful ruling on this question. But the decision rendered is suggestive for other areas. *Steele v. Louisville & Nashville R.R. Co.* has read into the Railway Labor Act and other cases have read into the Labor Management Relations Act a requirement that a certified union represent all persons within its bargaining unit without discrimination.[83] Without this limitation, the Court has held, serious Fifth Amendment due process questions would arise. One Supreme Court case, *Brotherhood of Railroad Trainmen v. Howard*,[84] holds that a certified union may not discriminate on racial grounds against members of another bargaining unit. These decisions suggest strongly what the Supreme Court of Kansas [85] and some individual judges [86] have said, namely, that the government-union connection imposes constitutional obligations on certified unions.

Quite apart from state aid and regulation, one asserting a private right can, in the last analysis, keep Negroes out only by personal force, or possibly with the aid of the courts and the police or other law en-

---

[81] Ming v. Horgan, 3 R.R.L.R. 693 (Cal. Super. Ct. 1958). This case and the issues it presents are discussed more fully pp. 297–300 *infra*.

[82] See pp. 85–86 *infra* for discussion of licensing in transportation; 175–186 (labor unions); 100 (liquor).

[83] Steele v. Louisville & N.R.R. Co., 323 U.S. 192 (1944) (Railway Labor Act); Syres v. Oil Workers Int'l Union, 223 F.2d 739 (5th Cir. 1955), *rev'd per curiam*, 350 U.S. 892 (1955) (Labor Management Relations Act); see also Railway Employees' Dep't, AFL v. Hanson, 351 U.S. 225, 232 n.4 (1956).

[84] 343 U.S. 768 (1952).

[85] Betts v. Easley, 161 Kan. 459, 169 P.2d 831 (1946).

[86] Justice Murphy; Judges Rives and Pope (see pp. 183–184 *infra*).

forcement officers who implement legal directives. To what extent does
this sort of participation invoke state action consequences? Here, too,
there are limitations with not yet fully defined outer bounds. *Marsh v.
Alabama*,[87] discussed above, is one guidepost. In *Shelley v. Kraemer*,[88]
private covenants not to sell property to Negroes were said to be
valid, but the courts were held constitutionally prohibited from enforcing them. In *Barrows v. Jackson* [89] these "valid" agreements were
ruled to have been so devitalized by *Shelley* that damages could not
be awarded for their violation, because, the Court pointed out, awarding damages would result indirectly in their enforcement. Therefore,
according to any meaningful sense of "right" in a legal system, the
covenantors had no right to enter into private agreements intended to
keep Negroes from buying property.

In *Marsh*, as we have said, a "trespasser" on company town property
was held immune from punishment; but in *State v. Clyburn*,[90] a recent
North Carolina decision, a Negro who entered an ice cream parlor
and refused to leave when the proprietor, solely because of race, ordered him to, was held guilty of a crime in the nature of trespass. May
not the difference be explained by the relative scope of restrictiveness
of the respective restraints? In covenant cases, to be sure, only single
parcels of property may be involved. A covenant, however, ties the
hands of both a willing seller *and* a willing buyer. Moreover, the
strangling effect of the covenant system on housing added great pressure against it in a judicial system traditionally biased against restraints
on alienation of real property. Would not the plaintiffs in the *Clyburn*
case have been in a much stronger position had they been ejected from
a large shopping center, the only one conveniently accessible, or from
an indispensable or near-indispensable fuel supply, or from a hospital? [91]
An ice cream parlor presents perhaps the least compelling case.

There is a penumbral area in which judicial enforcement or legal
recognition of private discrimination has not been clearly labeled
"state" or "nonstate." This expanse is typified by *Rice v. Sioux City*

---

[87] *Supra* note 71.   [88] *Supra* note 73.   [89] 346 U.S. 249 (1953).
[90] 247 N.C. 455, 101 S.E.2d 295 (1958).
[91] But see Eaton v. Board of Managers of James Walker Memorial Hosp., 261
F.2d 521 (4th Cir. 1958) (Negro doctors excluded from hospital; upheld on
ground that state involvement insufficient); *cert. denied*, 358 U.S. 948 (1959) (the
certiorari petition argued that petitioners should have been permitted to present at
a trial the detailed evidence necessary for making a decision on state action, that
such evidence existed, and that the broad generalities of the pleadings were sufficient). The Chief Justice and Justices Douglas and Brennan dissented from the
denial.

Memorial Park Cemetery.[92] The plaintiff sued for damages caused by the cemetery's refusal to bury her husband because he was an Indian. The contract of sale for her burial lot stated that "burial privileges accrue only to members of the Caucasian race." The Iowa courts dismissed the case, rejecting the claim that judicially to recognize this clause would amount to state action based on race forbidden by *Shelley*. The United States Supreme Court at first split 4–4, upholding the Iowa decision.[93] On petition for a rehearing before a full Supreme Court, it was discovered that the Iowa legislature had outlawed such clauses after this incident. This fact, it was held, would

> bar the ultimate question presented in this case from again arising in that State. In light of this fact and the standards governing the exercise of . . . discretionary power of review upon writ of certiorari, [the Court] considered anew whether this case [was] one in which "there are special and important reasons" for granting the writ of certiorari.[94]

A majority concluded that there were not and the writ was dismissed as improvidently granted. A similar indecisive result was achieved by dismissing a writ of certiorari previously granted in *Black v. Cutter Laboratories* [95] in which the Supreme Court was confronted with the issue of whether judicial recognition of a contract under which an employee was discharged, allegedly for Communist activity, was state action in the sense that Fourteenth Amendment restraints come into play. A number of lower court and state supreme court cases have inconclusively touched like questions. One case has held that a reverter in a deed operates by itself (not by action of the state) in shifting the ownership of property when it is occupied by Negroes; [96] another involving similar facts points the other way.[97]

    Another area in which state action has been found is voting, so important a governmental function that the courts are ever alert to prevent nominally private activities from imposing racial restraints on it. The first *Nixon* White Primary election case held in 1927 that state laws requiring primaries to discriminate were unconstitutional.[98] It

---

[92] 349 U.S. 70 (1955).   [93] 348 U.S. 880 (1954), *per curiam.*

[94] 349 U.S. at 73.

[95] 351 U.S. 292 (1956) (see particularly Mr. Justice Douglas's dissenting opinion at 300, 302).

[96] See Charlotte Park & Recreation Comm'n v. Barringer, 249 N.C. 311, 88 S.E.2d 114 (1955), *cert. denied,* 350 U.S. 983 (1956); Leeper v. Charlotte Park & Recreation Comm'n, 2 R.R.L.R. 411 (N.C. Super. Ct. 1957).

[97] Clifton v. Puente, 218 S.W.2d 272 (Tex. Civ. App. 1948); compare cases discussed pp. 281–285 *infra.*

[98] On this development see pp. 143–145 *infra.*

then became clear that the Fourteenth and Fifteenth amendments controlled primaries conducted under the aegis of state law even though the discrimination was required by party rule, not statute. The most recent pronouncement, *Terry v. Adams* (1953),[99] is that a private Southern county-wide association which held preprimary elections, the winners of which then ran and invariably triumphed in the Democratic primaries in the county (where nomination equaled election), could not exclude Negroes from voting.

What are the chief state action issues which will come to court in the near future? Most probably they will be of the following types.

1. *Cases of private school plans designed to evade the* School Segregation *decisions.* Because universal education can hardly be conducted without heavy state aid and careful control of one sort or another, these laws on their face are but devices to continue state-supported schooling under the name "private." They do not even pose a genuine state action question. Authoritative commentators are agreed that these schools will be held "public" in the constitutional sense.[100]

2. *Cases of "private" housing receiving governmental financial and other support.* This includes, primarily, Title I Urban Renewal and FHA-aided housing. Without substantial financial contributions from all the taxpayers, and detailed regulation of planning, construction, and other business aspects, this housing could not be continued—or at least not so profitably. Government's thumb weighs heavily here. Indeed, this kind of planning is now remaking the face of America's cities for generations to come, more effectively than zoning or restrictive covenants. The need for housing is great; the resentment of minority members at exclusion is sharp.[101]

3. *Cases of labor union discrimination*—particularly those involving exclusion of Negroes from membership. Unions must represent fairly all those within the bargaining unit and while what is a reasonable and fair discrimination may be debatable, for distinctions always must be made as between skilled and unskilled, experienced workers and newcomers, and so forth, clearly Negroes may not be treated in an invidious fashion. So far, no court has held that this duty encompasses admitting all to membership to participate in the formulation of policies, election of officers, acceptance or rejection of offers, and so forth.

[99] 345 U.S. 461 (1953).   [100] See pp. 240–243 *infra.*
[101] See pp. 286–300 *infra;* and see NAACP 49th Annual Convention Resolutions 18–20 (1958) (condemning city planning and other governmental activity which seeks to compartmentalize Negroes or supports private efforts to do so).

But there is growing authority for the proposition that there is a constitutional duty upon unions which would include the obligation to admit all to membership. The Supreme Court has not yet passed on the issue.[102]

Although it is impossible to predict what will move people to file suits, the manner in which cases will be handled, and what encouragement will be offered by the course of decision, the above sectors probably will see considerable activity because the need seems greatest and the thumb of government weighs so heavily there.

Under these pressures where may the state action doctrine and concomitant Fourteenth Amendment application stop? Perhaps the private school issue presents an example helpful to understanding. As noted above, Miller, in *Racial Discrimination and Private Education*,[103] has suggested that the amendment will not be applied to truly private education. But his conclusion rests as much on a feeling that the Supreme Court will avoid deciding such cases as on the merits. The Court, he says, will fear opening a "Pandora's box." Law does not, he points out, proceed rigorously and inevitably to its logical conclusion. But law also necessarily has responded, and in these matters is responding, to the pressures of society. One of the important policy questions a court will have to face, in addition to those pointed out by Miller, will be whether ignoring important state-"private" school contacts will cut off Negro students (or those of any other minority selected for ostracism) from an important area of education. On the graduate level the question may be clearer, as where a "private" university has a governmentally subsidized nuclear installation or medical training facility. At other levels it may be that unique educational experiences are available only in "private" schools which bar Negroes. Where the opportunity to attend such a school means enough, a court might begin to add up how much the school receives from all the citizens. The more important the educational offering and the more the school benefits from all, the greater will be the moral pressure that it be opened to all. In other words, we may ask as did John Stuart Mill, whether liberty is better served by leaving "private" constraints alone or by subjecting them to restraint. A questioning attitude of this sort does not construe statutes or constitutions or decide concrete cases, nor does it discrimi-

---

[102] See pp. 175–185 *infra;* and see Wellington, *Union Democracy and Fair Representation*, 67 YALE L.J. 1327 (1958); Cox, *The Role of Law in Preserving Union Democracy*, 72 HARV. L. REV. 609 (1959).

[103] *Op. cit. supra* note 69, at 262, 263.

nate between the roles of legislature, judiciary, and executive. But it does work, and as the law develops it may leave a mark.

We are, in any case, looking at a long-run development. Probably, while the courts continue to come to grips with the state action problem, state laws against discrimination will spread, even to the South (they are already beginning to appear in border municipalities). Negro economic and political power are also breaking down biased practices. Thus in time the Fourteenth Amendment will no longer be a primary weapon of defense for the colored minority. Should the need for federal correctives involving application of the state action concept diminish, there may be fewer cases to raise the issue. In these, judicial keenness to preserve civil rights may be tempered with the knowledge that the exercise of political freedoms is beginning to establish protections of its own. Justice Stone's famous footnote in *United States v. Carolene Products Co.*[104] perhaps suggests a clue to the point at which there may be a slowdown in Fourteenth Amendment growth to protect Negroes. He asked

whether legislation which restricts those political processes which can ordinarily be expected to bring about repeal of undesirable legislation, is to be subjected to more exacting judicial scrutiny under the general prohibitions of the Fourteenth Amendment than are most other types of legislation.

In other words, he felt that once political power exists the need for judicial protection may be less compelling. Political power, realistically viewed, however, consists of more than the mere right to vote and encompasses educational, economic, and social competence.

Both of the factors discussed above—the importance of the institution and the political self-sufficiency of the Negro community—are reflected in the *Girard College* case.[105] The so-called "private trust" was, as the suit began, administered by a municipal board. The United States Supreme Court held that there was state action. The state then

---

[104] 304 U.S. 144, 152–153 n.4 (1938). Note some of the cases not involving racial minorities in which assertions of denial of Fourteenth Amendment rights were rejected: Goesaert v. Cleary, 335 U.S. 464 (1948) (women bartenders prohibited); Kotch v. Board of River Port Pilot Comm'rs, 330 U.S. 552 (1947) (nepotistic standard of selecting river pilots); Williamson v. Lee Optical of Okla., 348 U.S. 483 (1955) (optometrists may not fit eyeglasses without prescription); Snowden v. Hughes, 321 U.S. 1 (1944) (plaintiff not certified as nominee; no denial of equal protection where discrimination not purposeful or directed against a class).

[105] Pennsylvania v. Board of Directors of City Trusts of Philadelphia, 353 U.S. 230 (1957), *on remand*, 391 Pa. 434, 138 A.2d 844 (1958), *app. dism.*, 357 U.S. 570 (1958).

conveyed the trust to "private" trustees, but there were still numerous other state contacts involved. Yet the Pennsylvania courts held that there was no state action. The Supreme Court dismissed the appeal, and, viewing it as a petition for certiorari, also denied certiorari in what was at least a debatable case deserving of argument over whether there was sufficient state action to invoke the Fourteenth Amendment. The granting of certiorari is motivated chiefly by policy considerations and it seems that two policies may have moved the Court: (1) Girard College presents a unique situation, legally and factually. It may have been thought that the welfare of minorities generally would depend little on the outcome. (2) Pennsylvania does not restrict Negro voters and they are in fact an influential electoral group there. The state has long had civil rights laws. Indeed, although the decisions do not discuss it, the state public accommodations law, which covers schools, may very well have controlled the *Girard* situation and have required admission of the plaintiffs. Pennsylvania has an FEPC law and Philadelphia has a similar ordinance. Both the city of Philadelphia and the state of Pennsylvania sided with the Negro plaintiffs. In this situation, remedies other than a finding of state action may have been available and if not, could possibly have been developed without great difficulty. Even today Pennsylvania or Philadelphia might enact legislation requiring that private schools like Girard College admit all without bias—if the state public accommodations law does not already demand this.

Does *Girard* portend that when or where the inequalities which Negroes suffer become no greater than those which life inevitably visits upon people at large—that is, when Negroes are able to defend themselves in the political arena without the disadvantages of special discriminations—then the courts may drop what seems to be a special alert? The problem is complicated, however, by the fact that the *Girard* case, although an aberration in Pennsylvania, may be a precedent for the Deep South in trying to preserve segregation by "private" public schools. Perhaps more explicit recognition of such factors as those outlined above would distinguish the cases, but it may be that these are factors which the courts would prefer not to use as a basis of decision and which would, if evidence were taken on them, open the door to endless proceedings. Maybe a tacit recognition of these factors on the part of the courts is unavoidable, but counsel might do well to argue them.

If this analysis has merit there may be a race on between the spread of civil rights legislation and equalitarian treatment generally on the one hand, and the expansion of the Fourteenth Amendment state action concept on the other. Perhaps it is tautologous to say that the courts will stop protecting minority rights when those rights no longer need protection. But the time of arrival of that condition may help to decide for how long the state action idea will continue to grow.

LEGAL METHODS OF DELAY
AND ENFORCEMENT

Intransigent state and local governments have adopted policies which they call "resistance by all lawful means." Their defense is carried on in a number of ways: by discouraging Negroes from enjoying clear rights; by deterring would-be plaintiffs from litigating; by prohibiting public officials from recognizing civil rights; by legislating and re-legislating to establish a body of laws which, it is asserted, must first be construed or invalidated before federal rights can be enjoyed; by raising dilatory procedural issues and exhausting every possible avenue of appeal, sometimes taking a case through the appellate courts several times. Every time admission of Negro children to a school system is prolonged beyond the beginning of a school year desegregation in that district probably has been frustrated until at least the following September. And when these methods fail, some individuals have resorted to violence, which "lawful" resistance at times has encouraged.

However, there are ways to combat these delays and to enforce legal obligations, even against those who would resort to the ultimate of lawlessness. This section considers some of the important time-consuming tactics, the more obstinate resistance, the legal issues they raise, and the means which the law provides for enforcing rights against those in opposition. Because the legal issues which deserve discussion occur most frequently in the South, the context will contemplate largely a Southern desegregation dispute. But there are no clear geographical boundaries for the legal problems and most have arisen at one time or another in the North as well.

REFERENCE TO STATE COURTS

It is a common defense tactic in segregation cases to urge that the cause should first be heard in the state courts,[106] where, with rare ex-

---

[106] See HART & WECHSLER, THE FEDERAL COURTS AND THE FEDERAL SYSTEM 869 et seq. (1953); Note, 14 WASH. & LEE L. REV. 266 (1957).

ceptions, the difficulties of the plaintiff will be multiplied. Even when the maneuver does not succeed, it is a stock issue which consumes the time, energy, and funds of complainants who can ill afford them. Where a federal court has jurisdiction, the plaintiff cannot automatically be shunted to the state courts for a prior determination of his case.[107] There are, however, certain issues which the federal judiciary deems best first considered in a state forum. These include cases in which it is reasonably likely that the state court may eliminate what appears to be a constitutional question (by, for example, construing a state statute), for it has long been the policy of the federal courts to avoid the decision of constitutional questions wherever possible.[108] In *Railroad Commission of Texas v. Pullman Co.* (1941) [109] the Supreme Court required a federal district court to decline exercise of its jurisdiction, but to retain the matter until after state court construction of the state law in question, since the state court could have construed the state law in a manner taking the constitutional question out of the case.[110]

But the federal judiciary is not deprived of jurisdiction pending state determination; it may remand to state courts but may not dismiss.[111] If there is remand, an appropriate step might be to hold the case under some arrangement which would protect the rights of the parties,[112] perhaps by placing a time limit on state procedures, keeping the federal courts open for recourse if necessary.[113] Actually, the remand rule seems properly applicable only to cases which Chief Justice Vinson characterized in *Alabama Public Service Commission v.*

[107] Lane v. Wilson, 307 U.S. 268 (1939).

[108] *E.g.*, Rescue Army v. Municipal Court of Los Angeles, 331 U.S. 549 (1947); see DOWLING, CASES ON CONSTITUTIONAL LAW 183 (5th ed. 1954).

[109] 312 U.S. 496 (1941).

[110] Other cases holding similarly are Spector Motor Serv. v. McLaughlin, 323 U.S. 101 (1944); Government & Civic Employees Organizing Comm., CIO v. Windsor, 353 U.S. 364 (1957), *per curiam;* Shipman v. DuPre, 339 U.S. 321 (1950), *per curiam. Compare* Burford v. Sun Oil Co., 319 U.S. 315 (1943), *with* Meredith v. Winter Haven, 320 U.S. 228 (1943) (diversity jurisdiction should be exercised although state law uncertain); and see Alabama Pub. Serv. Comm'n v. Southern Ry., 341 U.S. 341 (1951). The *Burford* case may represent a high point in the propensity to remand. The basis of the decision seems to be that the state was uniquely familiar with the intricacies of the regulation involved. In *Burford* Mr. Justice Frankfurter, perhaps the chief proponent of judicial self-restraint, dissented vigorously at 336 on the ground that in a diversity suit federal courts should afford remedies coextensive with those in state courts.

[111] Doud v. Hodge, 350 U.S. 485 (1956).

[112] See NAACP v. Patty, 159 F. Supp. 503, 534 (E.D. Va. 1958); *rev'd sub nom.* Harrison v. NAACP, 27 U.S.L. Week 4384 (U.S. June 8, 1959) (suggesting, possibly, constitutional constructions); *compare with* NAACP v. Bennett, 27 U.S.L. Week 3361 (U.S. June 22, 1959) (*vac'g* automatic remand to state court for consideration in light of *Harrison, supra*).

[113] Wilson v. Beebe, 99 F. Supp. 418, 421 (D. Del. 1951).

Southern Ry. as those involving "construction of a state statute so ill-defined that a federal court should hold the case pending a definitive construction of that statute in the state courts." [114] And this despite the fact that one may find such expressions as "it may be true that the statute in question is clear and unequivocal but this does not prevent us from exercising our discretion in requiring that it be submitted to the state court for interpretation," [115] and though in some Supreme Court decisions the *Pullman* doctrine may have been applied to laws which may have seemed clear.[116]

Recently, in *Public Utilities Commission of California v. United States* (1958),[117] the majority opinion, in passing on the constitutionality of a state statute not yet construed by the state courts, answered an assertion of the dissent's concerning *Pullman* by saying, "We *know* the statute applies to shipments of the United States. We *know* that it is unlawful to ship at reduced rates unless the Commission approves those rates" (italics added). And at the same term in *Chicago v. Atchison, Topeka & Santa Fe R.R. Co.* (1958) the Court held concerning a disputed law:

We see no ambiguity in the section which calls for interpretation by the state courts. . . . Remission to those courts would involve substantial delay and expense, and the chance of a result different from that reached below, on the issue of applicability, would appear to be slight.[118]

Moreover, in the segregation field itself, federal courts in Louisiana, Tennessee, and Virginia have shown no hesitation in dealing with school segregation provisions in the absence of state court construction, for there was no doubt about what the laws required.[119]

EXHAUSTION OF ADMINISTRATIVE REMEDIES

Another common ground for remand to state jurisdiction is for the purpose of exhausting administrative remedies.[120] While exercise of

[114] 341 U.S. 341, 344 (1951).
[115] Bryan v. Austin, 148 F. Supp. 563, 567 (1957).
[116] This was the reasoning underlying Judge Williams's opinion in Bryan v. Austin, *supra*, citing Government & Civic Employees Organizing Comm. v. Windsor, *supra* note 110, Albertson v. Millard, 345 U.S. 242 (1953), and other cases; see 148 F. Supp. at 565–567.
[117] 355 U.S. 534, 539 (1958).
[118] 357 U.S. 77, 84 (1958).
[119] Adkins v. School Bd. of the City of Newport News, 148 F. Supp. 430 (E.D. Va. 1957), *aff'd*, 246 F.2d 325 (4th Cir. 1957), *cert. denied*, 355 U.S. 855 (1957); Bush v. Orleans Parish Bd., 138 F. Supp. 336 (E.D. La. 1956), *aff'd*, 242 F.2d 156 (5th Cir. 1957), *cert. denied*, 354 U.S. 921 (1957) (statutes in each case invalid); Kelly v. Board of Educ. of Nashville, 159 F. Supp. 272 (M.D. Tenn. 1958) (administrative remedy inadequate).
[120] See HART & WECHSLER, *op. cit. supra* note 106, at 858 *et seq.*; *The Exhaustion*

federal jurisdiction may not be deferred to require exhaustion of a state judicial remedy,[121] there is, however, sometimes debate over whether a state court furnishes judicial or administrative-legislative relief. In rate-making cases, for example, some courts act "administratively," not "judicially." [122] But this facet of the rule has been of no real significance in race relations cases.[123]

Remand to the state administrative process is discretionary.[124] In exercising that discretion, the nub of the rule, at least in terms of our interest, is that plaintiff may not be remanded to an administrative exercise in futility. An administrative advisory ruling does not suffice to bar federal judicial action; an agency must be legally empowered to grant the requested relief [125] if the federal judiciary is to stay its own hand. Where, for example, the overriding state law is that schools must be segregated no matter what a board rules, the board is clearly powerless to furnish the relief requested and plaintiff will not be required to seek its aid.[126] Moreover, the administrative proceedings are not to be unduly burdensome; a remedy which takes over a hundred days to exhaust presents no valid reason for staying the

---

of *Administrative Remedies*, 2 R.R.L.R. 561 (1957); Davis, *Administrative Remedies Often Need Not Be Exhausted*, 19 F.R.D. 437 (1957); Note, *Obstacles to Federal Jurisdiction—New Barriers to Non-Segregated Public Education in Old Forms*, 104 U. PA. L. REV. 974 (1956); and see, *e.g.*, Davis v. Arn, 199 F.2d 424 (5th Cir. 1952); Peay v. Cox, 190 F.2d 123 (5th Cir. 1951), *cert. denied*, 342 U.S. 896 (1951); Cook v. Davis, 178 F.2d 595 (5th Cir. 1949), *cert. denied*, 340 U.S. 811 (1950).

[121] Lane v. Wilson, *supra* note 107.

[122] See, *e.g.*, Prentis v. Atlantic Coast Line Co., 211 U.S. 210 (1908) (question is "legislative"; required to go before courts); *compare with* Detroit & Mackinac Ry. v. Michigan R.R. Comm'n, 235 U.S. 402 (1914) (state constitution limits courts to *judicial* proceedings; final order sustaining commission *res judicata;* courts acted judicially); Mitchell v. Wright, 154 F.2d 924 (5th Cir. 1946), *cert. denied*, 329 U.S. 733 (1946) (state court powerless to substitute its order for administrator's; jury trial; court acted judicially).

[123] An exception was Peay v. Cox, 190 F.2d 123 (5th Cir. 1951), *cert. denied*, 342 U.S. 896 (1951) (would-be voter's appeal to Mississippi courts administrative; remedy must be exhausted).

[124] See Railroad & Warehouse Comm'n of Minn. v. Duluth St. Ry., 273 U.S. 625, 628 (1927) ("the requirement that state remedies be exhausted is not a fundamental principle of substantive law but merely a requirement of convenience or comity"); *compare with* Myers v. Bethlehem Shipbuilding Corp., 303 U.S. 41, 51 n.9 (1938) (concerning federal agencies: "the rule is one of judicial administration—not merely a ruling governing the exercise of discretion").

[125] See United States Alkali Export Ass'n v. United States, 325 U.S. 196 (1945); Montana Nat'l Bank v. Yellowstone County, 276 U.S. 499 (1928); see Davis, *supra* note 120, at 476.

[126] See School Bd. of City of Newport News v. Adkins; Orleans Parish School Bd. v. Bush, *supra* note 119.

federal courts.[127] At this writing plaintiffs in the Fifth Circuit need not invoke state administrative process when they merely ask that an unconstitutional policy be enjoined and do not request admission to a particular school; but in the Fourth Circuit even though a board is assigning on a racial basis plaintiffs must first have asked the board for reassignment to a specific school before going to court.[128] The Supreme Court most probably will have to resolve the conflict. In any event, when a segregation policy is in fact generally ended, should children then ask permission to particular schools, they might all be required to go before the board everywhere.[129]

The various pupil assignment plans treated in more detail in the education chapter of this book display facets of the administrative remedy requirement. Alabama's and North Carolina's pupil placement plans have been upheld, but with the *caveat* that the plaintiffs may later complain if it appears that the plan, in actual operation, is not a bona fide device for effecting transfers without regard to race.[130] In fact, Alabama and North Carolina officials always seem to assign Negro children to colored schools unless an application for transfer is made (and even then only a handful of Negro children have been admitted to white institutions in North Carolina and none have been admitted in Alabama). It may well be questioned whether such a plan, which operates on a base of initial assignments that in fact (though this is not required by the statute) are always segregated, is in operation nondiscriminatory. The South Carolina plan works similarly, although it appears that in a suit attacking it by a group known as "Turks," some of the "Turks" obtained administrative relief.[131] No South Carolina Negro child, however, has been assigned to a white school. If he were so assigned, as in North Carolina or Alabama, it would

---

[127] Adkins v. School Bd. of City of Newport News, *supra* note 119, 148 F. Supp. at 443.

[128] Gibson v. Board of Public Instruction of Dade County, 246 F.2d 913 (5th Cir. 1957); Holland v. Board of Public Instruction of Palm Beach County, 258 F.2d 730 (5th Cir. 1958); *compare with* Covington v. Edwards, 264 F.2d 780 (4th Cir. 1959).

[129] *Ibid.* This is, of course, tied up with the question of the validity of pupil assignment plans. See pp. 232–240 *infra*.

[130] Shuttlesworth v. Birmingham Bd. of Educ., 162 F. Supp. 372 (N.D. Ala. 1958), *aff'd*, 358 U.S. 101 (1958); Carson v. Warlick, 238 F.2d 724 (4th Cir. 1956), *cert. denied*, 353 U.S. 910 (1957); Carson v. Board of Educ. of McDowell County, 227 F.2d 789 (4th Cir. 1955); Covington v. Edwards, *supra* note 128.

[131] Hood v. Board of Trustees of Sumter County School Dist., 232 F.2d 626 (4th Cir. 1956), *cert. denied*, 352 U.S. 870 (1956). The briefs in this case indicate that some Turkish children have, in fact, been admitted to "white" schools.

only be upon challenge of a Jim Crow assignment. In Maryland suits the United States District Court has held that the state Board of Education is empowered to award relief in segregation disputes and has sent plaintiffs to it.[132] Now, however, the board apparently disclaims that power.[133] On the other hand, the Virginia pupil placement plan has been invalidated as a subterfuge to perpetuate segregation: [134] state law would permit no desegregation, and the remedy for segregation, pupil-placement, was onerously lengthy and complex. The Louisiana placement plan was knocked out on similar grounds.[135] In both states, the courts observed, the legislative aim was to frustrate, not to implement, the constitutional rule.

The need to exhaust administrative remedies has impeded the progress of some persons seeking relief against voting discrimination. The Civil Rights Act of 1957 now dispenses with administrative remedies as a prerequisite to filing suit in federal court in such cases.[136]

SUPERVENING LEGISLATION AND OTHER ISSUES

A dilatory tactic which some think might stave off desegregation is to pass new legislation after a suit has already determined rights (or after suit has been filed but not yet decided) for the purpose of creating the need to exhaust fresh administrative remedies and to undertake further litigation before compliance becomes necessary. The process, if allowable, could go on forever. But in *Cooper v. Aaron*, the Little Rock case, the Supreme Court held:

We are urged to uphold a suspension of the Little Rock School Board's plan to do away with segregated public schools in Little Rock until state laws and efforts to nullify our holding in *Brown v. Board of Education* have been further challenged and tested in the courts. We reject these contentions.[137]

[132] Robinson v. Board of Educ. of St. Mary's County, 143 F. Supp. 481, 490 (D. Md. 1956); Moore v. Board of Educ. of Harford County, 146 F. Supp. 91, 97 (D. Md. 1956); see same case 152 F. Supp. 114 (1957), *aff'd sub. nom.*, Slade v. Board, 252 F.2d 291 (4th Cir. 1958), *cert. denied*, 357 U.S. 906 (1958).
[133] See Board of Educ. of St. Mary's County v. Groves, 261 F.2d 527 (4th Cir. 1958); Hart v. Board of Educ. of Charles County, 164 F. Supp. 501, 502 (D. Md. 1958).
[134] School Bd. of City of Newport News v. Adkins, *supra* note 119.
[135] Orleans Parish School Bd. v. Bush, *supra* note 119.
[136] 42 U.S.C.A. § 1971. *But see* Darby v. Daniel, 168 F. Supp. 170, 190 (D. Miss. 1958) (some remedies at least must be pursued, though not "exhausted"; statute applies only to actions instituted by United States Attorney General).
[137] 358 U.S. 1, 4 (1958).

When the series of Virginia cases came to final hearings, the courts passed on lately enacted laws, holding them ineffective to prevent desegregation and refusing stays of execution.[138] Earlier, the Fourth Circuit had affirmed a district court decision which held that:

In its injunctive decree [entered in an earlier stage of the case] the court took notice of existing and future State and local rules and administrative remedies for the assignment of children to public schools. It directed conformance with them before the complainant should turn to the court. Of course, the decree only contemplated reasonable regulations and remedies. Defendants' position that the Pupil Placement Act is such a regulation is untenable. The procedure there described is too sluggish and prolix to constitute a reasonable remedial process.[139]

This ruling would not limit states or their subdivisions to unchangeable procedures, but would seem to place an equitable limit on the extent to which revisions can prejudice already determined rights.

There is no end to the issues, petty or important, by which obdurate defendants can protract litigation. Others include questioning whether the suit is properly a class action,[140] whether a bond was necessary,[141] whether the infant plaintiffs' guardians were properly designated for purposes of the suit,[142] to name a few. Then there are the delays because of real or pretended pressure of other business, health, need for time to research the issues, and so forth.

SUMMARY PROCEDURES AND THE STAY OF EXECUTION

When litigation is spun out merely to delay or new laws are passed for that purpose, the law possesses procedures which can be applied

[138] See Thompson v. School Bd. of Arlington County, 166 F. Supp. 529 (E.D. Va. 1958), aff'd sub nom. Hamm v. County School Bd., 263 F.2d 226 (4th Cir. 1959); on stays of execution see discussion infra.

[139] Thompson v. School Bd. of Arlington County, 2 R.R.L.R. 987, 988 (E.D. Va. 1957). Sometimes supervening rules of a university have posed similar problems. See Ward v. Regents of the Univ. of Ga., 2 R.R.L.R. 369, 599 (N.D. Ga. 1957) (admission rules changed after plaintiff applied; but during pendency of suit plaintiff enrolled elsewhere and became transfer-applicant to University of Georgia; he did not at earliest opportunity disclose shift in status to court; relief denied).

[140] See, e.g., Orleans Parish School Bd. v. Bush, 242 F.2d 156, 165 (5th Cir. 1957).

[141] Orleans Parish School Bd. v. Bush, 252 F.2d 253 (5th Cir. 1958), cert. denied, 356 U.S. 969 (1958).

[142] Board of Supervisors of La. State Univ. v. Tureaud, 225 F.2d 434, 435, 228 F.2d 895 (5th Cir. 1956); Bush v. Orleans Parish School Bd., 138 F. Supp. 337, 340 n.7 (E.D. La. 1956).

swiftly. Summary judgment [143] and the preliminary injunction [144] or temporary restraining order [145] are such remedies. In one of the bus segregation suits the Supreme Court seems to have indicated impatience, citing a case which allowed the appellee damages for a frivolous appeal by his opponent.[146] But in fact no such damages have been obtained in a segregation case, although a United States district judge in Virginia recently allowed punitive damages against a railway union which, well aware of its obligation to Negro firemen in the bargaining unit, persisted in refusing to represent them.[147]

Most effective as a spur to desegregation would be the denial of stays of execution. It does no good to multiply an infinite number of legal issues to gain delay if all the while desegregation is a fact. In what is a growing number of cases segregators have been denied stays.[148] These decisions accord with the general rule that an application for stay is to be granted or denied on the equities, among which one of the most important is the likelihood of success on appeal.[149] Moreover, since the principal question on the merits of a segregation

---

[143] See Rule 56, FED. R. CIV. P.; Thompson v. County School Bd. of Arlington, 144 F. Supp. 239, 240 (E.D. Va. 1956), aff'd 240 F.2d 59 (4th Cir. 1956), cert. denied, 353 U.S. 910 (1957).

[144] Board of Supervisors of La. State Univ. v. Wilson, 340 U.S. 909 (1951), aff'g 92 F. Supp. 986 (E.D. La. 1950).

[145] Ludley v. Board of Supervisors of La. State Univ., 150 F. Supp. 900 (E.D. La. 1957), aff'd, 252 F.2d 372 (5th Cir. 1958), cert. denied, 358 U.S. 819 (1958).

[146] South Carolina Elec. & Gas Co. v. Flemming, 351 U.S. 901 (1956), citing Slaker v. O'Connor, 278 U.S. 188 (1929).

[147] Order of the United States District Court for the Western District of Virginia in Clark v. Norfolk & W. Ry., Civ. Action No. 689, May 5, 1958.

[148] See Lucy v. Adams, 350 U.S. 1 (1955), per curiam (motion granted to vacate suspension of injunction ordering admission of Negro student to University of Alabama); Tureaud v. Board of Supervisors, 346 U.S. 881 (1953) (trial court had ordered applicant's admission to Louisiana State University, and he commenced attendance; court of appeals reversed; Supreme Court granted application for stay of court of appeals' judgment which was to be brought up by certiorari; therefore, applicant was permitted to continue attendance); in the Virginia elementary and high school suits final orders ultimately were entered by the district courts, stays denied; School Bd. of Warren v. Kilby, 259 F.2d 497, 498 (4th Cir. 1958); School Bd. of City of Norfolk v. Beckett, 260 F.2d 18 (4th Cir. 1958); compare with School Bd. of City of Charlottesville v. Allen, 263 F.2d 295 (4th Cir. 1959) (board and city council vote to cooperate in complying expeditiously with decree; stay granted); see also Aaron v. Cooper, 2 R.R.L.R. 940 (E.D. Ark. 1957) (board's stay application denied); in this case, the Little Rock suit, the Supreme Court was presented with the issue of stay during the Special 1958 Term, but went to the merits, Cooper v. Aaron, 358 U.S. 1 n.† (1958).

[149] Virginia Ry. v. United States, 272 U.S. 658 (1926); United States v. Ohio, 291 U.S. 644 (1934); United States v. United Liquor Corp., 1 L. Ed. 2d 32 (1956) (Mr. Justice Reed in chambers); Breswick v. United States, 100 L. Ed. 1510 (1955) (Mr. Justice Harlan in chambers).

suit is usually one of time, that is, when shall plaintiffs be admitted, the question of whether a stay shall be granted turns with peculiar appropriateness on considerations like those which determined the merits.

ENFORCEMENT

Most desegregation following legal change, we have observed previously, has not come about by direct compulsion of decree or other enforcement procedure. Rather, it has come because of general law-abidingness or because it has been known that further coercion is possible. The ultimate force of the state has been displayed in enough desegregation cases to exhibit a variegated arsenal of governmental enforcement weapons. Basically, the procedural approaches are three: criminal prosecution; private civil suit; and administrative and/or equitable implementation by governmental officials, exemplified particularly by state antidiscrimination commissions. The relative merits of these methods were discussed in the first chapter.[150] When any kind of a suit has gone to judgment, however, the question may arise of what to do in the face of opposition. Here we discuss some of the more important available resources.

PHYSICAL FORCE

In ordinary law enforcement the local police are basic and commonplace. They have been used in the desegregation of schools both as a routine precaution and to suppress or contain mob violence.[151] For major law enforcement problems beyond the competence of the police the states historically have called upon their national guards. These too have been detailed to keep order in a few major desegregation disturbances.[152] On the other hand, the national guard was used to combat the law in Little Rock.[153] Similarly the governor of Texas instructed its Rangers to transfer out of the school district students who might provoke violence when the court decree to desegregate the Mansfield schools became effective.[154] An important difference between the two

[150] See pp. 15–17 *supra*.
[151] On police action against antidesegregation violence see S.S.N., Nov. 4, 1954, p. 4 (District of Columbia); *id.* at 8 (Baltimore); on police preparedness see CARMICHAEL & JAMES, THE LOUISVILLE STORY 138 (1957).
[152] On National Guard protection of desegregation see S.S.N., Oct., 1956, p. 3 (Clay and Sturgis, Ky.); *id.* at 15 (Clinton, Tenn.).
[153] One of many descriptions of the Little Rock events appears in S.S.N., Oct., 1957, p. 1; see also Faubus v. United States, 254 F.2d 797 (8th Cir. 1958), *cert. denied*, 358 U.S. 829 (1958); Cooper v. Aaron, 358 U.S. 1 (1958).
[154] See S.S.N., Oct., 1956, p. 14.

is that the Little Rock act was challenged in the courts and held beyond the governor's power. In Texas the Negro children did not challenge the governor and his act stood unopposed.

But where state and local force is unwilling or insufficient to safeguard federal rights, the duty falls upon the federal government. For such a situation there are special statutory provisions. The power which the President exercised in sending troops to Little Rock emanated, in terms of statute, from 10 U.S.C.A. §§ 332, 333, and 334: [155]

§ 332: Whenever the President considers that unlawful obstructions, combinations, or assemblages . . . make it impracticable to enforce the laws of the United States in any State . . . by the ordinary course of judicial proceedings, he may call into Federal service such of the militia of any State, and use such of the armed forces, as he considers necessary to enforce those laws. . . .

§ 333: The President, by using the militia or the armed forces, or both, or by any other means, shall take such measures as he considers necessary to suppress, in a State, any . . . domestic violence, unlawful combination, or conspiracy, if it—

(1) so hinders the execution of the laws of that State, and of the United States within the State, that any part or class of its people is deprived of a right, privilege, immunity, or protection named in the Constitution and secured by law, and the constituted authorities of that State are unable, fail, or refuse to protect [the above]; or

(2) opposes or obstructs the execution of the laws of the United States or impedes the course of justice under those laws.

In any situation covered by clause (1), the State shall be considered to have denied the equal protection of the laws secured by the Constitution.

Section 334 provides that when the President considers it necessary to use troops he shall issue a proclamation ordering the insurgents to disperse. This he did in Little Rock.[156] He was implementing, of course,

---

[155] 10 U.S.C.A. § 331 provides that the President may summon troops upon request of the governor or legislature of a state. In Little Rock, obviously, the President did not invoke this section. The presidential act was sustained in Faubus v. United States, *supra* note 153. 42 U.S.C.A. § 1993 had provided for presidential use of military force to implement the civil rights laws, but was repealed as part of the Civil Rights Act of 1957, P.L. 85-315, 71 Stat. 637. See 56 MICH. L. REV. 249, 262 (1957).

[156] The order to disperse, Presidential Proclamation No. 3204, appears at 22 Fed. Reg. 7628 (1957), 2 R.R.L.R. 963 (1957); on the following day, when the order was not obeyed, the President ordered the Secretary of Defense to order into active service Arkansas National Guard units and such of the armed forces of the United States as he might deem necessary. Exec. Order No. 10730, 22 Fed. Reg. 7628 (1957), 2 R.R.L.R. 904 (1957). That day the Secretary called Arkansas National Guard units into active duty and authorized the Secretary of the Army to take steps to implement the Executive Order, 2 R.R.L.R. 965 (1957).

Article II, Section 3, of the Constitution, which confers on the President the duty to "take care that the Laws be faithfully executed."

Actually, Presidents have used similar force on other occasions to perform their duty of enforcing federal rights.[157] Under like provisions which were written on the statute books at the time of the Whiskey Rebellion of 1792, it was held that the authority to determine the appropriateness of invoking this power lies solely with the President.[158] President Jefferson used such authority to enforce the Embargo Acts. The Fugitive Slave Act, it was ruled, could be implemented by state and federal troops summoned by United States marshals. President Pierce stated that he was obliged to place United States forces in Kansas at the disposal of the United States marshal in connection with the civil war which occurred there in 1856. Lincoln, under this authority, called for 75,000 volunteers in 1861.[159]

The United States marshals also are an available force for compelling obedience when ordinary acquiescence does not follow a court order. The use of federal marshals was projected by the federal government for the second year of the Little Rock dispute (in lieu of troops), but the need to employ them never actually materialized.[160]

INJUNCTION OR SUPPLEMENTAL INJUNCTION

TO PROTECT DESEGREGATION

Before means so forceful are invoked, however, there are a number of remedies of intermediate coercive effect which may impress upon violators a duty to cease defying or interfering with court orders. One was used for the first time in a segregation dispute by the school board of Hoxie, Arkansas, which initiated desegregation, was beset by rioters

---

[157] *Cf. In re* Neagle, 135 U.S. 1, 64 (1890) concerning the extent of the rights protected. Justice Miller wrote: "Is this duty limited to the enforcement of Acts of Congress . . . by their *express terms*, or does it include the rights, duties and obligations growing out of the Constitution itself, our international relations, and all the protection implied by the nature of the government under the Constitution?" He indicated an affirmative answer.

[158] Martin v. Mott, 12 Wheat. 19 (1827); to the same effect see Consolidated Coal & Coke Co. v. Beale, 282 Fed. 934 (S.D. Ohio 1922), and *cf.* United States v. George S. Bush & Co., 310 U.S. 371, 379-380 (1940).

[159] The examples in the text are taken from THE CONSTITUTION OF THE UNITED STATES OF AMERICA 483 (Corwin ed. 1953).

[160] On the general power of United States marshals see 28 U.S.C.A. § 547; on appointment of deputies see 28 U.S.C.A. § 542; for the history of the service of process by marshals and a posse of 2,000 men against opposition in United States v. Peters, 5 Cranch 115, see Mr. Justice Douglas's article, entitled by that case's name, in 19 F.R.D. 185 (1957).

who forcefully tried to compel resegregation, and went to court for an injunction against them. The Eighth Circuit Court of Appeals held that board members had a Fourteenth Amendment–supremacy clause duty (and right) to desegregate, that this duty was intimately linked with the right of Negro children to nonsegregated schooling, and that the board could assert the children's right by obtaining an injunction against the mob. In response to argument that the defendants' action was not state action and hence was beyond federal jurisdiction the court held that the defendants' resistance threatened to deprive Negro children of their rights by trying to intimidate school board officials— state officers—and consequently was state action.[161]

In Clinton, Tennessee, where the school board commenced desegregating under court order, it secured a supplemental injunction against John Kasper and others when they began to provoke violent resistance.[162] In Little Rock the plaintiffs in the original desegregation suit and the United States as *amicus curiae* obtained supplementary injunctive relief against the Governor and the National Guard who were trying to stem desegregation.[163]

CONTEMPT

Contempt proceedings are a traditional mode of compelling obedience to judicial decrees. John Kasper's activities in Clinton, Tennessee, brought him into one contempt proceeding for violation of a supplemental injunction directed against him personally. He was tried and convicted without a jury.[164] Later he was tried and convicted of conspiring with others who were unnamed in any decree, but who with notice of a federal court desegregation order, attempted to obstruct it. This case was tried with a jury.[165] Actually, however, there has been relatively little use of the contempt power in race relations suits. Chiefly it has been significant as a threat.[166]

[161] Brewer v. Hoxie School Dist., 238 F.2d 91 (8th Cir. 1956).
[162] McSwain v. County Bd. of Educ., 1 R.R.L.R. 872, 1045 (E.D. Tenn. 1956).
[163] Injunction set out at 2 R.R.L.R. 957 (1957).
[164] Kasper v. Brittain, 245 F.2d 92 (6th Cir. 1957), *cert. denied*, 355 U.S. 834 (1957).
[165] See the court's charge to the jury in United States v. Kasper, 2 R.R.L.R. 795 (E.D. Tenn. 1957), Bullock v. United States, 265 F.2d 683 (6th Cir. 1959).
[166] For unsuccessful efforts to use the contempt power see Gainer v. School Bd. of Jefferson County, 135 F. Supp. 559 (N.D. Ala. 1955) (holding that the Eleventh Amendment bars fining defendants who disobeyed teachers' salary equalization decree); Lucy v. Adams, 2 R.R.L.R. 350 (N.D. Ala. 1957) (university board not in contempt for expelling plaintiff; reasons not racial). The best study of con-

Contempt may be of two sorts, criminal or civil. Proceedings to establish the former are clothed with many of the protections due in criminal cases. These include that the offense must be proved beyond a reasonable doubt, that it must have been willful, and that the defendant may not be compelled to be a witness against himself.[167] A conviction for civil contempt falls if the disobeyed order is ultimately reversed; one for criminal contempt stands,[168] which means that in the latter type of proceeding one acts defiantly at greater peril for even a reversal on the merits will not forgive disobedience.

The fundamental federal contempt statute is 18 U.S.C.A. § 401. It provides that:

A court of the United States shall have power to punish by fine or imprisonment, at its discretion, such contempt of its authority, and none others, as—

(1) Misbehavior of any person in its presence or so near thereto as to obstruct the administration of justice;

(2) Misbehavior of any of its officers in their official transactions;

(3) Disobedience or resistance to its lawful writ, process, order, rule, decree, or command.

The last subdivision is the one which would most likely be applied in a desegregation dispute.

Title 18 U.S.C.A. § 402 provides that the contempts specified in section 401(3), if the act is of such a character as to constitute also a criminal offense under federal law or the law of the state in which it occurs, shall be prosecuted before a jury.[169] In race relations cases especially this mode of proceeding may mean a greater chance of acquittal. The jury trial provision does not apply to contempts committed in the presence of the court or so near thereto as to obstruct the administration of justice, nor to contempts committed in disobedience of court orders in actions brought by the United States. These con-

---

tempt is Moskovitz, *Contempt of Injunctions, Civil and Criminal*, 43 COLUM. L. REV. 780 (1943); see also *Civil and Criminal Contempt in the Federal Courts*, 17 F.R.D. 167 (1955); Note, *Legal Sanctions To Enforce Desegregation in the Public Schools—The Contempt Power and the Civil Rights Acts*, 65 YALE L.J. 630 (1956); Note, *Implementation of Desegregation by the Lower Courts*, 71 HARV. L. REV. 486, 495 (1958); Note, *Contempt by Strangers to a Federal Court Decree*, 43 VA. L. REV. 1294 (1957).

[167] Gompers v. Bucks Stove & Range Co., 221 U.S. 418, 444 (1911); Michaelson v. United States, 266 U.S. 42, 65 (1924).

[168] See United States v. United Mine Workers of Am., 330 U.S. 258, 294 (1946).

[169] The method of prosecuting contempts under § 402 is set forth in 18 U.S.C.A. § 3691.

tempts are to be "punished in conformity to the prevailing usages at law," [170] or, as held by *Green v. United States* (1958), under familiar contempt *procedures,* that is, among other things, by the court rather than a jury.[171]

The jury trial provisions, however, as stated in *Green* have not been bestowed as a matter of constitutional right. It is Congress, wrote Mr. Justice Frankfurter in his concurrence in that case, which "has seen fit from time to time to qualify the power of summary punishment for contempt . . . by requiring in explicitly defined situations that a jury be associated with the court in determining whether there has been a contempt." [172] But although it has been suggested, as in *Michaelson v. United States* (1924),[173] that there are bounds beyond which congressional limitations on the contempt power may not go, because courts presumably are inherently endowed with the power to preserve their dignity, these bounds have never been precisely defined.

The Civil Rights Act of 1957 (which is limited to voting rights) by 42 U.S.C.A. § 1995 extends the jury trial exception further than preexisting statutes, with the apparent purpose, however, of remaining within acceptable bounds pointed out in *Michaelson.* The act does not curtail the courts' right "to deal summarily with contempts committed in the presence of the court or so near thereto as to obstruct the administration of justice," or the power to enforce mandatory decrees, which *Michaelson* may have insulated from legislation by defining them as inherent attributes of courts.[174] Civil contempt, which, as we shall see, may inflict as great, or a greater, penalty as criminal contempt remains untouched. The jury trial extension consists solely of a proviso in 42 U.S.C.A. § 1995 of the new act which states that if criminal contempt proceedings under that act are tried by a judge without a jury and the sentence is more than $300 or 45 days' imprisonment the accused may demand a trial de novo before a jury. But this privilege does not deprive the courts of their contempt power, by finding civil contempt, without a jury, to secure compliance with or to prevent obstruction of any lawful order in accordance with prevailing usages of law and equity—including the power of detention.

The severity or nature of sanction may differ according to the kind of contempt. Contempts tried before a jury are punishable, in terms of 18 U.S.C.A. § 402, by fine up to $1,000 or imprisonment up to six

[170] 18 U.S.C.A. § 402.   [171] 356 U.S. 165 (1958).   [172] 356 U.S. 189, 193 (1958).
[173] 266 U.S. 42, 65, 66 (1924).   [174] *Id.* at 65–66.

months. But the "prevailing usages" language, quoted above, does not freeze the power to sentence in cases other than those specified in the statute. Jail sentences or fines for criminal contempt tried without a jury may be imposed in the discretion of the court. The Supreme Court recently has upheld a three-year term (for Communists convicted under the Smith Act who fled rather than surrender for imprisonment).[175] The trial court must "exercise such an extraordinary power with the utmost sense of responsibility and circumspection . . . and appellate courts have here a special responsibility for determining that the power is not abused, to be exercised if necessary by revising themselves the sentences imposed." [176]

The sanction employed against civil contemnors is theoretically limitless, for it may

> be employed for either or both of two purposes: to coerce the defendant into compliance with the court's order, and to compensate the complainant for losses sustained. . . . Where compensation is extended, a fine is imposed, payable to the complainant. Such fine must of course be based upon evidence of complainant's actual loss.[177]

When a civil contemnor is placed in jail, he "carries the keys of his prison in his own pocket." [178] He may be kept there until he complies.

For these reasons it is important to identify civil as distinguished from criminal contempts, although "conduct can amount to both civil and criminal contempt," [179] and trial may be for both together. (Where the proceedings are combined, however, the enhanced protections for criminal cases apply.)

Gompers v. Bucks Stove and Range Co. points out some of the circumstances which mark a controversy as appropriate for one type of contempt proceeding rather than the other:

> If it is for civil contempt the punishment is remedial, and for the benefit of the complainant. But if it is for criminal contempt the sentence is punitive, to vindicate the authority of the court. . . . imprisonment for civil contempt is ordered where the defendant has refused to do an affirmative act required by the provisions of an order which, either in form or substance, was mandatory in character.[180]

[175] Green v. United States, *supra* note 171.   [176] 356 U.S. at 188.
[177] United States v. United Mine Workers of Am., 330 U.S. 258, 303–304.
[178] Gompers v. Bucks Stove & Range Co. *supra* note 167, at 442 (1911).
[179] United States v. United Mine Workers of Am., 330 U.S. 258, 298–299. See also Union Tool Co. v. Wilson, 259 U.S. 107, 110 (1922) (where fine is both for punishment and for compensating of complainant, criminal feature is dominant).
[180] *Supra* note 167, at 441–442.

Sometimes the identification may be made retrospectively, as the above quotation indicates. A reviewing court may look at what has been done and then decide that the trial court meant to impose one type of contempt sanction rather than the other. Another characteristic of the suit that the appellate judges look into is whether the proceedings were between the original parties and were instituted and tried as part of the main cause, which indicates civil contempt, or whether they were between the public and the defendant, and were not part of the original cause, indicating a criminal quality.[181] Sometimes it is a significant fact, tending to indicate criminal contempt, that the alleged perpetrators "were strangers, not parties." [182] Those contempts for which jury trial is required by statute are also criminal; [183] but as indicated above not all criminal contempts need be tried by jury.

PARTICIPATION BY THE UNITED STATES

Whatever the approach, the appearance of the United States is of great help to plaintiffs in segregation suits. Its resources are, of course, incomparable. Not only does it have a large, able legal staff, but it can also draw on the services of the Federal Bureau of Investigation. Its taking a position signifies that the country as a whole supports the action and should indicate that obstructive tactics probably are hopeless. The federal government, like the state governments, may proceed by criminal prosecution or by an administrative or injunctive route, though in the latter two regards its express authority is limited and has not been extensively employed. Criminal proceedings, which are what the present Civil Rights Acts contemplate, have the inherent limitations treated in other portions of this book and, moreover, the existing applicable civil rights laws suffer significant substantive shortcomings.[184] To the conventional modes of enforcement, however, should be added appearance by the United States as *amicus curiae.* The government has taken part in a number of important segregation cases in the Supreme Court as *amicus,* most notably in the *School*

[181] *Id.* at 444–445.

[182] Nye v. United States, 313 U.S. 33, 43 (1941).

[183] FED. R. CRIM. P. 42 (b) allows plaintiff's attorney to be specially appointed for the purpose of starting criminal contempt proceedings, something otherwise reserved for the United States Attorney. See also Michaelson v. United States, 266 U.S. 42, 65–66 (1924).

[184] For discussions of the Civil Rights Acts see pp. 135–138, 269–272, and 316–323 *infra.*

Segregation Cases and the Little Rock case,[185] but it also has intervened in this manner at the trial level.[186]

The President's office has issued a statement affirming that

although the Federal Government has no responsibility to initiate action to desegregate public schools or to formulate any plan for desegregation, the courts have made it clear that the Department of Justice, at the invitation of the Court, must participate in litigation involving public school desegregation for the purpose of assisting the Court.[187]

The propriety of such participation has been upheld in the courts.[188]

While proposed legislation would give the Attorney General the right to seek injunctions on behalf of civil rights other than voting [189]— the extent of his statutory authority under the Civil Rights Act of 1957—he probably, even without explicit statutory authority may use this procedure in nonvoting cases, as indicated by *In re Debs* (1895),[190] something, however, he has never attempted.

The *Debs* case perhaps outlines the extent to which the government can go to preserve federal rights. The case itself involved the validity of an injunction forbidding a railway strike because of its interference with the mails and interstate commerce. In the course of the strike the President dispatched troops. Although there was no statutory basis for the injunction, the Supreme Court upheld it on the ground that the government was empowered to protect its own property. But the opinion went further and stated:

Every government, entrusted by the very terms of its being with powers and duties to be exercised and discharged for the general welfare, has a

[185] Among other appellate cases in which the United States has appeared on the side of desegregation have been the *Restrictive Covenant Cases,* the *Sweatt, McLaurin,* and *Henderson* suits.

[186] The government appeared at the trial level in later stages of the Little Rock litigation. The district court's order directing the United States to appear there is at 2 R.R.L.R. 941 (1957). In Clinton, Tenn., the government appeared at the trial level, Kasper v. Brittain, 245 F.2d 97 (6th Cir. 1957).

[187] 2 R.R.L.R. 929 (1957).

[188] Faubus v. United States, 254 F.2d 797 (8th Cir. 1958), *cert. denied,* 358 U.S. 829 (1958), citing Universal Oil Prods. Co. v. Root Ref. Co., 328 U.S. 575, 581 ("after all, a federal court can always call on law officers of the United States to serve as *amici*").

[189] See discussion of the proposed civil rights bill of 1958, pp. 271–272 *infra.*

[190] 158 U.S. 565 (1895). For comparable power of a state attorney general to initiate suit for injunction without explicit statutory authorization see People *ex rel.* Bennett v. Laman, 277 N.Y. 368, 14 N.E. 2d 439 (1938) (New York Attorney General sues to enjoin quack). A superb study of the presidential power appears in Brief for the United States in Jackson v. Kuhn, 254 F.2d 555 (8th Cir. 1958).

right to apply to its own courts for any proper assistance in the exercise of the one and the discharge of the other. . . . whenever the wrongs complained of are such as affect the public at large, and are in respect of matters which by the Constitution are entrusted to the care of the nation, and concerning which the nation owes the duty to all the citizens of securing to them their common rights, then the mere fact that the government has no pecuniary interest in the controversy is not sufficient to exclude it from the courts, or prevent it from taking measures therein to fully discharge those constitutional duties.[191]

Therefore, there appears to be substantial power at local, state, and federal levels to compel desegregation where the law is not obeyed in the manner that laws customarily are followed.

---

[191] 158 U.S. at 584, 586. Congress, under Article IV, has been held authorized to deal with lawlessness which denies federal rights, Luther v. Borden, 7 How. 1 (1849). But under the inherent powers of which *Debs* speaks and the statutory powers described above, congressional power has become secondary. CORWIN, THE PRESIDENT, OFFICE, AND POWERS 164–166 (3d ed. 1948).

CHAPTER III

PUBLIC ACCOMMODATIONS AND SERVICES

A discussion of "public accommodations" encompasses such a variety of legal and social considerations that it touches in some degree on most of the issues treated in more or less detail in subsequent chapters. It is therefore an appropriate first chapter in the "vertical" presentation of the operation of law in race relations, that is, the presentation according to areas of life activity.

"Public accommodations" has been defined variously in statutes and cases. The usage of lawyers shares the nonlegal connotation: simply that the accommodation is "open to the public," although there has been much peripheral debate over whether this or that spot is within the term. Succeeding chapters concern places where people spend large blocks of time: schools, homes, jobs, for example. Public accommodations are interstitial: the bus that takes people to work, the park attended afterward, the cafeteria used for lunch, the store for shopping, the hospital, the library, the public auditorium, and so forth. Together they make up the medium in which life is lived, that which, generally, facilitates service to the larger, more demanding institutions. Usually public accommodations are thought of as privately owned facilities (like the typical theater, restaurant, hotel, or retail store), despite the fact that they often are governmentally operated (like libraries, parks, and hospitals).

Local or intrastate transportation is sometimes discussed in conjunction with interstate travel, but we shall consider it with public accommodations, for legally intrastate transit has largely the same status as public accommodations. The commerce clause, crucial for interstate transit, does not apply to purely local carriers. (The intrastate passenger on a carrier—or in its terminal—whose journey spans several states is treated with interstate travel, ch. IV). Almost every Southern state has travel separation laws. Segregated local travel has a tremendous impact on the average Negro's life. It rankles more than most other racial distinctions, is less solidly rooted in society than many, and is more amenable to legal attack and economic pressure.[1]

Relatively few racial distinctions in public accommodations or recreation are imposed by statute, but almost all such facilities, public and private, throughout the South and in many places in the North (parks, pools, beaches, golf courses, libraries, theaters, tennis courts, restaurants, hotels, and so on) either bar Negroes or are segregated, by custom, ordinance, or regulation. Yet in the Southern states it is extremely rare to find a public facility which Negroes may attend even nearly equal to the best available for whites, and nowhere in the South can Negroes choose from the variety open to whites. A 1954 survey showed no state park facilities for Negroes in Louisiana, Mississippi, and Texas, although those states had, respectively, 7,000, 10,972, and 58,126 acres for whites. In 1952 nine Southern states had 12 parks for Negroes against 180 for whites.[2] Litigation and some appropriations have changed this imbalance a little, but essentially it remains the same. The importance of access to such places increases with Southern industrialization, national automation, and the leisure accompanying them,[3] even though the work Negroes now obtain usually does not gain for them a proportionate share of this new freedom.

The importance of good hospitals and health facilities is obvious, but segregation in and exclusion of Negroes from them, in the North as well as in the South, is widespread. Not only state laws but hospital rules and medical association membership rules as well govern hospital admissions and treatment.

[1] See Popham, *Report on Bus Desegregation*, N.Y. Times, Feb. 3, 1957, § E, p. 8.
[2] See, McKay, *Segregation and Public Recreation*, 40 VA. L. REV. 697, 702–706 (1954); South Carolina operates 21 parks, 17 of which are for whites, Afro-American, Jan. 21, 1956, p. 2.
[3] See, Bendiner, *Could You Stand a Four-Day Week*, Reporter, Aug. 8, 1957, pp. 10, 11. Other than school and travel cases most civil rights suits have concerned public recreation and most often, golf courses; Negro professional and businessmen want to enjoy leisure as do their white peers and have funds to finance this litigation.

THE LEGAL FRAMEWORK

State-owned facilities are forbidden to discriminate by the Fourteenth Amendment. Privately owned accommodations, on the other hand, have been held insulated from the Fourteenth Amendment, which inhibits only state action. But when private proprietors discriminate because legally required to, even they come under the Fourteenth. The big issue in more and more cases is becoming the definition of what constitutes state action. Does the Fourteenth Amendment govern a franchise or license holder, impose standards on institutions supported jointly by the government and private interests, cover a business invested with public interest, or control police enforcement of discriminatory "private" rules? Can the state convey or lease its property and shed the duty of not discriminating on it?

The first Justice Harlan, as we observed in chapter II, would have placed most public accommodations under the control of the Constitution, for despite their nominally private character he believed them governmental for purposes of applying the Fourteenth Amendment. In the *Civil Rights Cases* his lone dissent, part of which was quoted earlier, stated:

In every material sense applicable to the practical enforcement of the Fourteenth Amendment, railroad corporations, keepers of inns, and managers of places of public amusement are agents or instrumentalities of the State, because they are charged with duties to the public, and are amenable, in respect of their duties and functions, to governmental regulation. It seems to me that, within the principle settled in *Ex Parte Virginia*, a denial, by these instrumentalities of the State, to the Citizen, because of his race, of that equality of civil rights secured to him by law, is a denial by the State, within the meaning of the Fourteenth Amendment. If it be not, then that race is left, in respect of the civil rights in question, practically at the mercy of corporations and individuals wielding power under the States.[4]

As we urged more fully in chapter II, Harlan's view is likely to gain greater acceptance as governmental protection, regulation, or privilege increases. But still, so long as an enterprise is called "private," the burden of getting it opened to all rests on those who say the Constitution forbids the enterprise to discriminate. The Civil Rights Acts, though sometimes applicable, have not been used by the government in the area of public accommodations.

[4] 109 U.S. 3, 58 (1883).

Apart from constitutional questions, some common law doctrines deserve attention in connection with public accommodations: for example, the innkeeper's obligation to serve all travelers, the common carrier's (or utility's) duty to treat the public without discrimination. Most important of all is the growing body of state civil rights statutes forbidding discrimination in places of public accommodation, which we shall examine.

INTRASTATE TRAVEL

At common law common carriers were bound to accept all passengers without discrimination, a duty now contained in the statutory law of most states.[5] But the Southern states of the United States made segregation an exception to this doctrine (actually they would argue that segregation is not discrimination). *Plessy v. Ferguson*,[6] the keystone of legally enforced segregation, was an intrastate travel case. Even after the *School Segregation Cases* strict constructionists continued to say that *Plessy* remained good law because while segregation might not be allowed in schools and other places where it had been specifically outlawed, it had not been prohibited in local transit.

All the Southern states (except Maryland, Missouri, West Virginia, and the District of Columbia) have segregation statutes for local travel (buses, trolleys, and trains), and many Southern cities also have such ordinances, or officially enforced practices, which often make of the driver a police officer to enforce segregation. (These are the same laws in the main which also have been applied to interstate travel, although there are a few statutes distinctly applying to intrastate carriers which were enacted after interstate travel separation was outlawed by application of the commerce clause of the Constitution and the Interstate Commerce Act.) [7] The validity of these statutes, attacked as unconstitutional for making unreasonable classifications forbidden by the due process and equal protection clauses, for creating inequality prohibited under the doctrine of equal protection, and for impeding freedom of locomotion, a "liberty" protected by due process,[8] was

[5] See C.J.S. *Carriers* § 538.   [6] 163 U.S. 537 (1896).
[7] For the statutes see appendix A1. For ordinances see MURRAY, STATES' LAWS ON RACE AND COLOR app. 5 (1950). Other practices are: Montgomery has separate cabs; police have put up cab stand signs "for white cabs only," none for Negroes, Afro-American, Feb. 11, 1956, p. 8; in Birmingham, the Harlem (colored) cab company has a franchise for Negro transfer passengers only at the Southern Railway station, *id.*, Dec. 15, 1956, p. 1.
[8] On due process and equal protection, generally, see pp. 32–46 *supra*; on free-

conclusively destroyed by a 1957 Supreme Court affirmance of a district court decree in *Browder v. Gayle*,[9] holding state-imposed bus segregation unconstitutional in Montgomery, Alabama. The theory of the decision was that legally enforced intrastate travel segregation denies due process and equal protection. The district court found that the spate of antisegregation decisions of recent years had implicitly overruled *Plessy*. Shortly thereafter the Justice Department called a conference of United States Attorneys in the Southern states to consider what measures it would be appropriate for the department to take in "securing observance of the 'United States Constitution and laws,' by common carriers of passengers." [10] Presumably violators could be guilty of breaching the Civil Rights Laws. It appears, however, that no departmental action ensued.

Although a number of bus lines ceased to require segregation without litigation directed specifically against them,[11] none of the Southern

---

dom of locomotion, see Edwards v. California, 314 U.S. 160, 178 (1941) (concurring opinion); Williams v. Fears, 179 U.S. 270, 274 (1900); Crandall v. Nevada, 73 U.S. 35 (1867).

[9] 142 F. Supp. 707 (M.D. Ala. 1956), *aff'd per curiam*, 352 U.S. 903 (1956). A few months earlier, Flemming v. South Carolina Elec. & Gas Co., 351 U.S. 901 (1956), dismissing an appeal from the Fourth Circuit's outlawry of bus segregation in South Carolina, 224 F.2d 752 (1955), was widely interpreted as high Court repudiation of *Plessy*. The decision had those overtones—it cited a case indicating the appeal was frivolous—but probably held that the appeal was not from a final order. At this point, many bus companies throughout the South announced desegregation, including Virginia Motor Transit (Richmond, Norfolk); Duke Power Co. (Durham, Greensboro); National City Lines (Jackson, Tampa, Mobile, Tulsa, Montgomery, Wichita Falls, Beaumont, El Paso), N.Y. Times, April 25, 1956, p. 1. Before *Browder v. Gayle* an Alabama judge held *Flemming* to be of no weight and enjoined the Montgomery bus company from desegregating, City of Montgomery v. Montgomery City Lines, 1 R.R.L.R. 534 (Montgomery County Cir. Ct. 1956); following *Browder v. Gayle* the injunction was regretfully dissolved, 2 R.R.L.R. 121 (1957). New Orleans bus segregation was enjoined in Morrison v. Davis, 252 F.2d 102 (5th Cir. 1958), *cert. denied*, 357 U.S. 944 (1958).

[10] N.Y. Times, Nov. 20, 1956, p. 1. As late as December, 1958, Evers v. Dwyer, 358 U.S. 202 (1958) outlawed Memphis's continued enforcement of bus segregation, holding that the fact that plaintiff may have boarded bus to start litigation was not significant.

[11] See Afro-American, March 23, 1956, p. 1 (Nashville); *id.*, Jan. 26, 1957, p. 12 (Knoxville: bus segregation "had never been a rigidly enforced rule. . . . that Knoxville College and the University of Tennessee are located in Knoxville is no little point in favor of the peaceful racial transitions"; Chattanooga: transition so slight and gradual that many unaware of change); *id.*, Jan. 19, 1957, p. 18 (following protest by Oklahoma NAACP, Lawton station and vehicle racial signs removed); *id.*, Jan. 19, 1957, p. 3 (Columbia, S.C.); *id.*, May 5, 1956, p. 1 (Richmond, Norfolk, Portsmouth, Charlotte, Roanoke, Lynchburg; in Richmond and Fredericksburg, at least, segregation had not been rigidly enforced for years; but litigation contesting intrastate travel segregation was pending in Virginia courts). 1 R.R.L.R.

travel segregation statutes has been repealed and many continue to be enforced [12]—either by explicit governmental directive or through the more subtle pressures of society. Sometimes violent, terroristic efforts have been made to retain the old system and these have been followed by governmental edict to maintain segregation for the purpose of keeping peace.[13] Some new laws forbid nonsegregation on intrastate carriers, although an equally important purpose appears to be to retain as much segregation as possible on interstate vehicles.[14] In a sense, therefore, segregation is "law" for local carriers in many Southern communities, as it is for other activities, notwithstanding legal pre-scripts to the contrary. However, as a result of court action and voluntary compliance many Negroes now sit in all sections of local buses. Yet in some places where they may sit wherever they please unmolested, many or most sit in the former Jim Crow sections. generally the rear.[15]

947 (1956) (mayor and council of Dallas believe public transportation issue for courts; suit filed to require bus company compliance with segregation laws dis-missed on ground that plaintiffs, taxpayers, had insufficient interest to sue, Frazier v. Dallas Transit Co., 2 R.R.L.R. 146 (Dallas County Dist. Ct. 1956)).

[12] N.Y. Times, Jan. 11, 1957, p. 13 (Atlanta Negro ministers who defied bus segregation arrested; the company, trying to avoid a clear-cut decision did not insist openly on segregation, but when Negroes boarded the vehicle, it was declared out of order and returned to garage for repairs); Afro-American, March 23, 1957, p. 3; N.Y. Times, Dec. 27, 1956, p. 1 (Birmingham police en-force bus segregation); see Birmingham Ordinance No. 1342-F, 2 R.R.L.R. 457 (1957), reaffirming bus segregation; Afro-American, Jan. 19, 1957, p. 2 (mayor of Pritchard, Ala., will enforce segregation notwithstanding bus company an-nouncement it will desegregate); N.Y. Times, Nov. 14, 1956, p. 22 (Florida At-torney General says state's bus segregation laws remain in effect).

[13] See, e.g., N.Y. Times, Jan. 11, 1957, p. 1 (Montgomery bombings). There-upon the Montgomery Board of Commissioners adopted resolutions curtailing bus service, 2 R.R.L.R. 223 (1957). Following threats of violence in Tallahassee, Florida's governor suspended and then permitted resumption of bus service, 2 R.R.L.R. 224 (1957). Tallahassee buses thereafter were nonsegregated in Negro sections, segregated in white sections, N.Y. Times, Sept. 27, 1957, p. 11. Seating is at the discretion of the driver who considers, among other things, weight dis-tribution; disobedience of his orders is a misdemeanor, Tallahassee Ordinance No. 741, 2 R.R.L.R. 459 (1957). The ordinance survived attack in Speed v. City of Tallahassee, 3 R.R.L.R. 37 (1958), cert. denied, 356 U.S. 913 (1958); in opposition to certiorari the state argued that defendants had used the wrong local procedure. Apparently encouraged by the Speed outcome, Birmingham has adopted an ordinance entrusting seating to the driver. See Cherry v. Morgan, 3 R.R.L.R. 1236 (1958).

[14] See pp. 127–129 infra.

[15] Shortly after Montgomery buses began desegregation "when whites and Negroes rode the same buses, the Negroes took seats from the middle of the bus back, while the whites stayed in the front. Habit, it seemed, still prevailed," N.Y. Times, Jan. 17, 1957, p. 25. Following oral Miami federal court ruling that bus segregation is unconstitutional, Miami Negroes continued riding as before,

The carrier's duty where there is no segregation law may be illustrated by what happened in Montgomery, Alabama, after bus segregation was declared illegal there. The Fourteenth Amendment requires merely that government shall not segregate; the interstate commerce clause does not apply to local travel. Following the Montgomery decision, a group of white citizens proposed to set up a private bus line, called the "Rebel Line." Its obvious purpose was to furnish transportation for white persons only, but not pursuant to a law or ordinance, since these had just been invalidated. The applicants asked the city for a franchise and the Board of Commissioners, in turn, filed a "petition for instructions" with the district court which had outlawed the segregation ordinance. They asked three questions of which the third was: "If such a franchise is granted, is it incumbent upon your Petitioners to see to it that in the course of the operation of this private enterprise the holder of such franchise does not discriminate between white and colored passengers?" The district court dismissed, holding that it had no power to "give advisory opinions, nor decide abstract, hypothetical, or contingent questions." But the *per curiam* opinion [16] stated that Judge Rives of the court of appeals and Judge Johnson of the district court "feel that it will be of some public service if they express their opinions as individuals, of which they presently entertain no doubt, namely, that the word 'private' as used in the third question is inappropriate, and that each of the three questions propounded should be answered 'yes.' "

It might be argued that because the petition was presented in a situation in which the city had already been enjoined, Judges Rives and Johnson were but closing loopholes in an existing decree; that, perhaps, without such a background a city might permit a "private" line to segregate so long as the segregation was not governmentally

---

ibid. (The order was entered in Garmon v. Miami Transit Co., 151 F. Supp. 953 (S.D. Fla. 1957), *aff'd*, 253 F.2d 428 (5th Cir. 1958).) In Chattanooga the old pattern tended to continue after segregation officially ended, N.Y. Times, Jan. 11, 1957, p. 1; Afro-American, Jan. 26, 1957, p. 12. In Columbia chiefly young people breached the segregation pattern, but number of others is increasing, *id.*, Jan. 19, 1957, p. 3. In Fredericksburg, where segregation has not been enforced for years, following bus decision "you just couldn't tell there had been a change . . . only one colored person sitting in . . . front . . . during . . . 15 trips," *id.*, May 5, 1956, p. 1. On first day of New Orleans bus desegregation a few Negroes sat in front, N.Y. Times, June 1, 1958, p. 41.

[16] See Browder v. Gayle, 2 R.R.L.R. 412 (M.D. Ala. 1957). N.Y. Times, Feb. 28, 1957, p. 14 (Rebel Club organized as means of combatting integration). The opinion accords with Public Utilities Comm'n v. Pollak, 343 U.S. 451 (1952) (transit company operating under commission tested by First and Fifth Amendments).

enforced. But such escape is doubtful. A bus line, if in reality public, is a common carrier, whatever it may be called; [17] its universally recognized duty is to serve all without discrimination. The new tactic then is merely asking for a judicial exception to replace the statutory one, *i.e.*, it asks the courts to say as a matter of common law that although private carriers may not otherwise discriminate, they may segregate Negroes. But common law racial distinctions are as unconstitutional as statutory ones. Moreover, such a rule would immediately involve the police in its enforcement. The question also would arise whether the invaluable exclusive franchise plus extensive regulation impose the obligation not to discriminate. The implication of the certified exclusive collective bargaining (labor union) cases (chapter VI) is that an exclusive governmental franchise will be construed as forbidding racial distinctions or will fall under constitutional restraint. The *Pollak* case, cited above, shows that there is virtually no question about the applicability of state action restraints to a regulated carrier.

Apart from rules of law, economics must be reckoned with too. The bus boycotts which have proliferated over the South have done as much as lawsuits to end racial separation on buses there. It is important to remember, however, that segregation continued in Montgomery in the face of an effective boycott until the Supreme Court decided the legal issue. Only then did the city accede to the bus company's decision to give in to the boycotters. [18]

Here we may note that public utilities, like carriers, generally are obliged to serve all without arbitrary distinctions. [19] But there is no

[17] See Morgan v. Fielder, 194 Ark. 719, 109 S.W.2d 922, 923 (1937) (fact that carrier bars Negroes and drunks does not make it private).

[18] On legal questions posed by these boycotts see 66 YALE L.J. 397 (1957). Montgomery enjoined the boycotters, City of Montgomery v. Montgomery Improvement Ass'n, 2 R.R.L.R. 123 (Montgomery County Cir. Ct. 1956); the boycotters unsuccessfuly attempted to obtain a federal court injunction against these state proceedings, Browder v. City of Montgomery, 146 F. Supp. 127 (M.D. Ala. 1956). See also N.Y. Times, June 5, 1956, p. 35 (Tallahassee bus company counters boycott by suspending services in Negro areas). Legal maneuverings in Tallahassee are set forth in City of Tallahassee v. Cities Transit Inc., 2 R.R.L.R. 135 (Leon County Cir. Ct. 1956) (city enjoins bus company); Cities Transit Inc. v. City of Tallahassee, 2 R.R.L.R. 137 (N.D. Fla. 1956) (enjoining city from revoking company franchise); the Tallahassee boycotters attempted to secure a federal court injunction against criminal prosecution which was denied in Inter-Civic Council of Tallahassee, Inc. v. City of Tallahassee, 2 R.R.L.R. 143 (N.D. Fla. 1956).

[19] Concerning public utilities generally see 73 C.J.S. *Utilities* § 7. The Southern

evidence that racial discrimination represents a separate legal problem in the application or enforcement of this doctrine to utilities.

INSURANCE

Similar issues are presented by the sale of insurance. The companies are regulated as closely as any public utility and are totally dependent on the state for the right to function. Most states—without mentioning race—forbid discrimination in the sale of insurance, although some have particular racial safeguards.[20] Because insurance rates are based upon predictions concerning members of classes (*e.g.*, age, sex, occupation) and because the life expectancy of Negroes as a class is less than that for whites, Negroes who have not been disadvantaged and personally may expect the same life expectancy as similarly situated whites have been offered insurance by some companies only at less advantageous terms than have been offered comparable white persons. This was held illegal in the case of the Wisconsin state-owned life insurance fund in *Lange v. Rancher*,[21] a decision which rested on an interpretation of the state's insurance law. Whether the *Rancher* rule would apply to private companies would depend partly on the legal effect of extensive state regulation and licensing as they contribute to answering the state action question.

HOSPITALS

Hospitals occupy approximately the same position of uniqueness and indispensability as utilities and the utility-like services considered above. But the law has not treated them in the same way.

Most Southern states have provided by law that at least certain public hospitals (usually specifically named institutions for mental illness and, less often, tuberculosis) shall be solely either for Negroes or for whites or segregated.[22] Beyond this, state laws do not require racial distinctions in hospitals, although practice often has. Veterans Administration hospitals throughout the country do not segregate, and the states have

---

Bell Telephone Co. has refused to segregate party lines (*i.e.*, whites or Negroes only on the same line), stating, "We are a public utility," Afro-American, May 5, 1956, p. 1.

[20] See 44 C.J.S. *Insurance* § 55 and statutes cited in appendix A2.

[21] 262 Wis. 625, 56 N.W. 2d 542 (1953). See Note, *The Constitutionality of Racial Classifications in Mortality Tables*, 11 RUTGERS L. REV. 757 (1956).

[22] See appendix A3.

made no overt effort to assert authority over their management. Mississippi has accepted an integrated VA hospital rather than have none at all.[23]

Apart from those covered by statutory law, however, separate hospitals or wings for Negroes are the general Southern practice.[24] Yet not all hospitals there make racial distinctions. The United Mine Workers, in 1956, opened seven hospitals in Kentucky, one in Virginia, and two in West Virginia which are operated on an integrated basis.[25] Opelousas, Louisiana, has a completely nonsegregated hospital.[26] But a Knoxville hospital under construction, which was supposed to be nonsegregated, was changed to segregated because of shifts in political power in that city.[27] The Charlotte Rehabilitation and Spastics Hospital is one of a number of Southern hospitals for crippled children which are nonsegregated.[28] A Houston clinic for a time did not segregate until pressure forced the director, who had employed this policy, to resign.[29] These, however, appear to be exceptional cases.

There has been discrimination in Northern hospitals as well. While many do not discriminate,[30] still some do not accept Negroes and others segregate.[31] Following findings of bias, Chicago has recently passed an ordinance outlawing discrimination against colored physicians in staff appointments.[32] A New York City Department of Wel-

---

[23] On VA hospitals see LOTH & FLEMING, INTEGRATION NORTH AND SOUTH 36 (1956); on Mississippi VA see ASHMORE, AN EPITAPH FOR DIXIE 131 (1958); see also Chicago Defender, Aug. 4, 1956, p. 3 (Mississippian's protest against non-segregation policy at Jackson, Miss., hospital).

[24] The only comprehensive, recent treatments of hospital discrimination are REITZES, NEGROES AND MEDICINE (1958), and the reports of physicians in 49 J. NATIONAL MEDICAL ASS'N 189-201, 272-273, 352-356, 429-433 (1957).

[25] LOTH & FLEMING, op. cit. supra note 23, at 82.

[26] 49 J. NATIONAL MEDICAL ASS'N, op. cit. supra note 24, at 355.

[27] LOTH & FLEMING, at 83; 49 J. NATIONAL MEDICAL ASS'N 431 (1957).

[28] N.Y. Times, Sept. 15, 1957, p. 59.   [29] N.Y. Daily News, Sept. 30, 1957.

[30] See 49 J. NATIONAL MEDICAL ASS'N 429, 432 (1957); REITZES, op. cit. supra note 24, at 47-187 passim.

[31] Ibid. See also 1 R.R.L.R. 1123 (1956) (Detroit: of 47 hospitals, 17 had few Negro patients, 20 segregated. Of those which did not segregate, 8 were governmental, 5 were Negro hospitals); LOTH & FLEMING, op. cit. supra note 23, at 36 (a Camden, N.J., hospital ended segregation only in 1954; a Cincinnati hospital first extended courtesies to a Negro physician in 1955); N.Y. Times, April 1, 1956, p. 42 (when the Catholic Queen of the World Hospital opened in Kansas City, Mo., in 1955, it was the only modern private hospital there to give Negro physicians staff privileges, although the city had a 16 percent Negro population); N.Y. Times, Nov. 3, 1957, p. 37 (Kansas City orders consolidation of municipal hospitals for Negroes and whites as of 1958).

[32] CHICAGO MUNICIPAL CODE § 137-13.1 (1956), 2 R.R.L.R. 697 (1957). Forty-six of fifty-six Chicago hospitals reported no colored physicians on attending staffs;

fare regulation[33] requires that private nursing homes which care for welfare recipients give proof that they do not practice discrimination if they wish to continue receiving such referrals.

Almost all hospital segregation in the South and a great deal of it in the North is the private action of doctors, hospital boards, and medical societies. It reflects the arrangement (discussed in chapter VI) which links the right to practice in a hospital to membership in the local medical society. Heretofore Negroes have been barred from the white societies in most Southern states, and even now membership is the exception, although a number of societies have lifted racial bars following an American Medical Association recommendation that these be reviewed.[34] Absence of an open policy of discrimination, however, has not meant that Negroes enjoy a proportionate share of hospital appointments. Most Negro patients in Southern white hospitals are the patients of white physicians and are billeted in separate wings or floors, but some Southern institutions have permitted Negro doctors to enter to treat their own patients. Where they may not the Negro physician gets the patients who cannot afford hospitalization, while patients who can pay go to white doctors who can use the best hospital.[35]

The small amount of existing law on the subject indicates that private hospitals may govern themselves like other private enterprises unless restrained by statute or other regulation.[36] If a private hospital offered some unique facility—as is undoubtedly true in many com-

---

five reported 16 colored staff physicians; five had had them in the past, but had none at the time. Fifty-five had colored patients but only 23 cases had been admitted as private patients of staff doctors. See Afro-American, July 30, 1957, p. 9.

[33] 2 R.R.L.R. 511 (1957); see N.Y. Times, Dec. 20, 1956, p. 16 (Nursing Home Association pledges support; agreement worked out with New York City Commission on Intergroup Relations; the homes receive $150–$200 per month per patient).

[34] In at least ten Southern states medical societies have admitted Negroes, although it is not clear that full status was accorded in all cases; in Virginia more than a score joined (as of the report of LOTH & FLEMING op. cit. supra note 23, at 80–81). See also 49 J. NATIONAL MEDICAL ASS'N, op. cit. supra note 24, passim.

[35] See 49 J. NATIONAL MEDICAL ASS'N, op. cit. supra note 24, at 354.

[36] See HAYT, HAYT & GROESCHEL, LAW OF HOSPITAL, PHYSICIAN AND PATIENT 241 (2d ed. 1952); 41 C.J.S. Hospitals § 8; the following states' civil rights statutes, cited in appendix A6, expressly cover hospitals: Massachusetts, New Jersey, New Mexico, New York, Pennsylvania, Rhode Island, Washington. ILL. STATS. ANN. ch. 120, § 500(7) provides that hospitals found by court adjudication to have denied admission for race shall not be tax-exempt. A policy of nonsegregation has been adopted by administrators of Maryland's State Department of Mental Hygiene, Afro-American, Aug. 17, 1957, p. 1; the Maryland State Department of Welfare does not segregate at its Clyburn Shelter, Afro-American, June 29, 1957, p. 1.

munities—it might be held to the standard of a monopoly. But a paucity of cases [37] on the duty of hospitals with respect to race probably stems from the fact that persons requiring hospitalization usually are in no position to litigate. They have to care for their illnesses where and as soon as they can; potential litigation then becomes moot. On the other hand, however, for the same reason, patients desiring segregation may be in no real position to object where hospitals decided to end it.

The term "private" is not really fully descriptive when applied to most hospitals which are so called. Probably all enjoy tax exemption; many receive other state or local assistance; and since 1946 more than 3,000 hospitals, including "private" ones, have been approved for aid under the federal Hill-Burton Hospital Construction Act.[38] That act contains a racial equity formula (like that of the Morrill Land-Grant College Act) which approves separate-but-equal facilities. To qualify for federal aid there may not be any racial distinctions in the state hospital plan "but," in the words of the act, "an exception shall be made in cases where separate hospital facilities are provided for separate population groups, if the plan makes equitable provision on the basis of need for facilities and services of like quality for each group." It has been suggested that the act's administrators could in practice read the equity formula out by overriding it with the Constitution's equal protection clause which, subsequent to Hill-Burton's passage, was held to bar segregation. But the Department of Health, Education, and Welfare (HEW) has not expressed an opinion on whether federal funds may be given to a Jim Crow hospital,[39] although HEW continues to make such grants. A suit filed in North Carolina has challenged the legality of excluding Negro physicians from a hospital in Wilmington which has received substantial federal aid, but has not assailed the segregation of patients.[40]

[37] See Johnson v. Crawfis, 128 F. Supp. 230 (E.D. Ark. 1955) (action to compel admission of insane Negro child to mental institution dismissed; no evidence to show racial discrimination); see note 40 *infra*.

[38] 42 U.S.C.A. § 291e(f); see 49 J. NATIONAL MEDICAL ASS'N, *op. cit. supra* note 24, at 191.

[39] Afro-American, Feb. 23, 1957, p. 3. (Louisiana attorney queries Secretary Folsom on legality of bond election to raise matching funds for construction of a segregated hospital, as well as constitutionality of federal Hill-Burton grants for such purpose. HEW spokesman says no application was made, *id.* at 6.)

[40] Eaton v. Board of Managers of James Walker Memorial Hosp., 261 F.2d 521 (4th Cir. 1958) *cert. denied*, 358 U.S. 984 (1959) (dismissed; but the Hill-Burton Act was not involved); see p. 55 *supra*.

DISCRIMINATION BY LAW IN RECREATIONAL FACILITIES

State laws provide no South-wide, coherent plan for segregating public accommodations or amusements. Such separation or exclusion statutes as there are on the books, or other such official rules, obviously are illegal, but these have been proclaimed as law. In Arkansas race tracks and gaming houses must be separate; in Georgia, poolrooms. Kentucky statutes until recently spoke of separate funds and boards for parks. Louisiana, which at one time required segregation only at circuses, recently passed a comprehensive law. Missouri empowers boards of education to provide separate libraries and parks (although it has repealed its general educational segregation laws). Oklahoma has authorized separate parks and telephone booths. North Carolina until recently had a law for segregating library reading rooms. South Carolina has provided for segregated poolrooms, public recreation (in cities of more than 60,000), and state parks. Tennessee has legislated generally to preserve "existing rights to provide separate accommodations." Texas statutes separate in libraries and parks. Virginia has a thoroughgoing law, segregating any place of public entertainment or public assemblage. Mississippi has a new comprehensive statute providing for separate places of public accommodation.[41]

There are also municipal ordinances,[42] but the state speaks in other ways too. For example, until forbidden by court decree a short while ago the Baltimore Board of Liquor Commissioners granted liquor licenses for colored or white patronage only, not both.[43] And administrators or managers have segregated without statutory direction.[44] The largest part of segregation, however, is enforced by custom or proprietors, who, so far as the law is concerned, need not segregate at

[41] For statutes described in text see appendix A4.

[42] For recent ordinances, see, e.g., Afro-American, April 14, 1956, p. 2 (Lipscomb, Ala.: public transportation, eating places, public assembly); id., Aug. 24, 1957, p. 9 (Bessemer, Ala.: tennis courts); 1 R.R.L.R. 733 (1956) (Delray Beach, Fla.: beach and pool ordinance); id. at 945 (Sarasota, Fla.: beach). Other ordinances are set forth in MURRAY, op. cit. supra note 7, at 615 et seq.

[43] De Angelis v. Board of Liquor License Comm'rs, 1 R.R.L.R. 370 (Baltimore City Ct. 1955); see Afro-American, July 14, 1956, p. 32 (upon invalidation of the rule "many of the establishments did change their policy . . . estimates . . . running in the hundreds"). In Montgomery there are separate state-owned liquor shops for Negro and white patrons, but in Birmingham both buy from the same state store, id., Feb. 11, 1956, p. 8.

[44] See Lonesome v. Maxwell, 220 F.2d 386 (4th Cir. 1955), aff'd sub nom. Mayor, etc., of Baltimore City v. Dawson, 350 U.S. 877 (1955) (involving state and city boards which segregated without specific statutory authorization).

all. On the other hand, there are instances of private businessmen in otherwise segregated communities who occasionally or regularly have departed from the pattern.[45] The policy of some groups to avoid holding conventions in segregated cities sometimes has been a successful force against segregation.[46] A more pervasive pressure has been the growing prosperity of the Negro market.

Laws or ordinances requiring segregation in places of public accommodation are as unconstitutional as other state segregation rules. They affect not only members of the public but businessmen, Negro and white, whose patronage is limited to one race. Such businessmen should be able to sue to restrain the city or state from keeping part of their trade away, but suit by a member of the public who had been discriminated against is more likely. The plaintiff would probably enjoin the government from enforcing segregation, but then if proprietors continued to make racial distinctions, the plaintiff's position in the community would be one where with no segregation laws proprietors discriminate voluntarily against him. This situation is the most prevalent, and may explain why there have been few suits involving state-required discrimination in privately owned facilities in the South.[47] There has, however, been a good deal of litigation involving Southern state-owned accommodations which cannot fall back on private prerogative as a defense.

In public recreation there has been little dispute over the law gov-

[45] See LOTH & FLEMING, *op. cit. supra* note 23, at 100-101 (reporting instances of nondiscrimination in public accommodations in Delaware, Kentucky, Maryland, Missouri, Oklahoma, Tennessee, Texas, West Virginia); Afro-American, May 12, 1956, p. 5 (Negroes admitted to Miami Beach hotels; attorney general says no law forbids); *id.*, Aug. 4, 1956, p. 28 (Baltimore department store cafeteria open to all); *id.*, March 30, 1957, p. 32 (Baltimore Sheraton Belvedere continues new nonsegregation policy); *id.*, Feb. 11, 1956, p. 8 (Baltimore stores do not permit Negroes to try on lingerie; Atlanta, Birmingham, Jackson stores do).

[46] *E.g.*, Afro-American, April 6, 1957, p. 1 (protest over Baltimore hotel segregation during convention of American Association of Anatomists); N.Y. Times, Feb. 16, 1957, p. 13 (Connecticut delegation boycotts Federal Old Age and Survivors Insurance Agency conference in Baltimore); *id.*, March 7, 1956, p. 24 (suit filed against VFW by members to restrain holding of convention in Dallas); Afro-American, April 6, 1957, p. 1 (American Association for the Advancement of Science resolution barring conventions in segregated cities); Chicago Defender, July 6, 1957, p. 4 (Baptists hit Texas hotel ban).

[47] See Bissell v. Commonwealth, 199 Va. 397, 100 S.E.2d 1 (1957) (violation of segregation at auditorium; Virginia Supreme Court refused to pass on constitutionality, reversing on ground of defective warrant); *compare with* Commonwealth v. Taylor, 3 R.R.L.R. 313 (Arlington, Va., Cir. Ct. 1958) (Virginia statute held unconstitutional); *cf.* County of Arlington v. Eldridge, 3 R.R.L.R. 737 (Arlington, Va., County Ct. 1958) (disorderly conduct charge not sustained).

erning racial distinctions since the *School Cases*. A Maryland federal district court in 1954 attempted to distinguish beaches and pools from schools to avoid the *School* rule. The opinion argued that beach attendance is voluntary and not as important as education, and that interracial contact at swimming places stirs intense opposition because it has erotic connotations. But the Court of Appeals for the Fourth Circuit reversed and was affirmed by the Supreme Court.[48] The high court at the same time summarily vacated a Fifth Circuit decision that an Atlanta municipal golf course might continue a program of separate days for Negroes and whites.[49]

Since then a considerable number (though small in proportion to the whole) of other public recreational facilities have been ordered to cease making racial distinctions; most have complied.[50] Pools and

[48] Lonesome v. Maxwell, 123 F. Supp. 193 (D. Md. 1954), *rev'd*, 220 F.2d 386 (4th Cir. 1955), *aff'd sub nom.* Mayor, etc., of Baltimore City v. Dawson, 350 U.S. 877 (1955). Following this decision park officials announced "transition had been effected without incident," Afro-American, July 7, 1956, p. 16.

[49] Holmes v. City of Atlanta, 350 U.S. 879 (1955), *vac'g* 223 F.2d 93 (5th Cir. 1955).

[50] Holley v. City of Portsmouth, 150 F. Supp. 6 (E.D. Va. 1957) (golf; opinion notes that Norfolk's golf course lessee has ended segregation following decision of *Tate* case, *infra* note 56); Ward v. City of Miami, 151 F. Supp. 593 (S.D. Fla. 1957) (golf; segregation ended); City of St. Petersburg v. Alsup, 238 F.2d 830 (5th Cir. 1956), *cert. denied*, 353 U.S. 922 (1957) (discrimination at municipal beach and pool unconstitutional; closed when Negroes tried to use it, N.Y. Times, June 6, 1958, p. 15); Hayes v. Crutcher, 137 F. Supp. 853 (M.D. Tenn. 1956) (golf; segregation ended); Fayson v. Beard, 134 F. Supp. 379 (E.D. Tex. 1955) (city parks; segregation ended); Moorehead v. City of Ft. Lauderdale, 152 F. Supp. 131 (S.D. Fla. 1957), *aff'd*, 248 F.2d 544 (5th Cir. 1957) (segregation unconstitutional, but golf course sold, see note 55 *infra*); Augustus v. City of Pensacola, 1 R.R.L.R. 681 (N.D. Fla. 1956) (municipal recreation, including golf); Detiege v. New Orleans City Park Improvement Ass'n, 252 F.2d 122 (5th Cir. 1958), *aff'd*, 358 U.S. 54 (1958) (the Louisiana law and New Orleans ordinance requiring segregation in city parks unconstitutional); Leeper v. Charlotte Park & Recreation Comm'n, 2 R.R.L.R. 411 (N.C. Super. Ct. 1957) (this is the *Barringer* case, discussed *infra* p. 284; after remand, commission purchased the reverter; segregation ended); Moorman v. Morgan, 285 S.W.2d 146 (Ky. 1955) (outlawing segregation in Louisville parks on authority of *Dawson;* segregation ended). For pre-*School Cases* decisions under separate-but-equal see: Draper v. City of St. Louis, 92 F. Supp. 546 (E.D. Mo. 1950), *app. dism. by appellants*, 186 F.2d 307 (8th Cir. 1950) (swimming pool; segregation ended); Lawrence v. Hancock, 76 F. Supp. 1004 (S.D.W. Va. 1948) (pool had been leased to private operator; unconstitutional); Williams v. Kansas City, 104 F. Supp. 848 (W.D. Mo. 1952), *aff'd*, 205 F.2d 47 (8th Cir. 1953), *cert. denied*, 346 U.S. 826 (1953) (Negro pool distant from general facilities). But some older cases merely required separate days for Negro use, *e.g.*, Rice v. Arnold, 340 U.S. 848 (1950), *vacating and remanding* 45 So. 2d 195 (1950) to the Supreme Court of Florida with general instructions to proceed in the light of *Sweatt* and *McLaurin* (see pp. 260–262 *infra*); but the Florida court ignored the clear implication, 54 So. 2d 114 (1951), *cert. denied*, 342 U.S. 946 (1952) (giving as reason adequate nonfederal grounds). A week

beaches in Maryland and Texas; parks in Kentucky, North Carolina, Maryland, and Texas; an amphitheater in Louisville; golf courses in most Southern states, including in Georgia, where an Atlanta case was the first antisegregation suit won in that state, have been desegregated. Some Southern recreational desegregation has come as a result of administrative or legislative action.[51] A number of Northern facilities have given up segregation or exclusion, sometimes under legal pressure.[52] But in most Southern communities Negroes are barred from public recreation as before.[53]

Public accommodations and recreation, though state-owned, often lend themselves to private operation and may be leased out for management.[54] But recently some governmental bodies have turned management over to private persons or have authorized such conveyance

---

after the *School* decisions the Supreme Court of the United States summarily disposed of two recreation cases: Beal v. Holcombe, 193 F.2d 384 (5th Cir. 1951), *cert. denied*, 347 U.S. 974 (1954) (lower court upheld separate-but-equal for golf course but city subsequently opened course without distinctions in belief that prevailing standards of equality made segregation impossible, McKay, *supra* note 2, at 699 n.11, 716 n.97); Muir v. Louisville Park Theatrical Ass'n, 202 F.2d 275 (6th Cir. 1953), *judg. vacated and remanded* for consideration in light of *School* cases and "conditions that now prevail," 347 U.S. 971 (1954) (shortly thereafter defendants voted to offer tickets to general public, McKay at 708 n.57).

[51] San Antonio Ordinance No. 22555, 1 R.R.L.R. 589 (1956) (opening pools, auditoriums, golf, tennis courts; litigation was pending but never came to judgment); Afro-American, April 7, 1956, p. 1 (Corpus Christi desegregates pool by vote of park and recreation board); 1 R.R.L.R. 971 (1956) (statement of Maryland State Commission of Forests and Parks, Nov. 29, 1955, following *Dawson:* "public parks and recreational facilities . . . henceforward operated on an integrated basis"); N.Y. Times, July 17, 1957, p. 24 (Greensboro City Council votes to continue exclusion from pools but opens libraries); *id.*, May 21, 1956, p. 19 (Delray Beach, Fla., ended segregation on its beach following filing of federal suit, which was then dismissed by agreement; however, following interracial friction an ordinance was passed prohibiting Negroes from using municipal beach or pool, *id.*, May 24, 1956, p. 26, 1 R.R.L.R. 733 (1956)); Afro-American, June 29, 1957, p. 1 (Camp Frances Wood, operated by Baltimore, accepted only Negroes in 1957 while planning integration for 1958).

[52] *E.g.*, Morton v. City Comm'rs of Parsons, 178 Kan. 282, 285 P.2d 774 (1955); Evansville, Ind., recreation board orders end of segregation in five municipal pools after suit filed, Afro-American, July 10, 1956, p. 1; segregation by private clubs using San Francisco municipal golf courses forbidden, *id.*, March 9, 1957, p. 1; following ruling one club ceased use of course, N.Y. Times, Feb. 28, 1957, p. 23.

[53] *E.g.*, Afro-American, Aug. 24, 1957, p. 9 (Negroes arrested and taken into "protective custody" after attempting to use tennis courts in Bessemer, Ala., public park). N.Y. Times, July 13, 1957, p. 8 (Negroes arrested for playing on Durham city tennis court).

[54] The facilities involved in City of Greensboro v. Simkins, 246 F.2d 425 (4th Cir. 1957), and in Muir v. Louisville Park Theatrical Ass'n, *supra* note 50, apparently were not in the first instance placed under private management to avoid desegregation.

primarily to avoid desegregation and some facilities have even been closed or their closing authorized for the same purpose.[55] Courts have held, however, that when such property is leased, the lessee may not discriminate;[56] nor may cities which manage their own facilities in a so-called "proprietary capacity."[57] The Fourth Circuit has informed Virginia that should it turn over to private persons a park which was the subject of a suit, it must, if there is a sale, offer the property without discrimination, and if a lease, see that the lessee makes no racial distinctions.[58] The Fifth Circuit, which has forbidden the lessee of a restaurant in a county courthouse to make racial distinctions, has also written in that case that where there is "no purpose of discrimination, no joinder in the enterprise, or express reservation of control by the county," and the property is surplus, a lessee may exercise the prerogative of a wholly private proprietor.[59]

All of these gambits present questions on which there has been but little litigation.[60] The cases on schools appear to be closest in point: in Virginia federal courts have ruled that the schools may not be

[55] See appendix A5. N.Y. Times, Aug. 29, 1957, p. 25 (residents of Marshall, Texas, vote to sell municipal pool after suit filed against segregation); N.Y. Times, July 10, 1957, p. 14 (Fort Lauderdale sells $1,000,000 course for $562,400 to evade federal court ruling that Negroes must be permitted to use municipal golf course); see Griffis v. City of Fort Lauderdale, 104 So. 2d 33 (Fla. 1958) (sale was pursuant to state law); Afro-American, Oct. 26, 1957, p. 6 (Asheville, N.C., pool built for $106,700 in 1925 sold for $8,500 to avoid desegregation). Id., April 28, 1956, p. 16 (Georgia state parks director leases nine of the parks to private citizens at average price of $2,000 per month to preserve segregation; Alabama, Mississippi, and South Carolina have approved similar measures).

[56] Derrington v. Plummer, 240 F.2d 922 (5th Cir. 1956), cert. denied, 353 U.S. 924 (1957); Tate v. Department of Conservation, 133 F. Supp. 53 (E.D. Va. 1955), aff'd, 231 F.2d 615 (4th Cir. 1956), cert. denied, 352 U.S. 838 (1956); City of Greensboro v. Simkins, supra note 54. See also Burton v. Wilmington Parking Authority, Civil No. 1029, New Castle County, Del. Ch., April 15, 1959 (forbidding exclusion from restaurant owned by parking authority). The Durham, N.C., city attorney holds that Negroes have no constitutional right to enter city theater or ball park leased to private operators, 2 R.R.L.R. 874, 877 (1957).

[57] City of St. Petersburg v. Alsup, supra note 50.

[58] Tate v. Department of Conservation, supra note 56; City of Greensboro v. Simkins, supra note 54.

[59] Derrington v. Plummer, supra note 56, at 925; but no case has so held. See Easterly v. Dempster, 112 F. Supp. 214 (E.D. Tenn. 1953) (municipal golf course leased one day prior to service of complaint; lessee not defendant; lease held bona fide and not to deprive plaintiffs of rights); see also ruling of the Durham city attorney, note 56 supra.

[60] See Clark v. Flory, 141 F. Supp. 248 (E.D.S.C. 1956), aff'd, 237 F.2d 597 (4th Cir. 1956) (prior to decision state legislature closed park; court declined to pass on constitutionality of the statutes, see appendix A5, although in oral argument the state conceded them to be unconstitutional). Tate v. Department of Conservation, supra note 56.

closed to avoid mixing of the races,[61] but the decisions have been based on the inequality of maintaining public education in some areas while having ended it in others. The cases have not made holdings on the issue of whether a public function may be abandoned to defeat rights in pending litigation, or those earned in the courts. A "bona fide" sale of a swimming pool planned in anticipation of a desegregation suit, however, has been upheld by a federal district court in North Carolina, but at this writing the issue of what is "bona fide" is still to be thrashed out in that suit.[62] As noted above, the Fourth Circuit may require arrangements to assure equal opportunity to purchase, but for Negroes such a right is probably illusory when large sums are involved.

DISCRIMINATION NOT REQUIRED BY LAW IN PUBLIC ACCOMMODATIONS

English common law bound innkeepers to receive and lodge all travelers and to entertain them at reasonable prices without any specific or previous contract, in the absence of reasonable grounds for refusal.[63] "Inn" has been defined as an establishment where the host offers food, shelter, and protection (but this would not include an apartment-hotel for nontransients). In England rejection of a guest was long ago made a crime and remediable by suit for damages.[64] The rule is viable there today, as witnessed by a recent case in which a renowned West Indian cricketer, a Negro, recovered (though only nominal damages) against a British hotel for refusal to receive him.[65] As a gen-

[61] James v. Almond, 170 F. Supp. 331 (E.D. Va. 1959); James v. Duckworth, 170 F. Supp. 342 (E.D. Va. 1959).

[62] Tonkins v. City of Greensboro, 162 F. Supp. 549 (M.D.N.C. 1958).

[63] Robins v. Gray, [1895] 2 Q.B. 501, 503; 18 HALSBURY's LAWS OF ENGLAND 136 (2d ed. 1935) ("an innkeeper is . . . a common innkeeper because, within the limits of his liability to receive and entertain guests, he is equally bound to receive and entertain all persons, and is not entitled to pick and choose between them or to accept certain persons as guests and refuse others"); and see *id.* at 141; STORY, BAILMENTS § 470 (9th ed. 1878). See 43 C.J.S. *Innkeepers* § 3; Davis v. Gay, 141 Mass. 531, 6 N.E. 549 (1886) (owner of an apartment-hotel, not an innkeeper); Curtis v. Murphy, 63 Wis. 4, 22 N.W. 825 (1885); STORY, *op. cit. supra*, § 477; BEALE, INNKEEPERS §§ 1-6 (1906); see also R. v. Higgins, [1947] 2 All E.R. 619, [1948] 1 K.B. 165. Alpaugh v. Wolverton, 184 Va. 943, 36 S.E.2d 906 (1946). The requirement that the guest be a traveler seems to have been abandoned. See, *e.g.,* Walling v. Potter, 35 Conn. 183 (1868).

[64] *Crime:* R. v. Ivens, [1835] 7 C. & P. 213; R. v. Rymer, [1877] 2 Q.B. 136; HALSBURY, *op. cit. supra* note 63, at 148; STORY, *op. cit. supra* note 63, § 476; *cf.* R. v. Luellin, [1701] 12 Mod. Rep. 445. *Damages:* Fell v. Knight, [1841] 8 M. & W. 269; Constantine v. Imperial Hotels, Ltd., [1944] 1 K.B. 693, 2 All E.R. 171 (no need to prove special damages; plaintiff recovered nominal damages only; punitive damages refused).

[65] Constantine v. Imperial Hotels, Ltd., *supra* note 64.

eral rule, it might be said that American law has received the English standard; only a minority of states, however, have spoken; [66] a few have explicitly rejected it.[67] In a state where an innkeeper case arose for the first time a court could refuse to recognize the common law duty of hospitality, or where the rule exists the state legislature might repeal it or the courts judicially overrule it.

Some of the reasons for the English doctrine on inns no longer exist. It was developed to protect the traveler in a day when the solitary inn between cities was a necessity on long, dangerous journeys. The inn was like a common carrier or public utility, and partook of their legal obligations. In our day this is no longer generally true, but in states where Negroes may expect to be turned away from all places reserved for whites, their position rather closely approximates that of the old English traveler: food, shelter, and protection are hard to come by. There are a few good Negro hotels or motels in the United States, but in most communities there are none, or those which do exist provide poor accommodations. Thus, shelter is usually sought in private homes, sometimes on Negro college campuses or in Negro Ys.

Since the innkeeper's duty at old common law extended to providing food, one was considered a guest if he merely dined at a hotel.[68] Following that law hotel dining rooms of today should be within the

[66] CAL. PENAL CODE § 365 (1955); and see California statutes in appendix A6; ME. REV. STATS. ch. 100, § 32 (1954); MASS. ANN. LAWS ch. 140, §§ 7, 8 (1957); MONT REV. CODE ANN. § 94-35-104 (1949); N.Y. PEN. LAW § 513 (1944); cf. the recent English Hotel Proprietors Act, 1956, ch. 62, PUBLIC GENERAL ACTS (1956). Several Southern states have innkeeper provisions: GA. CODE ANN. § 52-103 (1937) ("the innkeeper . . . is bound to receive as guests . . . all persons of good character offering themselves, who are willing to comply with his rules"); cf. LA. REV. STATS. § 4:3 (1951) (repealed, Acts 1954 No. 194, § 1); N.C. GEN. STATS. § 72-1 (1950) (but see State v. Steele, infra note 70). See Thomas v. Pick Hotel Corp., 224 F.2d 664 (10th Cir. 1955) (Kansas); Bowlin v. Lyon, 67 Iowa 536, 25 N.W. 766 (1885); Op. Att'y Gen. of Vt. No. 97 (1955). See also, STORY, op. cit. supra note 63, § 476; 43 C.J.S. Innkeepers § 9; Hartmann, Racial and Religious Discrimination by Innkeepers in U.S.A., 12 MODERN L. REV. 449 (1949).

[67] DEL. CODE ANN. tit. 24, § 1501 (1953) (innkeeper, restaurateur, etc., not obliged to furnish services to persons whose reception would be offensive to major part of his customers, and would injure his business); MISS. CODE ANN. § 2046.5 (1956 Supp.) (anyone in "public business" authorized to select patrons); TENN. CODE ANN. § 62-710 (1955) (common law rule expressly abrogated); FLA. STATS. ANN. § 509.092 (1958 Supp.) (public lodging and public food establishments declared private; owner has right to refuse service).

[68] See, e.g., Orchard v. Bush & Co., [1898] 2Q.B. 284, 287 ("I confess I do not understand why he should not be a guest if he uses the inn as an inn for the purpose merely of getting a meal there"). Dove v. Lowden, 47 F. Supp. 546, 548 (W.D. Mo. 1942) (relation of innkeeper and guest arose when plaintiff went to the lunchroom in defendant's hotel solely for refreshments); Kopper v. Willis,

rule and open even to nonresident patrons of the hotel. There is, however, a Virginia case holding that under some circumstances the rule may be otherwise.[69]

The innkeeper rule as now observed in some jurisdictions seems to contain exceptions which might be used against Negroes. For one, it has been held that if a guest is objectionable to other patrons it is reasonable to exclude him.[70] For another, an English dictum states that the host may reserve his premises for a specific class.[71] The traveler is not entitled to any specific accommodation. An old text, *Beale on Innkeepers*, states that segregation would not breach the innkeeper's obligation, though the authority it cites is dubious.[72] Delaware permits a proprietor to exclude anyone objectionable to a majority of his patrons; Mississippi and Florida have legislated the right of proprietors to choose their customers, and those who do not leave when ordered are guilty of a misdemeanor.[73]

A state court, however, could not adopt the innkeeper rule for whites, recognizing race as reasonable grounds to exclude Negroes, since the Fourteenth Amendment reaches all state action including that emanating from the courts. But if a state in no way requires that hospitality be extended at inns or hotels, it seems that the Fourteenth Amendment would not apply, except under the first Justice Harlan's view of state action.

Nowadays many travelers book reservations before undertaking their journeys. If a hotel gives a Negro a reservation by mail or telephone, but denies him a room when he arrives and it appears that he is colored, the question arises whether the reservation confers any right greater than the right at common law to be accommodated. The

---

9 Daly 460, 463–464 (1881) ("if the restaurant forms part of the establishment and the whole house [*i.e.*, hotel] is . . . under one . . . management" it is considered an inn; plaintiff entered solely to dine); Burton v. Drake Hotel Co., 237 Ill. App. 76 (1925) (plaintiff had checked in); 43 C.J.S. *Innkeepers* § 3(b); see the highly critical note in 4 WASH. & LEE L. REV. 107 (1946) (hotel dining rooms and coffee shops . . . have no distinguishing features from separate restaurants).

[69] Alpaugh v. Wolverton, *supra* note 63.

[70] State v. Steele, 106 N.C. 766, 782, 11 S.E. 478 (1860) (suggesting race as valid ground of exclusion); *cf.* Langford v. Vandaveer, 254 S.W.2d. 498, 501 (Ky. Ct. App., 1953). *But compare* 43 C.J.S. *Innkeepers* § 9(b) (grounds for refusal to receive a proposed guest are as a rule limited to lack of accommodations or the unsuitability of the guest).

[71] Johnson v. Midland Ry., 4 Ex. 367, 371, 154 Eng. Rep. 1254 (1849) (those arriving in own carriages). See STORY, *op. cit. supra* note 63, at 437 n.8.

[72] BEALE, *op. cit. supra* note 63, § 55.   [73] See note 67 *supra*.

answer in at least one case is yes, that there is a breach of contract.[74] Aside from this, denial of hospitality to a reservation holder is almost surely evidence of discrimination (it would be difficult to claim that some nonracial reason was the ground for refusal). But breaking the reservation per se may not conclude the matter, since a reservation might, in some cases, be argued to be a promise by the hotel only that accommodations will be provided if they are available and that the hotel expects them to be available, a prediction based upon experience with arrivals and departures under similar conditions, which sometimes is not borne out. The inquiry may have to be directed to the real reason for refusal—unfortunately for a plaintiff information peculiarly the knowledge of the hotel staff.

Actually "inns" represent only a small fraction of the total number of public accommodations, even those which are recreational in nature. Turning to some others, for which there are neither segregation nor civil rights statutes, a private theater owner, for example, and other proprietors of places of amusement legally may admit whom they please. And even where there are civil rights laws, it has been held that when a theater ticket holder is barred, liability is the price of the ticket, hardly making suit worth while (except, of course, where there have been other damages).[75] In some communities proprietors of certain hotels, restaurants, or theaters have desired to admit Negroes but have been required to exclude them by their trade association, as

---

[74] Thomas v. Pick Hotels *supra* note 66 (breach of innkeeper's duty is tort; but *arbitrary* refusal also violates reservation contract). See Bishop v. Hotels Statler, 4 CIVIL LIBERTIES DOCKET 37 (E.D. Mich. 1958) (reservation made in Detroit for Dallas not honored; settled).

[75] See Taylor v. Cohn, 47 Ore. 538, 84 Pac. 388 (1906) (plaintiff could recover only purchase price of theater ticket where owner unlawfully refused him admission, regardless of discrimination); Purcell v. Daly, 19 Abb. N. Cas. 301 (N.Y. 1886) (similar holding); Capital Theatre v. Compton, 246 Ky. 130, 54 S.W.2d 620 (1932) (plaintiff could not recover for humiliation of being expelled from defendant's theater); Bailey v. Washington Theatre, 218 Ind. 513, 34 N.E.2d 17 (1941) (plaintiff unlawfully excluded from theater in violation of Civil Rights Act restricted to statutory amount of recovery); De La Ysla v. Publix Theatres, 82 Utah 598, 26 P.2d 818 (1933) (measure of damages for wrongful exclusion from theater seat, price of ticket); *but cf.* Boswell v. Barnum and Bailey, 135 Tenn. 35, 185 S.W. 692 (1916) (defendant liable in tort where its servants were abusive toward plaintiff in assigning him to seat; $500 recovery); W.W.V. Co. v. Black, 113 Va. 728, 75 S.E. 82 (1912) (complaint upheld as sounding in tort against demurrer where cause of action for wrongful expulsion of ticket holder from theater was based on tort and breach of contract); Nance v. Mayflower Tavern, Inc., 106 Utah 517, 150 P.2d 773 (1944) (restaurant owner not held to common law duty of innkeeper); Alpaugh v. Wolverton, *supra* note 63.

for a time in Baltimore.[76] A remedy against such concerted pressure might be the antitrust laws, state or federal.[77]

On another tack, since almost all places of public accommodation enjoy one or more municipal or state licenses, does enjoyment of this privilege require that the licensee not discriminate? [78] This question has been mooted among civil rights lawyers a great deal. One type of license, the liquor license, seems to invite state control more compellingly than others. There is apparently no right to engage in the liquor business without explicit governmental permission. Most states issue only a limited number of licenses. Traffic among legal dealers is encouraged, other liquor trade discouraged. It may be held, therefore, that liquor dealers are like public utility monopolies, that they must use their governmentally granted franchise for the public at large. If this is so, the Fourteenth Amendment should also apply, for the monopoly has been conferred by government as in the case of a common carrier or as to a certified collective bargaining agent.

The usual remedy in many of the cases discussed above would be a suit for damages. It is not clear, however, what the standard of computing damages would be for all states, although it should allow at least the value of the denied accommodation, and some jurisdictions do allow compensation for humiliation and embarrassment suffered in wrongful ejection from a hotel.[79] But in any case, damages probably would not reach the $10,000 necessary for federal jurisdiction, assuming that the requisite diversity of citizenship could be shown, and suit would have to be brought in state court. Suit for damages would, of

[76] Afro-American, Jan. 19, 1957, p. 1 (official of hotel barring Negroes states, "Our policy follows the Hotel Association of Baltimore. . . . I think all the hotels follow the policy, individually because, after all they belong to it." Query: Is this individual or concerted action?) The Baltimore Sheraton Belvedere began admitting Negroes but stopped at the demand of the association, *id.*, March 30, 1957, p. 32. It then resumed nondiscrimination and was followed by others. But only the Sheraton honored all reservations throughout the hotel; others accepted only Negro athletes and convention-goers in small numbers, declaring restaurants and bars off-limits. The change was spurred by unfavorable publicity about baseball stars. An important catalyst was the Governor's Commission on Interracial Problems, *id.* July 20, 1957, p. 1; see N. Y. Times, July 14, 1957, p. 50.

[77] For a discussion of antitrust considerations see pp. 302-304 *infra*.

[78] See Bowlin v. Lyon, 67 Iowa 536, 539, 25 N.W. 766, 768 (1885): "We incline to think that he would [not be permitted to]."

[79] See, *e.g.*, DeWolf v. Ford, 193 N.Y. 397, 86 N.E. 527 (1908) (but no punitive damages); Milner Hotel v. Brent, 207 Miss. 892, 43 So. 2d 654 (1949) (punitive damages too); Jones v. Shannon, 55 Mont. 225, 175 Pac. 882 (1918); see Annot., 14 A.L.R.2d 715 (1950).

course, involve a jury, which is likely to reflect the mores of a prejudiced community. In any event, wherever damages could be deemed inadequate, equity probably would have jurisdiction where state law recognizes the common law right to be served or admitted. Some jurisdictions, however, grant equitable relief to protect only property rights, not personal rights.[80] The courts also apparently have not passed upon the availability of injunction to protect the common law right to enjoy privately owned public accommodations.

Because courts and juries in more prejudiced areas are hardly likely to create or enforce public accommodations rights, the common law remedies discussed above are hardly powerful civil rights weapons. Travelers, for example, would probably find it difficult to return to a distant community to press suit for small and problematical damages. In parts of the country where these rules might be expected to afford the most protection, there are usually civil rights statutes which are more clear and effective.

PUBLIC ACCOMMODATIONS LAWS

Private proprietors who serve the public and are not under duty to serve all (like carriers, inns, and perhaps other places suggested above) may discriminate on racial grounds unless forbidden by state or local law.[81] Twenty-six states have enacted such laws, including Alaska, California, Colorado, Connecticut, Illinois, Indiana, Iowa, Kansas, Maine, Massachusetts, Michigan, Minnesota, Montana, Nebraska, New Hampshire (covering advertising only), New Jersey, New Mexico, New York, Ohio, Oregon, Pennsylvania, Rhode Island, Vermont, Washington, Wisconsin, and Wyoming, as well as the District of Columbia.[82] Legislation forbidding bias in public accommodations has been actively sought in other states, chiefly Western ones, which lack such

[80] Compare 43 C.J.S. *Injunctions* § 19(b): "While it has been held in some cases . . . that injunctive relief is not limited to cases where property rights are involved, it has also been held that, in the absence of statutory provisions, injunction will not issue except in support of property rights" with the "adequacy" test, 4 POMEROY, EQUITY JURISPRUDENCE § 1338 (5th ed. 1941): "The incompleteness and inadequacy of the legal remedy is the criterion which . . . determines the right to the . . . injunction." See the excellent, celebrated opinion by Qua, J., in Kenyon v. City of Chicopee, 320 Mass. 528, 70 N.E.2d 241 (1946); Pound, *Equitable Relief Against Defamation and Injuries to Personality*, 29 HARV. L. REV. 640 (1916).

[81] See State v. Clyburn, 247 N.C. 455, 101 S.E.2d 295 (1958).

[82] See appendix A6 for citations.

laws, but whose official public policy may be antidiscrimination, notwithstanding the existence of widespread racial distinctions there.[83]
States unquestionably have the power to enact such legislation; [84] municipal competence is almost always broad enough, but depends on
the terms of the charter.[85]

The places covered by these laws are "public," and genuinely private clubs or sectarian institutions [86] are not required to alter biased
policies. As a consequence, one attempt at evasion has been to call

[83] See COMM. ON HUMAN RIGHTS FOR THE WESTERN STATES OF THE NATIONAL
BAR ASS'N, ANOTHER LOOK AT HUMAN RIGHTS FOR THE WESTERN STATES (pamphlet).
This compendium states that civil rights bills have been introduced recently in
Arizona, Montana, Nevada, New Mexico, Utah, and Wyoming. It notes passage
in Montana and New Mexico of declarations of policy opposed to discrimination
and an enforceable statute in Wyoming, cited in appendix A6, and describes considerable discrimination in Arizona, Idaho, Montana, Nevada (Las Vegas's mayor
refused to endorse civil rights legislation, stating, "The right to refuse service is
an inherent right"), New Mexico, North Dakota, South Dakota, Utah, and
Wyoming. For proposed ordinances in border cities see Afro-American, June 14,
1958, p. 4 (Baltimore), id., March 1, 1958, p. 6 (St. Louis), id., Sept. 14, 1957, p. 1
(Louisville).

[84] Bob-Lo Excursion Co. v. Michigan, 333 U.S. 28 (1948); Railway Mail Ass'n v.
Corsi, 326 U.S. 88 (1945). The New York law has been applied to an out-of-state
resort soliciting guests in New York, Kaplan v. Virginia Hot Springs, Inc.
(SCAD), 3 R.R.L.R. 113 (1958).

[85] For a discussion by the Supreme Court of the power of municipalities under
home rule charters to enact ordinances in the field of public accommodations, see
John R. Thompson Co. v. District of Columbia, 346 U.S. 100, 108 (1953); and for
a compilation of such ordinances see the same case at 203 F.2d 579, 599 (D.C. Cir.
1953). Chicago has enacted an ordinance largely duplicating the state public accommodations law, N.Y. Times, Oct. 11, 1957, p. 20. Kansas City, Kan., has been
held to be without such power. Op. Att'y Gen. of Kan., Feb. 19, 1957, 2
R.R.L.R. 557 (1957). See also Nance v. Mayflower Tavern, Inc., supra note 75
(Salt Lake City civil rights ordinance invalid as beyond delegated power of city).
The converse of the problem is presented when a state undertakes to legislate for a
city which by state constitution enjoys exclusive jurisdiction over the subject
matter. The Maryland Attorney General has ruled that a state statute forbidding
discrimination in Baltimore's hotels would be unconstitutional for this reason.
Afro-American, Feb. 16, 1957, p. 19.

[86] See, e.g., the civil rights statutes of the following states, cited in appendix A6,
all containing provisions to the effect that nothing in the antidiscrimination law
shall be construed to include or apply to any institution, bona fide club, or place
of accommodation which is in its nature distinctly private: New Jersey, New
York, Oregon, Pennsylvania. See also Op. Att'y Gen. of N.J. No. 42 (1955)
(sectarian summer camp excluded from New Jersey law's coverage as private;
but nature of facility rather than agency maintaining it determines status). The
YMCAs would pose a problem of whether they are public or sectarian. Although
Y national policy opposes discrimination, and most comply, a number practice
it. See, e.g., Afro-American, Dec. 29, 1956, p. 20 (District of Columbia YMCA
rejects motion to desegregate); id., June 8, 1957, p. 16 (Maryland Y camps remain
Jim Crow); id., Nov. 24, 1956, p. 6 (Trenton Y segregation). As of mid-1958,
87% of the Ys were integrated, 10% more had limited mixed programs, Chicago
Defender, March 29, 1958, p. 1.

accommodations "private" or "clubs" when in fact they are open to the public. In New York in 1953 a bathing and recreation park which admitted only "members" (really all who applied except Negroes) claimed that it was a club immune from the antidiscrimination statute. But the State Commission Against Discrimination (SCAD) held that the club label was a subterfuge, that anyone (except Negroes) could obtain "memberships," and that "members" had no control over the "club's" affairs, as in bona fide clubs. The commission ordered an end to the discrimination, and the court of appeals upheld the order.[87]

A proof problem, sometimes capitalized on by those who would evade, is to ascertain whether an employee who discriminated acted under the owner's orders. A prima facie case for the owner may be made by showing that the worker had received good-faith instructions to the contrary.[88] Typical evidence of discrimination is contemporaneous treatment of other patrons,[89] but sometimes past policy may help to reveal true current conduct.[90]

The public accommodations antidiscrimination statutes usually have been drafted in great detail, listing long series of places in which they forbid discrimination (*e.g.*, roller rinks, restaurants, bars, poolrooms, hotels, beaches, and so on). Few enumerate as many places as does New

[87] Castle Hill Beach Club v. Arbury, 2 N.Y.2d 596, 142 N.E.2d 186 (1957). See also American Jewish Comm. v. Flick d/b/a Westkill Tavern Club, 1953 N.Y. SCAD REPORT 22 (hotel, bar, and restaurant formerly known as Westkill Hotel "had thereafter been arbitrarily given its appellation of 'Westkill Tavern Club'", commission found it was a place of public accommodation, subject to the law against discrimination); to the same effect see Bash v. Anderson d/b/a Point Breeze Camp, *ibid.; cf.* McCarter v. Beckwith, 247 App. Div. 289, 285 N.Y. Supp. 151 (1936), *aff'd*, 272 N.Y. 488, 3 N.E.2d 882, *cert. denied*, 299 U.S. 601 (1936) (court looked behind corporate structure of beach "club" and held operation to be "sham").

[88] On the master-servant relationship, see Dean v. Chicago & Northwestern R.R., 183 Ill. App. 317 (1913) (acts within scope of employment, civil rights statute applied); Wilkinson v. Hart's Drive-In, Inc., 338 Ill. App. 210, 86 N.E.2d 870 (1949) (owner not liable where employee not authorized or instructed to discriminate); Jackson v. Imburgia, 184 Misc. 1063, 55 N.Y.S.2d 549 (1945) (on preliminary motion: where employee directly violated orders owner not liable; but burden on master to prove that he issued such orders); Goldsberry v. Kamachos, 255 Mich. 647, 239 N.W. 513 (1931) (owner not liable; waitress refused service contrary to orders); *But compare* A.L.I. RESTATEMENT OF AGENCY § 230 (1933) (forbidden acts may be within scope of employment).

[89] Wilson v. Razzetti, 88 Misc. 37, 150 N.Y. Supp. 145 (1914); Bailey v. Washington Theatre, 112 Ind. App. 336, 41 N.E.2d 819 (1942); but it has been held unnecessary to show that others actually were served, State v. Katz, 241 Iowa 115, 40 N.W.2d 41 (1949).

[90] State v. Katz, *supra* note 89; *cf.* Norris v. Alabama, 294 U.S. 587 (1935) (evidence showing no Negro had served on jury for at least a generation).

York's statute (about thirty), but that one shows the typical style of draftsmanship.[91] Phraseology in most public accommodations laws indicates, moreover, that coverage extends beyond the enumerated places. New York says that a place of public accommodation "shall be deemed to include" (then follows the list); Illinois states, after its catalogue, "and all other places of public accommodation and amusement."

Drafting of this sort invariably produces litigation when it encounters the case which the draftsman seems to have overlooked. The issue then arises whether the place in question is covered by the catchall phrase. In years past construction was usually narrow. New York's law at one time was held not to include golf courses,[92] beauty parlors,[93] and bootblack stands,[94] but amendments have now supplied the first two. Other states have had similar disputes.[95] Such suits are usually debated in terms of "legislative intent" or canons of statutory interpretation, but, as Karl Llewellyn has observed in a more general context, they are resolved "essentially, by means other than the use of the canon." [96] In the case of civil rights laws the leniency or strictness

[91] The Kansas statute, cited in appendix A6, is an exception; it applies only to certain lodging places and *licensed* places of public accommodation. See Stovall v. City of Topeka, 166 Kan. 35, 199 P.2d 516 (1948) (upholding repeal of Topeka's theater-licensing ordinance, permitting theaters to escape public accommodations law's coverage); Brown v. Meyer Sanitary Milk Co., 150 Kan. 931, 96 P.2d 651 (1939) (ice cream parlor not within Kansas law; invoking the rule that a penal statute should be strictly construed); see the District of Columbia, Vermont, and Wyoming statutes in appendix A6, all less detailed than usual.
[92] Delaney v. Central Valley Golf Club, 28 N.Y.S.2d 932, 935, *aff'd on other grounds*, 289 N.Y. 577, 43 N.E.2d 716 (1942).
[93] Campbell v. Eichert, 155 Misc. 164, 278 N.Y. Supp. 946 (1935).
[94] Burks v. Bosso, 180 N.Y. 341, 73 N.E. 58 (1905).
[95] *E.g.*, Evans v. Fong Poy, 42 Cal. App. 2d 320, 108 P.2d 942 (1941) (saloons within "other" places of public accommodation); Long v. Mountain View Cemetery Ass'n, 130 Cal. App. 2d 328, 278 P.2d 945 (1955) (cemeteries not); Coleman v. Middlestaff, 147 Cal. App. 2d 833, 305 P.2d 1020 (1957) (dentists not); Darius v. Apostolos, 68 Colo. 323, 190 P. 510, 10 A.L.R. 986 (1920) (bootblack stands within Colorado statute; doctrine of *ejusdem generis* held inapplicable since the enumerated businesses bear no relation to each other); Faulkner v. Solazzi, 79 Conn. 541, 65 Atl. 947 (1907) (barber shop not within Connecticut statute); Cecil v. Green, 161 Ill. 265, 43 N.E. 1105 (1896) (soda fountains not public accommodations; but amendment now includes them); Rhone v. Loomis, 74 Minn. 200, 77 N.W. 31 (1898) (saloons not included; but within act today); see also notes 92–94 *supra;* Alsberg v. Lucerne Hotel, 46 Misc. 617, 92 N.Y. Supp. 851 (1905) (hotel suites leased on annual basis not within statute); Rice v. Rinaldo, 119 N.E.2d 657 (Ohio App. 1951) (dentist not within statute).
[96] Llewellyn, *Remarks on the Theory of Appellate Decision*, 3 VAND. L. REV. 395, 401 (1950). Those favoring a more inclusive interpretation would urge the maxim *ejusdem generis* (general words following an enumeration are usually restricted to things of the same kind); those opposed would argue *inclusio unius est exclusio alterius* (inclusion of one is exclusion of the other).

of construction is likely to reflect public policy, which nowadays grows more favorable to persons claiming denial.

Two reasons for the detail in most public accommodations laws are: (1) that they are criminal statutes which to be constitutional should give sufficient notice of what acts are crimes; and (2) that when the pattern for the laws was set, it was during a time of general deference to the dogma that statutes in derogation of the common law, that is, those departing from common law standards, should be strictly construed. The latter idea has been waning; the former has always permitted some generality (there are quite broadly phrased criminal laws which have been upheld as constitutional). At any rate, the specificity of criminal law is not necessary in civil or administrative laws, remedies which are more favored these days. Apparently, however, since detailed penal statutes have long been on the books, draftsmen of new laws employing other remedies have thought that departing from the old mold would be confusing. Consequently New York's law giving its State Commission Against Discrimination jurisdiction over public accommodations incorporates the provisions of the civil rights laws by reference. The SCAD statute itself directs that it shall be liberally construed.[97]

Public accommodations laws differ from the innkeeper's rule in significant respects (some states have both).[98] The latter is confined to inns; the former cover a wide range of places listed in the laws. Some state statutes on public accommodations also may be used against those who incite discrimination;[99] the innkeeper's rule has not been thus applied so far. Neither does the innkeeper's duty require that he refrain from discriminatory advertising as do some public accommodations laws.[100] While the innkeeper's rule is perhaps limited to travelers, public accommodations laws flatly protect all persons, or sometimes all citizens.[101] It might be possible to construe the innkeeper's rule so as to recognize race or color as "reasonable" grounds for segregation or

[97] Exec. Law § 300; *but cf.* § 292(9) (jurisdiction limited to "such" places appearing in Civ. Rights Law § 40).

[98] See the statutes of California, Maine, Massachusetts, Montana, and New York cited in appendix A6 and note 66 *supra*. See Horn v. Illinois Cent. R.R., 327 Ill. App. 498, 64 N.E.2d 574 (1946).

[99] Piluso v. Spencer, 36 Cal. App. 416, 172 P. 412 (1918). Some states' statutes speak of inciting: *e.g.*, Massachusetts, Minnesota, and Ohio, cited in appendix A6.

[100] See, *e.g.*, Colorado, Illinois, New York, and Pennsylvania, cited in appendix A6. See, *e.g.*, Camp-of-the-Pines v. New York Times, 184 Misc. 389, 53 N.Y.S.2d 475 (1945) (newspaper refused to publish advertisement for "selected clientele"); Op. Att'y Gen. of Mich. No. 2524 (1956) ("gentile clientele" violative).

[101] "Citizen" was held to include "person" in Prowd v. Gore, 57 Cal. App. 458,

exclusion, although constitutional issues would then appear; the new laws forbid discrimination for reasons of race, color, creed, or national origin,[102] and sometimes segregation has been specifically forbidden.[103] But, of course, owners still may refuse service for nonracial reasons,[104] or may be inefficient or rude without racial animus.[105] This raises the proof problem: what was the real reason for different treatment?

Implementation, as appendix A6 indicates, varies. Most states employ a combination of means.[106] A growing number enforce administratively, in addition to employing more traditional sanctions. But an agency may draw upon the older means too: it may award damages as well as issue other corrective orders; [107] those obstructing its process may be guilty of a crime; violators ultimately may be cited for con-

---

207 P. 490 (1922). The distinction would be of little practical importance in cases involving Negroes, but more significant when certain national minorities, e.g., Mexicans are involved.

[102] New York also forbids discrimination against a white person because he is accompanied by a Negro, Hobson v. York Studios, 208 Misc. 888, 145 N.Y.S.2d 162 (1955). But its rule was once to the contrary: Cohn v. Goldgraben, 103 Misc. 500, 170 N.Y.S. 407 (1918).

[103] See the Connecticut statute, cited in appendix A6. Jones v. Kehrlein, 49 Cal. App. 646, 194 Pac. 55 (1920); Fruchey v. Eagleson, 15 Ind. App. 88, 43 N.E. 146 (1896); Ferguson v. Gies, 82 Mich. 358, 46 N.W. 718 (1890).

[104] Larson v. R.B. Wrigley Co., 183 Minn. 28, 235 N.W. 393 (1931) (plaintiff excluded because he was dirty); Shubert v. Nixon Amusement Co., 83 N.J.L. 101, 83 Atl. 369 (1912) (no averment that exclusion was for race); Madden v. Queens County Jockey Club, 296 N.Y. 249, 72 N.E.2d 697 (1947), cert. denied, 332 U.S. 761 (1947) (plaintiff barred on mistaken belief that he was a notorious gambler; no denial of rights); City of Chicago v. Corney, 13 Ill. App. 2d 396, 142 N.E.2d 160 (1957) (some defendants disorderly after refusal of restaurant owner to serve them because of their race); Woolcott v. Shubert, 217 N.Y. 212, 111 N.E. 829 (1916) (noted critic barred from defendant's theaters because of unfavorable reviews; no denial of civil rights); see also Annot., 1 A.L.R.2d 1165 (1948).

[105] See Williams v. Deer's Head Inn, 4 Misc. 2d 281, 158 N.Y.S.2d 666 (1956) (impatient and discourteous treatment by the employees); see Fitzgerald v. Pan Am. Airways, 229 F.2d 499 (2d Cir. 1956) (passenger bumped; airline claims mistake).

[106] E.g., Connecticut (administrative, criminal); New Jersey (administrative, civil, criminal); New York (administrative, civil, criminal); Oregon (administrative, civil); Washington, (administrative, criminal); Wisconsin (administrative, civil, criminal). See appendix A6.

[107] See 1955 N.Y. SCAD REPORT 61 (Feliciano v. Ben Fishman d/b/a Klein's Hillside; proprietor rejected Negroes after they had traveled to his resort on basis of reservations; commission awarded damages to reimburse travel expenses and issued other corrective orders). Compare with Scott v. Fred Wells Diner, 1953 N.Y. SCAD REPORT 45 ("no jurisdiction to require payment of penalty"). None of the statutes expressly provide for award of damages; some do provide that the commission is to "take such affirmative action, including, but not limited to . . ." (italics added), see New Jersey, New York, Rhode Island statutes, cited in appendix A6.

tempt. Criminal standards, as often is the case, may by implication indicate a duty, which, if breached, justifies civil suit by the injured party.[108] Damages may include punitive damages.[109] In some places an offender's license may be revoked.[110]

There has been division among the various jurisdictions on whether an injunction may be given without express statutory authority.[111] On one hand, it has been argued that equity cannot enjoin commission of a crime; that it protects only property rights; and that the legislature would have mentioned injunctions if it had intended that they be used.[112] On the other hand,[113] some say equity does guard personal rights; that it is not controlled by the fact that the breach is also a

[108] Civil actions for damages have been authorized notwithstanding absence of express statutory authorization: Bolden v. Grand Rapids Operating Co., 239 Mich. 318, 214 N.W. 241 (1927) (decided before present treble damage provision); Anderson v. Pantages Theatre, 114 Wash. 24, 194 Pac. 813 (1921) (statute penal only; civil action may be maintained); Ross v. Schade, 7 Conn. Supp. 443 (1939) (although supplements to Connecticut statutes had omitted inclusion of authority to sue civilly for double damages, formerly in § 5985 of 1930 Rev. there was no implied repeal); Humburd v. Crawford, 128 Iowa 743, 105 N.W. 330 (1905) (statute penal only; action for damages; question of whether civil damages would lie not discussed); see Everett v. Harron, 380 Pa. 123, 127, 110 A.2d 383, 386 (1955); see Note, 44 ILL. L. REV. 363, 373 (1949). Recently the Municipal Court of the District of Columbia decided that the District's public accommodations laws are criminal only and will not support civil suit, Tynes v. Gogos, 3 R.R.L.R. 37 (1958). Bailey v. Washington Theatre, *supra* note 75, holds that the Indiana statute does not permit cumulative common law and statutory damages.

[109] Perrine v. Paulos, 100 Cal. App. 2d 655, 224 P 2d 41 (1950) (Innkeeper liable in punitive damages for unlawful eviction of guests); *cf.* McCarthy v. Niskern, 22 Minn. 90 (1875) (plaintiff ejected from inn by defendant who was in drunken rage; new trial ordered; damages excessive); see also Greenberg v. Western Turf Ass'n, 140 Cal. 357, 73 Pac. 1050 (1903), 14 A.L.R.2d 715 (1950).

[110] District of Columbia, Illinois, Michigan (liquor license), cited in appendix A6. But the Minnesota Attorney General has ruled that a restaurant or hotel license may not be revoked for discrimination. Op. Att'y Gen. of Minn. No. 238-F, June 3, 1942. Op. Att'y Gen. of Mich. No. 3041, 2 R.R.L.R. 1046 (1957) (golf club purporting to be private but holding Class C liquor license evidencing that it was a public course within the civil rights act; if discrimination shown, might have license revoked).

[111] See *Availability of Injunctive Relief Under State Civil Rights Acts*, 24 U. CHI. L. REV. 174, 175 (1956).

[112] See, *e.g.*, Fletcher v. Coney Island, Inc., 165 Ohio St. 150, 134 N.E.2d 371 (1956) (statutory remedies exclusive, adequacy thereof for legislative determination).

[113] Everett v. Harron, *supra* note 108 (injunctive relief granted over arguments that equity will not enjoin a crime and will not act unless a property right is involved); Orloff v. Los Angeles Turf Club, 30 Cal. 2d 110, 180 P.2d 321 (1947) (injunctive relief granted; legal remedy under civil rights statute inadequate); Stone v. Board of City of Pasadena, 47 Cal. App. 2d 749, 118 P.2d 866 (1941) (mandamus against a superintendent of parks to enforce the civil rights statutes; mandamus, of course, would probably lie against a municipal officer for violation

crime; and that it should be guided by the adage "whenever there is a right there is a remedy." The choice of the controlling maxims is largely dictated by the judges' views of more fundamental issues.

The effectiveness of criminal and civil public accommodations laws has been questioned. Will Maslow has concluded that the attitude of district attorneys, who are preoccupied with crimes of violence and other major offenses, and the reluctance of juries to convict, has taught civil rights advocates that "civil rights laws should not be penal statutes." He observes further, however, that civil statutes, allowing little recovery for great trouble, have little deterrent effect and that "many hotels and restaurants . . . [will] pay whatever small penalties are assessed and then continue discriminating. These penalties become a license fee for discrimination rather than a means of preventing it." [114] To these shortcomings we may add that when a statute's enforcement rests on the initiative of underprivileged persons, who must complain to the prosecutor or file civil suit, action, understandably, will be slow.[115] In support of these views we may note that a California group which in 1957 supported 36 damage suits against Los Angeles hotels, and other places, announced a survey finding that " 'after having a civil rights law for 50 years . . .' less than 20 per cent of California's hotels and motels will accommodate Negroes." [116] The president of the Illinois NAACP in a 1957 survey of discrimination in that state, which for eighty years had had a public accommodations law, wrote that discrimination there was widespread and that the law was poorly

---

of the Fourteenth Amendment, statutory rights aside); *cf.* Neff v. Boomer, 149 Neb. 361, 31 N.W.2d 222 (1948) (if there were showing that plaintiff would be barred in the future injunction probably would issue); Note, *Civil Rights—Extent of California Statute and Remedies Available for Its Enforcement,* 30 CALIF. L. REV. 563 (1942).

[114] Maslow, The Enforcement of Northern Civil Rights Laws, Address at Fisk Institute on Race Relations, June 28, 1950 (mimeographed).

[115] An effort partially to overcome this hurdle by filing a class suit on behalf of a number of rejectees was decided adversely by the California courts in Kennedy v. Domerque, 137 Cal. App. 2d 849, 290 P.2d 85 (1955) (persons involved not too numerous to appear; no community of interest as required by class action procedure). Colbert v. Coney Island, Inc., 97 Ohio App. 311, 121 N.E.2d 911 (1954) (class action to enjoin denial of admission to plaintiffs and other Negroes similarly situated; the court by its own admission utilized a restrictive approach).

[116] Chicago Defender, April 27, 1957, p. 20. See Afro-American, March 23, 1957, p. 3 (two Negro patrons sue San Francisco restaurant for $2,000 for refusal to permit them to occupy booth with view of Fisherman's Wharf); N.Y. Times, Feb. 27, 1957, p. 19 (Vermont hotel bars student's girl friend although she had reservation; state Attorney General says Vermont law forbids discrimination in inns).

enforced.[117] But an examination of practices in New York City in 1954 found virtually no discrimination in restaurants. Although the state commission had had jurisdiction over public accommodations for almost four years, its administration had not been so pervasive and strong that it could claim the credit for the situation exclusive of the effect of prior law. But forces other than law—political and social—are vigorous in behalf of antidiscrimination in New York City, which therefore is not typical. Upstate New York presents a different picture; there discrimination has been more widespread.

Nowadays there are more reported civil and criminal findings for persons claiming that they were discriminated against than there used to be,[118] although the significance of the absolute numbers of decisions is unclear. The case of the District of Columbia, even though it is a special one because of presidential policy and national publicity, shows that a civil rights statute implemented by criminal proceedings can effect a great deal of change if supported by a forcible policy. After the United States Supreme Court held the District's civil rights law

[117] Chicago Defender, May 18, 1957, p. 12, May 25, 1957, p. 12 (police will not arrest on prima facie evidence, magistrates are reluctant to issue warrants; officers virtually refuse to serve them; prejudices of judge and jury usually govern trials; in Rock Island 95% of all accommodations discriminate; in Plainsville, Negro civic leader asked to leave town before nightfall; in Springfield, state capital, hotels opened to all only short time ago. Roadstands and other places along highways often not open to Negroes). See, Goostree, *The Iowa Civil Rights Statute—A Problem of Enforcement*, 37 IOWA L. REV. 242 (1952) (between 1939 and 1950 there were 22 criminal prosecutions under the Iowa civil rights law; of these 4 resulted in convictions—3 fines and 1 suspended sentence; but 8 cases were dropped after defendants agreed to cease discriminating; there were 6 acquittals. There were 14 damage suits, 8 of which paralleled criminal suits; 10 were dismissed on defendants' promises to cease discrimination; 3 were decided for defendant; in one, plaintiff recovered $1.00).

[118] Around the turn of the century there were many reported decisions. Among recent instances are: railroad terminal restaurant, Syracuse, N.Y., ordered to pay damages of $200.00 to two Negroes who were refused service, American Jewish Comm. Anti-Defamation League Joint Memorandum No. 201 May 20, 1957; Santa Monica Municipal Court awards $400 damages against motel which refused accommodations to Negroes; jury awards $100 against Mineola, N.Y., barber shops which refused to cut Negro child's hair, LOTH & FLEMING, *op. cit. supra* note 23, at 31–32. Nebraska v. Peony Park, Inc., 1 R.R.L.R. 366 (Neb. County Ct. 1956) (defendant pleads *nolo contendere*, fined $50); Holifield v. Paputchis, 1 R.R.L.R. 553 (Wash. County Ct. 1956) (plaintiff recovers $200); Central Amusement Co., Inc. v. District of Columbia, 121 A.2d 865 (1956) (conviction for barring Negroes from bowling alleys); Hobson v. York Studios, *supra* note 102 (two plaintiffs win judgment of $100 each); Browning v. Slenderella Sys. of Seattle, 2 R.R.L.R. 618 (Wash. Super. Ct. 1957) (plaintiffs, husband and wife, recover $750); Manley v. Murrillos, 2 R.R.L.R. 421 (Cal. Munic. Ct. 1957) ($200 damages); Teverbaugh v. El Rey Trailer Parks, 3 R.R.L.R. 222 (Cal. Super. Ct. 1958) ($1,100 damages from six trailer parks).

operative in 1953, the switch from discrimination to nondiscrimination was phenomenal. Now the District is almost like New York City so far as public accommodations are concerned.

The annual reports of the commissions which enforce public accommodations laws are not entirely clear to one who seeks to discover how much change they have brought about. Very few orders have been issued by the commissions. "Adjustment" usually has followed conciliation, which, of course, can imply that the state would use coercion if there was unwillingness to obey the law. It is doubtful that the commissions' reported achievements reflect the potential efficacy of administrative enforcement, but clearly, they have accomplished some changes, probably more than prior law during comparable time. Limitations of manpower, budget, and agency self-restraint seem now to be the most important hedges against this type of regulation. These inhibitions are amplified by the fact that some agencies, including New York's, are required to adhere to the traditional law enforcement pattern, demanding a complaint from an aggrieved person before proceeding, and cannot act on their own initiative or on the allegations of civil rights organizations. New York's SCAD has, however, acted on complaint by civil rights organizations involving discriminatory advertising.[119]

The Connecticut Commission on Civil Rights reported 46 complaints of discrimination in public accommodations for 1953–54, 66 for 1954–55, 35 for 1955–56, and 51 for 1956–57. Like the reports from other states, those from Connecticut do not describe the worthiness of the complaints, their disposition, or the future conduct of the party complained of. There are statements that complaints were filed against barbershops, taverns, restaurants, hotels, motels, taxi services, rooming houses, roller-skating rinks, and recreation parks.[120] We are told that some barbershops have changed their policies and no longer discriminate,[121] that a hotel ballroom has changed a biased policy,[122] and that far fewer complaints are received concerning restaurants, grills, hotels, and places of recreation and amusement.[123] The Connecticut commission clearly feels that the public accommodations situation has improved and apparently ascribes a large part of the change to its education policy. It has briefed police officers on their

---

[119] 1953 REPORT at 77.   [120] 1953–54 CONN. COMM'N ON CIVIL RIGHTS REPORT.
[121] *Id.* at 3.   [122] CONN. COMM'N ON CIVIL RIGHTS BULL., vol. 1, no. 12.
[123] 1954–55 CONN. COMM'N ON CIVIL RIGHTS REPORT.

duty under the penal portions of Connecticut law,[124] has enlisted the aid of the state Board of Barber Examiners,[125] has advertised,[126] and employed publicity about civil rights in all media.

New York's commission reports similar results. In 1954 it received 28 public accommodations complaints, in 14 of which it found probable cause, sustained and adjusted the complaint.[127] In 1955 it received 76 public accommodations complaints; in half of these illegal specifications in advertisements were alleged.[128] Only 32 of the cases were closed during the year, and of these about half sustained the complaint or forbade other discriminatory practices.[129] The facilities involved were like those in Connecticut. The New York commission is more explicit in describing the facts of cases and their disposition, but does so only on the basis of giving examples with no indication of what they mean to the over-all discrimination picture. The New York summaries come closer than any other commission's reports to approximating reported legal cases.[130] New York has an educational program as well, and one of its achievements is that the hotel industry in the state has become well briefed on the law's requirements.[131] Other state reports are generally more spare,[132] although all show a trend away from discrimination.

Clearly, administratively enforced laws have the potential of accom-

[124] *Ibid.*   [125] 1953–54 CONN. COMM'N ON CIVIL RIGHTS REPORT.
[126] 1955–56 and 1956–57 CONN. COMM'N ON CIVIL RIGHTS REPORTS.
[127] 1954 N.Y. SCAD REPORT 8, 14.   [128] 1955 N.Y. SCAD REPORT 5.
[129] *Id.* at 12.
[130] Typical N.Y. SCAD cases dealing with discrimination in places of public accommodation are: (1) Negro complainant refused admission to dance hall because of race. Respondent contended that admission was by invitation only. It appeared that invitations issued to whites as a matter of course and that no Negroes had ever been admitted. Upon a finding of "probable cause" conciliation was proposed and accepted by the respondent; it was agreed that full and unsegregated facilities, privileges, etc., of the dance hall would be extended to complainant whenever he seeks admission. A follow-up investigation was made by the commission to insure that the respondent was complying with the conciliation. Thomas v. Cain, 1954 N.Y. SCAD REPORT 54. (2) Complainants charged respondent barber with refusing to cut their hair because of their color. Respondent maintained that he did not have the proper tools to cut Negroes' hair satisfactorily. Respondent was advised by the investigating commissioner that the law obligates barbers to employ persons qualified to serve customers of every color. "If you feel that you . . . require different tools with which to cut the hair of Negroes, then you are duty bound to procure the same and also to qualify to service Negroes." Smith v. Calcagra d/b/a Broadway Barber Shop, *id.* at 57.
[131] 1955 N.Y. SCAD REPORT 70.
[132] See 1954 R.I. COMM'N AGAINST DISCRIMINATION ANNUAL REPORT 8, 9, 11, 12–13, 14; 1955, at 8, 11; 1956, at 6, 9, 11. 1954–55 MASS. COMM'N AGAINST DISCRIMINATION ANNUAL REPORT 5–6 (reviews advertising brochures; sends repre-

plishing more than penal statutes and private civil suits. But while it appears that they have done a great deal, one might question whether, for example, in New York in 1955 (when the commission adjusted about 15 public accommodations cases), there were not as many instances in which informal adjustments were achieved by police or district attorneys, private attorneys or social agencies. The efficacy of administratively enforced laws depends in largest part upon the energy and manpower with which the commission attacks the problem. By and large, however, the policies of the commissions have been conservative, and in such circumstances a number of civil rights attorneys and organizations have preferred filing court cases. There, some have felt, they can muster their own evidence and persuade judges or juries unhampered by go-slow policies. Moreover, in so doing, they have not been encumbered by unfavorable commission determinations which have sometimes impeded later attempts to secure courtroom relief. In New York, beginning with the Abrams administration of SCAD, some lawyers have believed that the proceedings of the commission offer a greater chance of success, and they have placed greater emphasis on filing complaints with SCAD.

CONCLUSION

There is a pressing demand for equal access to public accommodations and services both in the North and in the South—especially in view of the gross Negro-white disparity in facilities even by separate-but-equal standards, as American leisure increases and the economic position of Negroes improves. Relatively little of the inequality that exists is required by statute. More exists because states have furnished the best and the greatest number of accommodations for whites. But most exists because the great majority of facilities is privately owned and discrimination in them is the work of their proprietors. While there has been much litigation about public accommodations in the South, almost all of it has been directed against state action, to which the Fourteenth Amendment is limited. There is no established way of legally getting at private action without a civil rights law—the various common law rules have usually, as a practical matter, been nullified.

---

sentatives and communications to resorts in state); 1955–56 (same). Massachusetts does not even reveal how many public accommodations complaints it receives.

An index of the Negro demand has been the large number of recreation suits, particularly golf course cases. Negro business and professional men have the time, money, and desire to play golf and can afford to engage counsel. In Atlanta, the first court-enforced desegregation was on the golf course.

While in a few instances—chiefly those involving swimming places—there has been some violent resistance, most desegregation of publicly owned accommodations has been peaceful and effective, including that at beaches and pools. A favorite opposition tactic—used only a little, but threatened in more instances—has been to lease, sell, or close the place in question. But a private lessee of state-owned property may not discriminate, and even if legally valid, a question so far almost completely untested, sale and closing are not available as a general antidote, for it is questionable whether whites will long suffer being deprived of all public recreation just to keep Negroes out. However, until the Negro demand and the ability to sue intensify to such a pitch that there will be sufficient closure to affect whites severely, this gambit may temporarily defer some desegregation.

Increasing Negro economic strength and community organization are playing an important role in desegregation. This factor has had a telling effect on intrastate travel (where there is a clear legal duty), hotel accommodations (where the law is state, not federal, and often less helpful to those seeking equality), and retailing (where there will usually be no duty unless there is a civil rights law). Wherever legal and social forces are both strong and are combined, change has been greatest. Because bus passengers include a disproportionately large number of Negroes, after a showing in Montgomery of what a bus boycott can do, the judicial declaration that segregation on buses is illegal brought on considerable bus desegregation throughout the South. Although the innkeeper's rule and contractual duty to honor reservations may oblige hotels to receive colored persons, the pressure of conventions which refuse to meet in whites-only lodgings probably has been more effective in opening some of them. Even where there is no legal duty many retail stores which once discriminated against Negro customers in various ways now solicit their increasingly valuable trade and treat them with utmost courtesy. But there still remains the problem of responsiveness to the right: many Negroes still ride in the former Jim Crow section on buses; in some Southern or border communities where hotels have opened up, transients take advantage of the new rights, but almost all residents follow the old pattern.

The public accommodations issue remains important in Northern areas as well as in the South. Some states which have long had civil rights laws display widespread and open bias in privately owned public facilities. Because the Fourteenth Amendment applies only where there is state action, legal proceedings against privately owned public accommodations have been limited, although the question of what is "private" and what is "state" remains open and surely will be litigated frequently in the future. Perhaps the most important institutions to be faced by this issue will be the so-called private (but usually state- and federal-subsidized) hospitals, although the need for immediate hospitalization works against suing them.

In the North economic pressure has been telling, but political strength is most meaningful, for it has helped to get enacted state and municipal civil rights laws. These are undoubtedly the most effective ways to reach discrimination. Almost thirty jurisdictions have such such statutes and their enactment is being pressed elsewhere, chiefly in the West. However, experience shows clearly that a mere law on the books is meaningless. Criminal and civil damage statutes have lent themselves badly to policing the problem, though they can be used with effect if a prosecutor is willing (politics can be a stimulus to willingness) or civil rights groups support such a campaign.

Theoretically, the best way to upset privately imposed discrimination in public accommodations is by an administratively enforced statute—like the New York SCAD law—counterparts of which exist in a handful of other states. Enforcement is entrusted to experts, it can be systematic, the jury is dispensed with, and there need not be proof beyond a reasonable doubt. But a commission's effectiveness depends upon its diligence. Although they have effected change, many such commissions are obscure concerning what they have achieved. Political participation by minorities can stimulate firmness in their enforcement actions.

CHAPTER IV

INTERSTATE TRAVEL

Accommodations aboard interstate carriers are in most respects physically indistinguishable from those on local transport. But these farther-ranging conveyances involve legal and social considerations which, although in part the same as those presented by local transit, diverge in important respects. Therefore, while the intrastate travel discussion is still fresh we shall turn to the related subject of interstate commerce.

Segregation in travel has shallower roots than most other racial separation. At the turn of the century legally compelled segregation in transportation was hardly universal in the South. North Carolina, South Carolina, and Virginia enacted such laws only between 1898 and 1900. Before 1899 just three states required or authorized Jim Crow waiting rooms. But within a decade virtually all aspects of rail travel in the South came under laws requiring separation of the races. When interstate buses became numerous in the 1930s, they naturally fell into the pattern. Only the airplane escaped, for, as C. Vann Woodward has written, "even to the orthodox there was doubtless something slightly incongruous about requiring a Jim Crow compartment on a Lockheed Constellation or a DC-6." But Southern airports generally have been racially separate, as have been the limousines carrying passengers between terminal and city. Gunnar Myrdal has described Jim Crow travel as "resented more bitterly than most other forms of segregation." And this resentment has given rise to more lawsuits than that over any other civil rights problem except education.[1]

[1] Some of the background of travel segregation is set forth in WOODWARD, THE STRANGE CAREER OF JIM CROW 81–82, 103–104 (1957); JOHNSON, PATTERNS OF NEGRO SEGREGATION 48 (1943). The quotation about the DC-6 is from WOODWARD at 103; the quotation from MYRDAL is from AN AMERICAN DILEMMA 635 (1944).

The nature of interstate travel invites social and legal control of the race question that is often conflicting. The local terminal, an indispensable link in the distant journey, is very much a part of its community, staffed by local people, serving many neighboring citizens, amenable to local police. Negroes of the community who breach its patterns at the station, especially in small towns where they probably will be known, could invite social and economic reprisal when they come home. The carriers, however, are huge, impersonal enterprises, usually with distant headquarters. Power is even more centralized and insulated from local pressure in the Interstate Commerce Commission or the Civil Aeronautics Administration, which with a single order may require changes in thousands of terminals and carriers. And what happens in a terminal in Atlanta may touch as many Northerners as Southerners. The national scope of the problem is apparent. Travelers away from home are anonymous, fleeting personalities not responsive to ordinary pressures, often acting in ways they would not dare at home. Those segregationists who carry on as do some convention-goers would probably think nothing of leaving their social mold long enough to eat alongside a Negro in a dining car.

LAWS REQUIRING SEGREGATED TRAVEL

Presently, thirteen states have laws on the books requiring or authorizing segregated travel.[2] These specify that separate coaches or partitions on trains be provided or that all Negroes sit in one single section of a bus.[3] The conductor or driver, generally the arbiter of the situation, may assign the seats and usually is clothed with police power to enforce segregation.[4] The Florida provision asserts authority to "require the building or alteration of any and all passenger depots and terminal stations . . . to secure the separation of white and colored

[2] See appendix A1.
[3] E.g., "Railroad companies doing business in this State shall furnish equal accommodations, in separate cars or compartments of cars, for white and colored passengers," GA. CODE ANN. § 18-206 (1935). "All persons or corporations operating street railways and street or municipal buses carrying passengers in this state, and every common carrier by motor vehicle . . . shall provide equal, but separate, accommodations for the white and colored races," MISS. CODE ANN. § 7785 (1956).
[4] E.g., "The conductors of any train carrying passengers in this state are invested with all the powers, duties and responsibilities of police officers while on duty on their trains," FLA. STATS. ANN. § 352.02 (1958). Other statutes conferring express police power to conductors, drivers, etc., are: ALA. CODE ANN. tit. 48, § 198 (1940); GA. CODE ANN. § 18-207 (1935); N.C. GEN. STATS. ch. 60, art. 136 (1950); VA. CODE ANN. tit. 56, § 394 (1950).

passengers." [5] The statutes do not differentiate between interstate and intrastate travel, except that Alabama's speaks of both kinds and those of Georgia, Louisiana, and Mississippi expressly reaffirm intrastate segregation for the obvious purpose of deterring desegregation, including that on interstate carriers, as much as possible.[6]

Whether to call these statutes "law" depends on one's view of what law is, an observation which could be made continuously throughout these pages. Courts and the Interstate Commerce Commission, as discussed below, have held such travel enactments void. Therefore, what are called "laws" may be deemed empty words, voidable by higher authority. But some state officers have continued to enforce segregation statutes despite their invalidity. The issue reaches the courts in relatively few instances for a variety of reasons, such as ignorance, fear of reprisal, reluctance to litigate, the difficulty of appealing minor offenses, and the psychological momentum of decades of segregation. So, if we regard "law" as rules actually imposed by state officers, these statutes are still "law" in many places. In addition, apart from statute, ordinance, or police enforcement, ticket agents, conductors, bus drivers, station managers, and others sometimes segregate pursuant to company policy, or on their own, and by virtue of their lawful positions their acts are as enforceable as law. Moreover, we cannot ignore the Negroes who, following the pattern which the law long ago helped to shape, segregate themselves where no railroad or government official requires it. This self-segregation cannot be entirely divorced from the repudiated statute. Some would say that the law operates here too, not only in the sociological jurisprudential sense that "the centre of gravity of legal development lies not in legislation nor in juristic science, nor in judicial decision, but in society itself," [7] but also for the reason that positive law in the form of the once-valid statute helped to form these habits.

GOVERNING LEGAL PRINCIPLES

The legal principles most meaningful for this issue reflect the national policy which assures the free flow of commerce through the nation. The Fourteenth Amendment, which today condemns any segregation law, including those requiring segregated travel, was largely

[5] FLA. STATS. ANN. § 350.21 (1957).   [6] See appendix A1.
[7] FRIEDMANN, LEGAL THEORY 191 (3d ed. 1953), quoting Eugen Ehrlich, and see id., ch. 17.

by-passed in establishing desegregation of interstate travel to avoid the separate-but-equal doctrine, until recently a qualification on that amendment. Counsel arguing commerce cases relied mainly on the Constitution's commerce clause (Article I, Section 8). It contained no such condition, and was doubly attractive because it forbids both private and governmental burdens on interstate commerce while the Fourteenth controls only state action. The Interstate Commerce Act was important too. It requires equal treatment of travelers and permits decisions to be based on statutory grounds affording the courts welcome opportunity to avoid constitutional questions.

State antidiscrimination law has importance for interstate travel too. In the last chapter we pointed out the duty of common carriers to refrain from discrimination. This applies to interstate as well as to intrastate transportation. And there are the state civil rights laws, which, the Supreme Court has held, may properly forbid discrimination in interstate conveyances.[8] However, only the legal questions concerning interstate commerce require separate treatment here.

THE COMMERCE CLAUSE

Article I, Section 8, Clause 3, of the Constitution provides: "The Congress shall have Power . . . To regulate Commerce with foreign Nations, and among the several States, and with the Indian Tribes." In interpreting this clause, the Supreme Court has held that where uniformity is essential for the functioning of commerce, a state may not interpose its regulation.[9] The clause has been viewed, for example, as forbidding a state to regulate the length of freight trains, because of the burdensomeness of coupling and uncoupling cars from state to state.[10]

Travel segregation laws failed to pass the test of uniformity in *Morgan v. Virginia* (1946).[11] In 1944 a bus driver of the Richmond Greyhound lines tried to force a passenger traveling from rural Hayes Store, Gloucester, Virginia, to Baltimore, to move to the rear of the bus at Saluda, Virginia, to make room for a white passenger. Her refusal ended in a fight with the sheriff whom the driver summoned. She was convicted of violating Virginia's segregation law, which allowed shifting of seats to maintain segregation. When her case reached the

[8] Bob-Lo Excursion Co. v. Michigan, 333 U.S. 28 (1948); see Railway Mail Ass'n v. Corsi, 326 U.S. 88 (1945).
[9] Southern Pac. Ry. v. Arizona, 325 U.S. 761 (1945).
[10] *Ibid.*   [11] 328 U.S. 373 (1946).

Supreme Court of the United States, the Court pointed out the lack of uniformity among states on the segregation issue and the many opportunities for burdensome conflict. Eighteen states forbade segregation while ten required it. On top of this, the definition of Negro varied from state to state. In a nation in which racial regulations varied so greatly from state to state permitting such variant laws to stand could keep passengers in perpetual ferment during a long trip: they might sit where they pleased upon entering states without segregation laws, but would have to shift in states like Virginia with laws requiring segregation.

The Court held:

As there is no federal act dealing with the separation of races in interstate transportation, we must decide the validity of this Virginia statute . . . as a matter of balance between the exercise of the local police power and the need for national uniformity in the regulations for interstate travel. It seems clear to us that seating arrangements for the different races in interstate motor travel require a single, uniform rule to promote and protect national travel. Consequently, we hold the Virginia statute in controversy invalid.[12]

The *Morgan* decision, ironically, followed, though with opposite result, an 1878 case in which the Court struck down a Louisiana Reconstruction law *forbidding* segregation on steamboats, for the reason that

no carrier of passengers can conduct his business with satisfaction to himself, or comfort to those employing him, if on one side of a State line his passengers, both white and colored, must be permitted to occupy the same cabin, and on the other be kept separate. Uniformity . . . is a necessity in his business.[13]

But the Court was undoubtedly persuaded to its conclusion in *Morgan* by more than considerations of free commerce, as shown in 1948 in *Bob-Lo Excursion Co. v. Michigan.*[14] In an opinion considering a Michigan antidiscrimination law which had been applied against a steamboat operating between Detroit and a Canadian amusement park, it elbowed aside, to use Edward S. Corwin's characterization,[15] the 1878 steamboat case and held that the Detroit-Canada trip was essentially local—although actually foreign—and that conflict with Canada on the issue of discrimination was not to be anticipated. The Michigan

[12] *Id.* at 386.   [13] Hall v. DeCuir, 95 U.S. 485, 489 (1878).
[14] 333 U.S. 28 (1948).
[15] CONSTITUTION OF THE UNITED STATES OF AMERICA 230 (Corwin ed. 1953).

law, therefore, was upheld. The obvious conclusion is that the Court places a low value on the state's interest in segregation when balancing it against national uniformity, while placing a high value on nonsegregation in a similar equation.

The rule of *Morgan* has been applied to company regulation as well as law. Segregation ordered by a driver in Kentucky, which has no bus segregation law, was held to burden commerce as much as if it were imposed by law.[16]

Morgan has also been applied to rail travel, the Supreme Court of Virginia holding that buses and trains are indistinguishable for purposes of this issue.[17] A 1951 federal decision involving a passenger traveling from Philadelphia to Rocky Mount, North Carolina, held that Negro passengers on a North to South journey may not be segregated on entering the South, for segregating would require changing of seats. This case invalidated also the tactic of arresting for disorderly conduct instead of for violation of the segregation rule when the only "disorder" has been a refusal to be segregated. But it implied that segregation on a South to North journey would be valid, for passengers settled and segregated at the outset would at no time be required to move.[18] The decision augured development of baffling refinements in the law, but was never really elaborated or followed because not long thereafter the Interstate Commerce Act was held to condemn all interstate travel segregation.

THE INTERSTATE COMMERCE ACT

Section 3(1) of the Interstate Commerce Act makes it unlawful for a rail carrier "to subject any particular person . . . to any undue or unreasonable prejudice or disadvantage in any respect whatsoever." [19] So far as race is concerned, the act has generally been interpreted to impose the same standard as the Fourteenth Amendment.[20] In 1941, in a case brought by Congressman Arthur Mitchell (a Negro who had been denied Pullman accommodations), when separate-but-equal was law, the Supreme Court condemned the Illinois Central for assigning Negroes traveling first class to "lower 13," the drawing room (where they could not be seen), and if that were unavailable, to coaches. The

---

[16] Whiteside v. Southern Bus Lines, 177 F.2d 949 (6th Cir. 1949).

[17] Lee v. Commonwealth, 189 Va. 890, 54 S.E. 2d 888 (1949).

[18] Chance v. Lambeth, 186 F.2d 879 (4th Cir. 1951), *cert. denied,* 341 U.S. 941 (1951).

[19] 49 U.S.C.A. § 3(1).   [20] Mitchell v. United States, 313 U.S. 80, 94 (1941).

railroad defended on the ground that it would be financially ruinous to carry separate Negro Pullmans. Chief Justice Hughes wrote:

If facilities are provided, substantial equality of treatment of persons traveling under like conditions cannot be refused. It is the individual, we said, who is entitled to the equal protection of the laws, not merely a group of individuals, or a body of persons according to their numbers. . . . And the Interstate Commerce Act expressly extends its prohibitions to the subjecting of "any particular person" to unreasonable discriminations.[21]

The requirement that segregation yield to equality under separate-but-equal was obeyed by Southern roads as to Pullmans, but even that principle was not generally accepted. Dining cars remained segregated, as did coaches, and treatment was often very unequal. In 1950 the Supreme Court, following the *Mitchell* precedent decided *Henderson v. United States*[22] in a manner making dining car segregation impossible. *Henderson* held that Negroes might not be excluded from any empty seats in the diner, even if this meant violating a segregation rule. The Court did not have to address itself to the question of segregation per se, but it obliquely condemned the principle by criticizing "the curtains, partitions and signs [which] emphasize the artificiality of a difference in treatment which serves only to call attention to a racial classification of passengers."[23]

Nevertheless, most roads did not accept the Court's implication. There was an attempt to retain diner segregation by seating Negroes from one end of the car and whites from the other[24]—but, since no person could be required to stand while seats remained empty, in practice segregation broke down. At the same time coaches remained segregated as did station facilities, and in many respects accommodations for Negroes in both were quite unequal to those for whites. This was particularly true in the case of "through coaches."[25] White persons could board a "through coach" and ride it to its destination without changing. It was uneconomical to run Negro "through cars," and Negroes often had to wait or change at transfer points. Many bus

---

[21] *Id.* at 97.　　　　[22] 339 U.S. 816 (1950).　　　　[23] *Id.* at 825.

[24] Henderson v. Southern R.R., 284 I.C.C. 161 (1952). Other roads made rules that women should be seated with women, young people with young people, old people with old people, Negroes with Negroes. This too was inadministrable.

[25] A thoroughly detailed study, Segregation in Interstate Railway Coach Travel (mimeographed), was prepared by Professor Herman Long of Fisk University in 1952. It is referred to in the ICC'S opinion in NAACP v. St. Louis–San Francisco Ry., 297 I.C.C. 335, 338 (1955). Professor Long testified before the ICC concerning many of the experiences and conclusions related in his study.

drivers continued to segregate notwithstanding the *Morgan* decision. Thus the *Henderson* and *Mitchell* cases, and the refinement of *Morgan*, confused and dissatisfied many Negroes. The Interstate Commerce Commission noted that "some Negroes quite understandably have been unaware of the comparatively limited scope of those decisions, and upon encountering segregation as railroad passengers, have felt . . . their traditional resentment of passenger segregation [which] tends to produce friction." [26]

THE INTERSTATE COMMERCE COMMISSION'S
DECISIONS OF NOVEMBER 7, 1955

Carrier policy all along has been to interpret court and commission rulings narrowly and to yield no more than absolutely necessary. This moved the NAACP, in conjunction with individual complainants, to petition the Interstate Commerce Commission to ban segregation on thirteen major Southern rail carriers and in the Richmond Terminal. An individual court case might obtain relief for one person, or perhaps even establish a general principle; but a commission order, enforceable by the commission's continuing jurisdiction and supervision, would be far more effective. Violators of commission orders are punishable by a fine of $5,000 for each day of violation.[27] While an association cannot ordinarily file a court case on behalf of an individual's rights, the commission may hear the complaint of "any person," [28] and regularly hears chambers of commerce, trade associations, rate conferences, and other groups. It was under this principle that the NAACP was able to request an over-all ruling. If the association had lost before the commission, its right to appeal to the courts would have been highly questionable. The individual complainants, however, could have continued to pursue the matter.

In fact, the association did not lose. On November 7, 1955, the commission decided *NAACP v. St. Louis–San Francisco Ry. Co.*,[29] which ordered the end of segregation in interstate rail travel. The opinion rested heavily on the Supreme Court's decision in the *School Segregation Cases*. It held:

[26] NAACP v. St. Louis–San Francisco Ry., 297 I.C.C. 335, 346 (1955).
[27] 49 U.S.C.A. § 16(8).
[28] See Moffat Tunnel League v. United States, 289 U.S. 113 (1933). There are, however, other cases in which a person or association may file suit to vindicate the rights of another, see p. 281 *infra*.
[29] *Supra* note 26

The disadvantage to a traveler who is assigned accommodations or facilities so designated as to imply his inherent inferiority solely because of his race must be regarded under present conditions as unreasonable. Also, he is entitled to be free of annoyances, some petty and some substantial, which almost inevitably accompany segregation even though the rail carriers, as most of the defendants have done here, sincerely try to provide both races with equally convenient and comfortable cars and waiting rooms.[30]

The commission not only condemned segregation which was enforced directly, but ordered the Richmond Terminal to take down WHITE and COLORED signs, although they were not enforced, for they "are commonly understood to represent rules established by managers of buildings in which they are posted in the expectation that they will be observed by persons having due regard for the proprieties." [31] The commission was empowered to issue an order concerning stationary facilities because the Interstate Commerce Act places under its jurisdiction terminal facilities which are part of passenger service.[32] Under this principle the lunchroom in the Richmond Terminal, leased to a concessionaire, was exempted, for the evidence showed that it had been closed from 1933 to 1952, which was taken to be evidence of its nonessentiality and that it was not an integral part of passenger service.

In another decision handed down the same day, *Keys v. Carolina Coach Co.*,[33] the commission held that requiring "Negro interstate passengers [to] occupy space or seats in specified portions . . . of buses, subjects such passengers to unjust discrimination, and undue and unreasonable prejudice and disadvantage, in violation of Section 216(d) [of the Interstate Commerce Act], and is therefore unlawful." [34] The decision showed, incidentally, that the 1946 *Morgan* case had not ended bus segregation by 1955.

In *Keys* no ruling concerning bus terminals was requested or made. But apparently the decision has been interpreted correctly by at least some bus companies as requiring them to end segregation in their stations. The commission's jurisdiction over bus stations is narrower than that over rail stations. The motor portion of the Interstate Commerce Act governs only terminals operated or controlled by carriers [35]

---

[30] *Id*. at 347.   [31] *Id*. at 345.

[32] 49 U.S.C.A. § 1(3): "The term 'railroad' as used in this chapter shall include . . . terminal facilities of every kind used or necessary in the transportation of the persons or property designated herein."

[33] 64 M.C.C. 769 (1955).   [34] *Id*. at 772.

[35] 49 U.S.C.A. § 303 (19): "The 'services' and 'transportation' to which this chapter applies include . . . all facilities and property operated or controlled by

whereas the rail act governs all stations. However, since it appears that many bus terminals are company-operated, the *Keys* principle will have widespread effect.

A set of instructions following *Keys* was issued by its president to Southeastern Greyhound Lines personnel on January 4, 1956:

TO: ALL COACH OPERATORS AND STATION PERSONNEL
SUBJECT: SEGREGATION

The recent orders of the Interstate Commerce Commission compel us to issue the following instructions concerning the segregation of passengers on buses and in stations. Therefore, effective January 10, 1956, Executive Bulletin No. 50, dated August 16, 1955, will be modified to the following extent:

1. Interstate passengers must *not* be asked to seat themselves in any particular part of the bus.

2. Intrastate passengers may be courteously requested to comply with the law of that particular state, but if passenger refuses to comply, then no further action should be taken.

3. Existing signs and separation of waiting rooms and restaurants will be maintained as at present, but station personnel must not take *any* steps to enforce segregation in the use of these facilities.

I know you can be depended upon to handle this delicate situation with tact and understanding to the end that trouble and misunderstanding can be avoided.

Letters of inquiry by Professor Jack B. Weinstein sent at about the same time to other bus companies doing business in the South have indicated no affirmative action by them except in the case of the Carolina Coach Company which replied that

while we have a number of problems, due to a conflict between state and national laws, we have followed the regulations of the Interstate Commerce Commission and have instructed the drivers of our buses not to segregate passengers as required by state laws. We are having no difficulty whatsoever in the handling of our colored passengers on the buses.

Bus way stations, where stops are made for food and to permit use of rest room facilities, present another question. These are less frequently owned or operated by bus companies and in such cases the Motor Carriers Act would appear not to control. But although it has not been litigated, a commerce clause argument may very well apply to these stopping points too. It seems burdensome on commerce to

---

any such carrier or carriers, and used in the transportation of passengers or property in interstate or foreign commerce or in the performance of any service in connection therewith."

require some passengers to do without these conveniences on a lengthy journey, or to enjoy them on a restricted basis; it might be shown that denial of these comforts discourages bus travel. Therefore, such stop-overs may some day be held to enjoy a dual status: under state law they may choose their local patronage as they please (aside from statute and common law rules, as detailed in chapter III), but under federal law they may be required to serve all interstate bus passengers alike.

A United States court of appeals has held that a Northern carrier which sells a through ticket on a journey into the South is not liable for the segregation of a connecting carrier, even if that carrier is part of the original seller's system.[36] This ruling requires a bus segregation suit to be brought in the South when the segregating line does not do business in the North. And even when jurisdiction may be obtained against an offending carrier in the North, in at least one unreported case, applying the doctrine of *forum non conveniens*, it was required that the suit be heard where the wrong occurred.[37] Southern juries, of course, may be expected to be less sympathetic than Northern ones to such plaintiffs.

REACTIONS TO ICC'S RULINGS

The reactions to the ICC's rulings were not uniform, nor have they been fixed. We have noted the bus companies' response. Major rail carriers responding to a questionnaire of Weinstein's, inquiring about action taken in response to the decisions, replied as follows.

Atlantic Coast Line: "no instructions . . . other than those necessary to insure compliance with order of the Interstate Commerce Commission dated November 7, 1955."

Seaboard Air Line: A bulletin quoted from the ICC opinion and the Interstate Commerce Act provisions, setting forth penalty for their violation and stating to employees: "With respect to Negro interstate passengers, you will be governed accordingly."

Atchison, Topeka and Santa Fe: "all signs reading 'colored' or 'white' were removed from our stations, and employes were instructed not to attempt to segregate the races either on trains or in stations."

Illinois Central: "Except for more formal matters, we on the Illinois

[36] Spears v. Transcontinental Bus Sys., 226 F.2d 94 (9th Cir. 1955).
[37] Watson v. Eastern Airlines, 4 CIVIL LIBERTIES DOCKET 35 (N.D. Ga. 1958) (plaintiff ejected from bus carrying plane passengers after unscheduled stop).

Central give through our supervising officers oral instructions with respect to current changes in procedure. Subsequent to November 7, 1955, and prior to January 10, 1956, instructions were given to remove all 'Colored' and 'White' signs around stations and load all passenger trains without reference to the race of passengers. These instructions were promptly complied with over the system."

Southern: "We have not issued any written instructions or regulations to our employees as a result of this decision."

Missouri Pacific: "Our company has not issued any instructions in this matter subsequent to November 7, 1955, as we had been complying with the law in this matter to the best of our ability prior to that date."

Texas and Pacific: "This company has issued no such regulations or instructions since that date."

As we shall see, however, the problem of compliance is more complex than simply whether an order has been issued or not. But for purposes of legal analysis, carrier response falls into three principal categories:

1. *Full compliance.* In some places WHITE and COLORED signs have come down and there is complete desegregation. For example, in Louisville and Paducah, Kentucky, and at Broad Street Station, Richmond, there are no signs and no segregation. But policies are not even uniform within a single city. In October, 1956, in Charleston, South Carolina, the Atlantic Coast Line Station had no signs, but the Greyhound Terminal did; in Richmond at the same time the Southern station had a sign reading COLORED INTRASTATE PASSENGERS WAITING ROOM, the Richmond Terminal had no racial signs.

2. *Full defiance.* Governor Kennon of Louisiana announced his intention to enforce segregation on carriers. The Mississippi Public Service Commission announced a similar intention, and Mississippi officials have taken the same position. When carriers took down signs in Jackson, the city put up fresh ones. A Mississippi lawyer has reported that in one city the police arrested violators of segregation rules in the railroad stations, kept defendants in jail overnight, and released them upon a plea of not guilty; but some who have not known they would be released on a not guilty plea have pleaded guilty. South Carolina and Alabama have enforced the old law against interstate travelers, although one South Carolina case, involving the Florence rail station, was dismissed.[38]

3. *Compliance so far as is deemed absolutely necessary.* In many

[38] Afro-American, March 10, 1956, p. 1.

places "compliance" is effected in accordance with a narrow interpretation of the law. Three states require by statute,[39] others by practice, and some major Southern roads employ, a system of separating interstate from intrastate passengers and of segregating intrastate travelers in terminals. A 1956 trip taken by the author from Florida through Virginia showed that in most stations the old COLORED waiting rooms were then labeled COLORED INTRASTATE; this condition apparently continues. But many Negroes ignore these signs with impunity, although probably a larger number observe them. Inquiry among travelers and among railroad employees reveals that on trains many conductors seat Negroes with one another unless there is an objection. Upon objection, a Negro is seated elsewhere without question. One railroad has written to a passenger who protested this practice that it does not understand the ICC decision to require affirmative integration. As to buses, Negroes in the South say that segregation often depends upon the driver: some segregate and some do not, without apparent system.

A South Carolina lawyer of whom inquiry was made, replied in October, 1956:

> I have heard of no instance in which any railroad personnel has acted contrary to the regulation. They raise no objection to Negroes using the "white" waiting room; they courteously serve passengers who ignore the segregation patterns. Formerly, Negroes could not get travel reservations except on segregated coaches, even though there were accommodations in other cars. Now, Negroes can get reservations wherever same are available. True, though, they just attempt, without any fanfare, of course, to place Negroes all together.
>
> What are Negroes themselves doing in these communities?
>
> Very little. In isolated instances, Negroes are using formerly all-white waiting rooms, without opposition. (The Florence situation is an exception.) Almost invariably the average Negro will go where he always went; the "upper crust" of my people insist upon using accommodations. This applies, of course, only with respect to interstate travel. . . .
>
> With reference to bus travel, there has been absolutely no change in custom. The waiting rooms are still designated "white" and "colored"; Negroes still are seated in the back of buses, and the dining rooms are still segregated.

LEGALITY OF NEW LAWS AND PRACTICES

There has been little decision on the legality of the new practices, although the Fifth Circuit has held that suit for injunction may be

---

[39] See the Georgia, Louisiana, and Mississippi statutes in appendix A1. On Alabama see note 40 *infra*.

brought against the Alabama Public Service Commission, the Birmingham city commissioners, and the Birmingham Terminal Company to stop the practice of arresting, although not convicting, Negroes who refuse to be segregated at the station.[40]

Some things are clear under general principles, however.

1. If segregation is enforced by state officers, they are violating the Fourteenth Amendment, no matter whether inter- or intrastate travel is involved.[41] Moreover, state officers who enforce obviously invalid rules for the purpose of denying constitutional rights may be guilty of violating the federal Civil Rights Acts.[42]

2. In addition, it may well be held a burden on interstate commerce and an unnecessary expense to require carriers to maintain separate facilities for inter- and intrastate passengers and two types of space for the latter. The carriers themselves could best attack such rules on this basis, but they apparently prefer to avoid controversy. (Query, could a dissident stockholder bring such an action?)

3. There is no settled law on the practice of some carriers to separate intrastate from interstate passengers without being legally required to do so as a prelude to racially segregating the former group. It might be argued that this system perpetuates confusion like that upon which the ICC looked with disfavor in *NAACP v. St. Louis–San Francisco Ry.* and effects the same compulsion which the commission criticized in the Richmond Terminal, by deterring even some interstate passengers from enjoying their rights. The average passenger cannot be expected to distinguish between interstate and intrastate commerce (especially when judges sometimes disagree), for it is probable that many passengers do not understand the meaning of the words.

4. The system of segregating all passengers despite the law until there is an objection involves similar subtleties. Often a passenger will not know that he has been placed in an all-Negro section until he is on the train and it is too late to complain without inconvenience or

[40] Baldwin v. Morgan, 251 F.2d 780 (5th Cir. 1958).
[41] Browder v. Gayle, 142 F. Supp. 707 (M.D. Ala. 1956), *aff'd*, 352 U.S. 903 (1956), has held intrastate travel segregation laws unconstitutional under the Fourteenth Amendment. This surely governs interstate laws. But since interstate travel traditionally has been adjudicated under the commerce clause and the Interstate Commerce Act, it seems unlikely that there will be a Supreme Court Fourteenth Amendment holding on the validity of interstate travel laws. See also Baldwin v. Morgan, *supra* note 40.
[42] See p. 83 *supra*, pp. 269–272, 316–323 *infra*.

postponement of the journey. Some, "having due regard for the proprieties," [43] may prefer not to make an issue of the matter.

These arguments probably will be made against the new systems.

AIR TRAVEL

No state laws require segregation in airplanes, and state officials apparently have not tried to enforce any such rules. Neither have the air carriers themselves practiced segregation. But in a recent case [44] in which the singer Ella Fitzgerald charged that she had been "bumped" from a flight because of race, a federal court of appeals held that the Civil Aeronautics Act outlawed racial discrimination in the air. The Act's section on discrimination [45] is essentially the same as that of the Interstate Commerce Act. It is not necessary, however, that an air traveler be an interstate passenger to enjoy the immunities conferred by the Civil Aeronautics Act since federal dominion over the airways is complete.[46]

There has not been much litigation on segregation at airports.[47] Practices vary, but even where segregation is required, it is often—with the exception of terminal restaurants—not enforced. It is common to find a section of a Southern airport terminal labeled COLORED, but to see Negroes and whites sitting or standing indiscriminately throughout the building. One lower court case, relying on the due process clause of the Fifth Amendment, held that a federally owned airport may not segregate where Negro facilities are inferior to white ones.[48] The case

[43] NAACP v. St. Louis–San Francisco Ry., *supra* note 26, at 345.

[44] Fitzgerald v. Pan Am. World Airlines, 229 F.2d 499 (2d Cir. 1956).

[45] 49 U.S.C. § 484(b): "No air carrier or foreign air carrier shall make . . . or subject any particular person, port, locality, or description of traffic in air transportation to any unjust discrimination or any undue or unreasonable prejudice or disadvantage in any respect whatsoever."

[46] *Re* Veterans Air Express Co., 76 F. Supp. 684 (D.N.J. 1948); see Ballard, *Federal Regulation of Aviation*, 60 HARV. L. REV. 1235 (1947).

[47] See Nash v. Air Terminal Servs., 85 F. Supp. 545 (E.D. Va. 1949); Air Terminal Servs. Inc. v. Rentzel, 81 F. Supp. 611 (E.D. Va. 1949). Both cases involved Washington National Airport; regulation of the Administrator of Civil Aeronautics barring segregation there was valid. At this writing there are pending: Henry v. Greenville Airport Comm'n, Civil Action No. 2491, W.D.S.C., Jan. 20, 1959 (waiting room); Coke v. City of Atlanta, Civil Action No. 6733, N.D. Ga., Dec. 23, 1958 (restaurant).

[48] Nash v. Air Terminal Servs., *supra* note 47. A suit against Greensboro-Highpoint Airport (N.C.), which is owned by a government authority, for restaurant segregation there, alleging denial of Fourteenth Amendment rights, was answered by a denial of segregation and the assertion of a nondiscriminatory policy. Brisbane v. Greensboro-Highpoint Airport Authority, Civ. Action No. c-87G-57 (M.D.N.C. 1957).

was decided when separate-but-equal was still considered good law. Today it indicates that governmentally owned airports may not segregate at all. The overwhelming majority of airports are owned by municipalities, counties, authorities, or states, and therefore the principle of that case—or the broad requirements of due process and equal protection—largely govern the airport problem.

The Civil Aeronautics Act does not regulate airports to the extent that the Interstate Commerce Act governs rail stations, for airports are outside the act's definition of carriers.[49] But the administrator of the act has the power to encourage and foster the development of civil aeronautics,[50] and he probably could prohibit segregation as tending to discourage the patronage of a large segment of the population. This he has done recently in a limited way by ordering that no "Federal aid Airport Program funds will be made available for the development of separate facilities." [51] Airports may, of course, construct or maintain such facilities, but not with federal funds. For the fiscal year 1956, 524 airports received such funds; [52] for fiscal 1957 at least 368 projects have been benefited.[53] Not many of these grants involve the construction of buildings for which the antisegregation ruling would be meaningful, however, since most of them have been for land, runways, lights, and so forth.[54] Actually, even where an airport is not governmentally owned, and no federal funds are used for it, a commerce clause argument may apply against segregation: namely, that segregation burdens interstate commerce by inconveniencing Negro passengers. There has been no decision along these lines, however.

Neither has there been a case on discrimination in limousines which service airports. They are specifically exempted from the Motor Carriers Act.[55] If they were viewed as being in interstate commerce, the commerce clause would govern, but whether they are has not been decided. *United States v. Yellow Cab Co.*,[56] an antitrust case, has held that taxies regularly transporting passengers among Chicago railroad stations are in interstate commerce but that those which travel between the stations and other local points are not. The relation of the latter to interstate commerce is only casual and incidental. The Supreme Court

[49] 49 U.S.C. § 401 (2).   [50] 49 U.S.C. § 451.
[51] Airports Policy and Procedure Memorandum No. 41, April 6, 1956, U.S. Dep't of Commerce, CAA.
[52] U.S. Dep't of Commerce Release, CAA, Feb. 9, 1956, Aug. 10, 1955.
[53] U.S. Dep't of Commerce Release, CAA, June 12, 1956.
[54] See notes 52 and 53 *supra*.   [55] 49 U.S.C. § 303 (b) (7a).
[56] 332 U.S. 218 (1947).

held that so far as the rail travel in *Yellow Cab* was concerned, the common understanding was that "a traveler . . . begins his interstate movement when he boards the train at the station and that his journey ends when he disembarks at the station in the city of his destination." [57]

In some cities, however, certain taxis and buses furnish regular and sometimes exclusive service to airports. Moreover, unlike train travel, which terminates in the heart of town, accessible to local transportation, air travel ends in outlying sections and the connecting service is an essential part of the journey. Undoubtedly, for many, the understanding is that the trip ends at the terminal in town. Therefore, *Yellow Cab* may not always apply, and at least some airport motor service may be required to refrain from segregation. Looking a little into the future, helicopter taxis will be controlled by the exclusive federal dominion over the airways. In large cities, therefore, the taxi problem may become minimal.

INTERSTATE AUTOMOBILE TRAVEL

There do not appear to be any laws requiring segregation in private automobiles. The real problem in this area concerns the long trip on which overnight stops must be made. Negroes traveling through the South and in many parts of the North are often unable to find a suitable place to stay, and must put up with quarters far inferior to the large selection of hotels and motels for whites. Auto travelers try to cope with the difficulty by planning their itinerary carefully and consulting publications like *Travel-Guide* and *Go-Guide* or the Tourist Motor Club, which list accommodations where Negroes will be received.[58]

In some communities civil rights laws or rules of innkeepers' liability may apply (see chapter III) to restrain discrimination, but elsewhere, although the Fourteenth Amendment invalidates laws requiring discrimination in these facilities, the private actions of proprietors are immune. A commerce clause argument, however, is again conceivable: travelers are burdened by inability to find suitable overnight accommodations; this handicap burdens interstate commerce; therefore, it is illegal under the commerce clause. The problem, however, is essentially a local one and is more thoroughly discussed in the chapter

[57] *Id.* at 231.
[58] See full-page advertisement, Chicago Defender, Aug. 10, 1957, p. 6 ("Travel Without Embarrassment. . . . Would you like a vacation in *any* of the 48 states —minus rebuffs? Are you ready for any highway emergency—even in a hostile town? [Join] Tourist Motor Club").

on public accommodations. But recently heavy federal and state spending for highway construction has suggested the possibility of constitutional or statutory restraints, so far not actually imposed, against segregation in accommodations along the way.[59]

CONCLUSION

Law has invalidated the largest part of publicly and privately imposed discrimination in travel. While some legal problems remain undecided, including those raised by laws and practices designed to avoid the full effect of Supreme Court and ICC decisions, these restrictions probably will be outlawed if they ever come to litigation. Even as things stand, however, if all Negroes asserted their clear rights, not much would be left of interstate travel segregation. For example, the Southern roads will now change a Negro's seat to a nonsegregated car merely upon request, but the number of requests is relatively small.

The chief exception is in those states or communities where segregation in terminals is imposed by defiant state officers. Of course, local political changes could alter police practices, and this raises problems of why Negroes cannot or do not vote. But litigation probably will be necessary to enjoin what is already obviously illegal in these intransigent areas. Federal prosecution under the Civil Rights Acts is another possible remedy. Here too politics may be a spur to federal officials who have so far hardly used these statutes.

Social factors, however, have been most effective in deterring the full enjoyment of that freedom which is available. Educating and encouraging Negroes concerning their rights and creating an atmosphere in which they can assert their rights freely is now more important to the travel problem than further elucidation of the law. Yet forthright law enforcement may often be educational for the segregator and the segregated and encouraging to the latter group as well.

[59] "Plans to allow motels along the Blue Ridge Parkway [Va.]—which would involve the question of mixing the races—were reported uncertain yesterday," Washington Post, April 25, 1957, § B, p. 2. See Afro-American, Feb. 16, 1957, p. 19 (bill proposed to forbid discrimination in public facilities within 200 yards of state highway). Williams v. Howard Johnson's Restaurant, 4 CIVIL LIBERTIES DOCKET 36 (E.D. Va. 1958) (praying for ruling that restaurant adjacent to public highway is in interstate commerce).

CHAPTER V

ELECTIONS

In treating the law's capacity to affect race relations in chapter I, the role of political power in creating and enforcing civil rights legislation at state and federal levels was noted. In chapters III and IV on public accommodations and interstate travel we also observed particular instances where the ballot was, or could be, a telling force. That potential, and its realization, will be remarked many times in pages to follow. Negro leadership is making great efforts to develop this democratic energy, which in turn stands to profit by the sustenance of improved economic and educational conditions. The program is aided by the fact that no one in America, except the most unyielding racists, questions that all citizens should be free to vote. What does this Negro vote amount to, what role has law performed and what part can it play in its further development?

Negro votes provided the margin of Republican victory in Louisiana and Tennessee in the 1956 national elections. They were decisive in President Eisenhower's carrying the counties containing Birmingham, Mobile, and Montgomery, Alabama, and, some think, provided an impetus toward the creation of a two-party South by turning heavily Republican in Maryland, North Carolina, South Carolina, Virginia, Atlanta, Miami, Savannah and Tampa.[1] In twenty-three Southern cities Negro votes for President were 36.8 percent more Republican than in the previous presidential election.[2] Negroes themselves have been elected to public office in Atlanta, Augusta, Greensboro, Knoxville, Nashville, Richmond, San Antonio, Winston-Salem, and other Southern communities in recent years. But as late as 1944, before the

[1] N.Y. Times, Nov. 11, 1956, p. 60.
[2] Moon, *The Negro Vote in the Presidential Election of 1956*, 26 J. NEGRO EDUCATION 219 (1957).

Supreme Court struck down the White Primary, not a single Negro held public office in the South, unless one includes a few border states.[3]

In 1946 the Southern Negro vote was estimated at 750,000.[4] The number had grown to 1,238,000 in 1956, but that was still only 25 percent of its potential, compared to a 65 percent white registration. In 1958 the number rose to 1,266,488 despite purges of Negroes from voting lists in some states.[5] An over-all figure is misleading, however, in that it fails to reveal the high Negro urban participation, as in Atlanta, and the microscopic rural participation. Yet latent Negro voting strength still exists in urban centers where political organization is easiest, intimidation most difficult. There is at least 25 percent Negro population in over half of the fifty-eight major Southern cities. Potential of course exists in rural areas, too—for example, more Negroes than whites live in thirty-one Mississippi counties.[6] But Negro enrollment has been leveling off—only 210,000 new registrants appeared between 1952 and 1956 and there were fewer than 30,000 more between 1956 and 1958.

As some keen observers have warned, however, the right to vote and even its exercise do not assure political power. Wealth and leisure time, Samuel Lubell notes, are necessary for those who would practice politics successfully.[7] The Southern political power structure, centered on the office of the sheriff, as James M. Nabrit, Jr., has pointed out, does not respond solely to votes, but to a complex of social, economic, personal, and other factors as well.[8] The power of the ballot, it follows, would draw further strength from the end of discrimination in other areas, particularly employment and education (another example of the interdependence of all factors that we note time and time again).

THE CONSTITUTIONAL AND STATUTORY FRAMEWORK

The Constitution contains at least half a dozen provisions authorizing outlawry of voting discrimination or flatly condemning it. The Fifteenth Amendment is pinpointed on the problem and is clearest: "The right of citizens of the United States to vote shall not be denied

[3] Moon, *The Southern Scene*, 16 PHYLON 351, 357 (1955).
[4] *Id.* at 353.
[5] See N.Y. Times, Nov. 3, 1958, p. 41; *id.*, Nov. 5, 1956, p. 31.
[6] ASHMORE, THE NEGRO AND THE SCHOOLS 186 *et seq.* (2d ed. 1954).
[7] Lubell, *The Future of the Negro Voter in the United States*, 26 J. NEGRO EDUCATION 408, 415 (1957).
[8] Nabrit, *The Future of the Negro Voter in the South*, 26 J. NEGRO EDUCATION 418, 420 (1957).

or abridged by the United States or by any State on account of race, color, or previous condition of servitude." The Fourteenth Amendment's due process and equal protection clauses also have been employed to safeguard Negro suffrage. The Fourteenth's second section provides what could be the most potent sanction: reduction of the congressional representation of states in the proportion that they deny the right to vote. Article I, Section 4, which gives no express protection, authorizes Congress to "make or alter . . . Regulations" as to "the Times, Places and manner of holding Elections for Senators and Representatives." And finally, by Article I, Section 5, Congress is the "Judge of the Elections, Returns and Qualifications of its own Members."

These constitutional provisions have been implemented by a number of statutes, the most important of which is the Civil Rights Act of 1957. Most Reconstruction legislation expressly protecting voting was repealed in 1894, but there still remain 42 U.S.C.A. §§ 1971(a) and 1972. Section 1971(a), as couched before 1957, when new provisions were added by the Civil Rights Act of that year, provided: All citizens otherwise qualified may vote at any election in any State, Territory, district, county, city, parish, township, school district municipality, or other territorial subdivision, without racial distinction, any law to the contrary notwithstanding; and § 1972 states: No officer of the Army, Navy, or Air Force shall interfere with the exercise of the free right of suffrage in any State. The pre-1957 section 1971 is without sanction apart from being enforceable in a private civil suit, but in such cases it does not grant any rights not already conferred by the Fifteenth Amendment. Section 1972 is obviously of no practical import. The more recent Hatch Act (18 U.S.C.A. § 594), which also applies specifically to voting, makes it a crime to intimidate voters in federal elections, but by its own terms (§ 591) it does not apply to primaries, which is where political issues are usually settled in the South.

In addition, the general civil rights statutes apply to voting, among other rights. Title 42 U.S.C.A. § 1983 imposes civil liability on persons who, under color of state law, deprive United States citizens of federal rights, and often has been held to comprehend voting.[9] Title 42 U.S.C.A. § 1985(3) makes civilly liable those who conspire to intimi-

[9] Lane v. Wilson, 307 U.S. 268 (1939); Myers v. Anderson, 238 U.S. 368 (1915); Rice v. Elmore, 165 F.2d 387 (4th Cir. 1947), *cert. denied*, 333 U.S. 875 (1948).

date a citizen from supporting certain federal candidates or who injure a citizen while furthering a conspiracy to prevent him, by force or threat, from supporting such candidates. It would apply to private persons as well as to those acting under color of state law. But there is no reported instance of its having been invoked. Title 18 U.S.C.A. § 241—applying to all persons, private and governmental—which makes conspiracies to injure citizens in the exercise of federal rights criminal, has been used often to safeguard suffrage rights.[10] And 18 U.S.C.A. § 242, which makes it a crime to deprive citizens of federal rights under color of law, also protects elections.[11]

As with all federal legislation, civil rights laws must find some authority in a power delegated to Congress by the Constitution. Because the Fourteenth and Fifteenth amendments authorize outlawry of discrimination effected under color of law, these statutes may constitutionally apply to those who discriminate under color of law, whether in a state or a federal election. But as the *Civil Rights Cases* [12] declared, private action may not be regulated by those amendments. To reach nonofficial deeds the Civil Rights Acts find justification in Article I, Section 4 (empowering Congress to regulate elections for Senator and Representative) and in the implied power of the federal government to safeguard its own elections.[13] But this foundation supports only laws regulating federal elections (although incidental protection is afforded state elections conducted at the same time).[14] Consequently, there is a constitutional gap in the regulatory scheme which permits discrimination by private persons in state elections.[15]

Perhaps this omission is not too serious, for usually federal and state elections are conducted simultaneously and obstruction of one impedes the other. Moreover, some private action interfering with state elections may be reached. For example, a private person who conspires with a state officer to discriminate in elections is guilty of a conspiracy to commit an offense against the United States (18 U.S.C.A. § 371) and of aiding and abetting commission of a crime (18 U.S.C.A. § 2(a)). The influence of some private groups which run their own pre-primary elections may be so great that the courts will treat them as if

---

[10] United States v. Saylor, 322 U.S. 385 (1944); United States v. Classic, 313 U.S. 299 (1941); Guinn v. United States, 238 U.S. 347 (1915); United States v. Mosley, 238 U.S. 383 (1915); *Ex parte* Yarbrough, 110 U.S. 651 (1884).
[11] United States v. Classic, *supra* note 10.   [12] 109 U.S. 3 (1883).
[13] *Ex parte* Yarbrough, 110 U.S. 651, 657, 662 (1884).
[14] *Ibid.*   [15] United States v. Cruikshank, 92 U.S. 542, 555 (1875).

they were wielding state power and subject them to constitutional restraint, as in *Terry v. Adams* (p. 144 *infra*). Private action may be so widespread and powerful, as in the heyday of the Ku Klux Klan, that it could be viewed as virtually governmental in quality and treated the same way.[16]

There was, however, a perhaps more important lapse in the statutory scheme, prior to the enactment of the Civil Rights Act of 1957, for, apart from those covered by the Hatch Act, the only private acts which the pre-1957 statutes outlawed were conspiracies. An employer who alone, and not in concert with anyone else, told a Negro employee that he would be fired if he voted in the primary, did not violate federal law. Proof of conspiracy in such cases would have been close to impossible. But unlike the constitutional gap exempting private acts in state elections, this omission was remediable by legislation. One aim of the Civil Rights Act of 1957 was to correct this lapse, but probably the most serious matters to which that act was addressed were procedure and enforcement.

PROCEDURE AND ENFORCEMENT

Lane v. Wilson,[17] a leading case to secure the ballot, was a suit for damages, since earlier authority [18] had cast doubt on the power of a court to grant injunctions to protect "political" rights. Of course, damages—if a jury would award them—might be a deterrent to offend ing registrars, but they are not so effective as an injunction granted by a judge alone and enforceable by contempt proceedings. This was once a major procedural problem. But subsequent decisions, particularly *Davis v. Schnell,*[19] granted injunctions, and settled the question of whether courts can enjoin discrimination in voting at the suit of a private party.

The federal government, however, while it may prosecute criminally, could not before 1957 bring suits for injunctions. Prosecution, of course, involves trial before a jury, which could sympathize with a guilty defendant. Indeed, there have been instances of clear violations where grand juries have refused to indict.[20] Moreover, conviction

---

[16] Collins v. Hardyman, 341 U.S. 651, 662 (1951).
[17] Discussed in greater detail p. 140 *infra*.
[18] *E.g.,* Giles v. Harris, 189 U.S. 475 (1903).
[19] Discussed in greater detail p. 140 *infra*.
[20] See *Hearings on S. 83 Before the Subcommittee on Constitutional Rights of the Senate Committee on the Judiciary,* 85th Cong., 1st Sess. 242–243 (1957)

requires proof beyond a reasonable doubt, and is especially hard to obtain when defendants are popular public officials. And, a criminal conviction usually would come after the election; it would not actually secure the right to vote.

Suits by private parties have also had serious hurdles to overcome. As substantive defenses vanish, those who would preserve segregation rely more heavily on procedural defenses. Among these is the ubiquitous "administrative remedy." In *Peay v. Cox* (1951),[21] for example, where it was claimed that state law was misconstrued by a Mississippi registrar, who required white voters merely to read, but Negro voters to explain, parts of the Federal Constitution, the Fifth Circuit required a preliminary appeal to the state board of election commissioners and then, if necessary, to state courts as provided by state law. The victims of discrimination, often poor, rural Negroes, could not be expected to sue in every case of discrimination at the polls, especially when dilatory defenses postponed relief and compounded expenses.

THE CIVIL RIGHTS ACT OF 1957

The voting provisions of the Civil Rights Act of 1957[22] were designed to fill some of the breaches discussed above. Leaving existing protections of voting rights unrepealed, its first provision forbids any person from interfering with the right of another to vote in federal elections. Primaries are expressly included. It then provides, most significantly, that whenever the Attorney General believes that anyone has violated or is about to violate rights secured by the act, he may sue to prevent the wrong. (Of course, private civil suit and criminal prosecution are still available.) And federal courts may hear suits by the Attorney General and apparently by private individuals as well, even when administrative remedies have not been exhausted.[23]

(Louisiana Federal Grand Jury refuses to indict on clear evidence of denial of voting rights and does not desire to hear testimony in connection with certain voting cases).

[21] 190 F.2d 123 (5th Cir. 1951), *cert. denied,* 342 U.S. 896 (1951).

[22] 42 U.S.C.A. §§ 197(b)–(e). United States v. Raines, 27 U.S.L. Week 2530 (M.D. Ga. 1959) (statute held unconstitutional as authorizing suit against private persons, though instant defendants are officials).

[23] Darby v. Daniel, 168 F. Supp. 170, 190 (D. Miss. 1958), holds that the exhaustion provision applies only to actions commenced by the United States, relying on the fact that the statute dispenses with administrative remedies commenced under "this section." But "this section" (131 of P.L. 85–315), by its terms, amends 42 U.S.C. § 1971 and seems, therefore, intended to apply to all of it. H. R.

In cases brought under the 1957 act, federal courts are not inhibited from holding a defendant in civil contempt as before to compel obedience to the court's decree.[24] Criminal contempt penalities may be as great as a fine of $1,000 and imprisonment for six months. But although in criminal contempt proceedings the judge may try the defendant with or without a jury, if the court adjudges a fine of more than $300 or imprisonment for more than 45 days, the defendant may request a new trial before a jury. Any person charged with contempt under the new law may be represented by counsel and subpoena witnesses. The court must appoint counsel when the defendant cannot pay for his own.

GOVERNMENTAL RESTRAINTS ON VOTING IN GENERAL ELECTIONS

There has been no substantive problem with obvious restraints even when disguised in language purporting to have nothing to do with race. At the turn of the century laws in Oklahoma and seven other states—the grandfather clauses—required preregistration literacy tests of everyone except those qualified to vote in 1866 or their lineal descendants. Obviously in 1866 Negroes were not qualified to vote and the statute was but an Aesopian formula to bar them where whites were admitted. In *Guinn v. United States* (1915),[25] a federal prosecution of state officials under the Civil Rights Acts, the Supreme Court held the grandfather clauses unconstitutional.

Enforcement of the grandfather clause was abandoned in Oklahoma and elsewhere, but the conduct of individual registrars, as we shall see, is not completely predictable, and a similar North Carolina statute [26] was allegedly enforced recently by a registrar in Brunswick County, although apparently ignored in other parts of the state.[27] Later, in the wake of the debate over the Civil Rights Act of 1957, North Carolina repealed the grandfather provisions of its statutes which, when challenged in the courts, were then upheld by the Supreme Court.[28]

REP. No. 291, 85th Cong., 1st Sess. (1957), Pt. III, states that the amendment's purpose is to overrule Peay v. Cox, *supra* note 21, and Carson v. Warlick, 238 F.2d 724 (4th Cir. 1956), both suits by private persons.

[24] 42 U.S.C.A. § 1995. See also pp. 72–76 *supra*.

[25] *Supra* note 10.

[26] N.C. CONST. art. IV, § 4, and N.C. GEN. STATS. § 163-28 (1943), amended by N.C. Laws 1957, ch. 287, to retain literacy provisions but excise grandfather provision.

[27] *Hearings on S. 83, supra* note 20, at 513.

[28] Lassiter v. Northampton County Bd. of Elections, 27 U.S.L. Week 4405 (U.S. June 9, 1959).

When Oklahoma could no longer rely on the grandfather clause, it substituted a requirement that persons previously barred could qualify only by registering during a twelve-day period in 1916. (Those who had voted in the past continued to be qualified.) This new statute did not reach the Supreme Court until 1939, when presented in *Lane v. Wilson* [29] by a Negro who had not registered during the prescribed time. The claim was that the opportunity for registration had been so circumscribed that the grandfather clause, to all intents, remained in effect. Ruling that the Fifteenth Amendment bars "sophisticated as well as simple-minded modes of discrimination," Mr. Justice Frankfurter, in holding the twelve-day exception inadequate, realistically wrote that it "must be remembered that we are dealing with a body of citizens lacking the habits and traditions of political independence and otherwise living in circumstances which do not encourage initiative and enterprise." [30]

In 1946, Alabama attempted a different formula, the Boswell Amendment, which permitted registration only of persons who could "understand and explain" any article of the Federal Constitution, a standard so vague that registrars could accept or reject whomever they pleased. As enforced in one county where 36 percent of the population was Negro, only 104 Negroes were registered compared to 2,800 whites. *Davis v. Schnell* [31] (1949) held the Boswell Amendment unconstitutional. Citing the vague standards and their obvious purpose, a federal three-judge court said: "We cannot ignore the impact of the Boswell Amendment upon Negro citizens because it avoids mention of race or color; 'To do this would be to shut our eyes to what all others than we can see and understand.'" [32] The Supreme Court affirmed.

But other states retain similar legislation today. In Georgia one must be able to read and write the Constitution or to understand the duties and obligations of citizenship under a republican form of government. [33] Louisiana requires reasonable interpretation of the state or federal Constitution, an understanding of the duties and obligations of a citizen under a republican form of government, and good character. [34]

[29] 307 U.S. 268 (1939).   [30] *Id.* at 275, 276.
[31] 81 F. Supp. 872 (S.D. Ala. 1949), *aff'd*, 336 U.S. 933 (1949).
[32] *Id.* at 881, quoting in part from United States v. Butler, 297 U.S. 1 (1936).
[33] GA. CONST. (1945) art. II, § 2-704; GA. CODE ANN. § 34-117 *et seq.* (1955 Supp.). The standard questions are in §34-122.
[34] LA. CONST. (1921) art. 8, §§ 1(c) and (d); see also LA. REV. STATS. tit. 18, §§ 35 and 36 (1950).

The statute in Mississippi is substantially similar to that in Louisiana.[35] Georgia's law has thus far survived one test in the state courts (*Franklin v. Harper*, 1949).[36] However, although the court specifically upheld the constitutionality of the Voter's Registration Act of 1949, the case is susceptible of interpretation that the result did not rest on the statute's merits, but rather on the fact that the complaint failed to allege that the plaintiff had sought and was denied the right to register.

Today, however, one rarely encounters the gross statutory discriminations. Even where such laws are still on the books, they generally are not followed, although registrars often improvise their own discriminatory qualifications, and sometimes violence or economic pressure are used.

A recent issue of the *Journal of Negro Education* examines in detail Negro voting throughout the United States. This study and the 1957 Senate (and to a lesser extent, House) hearings on civil rights are the most thorough inquiries into Negro voting so far conducted.[37] In sum, they describe discrimination, where it exists, as largely a rural phenomenon effected by each board or community group in its own way, although sometimes inspired from above. No overt attempts to bar Negroes are described for Arkansas, Virginia, Tennessee, or Texas (except with regard to some county primaries). Some efforts at exclusion are pointed to for Florida, North Carolina, and South Carolina. But intensive discrimination appears to be the rule throughout Alabama, Georgia, Mississippi, and parts of Louisiana (although in the large cities of these states and the French-Catholic rural areas of Louisiana, Negroes generally vote freely).

Citing some examples of illegal practices, one Southern registrar has inquired, "How many bubbles . . . in a bar of soap?" [38] Another has asked, "How do you bring a case to trial?" [39] In Ouachita Parish, Louisiana, in 1956, White Citizens Council members filed unsworn challenges to over three thousand Negro voters, but virtually none to white voters. The registrar permitted the challenged Negroes to

[35] Miss. Const. (1942) art. XII, § 244. See also Miss. Code Ann. § 3213 (1956). The Mississippi statute contains a clause exempting those properly registered before 1954.

[36] 205 Ga. 779, 55 S.E.2d 221 (1949), *app. dism.*, 339 U.S. 946 (1950), "for want of a substantial federal question."

[37] See *Hearings on S. 83*, *supra* note 20; *Hearings on H.R. 140 Before Subcommittee No. 5 of the House Committee on the Judiciary*, 85th Cong., 1st Sess. (1957); 26 J. Negro Education, No. 3 (1957).

[38] N.Y. Times, May 3, 1956, p. 27.   [39] *Ibid.*

establish their qualifications only at the rate of fifty per day. Those admitted to the office were illegally denied the opportunity to call as witnesses persons who lived in another precinct or persons who had testified for another challenged voter. Consequently, the number of Negroes registered in Ouachita Parish was reduced from 4,000 to 694.[40] The Fifth Circuit has held that those who were purged have pleaded a good cause of action against the registrar.[41] In some North Carolina counties registrars have asked Negroes to write the Preamble to the Constitution from dictation, with all spelling, punctuation, and capitalization correct, or to name every candidate for office in the county, or to state whether they were members of the NAACP, but whites were registered upon fulfilling minimal objective standards.[42] Another tactic has appeared in Alabama, where a registration board, by resigning,[43] escaped a suit to compel registration of Negroes. Although its successors could undoubtedly have been brought under the decree, no successors were appointed immediately. The absence of registrars means that there are no defendants to sue. Therefore this approach not only attempts to stymie possible litigation but also tries to prevent registration. Such actions are just as lawless as if required by statute, but because of their uniqueness, the difficulty of proof, and the complexity of the litigation they provoke, they are harder to uncover and correct than a simple discriminatory law. That they are scattered makes attack even more difficult. While one lawsuit can invalidate a state-wide statute, the number of cases required to restrain intransigent registrars would be very large. When these actions are complicated by dilatory procedural tactics, the Negro voter, facing determined opposition, has a thorny and expensive task if he tries to win his right to register. The vigor with which the 1957 Civil Rights Act is applied will significantly affect the extent to which such practices will continue.

[40] Statement of the Attorney General, in *Hearings on S. 83, supra* note 20, at 4.

[41] Reddix v. Lucky, 252 F.2d 930 (5th Cir. 1958); attack on a similar purge in Georgia failed in Harris v. Echols, 146 F. Supp. 607 (S.D. Ga. 1956) (weight of evidence; procedural deficiencies). Another phase of the same situation is presented by Sharp v. Lucky, 165 F. Supp. 405 (W.D. La. 1958).

[42] Statement of the Attorney General, in *Hearings on S. 83, supra* note 20, at 4.

[43] Sellers v. Wilson, 123 F. Supp. 917 (M.D. Ala. 1954) (injunction will be granted if wrongdoers become board members again). In a suit by the United States under the 1957 Civil Rights Act the complaint was dismissed because registrars had resigned. United States v. Alabama, 27 U.S.L. Week 2645 (5th Cir. 1959) (suit may not be brought against state).

WHITE PRIMARIES

For a time Negroes were by law successfully barred from Southern Democratic primaries where the real choice of representatives is made. In *Nixon v. Herndon* (1927) [44] the Supreme Court invalidated such a Texas primary statute. Typically, some Southern states then began maneuvers to find something which would be immune from constitutional requirements and still perform the office of the primary. Texas first passed a law authorizing the party executive committee to adopt membership rules, whereupon the committee barred Negroes, but in *Nixon v. Condon* (1932) [45] this too was held state action. Because state laws were involved in both *Nixon* cases, the Fourteenth Amendment applied and the Court did not have to decide whether a primary is an "election" in the contemplation of the Fifteenth. Thereafter, in a further artifice the Texas party's state convention, without sanction of statute, embraced the White Primary once more. In *Grovey v. Townsend* (1935) [46] observing that no statute authorized the convention's action (therefore the Fourteenth Amendment was inapplicable) and holding primaries to be like elections of private clubs (therefore the Fifteenth was inapplicable), the Supreme Court upheld the ban.

But the Court now views the primary realistically. After deciding in *United States v. Classic* (1941) [47] (which did not involve racial discrimination) that stuffing a primary ballot box was criminal under the Civil Rights Acts because it denied the federal right to have one's vote counted, the Court applied the principle to Negroes in *Smith v. Allwright* (1944) [48] which involved a Texas primary once more. Pointing to the role in the electoral process which Texas law assigned to primaries [49] (the facts were essentially the same as in *Grovey v. Townsend*), the Court held the Fifteenth (and, inferentially, the Fourteenth) Amendment applicable, and overruled the *Grovey* case.

Since then the courts have been uncompromising in condemning racial restraints on voting. *Rice v. Elmore* (1947) [50] invalidated a ban on Negroes in the South Carolina Democratic primary which claimed immunity from the *Allwright* rule because South Carolina had repealed statutory references to primaries although they still performed the same function. The Fourth Circuit Court of Appeals pointed out:

[44] 273 U.S. 536 (1927).   [45] 286 U.S. 73 (1932).   [46] 295 U.S. 45 (1935).
[47] *Supra* note 10.   [48] 321 U.S. 649 (1944).
[49] See McCall, *History of Texas Elections Laws,* 9 TEX. REV. CIV. STATS. XVII (1951).
[50] 165 F.2d 387 (4th Cir., 1947), *cert. denied,* 333 U.S. 875 (1948).

Those who control the Democratic Party as well as the state government cannot by placing the first of the steps under officials of the party rather than of the state, absolve such officials from the limitations which the federal Constitution imposes. When these officials participate in what is a part of the state's election machinery, they are election officers of the state de facto if not de jure, and as such must observe the limitations of the Constitution.[51]

The South Carolina party then shifted to evasive phraseology. Said it, the primary did not purport to bar Negroes; it merely excluded those who refused to swear belief in segregation and opposition to a proposed Fair Employment Practice Commission bill. This was invalidated in *Brown v. Baskin* (1949).[52]

One of the latest Supreme Court voting cases, *Terry v. Adams* (1953),[53] makes clear that no stratagem, no matter how devious, will be held legal if it bars Negroes from what in fact is the electoral process. In Texas there was an association known as the Jaybird Party, ostensibly a private club. It held elections which almost always chose persons who then ran in the Democratic primary for nomination to county office and who were practically assured of victory in it and thus in the general election. A Negro who had been barred from voting in the club's elections sued. Mr. Justice Black, writing one of the majority opinions, held that the Jaybirds came under the Constitution by viewing the Jaybird-primary-election process as an integral continuum. He held that "it violates the Fifteenth Amendment for a state, by such circumvention, to permit within its borders the use of any device that produces an equivalent of the prohibited election." [54] Mr. Justice Frankfurter felt that the state was even more closely linked to the Jaybird's elections, pointing out that county officials charged with regulating the regular primaries "aid in this subversion of the State's official scheme of which they are trustees, by helping as participants in the scheme and by condoning it." [55] Mr. Justice Clark was less deterred by these conceptual problems. Perhaps as a Texan familiar with that state's electoral processes he had no doubt that the Jaybird operation was governmental and wrote that "the Fifteenth Amendment, as the Fourteenth, 'refers to exertions of state power in all forms.' " [56] Mr. Justice Minton, the lone dissenter, viewed the Jay-

---

[51] *Id.* at 391.
[52] 80 F. Supp. 1017 (E.D.S.C. 1948), *aff'd*, 174 F.2d 391 (4th Cir. 1949).
[53] 345 U.S. 461 (1953); see also Perry v. Cyphers, 186 F.2d 608 (5th Cir. 1951).
[54] 345 U.S. at 469.   [55] *Id.* at 470, 476.   [56] *Id.* at 477, 484.

birds merely as a highly successful pressure group and therefore immune from limitations imposed on government.[57]

The case was the first in which the Court overturned a ban on Negro participation in an election for state office. Mr. Justice Black pointed out that "the [Fifteenth] Amendment includes *any* election in which public issues are decided or public officials selected" (italics added).[58]

THE POLL TAX

The most renowned of the direct impediments to freedom of suffrage was once the poll tax, and it is still enforced as a prerequisite to voting in five states: [59] Alabama, Arkansas,[60] Mississippi, Texas, and Virginia. In Tennessee the law technically still exists [61] but is enforceable only as to taxes due in 1871 and otherwise has been made meaningless.[62] Although one of its chief original purposes was to disfranchise Negroes, the poll tax does not make a racial distinction on its face. However, because of the disproportionate number of poor Negroes, it discourages Negro voting in greater degree than it does white. It also works to deter those most unaccustomed to dealing with official procedures and record keeping, who are again often Negroes. With Negro social and economic progress, however, these effects of the poll tax have been diminished as a means of implementing racial bias. Attempts to outlaw the poll tax in the courts have failed, foundering on the reasoning that by Article I, Section 2, of the Constitution the states are empowered to establish voting qualifications—at least in so far as they do not conflict with federal requirements—and that poll taxing is within this competence.[63] The federal rule forbidding racial discrimination does not come into play either, for on the surface poll taxes fall upon all without regard to race.

Several states have repealed their poll tax laws in recent years: [64] Florida in 1941, Georgia in 1945, and South Carolina in 1951; while Tennessee in 1953 repealed its constitutional requirement that there

[57] *Id.* at 484.   [58] *Id.* at 468.   [59] See appendix A7.

[60] Some Arkansas Negro leaders have opposed ending its poll tax, feeling that payment of the one-dollar tax, tantamount to registration, is less burdensome than might be procedures which could be substituted. Cothran & Phillips, *Expansion of Negro Suffrage in Arkansas*, 26 J. NEGRO EDUCATION 287, 289 (1957).

[61] TENN. CODE ANN. § 67-401 (1955).   [62] See 7 VAND. L. REV. 763 (1954).

[63] Williams v. Mississippi, 170 U.S. 213 (1898); Breedlove v. Suttles, 302 U.S. 277 (1937); Pirtle v. Brown, 118 F.2d 218 (6th Cir. 1941), *cert. denied*, 314 U.S. 621 (1941).

[64] See appendix A7.

must be a poll tax. Whether this movement will continue is unclear. Arkansas voters rejected a constitutional amendment to repeal its poll tax in 1956.[65]

Federal anti-poll tax legislation has been proposed in past and present Congresses, it having been asserted that Congress can ban poll taxes as a prerequisite to federal voting under the broad authority of Article I, Section 4, and under the necessary and proper clause, to protect the national right to vote in federal elections.[66] But congressional power has also been questioned, it being argued that that power extends only to the "times, places and manner" of elections under Article I, Section 4, and that Article I, Section 2, otherwise endows the states with control over elections. One factor working to favor the exercise of federal power may be the past experience with corruption at the polls [67] attributed to such taxes. It would seem that Congress can legislate as much to cleanse federal elections from real or anticipated corruption as from violence (*Ex parte Yarbrough*) [68] or fraud (*United States v. Classic*).[69] An anti-poll tax constitutional amendment also has been advocated,[70] but if Congress already possesses the power, amendment would be unnecessary.

APPORTIONMENT

Where electoral districts are of unequal population but elect the same, or nearly the same, number of representatives, at least two theories could be used to secure for voters in the more populous district a vote of at least approximately the potency of that in the least populous district. First, there is the equal protection clause of the Fourteenth Amendment, which could apply to all elections, federal and state. Second, it may be argued that so far as congressional elections are concerned the framers of the Constitution desired all

[65] Cothran & Phillips, *supra* note 60, at 289.

[66] Proposed legislation and arguments favoring and opposing its constitutionality are discussed in Kallenbach, *Constitutional Aspects of Federal Anti-Poll Tax Legislation*, 45 MICH. L. REV. 717 (1947); Christensen, *The Constitutionality of National Anti-Poll Tax Bills*, 33 MINN. L. REV. 217 (1949), and Note, 53 HARV. L. REV. 645 (1940). See particularly *Hearings on H.R. 29 Before the Subcommittee on Elections of the Committee on House Administration*, 80th Cong., 1st Sess. (1947), and *Hearings* on same before the Senate Committee on Rules and Administration, 80th Cong., 2d Sess. (1948).

[67] See Christensen, *supra* note 66, at 235.   [68] *Supra* note 10.

[69] *Supra* note 10.

[70] See S.J. Res. 25, 83d Cong., 1st Sess. (1954) and *Hearings* thereon before Senate Judiciary Committee. See also Christensen, *supra* note 66, at 221.

votes to be of comparable strength.[71] In fact, however, neither of these theories has been widely accepted. But proponents of equality of ballot strength have had great enough incentive and enough encouragement to keep trying in the courts.

In 1929, a federal law lapsed which had required that congressional districts be approximately compact, contiguous, and equal.[72] Today, however, state legislatures are largely free, so far as federal statute is concerned, to carve out districts to suit their political views—in which the interests of rural areas bulk large.[73] Of course, to an extent this nation has also recognized as permissible, or even desirable, disproportionately greater political power in areas of small population. A fundamental example is the United States Senate, which has the same number of Senators from small as from large states. On the local or state-wide level the same imbalance often exists.[74] But where racial discrimination is practiced, in the Southern states which are of relatively small population, and in their more sparsely settled areas, this geographical favoritism becomes even further amplified. In such situations, solely because of racial discrimination, rural votes acquire an even larger say in electing public officers than do votes in either Northern or Southern urban communities where there is no discrimination.

The deference to rural areas has provoked some of the litigation mentioned above. A number of cases have involved the Georgia county unit system.[75] In Georgia the urban Negro is more likely to vote than are Negroes in rural Georgia, where education is inferior, political organization difficult, and intimidation flourishes. In Atlanta the Negro voting rate is not far below that for whites,[76] but the unit system takes

[71] The best article is Lewis, *Legislative Apportionment and the Federal Courts*, 71 HARV. L. REV. 1057 (1957). Lewis presents the historical evidence concerning the intention of the framers at 1071–1073. See also 17 LAW & CONTEMP. PROBS. 253–469 (1952); Dauer & Kelsay, *Unrepresentative States*, 44 NAT'L MUNIC. REV. 571 (1955).

[72] The statute requiring compactness, contiguity, and equality was Act of Aug. 8, 1911, 37 Stat. 13. It was succeeded by Act of June 18, 1929, 46 Stat. 26, 2 U.S.C.A. § 2a; see Wood v. Broom, 287 U.S. 1 (1932).

[73] AMERICAN POLITICAL SCIENCE ASS'N, REPORT OF THE COMMITTEE ON AMERICAN STATE LEGISLATURES 30 *et seq.* (Zeller ed. 1954).

[74] *Id.* at 37.

[75] South v. Peters, 339 U.S. 276 (1950); Cook v. Fortson, 68 F. Supp. 624 (N.D. Ga. 1946), *app. dism.*, 329 U.S. 675 (1946); Turman v. Duckworth, 68 F. Supp. 744 (N.D. Ga. 1946), *app. dism.*, 329 U.S. 675 (1946). See also Colegrove v. Green, 328 U.S. 549 (1946).

[76] See Bacote, *The Negro Voter in Georgia Politics Today*, 26 J. NEGRO EDUCATION 307, 310 *et seq.* (1957).

from the urban Negro the vote which social factors do not so readily touch. It assigns to each county from two to six "unit" votes for governor, senator, and other offices, the number of seats which the county has in the lower house of the general assembly. The candidate with the highest popular vote in each county wins all its units; the candidate with the most units becomes Democratic candidate for the office he seeks, and thus assured of election. In at least forty-five rural Georgia counties an individual's vote will be worth twenty to one hundred and twenty times that of a person in six-unit Fulton County, the location of Atlanta. The county unit system therefore "has . . . been called the 'last loophole' around [the Supreme Court's] decisions holding that there must be no discrimination because of race in primary as well as in general elections." [77]

Political remedies are not readily available, for, as is true of most states where nonurban areas have disproportionate power, the Georgia Constitution provides that the legislature shall be dominated by the same rural interests which profit from the unit system.[78] And the constitution may be amended only upon a two-thirds vote of the legislature.[79]

A related approach tried in Alabama has been to gerrymander Negroes out of a district where their vote may be important. The Alabama legislature has done this with Tuskegee; [80] it also has taken steps to abolish Macon County by redistributing it among the five surrounding counties so as to dilute the potency of the Negro ballot there.[81]

In Tennessee, where the Negro population is highly urban, proposals to redistribute the seats in the rural-dominated legislature have been opposed on the ground that "racial questions [might] develop if big cities gained additional representation." [82] Most recently, the Tennessee Senate defeated (20-12) such a bill in 1957.[83]

So far, the federal courts have refused to interfere. In *South v.*

[77] Douglas, J., dissenting in South v. Peters, *supra* note 75, at 278.

[78] GA. CONST. art. III, §§ 2-1501 to -1502 (largest counties have three seats, smallest, one); GA. CODE § 34-3212 (1955 Supp.) (winner of primary in each county wins two units for each seat county has in assembly).

[79] GA. CONST. art. XIII §§ 2-8101 to -8102.

[80] N.Y. Times, July 14, 1957, p. 51. See Gomillion v. Lightfoot, Mayor, 167 F. Supp. 405 (M.D. Ala. 1958) (dismissing complaint against this gerrymander).

[81] Afro-American, Sept. 14, 1957, p. 51.

[82] Valien, *Expansion of Negro Suffrage in Tennessee,* 26 J. NEGRO EDUCATION 362, 367 (1957).

[83] See Valien, *supra* note 82, at 366, 367.

Peters,[84] the Supreme Court would not pass on the issue, holding, "Federal courts consistently refuse to exercise their equity powers in cases posing political issues arising from a state's geographical distribution of electoral strength among its political subdivisions." [85] In 1958 a fresh assault on the county unit system by the mayor of Atlanta was again rebuffed. The precise issue was whether the question was substantial enough to warrant calling a three-judge district court. The Chief Justice and Justices Black, Douglas, and Brennan dissented. The significance of widespread disproportionate rural strength throughout the nation was reflected in the attempt of the United States Conference of Mayors to file an *amicus curiae* brief.[86] The argument for judicial abstention is that the question is "political," that intervention would involve the courts deeply in political matters and provoke excessive controversy between federal and state, as well as judicial and legislative, jurisdictions.

There is also the practical problem of what system of representation should prevail if the old is cast out until the legislature enacts a new one. Perhaps, notwithstanding judicial disapproval, it might reenact the old. Moreover, a rural-urban imbalance exists in a great number of places throughout the country, and the Court may fear a deluge of suits should it accept jurisdiction. Anthony Lewis urges, however, that if the judiciary defines an equitable standard (while still accepting reasonable self-imposed limitations on jurisdiction) it should not be assumed that the states will not generally hew to it.[87]

At any rate, these considerations have not inhibited the courts from acting in White Primary cases, as we have seen. And Tennessee's Supreme Court has outlawed that state's county unit system, holding that "devaluation of full participation in primary elections cannot be justified as a commonplace exercise of the police power." [88] Other state courts have not hesitated to intervene in similar situations.[89] Recently a federal district court ordered the Hawaiian legislature to reapportion the islands' legislative districts as required by statute, citing constitutional guarantees of due process along with the ter-

---

[84] *Supra* note 75.
[85] *Id.* at 277. See also Colegrove v. Green, *supra* note 75.
[86] Hartsfield v. Sloan, 357 U.S. 916 (1958).
[87] Lewis, *supra* note 71, at 1007. *Cf.* N.Y. Times, April 3, 1959, p. 15 (governor and two Georgia senators endorse larger unit vote for urban areas in belief that unit system will not withstand another judicial test).
[88] Gates v. Long, 172 Tenn. 471, 478, 113 S.W.2d 388, 391 (1938).
[89] A summary of the states' experience appears in Lewis, *supra* note 71 at 1066.

ritorial apportionment law.[90] However, the two cases noted involved no federal-state relationship: one was entirely within the state domain, the other entirely federal.

Nevertheless, in 1932, in *Smiley v. Holm*,[91] over objection that the question was "political," the Supreme Court reversed a state court ruling that the state legislature could create congressional districts without the governor's approval. Since there was no congressional direction as to an interim method of election, the Court prescribed election-at-large, pending enactment of a valid districting law. (Federal law had only provided for at-large election in the situation where following congressional apportionment a state might be awarded additional representatives and fail to create additional districts; otherwise, on this issue, it was silent.) Here, therefore, was a case of federal judicial "interference" with state "political" and "legislative" matters and federal judicial prescription of a method for electing representatives in place of the invalidated system.

Section 2 of the Fourteenth Amendment was enacted for the specific purpose of reducing a state's representation in Congress to the extent that it disfranchises Negroes. But for reasons like those asserted in the county unit cases, the courts have refrained from applying it.[92] Moreover, the practical problem is more complicated than that of setting up a new electoral system in one state, for to readjust properly proportions under Section 2 a court might have to redistrict the entire United States. Since the number of Congressmen is fixed, the question is who gets the seats taken away from the offenders. One answer may be that although perfect reapportionment is beyond judicial competence, greater justice will be achieved by simply denying seats to the offending states notwithstanding an ensuing imbalance.

But surely the remedy could be provided by Congress itself, which could either reapportion or refuse to seat a member on the ground that he was elected by a constituency from which Negroes were barred. Congressional power to judge the qualifications of its own members is unlimited, and has been exercised on a number of grounds, including that for the purpose of correcting wrongs wrought by dis-

[90] Dyer v. Kazuhisa Abe, 138 F. Supp. 220 (D. Hawaii 1956). Following the decision Congress laid out new legislative districts. Lewis, *supra* note 71, at 1089.

[91] 285 U.S. 355 (1932); see also Carroll v. Becker, 285 U.S. 380 (1932); Koenig v. Flynn, 285 U.S. 375 (1932).

[92] Saunders v. Wilkins, 152 F.2d 235 (4th Cir. 1945), *cert. denied*, 328 U.S. 870 (1946); Daly v. Madison County, 378 Ill. 357, 38 N.E.2d 160 (1941); *cf.* Dennis v. United States, 171 F.2d 986 (D.C. Cir. 1948), *aff'd*, 339 U.S. 162 (1950).

crimination. For example, in the Louisiana elections to the 54th Congress Negroes were barred from the polls or compelled to vote Democratic. The committee which investigated the charges held that

if fraud, violence, and intimidation have been so extensive and general as to render it certain that there has been no free and fair expression by the great body of the electors, then the election must be set aside, notwithstanding the fact that in some of the precincts or parishes there was a peaceable and fair election.[93]

The House declared the seat vacant.

In Rhode Island, in the 1884 congressional election, employers and their agents were stationed at the polls to ascertain how employees voted. It was possible to tell because each party used a different colored ballot. When the seat was contested, Congress, for this reason, declared it vacant.[94] Other cases involving similar facts have had similar results. This power of Congress is undoubted.[95]

The President, too, could aid in enforcing the Fourteenth Amendment's apportionment clause. He is by statute [96] obliged periodically to send to Congress a message setting forth the apportionment of Representatives according to law as calculated by him. If he were to read this statute in the light of the Constitution, he should make his computations pursuant to Section 2 of the Fourteenth Amendment as well as according to the mere arithmetical criteria ordinarily employed. But this he has never done. It might be that the Civil Rights Commission, one of whose functions is to study voting discrimination, could make these computations for him.[97]

[93] H.R. REP. No. 867, 54th Cong., 1st Sess. (Benoit v. Boatner), 11 (1896).

[94] CONG. REC., 49th Cong., 2d Sess., 1008–1028 (1887) (Rhode Island contested election); H.R. REP. No. 3617, 49th Cong., 2d Sess. (1887) (Page v. Pirce).

[95] CONG. GLOBE, 41st Cong., 2d Sess., 2850–2852 (1870) (Louisiana election case); H.R. REP. No. 806, 45th Cong., 2d Sess. (Richardson v. Rainey), 5, 48 (1878); CONG. GLOBE, 41st Cong., 1st Sess., 3–4 (1869) (seating of members from Georgia, Louisiana, Pennsylvania); H.R. REP. No. 1983, 47th Cong., 2d Sess. (Lee v. Richardson), 28–32 (1883). See also I HINDS, PRECEDENTS OF THE HOUSE OF REPRESENTATIVES 224–226 (1907) (Louisiana election case); II HINDS 163–164 (South Carolina case, Buttz v. Mackey).

[96] 2 U.S.C.A. § 2a.

[97] The commission was established by the Civil Rights Act of 1957. In late 1958 it began its first investigation—of Alabama voting discrimination—and immediately encountered intransigence. N.Y. Times, Dec. 9, 1958, p. 1. An Alabama civil rights leader has told the author that the commission's activity has encouraged Negroes, to some extent, to register.

STRICTURES ON NEGRO CANDIDATES

With the thought that publicizing a Negro candidate's race would discourage white persons from voting for him, Oklahoma required that "Negro" be placed after a Negro's name on the ballot. This has been held a denial of equal protection by the Tenth Circuit for the reason that members of no other group were required to designate their race or origin.[98]

What might be called a converse approach has been a recent North Carolina statute designed to dilute Negro bloc voting wherever a group of candidates compete for a relatively small number of seats, as on a city council, and a fixed number of those receiving the greatest number of ballots win. If Negroes voted only for a Negro candidate and cast no ballots for anyone else, the Negro candidate obviously would enjoy an advantage. This is called "single shot voting." The statute provides that "where an elector votes for any number of such group candidates less than the number of offices to be filled, such ballot shall not be counted" [99] Alabama has a similar law.[100]

CONCLUSION

The law has increased Negro participation at the ballot box, but a resurgence of discrimination calls for further legal effort. The Civil Rights Act of 1957 is designed to fill gaps in voting rights which existed before its passage. Its effect will, of course, depend upon the vigor with which it is enforced. But apart from its application its mere existence and the publicity attending its passage should spur Negro registration, even in areas where there has been no discrimination.

One of the largest problems in Negro voting, however, and indeed in voting in general, is that of bringing to the polls those whom none can keep away but themselves. Interviews with Negro leaders in Southern cities where discrimination at the polls is not substantial or is even nonexistent indicate concern over the fact that very many eligible Negroes fail to register, and if they do register, to vote. The *Journal of Negro Education* study, referred to earlier in this chapter, reports consistently concerning every Southern state that "apathy" is

[98] McDonald v. Key, 224 F.2d 608 (10th Cir. 1955), *cert. denied,* 350 U.S. 895 (1955).
[99] N.C. GEN. STATS. § 163–175(6) (1957 Supp.).
[100] ALA. CODE tit. 17, § 361 (1940).

a dominating force in Negro suffrage.[101] Of course, "apathy" is not an entirely fair term because it is superficial. The society of the South created conditions in which Negro voting was hardly encouraged and in which the education and economic status of Negroes worked against their full participation in community affairs. Where these factors are not so powerful, as in Louisville, we find Negro electoral participation about on a par with that of whites.[102] In Baltimore and some Maryland counties we find it not far off.[103] In both Louisville and Baltimore discrepancies may be accounted for by economic and educational factors. This demonstrates that given a freer climate and encouragement to vote so-called Negro "apathy" may dissipate.

The law can do nothing immediate about such self-restraint. Neither legislation, nor court order, nor administrative decree can rule it out. The law cannot directly overcome the ignorance with which Southern education has endowed Negroes in disproportionate share or the indifference with which Southern society has inculcated Negroes, in large measure by permitting them but small realization of the fruits of effort. However, law can create a condition which permits voting by those who desire to do so, and thus it can stimulate that desire in others. What will be realized from this political power depends on other factors, though, such factors as Negro prosperity, leisure, community organization, level of education, patterns of minority housing, and the whole host of variables which help to determine the scope and meaning of the right to vote. But as other chapters demonstrate law can contribute to changing racial patterns in these activities.

[101] See the following articles in 26 J. NEGRO EDUCATION (1957): Gomillion, *The Negro Voter in Alabama* 281, 285; Cothran & Phillips *supra* note 60, at 293; Bacote, *supra* note 76, at 308; Fenton, *The Negro Voter in Louisiana* 319, 322; Lewis, *The Negro Voter in Mississippi* 329, 346; Newton, *Expansion of Negro Suffrage in North Carolina* 351, 358; McCain, *The Negro Voter in South Carolina* 359, 360; Valien, *supra* note 82, at 367; McGuinn & Spraggins, *Negro in Politics in Virginia* 378, 387; Irving, *The Future of the Negro Voter in the South* 390, 391.

[102] Kesselman, *Negro Voting in a Border Community—Louisville, Kentucky*, 26 J. NEGRO EDUCATION 273 (1957).

[103] Some Maryland registration figures are:

	Colored Voters (In percent)	White Voters (In percent)
Dorchester County	66	78
Baltimore City	57	63
Caroline County	65	76

Afro-American Magazine, Sept. 14, 1957, p. 4. In 1958 over 100,000 colored citizens registered to vote in Baltimore, *id.*, Sept. 27, 1958, p. 1. In 1956 colored voters constituted 19.7% of Baltimore's electorate, in 1958, about 24%, *id.*, Oct. 18, 1958, p. 5.

CHAPTER VI

EARNING A LIVING

The ability to earn a living and the way it is earned help to determine not only how thoroughly any minority political potential can be realized, but also the fullness with which other qualities, including those of individual personality, can be developed. It is clear, however, that a Negro faces a far more difficult task than a white person in getting work suited to his abilities and in earning the money and leisure necessary for personal improvement and community participation.

The Negro-white disparity is substantial. In 1955 a larger proportion of the Negro population (62%) than of the white (57%) was in the labor force (more Negro women and both very young and old Negroes work). On one hand, of the nonwhites who worked only 12 percent were in professional, managerial, and white collar occupations (increased from 9 percent since the early postwar period); the comparable proportion among whites—about 42 percent in 1955—rose during the same period to a relatively smaller degree. On the other hand, the service and other unskilled nonfarm occupations employed about 47 percent of the nonwhite workers but only 14 percent of the whites. A much larger proportion of nonwhites worked part time, in many cases because of inability to find full-time jobs. Unemployment rates among Negroes were much higher; while they comprised only 10 percent of the work force, they constituted 20 percent of the unemployed.[1] This lack of well-paying jobs has produced a median urban white income almost double that for Negroes, a median rural white income almost three times the size of the Negroes'.[2]

[1] The statistics are from U.S. BUREAU OF THE CENSUS, DEP'T OF COMMERCE, SER. P-50, No. 66, CURRENT POPULATION REPORTS (March, 1956). See Afro-American, March 22, 1958, p. 5 (in 1958 depression twice as many Negroes unemployed as whites).

[2] 1957 STATISTICAL ABSTRACT OF THE UNITED STATES 313.

Their depressed position is not only detrimental to Negroes them-
selves, however, but to the nation as a whole. It inflicts loss on both
North and South, although more strikingly now on the South. In *The
Negro Potential*, Eli Ginzberg characterized the situation thus:

At present, a young Negro who has acquired skills in the armed services
and comes back even to such a metropolitan center as Atlanta finds it
difficult to obtain a job which uses his skills. Before long his availability is
made known to employment exchanges north of the Mason-Dixon Line,
and he is likely to be on his way. . . . Other costs are also implicit. . . .
Such a system inevitably results in excessive overhead and faulty utilization
practices since men must be assigned primarily according to their color
rather than the needs of the plant. The South will have to give up the
luxury of maintaining segregation in the work place and begin to make
progressive moves to abandon it, if it is to strengthen its position in the
never-ceasing competition for new plants.[3]

Harry Ashmore and James Dabbs have pointed out that such considerations are weighty in encouraging Southern racial change.[4] Moreover,
the fact that the Negroes' inferior economic position impairs the national potential [5] has furnished an argument for the President's Committee on Government Contracts, his Committee on Government Employment Policy, and for those supporting Fair Employment Practices
Codes and similar legislation to induce desegregation on the job.

Even where discrimination has receded, however, the inertia of past
bias weighs heavily. To qualify for skilled or professional employment
takes years of training and experience and those who did not prepare
when jobs did not exist cannot suddenly become capable when they
open. Law can aim directly at the unwillingness of employers to hire
members of minorities; it can only indirectly affect the ability of
minority members to do the job.

THE LEGAL FRAMEWORK

Very little employment discrimination is directly required by government—only a handful of laws, some of recent origin, demand segre-

[3] GINZBERG, THE NEGRO POTENTIAL 122 (1956). See also WEAVER, NEGRO LABOR
(1946); on the growing Negro middle class see FRAZIER, BLACK BOURGEOISIE (1957);
on national income distribution see U.S. DEP'T OF COMMERCE, PERSONAL INCOME
BY STATES 3 (1956) (Southeast per capita income as a percent of national average
is 70; Southwest is 86).

[4] ASHMORE, AN EPITAPH FOR DIXIE, esp. ch. 7 (1957); DABBS, THE SOUTHERN
HERITAGE ch. XIII (1958).

[5] On Negroes' disability to serve during the Second World War see SPECIAL
GROUPS, SPECIAL MONOGRAPH NO. 10, SELECTIVE SERVICE SYSTEM 166, 189, 191
(1953). See also GINZBERG & BRAY, THE UNEDUCATED (1955); GINZBERG & OTHERS,
THE INEFFECTIVE SOLDIER (3 vols. 1959).

gated facilities on the job—but a very great amount of employment is in fact discriminatory. Most discrimination in earning a living is privately inflicted, although even a good deal of employment by government itself is discriminatory in practice. Still, in many places public administration presents the best opportunity for nondiscriminatory advancement, safeguarded as it is by law against discrimination. Many states and cities have laws or regulations forbidding bias in state or municipal jobs. Similarly, the President's Committee on Government Employment Policy forbids discrimination in work for the United States. More fundamental, however, discriminatory laws and practices in government employment are interdicted by the Fifth and Fourteenth amendments. The duty of the nation and the states under these amendments extends as far as they participate in the employment relationship, and covers, for example, such preemployment activities as job referrals and apprenticeship training.

Of course, law is also involved in discrimination in employment, both public and private, to the extent that it has helped to create inferior education, living conditions, political position, and so forth, or has not prevented these conditions from continuing to exist. But this is tangential to the direct exertions of the law to end job discrimination.

Theoretically at least, the state and municipal FEPCs possess the most powerful weapons to abolish discrimination in private employment. In addition, the President's Committee on Government Contracts has been a legal influence against private job discrimination. And in the union-employee-employer relationship there is yet another legal force working against discrimination. In a sense the union contract is the law of the plant in which an employee works. Many such agreements contain nondiscrimination clauses, but unions also have an obligation not to discriminate which is imposed by law and stems from the Constitution, statute, and common law. There are other legal resources applicable to employment bias, including antitrust doctrine, which may impinge on restrictive practices of professional associations. To facilitate discussion of law and discrimination in employment, we shall look at the operation of government employment, then at private employment activities, and finally at the role of the President's Committee on Government Contracts and the FEPCs. But first we shall review the earliest of the efforts in this area, the laws against peonage, which, though a general problem, in greatest part has affected Negroes.

FORCED LABOR

The Thirteenth Amendment ("Neither slavery nor involuntary servitude . . . shall exist within the United States") supplied the basic protection against forced labor. Striking at state and private action alike, it cut to the core the slave tradition. It not only forbade slavery, but, implemented by legislation,[6] outlawed other statutory or contractual schemes to compel Negroes (and, of course, others) to labor against their will—the practice commonly known as peonage.[7] Federal law has raised "both a shield and a sword against forced labor because of debt," [8] making it a crime and invalidating state laws or other arrangements which would enforce it. Since 1939, the end of the depression, a widespread drop in peonage has occurred,[9] but as recently as 1956 the Civil Rights Section of the Department of Justice filed four peonage prosecutions, and in 1957 it filed two.[10]

Charges of involuntary servitude have been made against migrant farm operators who attract workers far away from their homes (often by false promises), frequently lodge them in uninhabitable dwellings, charge (or overcharge) their travel and living expenses against their earnings (leaving a minuscule balance or none), provide working conditions which are often onerous or even unbearable, exploit child labor, and use subtle or direct threats of violence against those who would depart while in debt, or indeed at any time during the farming season. Most of these workers are Negroes or Mexicans (the wetbacks).[11] A more favored remedy than prosecution for peonage (the crime would be difficult to establish and prosecuting for it could not strike at all the evils of migrant farms) is stricter enforcement of existing wage and social legislation and new enactments specifically designed for the migratory labor situation.[12] Therefore it is now out-

[6] 42 U.S.C.A. § 1994 (peonage abolished); 18 U.S.C.A. § 1581 (fine up to $5,000, imprisonment up to 5 years, or both). Military service under the draft has been held not to be involuntary servitude forbidden by the Thirteenth Amendment. Selective Draft Law Cases, 245 U.S. 366 (1917).

[7] The essence of peonage is compulsory service in payment of debt, Bailey v. Alabama, 219 U.S. 219, 242 (1911). See Pollock v. Williams, 322 U.S. 4 (1944) (Florida statute making it misdemeanor to obtain with intent to defraud advance upon agreement to render services and providing that failure to perform is prima facie evidence of such intent violates Thirteenth Amendment).

[8] 322 U.S. at 8.   [9] To SECURE THESE RIGHTS 29–30 (1947).

[10] 1956 ATT'Y GEN. ANN. REP. 362; see his 1957 REP. at 376; his 1955 REP. at 368.

[11] See N.Y. Times, Sept. 5, 1957, p. 59, Sept. 8, 1957, § E, p. 10, Sept. 11, 1957, p. 32; on Mexican laborers see GALARZA, STRANGERS IN OUR FIELDS (1956).

[12] See *Hearings on Migratory Labor Before the Senate Subcommittee on Labor*

side the main channels of job discrimination, for which other remedies are needed. Squarely in these channels is discrimination in government employment, which according to basic constitutional principle is illegal.

GOVERNMENT EMPLOYMENT

At the higher levels of government there is in a sense an "employment" problem for Negroes, but one for which only a political solution is conceivable. For example, no President has ever appointed a Negro cabinet officer (although a recent Assistant Secretary of Labor has been a Negro); there is only one Negro judge in the federal judiciary; in proportion to population Negro representation in Congress is insignificant. In some Northern states Negro participation in high governmental positions is more prominent, reflecting, of course, the strength of the Negro vote, but even there it is still slight. This slowness to recognize Negroes for important political posts permeates policy at other levels of government service and in private employment too by helping to reinforce and to perpetuate an image of them as persons not fit for higher responsibilities.

While some government jobs may perhaps occupy a penumbral area not accessible to conventional judicial remedies, it is clear that the Fifth and Fourteenth amendments may be invoked to interdict federal and state government efforts to use race as a factor in almost all of their own employment activities—including hiring, pay, promotion, access to work areas, and all the incidents of government service. There have been only a few reported cases in point, but *Alston v. School Board of the City of Norfolk* [13] makes clear that the rule is

---

and Labor-Management Relations, 82d Cong., 2d Sess. (1952); N.Y. STATE JOINT LEGISLATIVE COMM., REPORT ON MIGRANT LABOR (Leg. Doc. No. 51, 1955); N.Y. LABOR LAW §§ 212a–e; Comment, 1951 WIS. L. REV. 344. A model bill and discussion of the problem appears in PRESIDENT'S COMM., REPORT ON MIGRATORY LABOR (1956). Special provisions regulating transportation of migrant workers transported more than 75 miles, if such transport is across a state or foreign boundary, appear in pt. 198 Motor Carrier Safety Regulations (adopted by the ICC effective August 1, 1957).

[13] 112 F.2d 992 (4th Cir. 1940), *cert. denied,* 311 U.S. 693 (1940); other teachers' salary cases are McDaniel v. Board of Pub. Instruction for Escambia County, 39 F. Supp. 638 (N.D. Fla. 1941); Mills v. Board of Educ. of Anne Arundel County, 30 F. Supp. 245 (D. Md. 1939) (injunction against racial discrimination but not against paying colored teachers less than white; board entitled to exercise discretion on nonracial grounds); Thomas v. Hibbitts, 46 F. Supp. 368 (M.D. Tenn. 1942).

what one would expect: that race may not play any part in any aspect of employment by government. The school board of Norfolk was required to pay Negro teachers on the same basis as white ones; *i.e.*, race could not influence any individual teacher's compensation. Moreover, the fact that the Negro teachers had no contracts for the ensuing year (there was no tenure for teachers generally) did not bar a decree in their favor. They had a right, the case held, to equal terms if engaged. The *Alston* case was but one of scores of successful suits to equalize Negro teachers' salaries brought in the thirties and forties.[14] Other cases not involving race, also make clear that government may no more impose unconstitutional conditions in its employment practices than in its other activities.[15]

The federal government has implemented the constitutional standard for civil service by a statute which provides that "in the administration of this chapter ["Classification of Civilian Positions"], there shall be no discrimination with respect to any person, or with respect to the position held by any person, on account of sex, marital status, race, creed, or color." [16] This admonition refined the basic directive of the Civil Service Act of 1883 which provided that competitive examinations be given, that vacancies be filled from among those rated highest, and that appointments be made from among the highest eligibles as indicated by the results of such competitive examinations.[17]

[14] Perhaps most teachers' salary cases were settled, leaving no official report. On this litigation see 1936 NAACP ANNUAL REPORT 13 (Maryland); 1937, at 11-12 (Maryland, Virginia); 1938, at 11-12 (Florida, Maryland, Virginia); 1939, at 1-12 (Florida, Maryland, Virginia); 1940, at 18-20 (Kentucky, Maryland, Virginia); 1941, at 15-19 (Alabama, Florida, Kentucky, Louisiana, Tennessee, Virginia); and subsequent NAACP Annual Reports.

[15] Slochower v. Board of Higher Educ., 350 U.S. 551 (1956) (due process denied by discharge of teacher based upon inference of guilt drawn from exercise of self-incrimination privilege); Wieman v. Updegraff, 344 U.S. 183 (1952) (requirement that teacher take loyalty oath which did not provide that forbidden association was *knowing* denies due process); United Pub. Workers v. Mitchell, 330 U.S. 75 (1947) (government employees constitutionally may be forbidden to participate in politics but "Congress may not 'enact a regulation providing that no Republican, Jew or Negro shall be appointed to federal office, or that no federal employee shall attend Mass or take any active part in missionary work,'" at 100); see Bryan v. Austin, discussed *supra* pp. 19–20 and *infra* pp. 164–165, and Johnson v. Yeilding, discussed *infra* p. 164.

[16] 5 U.S.C.A. § 1074.

[17] 22 Stat. 403, § 2 (47th Cong., 2d Sess.). High points in the historical development have been: Exec. Order No. 8802, 6 Fed. Reg. 3109 (1941), establishing the President's Committee on Fair Employment Practice; Exec. Order No. 9346, 8 Fed. Reg. 7183 (1943), establishing a new FEPC. Between 1941 and 1946 when the FEPC was abolished, the Civil Service Commission received 1,871 complaints alleging discrimination; the complainant was upheld in 58. When postwar Civil

Today, not only the statutory mandates, but also the detailed Executive Order No. 10590 (1955),[18] is designed to prevent racial discrimination in every aspect of employment in the Executive Branch, almost all of which is in the civil service. (There is no similar directive governing other branches of the federal government, except, of course, the military.) The order established the President's Committee on Government Employment Policy (consisting of representatives of the Civil Service Commission, the Department of Labor, the Office of Defense Mobilization, the Department of Defense, and three public members appointed by the President),[19] which, in addition to advising the President, the Civil Service Commission, and the various department heads, reviews cases of discrimination referred to it and renders "advisory opinions" to department and agency heads. The order, however, it should be stressed, is directed primarily at the departments and agencies, making them principally responsible for keeping themselves free of discrimination.

The scheme of administration and review is largely decentralized. The head of each executive department and agency is required to designate an employment policy officer (who must not be connected with the agency's division handling personnel) [20] to operate immediately below him. The employment policy officer's duties include advising the department head concerning the executive order, receiving and investigating complaints, making recommendations for corrective orders, appraising the agency's personnel operations to assure adherence to the executive order's policy and making certain that within the agency there are fair hearings on complaints.[21] Although the em-

---

Service went back on a career basis, Exec. Order No. 9691, 11 Fed. Reg. 1381 (1946), forbade racial discrimination in temporary appointments. Two permanent regulations were issued: present § 04.2 (no racial discrimination may be practiced against employee, eligible or applicant) and § 9.101(2) (no discrimination in removal, suspension, demotion). Exec. Order No. 9980, 13 Fed. Reg. 4311 (1948) created the Fair Employment Board to enforce the policy of nondiscrimination in the Executive Branch. § 07.1 forbids the use of race as a standard in the exercise of discretion in appointing. The rules may be found in 5 C.F.R. (1954 Supp.).

[18] 20 Fed. Reg. 409 (1955).

[19] Exec. Order No. 10722, 22 Fed. Reg. 6287 (1957).

[20] Regulations and Procedure of the President's Committee on Government Employment Policy XIII.A. This corresponds to Exec. Order No. 10590 § 5.

[21] To aid him the committee has prepared two documents: Memoranda # 2 ("Procedures for Investigation of Complaints of Discrimination, June 3, 1955") and # 7 ("Duties and Responsibilities of Employment Policy Officers, Feb. 3, 1956").

ployment officer may enjoy a measure of independence because of his civil service status, he is the designee of his superior and is, of course, dependent on him for his personal situation. To some extent the employment officer is immune from pressure to support personnel policies in all events by the rule that he shall not be connected with the personnel department. While it may be questioned whether this assures complete freedom of action, either an agency or a complainant may refer cases to the President's Committee on Government Employment.

The committee will review a case if the complainant has followed prescribed procedure, prosecuted diligently, and cooperated in furnishing information. Prior to review issues first have to be thoroughly investigated and a hearing held, if requested by the complainant; an appraisal has to have been conducted of employment policies in the unit in question; and findings of fact have to have been made and a course of action recommended by the employment policy officer. If the committee needs additional information, it may request the complainant or his representative to appear; if evidence is inconclusive, the committee may request the agency head or his employment policy officer to furnish more, or may conduct its own inquiry. On all the evidence the committee drafts findings of fact and, when indicated, recommends corrective action to the department head.[22]

Perhaps the most important of the committee's regulations governing agencies—control is otherwise fairly loose—are that when a complaint is filed an appraisal must be undertaken [23] of employment practices in the questioned unit; and that, except in cases involving disciplinary action, the burden of developing sufficient facts to resolve the issues rests on the agency and not the complainant.[24] The first means that even though the particular complaint may be unwarranted other discrimination may be exposed, although its chief purpose, apparently, is to ascertain agency policy with respect to the minority involved in the complaint. The second relieves the complainant of the hardship of finding and developing evidence, all of which is probably in the agency files. However, this regulation does not appear to be the equivalent of placing the burden of proof on the agency, nor is it the same as discovery proceedings employed in regular litigation.

The committee does not on its own initiative ordinarily enter an

[22] Regulations and Procedures, *supra* note 20, VII.A *et seq.*
[23] *Id.* at IX.A.   [24] *Id.* at IX.B.

agency to ascertain whether discrimination is being practiced (the general review undertaken when a complaint is filed, however, leans in this direction), although other bodies in the field of implementing antidiscrimination policies have found that awaiting complaints is an unsatisfactory method for changing biased employment practices. It would, however, its executive director has stated, investigate any situation in which a question had arisen, and on at least one occasion has done so.[25]

While the Executive Order expressly authorizes the committee to issue "advisory opinions" only, excluding compulsion as a means of implementing its decisions, its status as a presidental committee endows it, in the opinion of those connected with its operation, with considerable power of persuasion. There apparently has never been a situation in which the committee and an agency deadlocked over a case, but we may ponder whether the committee might not be more insistent in its own determinations in specific cases, or whether the agencies might not be more compliant, if the committee possessed powers to enforce its determinations.

At this writing the committee has rendered its second report, announcing a total of 341 cases involving complaints of discrimination reported to it between May, 1956, and January, 1958, which included cases settled within the agencies and those appealed. Corrective action was taken in 53 cases at the agency level and 10 cases at committee level.[26] But the effect of the order and the committee is not limited to the adjudication of particular disputes. The committee also engages in various educational efforts, including calling meetings of agency heads and personnel officers to discuss the committee's goals and means

[25] Letter from Dr. Ross Clinchy, Executive Director of the President's Committee on Government Employment Policy, to the author, March 31, 1958.

[26] PRESIDENT'S COMM., SECOND REPORT ON GOVERNMENT EMPLOYMENT POLICY 20-21 (1958). At the lower level the complainant was satisfied with the explanation offered in 45 cases; in 28 he failed to prosecute; in 145 no finding of discrimination was made. Almost all cases involved Negroes. The nature of the complaints was about as follows: Failure of Appointment (83 cases); Failure of Promotion (67); Separation (48); Other (73). Seventy of the cases decided at agency level were referred to the committee; upon review discrimination was found in 10; in 9 cases the complaint was withdrawn; in 51 there was a finding of no discrimination. Almost all of the cases involved Negroes. The committee does not publish detailed reports of cases but has summarized about a dozen typical complaints and reviews for the edification of employment policy officers which may be obtained from the committee upon request. Some examples also are published as an appendix to the *Second Report*. The *First Report* contains comparable information, but indicates less activity.

of implementation and distributing substantial amounts of literature.

Unquestionably Negro employment in federal civil service has risen considerably since the committee began operating. Obviously general social and economic conditions have had much to do with the increase, but fair employment policy and the committee's operations seem to have influenced the change too. Some connected with the committee point to specific instances of its intervention having resulted in appreciable betterment in Negro employment, chiefly in border communities.

The committee has completed one of a series of surveys of federal Negro employment in Washington, D.C., Chicago, Los Angeles, St. Louis, and Mobile, designed to obtain an idea of the problem with which it is dealing. The first year's results (1956) have been assembled; follow-ups will show whether changes are occurring. While the study shows substantial numbers of Negro employees in each area, perhaps the most striking fact in the various tables prepared by the committee is the low degree of Negro participation in the higher grades of federal employment. In Washington, D.C., only 1.7 percent of Negroes in federal service were at Grade 6, 2.9 percent at Grade 7, 0.1 percent at Grade 8, and 1.1 percent at 9. There, between Grades 13 and 15 Negro participation was measured in hundredths of a percent, while more than 80 percent of Negro participation was in Grade 4 and below. Outside of Washington the Negro share of the higher grades was even lower. In Mobile no Negroes at all appeared above Grade 6 (for which the figure was 0.7 percent). Negroes in Grades 1 to 3 constituted over 84 percent of Negro federal employment there.[27] The committee acknowledges the role of discrimination in this situation, but points out that other factors are responsible too, namely, that Negroes have come into white-collar federal service in substantial numbers largely since the Second World War and that they have had limited educational opportunities.[28]

EMPLOYMENT IN STATE GOVERNMENT

Under the laws of many states discrimination in state employment is forbidden. The very theory of civil service laws should prohibit discrimination without even mentioning the racial question, but ob-

[27] A Five-City Survey of Negro-American Employees of the Federal Government (statistics as of June 30, 1956).
[28] Id. at 4.

viously notwithstanding the wide extent of state civil service, discrimination has occurred and, therefore, some states with civil service laws have specifically also forbidden racial bias. Some regulate the matter through general FEPC statutes,[29] some by statutes regulating governmental work or civil service,[30] and some by civil service rule or practice.[31] Certain states, it appears, cover the situation by a combination of methods, others have no law on the matter. The position of some states is that the law neither requires nor forbids discrimination—among these are states in the South where one might expect to find discrimination.[32] Only Oklahoma in reply to a questionnaire has stated that it uses a racial standard in state employment: "selective certification . . . on the basis of race and sex." [33]

Those who would evade prohibitions on discrimination—constitutional, statutory, or regulatory—may not have to show bias openly as, for example, in Birmingham, Alabama, where until recently police examinations were given to whites only.[34] In federal and often in state civil service appointments are made by the "rule of three": an appointing officer chooses from among the three highest scorers on an examination, and he might pass over a top-scoring Negro to take a white person.[35] True, on the federal level, if he did this often enough, a pattern would emerge and he then might be confronted with a finding of discrimination by the employment policy officer or the President's Committee on Goverment Employment, or the courts. On the state level there might be a suit based on the Fourteenth Amendment or an applicable bias statute, or possibly administrative hearings when statute or civil service rule so provide. But it takes a long time for a pattern to develop, aggrieved persons may never appeal, and there can be no certainty that administrative proceedings will develop all the facts or otherwise achieve a just result. The important role that subjective evaluations often play in employment compounds the difficulty.

We have in the first chapter mentioned one instance of a switch from overt to subtle tactics by repeal of South Carolina legislation

[29] See appendix A8.   [30] See appendix A9.
[31] See appendix A10.   [32] See appendix A11.
[33] Letter from Supervisor, Personnel Board, to Professor Jack B. Weinstein.
[34] Johnson v. Yeilding, 267 Ala. 108, 100 So. 2d 29 (1958); Johnson v. Yeilding, 165 F. Supp. 76 (N.D. Ala. 1958).
[35] See FIELD, CIVIL SERVICE LAW 14 (1939). Some states employ a different number. There have been charges of "rigged" civil service exams and unfair selection. Afro-American, Nov. 30, 1957, p. 4.

barring NAACP members from state employment and its replacement by a law requiring that state employees list the organizations to which they belong.[36] Similarly, the Birmingham police case, mentioned above, ended with the city abolishing the written rule that Negroes may not be hired. So far, however, none have been engaged and it is possible that the city is enforcing the old regulation under the guise of exercising discretion in each separate case. In Moberly, Missouri, upon desegregation of the schools, all the Negro teachers were fired, and only whites were retained in teaching positions. When suit was filed in federal court, the board defended on the ground that the white teachers were superior to the colored teachers in certain subjective respects. The trial court upheld the contention; [37] the case at this writing is on appeal.

Notwithstanding the effective use of subterfuges and outright violations, the law requiring nondiscriminatory governmental employment seems to have had some effect. According to a 1956 Bureau of the Census report Negroes and whites "now show similar proportions in the public administration field, indicating a considerable improvement in job opportunities for nonwhites in government work." [38] Of course, these reports average North with South, state employment with federal, and do not account for level of employment. Nonetheless, the statistic seems significant.

STATE PREEMPLOYMENT ACTIVITIES

The states not only employ workers of their own. They also refer workers to private companies through the state employment services which, supported in part by the federal government, continue to run the offices of the United States Employment Service (USES), whose property has been transferred to the states.[39] All of the services have been ordered to refuse discriminatory job orders by the federal departments,[40] but except where state law forbids job discrimination they appear to honor nonfederal requests for discriminatory referrals.

---

[36] Bryan v. Austin, 148 F. Supp. 563 (E.D.S.C. 1957), *app. dism. as moot,* 354 U.S. 933 (1957). See pp. 19–20 *supra.*

[37] Brooks v. Board of Educ. of the City of Moberly, Mo., 3 R.R.L.R. 660 (E.D. Mo. 1958), *aff'd,* No. 16,131, 8th Cir., June 17, 1959.

[38] 1956 BUREAU OF THE CENSUS POPULATION REPORTS, *op. cit. supra* note 1, at 3. See N.Y. Times, Jan. 22, 1959, p. 14 (one person in six is a government employee).

[39] On the USES and its relation to the state services see 29 U.S.C.A. ch. 4B.

[40] See 33 L.R.R.M. 96 (1954).

Referrals may be made on a discriminatory basis where state law permits either by a state on its own initiative or at the request of an employer. Before 1952, for example, when the Illinois State Employment Service was forbidden to honor discriminatory job specifications, more than 50 percent of its orders carried racial restrictions.[41]

In a letter of December 16, 1957, to the author, the Minority Groups Consultant of USES wrote:

Our Minority Groups Policy is stated below:
A. To promote employment opportunity for all applicants on the basis of their skills, abilities, and job qualifications.
B. To make definite and continuous effort with employers with whom relationships are established, to the end that their hiring specifications be based exclusively on job performance.
C. To assist the United States Civil Service Commission in effectuating Executive Order 10590 by not accepting discriminatory job orders from Federal establishments.
D. To cooperate with procurement agencies and other appropriate agencies of the Government in their efforts to secure compliance with nondiscrimination clauses in Government contracts.

However, the special assistant to the director of USES has stated concerning biased referral in the District of Columbia: "Unfortunately, we are required by law to accept job orders from private agencies which discriminate. Unlike agencies in states where discrimination is in violation of law, we cannot refuse to accept these job orders."[42] While there has been no reported litigation, these state services would seem to come under the Fourteenth (and, in view of federal participation and control, probably the Fifth) Amendment duty not to differentiate on the basis of race.

The states also often participate in apprenticeship programs. In this activity too they cannot, under the Constitution, make racial distinctions. New York has by statute suggested (but not required) that apprenticeship agreements contain a provision forbidding racial discrimination;[43] elsewhere there appear to be no such laws. The Cleveland Board of Education has prohibited discrimination in apprentice-training programs in the city schools to which unions, employers, and the city, state, and federal governments all contribute.[44]

[41] CHICAGO COMM'N ON HUMAN RELATIONS, FOURTH CHICAGO CONFERENCE ON CIVIC UNITY 101 (1952).
[42] See Afro-American, Oct. 27, 1956, p. 13.   [43] N.Y. LABOR LAW § 814(5).
[44] Afro-American, Nov. 17, 1956, p. 19.

PRIVATE EMPLOYMENT AND
THE PROFESSIONS

As there are not many statutes imposing racial distinctions in private employment or the professions,[45] most private job discrimination is practiced voluntarily. Some statutes have discriminated on bases related to race, but a number which have been contested have been struck down on grounds which indicate that racial rules would fare the same way. A leading Supreme Court case involving aliens, *Truax v. Raich* (1915),[46] held that a statute requiring that employers of more than five workers employ not less than 80 percent qualified electors or natural-born citizens denies equal protection of the laws. West Coast alien land and occupation laws aimed at Orientals have been held to deny equal protection to United States citizens of Oriental descent and to resident aliens.[47] Consonant with these decisions the Texas Court of Civil Appeals has held unconstitutional, as a denial of equal protection, a Texas law forbidding white and Negro professional boxers to fight against one another.[48] The Supreme Court—in cases not involving race in any sense—has held that states may not arbitrarily deny the opportunity to take a bar examination or refuse to certify an applicant who has passed the examination, as such an unreasonable disqualification denies due process.[49]

States often delegate licensing for skilled (and sometimes for not very skilled) occupations to boards of practitioners of these callings.[50]

---

[45] See appendix A12.   [46] 239 U.S. 33 (1915).

[47] See Oyama v. California, 332 U.S. 633 (1948); Takahashi v. Fish & Game Comm'n, 334 U.S. 410 (1948).

[48] Harvey v. Morgan, 272 S.W.2d 621 (1954), writ of error dismissed or refused (unreported); but Louisiana continued enforcing a similar restriction for baseball (Afro-American, Oct. 27, 1956, p. 15) and boxing (*id.*, April 6, 1957, p. 1). The Louisiana legislation was held unconstitutional in Dorsey v. State Athletic Comm'n, 168 F. Supp. 149 (E.D. La. 1958), *aff'd* 27 U.S.L. Week 3339 (U.S. May 26, 1959). See also Chaires v. City of Atlanta, 164 Ga. 755, 139 S.E. 559 (1927) (ordinance prohibiting colored barbers from serving white women or children invalid under state and federal constitutions as unreasonable classification).

[49] Schware v. Board of Bar Examiners of N.M., 353 U.S. 232 (1957) (use of aliases, arrests, former membership in Communist party do not justify exclusion from bar in light of overwhelming other evidence of good moral character); Konigsberg v. State Bar of Cal., 353 U.S. 252 (1957) (inferences of bad moral character drawn from petitioner's refusal to answer questions about political associations unwarranted; exclusion from bar denies due process).

[50] See generally GELLHORN, INDIVIDUAL FREEDOM AND GOVERNMENTAL RESTRAINTS (1956); see Afro-American, March 2, 1957, p. 8 (after 15-year dispute Maryland State Board of Plumbers allows Negroes to take exam to become licensed

These boards, usually representing the interests of incumbents who desire to keep competition down, have sometimes practiced racial discrimination. While the decisions of such boards ordinarily are difficult to reverse judicially, they should not be able to stand where racial discrimination has been established. But the problem is one of proof. Avowed discrimination or a pattern of biased rejections would support a suit against these bodies, for as state agencies exercising governmental power they are obviously subject to the Fourteenth Amendment. However, it takes time to establish a pattern, and boards which discriminate on racial grounds cannot be expected to say so.

THE PROFESSIONS

Many professional persons do not have to work for anyone; rather, they have their own practices. In this sense racial discrimination cannot directly affect them in earning a living. Discrimination probably hits Negro doctors and lawyers most severely at one remove, namely, to the extent that it diminishes the earning power of the potential Negro clientele to which they are largely confined. There are other ways too, however, in which discrimination operates against Negro professional persons.

One example of overt present-day professional discrimination by government is the practice of Alabama which admits to the bar without examination graduates of the University of Alabama Law School; [51] but the law school, notwithstanding *Sweatt v. Painter*,[52] does not admit Negroes. A suit of four Negro Alabama residents who were out-of-state law school graduates seeking admission to the bar without examination was dismissed by the state courts on the ground that by accepting state funds for out-of-state legal education and not applying to the University of Alabama Law School they went out of state of their own free will.[53]

Where there is discrimination in hospitals against Negro doctors (see Chapter III), they frequently must lose their patients to white physicians, for "white" hospitals are by far the best equipped. This bias is usually

---

plumbers). *Compare with* Kotch v. Board of River Pilots, 330 U.S. 552 (1947) (unfettered discretion of river pilots to select apprentices almost always exercised in favor of relatives and friends not denial of equal protection, although apprenticeship prerequisite to appointment as pilot). But *Kotch* has never sustained a racial classification, although cited in its support many times.

[51] ALA. CODE tit. 46, § 26 (1940).   [52] 339 U.S. 629 (1950).

[53] *Ex parte* Banks, 254 Ala. 117, 48 So. 2d 35 (1950).

connected with medical society and hospital arrangements. Hospitals will admit only society members and the societies often will not accept Negroes, although this restriction has been waning in some places.[54] Inability to participate in medical association meetings and to work in the best hospitals also impairs professional training. This discrimination has had a striking impact. Dietrich Reitzes's study, *Negroes and Medicine*, reveals that while the Negro population of New Orleans, Atlanta, and Nashville are increasing at a rapid rate the number of Negro doctors in these cities is decreasing substantially. This has been caused by the inability of Negro doctors to secure postgraduate training there along with their white peers and by the bar against Negro doctors treating their patients in the best hospitals.[55] Medical association restrictions raise, among other things, antitrust questions, and when considered with the hospital tie-up, raise issues of how much state involvement (as with government-aided, tax-exempt hospitals) constitutes state action under the Fifth and Fourteenth amendments.[56]

While racial restrictions on bar association membership do not similarly affect a lawyer's representation of his clients, they do impair professional training and contact, important for professional development.[57] Moreover, the bar associations, in an often informal but always real sense, contribute effectively to the law-making process. Legislatures look to the organized bar for recommendations, particularly concerning, but hardly limited to, procedural reform. In addition, the associations may perform quasi-judicial functions, in passing on grievances and charges of unprofessional conduct. Thus a Negro attorney brought before an all-white association's grievance committee could be tried (and possibly disbarred) by a body from which members of his race have been excluded. The associations also often pass on admissions to the bar and are, in addition, important in recommend-

---

[54] On hospital and medical association discrimination see also pp. 87–90 *supra*.

[55] REITZES, NEGROES AND MEDICINE, 272, 295, 316 (1958).

[56] For a comprehensive study on legal limitations on organized medicine see Note, 63 YALE L.J. 937 (1954). See also the discussion of antitrust and housing, pp. 302–304 *infra*. Eaton v. Board of Managers of James Walker Memorial Hosp., 261 F.2d 521 (4th Cir. 1958), appears to be the only case involving the right of Negro doctors to have access to a hospital. On May 4, 1959, the Supreme Court denied certiorari in *Eaton*, the Chief Justice and Justices Douglas and Brennan dissenting. The petition had rested principally on *Conley v. Gibson*, 355 U.S. 41 (1957), arguing that the broad generalities of the complaint warranted a trial on the merits.

[57] Sweatt v. Painter, *supra* note 52, at 634.

ing or disapproving appointments to the bench. These considerations might be advanced in a suit challenging a bar association's exclusion policy, or they might be used as a defense to disciplinary proceedings.[58] But there has been no reported litigation meaningful for race relations involving discrimination by professional organizations.

THE UNION-EMPLOYER-EMPLOYEE RELATIONSHIP

The traditional common law view is that a union ordinarily may not be compelled to accept anyone as a member: it is as free as a social club to admit or reject. Similarly, an employer is permitted to discriminate in choosing his workers under common law. But when an employer contracts with a union, the situation may change. The employer may agree with the union not to discriminate among its members, or not to discriminate at all in his employment. The law may compel a union to enter into nondiscriminatory agreements, or may read into agreements which are silent on the subject certain obligations not to discriminate which affect union and employer alike. Once a worker is a union member rights vest in him and he must be treated by it according to certain canons of fairness which also affect his rights and duties vis-à-vis management. Some cases hold that where a union has a monopoly on employment in an area or a plant, it may not discriminate on racial grounds between members and nonmembers who work in the bargaining unit. But these cases have not helped the nonmember not yet employed in the bargaining unit who is kept from getting a job there by racial bias.

The benefit which unions derive from federal certification has led the Supreme Court to hold, under interpretations of the National Labor Relations Act and the Railway Labor Act, that they may not discriminate against Negroes in the bargaining unit. It has not been established, however, that this statutory duty confers the right upon Negroes not to be excluded from membership because of race, although it has been argued that there can be no equal representation

[58] See Afro-American, Sept. 14, 1957, p. 5 (District of Columbia Bar Association excludes Negroes; uses rent-free quarters in courthouse; white attorneys sit in judgment on charges of misconduct of colored attorneys; association prepares bar examinations); see Goshorn v. Bar Ass'n of Dist. of Columbia, 152 F. Supp. 300 (D.D.C. 1957) (Bar Association vote to admit Negroes invalidated; method of voting violated by-laws). By a subsequent vote Negroes were admitted, N.Y. Times, Oct. 16, 1958, p. 29. Baltimore City Bar Association desegregated by vote of its members, Afro-American, June 22, 1957, p. 4; N.Y. Times, May 30, 1956 (American Bar Association drops inquiry concerning applicant's race).

without equal participation. Moreover, a constitutional argument derives from the labor act cases, *i.e.*, that the action of the union is "state action." If this is so, as "state" agencies unions may not discriminate racially at all—in admission to and participation in membership, in pay, working conditions, or otherwise.

COMMON LAW. Although the traditional common law view has been that one may not compel a union to accept his membership,[59] there is a kind of common due process of law governing membership in associations generally, including unions, which applies to members or to those with affiliation like membership. They may not be deprived of membership rights (*e.g.*, by expulsion) without proceedings in accordance with the association's constitution, by-laws, or rules.[60] Sometimes this doctrine has been extended to confer equality (though not in race cases) expressly denied by an intra-association arrangement. In *Cameron v. International Alliance* [61] the New Jersey Supreme Court gave the plaintiffs, "junior members," a more inclusive status of membership than had been expressly provided for in the "contract of membership" by which they had neither the vote, the right to meet outside the presence of senior members, nor the right to participate in collective bargaining or other membership activities. The court's theory was that an implied agreement arose with admission to the junior department, to which the written document was subsidiary.

[59] See Frank v. National Alliance of Bill Posters, 89 N.J.L. 380, 99 Atl. 134 (1916); Feinne v. Monohan, 196 Misc. 407, 92 N.Y.S.2d 112 (1949); Walter v. McCarvel, 309 Mass. 260, 265, 34 N.E.2d 677, 680 (1941). But for a well-developed argument that the old law of associations, on which these cases rest, is inappropriate to resolve issues raised by union exclusion in today's industrial society, see Hewitt, *The Right to Membership in a Labor Union*, 99 U. PA. L. REV. 919 (1951); see also Summers, *The Right to Join a Union*, 47 COLUM. L. REV. 33 (1947); Wellington, *Union Democracy and Fair Representation*, 67 YALE L.J. 1327 (1958).

[60] See generally 7 C.J.S. *Associations* 18, 55-68; Summers, *Legal Limitations on Union Discipline*, 64 HARV. L. REV. 1049 (1951).

[61] 118 N.J. Eq. 11, 176 Atl. 692 (1935); for cases involving rights of members of the international union to join a local see, Havens v. Detroit Motion Picture Projectionists, 338 Mich. 418, 423, 61 N.W.2d 790, 792 (1953) (local did not act arbitrarily; but "if the local has arbitrarily taken from the plaintiff his right to employment through the implement of a closed union, then it has taken from the plaintiff one of his assured and fundamental rights as a citizen"). Mandracio v. Bartenders Union, 41 Cal. 2d 81, 256 P.2d 927 (1953) (local may not deny holder of travel card admission to membership); Seligman v. Toledo Moving Pictures Operators Union, 88 Ohio App. 137, 98 N.E.2d 54, 59 (1947) (local operating under a closed shop agreement could not deprive member of the international union of his constitutional right to work, citing OHIO CONST. arts. 1 *et seq.* and U.S. CONST. amends. I *et seq.* in the N.E.2d report; but the Ohio App. report gives no such citations).

This implicit agreement stemmed from the same work, wages, and identical cards (except for the words "junior department"). The written contract of membership was dismissed as but a group of rules defining collateral relationships. There are other cases—none involving race—supporting the view that a union's control over its members' right to work must be exercised in a cooperative and democratic way.[62]

The most stringent common law standards appear to cover union discrimination against nonmembers who seek to work within the ambit of the union's power. The Restatement of Torts declares (§ 810): "Workers who in concert procure the dismissal of an employee because he is not a member of a labor union satisfactory to the workers are . . . liable to the employee if, but only if, he desires to be a member of the labor union but membership is not open to him on reasonable terms." Apparently only the California courts have actually applied the doctrine where race is concerned. (New York has employed it, but in nonracial situations.[63]) In *James v. Marinship Co.*[64] the Supreme Court of California held that a union with a work monopoly in an area could not enforce a closed shop contract against Negroes whom, because of race, it would not admit to membership on terms of equality with other workers. The decision cited cases like those discussed above, the fact that other states (although *not* California) had by statute forbidden unions to discriminate, and section 810 of the Restatement of Torts. From this vantage point, in *Williams v. International Brotherhood*[65] the California Supreme Court extended the ruling to a closed shop union having no monopoly in its locality that

[62] Chalghian v. International Bhd. of Teamsters, 114 N.J. Eq. 497, 169 Atl. 327 (1933) (court has authority to appoint receiver where officers have misappropriated funds and otherwise violated trust); Local No. 11 v. McKee, 114 N.J. Eq. 555, 169 Atl. 351 (1933) (similar); Harris v. Geier, 112 N.J. Eq. 99, 108, 164 Atl. 50, 53 (1932) ("the policy of New Jersey approves of the organization of employees in trade unions which are governed on democratic principles and membership in which is open, on reasonable and equal terms, to all persons of good character and of skill in the trade"); Bricklayers', Plasterers' & Stonemasons' Union v. Bowen, 183 N.Y. Supp. 855, 859 (1920), *aff'd*, 189 N.Y. Supp. 938 (1921) (provision in constitution of a general union for removal without hearing of officers and members of subordinate union for violation of union rule invalid); *but cf.* Shein v. Rose, 12 N.Y.S.2d 87 (Sup. Ct. 1939) (the holder of temporary membership may be arbitrarily refused full status). See Kovner, *The Legal Protection of Civil Liberties Within Unions*, 1948 Wis. L. Rev. 18.

[63] See Clark v. Curtis, 273 App. Div. 797, 76 N.Y.S.2d 3 (2d Dep't 1947) (injunctive relief sought either to compel defendant union to admit plaintiff-employees or to enjoin the closed shop agreement), *aff'd*, 297 N.Y. 1014, 80 N.E.2d 536 (1948); see discussion of *Clark* in Wilson v. Hacker, 200 Misc. 124, 129, 101 N.Y.S.2d 461, 467 (1950).

[64] 25 Cal. 2d 721, 155 P.2d 329 (1944).   [65] 27 Cal. 2d 586, 165 P.2d 903 (1946).

demanded Negroes join auxiliary lodges which conferred no real membership rights. The California high court pointed out that *James* involved

only an aggravated phase of the general problem. The individual worker denied the right to keep his job suffers a loss, and his right to protection against arbitrary and discriminatory exclusion from union membership should be recognized wherever membership is a necessary prerequisite to work. A closed shop agreement with a single employer is in itself a form of monopoly, giving a third party, the union, control over at least the plant of the signatory employer, and although such a labor monopoly is not in itself improper, it carries with it certain responsibilities, and the public clearly has an interest in preventing any abuse of it.[66]

The decision asserted that states have power to regulate unions by citing *Railway Mail Association v. Corsi*,[67] upholding New York's anti-discrimination statute. It rested too on citations of *Steele v. Louisville & Nashville R.R.*[68] and NLRB rulings that unions may not compel the discharge of employees who are discriminatorily denied membership. But it probably most clearly spelled out a rationale in citing the Restatement of Torts, section 810, quoted above.

THE UNION CONTRACT. The collective bargaining contract has been likened to a statute regulating the rights and obligations of the workers subject to its terms. To the extent that unions can negotiate contracts with employers forbidding discrimination, there is a legally enforceable duty upon the employer not to discriminate. Conversely, to the extent that unions negotiate discriminatory agreements, workers must labor under those terms unless and until legal relief is obtained, or else they must be excluded from labor. Sometimes the racial aspect of an "agreement" may be a tacit understanding or a mutually acceptable practice, which is, however, just as harmful as an open agreement.

The AFL-CIO constitution declares that an object and principle of the merged body is "to encourage all workers without regard to race, creed, color, national origin or ancestry to share equally in the full benefits of union organization." [69] It empowers the executive council,

[66] 27 Cal. 2d at 591, 165 P.2d at 906. Following *James* and *Williams* the California Supreme Court in Thormon v. International Alliance of Theatrical Stage Employees, 49 Cal. 2d 638, 320 P.2d 494 (1958), ordered an individual admitted to union membership where there was a closed union and closed shop.
[67] 326 U.S. 88 (1945). [68] Discussed pp. 175–177 *infra*.
[69] Art. II(4). See generally Chicago Defender, May 11, 1957, p. 11. ("Organized Labor and the Negro"); *id.*, June 1, 1957, p. 11 ("Why Jim Carey Quit," charging "go slow" policy in implementing civil rights).

in carrying out its authority, to "recognize . . . that all workers whatever their race, color, creed or national origin are entitled to share
in the full benefits of trade union organization," [70] and establishes a
committee on civil rights with the duty and responsibility of assisting
the executive council in bringing about effective implementation of
these nondiscrimination provisions.[71] And railroad brotherhoods which
have applied for AFL-CIO affiliation, have given pledges to abandon
policies of racial bias.[72]

The International Constitution of the United Steelworkers of America is more explicit. In addition to an article stating that the object of
the union is to "unite . . . regardless of race, creed, color or nationality, all workers . . ." in work related to steel production,[73] it provides that "all working men and working women [in the industry],
regardless of race, creed, color or nationality . . . are eligible to membership." [74]

About 18 percent of the contracts between unions and employers
forbid management to discriminate on racial grounds; about three-
fourths as many forbid unions so to discriminate.[75] A typical nondiscrimination clause reads:

The Company and the Union shall not . . . be discriminatory of any employees because of nationality, race, sex, political or religious affiliation or
membership in any labor or other lawful organization.[76]

The United Auto Workers has arranged with the National Urban
League cooperatively to handle claims of racial grievances in all in-

---

[70] Art. VIII, § 9.

[71] Art. XIII, § 1(b). See also Policy Resolutions of the AFL-CIO 22 (Dec.,
1955) (civil rights: "The AFL and the CIO have always believed in the principle
and practice of equal rights for all, regardless of race, color, creed or national
origin"). See FLEISCHMANN & RORTY, WE OPEN THE GATES (1958) for case
studies of union action against discrimination.

[72] N.Y. Times, Aug. 27, 1957, p. 28. But two brotherhoods have been admitted
while still practicing racial bias, id., May 22, 1958, p. 21. See also id., Jan. 6, 1957,
p. 76 (American Federation of Teachers orders Southern locals to end segregation); id., Jan. 14, 1957, p. 1 ("Union Leaders Vow State Fight on Bias"); id.,
Jan. 15, 1957, p. 28 (editorial); id., May 14, 1956 (textile workers unions condemn
discrimination despite Southern members' pleas).

[73] Art. II. First.

[74] Art. III, § 1; see N.Y. Times, Dec. 24, 1957, p. 26 (half of 54 important
Chicago locals have written nondiscrimination clauses).

[75] COLLECTIVE BARGAINING NEGOTIATIONS & CONTRACTS § 95:481.

[76] Contract between Caterpillar Tractor Co. & Auto Workers, exp. July, 1958,
quoted ibid. See id. at § 55:12 (clauses covering hiring), § 93:602 (clauses covering
wage differentials). See also LABOR RELATIONS EXPEDITER (L.R.X.) 90, 391.

dustries where the union has agreements.[77] Nondiscrimination clauses are nowadays one of the items traded back and forth in the give and take of bargaining, but it is interesting to note that during the Second World War the War Labor Board in some instances ordered that nondiscrimination clauses be written into labor contracts.[78]

In at least one reported case, *Syres v. Oil Workers International, Local No. 23*,[79] an international union opposed one of its locals which practiced discrimination, the international participating as *amicus curiae* on the side of Negro workers who brought suit to enjoin the local from practicing bias. Most often, however, international unions and the AFL-CIO operate through union channels in an effort to achieve implementation of nondiscrimination.

A union policy opposed to discrimination, voluntarily adopted or imposed by law, would be most effective in a closed shop. For the employer—if the union is faithful to its duty—must then hire from an unbiased source, and pay and promote without regard to race. Where there is no closed shop and the employer hires whites only, or only a few Negroes, union policy may mean little, since the nondiscrimination provision will have few or no Negroes to operate upon in the shop and little or no control over the selection of workers. The closed shop, however, is not legal under the Labor Management Relations (Taft-Hartley) Act.[80]

THE LABOR MANAGEMENT RELATIONS ACT AND

THE RAILWAY LABOR ACT

The Labor Management Relations Act (LMRA) and the Railway Labor Act do not deal with race in specific terms. Yet because they

[77] N.Y. Times, July 11, 1957, p. 14. Recently Westinghouse refused to accede to a union demand that a nondiscrimination clause be placed in the contract, reportedly because it would harm the union's competitive position, Afro-American, Nov. 30, 1957, p. 3.

[78] *In re* Montgomery Ward & Co. *and* Int'l Longshoremen's Union, 18 War Lab. Rep. 371, 15 L.R.R.M. 1524 (1944). See also Zellerbach Paper Co. *and* Int'l Longshoremen's & Warehousing Union, 20 War Lab. Rep. 598, 15 L.R.R.M. 1807 (1944); *In re* Miami Copper Co. *and* Int'l Union of Mine, Mill & Smelter Workers, 15 L.R.R.M. 1538 (1944). See Sunken Gardens Restaurant *and* Hotel & Restaurant Employees' Int'l Alliance, 20 War Lab. Rep. 101, 15 L.R.R.M. 1775 (1944) (union requests clause freezing certain jobs for men, women, whites, Negroes; denied).

[79] 223 F.2d 739, 741 (5th Cir. 1955), *rev'd per curiam*, 350 U.S. 892 (1955). See Butler v. The Celotex Corp., 3 R.R.L.R. 503 (E.D. La. 1958) (consent decree to abandon segregated lines of seniority; international joins agreement).

[80] 29 U.S.C.A. § 158(a)(3).

confer great power on unions and—race questions aside—have required fair representation, they are in some ways applicable to discriminatory union and union-employer policies.

THE DUTY TO REPRESENT. The bedrock requirement of both acts, for purposes of this inquiry, is the obligation of exclusive bargaining agents to represent all persons within the bargaining unit.[81] As early as 1944, *Steele v. Louisville & Nashville R.R.* [82] established that Negroes within the unit but barred from the union were nevertheless entitled to union representation. The Supreme Court found the right implicit in the Railway Labor Act, observing that if the rule were to be otherwise, serious Fifth Amendment due process questions would arise, for the union's power stemmed substantially from rights conferred by statute. It had been assumed that the doctrine stated in *Steele* applied to the LMRA as well,[83] and in 1955 this became explicit in *Syres v. Oil Workers International Union.*[84] The Supreme Court summarily reversed the court of appeals which had dismissed allegations that union-employer discrimination was forbidden by the act. The high court

[81] Labor Management Relations Act, 29 U.S.C.A. § 159; Railway Labor Act, 45 U.S.C.A. § 151 Sixth, § 152 as interpreted in Steele v. Louisville & N.R.R., 323 U.S. 192, 199-200 (1944).

[82] *Ibid.* Other Railway Labor Act cases are: Central of Ga. Ry. v. Jones, 229 F.2d 648 (5th Cir. 1956), *cert. denied*, 352 U.S. 848 (1956) (injunctive and other relief granted against enforcement of contract between union and railroad which discriminated against Negroes); Richardson v. Texas N.O.R.R., 242 F.2d 230 (5th Cir. 1957) (acts complained of were breach of bargaining representative's implied statutory duty of impartial representation, notwithstanding absence of allegation that agreement was discriminatory on face); Rolax v. Atlantic Coast Line R.R., 186 F.2d 473 (4th Cir. 1951) (union-railroad agreement depriving Negroes of seniority and employment rights under cloak of innocuous term, "non-promotable firemen," held void); Graham v. Southern Ry., 74 F. Supp. 663 (D.D.C. 1947) (injunction granted restraining union from discriminating in hiring practices); *but cf.*: Davis v. Brotherhood of Ry. Carmen, 272 S.W.2d 147 (Tex. Civ. App. 1954) (existence of separate locals for whites and Negroes not discriminatory per se in the absence of discriminatory acts; administrative remedies had not been exhausted); Brotherhood of Ry. & Steamship Clerks v. United Transport Serv. Employees, 320 U.S. 715 (1943) *per curiam, rev'g* 137 F.2d 817 (D.C. Cir. 1943); Washington v. Central of Ga. Ry., 3 R.R.L.R. 680 (M.D. Ga. 1958) (discrimination not proved); see Comment, *Judicial Regulation of the Railway Brotherhoods' Discriminatory Practices*, 1953 WIS. L. REV. 416.

[83] In 1944, Wallace Corp. v. NLRB, 323 U.S. 248, 255 (1944), involving discrimination against members of a rival union, held: "By its selection as bargaining representative, . . . [the union] has become the agent of all the employees, charged with the responsibility of representing their interests fairly and impartially."

[84] *Supra* note 79. See *id.* at 257 F.2d 479 (5th Cir. 1958), *cert. denied*, 358 U.S. 929 (1959) (plaintiffs must prove individual personal loss; recovery denied).

merely cited *Steele* and two related cases. In 1957, *Conley v. Gibson* held that the duty to represent without discrimination extends to day-to-day adjustments in the contract and other working rules, resolution of new problems not covered by existing agreements, and the protection of employee rights already secured by contract.[85]

How far does *Steele-Syres* reach as a statutory standard? What is the nature of the obligation to those in the unit and to those outside? *Syres* itself involved essentially an intraunion dispute, though there were actually two unions involved. The Negro and white workers, members of different unions, were by their own agreement in the same bargaining unit and represented by one negotiating committee. Violating a pact between the unions, this committee negotiated separate Negro-white lines of seniority which barred Negroes from rising above menial jobs. The legal picture is somewhat more fully drawn by *Ford Motor Co. v. Huffman* (1953),[86] which, though not a race relations case, upheld as reasonable and permissible under the LMRA a contract between Ford and the union granting certain war veterans seniority rights at the expense of others for time spent in the armed forces, but, the opinion stated, although "a wide range of reasonableness must be allowed a statutory bargaining representative in serving the unit it represents," the representative must "make an honest effort to serve the interests of all of those members, without hostility to any." [87] *Brotherhood of Railroad Trainmen v. Howard* (1952) [88] involved Negro and white workers who were in distinctly separate unions and separate bargaining units. The white organization, which was more powerful, threatened to strike to win a contract abolishing the Negroes' jobs. The Supreme Court, citing *Steele*, held plaintiffs entitled to enjoin enforcement of the contract. The opinions did not say so but under *Steele-Syres*, as illuminated by *Huffman* and *Howard*, the labor acts define a union's duty as follows: it may differentiate among classes so long as the classifications are not unreasonable, somewhat in the manner of legislatures. As with legislatures, racial discrimination is forbidden.

INDIVIDUAL PRESENTATION OF GRIEVANCES. Notwithstanding the exclusive duty and power of the certified bargaining agent to nego-

---

[85] 355 U.S. 41 (1957).   [86] 345 U.S. 330 (1953).
[87] The quotations are taken from *id*. at 337, 338, respectively.
[88] 343 U.S. 768 (1952); see Note, 52 COLUM. L. REV. 1058 (1952).

tiate, a victim of discrimination by the union may in theory by-pass it and go directly to the employer with his grievance. Section 9 [89] of the LMRA contains a proviso that

any individual employee or a group of employees shall have the right at any time to present grievances to their employer and to have such grievances adjusted, without the intervention of the bargaining representative, as long as the adjustment is not inconsistent with the terms of a collective-bargaining contract or agreement then in effect: *Provided further*, That the bargaining representative has been given opportunity to be present at such adjustment.

FAVORING UNION OVER NONUNION MEMBERS. Sections 8(a)(3) and 8(b)(2),[90] also, of the LMRA specifically forbid racial discrimination in some situations. These sections provide, respectively, that it is an unfair labor practice for an employer by discrimination in hire, tenure, or any term or condition of employment to encourage or discourage membership in any labor organization, and that it is an unfair labor practice for a labor organization to cause an employer so to discriminate. In terms of racial problems this means that the union may not negotiate terms for members more favorable than those for nonmembers when whites are in the union and Negroes out. If such a discriminatory contract were negotiated, it would, of course, encourage union membership, for nonmembers would naturally desire the more favorable terms and want to join to secure them. *Radio Officers' Union of Commercial Telegraphers Union, AFL v. NLRB* (1954) [91] holds that there need be no motive to encourage [92] and that the courts should not inquire into whether the discrimination actually does encourage [93] union membership for a discriminatory contract to be illegal. Indeed, one of the situations involved in the opinion concerned workers barred from the union by a nepotistic policy. In this case discrimination could not have "encouraged," let alone augmented, union membership—as nonrelatives the workers could no more have joined than Negroes could enter a lily-white union. It is enough if the courts can see a natural tendency, said the Court, noting that since union policies and politics are fluid, encouragement today, though nothing may come of it, may bear fruit in the future.

The *Radio Officers* rule has not been applied to race relations problems in any reported case, but Judge Pope (Ninth Circuit) has indi-

[89] 29 U.S.C.A. § 159(a).
[90] 29 U.S.C.A. §§ 158(a)(3) and 158(b)(2), respectively.
[91] 347 U.S. 17 (1954).   [92] *Id.* at 45.   [93] *Id.* at 52.

cated that it might control in racially discriminatory situations, as where a union hiring hall sends out only non-Negro members on referrals.[94]

THE UNION SHOP. There is a statutory exception in section 8(a)(3). There may be a union shop agreement between union and employer requiring employees in the unit to join the union or be fired. But there are qualifications contained in this rule which could protect Negroes. The employer cannot justify dismissal of a nonjoiner "if he has reasonable grounds for believing that such membership was not available to the employee on the same terms and conditions generally applicable to other members"; or if "he has reasonable grounds for believing that membership was denied or terminated for reasons other than the failure of the employee to tender the periodic dues and the initiation fees uniformly required." [95] Some states have enacted "right-to-work" laws which outlaw the union shop,[96] and in such areas the matter treated above would of course be irrelevant.

CERTIFICATION AND DECERTIFICATION. The Labor Management Relations Act authorizes the National Labor Relations Board (NLRB) to certify unions as exclusive collective bargaining representatives if designated or selected by a majority of the employees in the appropriate unit. The board could refuse to certify a union which discriminates against members of the bargaining unit and could also, on such grounds, decertify an already certified union. The act provides in specific terms for decertification under certain circumstances. Section 9(c)(1) [97] states that whenever a petition shall have been filed assert-

[94] NLRB v. Pacific Am. Shipowners Ass'n, 218 F.2d 913, 914, 917 n.3 (separate concurring opinion) (9th Cir. 1955), cert. denied, 349 U.S. 930 (1955) sub nom. National Union of Marine Cooks & Stewards v. NLRB; see also NLRB v. Philadelphia Iron Works, 211 F.2d 937, 943 (3d Cir. 1954) (referral system discriminating against nonmembers would be illegal).

[95] 29 U.S.C.A. § 158(a)(3); cf. NLRB v. Pape Broadcasting Co., 217 F.2d 197, 199 (5th Cir. 1954).

[96] "Right to work" laws are basically provisions prohibiting making union membership a condition for obtaining or holding a job. § 14(b) of the Taft-Hartley Act (29 U.S.C.A. § 164(b)) permits the states to legislate in this area which otherwise would be preempted by the federal government. About one third of the states have adopted such laws: see Teple, A Closer Look at "Right to Work" Legislation, 9 W. RES. L. REV. 5 (1957). These laws have been sustained against constitutional attack, Lincoln Fed. Labor Union v. Northwestern Iron & Metal Co., 335 U.S. 525 (1949); AFL v. American Sash & Door Co., 335 U.S. 538 (1949), esp. Frankfurter, J., concurring at 542 et seq. But where a union shop agreement is executed pursuant to federal statutory authority under the Railway Labor Act, it is valid notwithstanding a state's "right to work" law. Railway Employees' Dep't, AFL v. Hanson, 351 U.S. 225 (1956).

[97] 29 U.S.C.A. § 159(c)(1).

ing that the certified agent is no longer the representative of the bargaining unit, the board shall investigate. If it reasonably believes a question of representation exists it shall provide for a hearing. If it finds that there is a question of representation, the board shall direct an election. Section 9(e) [98] provides, moreover, that if at least 30 percent of the employees in a unit file a petition with the board alleging their desire that the bargaining agent's authority be rescinded, the board shall conduct an election.[99]

As expressed in its *Tenth Annual Report* in 1945 (no alteration has appeared since), however, the standard of the NLRB has been essentially separate-but-equal:

Neither exclusion from membership nor segregated membership *per se* represents evasion on the part of a labor organization of its statutory duty to afford "equal representation." But in each case where the issue is presented the Board will scrutinize the contract and conduct of a representative organization and withhold or withdraw its certification if it finds that the organization has discriminated against employees in the bargaining units through its membership restrictions or otherwise.[100]

Yet, at the same time, unless a difference of function can be shown, the board has held, bargaining units may not be determined on the basis of race.[101] It has rejected argument that unless Negroes are in a separate unit they will be outvoted by whites.[102] On the other hand, the mere fact that a union is entirely composed of members of one race does not disqualify it, at least where the union policy is opposed to discrimination.[103]

[98] 29 U.S.C.A. § 159(e)(1).

[99] See Krislov, *Union Decertification*, 9 IND. & LAB. REL. REV. 580 (1956), esp. Table I, at 590. DISPOSITION OF DECERTIFICATION PETITIONS, 1948-1955, from which the following is excerpted:

	1950	1951	1952	1953	1954	1955
Elections held	112	93	101	142	150	157
Elections resulting						
in decertification	75	66	74	97	102	102

[100] At p. 18. The Report discusses most of the pertinent decisions as of that date: Matter of Larus & Brother Co., Inc., 62 N.L.R.B. 1075 (1945); Matter of Atlanta Oak Flooring Co., 62 N.L.R.B. 973 (1945); Matter of Henri Wines, 44 N.L.R.B. 1310 (1942); Matter of Rutland Court Owners, Inc., 44 N.L.R.B. 587 (1942), 46 N.L.R.B. 1040 (1943); Matter of Wallace Corp., 50 N.L.R.B. 138 (1943); Matter of Bethlehem Alameda Shipyard, 53 N.L.R.B. 999 (1943).

[101] Andrews Indus., Inc., 105 N.L.R.B. 946 (1953); Matter of United States Bedding Co., 52 N.L.R.B. 382 (1943); Matter of Union Envelope, 10 N.L.R.B. 1147 (1939).

[102] See NLRB v. Pacific Am. Shipowners Ass'n, *supra* note 94; *cf.* Matter of Colorado Fuel & Iron Co., 67 N.L.R.B. 100, 103 (1946).

[103] Matter of United States Bedding Co., *supra* note 101, at 388; see Matter of

The board has in no case decertified or refused to certify a union because of racial practices, although in a number of cases, the most thoroughly considered of which was *Larus & Brother*,[104] it has stated or implied the threat. In *Larus* the white union and the company had conducted negotiations but required Negro employees to maintain membership in and pay dues to a Negro local which had no standing. By the time of decision in the case, however, the union contract had expired and the white union was willing to relinquish certification, asking then for a new election. The board stated that a petition for such action in the name of the white and colored locals would be accepted.

In at least two cases, partly because the bargaining unit was based on race, the board has held that an existing contract did not bar an election to determine representatives.[105] In one of these cases it designated an industrial unit as the appropriate collective bargaining unit over the objection of craft unions. The decision rested in part on the ground that some of the craft unions excluded Negroes, notwithstanding the fact that the employer's policies were applicable to them.[106] The board has also entered into a consent decree requiring shipping companies not to discriminate against employees or applicants for employment on grounds of "sex, race, creed, color, national origin, political views or affiliations, or legitimate union activity." [107] And it has condemned the use of racial prejudice and segregation of white from

---

Taxicabs of Cincinnati, 82 N.L.R.B. 664, 667 (1949), 83 N.L.R.B. 1150 (1949) (supplemental decision) (separate bargaining units based in part on color found appropriate although single unit containing whites and Negroes also would be appropriate).

[104] *Supra* note 100. See also Matter of Carter Mfg. Co., 59 N.L.R.B. 804, 806 (1944) (certification will be rescinded if equal representation denied on racial grounds); in Matter of Bethlehem Alameda Shipyard, *supra* note 100, at 1016, the board expressed doubt whether a union which discriminatorily denies membership on the basis of race can bargain fairly for a unit including Negro nonmembers; there was no decision on the merits because the union changed policy. The board has held that segregation into separate locals is not unequal representation. Matter of Atlanta Oak Flooring Co., *supra* note 100. See also Matter of General Motors Corp., 62 N.L.R.B. 427 (1945); Matter of Southwestern Portland Cement Co., 61 N.L.R.B. 1217 (1945).

[105] Matter of Columbian Iron Works, 52 N.L.R.B. 370 (1943) (union excluded Negroes); Matter of Crescent Bed Co., Inc., 29 N.L.R.B. 34 (1941) (union members all Negro).

[106] Matter of Hughes Tool Co., 33 N.L.R.B. 1089 (1941).

[107] Jones v. American President Lines, 149 Cal. App. 2d 319, 321, 308 P.2d 393, 394 (1957) (Negro cook, alleging denial of employment contrary to contract rights given him and preserved by NLRB decree, may bring damage suit in state court).

colored workers to sway voters in union elections, although more recent rulings seem to look the other way.[108]

Board tolerance of segregation became a policy prior to the Taft-Hartley Act. It was based in part on the fact that the NLRA as then written did not permit orders to be issued against unions. Under the Taft-Hartley Act that is no longer true, but there has been no board decision on whether this legal change affects the foundation of the earlier argument. However, the board's general counsel has sustained refusals to issue complaints against employers and unions where Negro workers could not be promoted to certain jobs, a practice in which the unions apparently acquiesced. The general counsel held that the unions were not obliged to question such policy.[109]

Decertification or refusal to certify is a technique of dubious worth against discrimination. A decertification investigation or petition can result only in a new election; refusal to certify means no union representation or another election. A biased union might win on the new vote or the voters' choice might be for no union representation. Should the board refuse to certify a winner because of its racial policies, the result also might well be no union representation at all.[110] While an employer without a union could be more impartial than one with a union contract, experience does not suggest this as probable. Nevertheless, a biased union might change its policies if it knew that notwithstanding electoral victory it could not become certified until it

[108] Matter of Edinburg Citrus Ass'n, 57 N.L.R.B. 1145, 1157 (1944) (statement that if union came in Mexicans would be ruling workers and taking their jobs); Matter of Bibb Mfg. Co., 82 N.L.R.B. 338, 357-358 (1949) (statement to white employee that he could join union if he wanted to work with Negroes); cf. Matter of Rapid Roller Co., 33 N.L.R.B. 557, 566-567 (1941); Matter of American Thread Co., 84 N.L.R.B. 593, 601 (1949). For cases holding segregation of white from colored workers to be interference with legitimate union activities, such as collecting dues, membership drives, etc., see Matter of American Cyanamid Co., 37 N.L.R.B. 578 (1941); Matter of Ozan Lumber Co., 42 N.L.R.B. 1073 (1942). Compare Chock Full O'Nuts and United Bakery Workers, 120 N.L.R.B. No. 172 (1958) (does not find that injection of racial issue sufficient ground for invalidation); Sharney Hosiery Mills and Textile Workers Union, 120 N.L.R.B. No. 102 (1958) (rely on good sense of voters); Westinghouse Elec. Corp. v. IUE, 119 N.L.R.B. No. 26 (1957) (motion for reconsideration alleging use of prejudice in election: denied); charges of such tactics continue. N.Y. Times, Nov. 10, 1957, p. 57 ("Labor Chief Says Southern Employers Exploit Racial Bias in Fighting Union").
[109] Case No. 1047, Nov. 5, 1954, 35 L.R.R.M. 1130; Case No. K-311, March 22, 1956, 37 L.R.R.M. 1457.
[110] Cf. Pacific Maritime Ass'n, 112 N.L.R.B. 1280, 1282 (1955) (board rejects contention that racially discriminatory union should not be certified, but will police certification).

stopped discriminating. In some situations where a discriminating and a nondiscriminating union were in competition, and employees opposed to discrimination constituted a balance of power, fear of losing the election might stimulate changes in the attitude of the anti-Negro organization.[111] Notwithstanding these limitations, decertification seems to have been effective in at least a few cases as an unrealized threat where, pending board consideration, unions reversed their racial policies.[112] But, as noted above, the board has never actually applied the sanction.

THE CONSTITUTION AND UNION MEMBERSHIP

The *Steele-Syres* rule, nominally statutory, emits constitutional overtones at least. Some of its manifestations can be explained best by viewing it as a constitutional standard; some jurists have seen it as constitutional, not merely legislative. In *Steele* itself Justice Murphy concurred on constitutional grounds.[113]

The *Howard* decision is most readily explainable if we view it as actually applying a constitutional standard, notwithstanding its citation of the nominally statutory *Steele* case as authority. Under the statutory view of *Steele* a union merely owes allegiance to all within the bargaining unit. It need not, so far as the express rationale goes, negotiate for or show fairness toward members of other unions outside the unit. To the contrary, it might be argued that it is obliged to get all it can for its members, even at the expense of other unions. Therefore, the question is raised as to where the duty imposed by *Howard*—which forbade discrimination against another union—comes from. It would seem that the rule might be justifiably stated somewhat as follows: while the labor acts require only fair treatment of those within the unit, unions enjoying power conferred by the acts are in

[111] *In re* Arbitration Between Layne & Bowler, Inc. *and* SWOC (CIO), 10 L.R.R.M. 1178 (1942) (AFL unions which did not accept Negroes commenced admitting them when the rival SWOC, which admitted Negroes, entered the picture).

[112] *Cf.* Matter of Bethlehem Alameda Shipyard, *supra* note 100, at 1016 (following hearing council accords Negro auxiliaries same rights of affiliation as other locals); Matter of Larus & Brother, *supra* note 100, at 1085 (AFL voluntarily gives up certification and is willing to accept conditions board may impose; board permits filing petition in name of colored and white locals); Matter of Virginia Smelting Co., 60 N.L.R.B. 616, 617 (1945) (AFL would admit Negroes barred by its constitution); Matter of General Motors Corp., *supra* note 104, at 431 (IAM and IBEW state they will admit Negroes).

[113] 323 U.S. at 208.

a constitutional sense governmental agents, whose duty thus reaches further. The Constitution forbids a governmental agent—here, the union—to discriminate against anyone whether within the unit or outside it. This analysis of *Howard* may, of course, be tempered by assuming that the Court realistically viewed the plaintiffs there as members of the same bargaining unit as the defense. The work was identical for both sides, and were it not for race, all the workers concerned would have been in the same union. Yet the opinion does not offer this as the reason for the decision.

In the court of appeals handling of *Syres,* Judge Rives wrote a lengthy dissent (at least partly vindicated by the Supreme Court's reversal) stating that he would hold the bargaining agent under constitutional duty not to discriminate.

If . . . the contract is the product not merely of private agreement, but also of the provisions of the law [citing *Steele* and *Howard*] or if the law is called on for the enforcement of the contract [citing *Shelley*] or, it seems to me to follow as a necessary consequence, if the law provides automatic sanctions for the observance of the contract, then there can be no discrimination based on race or color.[114]

He wrote also that since the LMRA makes the union the exclusive collective bargaining agent for all the workers in a given unit, this "impliedly, but clearly imposes a duty on a certified bargaining agent not to abuse the bargaining prerogative by resorting to unconstitutionally discriminatory practices." [115] Judge Pope of the Ninth Circuit may see a constitutional rule too, for he has suggested, citing *Shelley v. Kraemer,* that discriminatory contracts may not be enforceable by the NLRB.[116]

The Supreme Court of Kansas, moreover, has flatly held that board certification places the agent under constitutional obligation. *Betts v. Easley* (1946) [117] decided that a railway union had a Fifth Amendment due process duty to Negro employees forced to join a separate auxiliary lodge under the white union's jurisdiction with no right to participate in elections, fixing of dues, formulation of policies on collective bargaining, and other issues. The white union was required to represent all employees in the bargaining unit.

[114] 223 F.2d at 745.   [115] *Id.* at 747.
[116] NLRB v. Pacific Am. Shipowners Ass'n, *supra* note 94.
[117] 161 Kan. 459, 169 P.2d 831, 166 A.L.R. 342 (1946).

THE RIGHT NOT TO BE BARRED FROM UNION MEMBERSHIP
BECAUSE OF RACE

A number of states have enacted statutes other than FEPC laws forbidding unions to discriminate on racial grounds.[118] Apart from these, we may ask what right to union membership the Constitution and common law afford. The California courts, as indicated above, will in some circumstances order admission to membership. Moreover, should the constitutional potential of *Steele-Syres* become fully developed, it would seem logical that a union could not bar Negroes from membership because of race. Thus far, no court has so held. In a recent case presenting this question, *Oliphant v. Brotherhood Locomotive Firemen and Enginemen,* the lower federal courts held that the railway union involved was not a governmental agent. While the United States Supreme Court denied certiorari, it was careful not to foreclose the issue and appended to its denial the unusual notation that review was refused because of the abstract state of the record.[119]

Established doctrine which protects against discriminatory union action—under the labor acts and common law—does not appear to go far enough actually to require full membership status for those barred on racial grounds. The theory seems to be that it is enough to forbid union discrimination against nonmembers. But can a union which excludes Negroes afford them equal representation? Representation does not consist merely in the representative's objective (if it can be objective) assertion of the interests of employees against the employer; it also involves a division of the employer's work, funds, and other benefits among the workers. In this they often have conflicting interests, and intraunion political conflict usually helps to decide who gets what. Nonmembers are hardly so situated as to be represented fairly since they cannot participate in union affairs.[120]

We should also note the applicability of the federal antitrust laws in this area. In 1958, for probably the first time, a consent decree was

[118] See appendix A13.

[119] 359 U.S. 935 (1959); *cf.* Taylor v. Brotherhood of Ry. & Steamship Clerks, 106 F. Supp. 438, 440 (D.D.C. 1952) ("the union shop agreement does not seek to insure admission to all employees who apply . . . nor does *Steele* case make unlawful a failure to do so"); *cf.* also Davis v. Brotherhood of Ry. Carmen, *supra* note 82.

[120] See TELLER, A LABOR POLICY FOR AMERICA 152 (1945); PHILIP TAFT, ECONOMICS AND PROBLEMS OF LABOR 281 *et seq.* (1948); ACLU, DEMOCRACY IN LABOR UNIONS (pamphlet 1952); see also CAYTON & MITCHELL, BLACK WORKERS AND THE NEW UNIONS (1939); LIPSET, TROW & COLEMAN, UNION DEMOCRACY (1956).

obtained in an antitrust action against a local of the Wood, Wire, and Metal Lathers International Union of Chicago and vicinity, forbidding the union to discriminate racially. Damages and attorneys fees were paid too.[121]

PRIVATE EMPLOYERS AND ANTIDISCRIMINATION CLAUSES IN GOVERNMENT CONTRACTS

The duty of unions not to discriminate, whether self- or legally imposed, generally has real meaning for race relations only for those within the bargaining unit. And beyond this, except where there is a closed shop, workers usually come to their jobs through channels other than union ones. Therefore, if an employer practices discrimination, there will not be many Negroes in the unit upon whom a union's nondiscrimination policy—voluntary or enforced by law—can work. Thus we must now inquire what is the duty of a private employer not to make racial distinctions.

Apart from states and cities with fair employment and kindred laws (which will be discussed in the next section), the chief duty on private employers not to discriminate is that imposed by the uniform antidiscrimination clause in all federal contracts, which requires that there be no discrimination on the part of government contractors and their subcontractors. Every federal government contract (with a few minor exceptions) [122] must contain the following provision required by Executive Order No. 10557:

In connection with the performance of work under this contract, the contractor agrees not to discriminate against any employee or applicant for employment because of race, religion, color, or national origin. The aforesaid provision shall include, but not be limited to, the following: employment, upgrading, demotion, or transfer; recruitment or recruitment advertising; layoff or termination; rates of pay or other forms of compensation; and selection for training including apprenticeship. The contractor agrees to post hereafter in conspicuous places, available for employees and applicants for employment, notices to be provided by the contracting officer setting forth the provisions of the non-discrimination clause.

The contractor further agrees to insert the foregoing provision in all subcontracts hereunder, except subcontracts for standard commercial supplies or raw materials.[123]

[121] Menifee v. Local 74, 3 R.R.L.R. 507 (E.D. Ill. 1958); Chicago Defender, March 15, 1958, p. 1. See the discussion of antitrust and housing, *infra* pp. 302–304.
[122] The exceptions are set forth in 21 Fed. Reg. 1193 (1956) (Contract Committee's Interpretive Rule of Feb. 15, 1956).
[123] Exec. Order No. 10557, 19 Fed. Reg. 5655 (1954). A series of related predecessor Executive Orders is catalogued in PRESIDENT'S COMM. ON GOVERNMENT

Because goods and services furnished pursuant to federal government contracts constitute a major part of our economy, compliance with the contract clause could work substantial changes in employment policy. In fact, however, it is common knowledge that many firms discriminate without regard to whether they enjoy government contracts. In 1953 the Committee on Government Contract Compliance concluded that contracting agencies have followed a line of least resistance in enforcement of the clause.[124]

Executive Order No. 10479 [125] established in 1953 the Government Contract Committee (popularly called the "President's Committee on Government Contracts"), which succeeded to and carried on in expanded form the work of the Committee on Government Contract Compliance (established by Executive Order No. 10308 in 1951).[126] Its chairman has been Vice President Nixon; its vice chairman is the Secretary of Labor; and industrial, labor, and civic leaders constitute its membership. The order provides that the committee shall make recommendations to the contracting agencies for improving and making more effective the nondiscrimination provisions of government contracts; it directs all contracting agencies of the government to cooperate with the committee; and it authorizes the committee to receive complaints of alleged violations of the nondiscrimination provisions of government contracts. Upon receipt of a complaint the committee directs it to the appropriate contracting agency to be processed in accordance with its procedure. Each agency is required to report to the committee the action taken with respect to these and other complaints of discrimination. The committee is then to review and analyze the reports submitted by the contracting agencies.

Contrary to what seems to be the popular belief, the committee operates principally through the compliance officers of the various contracting agencies, *e.g.*, the Atomic Energy Commission, the Department of Agriculture, Department of Commerce, Department of Defense. It is the agencies which have the power to effect compliance; the committee actually has little power to require action. By its mandate it may exhort, consult, and prod, and although its authority is enhanced by the fact that the Vice President is its chairman, with all

---

CONTRACTS, EQUAL JOB OPPORTUNITY PROGRAM 1-6 (1956). For a thorough treatment of this area see Pasley, *The Non Discrimination Clause in Government Contracts*, 43 VA. L. REV. 837 (1957).

[124] PRESIDENT'S COMM. ON GOVERNMENT CONTRACT COMPLIANCE, REPORT ON EQUAL ECONOMIC OPPORTUNITY 14-15 (1953).

[125] 48 Fed. Reg. 4899 (1953).   [126] 16 Fed. Reg. 12303 (1951).

the implications which flow from his powerful political position, in the last analysis it alone cannot declare that either a violator must comply or sanctions will be imposed. It has to rely on persuasion, conciliation, mediation, and an extensive educational program involving the distribution of literature, posters, and motion pictures and the establishment of high-level contacts between important government officials and leaders of industry.

As part of its educational–public relations program the committee also encourages programs by voluntary nongovernmental groups (management, labor, civic, religious, and so forth) to reduce the basic causes of discrimination in employment and to establish and maintain cooperative relationships with state, local, and nongovernmental bodies to achieve the purposes of the Executive Order. Its effectiveness could be enhanced by participation in private litigation against discrimination (it has at least once taken part in the negotiation of a settlement ending discrimination by a union-employer contract),[127] but this obviously is not a major part of its program.

The nature of the committee's authority and the chain of its operation make for difficulties in securing adherence. Contracting officers are by training and interest most often primarily concerned with the materials and services for which they negotiate. Some may even tend to regard the nondiscrimination clause as simply another impediment to getting the job done. In difficult negotiations they may not want to "rock the boat" by focusing too insistently on matters such as discrimination that they do not care too much about in relation to their desire successfully to conclude a contract. In many cases, chiefly those involving public utilities or those where alternative sources of supply are difficult or impossible to obtain, a contracting officer may not be in a sufficiently strong position to insist on observance of the clause by an intransigent supplier.[128] Because there is no specific provision for enforcement, biased suppliers may feel, with some justification, that they will not be penalized if they do not comply. Few have flatly refused to cooperate with the committee, but cases of fruitless, protracted negotiations are fairly common.

Despite lack of specific provision for enforcement, however, some

[127] Holt v. Oil Workers Union, 36 L.R.R.M. 2702 (Harris County, Texas, Dist. Ct. 1955).

[128] Pasley, *supra* note 123, at 855, sets forth one method used to avoid the clause in this situation: an "order" is issued instead of a contract. But Pasley concludes that the subterfuge probably is illegal.

means may be found in other general legal authority. In 1953, the present committee's predecessor listed seven possible means of achieving compliance when conciliation fails.[129]

1. *Disqualification from future contracting.* The old committee concluded, "It appears that the language of the legislation [governing procurement activities] would allow an agency to establish administrative disqualifying procedures directed against irresponsible bidders whose past performance has been detrimental to the Government's interest." [130] In practice this sanction has not been used. But the *Fourth Annual Report* urges contracting agencies to deny awards to noncomplying contractors.[131]

2. *Termination of contract.* Each contract contains a standard provision that the government may terminate the whole contract or any part thereof if the contractor fails to perform under any provision and does not rectify the failure within a specified period of time. Violation of the nondiscrimination clause might be considered a material breach and the termination remedy could be applied. The committee called this the most potent sanction, noting, however, that for military or economic reasons it sometimes might not be feasible. To date, it appears, no contract has ever been terminated for failure to comply with the antidiscrimination clause.

3. *Injunctive relief.* The government might sue for specific performance of the nondiscrimination clause. Failure of a contractor to comply is in many cases, at least, hardly measurable in monetary damages. The inadequacy of damages supports suit for injunction. The committee, while apparently believing that injunction is an available remedy,[132] did have one question about it. It stated that "the fact that traditionally the adequacy test has been concerned with the main objective of the contract, *i.e.*, goods and services, and not with a collateral objective, *i.e.*, full utilization of manpower, leaves some doubt as to whether injunctive relief is an available remedy." [133] But in many instances may we not ask whether the latter objective is not equally or more important than the former?

4. *Arbitration.* The committee suggested arbitration as a remedy of

[129] President's Comm. on Government Contract Compliance, Report on Equal Economic Opportunity, *op. cit. supra* note 124, at 36-41.
[130] *Id.* at 37.
[131] 1957 Fourth Annual Report on Equal Job Opportunity 6.
[132] Report on Equal Economic Opportunity, *op. cit. supra* note 124, at 70.
[133] *Id.* at 39.

considerable value. It noted that an agreement to arbitrate could embrace preliminary processes of conciliation and mediation. However, it observed that supporting legislation probably was necessary to make an arbitration award enforceable in the courts under the United States Arbitration Act of 1925, and thought that doubt existed whether government agents may submit to arbitration. It recommended legislation as the only effective basis for establishing arbitration as a compliance device. No move appears to have been made to write this recommendation into law.

5. *Liquidated damages.* The committee suggested that liquidated damage provisions might be inserted in contract agreements. It pointed out, however, that the validity of a liquidated damage provision is contingent on whether it represents a good faith estimate of probable actual injury. If not, it will be viewed as a penalty and invalid. The committee concluded that although liquidated damage provisions "have been upheld by the courts many times where injury or the extent thereof was difficult to assess . . . the safer course is to obtain congressional authorization." [134] Apparently no move has been made to secure this legislation either.

6. *Third-Party Beneficiary.* The committee concluded that "there is only a remote possibility that the injured party could qualify as a beneficiary with enforceable rights under the nondiscrimination provision," and observed that a specific clause conferring third-party beneficiary rights would obviate some of the apparent difficulties. "However," it suggested, "only legislative action would provide solid ground for its use." [135] Nevertheless, we may note that there are cases, of which the committee seemingly was unaware, holding that a clause inserted in a government contract requiring the contractor to comply with an Executive Order governing overtime is enforceable by the employees.[136] Yet a third-party beneficiary theory invoking Executive Order Nos. 10479 and 10557 has never been applied in a reported case.

7. *Certificate of compliance.* The contractor could be required to file a certificate of compliance to obtain payment. Execution of a false certificate is a crime punishable by a fine up to $10,000, or imprisonment up to five years, or both. But the committee expressed a feeling that possible criminal liability might interfere with procurement

---

[134] *Id.* at 40.   [135] *Ibid.*
[136] Young v. Kellex Corp., 82 F. Supp. 953 (E.D. Tenn. 1948); Crabb v. Welden Bros., 65 F. Supp. 369 (S.D. Iowa 1946), *rev'd in part on other grounds,* 164 F.2d 797 (8th Cir. 1947).

activities, concluding that "such possible criminal liability is not consonant with the philosophy of voluntary compliance sought under the nondiscrimination provision." [137]

In addition, it has been suggested that the plant seizure provisions of the Selective Service Act which authorize the President to seize facilities which refuse to fill orders placed by the Armed Services, or the Atomic Energy Act "could be brought into play where a contractor, by refusing to comply with the non-discrimination clause, refuses, in effect to accept the contract." [138]

Refusal to use or to try to develop coercive weapons in the case of open violators and failure to report on complaints for sometimes as long as two years after filing have prompted serious criticism of the committee.[139]

Although it receives complaints and refers them for review and corrective action the committee also utilizes "compliance reviews." During the year beginning July 1, 1956, compliance reviews covered more than 500 businesses in about twenty-five metropolitan areas with large minority populations. Most of the facilities involved were those of the largest government contractors. The committee has observed that "contractors report their inability to find members of minority groups among qualified applicants for employment" and "members of minority groups usually are reluctant to apply for positions unless they have positive knowledge that the company employs without regard to race, religion or national origin." [140]

While the committee has no definite statistics on the amount of social change achieved by its activities, there are doubtless a number of Negroes in jobs today which they would not have if it were not for the committee. These include positions in transportation and telephone companies, atomic energy installations, chemical works, electrical equipment manufacturing plants, aircraft factories, building trades. Other factors, including economic and social change as well as activities of state and private groups pressuring for desegregation, have, of course, played a role here too. On the other hand, lacking quantitative information which the committee does not issue, there is no basis to say whether the numbers are significant in relation to the

[137] REPORT ON EQUAL ECONOMIC OPPORTUNITY, *op. cit. supra* note 124, at 41.
[138] C.C.H. GOVERNMENT CONTRACTS REPORTER ¶ 6325.
[139] Kempton, *The Conscience of Our Servants*, N.Y. Post Magazine, June 28, 1958.
[140] 1955-1956 THIRD ANNUAL REPORT ON EQUAL JOB OPPORTUNITY 9-10.

magnitude of the problem. Moreover, it is not mere employment that is important, but positions attained and upgrading procedures. It is here that change has been slowest. The committee's *Fourth Annual Report* (covering through mid-1957) reveals that in 21 auto assembly plants Negroes comprised nearly 12 percent of the total work force, but constituted less than one fifth of one percent of the 5,171 employees in professional-technical and clerical jobs. However, Negroes did show a higher participation in apprenticeship and on-the-job training (7 percent) in many industries, indicating that their share of skilled jobs (now 4.2 percent) could increase in the near future.

A number of states have contract clause statutes substantively like the presidential Executive Order although the state laws have no provisions for administrative implementation.[141] There is no reported information concerning the extent of their enforcement, if any, and the best indications are that there is no enforcement.

FAIR EMPLOYMENT PRACTICE COMMISSIONS

The strongest of all legal devices against discrimination in private employment are the fair employment practice commissions or state commissions against discrimination. Before the Second World War such commissions did not exist. The first was the Fair Employment Practice Committee, established in 1941 by Franklin D. Roosevelt under his wartime powers as commander in chief. As national FEPC faded, a number of states and municipalities began to enact fair employment laws, just as when federal enforcement of civil rights retreated under post–Civil War repealers and court reversals, some states filled in with their own public accommodations legislation.

New York was first with a fair employment law in 1945. The "Purposes" section of the New York statute sketches in general terms the purpose of all the FEP-type statutes so far as employment is concerned:

§ 290. A state agency is hereby created with power to eliminate and prevent discrimination in employment because of race, creed, color or national origin, either by employers, labor organizations, employment agencies or other persons.

[141] See appendix A14. See Chicago Defender, May 24, 1958, p. 9 (Negro artisans denied employment on public construction; no procedure for processing complaints).

But many of the state commissions now also enforce nondiscrimination rules in public accommodations, housing, and education.[142] Today there are enforceable statutes in [143] Alaska, California, Colorado, Connecticut, Massachusetts, Michigan, Minnesota, New Jersey, New Mexico, New York, Ohio, Oregon, Pennsylvania, Rhode Island, Washington, and Wisconsin. These states include about 50 percent of the nation's total population and about 25 percent of its Negro population. Indiana and Kansas, with about 4 percent of the national and 1.6 percent of the Negro population,[144] have hortatory fair employment laws with no sanction for violation.

More than a score of municipalities have ordinances similar in aspiration. These include Baltimore, Chicago, Cleveland, Duluth, East Chicago (Ind.), Ecorse (Mich.), Erie and Farrell (Pa.), Gary (Ind.), Hamtramck (Mich.), Milwaukee, Minneapolis, Monessen (Pa.), Philadelphia, Pittsburgh, River Rouge (Mich.), St. Paul, San Francisco, Sharon (Pa.), Toledo, Warren and Youngstown (Ohio).[145] Most of the ordinances, but not all, overlap state laws. A number of the ordinances are unenforceable; if enforceable, criminal rather than injunctive or administrative procedure is customary.

There is no question about a state's constitutional power to enact such laws, nor, questions of specific municipal charters aside, of the competence of municipalities.[146] The statutes implement a policy

---

[142] See pp. 110–112 *supra* (public accommodations), 246–255 *infra* (education), 309 *infra* (housing).

[143] The FEP statutes, enforceable and unenforceable, are cited in appendix A15. The California and Ohio statutes, enacted as these pages went to press, are not discussed in the ensuing summaries in the text, but they are cited in appendix E. On FEPCs generally, see Meiners, *Fair Employment Practices Legislation*, 62 DICK. L. REV. 31 (1957); Morgan, *An Analysis of State FEPC Legislation*, 8 LAB. L.J. 469 (1957); Note, 68 HARV. L. REV. 685 (1955). On individual states see, *e.g.*, Carter, *New York Law Against Discrimination*, 40 CORNELL L.Q. 40 (1954); Le Breton, *Michigan Fair Employment Practices Act*, 34 U. DET. L.J. 337 (1957); Leland, *"We Believe in Employment on Merit, But . . ."*, 37 MINN. L. REV. 246 (1953); Note, 17 U. PITT. L. REV. 438 (1956); Annot., 44 A.L.R.2d 1138 (1955). On wartime FEPC see RUCHAMES, RACE, JOBS AND POLITICS (1953). On proposed federal FEPC see Maslow & Robison, *Civil Rights Legislation and the Fight for Equality, 1862–1952*, 20 U. CHI. L. REV. 363, 394 (1953).

[144] The population statistics for both types of states are taken from CONFERENCE OF GOVERNORS OF CIVIL RIGHTS STATES, REPORT ON FAIR EMPLOYMENT PRACTICES AT WORK IN TWELVE STATES 4 (1958), and from REPORT ON EQUAL ECONOMIC OPPORTUNITY, *op. cit. supra* note 124, at 102. But since the publication of these figures there has been steady and substantial northward migration of Negroes, see p. 275 *infra*.

[145] For FEP-type ordinances see appendix A16.

[146] See Railway Mail Ass'n v. Corsi, *supra* note 67; Bob-Lo Excursion Co. v. Michigan, 333 U.S. 28 (1948); District of Columbia v. Thompson Restaurant Co., 346 U.S. 100 (1953).

against discrimination in employment (and many include accommodations, some housing and education) on grounds of race, color, creed, or national origin. A few laws include ancestry, age (Massachusetts, New York, Pennsylvania), and service in the armed forces (New Jersey), while Pennsylvania has a proviso that an employer may favor "the individual . . . best able and most competent to perform the services required." Most of the complaints have involved employment, and the overwhelming number of these have alleged racial bias.

A number of states expressly define discrimination to include segregation (Connecticut, Kansas, Michigan, Minnesota, New Mexico, Pennsylvania, Rhode Island), although administrative and judicial interpretation doubtlessly would reach the same result. All cover hiring, discharge, upgrading, and pay; all apply to employers, employment agencies, and unions. Most govern referrals by employment agencies; some (Colorado, Minnesota, Rhode Island) cover compliance with a biased request for referral. Almost all ban discriminatory inquiries [147] and advertising. Most try to preserve the integrity of enforcement by forbidding discrimination against complainants for having complained; by outlawing the aiding or inciting of violators; and by banning attempts at obstructing and obstruction of the commissions' process. A few permit employers to complain against employees or unions that interfere with fair employment policies.

Exemptions are fairly standard. All statutes but Wisconsin's except employers of specified small numbers of employees (*e.g.*, Pennsylvania, 12, the highest; New York, 6; Rhode Island, 4, the lowest). Other employees not covered are domestic workers (all states but Oregon and Wisconsin); farm workers (Pennsylvania); and immediate family members (Connecticut, Massachusetts, Minnesota, New Jersey, New York, Pennsylvania, Rhode Island, Washington, Wisconsin). The family provision is not really an exception, for if an employer favors an employee because of relationship, he is not discriminating against another because of race.

All statutes grant religious or nonprofit institutions the privilege of using religion or membership as a factor in selection, some by sweeping exemption for nonprofit or religious organizations, some by permitting preference for members. A few permit inquiry concerning

---

[147] For rules on preemployment inquiries see, *e.g.*, N.Y. Exec. Law § 296(1)(c) (1958 Supp.); Pa. Stats. Ann. § 955(b)(1) and (2) (1957 Supp.). Concerning photographs see Op. Att'y Gen. of Minn., 1 R.R.I.R. 1161 (1956) (permissible only where bona fide occupational qualification); concerning inquiry about attendance at house of worship see Op. Att'y Gen. of Ore., *id*. at 1163 (prohibited).

religion to the extent that adherence to a particular faith is a genuine job specification (*e.g.*, Colorado, Massachusetts, Michigan). Minnesota exempts religious and fraternal corporations with respect to qualifications based on religion, when religion is a bona fide occupational qualification for employment in such organizations. A number of statutes expressly cover state agencies, while others may do so by implication.[148]

The enforceable statutes all provide that aggrieved persons may complain to the commission, which then may investigate. If there is substance to the complaint, commission conciliation efforts follow. If these do not terminate the dispute, a formal hearing may be held. But in practice hearings have been rare: of the thousands of complaints presented to its commission since 1945, New York has had only about twenty come to hearing, while a few other states have had one or two.[149] When there has been a hearing, an order may issue requiring hiring, upgrading, posting of notices, an award of back pay, or the like, or perhaps dismissal of the complaint. The order need not be confined to the precise instance of discrimination raised in the complaint. The commission may proceed against any biased practices it finds in enterprises which have been the subject of complaint.[150] Edicts of the commissions may be enforced by court order. But court cases have been very unusual.[151] In at least Michigan, New Jersey,

[148] See appendix A8.

[149] REPORT ON FAIR EMPLOYMENT PRACTICES, etc., *op. cit. supra* note 144, at 8.

[150] For typical FEPC orders, see DIV. AGAINST DISCRIMINATION, N.J. DEP'T OF EDUCATION, ANNUAL REPORT 14 (July 1, 1955–June 30, 1956) (after hearings cease and desist order issued requiring Erie R.R. not to discriminate against employees because of race in initial employment, upgrading, consideration for new positions which may be created, etc.; also ordering wage adjustment); but after further hearings commissioner ruled that no wage differential was due, ANNUAL REPORT 13 (July 1, 1956–June 30, 1957); 1952 N.Y. SCAD REPORT 53, Westreich v. Wall St. Employment Bureau (respondent agreed to cease and desist order prohibiting inquiries respecting race, etc., when interviewing or receiving applications and prohibiting acceptance of discriminatory job orders).

[151] See Holland v. Edwards, 307 N.Y. 38, 119 N.E.2d 581 (1954) (affirming a SCAD cease and desist order against employment agency with respect to unlawful inquiries; this was the first litigated controversy after hearing under the New York FEP law); Ross v. Arbury, 206 Misc. 74, 133 N.Y.S.2d 62 (1954), *aff'd*, 285 App. Div. 886, 139 N.Y.S.2d 245 (1st Dep't, 1955) (power of SCAD to require posting notices in employment agencies concerning objectives of FEP law upheld); International Bhd. of Elec. Workers v. Commission on Civil Rights, 140 Conn. 537, 102 A.2d 366 (1953) (cease and desist order against union prohibiting exclusion of complainant because of race upheld); Draper v. Clark Dairy, Inc., 17 Conn. Supp. 93 (1950) (cease and desist order prohibiting private employer from discriminating upheld); see Annot., 44 A.L.R.2d 1138 (1955); *cf.* Ross v. Ebert, 275 Wis. 523, 82 N.W.2d 315 (1957), holding that Wisconsin FEP law did not authorize judicial enforcement; but *Ross* has been overruled by amendment, see appendix A15.

New York, Pennsylvania, and Washington, a complainant may obtain judicial review of a finding of no probable cause.[152] At least the Connecticut, Michigan, New York, and Wisconsin commissions review cases three to six months after they have been closed.[153]

One hurdle to enforcement of civil rights law, including that on employment, is the ineffectiveness of proceeding solely upon complaints, as we have noted before (although over a period of years, New York's coverage has been fairly comprehensive).[154] Regarding employment, potential complainants often will not waste time in seeking work from biased employers. Moreover, complete industries rarely are covered, resulting in different policies for essentially similar, competing enterprises. A public matter, therefore, hinges on the *ad hoc* activities of individual job seekers.

To overcome this problem eight states permit their commissions to act without a complaint (all but Alaska, Michigan, New Jersey, New Mexico, New York, Oregon), and eight states (all but Alaska, Connecticut, Michigan, Minnesota, Rhode Island, Washington) empower a public official (*e.g.*, attorney general, industrial commissioner) to file complaints. It seems that all states may investigate informally without a complaint, but there sometimes is a question of whether a court-enforceable order may be issued in such cases.[155] The Rhode Island and Wisconsin statutes permit complaints to be filed by nongovernmental civil rights organizations. In New York these organizations may lodge complaints concerning such activities as advertising with general prospective application as distinguished from a particular charge on behalf of an individual.[156] Organizations everywhere, of course, may and do refer complainants.

Most of the city ordinances are enforceable by criminal prosecution, and the penalties usually are in the light misdemeanor range (*e.g.*, Cleveland, $100; Chicago, $200; Milwaukee, $10; Minneapolis, $100,

---

[152] That orders dismissing complaints without formal hearing are reviewable in New York may be seen in Jeanpierre v. Arbury, 4 N.Y.2d 238, 173 N.Y.S.2d 597 (1958); on the *Jeanpierre* case, see N.Y. Times, May 8, 1957, p. 29.

[153] REPORT ON FAIR EMPLOYMENT PRACTICES, etc., *op. cit. supra* note 144, at 9.

[154] See N.Y. Times, Nov. 25, 1957, p. 28 (New York commission has dealt with 78% of firms employing 1,000 or more persons during past 12 years).

[155] REPORT ON FAIR EMPLOYMENT PRACTICES, etc., *op. cit. supra* note 144, at 8.

[156] See 1956 N.Y. SCAD REPORT 5: "In addition to acting on formal complaints, the Commission's regulatory activities include industry-wide studies based on information about specific situations brought to the Commission's attention by individuals or groups." However, in these cases the commission "has no power to order public hearings or to utilize other enforcement procedures."

90 days, or both). A few may be implemented by action to "secure enforcement," presumably injunctive proceedings (*e.g.*, Monessen, Philadelphia, Pittsburgh). San Francisco has no penalty, but authorizes injunctive relief and up to 90 days' back pay. Some have no sanction at all (*e.g.*, Baltimore).

Minnesota and Pennsylvania allow their municipal fair employment practice bodies to operate autonomously in cooperation with the state commission and have set up a referral procedure.[157] New Jersey holds city commissions powerless to compel compliance.[158] Although New York City has no such commission, the City License Commissioner, in his regulation of employment agencies, works in cooperation with the State Commission Against Discrimination.[159] The city also has a Commission on Intergroup Relations which administers the municipal law governing discrimination in housing and is concerned with race relations in the community generally. Almost all of the state commissions have cooperated with one another, sometimes in cases involving multistate enterprises;[160] there is now a Continuing Committee of Governors on Civil Rights, one of whose main purposes is to foster interstate cooperation.[161]

The commissions look upon education, defined broadly, as a function equal or prior to compelled enforcement. In Minnesota, two thirds of the time of the agency's two professionals is spent on educational activities. Colorado, Connecticut, Michigan, Oregon, Rhode Island, Washington, and Wisconsin reportedly spend a larger proportion of staff and budget on education; Massachusetts, New Jersey, New York, and Pennsylvania, a smaller proportion. The educational process includes conciliation; conferences with unions, employers (often, particularly, new ones), and personnel managers; and public information programs (literature, films, lectures, advertisements, and so forth). New York has an extensive network of councils to advise the com-

[157] 1956 MINN. FEPC ANNUAL REPORT 4; PA. FEPC ANNUAL REPORT 5. See *Memorandum of Agreement Between the Erie Commission and the State*, in 1957 ERIE COMM'N REPORT app. II.

[158] 1955 DIV. AGAINST DISCRIMINATION, N.J. DEP'T OF EDUCATION, ANNUAL REPORT 14. See Op. of City Attorney that San Francisco ordinance would conflict with state law then being proposed, 2 R.R.L.R. 750 (1957). See Op. Att'y Gen. of Mich. No. 2880, 1958 (state statute has preempted field).

[159] N.Y. Times, Oct. 12, 1956, p. 31.

[160] REPORT ON FAIR EMPLOYMENT PRACTICES, etc., *op. cit. supra* note 144, at 15. See N.Y. Times, Dec. 11, 1956, p. 46 ("Hiring Bias Ended by 18 Rail Lines"; New York and New Jersey commissions cooperated with one another).

[161] REPORT ON FAIR EMPLOYMENT PRACTICES, etc., *op. cit. supra* note 144, at 19-24.

mission and the public; most other states employ a similar but not so highly developed system of affiliates. A few work with already established agencies. Most states, too, engage in and publish some research.[162] "Education" and "enforcement," however, are often inseparable. Each helps to advance the function of the other; implicit in every conciliation conference is the power to invoke force where persuasion fails, and where practice is forced, the process of doing may be educational.

In evaluating whether the commissions have created any change, and if so, how much, probably their nation-wide impact is most meaningful. As of 1957, the New York commission, since its inception, has had 4,213 employment complaints; New Jersey's, 1,664; Connecticut's, 715; and Michigan's, 435. Even in states where the commissions also cover other matters, by far the greatest number of charges have involved employment.[163] (Of course, we must bear in mind that "complaint" is defined from state to state as a term with varying degrees of specificity, ranging from a notarized charge to commission observation of a biased newspaper advertisement.) On the average the states seem to make adjustments (whether that means sweeping or slight change) where probable cause is found or other discriminatory practice is uncovered in about half of the cases presented (e.g., Minnesota, 57 percent; Connecticut and Pennsylvania, 51 percent; New York, 46 percent; New Jersey, 37 percent).[164] While it is hardly comprehensive, there is evidence of a substantial number of large enterprises having changed their employment policies because of the law or commission action.[165] A 1958 survey of major insurance companies' employment in New York has shown "dramatic increases" since passage of the SCAD statute. One firm was said to have

---

[162] Id. at 10-11. The states report the following amounts of their 1957 budgets exclusive of salaries allocated to educational activities or materials: New York, $25,000; Michigan, $10,820; New Jersey, $10,000; Connecticut, $7,790; Colorado, $5,000; Minnesota, $4,000; Washington, $2,500; Rhode Island, $2,200; Oregon, $1,350. Massachusetts, Pennsylvania, and Wisconsin do not indicate specific amounts of money available for this purpose.

[163] Id. at 9.   [164] Id. at 31.

[165] For illustrative reports of changes see, e.g., Michigan FEPC "Information," Sept., 1956, p. 1 ("In many instances where adjustments have been reached employers have agreed to promulgate statements of policy indicating merit employment programs in keeping with the spirit as well as the letter of the Michigan FEP Act. Patterns of exclusion have become patterns of merit employment"); 1957 MINN. FEPC ANNUAL REPORT 13 (Case No. 2: Negro employee applied for membership in railway union and was rejected. Case complicated by question of whether union had jurisdiction over applicant's position and what proper seniority date should be. Conferences with employer and union resolved these questions; applicant enrolled as member; case closed as satisfactorily

doubled the number of Negro employees in eight years. Another was found to have hired 50 Negroes in a group of 499 high school graduates given jobs. Fourteen companies were shown to have improved their "employment patterns" and three were said to have hired Negroes for the first time after employment discrimination complaints were filed against them. More than forty of the companies had had complaints filed against them.[166]

The commissions themselves believe that they have been effective. Those in New Jersey, Oregon, and Wisconsin assert a high degree of effectiveness, while the others claim that the law has been "effective" or "fairly effective." [167] Civil rights groups representing minorities which would benefit from changes in employment patterns continue to press for fair employment laws in states that do not have them. Therefore, while we cannot measure how much change the commissions have brought about, it seems that they have exerted a steady, although perhaps geographically and temporally uneven, pressure toward achieving equal employment opportunity.

Today, however, the questions posed in Morroe Berger's thorough 1952 study of New York's SCAD remain largely unanswered.

How many employers, employment agencies and labor unions have reduced or eliminated discriminatory practices merely because the law had been enacted? How many employers have voluntarily gone far beyond the law's requirements in eliminating employment discrimination, and how far have they gone? How many employers have eliminated discrimination as a result of their knowledge of the Commission's work, without ever becoming parties to a case? How many employers, once in contact with the

---

adjusted). DIV. AGAINST DISCRIMINATION, N.J. DEP'T OF EDUCATION, ANNUAL REPORT 12 (July 1, 1954-June 30, 1955) (Negro carpenter refused employment; employer feared that white workers would quit; through conciliation employer was persuaded that white workers would not leave; complainant then would not take job; another Negro subsequently hired); 1952 N.Y. SCAD REPORT 51 (Johnson v. S.S. Kresge Co.: company changed its previous employment policy after finding of probable cause by the Investigating Commissioner; previously respondent had not employed a single Negro; shortly thereafter hired three Negro salesgirls and a Negro stockman); 1956 R.I. COMM'N AGAINST DISCRIMINATION REPORT 5 ("during the entire year, not one complaint was processed, alleging termination in the field of employment, which could be supported by evidence, as being based on discrimination. . . . A notable gain during this past year was the appearance of colored drivers in interstate bus transportation"). On the New York commission's campaign against discrimination by the airlines in flight positions, see N.Y. Times, Dec. 29, 1957, § X, p. 25 ("Aviation: Stewardess; First Negro Girl To Obtain a Position as Air Hostess Hired by Mohawk"). See also N.Y. Times, Dec. 27, 1957, p. 25.
[166] N.Y. Times, Oct. 13, 1958, p. 31.
[167] REPORT ON FAIR EMPLOYMENT PRACTICES, etc., op. cit. supra note 144, at 12–13.

Commission, manage to continue to discriminate illegally? Some of these questions can be given approximate answers, but only after a lengthy field study using data which SCAD regards as confidential, while others are hardly answerable at all in the present state of social science.[168]

As a simple measuring device, Berger suggested an annual survey to report employers admitting minority members for the first time; no such studies are being made. Some of the states' reports are vague in the extreme. To an extent this may be necessary because the statutes require confidential treatment of those with whom the commissions deal, but much could be told without revealing identities. A number of states lump together reports of complaints about employment, housing, and public accommodations or reports of their disposition. For example, Rhode Island's 1956 *Report* (like others for that state) sets forth the number of complaints, enumerates types of respondents (*i.e.*, employers, public housing, hotels, and so forth), the number of cases in which discrimination existed and where no probable cause was found, the number and types of unlawful practices in employment and public accommodations, the bases of alleged discrimination, the number of cases in which there was satisfactory adjustment, and the number in which there was lack of evidence. So it is completely unclear, for example, whether all of the cases in which there was lack of evidence were employment cases or others. Moreover, we do not know what constitutes a "satisfactory adjustment," as we do not know what the agency's standard of proof was, whether it was easy or hard to persuade the agency that there was no discrimination, whether the complainant was hired, how many Negroes were hired, or whether the complainant decided to accept a poor explanation and forget about the matter.

Connecticut and Massachusettes are just about as vague as Rhode Island. Apart from a few general statements of policy and activities and perhaps two or three isolated examples of cases in which the commission has engaged, Connecticut's information is set forth annually in a table like the following in its 1956–1957 *Report*.

STATISTICAL SUMMARY

ENFORCEMENT				EDUCATION			RESEARCH				
FEP	PA	O	Total	PS	MS	Total	IS	RC	PP	DS	Total
87	51	135	273	800	1131	1931	2	9	23	1028	1062

Code: FEP—Fair Employment Practices; PA—Public Accommodations; O—Other; PS—Personal Services; MS—Material Services; IS—Study Interviews; RC—Research Consultation; PP—Program Participation; DS—Distribution of Studies.

[168] Berger, Equality by Statute 117 (1952).

Minnesota also uses the phrase "satisfactory adjustment," although it has published a number of case histories which give an indication of what the commission does. Pennsylvania's first annual report (1957) uses the phrase "discrimination found and adjusted." Michigan reported in its April–May, 1957, *FEPC Information Bulletin* that of 272 claims filed with the commission 90 had been "adjusted." Many of the "adjustments," the report stated were "open ended"—*i.e.*, they called for consideration for a "next vacancy" or future vacancies, or they involved changes in the respondent's practice which were to be observed over a period of time. All provided for commission review. New York publishes the most detailed report. It provides, among other things, specific breakdowns of the basis of complaints and cases in which probable cause was found, an analysis of complaints by act and by area of activity in which the acts have occurred, and tables showing where discrimination was found and adjusted (including breakdowns of economic activities), all in considerable detail. It also provides interpretations and rulings and analyzes patterns of conciliation. There is a fair number of summary case histories (with names of complainants and respondents), selected with a view to explaining the meaning and operation of New York's law. New York recently has commenced publishing surveys of the long-range effect of the SCAD law.[169] Yet, it must be said, in sum, the reports of the FEP states are generally not very illuminating.

An important need for all commissions continues to be a uniform, informative reporting system. One may suspect that the obscurity stems from a desire to please all factions. Those who favor vigorous enforcement are denied an official basis for attacking the commissions; those who want weak implementation are similarly without factual foundation. Perhaps the Continuing Committee of Governors on Civil Rights could devise and adopt a uniform, or at least a minimal, reporting system to overcome this deficiency.

Some of the municipal agencies have been quite active, especially when allowance is made for relatively small populations. Philadelphia's Commission on Human Relations has been the busiest. In 1956 it investigated 99 cases of discrimination in employment (16 of which were initiated by the commission); 117 complaints were closed during the year; in 33 an unlawful practice was established and an adjustment made.[170] Philadelphia's reports convey more information (including a

[169] See text at note 166.
[170] 1956 Philadelphia Comm'n on Human Relations Annual Report 10.

substantial number of meaningful case histories) than those of most state commissions. Minneapolis's Fair Employment Commission had 33 complaints between November, 1955, and February, 1957, of which 12 resulted in "satisfactory adjustment" of the complaint and 4 in a commitment to follow a nondiscriminatory policy.[171] St Paul's commission administered 54 cases in 1956–57. Fifteen were terminated by conciliation, 27 were held to involve insufficient evidence. In one case which was brought to prosecution, the employer was found guilty and sentenced to $100 or 10 days in jail, which was suspended contingent upon compliance.[172] Cleveland's Community Relations Board has ordered a union to cease discrimination.[173] Other municipal commissions, however, have shown somewhat less activity and a number have done little or nothing.[174]

Some municipal budgets have been: Philadelphia (1956 *Report*): $136,000; East Chicago (1955 *Report*): $2,700; Youngstown (1954 *Report*): $9,593.40; Gary: $9,450; Erie: $10,000 (the latter two set forth in Youngstown's 1954 *Report*).[175]

A key factor in a commission's effectiveness is the vigor of its policy toward approaching its task. Of course, this is tied to the size of the staff, the funds available, and the scope of the commission's jurisdiction, in short, its total resources. The state budgets for 1956 give some indication of financial resources available.[176]

[171] 1956 MINNEAPOLIS FEPC ANNUAL REPORT 13.

[172] CITY OF ST. PAUL FEPC INTERIM REPORT 4 (July, 1956–July, 1957). Release of St. Paul FEPC, Feb. 5, 1957, 2 R.R.L.R. 625 (1957).

[173] Pinkston v. IBEW (June 18, 1956), No. A-123, 1 R.R.L.R. 979 (1956).

[174] See 1957 YOUNGSTOWN FEPC REPORT 5–6 (15 formal complaints; 12 dismissed for lack of probable cause; two satisfactorily adjusted); 1957 ERIE COMMUNITY RELATIONS THIRD ANNUAL REPORT 5 (from Jan., 1954, to Dec., 1956, 23 complaints; probable cause found in 14; 7 of these "adjusted," 7 under conciliation; no probable cause but other discrimination found in 3, 1 "adjusted," 2 under conciliation); 1955 EAST CHICAGO, IND. FEPC REPORT 6 (29 complaints to Sept., 1955; 13 "satisfactorily settled"); DULUTH FEPC REPORT (June, 1957) ("no formal complaints . . . during the past year"). See CHICAGO COMM'N ON HUMAN RELATIONS, MERIT EMPLOYMENT IN CHICAGO 17 (1956) (Chicago's was the first municipal ordinance, MUNICIPAL CODE ch. 198.7A; it did not establish an agency with investigative or enforcement powers; it had been alleged that the city council was without power under state law to enact even the law it did and the "ordinance has been of almost no effect"); Letter from City Attorney of Hamtramck to author, Nov. 8, 1957 ("F.E.P.C. Commission has had no cases before it since its inception"); Letter to author in reply to inquiry about Johnstown, Pa., FEPC Commission, Nov. 19, 1957 ("never activated").

[175] 1956 PHILADELPHIA REPORT 16; 1955 EAST CHICAGO REPORT 6; 1954 YOUNGSTOWN REPORT 19 (includes the Gary and Erie figures).

[176] The table is taken from REPORT ON FAIR EMPLOYMENT PRACTICES, etc., *op. cit. supra* note 144, at 30; statistics for Indiana, Kansas, and New Mexico, however,

Activity and effectiveness, however, are not determined merely by budget, but to a great extent reflect the attitude of the guiding personnel. Nowhere has this been made so clear as in New York, with the jump in caseload upon commencement of Charles Abrams's administration of SCAD. Between 1955 and 1957 the number of complaints in New York increased sharply.[177] Obviously, discrimination in the state could not have grown so markedly during this time. Rather, the change must have emanated in good part from recognition of the fact that Abrams was pledged to a firmer enforcement policy, despite the fact that new responsibilities conferred upon the commission by amendments to the law also brought new complaints. Growing awareness of the law, expanded commission responsibility, and enhanced vigor of enforcement apparently account for a slow but steady increase in complaints in all states. Expanding Negro populations probably are responsible also. But even the invigoration of the New York law has

are taken from reports of those states. New Mexico was not included in the FEP survey, possibly because of its slight activity. The latter two were not included presumably because their statutes are unenforceable.

State	1956 Population	Current Twelve-Month Budget in Dollars	Per Capita Expenditure in Dollars
Colorado	1,612,000	41,224	.0255
Connecticut	2,232,000	90,000	.0403
Massachusetts	4,812,000	80,440	.0167
Michigan	7,516,000	137,218	.0182
Minnesota (large number of complaints handled by municipal agencies)	3,241,000	31,000	.0095
New Jersey	5,403,000	114,093	.0211
New Mexico	815,000	2,000	.0025
New York	16,195,000	636,668	.0393
Oregon	1,718,000	20,000	.0116
Pennsylvania	10,964,000	112,500	.0102
Rhode Island	828,000	37,495	.0452
Washington	2,667,000	39,700	.0148
Wisconsin	3,764,000	16,480	.0044
Total	61,767,000	1,358,818	.0199
Indiana	4,413,000	30,000	.0068
Kansas	2,103,000	15,000	.0071
Total	6,516,000	45,000	.0070

[177] 562 complaints were filed in 1956 compared to 397 in 1955, 318 in 1954. See 1956 N.Y. SCAD REPORT 4: "Indications are that this upward trend will continue." See Governor Harriman's Annual Message to the Legislature, N.Y. Times, Jan. 9, 1958, p. 26: "In 1956, the commission received 562 cases, more than double the number three years earlier, and in 1957 the number was more than 40 per cent higher than in 1956."

not dissuaded the American Jewish Congress, a proponent of the fair employment practice concept, from criticizing SCAD severely (on the occasion of a commission announcement that anti-Semitic discrimination is on the wane). An editorial in *Congress Weekly* stated:

It is hard to avoid the conclusion that the declining number of complaints to SCAD, rather than indicating a waning of discrimination against Jews in New York (which, we repeat, may be the case), merely reflects a deepening skepticism about SCAD's ability to extend meaningful aid to the complainant. The SCAD report indicates that there has been a falling off in complaints about discrimination by employment agencies. Yet there are strong indications that there has been no decline in these agencies' discrimination.

We are far from blaming SCAD wholly for the situation today. The Commission is undoubtedly hampered by the fact that it must wait for complaints and does not have the power to initiate investigations.[178]

Chairman Abrams's reply [179] to this editorial agreed with the need for commission power to initiate complaints, but stood by the trustworthiness of his earlier assertions. In particular, he stated, the alleged evidence concerning employment agencies had never been brought to the commission's attention.

New York's recent survey of state commissions prepared for the conference of governors of civil rights states reports agreement on several major difficulties in enforcement: (1) "the failure of members of minority groups to file complaints, particularly in connection with problems of upgrading and promotion, and . . . the more highly paying jobs"; (2) the "small staff of the agency and . . . the vast areas involved in some of the states"; (3) "the small percentage of members of minority groups with any substantial vocational skills. Most members of minority groups are not prepared to challenge the discriminatory barriers except in unskilled classifications where discrimination is the least prevalent." Other problems cited by various states were those of creating public awareness; making housing available for Negroes near job openings; the difficulty of obtaining training in the skilled trades for Negroes; the lack of communication with newer nonwhite populations.[180]

[178] Congress Weekly, April 14, 1958, p. 3.
[179] Congress Weekly, April 28, 1958, p. 15.
[180] See Background Information for the Conference of Governors of Civil Rights States, New York City, December 12, 1957—An Analysis of the Questionnaire Returns by the Twelve Participating States 10–11 (mimeographed). This

Some of these enforcement problems may be remediable by amendment [181] to existing laws, although others would respond better to invigorated enforcement. New York's SCAD has pressed for power to commence proceedings on its own initiative, leading to enforceable orders (a power already possessed by the commissions of most states), whereby systematic enforcement could be undertaken without awaiting unpredictable, uncoordinated complaints. The proposal has been opposed on the ground that it would be an improper intrusion for the commission to act where no individual had been aggrieved. Such an amendment was defeated in a politically acrimonious dispute in which the governor vetoed an appropriation which had been requested for the purpose of strengthening the attorney general's power to file complaints with SCAD [182] (the attorney general and the governor were members of opposing political parties; civil rights organizations supported a bill to confer new powers on SCAD, opposed the proposal to invest the attorney general with new power). Connecticut's commission may not order job reinstatement or back pay awards. It desires amendments to confer this authority. Michigan's commission requests subpoena power, and also would like to have its orders reviewed in the same manner as those of administrative agencies generally, *i.e.*, upheld if supported by any reasonable evidence. Appellate review of fair employment orders there is now on a de novo basis, *i.e.*, the courts make an independent finding of fact. The Massachusetts, New York, Oregon, and Washington commissions wish to extend coverage to employers who are now exempt because of the small number of their employees; the New York and Massachusetts commissions suggest reconsideration of the charitable, sectarian, and private exemptions; Pennsylvania, of the agricultural exemption. The commissions of other states have not been advancing amendments.

At the same time there appear to be no organized opposition movements to existing fair employment legislation, and seven commissions state that there would be no, or little, opposition to extending present coverage. (While the statutes were first pending there was opposition, in some instances strong opposition.) Minority group organizations

---

study provided the basis for preparation of REPORT ON FAIR EMPLOYMENT PRACTICES, *op. cit. supra* note 144, and is in some respects more detailed.

[181] Amendments sought by the state commissions are reported in REPORT ON FAIR EMPLOYMENT PRACTICES, etc., at 13–14.

[182] S.B. 3816 vetoed April 24, 1957, reported in 2 R.R.L.R. 712 (1957).

are generally satisfied with the statutes and their implementation, except in New York and New Jersey where they say that the laws need strengthening.[183]

CONCLUSION

Law has played an important role in helping to reduce discrimination in employment: peonage has dwindled; government employment has seen a decrease in bias, and indeed, Negroes are employed in government in the ratio that they appear in the population (although hardly in as good jobs as whites); some unions have ceased to discriminate under the spur of law and others have reinforced antidiscrimination policies by invoking law against recalcitrant locals; the President's Committee on Government Contracts, while hardly equipped with effective legal weapons, has brought about some change in racial labor patterns; and Fair Employment Practice Commissions, in proportion to their budgets and assiduity, have achieved change in employment policy in states and cities containing close to half our national population. And all this despite the fact that some doctrine has not yet been developed to its full potential, particularly that of the right to join a union, that of the right of the individual to compel enforcement of the standard federal contract clause, and that of the right of professional persons to join professional associations.

Yet law is only one element in the picture. We must remember, for example, how much the decline in peonage was affected by changes in Southern agricultural techniques and a widespread move from farm to city. This was the framework in which the law operated. And we must remember how much of the current improvement in job discrimination would not have occurred had there not been sufficiently steady employment for Negroes to acquire skills and seniority. If jobs are hard to get, fair employment laws and other rules with the same objective will probably not be so effective.

Moreover, law alone cannot create a sufficient number of colored persons willing and able to take on better positions. Generations of a depressed standard of living have curtailed the size of this group in the minority population. Consider engineering, a discipline for which a high degree of professional training and interest is necessary. A recent study of Negroes in the engineering field concludes that while discrimination against Negroes in engineering is decreasing, there "is a

[183] REPORT ON FAIR EMPLOYMENT PRACTICES, etc., at 15.

lack of Negro applicants for available engineering jobs, and there are virtually no unemployed Negro engineers." The study states that "the nation-wide shortage of engineers represents an opportunity for an increasing number of Negroes to find employment in the engineering professions," but that "the availability of a supply of trained Negro engineers is necessary before the numbers of Negroes in engineering can be increased considerably." [184] Eli Ginzberg characterized this aspect of the problem generally in striking fashion in *The Negro Potential:*

Consider . . . a young Negro who leaves his father's farm in the deep South and finds a job as a service station helper in Atlanta or as a laundry worker in New York. He is probably on the road to substantial improvement in his economic position, especially if the prosperity of the last fifteen years continues. Still, there are definite limits to what this former farm laborer will be likely to accomplish in his new urban environment. Poorly educated, he will probably be rejected for military service. With no particular aptitudes or skills and with little opportunity for training, he will not rise above a laborer's job. The crucial question is what will happen to his children and his grandchildren.[185]

In considering the law's effect on employment discrimination, we must weigh the multitude of ways in which various discriminations are related, in which the inequalities of schooling, of housing, and of other aspects of life, as well as segregation generally, both North and South, are intertwined. Law, to be sure, has a role to play in abolishing employment bias and the other discrimination and segregation which support it. But, as we have noted before, it can work better if at the same time it helps to produce better schools, better housing, political participation, and the welfare of society on behalf of all.

[184] Kiehl, Preparation of the Negro for his Professional Engineering Opportunities 98–105 (Ph.D. dissertation, Rutgers University School of Education, 1957) (mimeographed). See also Kiehl, *Preparation of the Negro for His Professional Engineering Opportunities*, Negro History Bulletin, Nov., 1957, p. 40. Reitzes makes a similar finding concerning medical school admissions: "the basic problem today is not discriminatory admission policies and/or practices, but rather the preparation of young Negroes for medical school. . . . It is to be expected that as a result of the Supreme Court's decision on segregation in public schools and the general trend toward equal opportunities the group differences will be reduced, but this will not become apparent in the near future," NEGROES AND MEDICINE at xxii–xxiii (1958).
[185] GINZBERG, THE NEGRO POTENTIAL 82–83 (1956).

CHAPTER VII

EDUCATION

Among the interlocking abilities which help to create a personality equipped for success in mid-twentieth-century life, none is more important than education. In the *School Segregation Cases*, Mr. Chief Justice Warren described its significance in America today.

Today, education is perhaps the most important function of state and local governments. Compulsory school attendance laws and the great expenditures for education both demonstrate our recognition of the importance of education to our democratic society. It is required in the performance of our most basic public responsibilities, even service in the armed forces. It is the very foundation of good citizenship. Today it is a principal instrument in awakening the child to cultural values, in preparing him for later professional training, and in helping him to adjust normally to his environment. In these days, it is doubtful that any child may reasonably be expected to succeed in life if he is denied the opportunity of an education.[1]

Few would deny that this is true, and there has been no challenge to the Chief Justice's next sentence: "Such an opportunity, where the state has undertaken to provide it, is a right which must be made available to all on equal terms."[2] Segregationists, however, have insisted that separation and equality are compatible, but the Supreme Court, in the *School Cases*, capped a line of precedents which, since at least 1938, had been pointing to the conclusion that separate public schools could not provide equal protection of the laws.[3]

Segregation, the decision held "generates a feeling of inferiority

---

[1] 347 U.S. 483, 493 (1954).   [2] *Ibid.*

[3] See pp. 32–46 *supra* for the general development and 260–266 *infra* for discussion of the higher education cases, particularly *Sweatt v. Painter* and *McLaurin v. Oklahoma State Regents*, which augured the *School Cases*' result. For an excellent and prescient article on school segregation published shortly before the *School Segregation* decision see Leflar & Davis, *Segregation in the Public Schools—1953*, 67 HARV. L. REV. 377 (1954).

. . . and may affect [Negroes'] hearts and minds in a way unlikely ever to be undone." [4] Apart from the intangibles of schooling, however, there patently never was equality under the separate-but-equal regime. Often the gap was extremely large, though in recent years not as great as before. In vast educational sectors, markedly on the higher levels, Negroes did not have any facilities comparable to those offered whites.[5] At the time the *School Cases* were before the United States Supreme Court, the Department of Health, Education, and Welfare reported to the Department of Justice that to equalize Negro schools

if expenditures per classroom unit are to be continued at current levels for white children, an additional annual expenditure of over 160 million dollars will be required in the states involved and the District of Columbia. In respect to pupil transportation services, the estimated capital outlay is 40 million dollars. And the estimated cost of "equalizing" Negro schools is in excess of two billion dollars.[6]

One effect of the *School* suits has been to stimulate the nourishment of separate schools, those who want to keep segregation hoping that if Negroes are given good, attractive institutions they will not press for desegregation. The new construction often is deep in Negro sections to assure *de facto* separation even where legal segregation is decreed impermissible.[7] But, on the other hand, it has long been recognized that a dual school system is more expensive than a unified one and this factor has encouraged desegregation. In fact, some places have experienced substantial savings under the new order.[8] A further

[4] 347 U.S. at 494.
[5] A thorough analysis of the disparity, which also traces a trend in the direction of equalization, is PIERCE & OTHERS, WHITE AND NEGRO SCHOOLS IN THE SOUTH (1955). For a compendium of comparative Negro-white school statistics as of about the time of the *School Cases* see ASHMORE, THE NEGRO AND THE SCHOOLS (1954), esp. pt. Two; see also the 1935, 1945, and 1947 YEARBOOKS of J. NEGRO EDUCATION; GINZBERG & BRAY, THE UNEDUCATED (1953).
[6] Brief of the United States on the Further Argument of the Questions of Relief, in Brown v. Board of Educ., Nos. 1, 2, 3, 4, 5, U.S. Sup. Ct. Oct. 1954 Term, p. 17.
[7] See, *e.g.*, S.S.N., Feb., 1958, p. 5 (27 million dollar equalization program in Mississippi mostly for Negroes); S.S.N., Jan., 1958, p. 11 (Mississippi appropriation to secure accreditation for Negro colleges); S.S.N., Jan., 1958, p. 5 (in decade Louisiana appropriations for Negro schools up 400%); S.S.N., Jan., 1958, p. 3 (Negro Civic League warns that unless improvements are made they will move to desegregate high school); S.S.N., Dec., 1957, p. 9 (Nashville building 1,000-student school in Negro section); S.S.N., Nov., 1957, p. 15 (two Richmond, Ky., schools being built, one in white area, one in Negro, although single centrally located school would suffice).
[8] On Oklahoma savings see S.S.N., April, 1958, p. 7; Louisville, *id.* at 8; Montgomery County, Md., see S.S.N., Feb., 1958, p. 3; Kentucky counties, *id.* at 14;

financial incentive in the form of federal contributions to desegregating units has been proposed.[9]

In resolving the school segregation complex, racial factors have been found to be intertwined with nonracial ones in still other ways. Among these is the matter of achievement. There is general agreement that there are no innate racial psychological differences, but it is also clear that while on standard educational tests many Negroes achieve higher scores than the average white and many whites achieve lower scores than many Negroes, on the average Negroes have done more poorly in terms of these indicators.[10] Failure to respond well is not attributable to schooling alone—there are also other types of segregation and inequality which bear influence—but a lower testing level obviously reflects deficient education. Indeed, there is evidence that Negro children do better following admission to formerly white schools.[11] At any rate, the fact that Negroes on the average have performed less well than whites has been used as an argument for denying or deferring desegregation, although some systems have treated achievement standards on a nonracial basis, grouping bright, dull, or average Negro and white youngsters with their intellectual peers without regard to race.[12]

The school segregation question also is compounded by housing segregation North and South. Even in Northern communities which may try hard to have not even *de facto* segregated schools, housing patterns may dictate that result, and not an inconsiderable factor is

---

West Virginia economies, S.S.N., June, 1957, p. 3. Maryland desegregation has proceeded fastest where per pupil costs of Negro schools exceeded those of white schools, S.S.N., Aug., 1958, p. 7. Generally Negro population is smallest in these areas.

[9] See pp. 271–272 *infra.*

[10] On the issue of inherent differences see KLINEBERG, RACE AND PSYCHOLOGY (UNESCO publication 1951), which sets forth the generally accepted scientific views. Dissenters have been McGurk, U.S. News and World Report, Sept. 21, 1956, pp. 92–96, and SHUEY, THE TESTING OF NEGRO INTELLIGENCE (1958). But see the rebuttal to McGurk of Long, *The Relative Learning Capacities of Negroes and Whites,* 26 J. NEGRO EDUCATION 121 (1957), and to Shuey of Bond, *Cat on a Hot Tin Roof,* 27 J. NEGRO EDUCATION 519 (1958). On the overlap shown by recent testing see S.S.N., Sept., 1957, p. 16 (Atlanta survey).

[11] See S.S.N., Feb., 1958, p. 12 (Hoxie, Ark., Negro students closing the gaps); N.Y. Times, Sept. 15, 1957, p. 54 (Negroes in District of Columbia testing higher). See Albright, *What Are "Standards"?* S.S.N., June, 1958, pp. 1, 2. See N.Y. Times, March 6, 1959, p. 17 (slight improvement in achievement of both races in Wilmington and Washington).

[12] See N.Y. Times, Oct. 7, 1956, § IV, p. 11 (problem handled in District of Columbia and St. Louis by smaller classes, better supervision, remedial teachers, homogeneous grouping).

the rapid rate at which many urban centers are becoming more colored.[13] In this context a problem arises, as in other areas of law and race relations, from the fact that a permissible standard may cloak a forbidden one. For example, district lines may be racially gerrymandered, but officials may claim that the lines were drawn to avoid traffic hazards or to reduce distances between homes and schools. Moreover, despite apparent freedom of choice, social and economic pressures, sometimes cultivated and aggravated by prosegregationists, may shunt Negroes to segregated schools.

All but a hard core of Southern states, after a string of lawsuits, now permit Negroes to enter formerly white public academies of higher learning, and many private Southern institutions have opened because they no longer fear prosecution. But inferior education of Negroes at lower levels and other social factors have severely cut down the number of Negroes qualified to study at higher levels. The National Scholarship Service and Fund for Negro Students (NSSFNS), a unique organization which seeks to identify and aid as early as possible Negro students with the potential to go on and do well in college, stated in its 1954 report that "the annual number of Negro high school seniors, qualified and prepared under present conditions to do college work in accordance with national standards, would range from 1,200 to 2,000, out of a total of 45,000 Negroes graduating from high schools in those [the Southern] states." The report went on to say that these statistics reflect the ineffectiveness of the Southern dual school system to prepare for college as well as "the serious handicaps which students from the lower socio-economic brackets must overcome." For the North it described a survey of 50 leading Northern high schools with a 30 percent Negro enrollment, pointing out that "Negroes constituted less than $2/10$ of 1% of the graduating seniors who could meet the minimum college entrance and scholarship standards." It concluded: "The causes are complex. They include lack of motivation, family influence, inadequate counseling, economic disadvantagement, and *de facto* segregated schools on the elementary and junior high school levels." [14]

The poverty of Negro education has meant an immense national loss, and a particular loss to the South. During the Second World War more men were rejected for failure to pass Army I.Q. tests primarily

[13] See p. 275 *infra.*
[14] See Plaut, *Racial Integration in Higher Education in the North,* 23 J. NEGRO EDUCATION 310 (1954), which contains much of the same information. The 1956 NSSFNS REPORT finds the present lag to be less than that of 1954.

because of educational deficiency than the nation suffered war casualties. The rejectees reflected heavily the poor Negro showings on the tests.[15] Industrial development and proper preparation for citizenship also lag to the extent that educational standards are depressed.[16] Where the alternatives are, on the one hand, disorder and lack of education, and on the other, education and tranquility, society has a real incentive to attain the latter.

THE LEGAL FRAMEWORK

The equal protection clause of the Fourteenth Amendment has been the fundamental constitutional objection to state-maintained segregated public education. The Fourteenth also outlaws state segregation as a denial of liberty without due process of law. The Fifth Amendment's due process clause has imposed the same standard on the federal government. Because in higher education equality was interpreted as encompassing such intangibles as the opportunity to mingle and exchange ideas with white students, segregation was declared illegal at that level. Because "separate educational facilities are inherently unequal," the Supreme Court, in the *School Segregation Cases,* ruled "that in the field of public education the doctrine of 'separate but equal' has no place." [17] The unsubstantiated social-psychological assumptions of *Plessy v. Ferguson* [18] ("We consider the underlying fallacy of the plaintiff's argument to consist in the assumption that the enforced separation of the two races stamps the colored race with a badge of inferiority") were held inapplicable to public education.

Yet the constitutional rule does not completely dispose of the issue. Because the transition from segregation to desegregation will require complex changes in the communities involved, the Supreme Court framed the "with all deliberate speed" rule of 1955. Moreover, opposition to desegregation has brought about the enactment of a congeries of laws and the invention of other tactics, the ultimate bulwark of which is the threat of closing the public schools and the establishment of so-called private school systems, which raise, of course, questions as to what the "state action" is that the Fourteenth Amendment forbids.

[15] See generally SPECIAL GROUPS, SPECIAL MONOGRAPH NO. 10, SELECTIVE SERVICE SYSTEM, esp. ch. X (1953).
[16] See generally ASHMORE, AN EPITAPH FOR DIXIE (1957); GINZBERG, THE NEGRO POTENTIAL (1956).
[17] 347 U.S. at 495.   [18] 163 U.S. 537, 551 (1896).

The Civil Rights Acts also have some application, as in all areas where constitutional rights are assailed.

In Northern areas the legal arsenal against segregation is more diversified. Statutes and state constitutional provisions expressly forbid school segregation, and some general statutory language also evokes the same result. Moreover, some non-Southern districts have begun to grapple with the problem of affirmative school integration in the face of residential segregation. Some boards have designed and used various techniques to achieve heterogeneous school populations; others have proclaimed integration as a goal. Here, since the fount of doctrine has been almost exclusively legislative, the chief impetus to this sort of integration must be political. Lawyers, however, having done little by way of asking courts for such integration on the basis of existing statutory or constitutional prohibitions, have far from exhausted possible efforts at creative advocacy.

SOUTHERN PUBLIC ELEMENTARY AND HIGH SCHOOLS

The symbol of the desegregation issue has been the Southern elementary and high schools. Indeed, the terms "integration" and "desegregation," if used without further explanation are commonly understood to contemplate a Southern school situation. Even in the North, where the legal situation is different, it has been the Southern school issue that has spurred reexamination of racial patterns.

THE SCHOOL SEGREGATION CASES

The best-known constitutional prescript of this generation is that of *Brown v. Board of Education* (1954), which, resting on the Fourteenth Amendment's equal protection clause, held "that in the field of public education the doctrine of 'separate but equal' has no place. Separate educational facilities are inherently unequal." [19] Less publicized but of wider legal import are the companion words of *Bolling v. Sharpe*

[19] 347 U.S. 483, 495 (1954). The Supreme Court reviewed three district court decisions, Brown v. Board of Educ. of Topeka, 98 F. Supp. 797 (D. Kan. 1951); Briggs v. Elliott, 103 F. Supp. 920 (E.D.S.C. 1952) (involving Clarendon County, S.C.); Davis v. County School Bd. of Prince Edward County, Va., 103 F. Supp. 337 (E.D. Va. 1952); it also passed on the decision of the Supreme Court of Delaware (which ordered desegregation on separate-but-equal grounds) in Gebhart v. Belton, 33 Del. Ch. 144, 91 A.2d 137 (1952).

(1954), the District of Columbia *School Segregation* decision, which involved the Fifth Amendment's due process clause. It said: "Liberty under law extends to the full range of conduct which the individual is free to pursue, and it cannot be restricted except for a proper governmental objective. Segregation in public education is not reasonably related to any proper governmental objective." [20] That Fourteenth Amendment due process covers the same ground was demonstrated in *Cooper v. Aaron* (1958).[21]

But with the delivery of these opinions the Supreme Court requested of counsel further argument on how and when the constitutional principles should be realized. Whatever the implementation decision, it would of course greatly determine the meaning of the substantive rule.

Without waiting for the procedural formula, however, some communities started or completed desegregation. These included Topeka and Washington, D.C., both parties to the cases and bound by their outcome but not forced to proceed until a decree actually issued. The school districts in the Delaware suits desegregated before the cases reached the Supreme Court for the first argument. The state courts had already ordered desegregation because of inequality under separate-but-equal and the Delaware chancellor's decree which ordered desegregation at the trial level was operative because it had not been stayed.[22] Other districts, not involved in the *School Cases*, also started mixing classes before the implementation ruling providing a practical demonstration of how desegregation could be worked out.[23] Most of these had not been sued, although suits were pending in Baltimore which began voluntary desegregation. Wilmington was also indirectly before the courts at the time it began its transition. It was involved in the Delaware cases because plaintiffs in the high school suit emanating from that state attended Howard High School in Wilmington instead of in Clayton, their home community which had no colored high school, and to whose white high school they sought admission. But

[20] 347 U.S. 497, 499 (1954). For a compendium of Southern official recognition that the Supreme Court decision is the law of the land, see McKay, "*With All Deliberate Speed*," *A Study of School Desegregation*, 31 N.Y.U.L. REV. 991, 1039 nn.290–292 (1956); and see *infra* notes 76–78; Missouri repealed Mo. ANN. STATS. § 163.130 (1949) and other provisions requiring school segregation by Mo. L. 1957, p. 452.

[21] 358 U.S. 1, 19 (1958).

[22] See Brown v. Board of Educ., 349 U.S. 294, 299 (1955), *aff'g* Gebhart v. Belton, *supra* note 19.

[23] See appendix C on the course of Southern school desegregation.

Wilmington was not sued, and as the case stood could not have come under a desegregation decree.

THE IMPLEMENTATION DECISION

On May 31, 1955, the Supreme Court delivered its opinion on how and when desegregation would be required. The key features were:

All provisions of federal, state, or local law must yield to this [the holding of the *School Cases*] principle.

Full implementation of these constitutional principles may require solution of varied local school problems.

. . . the courts will require that the defendants make a prompt and reasonable start toward full compliance with our May 17, 1954, ruling.

Once such a start has been made, the courts may find that additional time is necessary to carry out the ruling in an effective manner.

The *burden rests upon the defendants* to establish that such time is necessary in the public interest and is consistent with good faith compliance at the earliest practicable date.

Factors which might be considered in a plea for more time could include: problems of administration, arising from the physical condition of the school plant, the school transportation system, personnel, and revision of school districts and attendance areas into compact units to achieve a nonracial public school admission system; revision of local laws and regulations and the adequacy of defendants' proposed plans to effect the transition. But, the Court added, "it should go without saying that the vitality of these constitutional principles cannot be allowed to yield simply because of disagreement with them." The district courts were directed to "take such proceedings and enter such orders and decrees consistent with [the above] as are necessary and proper to admit to public schools on a racially nondiscriminatory basis *with all deliberate speed* the parties to these cases" (italics added).[24]

Yet "deliberate speed" is a term which, as used in judicial decisions prior to the May 31 opinion, conveyed little specific meaning for school desegregation. In *Virginia v. West Virginia* Justice Holmes used the expression in treating the controversy between those two states over the amount which West Virginia had to pay as its share of the public debt of the original state of Virginia.

[24] Brown v. Board of Educ., *supra* note 22, at 298-301. The excerpts in the text do not entirely follow the order of their presentation in the opinion.

A question like the present should be disposed of without undue delay. But a state cannot be expected to move with the celerity of a private businessman; it is enough if it proceeds, in the language of the English Chancery, with all deliberate speed.[25]

This writer, however, and others whom he knows, have extensively researched the English precedents and have found nothing to elucidate the term's meaning.

The phrase appears in modern Supreme Court opinions, notably, as one commentator has pointed out, in those of Mr. Justice Frankfurter.[26] But these, too, indicate nothing precise for the school problem. Perhaps, then, more light is shed on it by the lines of Francis Thompson's "Hound of Heaven" than by judicial decisions:

> I fled Him, down the nights and down the days;
>   I fled Him, down the arches of the years;
> I fled Him, down the labyrinthine ways
>   Of my own mind; and in the mist of tears
> I hid from Him, and under running laughter.
>   Up vistaed hopes I sped;
>   And shot, precipitated
> Adown Titanic glooms of chasmed fears,
>   From those strong Feet that followed, followed after.
>   But with unhurrying chase,
>   And unperturbèd pace,
>   Deliberate speed, majestic instancy,
>   They beat—and a Voice beat
>   More instant than the Feet—
> "All things betray thee, who betrayest Me." [27]

Suggestively, the Court itself cited no precedents for the meaning of "deliberate speed." It desired, apparently, that court control of

[25] 222 U.S. 17, 19-20 (1911).

[26] Lewis, *An Appreciation of Justice Frankfurter*, N.Y. Times Magazine, Nov. 10, 1957, p. 25. The opinions are Radio Station WOW v. Johnson, 326 U.S. 120, 132 (1945); Addison v. Holly Hill Co., 322 U.S. 607, 619 (1944); Chrysler Corp. v. United States, 316 U.S. 556, 564, 568 (dissenting opinion) (two years delay in bringing suit not "deliberate speed" under the circumstances). I am grateful to Mr. Lewis for pointing out these references.

[27] The allusion was first called to this author's attention by Bickel, *Integration, the Second Year in Perspective*, New Republic, Oct. 8, 1956, pp. 12, 14. Bickel was Mr. Justice Frankfurter's clerk during argument of the *School Cases*. See his *Original Understanding and the Segregation Decision*, 69 HARV. L. REV. 1, n.† (1955). But see Freund, *Storm Over the American Supreme Court*, 21 MODERN L. REV. 345, 351 (1958): "The critical terms of the decree are, of course, 'deliberate speed'—a phrase taken from English Chancery practice and not, as some litterateurs believed, from the refrain in Francis Thompson's 'Hound of Heaven.'"

desegregation be guided by the light of unfolding experience, by the nature of the right and the difficulties tagged as pertinent in the opinion, not by abstract doctrine. Therefore, we must look to local school plans and judicial treatment of them for illumination.

Since May 31, 1955, other school districts have commenced desegregation for the 1955, 1956, 1957, and 1958 school years, some with no case having been filed against them.[28] Certain districts mixed classes or moved in that direction under the prod of legal proceedings; others did so under duress of a decree, but suits or decrees in single districts or situations have elicited action from others elsewhere.[29]

TYPES OF PLANS

So far as time was concerned, large systems which desegregated generally did so rapidly. Baltimore made a complete switch at the beginning of a school year,[30] and so did Louisville.[31] St. Louis high schools all changed during one semester, elementary schools during the next year.[32] Washington, D.C., went through a similar brief, two-stage process,[33] as did Wilmington, Delaware.[34] These quick conversions of big, complex units showed that administrative problems listed in the Supreme Court's opinion ordinarily should not be a serious impediment. Where they have been advanced as reasons for protracted delay, they probably conceal opposition to the idea of desegregation itself—which the Supreme Court has pointed out is not a valid justification for delay.

While many smaller districts which moved from segregation did so just as quickly, e.g., in West Virginia [35] and Missouri,[36] a number devised plans taking from one to twelve years. These included "stair-

[28] For the course of desegregation, see appendix C.

[29] See, e.g., S.S.N. Aug., 1956, p .1.

[30] S.S.N., Oct. 1, 1954, p. 8. See generally WEY & COREY, ACTION PATTERNS IN SCHOOL DESEGREGATION (1959).

[31] S.S.N., July 6, 1955, p. 8, Dec., 1955, p. 10, Sept., 1956, p. 5. See CARMICHAEL & JAMES, THE LOUISVILLE STORY (1957).

[32] S.S.N., Oct. 1, 1954, p. 10. See VALIEN, THE ST. LOUIS STORY (Anti-Defamation League pamphlet 1956).

[33] S.S.N., Sept. 3, 1954, p. 4, Oct., 1957, p. 14.

[34] S.S.N., Sept. 3, 1954, p. 3; see Shagaloff, Desegregation of Public Schools in Delaware, 24 J. NEGRO EDUCATION 188, 192 (1955).

[35] S.S.N., Sept. 3, 1954, p. 14 (Randolph County), Sept., 1957, p. 13 (Hancock County).

[36] S.S.N., Sept., 1955, p. 11 (St. Charles public schools desegregated in 1954, high schools in 1955).

step" plans (*i.e.*, one or more semesters or grades desegregated per year);[37] some commenced racial mixing in certain parts of a district and later moved to others;[38] some were "open-ended" (*i.e.*, desegregation was started, completion was left for later determination);[39] and some plans were selective, admitting certain Negro children on an individual basis to white schools and excluding others.[40] In one Texas community some classes and activities in the school were segregated, others not.[41] Nashville [42] (first grade desegregated in 1957; others to be considered later) and Little Rock [43] ("stair-step" over perhaps six years) were the chief large centers which proceeded slowly. Harford County, Maryland, used a composite of most of these techniques.[44]

General standards of school assignment varied, too, with varying consequences for desegregation. Baltimore continued its historic freedom of choice policy: white children had long been permitted to attend almost any white school they wanted; all children were now given the right to enroll in almost any school without regard to race.[45] Washington, D.C., and Wilmington established zones; all children were sent to schools in their districts.[46] States with pupil assignment laws—of which only North Carolina has produced a scintilla of de-

[37] See, *e.g.*, Charles County, Md. (first grade desegregated in 1956, second grade in 1957), and Howard County, Md. (grades one to five desegregated in 1956, sixth grade in 1957), S.S.N., Sept., 1957, p. 7; Dorchester County, Md., desegregates from top down, S.S.N., Sept., 1957, p. 7; Wyoming County, W. Va. (one grade per year), Sept., 1957, p. 2.

[38] See Moore v. Board of Educ. of Harford County, 146 F. Supp. 91 and 152 F. Supp. 114 (D. Md. 1957) (Harford County, Md.), *aff'd sub nom.* Slade v. Board of Educ. of Harford County, 252 F.2d 291 (4th Cir. 1958), *cert. denied*, 357 U.S. 906 (1958).

[39] *E.g.*, Nashville, see note 42 *infra*.

[40] See, *e.g.*, the "selective integration" approach of Montgomery County, Md., S.S.N., Nov., 1956, p. 4. Little Rock in fact proceeded in this manner, too, although the terms of the plan involved no such individuation.

[41] S.S.N., Feb., 1958, p. 3 (Dimmit, Texas).

[42] S.S.N., Aug. 19, 1957, p. 6, Sept., 1957, p. 3. See Kelly v. Board of Educ. of the City of Nashville, 2 R.R.L.R. 21 (1957); the same case at later stages is Nos. 13,748, 13,749, 6th Cir., June 17, 1959 (upholding twelve-year plan).

[43] For the Little Rock program see Aaron v. Cooper, 143 F. Supp. 855 (E.D. Ark. 1956), *aff'd*, 243 F.2d 361 (8th Cir. 1957); for later legal developments in Little Rock see 2 R.R.L.R. 929-965 (1957), part of which is officially reported as Aaron v. Cooper, 156 F. Supp. 220 (E.D. Ark. 1957). The Little Rock matter culminated in Cooper v. Aaron 358 U.S. 1 (1958); a further development was Aaron v. Cooper, 261 F.2d 97 (8th Cir. 1958) (enjoins leasing public schools to private corporation). See 169 F. Supp. 325 (E.D. Ark. 1959) (on remand); and see Aaron v. McKinley, *supra* note 126.

[44] See note 38 *supra* and quotation from the opinion *infra* pp. 223-224.

[45] See Jones, *City Limits*, in WITH ALL DELIBERATE SPEED 82 (Shoemaker ed. 1957).

[46] S.S.N., Sept. 3, 1954, p. 4 (D.C.); Shagaloff, *supra* note 34 (Wilmington).

segregation—require those who want change to apply specifically for transfer, or else (by regulation or custom) to continue attending the schools they have been attending. New Negro registrants are either referred to Negro schools or it is made clear, perhaps informally, that they are expected to attend these schools unless transfers are granted. Paducah, Kentucky, has an unusual plan: it permits free transfers but names some schools "Negro teacher schools" and so staffs them, while others are called "white teacher schools." Although no overt compulsion is applied, it is understood that Negroes will apply to Negro teacher schools, and that is what has occurred almost entirely.[47] One aim of a plan like this one is to enlist Negro teachers behind segregation for fear of losing their pupils. Apart from officially naming schools in this manner, administering them as Negro or white teacher schools tends to create the same result where there is pupil choice in school assignment. Some of the most thorough integration has taken place where teachers, too, have been mixed [48]—although, obviously, there is no clear cause and effect relationship. A willingness to integrate teachers shows a favorable disposition towards desegregation generally.

Desegregation in many instances has not meant an end to all-Negro schools. Where district lines are drawn on a neighborhood basis some remain entirely colored because of the composition of the surrounding homes (a growing focus of attention in the North and one bound to become important in the South). In Baltimore, where there are no lines,

[47] S.S.N., April, 1956, p. 16. Cf. Jefferson v. McCart, 3 R.R.L.R. 1154 (E.D. Okla. 1958) (injunction sought against Negro principal, to restrain from persuading Negro parents to send their children to his school instead of to desegregated school; denied).

[48] See generally N.Y. Times, Oct. 21, 1956, p. 54 (survey of Negro teachers conducting mixed classes); S.S.N., March, 1958, p. 12 (Wilmington: ⅛ of Negro teachers in white schools); S.S.N., Dec., 1957, p. 16 (St. Louis elementary school with 80 percent Negro and 20 percent white students has a faculty which is half Negro, half white); S.S.N., Oct., 1957, p. 13 (Kansas City has mixed faculties at 12 schools).

Dr. John W. Davis, former president of West Virginia State College, and now director of the Department of Teacher Information and Security at the NAACP Legal Defense and Educational Fund, has informed the author that the greatest difficulty in maintaining employment or status during desegregation has been experienced by Negro principals and supervisors. Upon merger or abolition of schools it is almost invariably the white principal who assumes charge. Negro elementary school teachers in Oklahoma have been the only ones to lose their jobs in numbers, occasioned by the closing of numerous small Negro schools. Most have, however, been absorbed in other state employment. In Oklahoma and West Virginia, Dr. Davis states, projected litigation, which never came to trial, probably spurred absorption of Negro teachers. Elsewhere, teacher tenure laws, and, more important, the teacher shortage, has prevented any appreciable displacement of Negro teachers upon desegregation.

the distance between the heart of Negro and white neighborhoods often is so great that many schools are populated by one race only. And apart from geography the social inertia of segregation keeps many Negro children where they have been. As the past's hold weakens, however, desegregation increases (the number of Baltimore Negro children in formerly white schools has about trebled since desegregation began).[49] Where school boards have desegregated but are not cordial to the idea, this, of course, will discourage Negroes from taking advantage of the opportunity. They may be made to feel unwelcome, for example, by refusing to allow them to ride on the "white" school bus.[50] Especially where specific transfers are required, the formerly all-colored schools remain the same while some Negroes go into "white" schools (it is almost unheard of for whites to apply to institutions formerly limited to colored children, although on the college level two-way desegregation has occurred).

Various forms of an option plan—often not expressly derived from statute—have been used in some jurisdictions,[51] although others have eschewed it.[52] While such a privilege may be administered entirely objectively, it may also have an open or well-understood racial basis, *i.e.*, to permit students to select public schools because of their classmates' race. In the District of Columbia, for example, transfers for "psychological" reasons have been thought to hide racial animosities.[53] To the extent that such plans tend to perpetuate segregation, or where they

[49] The number of Negro pupils in former white schools increased from 4,601 in the fall of 1955 to 14,826 in the fall of 1957, S.S.N., April, 1958, p. 16. But 80% of the Negro children continue to attend all-colored schools, S.S.N., Feb., 1958, p. 13.

[50] Hart v. Board of Educ. of Charles County, 164 F. Supp. 501 (D. Md. 1958). Sometimes an applicant may be deterred by the need to face an interview with school officials to secure desegregation. *Cf.* Holt v. Raleigh City Bd. of Educ., 265 F.2d 95, 96 (4th Cir. 1959). See also Joyner v. Board of Educ., 244 N.C. 164, 92 S.E.2d 795 (1956); Groves v. Board of Educ. of St. Mary's County, 164 F. Supp. 621, 622 (D. Md. 1958), *aff'd*, 261 F.2d 527 (4th Cir. 1958). See also S.S.N., April, 1958, p. 2 (Cabell and Raleigh counties, W. Va., boards' attitude discourages desegregation).

[51] On Wilmington, Del., see S.S.N., March, 1958, p. 12; Louisville, see 1 R.R.L.R. 779 (1956). For Louisville's transfer form see S.S.N., April, 1956, p. 16; for a description of the Louisville free-choice program in operation see Jones, *supra* note 45, at 83; CARMICHAEL & JAMES, *op. cit. supra* note 31, at 84; concerning Topeka see Brown v. Board of Educ. of Topeka, 139 F. Supp. 468, 470 (D. Kan. 1955). In Oklahoma City pupils may transfer to schools where their race predominates, S.S.N., Jan., 1958, p. 10; Fort Smith, Ark. (similar), S.S.N., Sept., 1957, p. 6. For Nashville see Kelly v. Board of Educ. of the City of Nashville, *supra* note 42.

[52] See VALIEN, *op. cit. supra* note 32, at 28.   [53] S.S.N., Nov., 1957, p. 11.

do not permit a Negro child the same transfer privileges that are given to white pupils similarly situated,[54] their constitutionality may be questioned.

Actually, where allowed, relatively few white children have picked up the option.[55] The United States district court which received the Topeka case on remand held that it "does not look with favor upon such a rule," [56] but allowed options for the time being.

COURT TREATMENT OF PLANS

The Supreme Court itself to the time of this writing has elucidated the standards of its May, 1955, opinion only in *Cooper v. Aaron* (1958), the Little Rock case, which dealt chiefly with the significance of violent opposition and the state's recalcitrance. The Court held:

Of course, in many locations, obedience to the duty of desegregation would require the immediate general admission of Negro children, otherwise qualified as students for their appropriate classes, at particular schools. . . . [But] a District Court, after analysis of the relevant factors (which, of course, excludes hostility to racial desegregation), might conclude that justification exists for not requiring the present nonsegregated admission of all qualified Negro children. In such circumstances, however, the courts should scrutinize the program of the school authorities to make sure that they had developed arrangements pointed toward the earliest practicable completion of desegregation, and had taken appropriate steps to put their program into effective operation. It was made plain that delay in any guise in order to deny the constitutional rights of Negro children could not be countenanced, and that only a prompt start, diligently and earnestly pursued, to eliminate racial segregation from the public schools could constitute good faith compliance. State authorities were thus duty bound to devote every effort toward initiating desegregation and bringing about the elimination of racial discrimination in the public school system.[57]

The Little Rock case, therefore, states that there is an affirmative duty on school boards to go forward.

[54] See S.S.N., Nov., 1957, p. 2 (Nashville: 11 Negroes in white areas stay in white schools, 105 transfer out); on how the Little Rock plan, including its transfer features, was devised to capitalize on social factors to perpetuate as much segregation as possible see S.S.N., May, 1957, pp. 2-3. See CARMICHAEL & JAMES, *op. cit. supra* note 31, at 90, concerning Louisville ("but most of them [the prosegregation parents] generally eased whatever their objections were by requesting transfers for their children to schools where they hoped there would be few or no members of the other race").

[55] See, *e.g.*, Wilmington's experience, S.S.N., March, 1958, p. 12 (of the thousands of requests that could have been filed, fewer than one hundred actually received).

[56] 139 F. Supp. at 470.   [57] 358 U.S. 1, 7 (1958).

On this point, some district and appellate tribunals have been quite specific. A number have been highly intolerant of procrastination. In the Fourth Circuit, federal district courts in West Virginia have ordered desegregation by the school term, or year following trial, whereas school boards' plans called for waiting up to perhaps twelve years. Reasons advanced for delay had included overcrowding, fiscal problems, and the need for time for consideration.[58]

The Sixth Circuit Court of Appeals rejected a 1954 plea of an Ohio board to defer desegregation until 1957 when a building program would alleviate classroom shortages.[59] It required immediate admittance of Negro children then not in school (some had refused to attend Jim Crow schools) and complete desegregation by the next school year. Judge Potter Stewart (now on the United States Supreme Court), concurring, wrote that "overcrowded classrooms, however, are unfortunately not peculiar to Hillsboro, and the avoidance alone of somewhat overcrowded classrooms cannot justify segregation of school children solely because of the color of their skins." [60] Ohio's own law forbids segregation, but the court of appeals relied chiefly on the Federal Constitution.

In the case of Tennessee's colleges the same court rejected a five-

[58] Shedd v. Board of Educ. of the County of Logan, 1 R.R.L.R. 521, 522 (1956) (district court rejected plan, alleging overcrowding, to desegregate grades one to six by the next term and defer further desegregation to an indeterminate date which, plaintiffs charged, S.S.N., April, 1956, p. 14, might be 10 to 12 years distant; for the September semester high school classes were not to be disturbed; if additional space became available students were to be admitted without regard to race, first-come-first-served. At the spring semester segregation was to be eliminated "by the establishment of attendance areas and [by] . . . permitting students from those areas to attend the schools that are convenient to those areas." Complete high school desegregation was postponed because of a building program; to change earlier would have meant two mass transfers in a year). See also Pierce v. Board of Educ. of Cabell County (S.D.W. Va. 1956) (unreported), discussed in S.S.N., June, 1956, p. 11, Nov., 1956, p. 10 (plan takes from 1954 through 1957; suit filed; defendants agree to complete desegregation by next school term; case remains on docket). Taylor v. Board of Educ. of the County of Raleigh, 1 R.R.L.R. 321 (S.D.W. Va. 1956) (board agreed to abolish segregation at such time as the court might direct. It ordered complete desegregation by next September and, prior to that, admission without regard to race of students for whom there might be room; no injunction entered; jurisdiction retained). See Dunn v. Board of Educ. of Greenbrier, 1 R.R.L.R. 319 (S.D.W. Va. 1956) (similar to *Taylor*); Anderson v. Board of Educ. of the County of Mercer, 1 R.R.L.R. 892 (S.D.W. Va. 1956) (complete desegregation by September; consent order entered).

[59] Clemons v. Board of Educ. of Hillsboro, 228 F.2d 853 (6th Cir. 1956), *cert. denied*, 350 U.S. 1006 (1956).

[60] *Id.* at 858, 860.

year "stair-step" plan, reaffirming that race may not be used to remedy overcrowding.[61] A number of Kentucky cases in that circuit have taken a similar expeditious approach.[62]

The Fourth Circuit has held that the "stair-step" plans of Harford and St. Mary's counties, Maryland, do not justify excluding a qualified individual applicant and has required that such persons be admitted notwithstanding a more gradual schedule applicable to the school population at large.[63] This issue has not arisen elsewhere.

But at the same time, the Little Rock plan (six-year or more "stair-step") was approved by the Court of Appeals for the Eighth Circuit.[64] A host of administrative problems, undoubtedly common in the large cities which desegregated quickly, were nonetheless held to justify delay.

The Fourth Circuit has approved the Harford County, Maryland, plan for desegregation, resting on Judge Thomsen's opinion below which held:

Eleven out of the eighteen elementary schools in Harford County will be completely desegregated in September, 1957, three months from now. Three more will be completely desegregated in 1958, and the remaining

[61] Booker v. Tennessee Bd. of Educ., 240 F.2d 689 (6th Cir. 1957), *cert. denied*, 353 U.S. 965 (1957). The university at Memphis had not, by 1959, admitted Negroes, and delays at the district court level prompted plaintiffs to mandamus the judge for an early hearing, which was denied in Prater v. Boyd, 263 F.2d 788 (6th Cir. 1959).

[62] See Willis v. Walker, 136 F. Supp. 177, 181 (W.D. Ky. 1955) ("no white children either before or after the application for admission of the plaintiffs, were denied admission. . . . good faith alone is not the test. There must be 'compliance at the earliest practicable date.'" Defendants had no definite plans for desegregation, pleading that they were planning construction to alleviate overcrowding). See also Mitchell v. Pollock, 2 R.R.L.R. 305 (W.D. Ky. 1957) (12-year "stair-step" plan disapproved; "stair-step" scheme terminating in 1960 substituted; relocation would not involve too much difficulty; primary grounds for delay were social problems; immediate desegregation ordered). In Gordon v. Collins, 2 R.R.L.R. 304 (W.D. Ky. 1957), the court rejected alleged reasons for delay which included overcrowding, transportation difficulties, reallocation problems, need for time to study the problem, unfavorable social conditions (this position of defendants is unreported); thereupon they came into court with a plan for immediate desegregation; the court approved. Similar is Garnett v. Oakley, 2 R.R.L.R. 303 (W.D. Ky. 1957) (plan was for 9th to 12th grades to be desegregated between 1957 and 1959; the court's order is unreported). See Dishman v. Archer, 2 R.R.L.R. 597 (E.D. Ky. 1957) (plan was for grades nine to twelve to be desegregated in 1957, for remainder, wait-and-see; complete integration ordered beginning Sept., 1957; immediate admission, Jan., 1957, denied; position of defendants unreported).

[63] Moore v. Board of Educ. of Harford County, *supra* note 38; Groves v. Board of Educ. of St. Mary's County, *supra* note 50.

[64] Aaron v. Cooper, 243 F.2d 361 (8th Cir. 1957).

four in 1959. The reason for the delay in desegregating the seven schools is that the county board and superintendent believe that the problems which accompany desegregation can best be solved in schools which are not over-crowded and where the teachers are not handicapped by having too many children in one class. That factor would not justify unreasonable delay; but in the circumstances of this case it justifies the one or two years delay in desegregating the seven schools. . . .

With respect to the high schools, other factors are involved. . . . A Negro child transferring to an upper grade at this time would not have the benefit of older brothers, sisters or cousins already in the school, or parents, relatives or friends who have been active in the P.T.A. High school teachers generally, with notable exceptions, are less "pupil conscious" and more "subject conscious" than teachers trained for elementary grades, and be-cause each teacher has the class for only one or two subjects, are less likely to help in the readjustment. The Harford County Board had sound reasons for making the transition on a year to year basis, so that most Negro children will have a normal high school experience, entering in the seventh grade and continuing through the same school.

While the court "was unwilling . . . to approve a plan which would prevent all Negro children now in the sixth grade or above from ever attending a desegregated high school," it felt that this flaw was met by the provision for selective certification of Negro children, based on qualification by examination, interview, and so forth, for admission to any grade in the white high schools notwithstanding the "stair-step." [65]

An open-end plan in Nashville, commencing with the first grade, and deferring other changes for an indeterminate time was approved as to its beginning. However, the defendants were required to make more definite provisions for the future. They came back with a twelve-year "stair-step" program which the district court approved and which the court of appeals affirmed.[66]

COURT ACTION WHERE THERE HAVE BEEN NO PLANS

Where defendants have prepared no plans for desegregation, the question facing the courts is more one of "prompt and reasonable start" than of "deliberate speed." As we approach a plateau in the

[65] 152 F. Supp. at 118–119.
[66] Kelly v. Board of Educ. of the City of Nashville, 2 R.R.L.R. 21 (1957), 159 F. Supp. 272 (M.D. Tenn. 1958); see also note 42 *supra* (court of appeals opinion). A similar twelve-year plan for the state of Delaware was approved in Evans v. Buchanan, 172 F. Supp. 508 (D. Del. 1959).

rate of desegregation with only the hard-core states refusing to move, the *start* rather than the full realization becomes a more pressing legal issue for the time being.

The Supreme Court of Kansas in 1957 ordered a noncomplying district to cease maintaining a colored school by the beginning of the next school year.[67] In cases involving Arlington, Charlottesville, Newport News, Norfolk, and Front Royal, all in Virginia, district judges have ordered desegregation by the start of the next school year or term and the court of appeals has affirmed.[68] The trial judges noted defiance at the state level and total refusal to make any progress, but the memorandum opinion of one judge stated that the court would reconsider the immediacy of his order if defendants would come in with a concrete plan to desegregate.[69] The judges who sat on each case observed that children were only to be assigned without regard to race and that nonracial administrative remedies and transfer procedures remained valid, that is, the normal rules which traditionally have governed school administration could still legally be applied. Therefore, the courts implicitly pointed out, geographical zoning, if not gerrymandered, or other regular standards might keep many Negroes from formerly white schools. But, of course, any fair system would almost inevitably require at least some desegregation in fact. When the Virginia boards did nothing, the courts, in some instances made individual assignments themselves. The effective dates of orders in the Virginia litigation, which had been stayed pending appeals, finally arrived, and the orders were reinstituted; when further stays were denied some schools were closed pursuant to state law to avoid desegregation.[70]

[67] Cameron v. Board of Educ. of the City of Bonner Springs, 182 Kan. 39, 318 P.2d 988 (1957).

[68] Thompson v. County School Bd. of Arlington County, 144 F. Supp. 239 (E.D. Va. 1956), aff'd, 240 F.2d 59 (4th Cir. 1957), cert. denied, 353 U.S. 910 (1957), supplemental decree granted, 159 F. Supp. 567 (E.D. Va. 1957), aff'd, 252 F.2d 929 (4th Cir. 1958), cert. denied, 356 U.S. 958 (1958); Allen v. School Bd. of the City of Charlottesville, 1 R.R.L.R. 886 (1956), aff'd, 240 F.2d 59 (4th Cir. 1957), cert. denied, 353 U.S. 910 (1957); Adkins v. School Bd. of the City of Newport News, 148 F. Supp. 430 (E.D. Va. 1957), aff'd, 246 F.2d 325 (4th Cir. 1957), cert. denied, 355 U.S. 855 (1957). Beckett v. School Bd. of the City of Norfolk, 2 R.R.L.R. 337, 340 (E.D. Va. 1957).
On the Arlington board's imposition of a pupil assignment test see Hamm v. County School Bd. of Arlington, 263 F.2d 226 (4th Cir. 1959) (order to admit four of twenty-six applicants affirmed).

[69] Beckett v. School Bd. of the City of Norfolk, *supra* note 68, at 340.

[70] See pp. 240–243 *infra*, on school closings, where this aspect of the Virginia cases is more fully discussed. The schools reopened pursuant to court order follow-

After having been reversed twice by the Fifth Circuit Court of Appeals for failing to require desegregation, a Texas federal district court ordered Dallas completely desegregated by the forthcoming mid-winter term. This ruling was then reversed because the court had held no hearing on the time and manner of transition.[71]

Undoubtedly the most extensive desegregation order has been entered by the United States District Court for the District of Delaware. Under state law the state Board of Education has supervisory power over local districts, and the state Supreme Court in an earlier case had held that the districts might not proceed until the state board approved their plans. On one hand, the board ordered submission of plans, but without result. On the other hand, the districts were reluctant to move until a uniform plan was formulated by the state board, some taking the position that they did not want to undertake action shunned by their neighbors. The federal district court ordered the state board to submit within sixty days a desegregation plan providing for state-wide integration for the fall of 1957.[72] The Third Circuit Court of Appeals affirmed. The United States Supreme Court has denied certiorari. But on remand to the district court a twelve-year "stair-step" plan was approved. It is now on appeal.

In contrast to the above there are district courts in South Carolina and Virginia, which, on remand of the original school cases, merely ordered desegregation from and after the time that a plan should be prepared for that purpose.[73] But the Virginia ruling was reversed by

---

ing James v. Almond, 170 F. Supp. 331 (E.D. Va. 1959); James v. Duckworth, 170 F. Supp. 342 (E.D. Va. 1959); Harrison v. Day, 106 S.E.2d 636 (Va. 1959).

[71] Borders v. Rippy, 2 R.R.L.R. 985 (1957), rev'd, 250 F.2d 690 (5th Cir. 1957).

[72] Evans v. Members of the State Bd. of Educ., 145 F. Supp. 873 (D. Del. 1956), 149 F. Supp. 376, 379 (D. Del. 1957); Evans v. Buchanan, 152 F. Supp. 886, 888, 889 (D. Del. 1957), aff'd, 256 F.2d 688 (3d Cir. 1958), cert. denied, 000 U.S. 000 (1958). The relationship between state and local authority, particularly vis-à-vis desegregation, is also described in Steiner v. Simmons, 111 A.2d 574 (Del. Sup. Ct. 1955) (Milford's admission of Negro students without state board approval violates state law). The decision on remand is Evans v. Buchanan, 172 F. Supp. 508 (D. Del. 1959).

[73] Briggs v. Elliott, 132 F. Supp. 776 (E.D.S.C. 1955); Davis v. County School Bd. of Prince Edward County, 1 R.R.L.R. 82 (1956); see same case at a later stage, 149 F. Supp. 431 (E.D. Va. 1957), rev'd sub nom. Allen v. County School Bd., 249 F.2d 462 (4th Cir. 1957), cert. denied, 353 U.S. 953 (1958), on remand sub nom. Allen v. County School Bd., 164 F. Supp. 786 (E.D. Va. 1958), rev'd, 27 U.S.L. Week 2565 (4th Cir. May 5, 1959) (opinion states that district court shall require exhaustion of administrative remedies).

the Fourth Circuit for holding that defendants need make no progress because of community opposition. The district judge then ordered desegregation to commence within seven years, and that ruling was upset too. The Fourth Circuit's requirement that defendants move undoubtedly governs South Carolina (which is in the same circuit) too, but plaintiffs there have made no other application for relief since the Supreme Court decision.

The New Orleans desegregation order stated that desegregation would not be "ordered overnight, or even in a year or more," although defendants should take steps in that direction.[74] Instead of yielding, the defendants appealed twice to the United States Supreme Court. The first time they raised issues as to whether administrative remedies had been exhausted, claimed that the suit was not a true class action, and that suit against the state is barred by the Eleventh Amendment. The second time they urged that the order was defective because plaintiffs had not posted a bond. All of these contentions have been rejected. Similarly, a suit involving Houston in the same circuit produced an order no more definite than to desegregate "with all deliberate speed." [75]

No matter what the ultimate definitive meaning of "deliberate speed" may be—and it probably will never be defined with precision—South-wide desegregation will be gradual. Except in situations such as Delaware's, decrees will not cover more than a school district or a county at a time. Desegregation will, therefore, be paced by the rate of voluntary obedience of school officials and the celerity of deprived Negroes to claim their constitutional rights. Both of those responses are governed at least as much by social as by legal forces. But law could affect the social situation by lending encouragement and protection, by absorbing the economic burden of implementation, and by consistently making clear the vitality and urgency of the rights involved.

[74] Bush v. Orleans Parish School Bd., 138 F. Supp. 337, 341 (E.D. La. 1956), aff'd, 242 F.2d 156 (5th Cir. 1957), cert. denied, 354 U.S. 921 (1957); on the second appeal see 252 F.2d 253 (5th Cir. 1958), cert. denied, 354 U.S. 921 (1958). On defendant's further motion to dismiss see 163 F. Supp. 701 (E.D. La. 1958) (denied). Other Louisiana suits await the outcome of Bush, Davis v. East Baton Rouge Parish School Bd., Angel v. State Bd. of Educ., see S.S.N., Nov., 1957, p. 16.
[75] Ross v. Rogers, 2 R.R.L.R. 1114 (S.D. Tex. 1957).

ATTACKS ON DESEGREGATION IN STATE COURTS

In Arkansas, the District of Columbia, Maryland, North Carolina, Tennessee, and Texas some who favor segregation have turned to their state courts for rulings that desegregation is illegal.[76] All of these efforts have been rebuffed at the outset except in Arkansas, where a state court of equity enjoined Little Rock's School Board from carrying out the plan approved by the federal courts. Immediately, however, the federal court enjoined state interference in the national legal domain.[77]

Apart from this, the desegregation issue has come to state courts chiefly on the question of the validity of bond issues or appropriations for nonsegregated schools. While a variety of motives may prompt such litigation, desegregation would have a harder road to travel if no public money could be spent for mixed schools. Efforts to make desegregation responsible for bond issue failures and, thereby, for spiking education generally are akin to the school closing laws in motivation. The state courts, however, have rejected all such efforts against bond floatations and public expenditures.[78]

[76] Heintz v. Board of Educ. of Howard County, 213 Md. 340, 131 A.2d 869 (1957) (U.S. Constitution controls); Burr v. Sondheim, 1 R.R.L.R. 309 (Baltimore Super. Ct. 1954) (similar); Sabine v. Sharpe, 1 R.R.L.R. 305 (E.D.D.C. 1954) (Supreme Court's decision may be put into effect pending final decision on implementation); McKinney v. Blankenship, 154 Tex. 632, 282 S.W. 2d 691 (1955) (segregation provisions of state law voided by Supreme Court decision); Applications for Reassignment of Pupils, 247 N.C. 413, 101 S.E.2d 359 (1958) (remedy of dissenting white child is to apply for reassignment for himself, not challenge the assignments of Negroes); Roy v. Brittain, 297 S.W.2d 72 (Tenn. 1956) (Tennessee segregation laws invalidated by *School Segregation Cases;* state funds may be spent for nonsegregated schools).

[77] Thomason v. Cooper, 2 R.R.L.R. 933 (Pulaski County, Ark., Ch. 1957) (desegregation enjoined for the purpose of preserving the peace); the United States District Court enjoined enforcement of this decree in Aaron v. Cooper, 2 R.R.L.R. 935 (E.D. Ark. 1957), *aff'd sub nom.* Thomason v. Cooper, 254 F.2d 808 (8th Cir. 1958).

[78] Board of Pub. Instruction of Manatee County, Florida v. Florida, 75 So. 2d 832 (1954) (school bond issue not invalid because issued in contemplation of segregated schools); Florida v. Special Tax School Dist. No. 1 of Dade County, 86 So. 2d 419 (1956) (segregation question has no place in discussion of bond issue; desegregation will require more and better schools); Constantian v. Anson County, 244 N.C. 221, 93 S.E.2d 163 (1956) (bond issue valid; United States Constitution invalidates North Carolina provisions requiring segregation); Matlock v. Board of County Comm'rs of Wagoner County, 281 P.2d 169 (Okla. 1955) (school bond issue found valid); School Bd. of Hanover County v. Shelton, 198 Va. 226, 193 S.E.2d 469 (1956) (bond issue valid); and see Note, *Effect of Desegregation on Public School Bonds in the Southern States,* 10 VAND. L. REV. 580 (1957). See also Davidson v. Cope, 1 R.R.L.R. 523 (Davidson County, Tenn.,

COMMUNITY HOSTILITY

The Supreme Court's implementation decision barred disagreement as grounds for devitalizing the constitutional principles of the *Brown* decision. The Little Rock decision adhered to this principle under the most extreme provocation, for the Court upheld desegregation notwithstanding a threat, later executed, to close the schools. The Court's position was entirely consistent with precedents of long standing.[79] Nevertheless, at least one commentator has written that judicial decisions in the desegregation field "manifest sub silentio consideration of hostile community attitudes." [80] Argument of this sort takes color from the fact that cases in which there has been failure to progress have emanated from communities like Clarendon County, South Carolina, Prince Edward County, Virginia, Houston, and New Orleans and that slow-moving plans, which have been judicially approved, have come from places like Little Rock and Nashville.

But even an a priori appraisal finds notable inconsistencies in seeking support for such a rationale. Some of the Virginia cases have required immediacy in the face of "massive resistance." On the other hand one of the Maryland suits (Harford County) countenanced a plan of perhaps six years in a state which stands squarely behind the law. Moreover, the courts have not backed down in the face of actual violence. In cases involving Little Rock and Hoxie, Arkansas, Clay and Sturgis, Kentucky, and Clinton, Tennessee, where there had been mob action, litigation concluded by ruling with the Negro applicants. Suits by prosegregationist groups in Baltimore and Washington which accompanied rioting there failed.[81] A legal realist viewing the outcomes apart from the judicial reasoning underlying them would conclude that violence did not influence the results. In two cases, the *Lucy* suit

---

Ch. 1956) (legislature impliedly authorized spending public funds for non-segregated colleges).

[79] See Buchanan v. Warley, 245 U.S. 60 (1917); Youngstown Sheet & Tube Co. v. Sawyer, 343 U.S. 579 (1952); *Ex parte* Endo, 323 U.S. 283 (1944); Morgan v. Virginia, 328 U.S. 373 (1946).

[80] Note, 71 HARV. L. REV. 486, 490–491 (1958).

[81] On Little Rock, see note 43 *supra;* on Hoxie, see Brewer v. Hoxie School Dist., 238 F.2d 91 (8th Cir. 1956); on Clay, Ky., see Gordon v. Collins, *supra* note 62; on Sturgis, Ky., see Garnett v. Oakley, *ibid.;* on Clinton, Tenn., see Kasper v. Brittain, 245 F.2d 92 (6th Cir. 1957), *cert. denied,* 355 U.S. 834 (1957). On Baltimore, see Burr v. Sondheim, *supra* note 76; on Washington, D.C., see Sabine v. Sharpe, *ibid.*

involving the University of Alabama and the *Steiner* [82] case, which concerned Milford, Delaware, the results at least did not favor the colored students. But the reasoning in these cases hardly catered to the disorder. While in the sense that they achieved a result which the rioters would have approved these decisions can be scored as acknowledging lawlessness, the grounds of the opinions offer explanations for the results at least as plausible.

In order to understand the uneven course of judicially approved desegregation two important factors must be weighed. These are the traditional predisposition of courts to accept administrative determinations, unless they are overbalanced by evidence, and the uneven manner in which different parties have pressed for final relief. These matters, of course, may be somewhat related to community hostility, but hardly in a sense which permits a simple generalization that courts have sub silentio based their decisions on such attitudes. So far as the role of administrative determinations is concerned, it seems obvious that an effort to pacify the opposition is what has slowed school boards in many places. In some suits the boards have not argued that they must acquiesce in opposition (although this is what probably concerned them), but have urged the need for time to work out "administrative" problems. Even where opposition is a ground of argument, "administration" also is advanced. So far, it appears that in no case approving a lengthy plan did the plaintiffs put on opposing evidence to show that the alleged administrative grounds were insufficient. In the Little Rock case no such evidence was put on at all. In the Harford County case some indication that less time was needed for administration was elicited through cross examination and exhibits prepared by the school board. Yet, the court deferred to the board's administrative determination, not looking behind it. We may ask thus whether the courts could not override the evidence of school boards that six or more years are needed for school desegregation by taking judicial notice of the fact that large, complicated school systems have desegregated in far less time. Probably yes, and if there has been a silent recognition of hostility, it has assumed the form of refusal to take such notice. But in view of the customary deference to administrative findings this is hardly the same as saying that the courts have surreptitiously based their decisions on hostility. In the Delaware case, *Evans v. Buchanan*, a twelve-year plan was approved despite testimony of of-

[82] On *Lucy*, see 2 R.R.L.R. 350 (N.D. Ala. 1957); on *Steiner* see note 72, *supra*.

ficials about how some Delaware districts had desegregated promptly. The court referred to community hostility. That ruling now is on appeal.

The second factor, the varying militancy of different Negro litigants may be related to hostility, although prediction concerning the nature of the relationship would be hazardous. Hostility could cause the minority group to tread lightly; but it also could, as in Virginia, reinforce its resolve. At any rate, Negroes in Clarendon County, New Orleans, Dallas, and Houston have moved for a deadline in a most deliberate way. Now, however, the Texas and New Orleans plaintiffs have moved for further relief. Undoubtedly, one reason for the delay has been a desire to await the unfolding of precedent in Virginia, the focus of the legal struggle. Therefore, it appears that no trustworthy generalization can be made concerning the inner workings of the judicial mind with respect to hostility until a number of cases present a full record of evidence concerning administrative problems in the district under examination and the Negro community presses for a speedy desegregation based on that evidence. There have not yet been cases on which to make the judgment. Even then, as in any case, it would be risky to try to divine hidden reasoning. Until evidence to the contrary appears the governing law is that of the Little Rock case: "hostility to desegregation" is not a relevant factor. And in view of the unanimity and forthrightness of that decision it is unlikely that the Supreme Court will retreat from it.

RESISTANCE LAWS

States opposing desegregation have embraced various statutes which they hope will slow or prevent racial mixing in the schools. These include open or thinly veiled reaffirmance of segregation rules, pupil assignment statutes with standards which could conceal segregation, administrative remedies which may be burdensome to exhaust, projected private school arrangements to avoid Fourteenth Amendment control of state action, threats to close schools, abolition of compulsory attendance rules, and like measures. Connected, too, is the large body of legislation designed to impede civil rights proponents from encouraging or implementing desegregation, the affirmations of interposition, nullification, and "police power," which, it is hoped, will insulate state rules from federal control. The combination of measures adopted—differing from state to state—bears on the legality of specific laws, showing perhaps the legal impossibility of desegregation under state law, or indicating a prosegregation policy which coupled with vague assignment standards would permit its retention under other alleged justifications.[83]

The enactments of some states are clear in announcing a resolve to keep pre-1954 racial groupings intact: Georgia, Louisiana, Mississippi, South Carolina, and Virginia, by specific statutory provision, have refused to permit nonsegregated public schools to come into being.[84] Minor supplements to such over-all legislation have been a few laws forbidding interracial athletic events [85] and one that teachers may instruct members of their own race only.[86] This open refusal invites court condemnation, which the draftsmen should have foreseen. Doubtlessly, however, they hoped to buy the time of litigation and, by affirming state hostility to desegregation, to muster political power against civil rights. Probably, too, these laws express outrage without thought of consequence.

A variation of the flat segregation rule is one which gives an option to those in opposition: if they do not desire to attend mixed schools, they may go to those for members of their race only. Tennessee is the only state which by statute has, for this purpose, expressly provided for three sets of institutions.[87] Others, while not so explicit, perhaps contemplate the possibility of two or three types of schools. These include Alabama, Arkansas, North Carolina, and Texas, which in essence say that no child need attend a biracial place of instruction.[88] Tennessee's option statute has already been condemned by a federal district court.[89]

ADMINISTRATIVE REMEDIES AND PUPIL ASSIGNMENT

Many schools systems traditionally have provided for some administrative review of the local determinations of principals, superintendents,

---

[83] See Adkins v. School Bd. of the City of Newport News, and School Bd. of the City of Charlottesville v. Allen, *supra* note 68; Bush v. Orleans Parish School Bd., *supra* note 74.

[84] See appendix A17. In what apparently was a friendly suit the Georgia Attorney General petitioned state court to enjoin the Valdosta School Board from considering desegregation in response to a petition by Negroes, Cook v. Valdosta Bd. of Educ. (Lowndes County Super. Ct. 1956); when Negroes intervened to demand desegregation, the state dropped the suit.

[85] LA. REV. STATS. § 4:451 (1957 Supp.); H.J. Res. No. 96, Va. House of Delegates (1956); Op. Att'y Gen. of Ga., 2 R.R.L.R. 266 (1957).

[86] LA. REV. STATS. § 17:345 (1957 Supp.); see also the Paducah Plan, supra note 47.

[87] TENN. CODE ANN. § 49-3704 (1958 Supp.).   [88] See appendix A18.

[89] Kelly v. Board of Educ. of the City of Nashville, *supra* note 66.

boards, or other officials. In Alabama, Arkansas, Florida, Louisiana, Mississippi, North Carolina, South Carolina, Tennessee, Texas and Virginia these provisions have been elaborated in varying degrees to create pupil assignment plans,[90] which usually provide standards for assignments and transfers and grant appeals. Some kind of pupil assignment standard is inevitable in any school system even if it takes the form of Baltimore's simple free choice plan. The legality of an assignment plan and its effect on race relations depend on its terms, purpose, and operation. But in gauging any such plan's ultimate effect, it should be noted that only those states which have complied little or not at all have passed these statutes.

The pupil assignment schemes involve two basic factors: the standards of assignment and the method of review. The Alabama criteria are typical of those used also by Arkansas, Florida, Tennessee, and Texas. Virginia's law originally was similar, but after judicial condemnation was rewritten to resemble North Carolina's. They include: available room; teaching capacity; transportation; effect of admission of new pupils on established or proposed academic programs; suitability of established curricula for particular pupils; adequacy of pupils' academic preparation for admission; scholastic aptitude and relative intelligence; mental energy or ability of individual pupil; psychological qualification of pupil for type of teaching and associations involved; effect of admission of pupil upon academic progress of others; effect of admission on academic standards; possibility of threat of friction or disorder among pupils or others; possibility of breaches of the peace or ill will or economic retaliation within the community; home environment of the pupil; maintenance or severance of established social and psychological relationships with other pupils and teachers; choice and interests of the pupil; morals, conduct, health, and personal standards of the pupil; request or consent of parents or guardians and the reasons assigned therefor. Such exceedingly wide scope given to school boards and the vagueness of many of the specified criteria raise the question of whether the delegation of power is unconstitutionally vague and but a pretence of legality to cover up segregation. But in passing on the Alabama statute in 1958 the Supreme Court upheld it on the explicitly narrow ground that the law is not unconstitutional on its face.[91] Desegregation can theoretically occur in

[90] See appendix A19. Statutes referred to on pp. 232–240 *infra*, unless otherwise cited, are cited in this appendix.

[91] Shuttlesworth v. Birmingham Bd. of Educ., 162 F. Supp. 372 (N.D. Ala. 1958), aff'd, 358 U.S. 101 (1958). *Compare with* Yick Wo v. Hopkins, 118 U.S. 356

Alabama within the framework of its statutory language. Under this ruling an opportunity is afforded the state to show that desegregation can be accomplished; the implication is that the courts will act if experience belies the assumption.

Arkansas and Texas explicitly provide along with yardsticks like those above that race shall *not* be a standard.[92] It is unlikely, however, that this self-serving declaration would insulate a segregating district from a court's decree. Louisiana, on the other hand, has proclaimed race as a fixed guidepost, while Virginia has employed "efficiency" as a key test and defined a mixed school as inefficient.[93] The Louisiana and Virginia statutes have been held unconstitutional, partly because of these provisions.[94]

North Carolina uses relatively simple bases of selection: boards shall make assignments to provide for the orderly and efficient administration of the public school system and for the health, safety, and general welfare of pupils, and may adopt reasonable rules and regulations. One Virginia amendment emulated North Carolina, though not to the extent of giving up "efficiency," which, of course, nullified the capacity of the plan to permit nonracial transfers. South Carolina and Mississippi do not prescribe as much as North Carolina; officially they leave boards with virtually unfettered discretion, although in other provisions they do forbid desegregation.

In addition to other provisions, South Carolina has a law that children may be peremptorily reassigned from one school to another.[95] Similarly, the Governor of Texas, upon threatened desegregation of Mansfield's school, instructed the district's president to transfer out students whose presence threatened violence— that is, Negroes.[96]

Alabama, Tennessee, and Texas have provided that children may be assigned on the basis of sex.[97] But these laws still contemplate racial segregation as well. Placing boys and girls in separate classes, if not compounded by racial discrimination, seems constitutionally

(1886); Davis v. Schnell, 81 F. Supp. 872 (S.D. Ala. 1949), *aff'd,* 336 U.S. 933 (1949); Bush v. Orleans Parish School Bd. *supra* note 74.

[92] ARK. STATS. ANN. § 80-1522 (1957 Supp.); TEX. REV. CIV. STATS. art. 2900a (1957 Supp.).

[93] VA. CODE § 22.188.31 (1958 Supp.).   [94] See notes 73 and 74 *supra.*

[95] S.C. CODE § 21-846.1 (1957 Supp.) (sheriff may remove and transfer at direction of superintendent).

[96] 1 R.R.L.R. 885 (1956). See GRIFFIN & FREEDMAN, MANSFIELD, TEXAS—A FIELD REPORT ON DESEGREGATION IN THE SOUTH (Anti-Defamation League pamphlet).

[97] ALA. CODE tit. 52, § 61(4) (1957 Supp.); TENN. CODE ANN. § 49-1742 (1958 Supp.); TEX. REV. CIV. STATS. art. 2901(a), § 4 (1958 Supp.).

unexceptionable—a normal grouping widely used despite debate over its wisdom.

The schemes of review vary. Virginia's law originally [98] was drafted to permit 105 days of appeals, commencing with the state-wide Pupil Placement Board (or its agent), proceeding to the governor, then to the circuit court, and finally to the Supreme Court of Appeals. "Interested parties," *i.e.*, parents having custody of children in affected schools, might intervene in the proceedings. North Carolina originaly provided for both administrative and judicial review, but the court of appeals has pointed out that judicial remedies need not be exhausted.[99] Now a North Carolinian may apply for reassignment within ten days after notification of assignment. If this application is disapproved, the board shall notify the applicant who then is "entitled to a prompt and fair hearing on the question of reassignment." [100] The board must render prompt decision. Thereafter, state law no longer may be asserted as a bar to filing suit in federal court. But this apparently summary remedy may impose a real burden. If notification of assignment did not come until late summer (often the case), judicial relief would have to be speedy indeed to secure desegregation by the opening of the fall school term.

The basic rule concerning administrative remedies applies—they need be exhausted only where, without unreasonable burden, they furnish relief.[101] The prolixity of Virginia's review system helped to invalidate its legislation (but besides that, the law forbade desegregation). Louisiana's assignment law has been knocked out because there was no chance of relief under it.[102] Although South Carolina is as dead-set against desegregation as the last two states, its assignment plan was upheld vis-à-vis a group of so-called "Turkish" children who in some communities there attend a third school system, but who, experience has shown, actually may obtain desegregation; [103] with Negroes it is otherwise.

Alabama's and North Carolina's statutes were also upheld, but in

[98] Va. Acts, 1956 Extra Sess., ch. 70, §§ 6 *et seq.* As amended the administrative appeal process has been shortened somewhat by removing the governor from the scheme of review. See VA. CODE §§ 22.232.9 (repealed) and 22.232.10 (1958 Supp.).

[99] Carson v. Warlick, 238 F.2d 724, 729 (4th Cir. 1956), *cert. denied*, 353 U.S. 910 (1957).

[100] N.C. GEN. STATS. §§ 115-178 to -179 (1957 Supp.).

[101] See pp. 63–66 *supra*.   [102] See notes 73 and 74 *supra*.

[103] Hood v. Board of Trustees of Sumter County, 232 F.2d 626 (4th Cir. 1956), *cert. denied*, 352 U.S. 870 (1956). Information that some "Turks" had been integrated appears in the briefs in this case, but not in the opinions.

suits in which the Supreme Court and the Fourth Circuit Court of Appeals, respectively, observed that there had been no actual test of the plans' operation.[104] If the gloss of experience shows that the plans are but sophisticated modes for segregating, they should fall. However, the question remains of how long denial in North Carolina and Alabama must continue until time demonstrates discrimination and of how realistic are the rights of those whose separation merely furnishes evidence upon which others can sue.

We have observed that a person seeking desegregation need not exhaust a remedy which forbids desegregating. The Fifth Circuit and a district court in Tennessee have held that neither need he use the remedy in a system which, apart from the explicit terms of statutes, is committed to segregation; in the Fourth Circuit, however, the rule is to the contrary.[105] In Florida and Tennessee, therefore, it was held that plaintiffs were entitled to general desegregation orders although they had not claimed the right to enter particular schools under the assignment laws. The Florida law is like Alabama's. One Florida opinion, involving Palm Beach,[106] was written by Judge Rives, senior judge at the trial of the Alabama case discussed above, in which he makes clear that if the Alabama plaintiffs had established that there existed and had then attacked a policy of segregation instead of the Alabama statutory language, they would have won. The Fourth Circuit's opinions, involving the North Carolina statute and local Virginia plans, have not commented on the Fifth's treatment of policy, as distinguished from statute, and merely have upheld the assignment law. Under the Fifth Circuit's holding, however, once a general policy of nonsegregation came into being anyone in such districts, claiming denial might have to pursue the administrative course.

PUPIL ASSIGNMENT COMBINED WITH A "GRANDFATHER CLAUSE"

The most thorough desegregation has been in cities where no all-Negro schools—as such—are maintained, the cities of Louisville, Wil-

[104] Shuttlesworth v. Birmingham Bd. of Educ., *supra* note 91; Carson v. Warlick, *supra* note 99; Carson v. Board of Educ. of McDowell County, 227 F.2d 789 (4th Cir. 1955).

[105] Gibson v. Board of Pub. Instruction of Dade County, 246 F.2d 913 (5th Cir. 1957); Kelly v. Board of Educ. of the City of Nashville, *supra* note 42; *compare with* Covington v. Edwards, 264 F.2d 780 (4th Cir. 1959); Holt v. Board of Educ. of the City of Raleigh, 265 F.2d 95 (4th Cir. 1959). The Virginia cases, involving the plans of the school boards themselves, are in the same vein: Allen v. County School Bd. of Prince Edward County, *supra* note 73; Hamm v. County School Bd. of Arlington, *supra* note 68.

[106] Holland v. Board of Pub. Instruction, 258 F.2d 730 (5th Cir. 1958).

mington, St. Louis, and Washington, D.C., where zones have been drawn and objective standards set.[107] In these places one usually cannot choose segregation or be pressured into it.

But many districts purporting to have no racial requirements maintain a fundamentally segregated system in which individual transfers merely are permitted. Tennessee and Virginia have expressly required that children shall continue to attend the schools in which they have been previously enrolled; [108] Florida's state Board of Education has recommended this as the key assignment standard; [109] other jurisdictions, including North Carolina districts, as well as some in Maryland, Kentucky, West Virginia, and elsewhere, have in fact employed this as the main or only basis of designating school assignments.[110] Such a standard of allocation, whether derived from statute, board regulation, or practice, is in reality of a "grandfather clause" type,[111] importing the now forbidden status of the past into present regulation. Although the Little Rock case states that there is a duty on school boards to desegregate, pupil assignment plans maintain segregation and place the burden on the minority.

This mode of mixing limits desegregation by making it contingent on available space in the white schools on which white children have first call. In addition, it musters prosegregation social forces and encourages efforts at intimidation. Fear, poverty, ignorance, inertia, leadership failings, and so forth, must be overcome by those whose

[107] See VALIEN, *op. cit. supra* note 32; S.S.N., April, 1958, p. 3 (St. Louis); Shagaloff, *supra* note 34 (Wilmington); S.S.N., Sept. 3, 1954, p. 4 (District of Columbia); CARMICHAEL & JAMES, *op. cit. supra* note 31 (Louisville).

[108] TENN. CODE ANN. § 49-1743 (1958 Supp.); VA. CODE § 22.232.6 (1958 Supp.); see TEX. REV. CIV. STATS. art. 2901a, § 3.

[109] Memorandum of Florida Superintendent of Public Instruction, 1 R.R.L.R. 961 (1956).

[110] See, *e.g.,* S.S.N., Aug., 1957, p. 3 (12 Negroes assigned to North Carolina previously all-white schools); S.S.N., May, 1957, p. 16 (Charlotte, N.C., school board tells Negroes that the initiative for desegregated schools rests with individuals); see Mitchell v. Pollock (Ky.), *supra* note 62, at 308 ("by the Court: . . . We are not forcing negro children to attend white schools, and we are not forcing white children to attend negro schools. It's a permissive order."); S.S.N., June, 1957, p. 12 ("after two years of voluntary or free choice desegregation, only 30 of Lexington's 2,750 Negro school pupils are attending mixed classes"); S.S.N., Oct., 1957, p. 10 (1 Negro transfers in Hopkins County, Ky., none transfer in Clay, 18 transfer in Sturgis, Ky.); see Slade v. Board of Educ. of Harford County (Md.), *supra* note 38; S.S.N., Dec., 1957, p. 6 (seven Maryland counties have desegregation policies but no Negro applicants for transfer); S.S.N., Oct., 1957, p. 11 (Hugo and Fort Towson, Okla., have official desegregation policies, no Negro applicants); S.S.N., April, 1958, p. 3 (similar experiences in some West Virginia counties).

[111] *Cf.* Guinn v. United States, 238 U.S. 347 (1915).

rights are denied; only those immune to intimidation and retaliation—
e.g., the self-employed, those who work for Negro-owned businesses,
individuals of unusual personal courage—can freely take the initiative.
The effectiveness of social forces as a way of keeping Negroes in all-
colored schools is accented in North Carolina, which has ruled that
applications under the pupil assignment law are individual and that no
administrative class proceedings may be conducted under it.[112] Similarly, in a recent Maryland case the local school board insisted on
interviewing each Negro parent applicant alone and rejected the plea
for a general meeting.[113] Other deterrents which may be effective in
the implementation of such a pupil assignment regimen have been the
refusal to allow Negro children the privilege of riding on the white
bus to the white school [114] and the establishment of "Negro-teacher"
schools.[115] While the average individual might readily go along with
a group, he is much less likely to step forward and claim his rights
alone, especially when it is made clear by officials that he is unwelcome.
Moreover, as pupil assignment is administered, of those who use the
process only a small percentage are afforded escape from segregation,
and then perhaps only after lengthy litigation.

Now that some Negro children have been admitted to a few
formerly white schools in a handful of North Carolina's districts—
although the bulk of Negro children are excluded—the position will no
doubt be taken that these boards are no longer committed to segregation.[116] And should objections be voiced against such an assignment
plan, which is based on preliminary segregation, the obvious retort is
that constitutional rights are personal and that the plan offers a way
to gain them. The courts, it will be said, will not safeguard rights of
those who willingly forego them. The original School case, Briggs v.
Elliott, on remand to the district court, evoked this comment from the
bench:

[The Supreme Court] has not decided that the federal courts are to take
over or regulate the public schools of the states. It has not decided that
the states must mix persons of different races in the schools or must require

[112] Joyner v. Board of Educ., 244 N.C. 164, 92 S.E.2d 795 (1956).
[113] Slade v. Board of Educ. of Harford County, supra note 38; this aspect of the
case is unreported.
[114] Hart v. Board of Educ. of Charles County, supra note 50.
[115] See the Paducah Plan, note 47 supra.
[116] See S.S.N., Aug., 1957, p. 3 (lawyers predict that assignment of a few Negroes will bolster the legal position of the state's pupil assignment act and Pearsall
Plan—antidesegregation statutes); S.S.N., July, 1957, p. 10 (Alabama's placement
law held principal defense against forced integration).

them to attend schools or must deprive them of the right of choosing the schools they attend. . . . The Constitution, in other words, does not require integration. It merely forbids discrimination. It does not forbid such segregation as occurs as the result of voluntary action.[117]

Does this mean that a segregation rule constitutionally may be retained, but that colored children with the courage to break the mold may apply to white schools and that they alone among Negroes may attend these schools? Although the courts have not fully explored this question, it would seem that "freedom of choice" can confer equality only where there is no racial standard involved. Where there is, for example, zoning into school districts and a segregation rule which Negroes may escape only by affirmative act, the zoning tends to be nullified by the racial rule which in the mind of Negroes and whites may be the dominant standard. The racial rule, which is the only rule for nonobjectors, causes the isolated dissenter to attend school as a lone Negro or one of a few—a freakish situation which would not exist but for the retention of Negro schools as such. (To argue that white children are free to attend the colored schools is obviously unrealistic.) The right to desegregated education should be the right to attend school in a system in which no racial standards are employed.[118]

In this context continuation of all-Negro schools recalls retention of Jim Crow waiting rooms and signs at railway stations, where Negroes theoretically are permitted to use white waiting rooms, but of which the Interstate Commerce Commission has written:

Signs such as "white" and "colored," as displayed in the Broad Street Station, are commonly understood to represent rules established by managers of buildings in which they are posted in the expectation that they will be observed by persons having due regard for the proprieties. It is reasonable to believe that such was the original purpose of these signs, and that this is still true, despite the Terminal's acquiescence in disregard of the signs.[119]

Moreover, the jury discrimination precedents may be recalled: Bias may be presumed from a consistently segregated result; a token number

[117] 132 F. Supp. at 777. To the same effect see Brown v. Board of Educ. of Topeka, 139 F. Supp. at 470: "Desegregation does not mean that there must be intermingling of the races in all school districts. It means only that they may not be prevented from intermingling or going to school together because of race or color."

[118] See Cameron v. Board of Educ. of the City of Bonner Springs, *supra* note 67 (defendants argued that they maintained an all-colored school but "did not force said Negro children to attend" it; Kansas Supreme Court rejected this plea on federal and state grounds).

[119] NAACP v. St. Louis & San Francisco Ry., 297 I.C.C. 335, 345.

of Negroes may be legally equivalent to none.[120] If, however, in education there were complete freedom of choice, or geographical zoning, or any other nonracial standard, and all Negroes still ended up in certain schools, there would seem to be no constitutional objection.

ABOLITION OF PUBLIC EDUCATION

The abolition of public education, repeal of requirements that public schooling be maintained, cutoff of state funds for desegregated schools, suspension of compulsory school attendance laws, and closing, sale, or lease of schools have been authorized by some states, including Alabama, Arkansas, Florida, Georgia, Louisiana, Mississippi, North Carolina, South Carolina, Texas, and Virginia.[121] In certain of these jurisdictions—Alabama, Arkansas, Georgia, Louisiana, North Carolina, and Virginia—various stand-by systems of "private" education have been projected to fill the gap.[122] But in reality these systems contemplate what amounts to government subsidy. No ordinary community could sustain a system of private schools at an adequate educational level without public funds. While the private school gambit might accommodate a handful of objectors (who might receive grants-in-aid), it could not very well supply the needs of large numbers unless it perpetuated the public schools with open or surreptitious subsidies. From the outset commentators have agreed that such private schools could not escape being dubbed "state" and that the Fourteenth Amendment would apply.[123] The source of financial support, the intent, the supervision, the meshing into existing educational programs, all contribute to this end.

The Supreme Court confirmed these predictions and by broad generalization doomed any state aid to "private" schools set up to avoid

[120] See pp. 323–327 infra.

[121] See appendix A20. The Supreme Court of Virginia has held that a Negro parent may not be prosecuted under the compulsory school laws for keeping his child out of school after the child had been rejected by a superior white school. Dobbins v. Commonwealth, 198 Va. 697, 96 S.E.2d 154 (1957).

[122] See appendix A21. On attendance at private schools in Virginia see S.S.N., Jan., 1959, p. 9 ("Where Are They Now . . ."); for Arkansas see id. at p. 14 ("Where Are They Now . . ."); see also S.S.N., April, 1958, p. 2 (white citizens of Prince Edward County pledge $200,000 for private schools); S.S.N., March, 1958, p. 8 (private school in Union County, Ky., for anti-integrationists; tuition is two dollars per week).

[123] See Nicholson, The Legal Standing of the South's School Resistance Proposals, 7 S.C.L.Q. 1 (1954); McKay, "With All Deliberate Speed"—Legislative Reaction and Judicial Development 1956–1957, 43 VA. L. REV. 1205, 1226 (1957). Comment, Legality of Plans for Maintaining School Segregation, 54 MICH. L. REV. 1142 (1956); Note, 57 COLUM. L. REV. 537 (1957); Murphy, Can Public Schools Be Private? 7 ALA. L. REV. 48 (1954).

desegregation in *Cooper v. Aaron,* the Little Rock case, in which it held, in response to the board's assertion that some Arkansas anti-desegregation laws were yet to be tested: "State support of segregated schools through any arrangement, management, funds, or property cannot be squared with the Amendment's command that no State shall deny to any person within its jurisdiction the equal protection of the laws." [124] The Eighth Circuit Court of Appeals made this prohibition explicit when in the next stage of the same suit it forbade the Little Rock board to lease its schools to a private segregated school system which was formed to take over schools closed by the governor to evade desegregation.[125]

In theory, the possibility of complete shutdown is the ultimate question. In the Little Rock case, however, the Supreme Court held that threats of violence and the possibility of closing the schools were no grounds for denying constitutional rights to equal educational opportunity. This view also was implemented by the Eighth Circuit in the next stage of the case when it held, in connection with the schools which were then closed: "[The Board] shall take such affirmative steps as the District Court may hereafter direct, to facilitate and accomplish the integration of the Little Rock School District in accordance with the Court's prior orders." [126] Obviously desegregation could not be accomplished unless these steps included reopening of the schools.

The Fourth and Fifth Circuit Courts of Appeals previously had held that the threat of closing does not justify refusing to desegregate.[127] An action brought by white parents in Norfolk seeking reopening of the Norfolk schools which had been closed to avoid desegregation brought a three-judge district court opinion that Virginia's school closing laws are unconstitutional and that the local boards must proceed to comply with prior decrees requiring desegregation.[128] A suit brought by the State of Virginia in the state Supreme Court evoked a decision that the school closing laws violated the state constitutional requirement that an efficient system of free public schools be maintained.[129]

---

[124] 358 U.S. 1, 19 (1958).   [125] 261 F.2d 97 (8th Cir. 1958).
[126] *Id.* at 108. On remand, however, the district judge took the view that reopening was not demanded by the court of appeals opinion, 169 F. Supp. 325 (E.D. Ark. 1959). But thereafter a three-judge district court ordered desegregation to proceed, Aaron v. McKinley, Civ. No. 3113, E.D. Ark., June 18, 1959.
[127] Allen v. County School Bd. of Prince Edward County, *supra* note 73; Borders v. Rippy, 247 F.2d 268, 272 (5th Cir. 1957) (on rehearing).
[128] James v. Almond; James v. Duckworth, *supra* note 70.
[129] Harrison v. Day, *supra* note 70.

The first legal argument against closing has been that it is a step taken to defeat a clear constitutional right. This appears to underly the Eighth Circuit's ruling that the schools may not be leased and that appropriate steps to proceed with desegregation should be taken. Moreover, closing plans contemplate sealing only a single desegregated institution or that one and others in the same district. Other schools in the state remain open. The denial of equal protection vis-à-vis the rest of the state is obvious. The Norfolk opinion devoted most attention to this aspect of the issue. As what happened in Norfolk has demonstrated, this is a theory on which whites as well as Negroes may proceed.

Moreover, school closing is questionable under other legal principles. Can a state say to its Negro children, "Take what we give you, even though it is unconstitutional, or nothing at all"? It would seem that the doctrine of unconstitutional conditions, in this context probably but another way of phrasing the interdict against defeat of clear constitutional rights, bars such a choice.[130]

It might also be argued that education has become so integral a part of American life that the state may not take it away. The case of *Truax v. Corrigan* (1921) provides something of an analogy which, in view of the importance of education, may lend weight to this approach. The state had by statute overruled a common law rule which had provided a remedy against picketing. Of this divestiture the Supreme Court said:

It is true that no one has a vested right in any particular rule of the common law, but it is also true that the legislative power of a state can only be exercised in subordination to the fundamental principles of right and justice which the guaranty of due process in the 14th Amendment is intended to preserve, and that a purely arbitrary or capricious exercise of that power, whereby a wrongful and highly injurious invasion of property rights, as here, is practically sanctioned and the owner stripped of all real remedy, is wholly at variance with those principles.[131]

In opposition, however, might be cited the recreation cases that have tolerated closing or sale of swimming facilities.[132] But recreation, while

[130] See, *e.g.*, Frost Trucking Co. v. Railroad Comm'n, 271 U.S. 583 (1926); Alston v. School Bd. of City of Norfolk, 112 F.2d 992 (4th Cir. 1940), *cert. denied,* 311 U.S. 693 (1940).

[131] 257 U.S. 312 (1921). See also Lynch v. United States, 189 F.2d 476 (5th Cir. 1951), *cert. denied,* 342 U.S. 831 (1951) (officer's inaction while prisoner beaten); Catlette v. United States, 132 F.2d 902 (4th Cir. 1943) (similar).

[132] Clark v. Flory, 237 F.2d 597 (4th Cir. 1956); Department of Conservation & Dev. v. Tate, 231 F.2d 615 (4th Cir. 1956), *cert. denied,* 352 U.S. 838 (1956); Tonkins v. City of Greensboro, 162 F. Supp. 549 (M.D.N.C. 1958).

important, does not rise to the significance of education. Moreover, because it is not maintained by states on a universal basis, the same equal protection issues do not arise.

At any rate, the fundamental issue is not primarily legal. It is whether school closings can be sustained in mid-twentieth-century America with its emphasis (especially its post-Sputnik emphasis) on education. The realities of the world in which Americans today live indicate that the answer is no. White groups are beginning to voice their opposition to closings in the deepest South. The suit filed by Norfolk white parents to reopen the schools was undoubtedly but the first concrete step to be taken by Southern whites to maintain public education notwithstanding desegregation.

Besides the constitutional question there is the practical or procedural one. Assuming that one has a right to prevent the closing of one's school system in these circumstances, how is that right to be enforced? Presumably an injunction or a supplemental injunction could be sought against those who have control of school funds and who would expend them in line of duty but for the resistance law. In other words, those persons might be enjoined to make payments as if no racial conditions were attached to the funds they disburse. An alternative remedy would be to forbid any expenditures at all unless made without regard to race. While *Cumming v. County Board of Education* (1899) [133] frowned on such an outcome—its rationale was that Negro children are done no good by taking education away from whites— that case presupposed some other remedy. But if there were no other remedy, *Cumming* might not apply. Clearly, however, it is not to be assumed that the federal courts, if faced squarely with this question by persistent, willful evaders, would permit frustration of a constitutional rule because obstructionists had maneuvered the issue into such a posture.

INTERPOSITION AND LIKE MEASURES

Other legislation warrants little discussion for purposes of this study because it has received scarcely a moment's consideration in the courts and promises to attain no more regard in the future. Some seek to identify power to segregate with a source which, it is hoped or believed, will insulate racial separation from federal law. Alabama has authorized the designation of school boards as "judicial" bodies; [134]

[133] 175 U.S. 528 (1899).
[134] ALA. CODE tit. 52, § 61(11) (1957 Supp.). See Johnson v. Yeilding, 267 Ala.

thereby, it is supposed, they will become immune to suit. Interposition declarations [135] and invocations of the state's police powers are related efforts of this type; [136] entrusting the governor with power to determine or enforce segregation is another. [137] None of these which has been tried in the courts has been successful. Interposition has played no courtroom role in cases striking down segregation rules in Arkansas, Florida, Louisiana, Tennessee, Texas, and Virginia, yet all of these states have some form of that protestation. Concerning the Alabama interposition resolution a federal district court has held that it "amounted to no more than a protest, an escape valve through which the legislators blew off steam to relieve their tensions." [138] In Arkansas, Louisiana, Texas, and Virginia the federal courts have, notwithstanding "police power," struck down segregation. Invocation of the word "governor" did not help the Arkansas, Louisiana, or Virginia statutes. Texas will allow desegregation only following the approval of local elections, and by the same method desegregation may be ended in districts where it was introduced before the law's passage. This statute has blocked some districts which were prepared to desegregate prior to its adoption.[139]

Most of these statutes are of a piece with laws which try to discourage civil rights organizations from operating in Deep Southern states [140] and with other intimidation. Akin are threats to the Negro teacher

108, 100 So. 2d 29 (1958) (personnel board judicial body; may not be sued for refusing to hire Negro).

[135] See generally *Interposition vs. Judicial Power*, 1 R.R.L.R. 465 (1956), and bibliography listed therein. McKay, *"With All Deliberate Speed," a Study of School Desegregation*, 31 N.Y.U.L. REV. 991, 1017 (1956).

[136] ARK. STATS. ANN. § 80-1520 (1957 Supp.); LA. REV. STATS. § 17:331 (1957 Supp.); TEX. REV. CIV. STATS. art. 2901a, § 1 (1957 Supp.); VA. CODE § 22-188.5 (1958 Supp.).

[137] Ark. Act No. 4, 2d Extraordinary Sess., 61st Gen. Ass'y, 1958, (governor may close schools); GA. CODE ANN. § 32-805 (1957 Supp.) (governor may close schools); LA. REV. STATS. §§ 17:336 et seq. (1958 Supp.) (governor authorized to close); TEX. REV. CIV. STATS. art. 2906-1, § 2 (1958 Supp.) (similar); VA. CODE §§ 22-188.3 et seq. (governor may operate school system).

[138] Shuttlesworth v. Birmingham Bd. of Educ., *supra* note 91, at 381.

[139] TEX. REV. CIV. STATS. § 2900a (1957 Supp.). See Dallas Independent School Dist. v. Edgar, 255 F.2d 421 (5th Cir. 1958) (no federal jurisdiction over district's suit for declaration whether it should obey desegregation decree notwithstanding that election had not been held); S.S.N., Nov., 1957, p. 5 (Galveston and Port Arthur postpone plans to desegregate because of this statute); N.Y. Times, Nov. 10, 1957, p. 60 (Pleasonton votes to desegregate).

[140] See, *e.g.*, Robison, *Protection of Associations From Compulsory Disclosure of Membership*, 58 COLUM. L. REV. 614 (1958); Winter, *Recent Legislation in Mississippi on the School Segregation Problem*, 28 MISS. L.J. 148, 151 (1957); McKay, *supra* note 123, at 1235 et seq.; S.S.N., Jan., 1957, p. 1.

of loss of employment should desegregation come, designed to enroll in behalf of segregation the important community status which colored teachers enjoy. Related are special appropriations for fighting segregation suits which undoubtedly enhance some lawyers' eagerness for prolonged litigation. Such moves try to serve their framers by stirring up opposition, consuming time in court, and frightening civil rights advocates. And, of course, we are not able to ignore the sheer violence that has marked some desegregation.[141] When we add all this intimidation to the burdens of commencing and sustaining litigation, it is not surprising that in a number of states there has been little litigation to desegregate schools and that many desegregation petitions have not been pressed to conclusion in court.[142] In many places the implementation of desegregation will have to start by securing the fundamental liberty to seek desegregation freely.

NON-SOUTHERN PUBLIC SCHOOLS

A recent federal suit referred to above, involving Hillsboro, Ohio, where there had been gerrymandered segregated schools, has emphasized that the Federal Constitution applies North as well as South and that geography alone does not determine racial patterns.[143] The constitutional rule of course dominates, but in addition, a number of states have their own statutes or constitutional provisions expressly forbidding school segregation. They are Colorado, Connecticut, Idaho, Illinois, Indiana, Massachusetts, Michigan, Minnesota, New Jersey, New York, Oregon, Pennsylvania, Rhode Island, Washington, and Wisconsin.[144] Others, by judicial decision interpreting more general provisions, have held segregation illegal.[145] And there are places where

[141] See particularly the Anti-Defamation League series of pamphlets entitled, "Field Reports on Desegregation in the South."

[142] See, STATUS OF SCHOOL SEGREGATION-DESEGREGATION IN THE SOUTHERN AND BORDER STATES, *passim* (Southern School News publisher Oct., 1958): Alabama has had 15 petitions; Arkansas, 15; most Florida boards have received them; Georgia has had 6; Louisiana, 5; Mississippi, 5; North Carolina, 22; South Carolina, 13; Virginia, 7. All of these states have had far fewer suits. The numbers of petitions is much smaller than the number of segregating districts in these states.

[143] *Supra* note 59. An excellent article is Ming, *The Elimination of Segregation in the Public Schools of the North and West*, 21 J. NEGRO EDUCATION 265 (1952). We have treated Delaware—which geographically and socially is partly Northern—with the Southern states because it required segregation by state law at the time of the *School Segregation Cases*.

[144] See appendix A22.

[145] See, *e.g.*, Iowa CONST. art. IX, 1st, § 12, as interpreted in Clark v. Board of Directors of the City of Muscatine, 24 Iowa 266 (1868); Board of Educ. v. State,

segregation has long been abolished, where the legal issue apparently never has arisen, or where no evidence of school segregation has been brought to light.[146] Kansas, Arizona, New Mexico, and Wyoming had, prior to the *School Segregation* decisions, permitted segregation on an optional basis, but those statutes have been repealed or locally ruled invalid.[147]

Many of these anti-school discrimination provisions are just declaratory and prescribe no specific implementation. Private civil suit, however, should be appropriate in such cases. But state law means little if it only repeats federal law. It is useful beyond federal law only to the extent that it provides other remedies. Illinois, Minnesota, New Jersey, New York, Pennsylvania, Rhode Island, Washington, and Wisconsin have criminal penalties (which appear never to have been applied) in the misdemeanor range for offending officials. Illinois and Minnesota are authorized to withhold state financial aid from transgressing districts, and in one instance funds were withheld in Illinois.[148] The Governor of Pennsylvania has made a similar threat,[149] although that state's statutes have no such express provision. New Jersey enforces through its Division Against Discrimination (DAD) in the typical administrative fashion (the division, incidentally, is part of the state Education Department). Washington's commission may regulate similarly. While New York's public accommodations law expressly in-

---

45 Ohio St. 555 (1880); Board of Educ. of School Dist. of City of Dayton v. State, 114 Ohio St. 188, 151 N.E. 39 (1926); ALASKA COMP. LAWS ANN. § 37-1-1 (1949), as treated in Jones v. Ellis, 8 Alaska 146 (1929); *cf.* Westminster School Dist. v. Mendez, 161 F.2d 774 (9th Cir. 1947) (Cal.).

[146] *E.g.*, Maine, Montana, Nebraska, Nevada, New Hampshire, North Dakota, South Dakota, Utah, Vermont. The views and deeds of these and the other states on school segregation around the time of the Fourteenth Amendment's passage are discussed in detail in the briefs in the *School Segregation Cases.* See Brief of Appellants, etc., in Nos. 1, 2, 4, and 10, Oct. 1953 Term, pp. 142-186; Brief of Appellees therein, pp. 28-47, and app. B; and Brief of the United States as *amicus curiae*, pp. 57-64, 86-104 and app. pp. 160-390.

[147] *Kansas:* Kan. L. 1957, ch. 389, repealed § 72-1724 of KAN. GEN. STATS. (1949) (the statute involved in *Brown v. Board of Educ.*; Kansas had permitted segregation in cities of the first class and in Kansas City high schools); *New Mexico:* N.M. L. 1955, ch. 169, § 1, deleted the optional provisions of N.M. STATS. ANN. §73-13-1 (1953); see Op. Att'y Gen. of N.M. No. 6080 (1955-56) (Supreme Court decisions invalidated segregation provisions); *Wyoming:* COMP. STATS. § 67-624 was repealed by Wyo. L. 1955, ch. 36; *Arizona:* for a discussion of unreported litigation (antedating *Brown v. Board of Educ.*) which invalidated the Arizona permissive statute see WILLIAMS & RYAN, SCHOOLS IN TRANSITION 161 (1954); S.S.N., Oct., 1954, p. 15.

[148] Shagaloff, *A Study of Community Acceptance of Desegregation in Two Selected Areas*, 23 J. NEGRO EDUCATION 330, 333, 336 (1954).

[149] See note 150 *infra*.

cludes schools within its definition of "public accommodations," the SCAD statute excludes schools from surveillance of the commission, on the premise, presumably, that Board of Regents supervision is enough. New York also governs postsecondary and certain vocational schools through its Fair Educational Practices Law, which seems, however, to be directed primarily at private schools. The New York State Commissioner of Education, under his general authority, has taken specific steps against segregation in public schools at all levels. Massachusetts superintends through administrative procedures; its law also seems tailored chiefly to fit the private school. Oregon's Bureau of Labor oversees its vocational, trade, and professional school provisions, enforceable by suspension of license; this law, too, aims chiefly at private schools.

Notwithstanding these laws, many of which have long been on the books, a number of these jurisdictions have had legal disputes of late arising out of the racial composition of schools. Indeed, desegregation in some places long subject to antisegregation standards has come about only in recent years. In some non-Southern districts racial distinctions still exist. The realms of contention or concern are chiefly three, though often they blend together: (1) open segregation, as by gerrymandering or racial assignments; (2) "*de facto*" segregation, growing out of ordinary zoning, which coincides with segregated residential areas; and (3) the deteriorated state of *de facto* separate schools for Negroes, which is related to their typically run-down locations and sometimes to the fact that where minorities predominate officials may treat the school as a whole according to lower, stereotyped standards.

AVOWED SEGREGATION

Despite state law some schools in California, Illinois, Ohio, New Jersey, Pennsylvania, and perhaps other places in recent years have been segregated by rule.[150] In southern Illinois, at least, some are so segre-

---

[150] *California:* In Pasadena white children had been permitted to transfer freely in a manner which created all-Negro schools; Los Angeles corporation counsel called this illegal and it was stopped. NAACP LEGAL DEFENSE & EDUCATIONAL FUND REPORT 8 (Sept., 1954). See also Marshall, *Concrete Curtain—The East Palo Alto Story,* Crisis, Nov., 1957, p. 543. *Ohio:* See Clemons v. Board of Educ. of Hillsboro, *supra* note 59; WILLIAMS & RYAN, *op. cit. supra* note 147, ch. 3 (1954). *Illinois:* See WILLIAMS & RYAN, ch. 5; Valien, *Racial Desegregation of the Public Schools in Southern Illinois,* 23 J. NEGRO EDUCATION 303 (1954); Shagaloff, *supra* note 148. *New Jersey:* See WILLIAMS & RYAN, chs. 7 and 8;

gated today.[151] There has been gerrymandering, direct racial assignment, and such techniques as permitting white children the option of transferring while denying it to Negroes, leaving the latter in all-colored schools.

New Jersey's experience suggests the effectiveness of administrative action as a mode of changing such conditions to conform with the law. Although 43 communities there had schools separated by official rule as late as 1948, within a year after the DAD attacked the problem 30 agreed to desegregate promptly. All but 4 of the remainder acceded to persistent tactful negotiation. Three capitulated quickly, one with slow reluctance, following a refusal of Negro parents to send their children to an all-Negro school. A widely used New Jersey method has been the "Princeton Plan," named after the town where it has been employed. Where two schools exist, one in a Negro, the other in a white neighborhood, one is assigned to children from, for example, kindergarten to third grade, the other to children from fourth to sixth grades. Children of both races then will attend each school. This plan has also been used by Benton Harbor, Michigan, Willow Grove, Pennsylvania, and other communities.[152] Of course, the Princeton Plan can operate against *de facto* segregation as well.

The effectiveness of an administrative approach is that it can be thorough and systematic, investigating and working district by district, as in other areas of civil rights. It relieves the minority of at

---

Wright, *Racial Integration in the Public Schools of New Jersey*, 23 J. NEGRO EDUCATION 282 (1954). *Pennsylvania:* In 1957 the governor of Pennsylvania reported official segregation in three of that state's districts and threatened to cut off state funds, apply legal sanctions, N.Y. Times, Aug. 26, 1957, p. 1. See also note 170 *infra*. See NAACP LEGAL DEFENSE AND EDUCATIONAL FUND REPORT 9 (Summer, 1954) (Chester, Pa., board agrees to desegregate upon being petitioned), and REPORT (Sept., 1954) (mode of Chester's desegregation). See also LOTH & FLEMING, INTEGRATION NORTH AND SOUTH 7-10 for some Northern districts desegregating between mid-1954 and 1956.

[151] Chicago Defender, Oct. 5, 1957, p. 12 (Centerville schools on double session, white children morning, Negro children afternoon); *id.*, July 27, 1957, p. 20 (following board vote to integrate Colp, Ill., schools, county trustees allow petition to detach white portion of Colp district and annex it to all-white Carterville; Carterville board's president says limitation on numbers selected from Colp dictated by considerations of space); *id.*, Sept. 7, 1957, p. 1 (upon court challenge to annexation white children boycott Colp schools); *id.*, Oct. 5, 1957, p. 5 (NAACP spokesman says segregation in Colp, Phoenix, and Centerville "are typical of . . . general condition"); *ibid.* (100,000 children allegedly attending all-Negro schools in Illinois as result of *de facto* and *de jure* segregation).

[152] On Benton Harbor see NAACP LEGAL DEFENSE AND EDUCATIONAL FUND REPORT 8 (Jan., 1957); on Willow Grove see *ibid.* and Crisis, March, 1955, p. 169.

least some of the need for taking the initiative, which for obvious reasons may be burdensome and slow to arise.

The real, pressing racial problem in Northern education is becoming that of what must be called *"de facto"* segregation.[153] As a practical matter, we may subsume much of the Northern *de jure* segregation inquiry under this heading, for administrators may be reluctant to admit using a racial standard even if they do, claiming that all-Negro or all-white schools have been created by housing, despite fair zoning and assignment standards. Sometimes this assertion cloaks purposeful separation; sometimes it is true; often it is impossible to tell.[154] It is also sometimes said that separate Negro schools are maintained because Negroes want them.[155] Whatever the truth is, in many places an all-Negro area is so vast that some segregation in fact will be unavoidable.

The dimensions of the problem are emphasized by a 1957 survey made by the American Jewish Committee,[156] which presented the following percentages of public schools having a nonwhite majority of pupils in eight Northern cities: Chicago, 19.7 percent (77 of 390 schools); Cincinnati, 43.2 percent (38 of 88); Cleveland, 22 percent (34 of 157); Detroit, 21.4 percent (48 of 224); Los Angeles, 15.1 percent (70 of 465); New York, 19.8 percent (126 of 639); Philadelphia, 26.9 percent (65 of 241); San Francisco, 7 percent (8 of 111); and in Manhattan, two thirds of the school children are Negro or Puerto Rican.[157] The Southern Negro migration northward is increasing these proportions. The population ratios in education are in many places accentuated by relatively heavy white attendance at private and parochial schools.

Assuming a school segregation situation which reflects housing patterns, and that there has been no affirmative effort to separate pupils racially, some have urged that nevertheless steps should be taken to

[153] See generally AMERICAN JEWISH CONGRESS, CHILDREN, TOGETHER 26-35 (pamphlet 1957); N.Y. Times, Feb. 10, 1957, § IV, p. 11 ("Northern Cities Confront the Problem of De Facto Segregation in the Schools").

[154] See Marshall, *supra* note 150 (gerrymandering alleged and denied; rezoning effects partial, but allegedly insufficient, integration).

[155] *Cf.* Cameron v. Board of Educ. of the City of Bonner Springs, *supra* note 67.

[156] Mimeographed release, October 25, 1957.

[157] N.Y. Times, July 28, 1957, § E, p. 9.

alleviate the racial bunching, in other words, that school officials have a duty to counteract, where possible, the effects of residential bias. Those who urge affirmative integration point to the psychological harm of segregation and the depressed condition of schools attended wholly or largely by Negroes. They have been aided by the Supreme Court's having focused on the psychological issue and the attention which the Southern problem has directed to racial factors in schooling throughout the nation. Advocacy of affirmative integration has raised, among other things, the issue of whether quotas should be employed to create balanced racial school populations. Some say it is the only way to assure nonsegregation, at least until housing and other social impediments to integration recede. Others fear that quotas may limit opportunity, rather than expand it, urging that qualified persons in excess of a quota may be excluded by it and that the principle, once established, may become entrenched to the detriment of individual liberty. There has been similar controversy over quotas in the armed forces and housing.[158]

Objections raised to "*de facto*" segregation have influenced at least the New York City and State Boards of Education, the New Jersey Attorney General, the Governor and State Board of Education of Pennsylvania, and some officials in other areas.[159] While they have not gone far in implementing their espousals, we must recognize the relative newness of the proposition and the political and administrative problems it sometimes poses. Besides, unlike officially enforced segregation which is concededly subject to courtroom attack, there has so far been no clearly recognized way of achieving affirmative integration other than by persuading, through ordinary political means, officers of government. A recent case involving Pontiac, Michigan, where plaintiffs charged that school site selection had been dictated by a desire to achieve racial segregation, was dismissed, the court holding that the board

may consider such factors in selecting sites that it considers relevant and reasonable and, in the absence of a showing that the standards for selection are not relevant and reasonable and that in reality they were adopted as a sham or subterfuge to foster segregation, or for any other illegal purpose, their use is within the administrative discretion of the school board. The

[158] See pp. 291–292, 360, *infra.*
[159] See N.Y. Times, Aug. 26, 1957, p. 1 ("North Moves To Eliminate Color Line in Its Schools").

fact that in a given area a school is populated almost exclusively by the children of a given race is not of itself evidence of discrimination.[160]

To achieve change through inducing rezoning by the school board is usually rather more difficult to do than hiring a lawyer and filing a suit; in addition, it is subject to political counterpressure.[161]

A thoughtful argument discussing, evaluating and speculating about affirmative integration has been made by the New Jersey Attorney General in a case before the state DAD involving the community of Englewood. It is set forth here in some detail because it is the most fully articulated legal exposition of this position.

The question arises whether the Law goes further and prohibits a board of education from permitting the existence of segregation-in-fact when it can reasonably be eliminated. We believe that the Law Against Discrimination should be so construed.

In determining the meaning of a statute, we must look to the mischief which the law is designed to overcome. . . .

[The] harmful effect of segregation-in-fact was . . . implicit in the reasoning of the U. S. Supreme Court in the *Brown* case . . . where the court . . . noted that the impact of the segregation was "greater when it has the sanction of law"; but by the same token, when it has the sanction of the agency charged with administering the law, the impact on the pupils involved would be at least as damaging. . . .

. . . the term "discrimination on account of race" as used in the Law Against Discrimination, and the term "segregation because of race" as used in the New Jersey Constitution, should not be narrowly confined to cases where a harmful division of the races has resulted from a deliberate purpose or intent to bring it about. Those terms must be construed in the light of the statutory responsibility of the Board . . . to furnish suitable educational facilities for all public school children in the district, and in the further light of the constitutional responsibility of the Board to provide such facilities to all children on an *equal* basis, *psychological as well as physical*, so far as reasonably possible (italics in original).

But what is the remedy and when should the board act? The Attorney General urged:

We do not maintain here that complete integration must be achieved at all costs, so that in every school the pupils would represent a fair cross section of all races in the district. Financial, transportation and other prob-

[160] Henry v. Godsell, 165 F. Supp. 87, 90 (E.D. Mich. 1958); see also Smith v. Lower Gwynedd Township School Bd., 72 Montg. Co. (Pa.) 266 (1955) (segregation was *de facto* and in process of being ended; relief denied to those temporarily in all-Negro school).

[161] On opposition in Queens County, N.Y., see note 178 *infra*.

lems involved in such a program might be insuperable. We do not believe that the constitutional requirement of de-segregation necessitates a disregard of physical and financial conditions in the school district.

The guiding principle, we submit, is that the Board of Education should establish, and where necessary alter, zones of attendance in such a manner as to eliminate racial segregation so far as possible consistently with due regard for physical and economic factors. This principle requires the Board to act whenever necessary to prevent segregation-in-fact from becoming entrenched; and it further demands that whenever the Board does take any action to construct new schools, change attendance zones, or otherwise to determine where children shall go to school, such action must be taken in accordance with the de-segregation objective.

The application of these basic rules to any particular case involves the determination of how far the predominance of Negroes in a school may be allowed to progress before the due to de-segregate arises. For example, must the Board act after the ratio of colored to white is more than one-half? Or more than 80 percent?

The solution to this problem would seem to be this: The Board must act whenever, under the particular circumstances, the ratio has become such that the Negro children are being denied educational facilities which are equal, intangibly as well as tangibly, with those afforded to the whites. The controlling object is always to provide all children with the best possible opportunity for psychological and personality development. Just when the injuries of racial segregation begin to be inflicted is a question which, in the first instance, must be decided by the Board in each case in the honest exercise of reasonable judgment, with the help of such expert advice as may be available. So long as reasonable men might differ in judging a particular situation, the discretion of the Board should not be disturbed.

Where, however, a school has become all Negro but for one or two children, while there are other schools nearby which are predominantly white, the harmful effect on the pupils of the colored school can no longer be disputed. Furthermore, where the State authorities have advised the Board that the racial segregation in its schools is unreasonable and should be remedied, the Board should abide by the judgment of the State authorities unless it proves that the State is wrong. In the case of Englewood, therefore, one can no longer doubt the Board's duty to remedy the situation if at all possible.[162]

The Commissioner of Education decided for the complainant but did not touch on the question of the validity of the Attorney General's argument. Instead, he ruled on bases that promoted some desegregation

[162] Brief on Behalf of Complainants in the State of New Jersey Department of Education, Division Against Discrimination, *Walker v. Board of Educ. of the Borough of Englewood,* pp. 29-33 (1954).

in Englewood, that in some cases could have as wide an effect to desegregate, but that in others might work the other way. He held that [163]

without impugning the motives of the Board of Education in fixing
boundary lines, it is the opinion of the Commissioner that if the drawing
of a straight line causes a pupil to be transferred in contravention of the
principles set forth above [*i.e.*, pupils should attend nearest school; if there
is overcrowding, transferees should be those required to travel least additional distance except for factors like safety, special grouping, special educational needs, etc.] the result is discrimination, regardless of intent or motivation. Furthermore, from the standpoint of school administration, it is
doubtful in these days of increasing and shifting population and overcrowding of schools whether district lines can be established to last very far into
the future.[164]

(Sometimes, however, where there are residential racial concentrations
those who urge affirmative integration may propose that to counteract housing segregation some pupils *not* attend the nearest school.)

Concerning alleged discrimination by maintenance of a separate,
virtually all-colored junior high school attended by residents of the
Lincoln School District in Englewood, the commissioner wrote:

The maintenance of a separate junior high school in the Lincoln school
district cannot be justified on any sound principles of school organization
or administration. The pupils of the Lincoln Junior High School are
entitled to attend classes and to participate in school activities with other
pupils of the city of their age. The Commissioner is convinced that these
pupils, denied such a right, are being discriminated against.[165]

New York State also has taken affirmative administrative steps. That
state has in recent years had a number of cases and administrative proceedings on segregation and integration, often involving charges of
gerrymandering. The NAACP reports [166] requests for aid on such
issues in Amityville, Buffalo, Freeport, Hempstead, Hillburn, Jamaica,
Lackawanna, New Rochelle, New York City, and Yonkers. The community in which the question seems to have stimulated most discussion

---

[163] Walker v. Board of Educ. of the Borough of Englewood, Department of
Education, Division Against Discrimination, State of New Jersey No. M-1268, May
19, 1955, 1 R.R.L.R. 255, 259 (1956).

[164] *Id.* at 259.   [165] *Id.* at 260.

[166] See N.Y. Times, March 3, 1957, p. 67 (state superintendent also reports that
influx of new residents into suburban area has created racial and religious issues
there for first time). On New Rochelle see *id.*, March 23, 1957, p. 21, April 2,
1957, p. 33 (head of Division of Intercultural Relations of State Board says:
"many instances where the boundary seemed to be neither reasonable nor
consistent").

is Brooklyn, where racial concentrations are great, Negro-attended schools often deficient, and Negro leadership militant.[167] In a number of these jurisdictions the issues have been met by decisions which conclude that while a segregation rule would be illegal, there has been no intentional racial separation (although reallocation of Negro and white pupils sometimes has been ordered on other grounds). Unfortunately, the cases provide no clear statement of a school board's duty when faced with a *de facto* segregation problem.[168]

The controversies have involved placement of school zone boundaries, school site selection, permissive transferring where relatively few white children live in mostly Negro sections, and continuation of zone lines where population had shifted, thus creating underutilized Negro-occupied schools near crowded white ones. Because the disputes show no sign of abating, the New York State Department of Education in 1957 created a Division of Intercultural Relations by expanding its unit which administers the Fair Educational Practices Act. The new body, apparently the first of its sort in the nation, is charged with assessing conditions and furnishing consultative services in the field of intercultural relations to achieve "true integration of all ethnic groups in our schools." [169]

In a Pennsylvania dispute in which gerrymandering was alleged, but which, at any rate, concerned *de facto* segregation, the Governor ap-

[167] On New York City's treatment of this issue, see p. 255 *infra*. Concerning suit filed against the city challenging zoning, apparently chiefly on the basis of the inequality of schools in Harlem, see N.Y. Times, July 18, 1957, p. 1, and July 21, 1957, § E, p. 7.

[168] On Hillburn, see Matter of Central School Dist. No. 1, Town of Ramapo, 65 St. Dep't Rep. 106 (1943) (school made all-Negro by zoning when state repealed statute authorizing segregation in 1938; closed as uneconomical). On Yonkers, see Matter of W. Scott Davis, 75 St. Dep't Rep. 57 (1954) (school which had been made all-Negro by zoning closed; its students assigned to "white" schools; protestant who favored expansion of "white" zone to other "white" areas overruled). On Hempstead, see Matter of School Dist. No. 1, Village of Hempstead, 70 St. Dep't Rep. 108 (1949) (irregularly drawn line susceptible to charge that its purpose is segregation, but mere concentration of Negro students not illegal per se; rezoning ordered; later, however, children were permitted to continue in school they had been attending; brothers and sisters permitted to follow them—latter aspect of case unreported). Concerning Freeport, see Matter of School Dist. No. 9, Town of Hempstead, 71 St. Dep't Rep. 166 (1950) (white children live in two noncontiguous areas considered as one zone and attend "white" school although one of the areas is closer to Negro school; zoning upheld on ground that separation is not purposeful, is related to topographical factors and Negro school equals white). On Amityville, see Matter of Alyce Bell, 77 St. Dep't Rep. 37 (1956) (site selection upheld; appeal too late; projected lines reasonable in view of traffic).

[169] N.Y. Times, Jan. 26, 1957, p. 13.

peared before the state Council of Education and stated that, relying on the advice of the Attorney General, he viewed the matter as "very serious" and advised that the council "should act against even the suspicion of racial segregation in the public schools." The council, which had previously approved the districting plan in question, withdrew its approval. The press reported that the special counsel for the state council said that the district judge had told him that unless the state council rejected the proposed zoning "it was likely a court would rule that it was unconstitutional." [170] The remaining aspects of the situation were found by a United States district court and the Third Circuit Court of Appeals not to involve discrimination.[171] If the Attorney General's stricture not to countenance the "suspicion" of segregation were to become a state-wide policy, it might be implemented to remove much *de facto* segregation.

NEW YORK CITY SCHOOLS

While the Englewood experience suggests the fullest development so far of the integration concept as found in interpretation of a state statute, New York City exhibits the greatest number of facets of the issue and the wide panoply of governmental approaches available to deal with it.[172] The Public Education Association (PEA) [173] has studied New York City schools in detail at the request of the president of the city's Board of Education to find "the relative position, with respect to educational opportunities received, of Negro and Puerto Rican schools . . . and . . . the status of Negro and Puerto Rican integration." It has reported that of the city's 639 elementary schools 445 enroll either 90 percent or more Negro and Puerto Rican children or 90 percent or more children of other origins. In terms of measurable

[170] See Philadelphia Inquirer, Nov. 21, 1957, and Upper Darby, Pennsylvania, News, Nov. 28, 1957, p. 1, concerning the situation which gave rise to Sealy v. Department of Pub. Instruction, 159 F. Supp. 561 (E.D. Pa. 1957), aff'd, 252 F.2d 898 (3rd Cir. 1958), *cert. denied*, 356 U.S. 975 (1958).

[171] *Ibid*.

[172] A lengthy and detailed analysis of some important aspects of the New York City experience appears in N.Y. Times, Oct. 31, 1957, p. 1. The Chicago situation appears to be similar to New York's. See Chicago Defender, Sept. 21, 1957, p. 5 (70% of Chicago high school students are in all-Negro or all-white schools). *Id*., Dec. 15, 1956, p. 10 (NAACP leader asks Chicago Board of Education to adopt policy like New York's). *De Facto Segregation in the Chicago Public Schools*, Crisis, Feb., 1958, p. 87.

[173] See PEA, THE STATUS OF THE PUBLIC SCHOOL EDUCATION OF NEGRO AND PUERTO RICAN CHILDREN IN NEW YORK CITY (pamphlet 1955). The quotations and references to the PEA's findings in the text come from this pamphlet.

factors, the Negro–Puerto Rican institutions had, among other inferi-
orities, generally older and less adequate plants than the others, less
maintenance, less competent teachers and higher faculty turnover, and
fewer classes for gifted pupils. About 90 percent of the Negro–Puerto
Rican schools are in the "difficult" category. At the elementary level
the average class size in the "difficult" minority group schools was, at
the time of the report, five pupils per class more than in other difficult
schools and four more than in typical schools. The children in the minority group schools did not test as high on reading and arithmetic
achievement tests.

On purposeful segregation, the PEA concluded: "There is no significant evidence to indicate that ethnic separation is seriously considered
in drawing school district boundary lines." It noted, however, and
recommended against permissive zones in fringe areas between racial
housing concentrations and the practice of some parents of evading
zoning regulations for ethnic reasons. It found, too, that "in general the
principles followed in zoning school districts ignore both the possibility
of separation and integration of ethnic groups," and that "it is not
overall school policy to encourage integration through zoning." The
PEA then suggested that "whenever a superintendent can further integration by drawing district lines he should do so."

The Board of Education on December 23, 1954, adopted the following resolution expressing its policy on this issue: "This Commission
affirms that it is desirable policy to promote ethnic integration in our
schools as a positive educational experience of which no child in the
city should be deprived." At the same time the board avowed that "it
is now the clearly reiterated policy . . . to devise and put into operation a plan which will prevent the further development of [racially
homogeneous] schools and would integrate the existing ones as quickly
as practicable."

Steps have been taken or policy adopted to remedy shortcomings
pointed out by the PEA and to implement these resolves.[174] The board's
Commission on Integration has made proposals, which have largely
been accepted by the board itself, with the aim of achieving more
integration, where possible, through rezoning and site selection, of
raising standards in those schools where integration cannot be achieved,

___

[174] The board has, in question and answer form, discussed many of the controversial aspects of its integration policy including rezoning, neighborhood schools,
student "bussing," permissive zoning, teacher assignment, N.Y. Times, Feb. 26,
1957, pp. 2-3; 2 R.R.L.R. 507 (1957).

and of assuring equitable distribution of qualified teachers and improving community relations. The proposals are:

1. That the objective of racial integration should be one of the cardinal principles of zoning.

2. That a master zoning plan should be formulated, a central zoning unit set up, an advisory council on zoning established, special assistant superintendents for zoning appointed, and a connected community relations program instituted.[175]

3. That difficult schools should get more teachers, smaller classes, psychiatric assistance, and better facilities, and that appointments should be made on a nondiscriminatory basis; teacher training, it is proposed, should include human relations courses.[176]

4. That special guidance, educational stimulation, and placement programs should be instituted in the difficult schools.

5. That various community and school relations programs should be undertaken.[177]

The purpose of the first two suggestions is to introduce uniformity in zoning standards for the entire city and apparently to remove the issue, so far as possible, from local pressures. The advisory council would bring to school zoning the experience of other government departments, *e.g.*, housing, traffic, and presumably enable them to account for educational factors in their own planning.

The superintendent has reported that a tentative master zoning plan has been formulated based on these criteria: distance from home to school, maximum utilization of school space, racially integrated schools, transportation, and topographical barriers. He states that there have been zoning changes to promote integration. He has not, however, identified the schools involved or meaningfully described the revisions. (One alleged problem connected with publicizing alterations is that this might provoke opposition.) [178] The zoning program contemplates

[175] See N.Y. Times, Dec. 14, 1956, p. 1. Other techniques for achieving integration suggested by the Subcommittee on Zoning of the Commission on Integration were: permissive zoning, selective use of bus transportation over reasonable distances, change of school organization (such as converting a junior high school to an elementary school). See also N.Y. Times, July 11, 1956, p. 27 (contemplated central zoning unit). For the text of the board's report see N.Y. Times, July 27, 1957, pp. 1 and 8. See 2 R.R.L.R. 231 (1957) (Report of the Subcommittee on Zoning); 2 R.R.L.R. 1037 (1957) (tentative zoning plan).

[176] For the recommendations on teacher policies see N.Y. Times, March 1, 1957, p. 9.

[177] See N.Y. Times, May 14, 1957, p. 37.

[178] For clarification of zoning and permissive zoning policies in New York City see N.Y. Times, April 20, 1957, p. 19. For the sharp dispute over whether it is

continuation of the "neighborhood school" concept. It has not been proposed to transport children over great distances to achieve school integration; rather, such transporting as would occur under this system would be no greater than has already been going on to achieve full space utilization.[179] Between 1954 and the end of 1957, 71 of the 134 schools planned, according to the board, were located to help the integration program, stress having been placed on site selection in fringe areas.[180]

The most controversial portion of the third phase of the recommendations has been the suggestion that teachers be assigned to schools on the basis of the needs of the school, not on the preference of the teachers. One reason that difficult schools—populated chiefly by minorities—give poorer instruction is that the more experienced teachers, as soon as possible, seek transfers to more pleasant neighborhoods and easier teaching experiences,[181] leaving minority group schools with a higher proportion of inexperienced and substitute teachers. The teachers' representatives have opposed this aspect of the proposals although otherwise endorsing them.

No assignment rule designed to assure more seasoned or steadier teaching in "colored" schools has been adopted. Funds have been allotted for accomplishing some of the other recommendations, however, including more teachers and supervision in difficult schools, improving pupil-teacher ratios, and rehabilitating the schools in question.[182] The superintendent has not replied to the demand for reallocating teachers other than to state that it has always been board policy not to discriminate in appointments.

Little has been done to implement the proposition that special pro-

---

possible to integrate Brooklyn P.S. 258, see N.Y. Times, Nov. 2, 1956, p. 29, Nov. 3, 1956, p. 25, Nov. 5, 1956, p. 33, Nov. 6, 1956, p. 37, Nov. 10, 1956, p. 17, Nov. 22, 1956, p. 35. On opposition of Queens Chamber of Commerce see N.Y. Times, March 8, 1957, p. 49. Of 2,000 letters opposing program, 90% were from Queens where there are relatively few Negroes, N.Y. Times, March 23, 1957, p. 21.

[179] N.Y. Times, Feb. 28, 1957, p. 15.

[180] N.Y. Times, Dec. 4, 1957, p. 41. On building (also zoning and assignment) see N.Y. Times, April 17, 1957, p. 1.

[181] On teacher opposition see N.Y. Times, Jan. 18, 1957, p. 13. See N.Y. Times, Jan. 21, 1957, p. 24 (editorial urging service in difficult schools; compulsory assignment if necessary), and March 4, 1957, p. 26 (editorial indorsing integration program); April 18, 1957, p. 28 (similar). See id., Feb. 25, 1959, p. 23 (as of September, 1959, new teachers to be assigned; experienced teachers not obliged to transfer).

[182] N.Y. Times, March 9, 1957, pp. 14 and 21, March 22, 1957, p. 21.

grams be undertaken in the difficult schools, and not much has been done to realize the proposal that community and school relations programs be instituted.

The teacher allocation disparity between "white" and "colored" schools was, at the end of 1958, the basis of a decision by Justice Polier of the New York City Domestic Relations Court. She found parents of Negro children who refused to send them to two all-colored junior high schools in Harlem not guilty of neglect. Relying heavily on the PEA report, Justice Polier's decision rested primarily on the deficiency of the instructional staffs in the colored schools. She wrote:

As of September 11, 1958, the average percentage of vacancies [positions not filled by regularly licensed teachers] in the X Schools (over 85% Negro and Puerto Rican students) was 49.5%, while the average percentage of vacancies in the Y Schools (over 85% white students) was 29.6%. In the two schools to which the children of the respondents were assigned, there were over 50% vacancies in one and 51% vacancies in the other. . . .

The Assistant Superintendent in charge of personnel in the Junior High School Division testified that the Board of Education had given her no power to transfer regularly licensed teachers once appointed. The Principal of Junior High School 136 testified that only one regularly licensed teacher had transferred voluntarily to his school. . . .

What the Board did was to let the teachers themselves establish the discriminatory pattern. But this was action by the Board's employees, and action by employees who, as regularly licensed teachers, were subject to such assignments as the Board chose to make. . . .

[It is not] the function of this Court to say how the Board should go about effecting a change in the present lamentable situation, whether by compulsory assignments of veteran teachers to X schools for a period of years, by paying a special bonus to teachers to induce them to accept such assignments, or by providing additional services and facilities in such schools, as, for example, additional administrative personnel, to make them more attractive to teachers now working in less difficult schools. . . .

I hold the defense on grounds of inferior educational opportunities in those schools by reason of racial discrimination to be established and to bar an adjudication of neglect.[183]

In another prosecution for the same offense before another judge, however, the defense of inferior education was held inadmissible and the defendants were convicted. There was no written opinion. So far there has been no reconciliation of the two decisions, although at this

[183] In the Matter of Charlene Skipwith, No. 3913/58 New York City Dom. Rel. Ct., Child. Ct. Div., New York County (unreported).

writing the Board of Education is considering whether appeals should be taken or the entire matter resolved by efforts to improve the X schools.

The approaches to the Northern school desegregation problem set forth above are but some of the possible treatments of this many-faceted issue. Others undoubtedly will develop as the significance of this area of law and school administration is better understood. As official segregation rules fade in the South, these "Northern" issues will come alive there.

PUBLIC HIGHER EDUCATION

Sweatt v. Painter, involving the University of Texas Law School,[184] and *McLaurin v. Oklahoma State Regents*, involving the University of Oklahoma graduate school [185] (both 1950), while neither rejecting nor considering the question of separate-but-equal's validity, measured factors which make it impossible for a colored school to equal a white one: tradition, prestige, and the opportunity to associate in school with members of the dominant (white) group. Considered, too, were the tangibles of wealth, size, and facilities, in which Negro higher education also was patently inferior but in which, perhaps, theoretical equality could be achieved. This, however, was an inconsequential part of the decision. Thereafter, no colored higher institution could legally "equal" a white one, and in fact, no such case since then has found equality. This balancing of impalpable, though meaningful, qualities was a forecast of the *School Segregation* decision of 1954.

After the *School Cases* it even became unnecessary to use the formula of equality. Segregation itself was viewed as denying equal protection. *Frasier v. Board of Trustees of the University of North Carolina* held:

[184] 339 U.S. 629 (1950).
[185] *Id.* at 637. *Sweatt* and *McLaurin* were preceded by Missouri *ex rel.* Gaines v. Canada, 305 U.S. 337 (1938), which held that where the state had a law school for whites and none for Negroes equal protection was not afforded by an out-of-state scholarship; to the same effect see Pearson v. Murray, 169 Md. 478, 182 A. 590 (1936); see also Sipuel v. University of Okla. p. 264 *infra*. Following *Sweatt* and *McLaurin* but prior to the *School* cases there were decided, *inter alia*, Wilson v. Board of Supervisors, 92 F. Supp. 986 (E.D. La. 1950), aff'd, 340 U.S. 909 (1951) (Louisiana State University law school); Gray v. Board of Trustees of Univ. of Tenn., 342 U.S. 517 (1952) (graduate and law schools); Wilson v. City of Paducah, 100 F. Supp. 116 (W.D. Ky. 1951) (Paducah, Ky., Junior College); Swanson v. University of Va., Civ. Action No. 30 (W.D. Va. 1950) (unreported) (law school); see Editorial Comment, 21 J. NEGRO EDUCATION 3 (1952), for list of states where Negroes attended Southern "white" state graduate and professional schools in 1952.

In view of these [the *School Cases'*] sweeping pronouncements, it is needless to extend the argument. There is nothing in the . . . statements of the court to suggest that the reasoning does not apply with equal force to colleges as to primary schools. Indeed, it is fair to say that they apply with greater force.[186]

Other levels of higher education are under the same standard, including colleges [187] and junior colleges.[188] The availability of education at Southern regional schools, which are institutions supported cooperatively by a number of states, does not excuse barring Negroes from indigenous academies.[189] And while there has so far been no decision concerning the practice of admitting resident and nonresident whites but rejecting nonresident Negroes, the language and purpose of the equal protection clause would not seem to tolerate this exception.[190]

One study in *With All Deliberate Speed* (1957) presents a thorough recent survey of desegregated schools of higher education. It reports that in the District of Columbia and twelve Southern states with some desegregation, 109 of 149 tax-supported formerly "white" institutions accepted Negroes, of whom about 2,400 attend these schools. In five other holdout states, there were 53 white state-supported colleges and universities, none of which accepted colored applicants.[191] In virtually every state where these schools are open, however, there have been

[186] 134 F. Supp. 589, 592 (M.D.N.C. 1955), *aff'd,* 350 U.S. 979 (1956).

[187] Frasier v. Board of Trustees of the Univ. of N.C., *supra* note 186; Parker v. University of Del., 31 Del. Ch. 381, 75 A.2d 225 (Del. Ch. 1950); Tureaud v. Board of Supervisors of L.S.U., 347 U.S. 971 (1954), for the *Tureaud* case on remand and discussing other issues see Board of Supervisors of L.S.U. v. Tureaud, 225 F.2d 434 (5th Cir. 1955), and see 228 F.2d 895 (5th Cir. 1956), *on rehearing, cert. denied,* 351 U.S. 924 (1956); Lucy v. Adams, 134 F. Supp. 235 (N.D. Ala. 1955), *aff'd,* 228 F.2d 619 (5th Cir. 1955), *cert. denied,* 351 U.S. 931 (1956) (University of Alabama); Atkins v. Matthews, 1 R.R.L.R. 323 (E.D. Tex. 1956) (North Texas State College); White v. Smith, 1 R.R.L.R. 324 (W.D. Tex. 1956) (Texas Western College).

[188] Whitmore v. Stilwell, 227 F.2d 187 (5th Cir. 1955) (Texarkana, Texas, Junior College).

[189] McCready v. Byrd, 195 Md. 131, 73 A.2d 8 (1950), *cert. denied,* 340 U.S. 827 (1950). This practice seems but a variation of the out-of-state scholarship substitute held inadequate in *Gaines, supra* note 185.

[190] See Afro-American editorial, April 26, 1958, p. 4, criticizing this practice of the University of Maryland.

[191] At p. 164. See N.Y. Times, May 26, 1957, § E, p. 60 ("Integration Is Gaining at the College Level"). But in 1957 a majority of Virginia's state-supported colleges still did not have Negroes, S.S.N., Nov., 1957, p. 10. All North Carolina University schools have Negroes, Afro-American, Sept. 29, 1956, p. 3. Subsequent to the WITH ALL DELIBERATE SPEED survey the University of Florida was opened, Hawkins v. Board of Control, 162 F. Supp. 851 (N.D. Fla., 1958). Early in 1959 the University of Georgia was ordered to desegregate, Hunt v. Arnold, 4 R.R.L.R. 79 (N.D. Ga. 1959).

one or more lawsuits for that purpose,[192] but probably most obedient institutions and certainly most Negro students in them have not been involved in litigation. While many of those enjoying equal protection at schools of higher learning have been favored by decisions in class actions, the defendants did not exhaust every legal avenue of resistance as to each scholar who might have at least been put to the trouble of proving himself a member of the class; and there has been no admission under the immediate coercion of contempt.

Deficient preparation continues to curtail the number of Negroes qualified for college. The University of Tennessee, recently required to desegregate, has authorized imposition of entrance requirements which applied without regard to race, and which, it believed, would keep down Negro enrollments.[193] Desegregated and enriched lower education in time should work to allay this limitation.

Most states which admit Negro students to "white" colleges and graduate schools continue to maintain colored ones which Negro students may attend. The Morrill Federal Land-Grant College Act recognizes maintenance of racially separate land-grant colleges as "compliance with the provisions of this act if the funds received . . . be equitably divided" as provided in the statute. The formula is more or less a separate-but-equal one.[194] Many Southern states provide out-of-state tuition so that Negroes may go elsewhere to take courses offered only to whites in their home state schools.[195] The very existence of all-Negro schools serves to attract Negro students who might otherwise apply to "white" institutions, but sometimes considerable effort is exerted to draw them there. Delaware State College for Negroes, for

[192] See notes 184-189 *supra* for some of the cases; there are others, reported and unreported. The University of Arkansas was opened following threat of suit but no case was filed, WITH ALL DELIBERATE SPEED at 165.

[193] The Tennessee case is Booker v. Tennessee Board of Educ., *supra* note 61. The examination policy is discussed at S.S.N., Dec., 1957, p. 9; S.S.N., March, 1958, p. 14.

[194] 7 U.S.C.A. § 323. But grants made under federal contracts must have a clause forbidding racial distinctions, see pp. 186-192 *supra*. For this reason Clemson College, S.C., refused to accept a federal grant for nuclear studies. S.S.N., Feb., 1958, p. 7; but the University of Florida accepted such a grant, S.S.N., Oct., 1957, p. 11.

[195] See appendix A23. The nonexistence of a statute does not mean that such scholarships are not granted. Florida apparently has not recognized out-of-state scholarships by statute but has authorized them, State *ex rel.* Hawkins v. Board of Control, 47 So. 2d 608, 610 (1950); *cf.* S.S.N., Dec., 1957, p. 12 (75 Florida out-of-state scholarships). On the other hand, it is questionable whether these laws are meaningful in border states which freely admit Negroes to all institutions of higher learning.

example, has experienced its greatest enrichment since the University of Delaware was ordered to desegregate; in fact, only thereafter did it become accredited.[196] Out-of-state scholarship arrangements similarly relieve pressure on "white" schools.

Yet there has been "two-way" integration too: some good "Negro" schools conveniently located at urban centers have enrolled substantial numbers of white students and have become genuine community colleges.[197] Desegregation has perforce raised the standards of Negro colleges which must now (and in the future, to an increasing extent) compete in the general collegiate market.[198]

The *McLaurin* decision makes clear that once a Negro student is admitted he must be afforded all of the university's facilities on the same basis as if he were white. There have, however, been some nonlitigated differences of opinion over how far this requirement extends. Louisiana State University apparently has tried to differentiate among the various aspects of university life. It has declared that Negro students may live in the regular dormitories without restriction as to rooms, bathrooms, eating areas, dining utensils, drinking fountains, and classrooms. But it would bar Negroes from student convocations, plays, lectures, musical programs, and so forth, if their purpose is entertainment, though not if they are presented as educational functions. Negro students may join an honor society, but not attend its banquet; they may not attend university-wide dances or use the pool; while they may be integrated at the commencement, their guests may not. Negro students must be seated separately at athletic events, but not among other Negro spectators generally.[199] Whether these rules would stand up in court to the extent that these events are conducted on university property or by the university is dubious. But informal social pressures as well as regulations work here, and there has been no legal test.

[196] See S.S.N., July, 1957, p. 8, June, 1957, p. 7. Redding, *Desegregation in Higher Education in Delaware*, 27 J. NEGRO EDUCATION 253 (1958).
[197] See WITH ALL DELIBERATE SPEED, at 174 (over 1,000 whites at West Virginia State College, 300 whites at Lincoln University, Mo.); S.S.N., Jan., 1958, p. 3 (Kentucky State College, Frankfort, Ky., reports increased white evening enrollment); S.S.N., March, 1958, p. 16 (if Langston is moved to Tulsa or Oklahoma City it is expected substantial number of whites would attend).
[198] See Hill, *The Negro College Faces Desegregation*, College and University, April, 1956, p. 291. S.S.N., Feb., 1958, p. 11 (18 Negro colleges admitted into Southern Association of Colleges and Secondary Schools for first time; 45 others accredited).
[199] 1 R.R.L.R. 970 (1956); for other nonclassroom treatment of Negroes see WITH ALL DELIBERATE SPEED, at 179-182. See S.S.N., July, 1957, p. 11 (Negro girl removed from school opera because she was to sing opposite white boy).

In the matter of how quickly equal higher educational opportunity is to be opened to colored applicants—or, in other words, whether there is a "deliberate speed" palliative—it is noteworthy that the upper school cases were marked by the swiftness of their remedy. *Sipuel v. Oklahoma State Regents* (1948) was decided with unfamiliar speed, over the weekend following argument, and held that: "The State must provide [legal education] for her in conformity with the equal protection clause of the Fourteenth Amendment and provide it as soon as it does for applicants of any other group." [200] Then the question arose as to whether the elementary *School* prescript of "deliberate speed" modified the rule for promptness in *Sipuel* and other university suits. The Supreme Court's opinion in *State of Florida ex rel. Hawkins v. Board of Control* stated that the pre-1954 higher learning rule remains intact.

On May 24, 1954. . . . We directed that the case be considered in light of our decision in the Segregation Cases. . . . In doing so, we did not imply that decrees involving graduate study present the problems of public elementary and secondary schools. We had theretofore, in three cases, ordered the admission of Negro applicants to graduate schools without discrimination because of color [citing *Sweatt, Sipuel,* and *McLaurin*]. Thus, our second decision in the Brown case . . . which implemented the earlier one, had no application to a case involving a Negro applying for admission to a state law school. . . .

As this case involves the admission of a Negro to a graduate professional school, there is no reason for delay. He is entitled to prompt admission under the rules and regulations applicable to other qualified candidates.[201]

The Sixth Circuit Court of Appeals has similarly rejected a five-year stair-step plan of the University of Tennessee.[202]

Among the so-far impersuasible states has been Georgia. In the case of Horace Ward, a Negro applicant to that state's law school, first a series of administrative appeals was required; then Ward was drafted; upon his release he was required to take tests for admission which had

[200] 332 U.S. 631, 633 (1948).

[201] 350 U.S. 413-414 (1956). The Florida court evaded this mandate, and upon a fresh petition the United States Supreme Court denied certiorari without prejudice to petitioner's seeking relief in an appropriate United States district court; presumably the thinking was that in the federal system there would be no disposition to evade and that appellate control over the inferior court would not present as many difficult questions of federal-state relationships. See 93 So. 2d 354 (1957), *cert. denied,* 355 U.S. 839 (1957). The district court awarded relief, Hawkins v. Board of Control, 162 F. Supp. 851 (N.D. Fla. 1958).

[202] See notes 61 and 193 *supra.*

not been required when he first applied, and this he refused to do. In the meantime, becoming impatient, he proceeded with his law training at a Northern university, which changed his status at the Georgia school to that of an applicant for transfer and made the case moot. Another case would have to be brought, it was held, alleging the new facts. Thus by dilatory administrative and judicial tactics the university accomplished what it could not have achieved on the issue of segregation's validity.[203]

The University of Georgia also requires that all applicants obtain certificates of good moral character from alumni, or in some cases, certain public officials. It would be difficult, if not impossible, for a Negro to obtain certification from alumni who are all white. Should the candidate meet admission standards, and pass examinations—including perhaps some subjective ones—the university system still retains the right to refer his request to another (presumably Jim Crow) school.[204] But early in 1959 the exclusionary rule, including the alumni certificate requirement, was invalidated by a United States district court.[205] Georgia fought this suit primarily by attempting to prove that the applicants were unqualified, but the court held merely that they had the right to have their applications considered on the same basis as whites. Finally, Georgia has provided that if a Negro wins admission to a white unit of the state university, appropriations will be suspended.[206] At this writing, however, no effort has been made to invoke this threat. Despite the decision no Negro student actually attends the university.

A devious, two-step credential requirement of Louisiana State University directed against desegregation was recently nullified by the federal courts. One statute had ordered that no student be admitted to a state university without a certificate of good moral character addressed to the particular university. Negro high schools were fur-

---

[203] Ward v. Regents of the Univ. Sys. of Ga., 2 R.R.L.R. 369, 599 (1957). The *Hawkins* case, *supra* note 201, followed a similar path. When it began to appear doubtful that the university could continue to justify exclusion on racial grounds or because, allegedly, a Negro would provoke riots, the state shifted to an attack on Ward's qualifications for admission other than race, N.Y. Times, May 17, 1958, p. 39.

[204] Resolution of the Board of Regents of the State of Georgia, May 9, 1956, 1 R.R.L.R. 968 (1956).

[205] Hunt v. Arnold, Civ. Action No. 5781 (N.D. Ga.). The university now uses criteria like those in the pupil placement laws to keep out Negroes. N.Y. Times, April 23, 1959, p. 8.

[206] Ga. L. 1956, Act No. 454, § 7(d).

nished only with certificates addressed to Negro colleges. Another law, which operated in combination with the first, provided that any teacher who performed an act to further racial integration should be dismissed; issuing a certificate to enable a Negro to go to a white school would be such an act.[207]

South Carolina has by statute promised to close any school of higher learning should a student attempt to attend under a court order. As part of the law the state's Negro college must then close too.[208] Appropriations to the state university, The Citadel, Clemson College, and other state institutions of higher learning are tagged "on a racially segregated basis only." [209]

The Alabama legislature has commended the state university for barring a Negro student (Autherine Lucy) whose admission under court order was the occasion for rioting.[210] While Alabama's state law school keeps out Negroes, the state, as we noted earlier, grants only to that school's graduates the right of membership in the bar without examination. Alabama Negroes who went out-of-state on tuition grants were denied the privilege, the Alabama Supreme Court noting that they had not applied to the state school.[211]

By way of contrast, some states forbid by statute discrimination in whole or in certain aspects at upper public educational levels. California, Illinois, Kansas, Massachusetts, Montana, Nevada, New Jersey, New York, Pennsylvania, and Washington do so,[212] and the language of some of the public school statutes cited in appendix A22 also may cover institutions of higher learning. New York's administratively enforced Fair Educational Practices Law has been considered responsible for a substantial decrease in discrimination in that state's colleges and in its graduate and professional schools.[213]

[207] See Ludley v. Board of Supervisors of L.S.U., 150 F. Supp. 900 (E.D. La. 1957), aff'd, 252 F.2d 372 (5th Cir. 1958), cert. denied, 358 U.S. 819 (1958).

[208] S.C. CODE §§ 22-3 and 22-3.1 (1957 Supp.).

[209] S.C.A. & J.R. 1958, No. 855, §§ 12-17.

[210] Ala. Acts, 1956 Spec. Sess., No. 118.   [211] See p. 168 *supra*.

[212] CAL. ED. CODE ANN. § 21701 (1958 Supp.) (state college scholarships awarded without regard to race); ILL. STATS. ANN. tit. 122, § 37-6(c) (1957 Supp.) (similar to California), tit. 48½, § 36(3) (in licensing engineers no school which excludes on racial grounds may be considered to be in good standing); KAN. GEN. STATS. § 76-307 (1949) (no exclusion from state university because of race); MONT. REV. CODE § 75-603 (1947) (School of Mines open to all residents without regard to race); NEV. REV. STATS. § 396.530(1) (1957) (University of Nevada not to discriminate in admission of students); on Massachusetts, New Jersey, New York, Pennsylvania, and Washington, see appendix A22. See Note, *Fair Educational Practices Acts—A Solution to Discrimination?* 64 HARV. L. REV. 307 (1950).

[213] BIENSTOCK & COXE, PROGRESS TOWARD EQUALITY OF OPPORTUNITY IN NEW YORK STATE COLLEGES (The University of the State of New York 1950).

Many colleges have been grappling with the problem of what to do about the discrimination practiced by certain fraternities, and some have forbidden it.[214] In a case involving state-operated schools in New York a federal district court held that the state Board of Regents was within its power in banning "social organization[s which] in policy or practice . . . operate under any rule which bars students on account of race, color, religion, creed, national origin or other artificial criteria." The United States Supreme Court dismissed the appeal for want of a substantial federal question.[215]

PRIVATE EDUCATION

Private schools [216] which once could be required to segregate or bar Negroes through threat of criminal prosecution or other sanction under state law [217] need no longer do so according to the rationale of *Sweatt*, *McLaurin*, and the *School Cases* even though such prohibitions remain on the books.[218] Although these cases did not deal with private schools, their pertinence is obvious. It has been emphasized by the fact that since these decisions many private institutions have been opened to both races with no action taken against them. Some of this has occurred in states without any other mixing of the races in education.[219]

[214] See generally LEE, FRATERNITIES WITHOUT BROTHERHOOD (1955).

[215] Webb v. State Univ. of N.Y., 125 F. Supp. 910, 911 (N.D.N.Y. 1954), *app. dism.*, 348 U.S. 867 (1954). The trustees of the University of Massachusetts have forbidden establishment of fraternities which discriminate on racial grounds and have ordered those with such rules to eliminate them by 1960, 2 R.R.L.R. 510 (1957). Concerning University of Vermont sororities see Chicago Defender, July 13, 1957, p. 20; on Rutgers see Afro-American, April 13, 1957, p. 11; Stanford, Afro-American, May 4, 1957, p. 12; Amherst, Afro-American, Jan. 26, 1957, p. 1; Williams, N.Y. Times, July 7, 1957, p. 38. There is also the question of whether fraternities at state universities may discriminate under the Fourteenth Amendment. See, Horowitz, *Discriminatory Fraternities at State Universities—A Violation of the Fourteenth Amendment?* 25 So. CALIF. L. REV. 289 (1952). The California Attorney General holds that state-supported colleges may not subsidize discriminatory fraternities, N.Y. Times, Jan. 3, 1959, p. 10.

[216] See, generally, the thorough, scholarly study MILLER, RACIAL DISCRIMINATION AND PRIVATE EDUCATION (1957).

[217] See Berea College v. Kentucky, 211 U.S. 45 (1908). The statute involved in *Berea College* was amended in 1950 to permit admission of Negroes to white schools where no equal instruction is offered at Kentucky State College. KY. REV. STATS. § 158.021 (1955); see § 159.990 (fine and imprisonment).

[218] For discussion of governmental sanctions against desegregation in private education see Miller, *op. cit. supra* note 216 at ch. 2. He points out that the Louisiana and Mississippi legislatures have been poised to act against desegregating private schools and that perhaps only the relatively light degree of private desegregation has stayed state retaliation.

[219] See WITH ALL DELIBERATE SPEED, at 166; LOTH & FLEMING, INTEGRATION NORTH AND SOUTH 62-67. Clark, *Desegregation—An Appraisal of the Evidence,* 9 J. SOCIAL ISSUES 17 (1953). The Association of American Law Schools has voted

However, reprisal, other than that specified by statute, is possible. In South Carolina a Negro school which admitted a Hungarian refugee and was accused of harboring "left-wingers" on its faculty found itself in trouble with the state accrediting authorities (loss of accreditation means that graduates cannot automatically qualify as teachers in the state system).[220] Enforcement of other regulations, *e.g.*, building, sanitary, safety, in an arbitrary manner is in the opinion of one expert an even more effective way for the state to retaliate.[221] It is suggestive that as part of a package of laws to preserve segregation Georgia enacted that no private school may be operated without a certificate of the state Fire Marshal that the school building is not a fire hazard.[222] Private intimidation is a weapon too.[223]

The laws of some states, however, prohibit discrimination in private schools at various levels,[224] and administrative enforcement of such rules has been effective.[225] The principal targets of the administratively implemented laws are the private institutions.

We have mentioned the right of state colleges to regulate fraternities with respect to discrimination. Private schools have undertaken such control too, undoubtedly with propriety, given their broad authority to discipline, including the generally recognized right to forbid fraternity membership altogether.[226]

A more intriguing legal question is that of the extent to which the Fourteenth Amendment applies to the admission policies of private schools. (The word "private" here does not comprehend the plans designed to avoid the requirements of the *School Segregation Cases*, which present a quite different issue.) Private schools are extensively regulated by the states and enjoy many governmental benefits, not the least of which is tax exemption.[227] "State action" has been found

---

to censure member institutions which bar applicants because of race, N.Y. Times, Dec. 31, 1957, p. 9.

[220] See S.S.N., Oct., 1957, p. 13; Afro-American, Sept. 28, 1957, p. 1 (Hungarian student will not leave); but see S.S.N., Oct., 1958, p. 18 (same student refused re-enrollment).

[221] MILLER, *op. cit. supra* note 216, at 34-37.

[222] GA. CODE ANN. § 32-811 (1957 Supp.).

[223] MILLER, ch. 3. S.S.N., April, 1958, p. 5 (Citizens' Council severely criticizes Mississippi College for permitting antisegregation address on campus).

[224] Massachusetts, New Jersey, New York, Oregon, Washington; statutes cited in appendix A22.

[225] See note 213 *supra* and discussion of administrative enforcement in employment, pp. 192–206 *supra*, public accommodations, pp. 106–112 *supra*, and housing, pp. 308–310 *infra*.

[226] AM. JUR., *Universities and Colleges*, §§ 19, 20 (1946).

[227] See BEACH & WILL, THE STATE AND NONPUBLIC SCHOOLS (1958), for a study

in other activities because of sufficient state-private nexus, and perhaps, it has been suggested, the linkage between a private school and the government may be substantial enough to invoke constitutional control. In the first phase of the *Girard College* case [228] the requisite connection was found in the fact that the college was administered by public officials. But such administration is not a commonplace characteristic of private schools. There has been little other decisional law on state action in the precise area of private schooling, and to form any prediction about it we must look to how the courts have treated the state action issue in connection with other activities, treated more fully as a general proposition in chapter II.

There, the proposition is advanced that pressure exists for the state action concept to expand, although the courts may try to avoid definitive decision on the issue. But the countervailing weight will lie in how significantly private school arrangements, *with the help of government*, tend to perpetuate a caste system in our society. If the courts make their decisions in terms of state-private contacts, but in addition weigh the social role of the private education under examination, wide, general rulings will be avoided and the sense of the state action concept preserved. Therefore, the extent to which private schools accommodate themselves voluntarily to a nondiscriminatory regime and the importance of private education in America may count more toward deciding questions of constitutional control than labels of "private" and "public."

FEDERAL LEGISLATION, ACTUAL AND PROPOSED

The Civil Rights Acts theoretically could provide a remedy against school segregation. Title 18 U.S.C. § 242 is violated by one who under color of law willfully deprives another of the equal protection of the laws. Even when separate-but-equal was deemed to be the law, section 242 was held to cover denial of equality in schools,[229] and thus

---

of private school enrollments, state regulation of such schools, state aid required and forbidden them, state department of education responsibilities, etc. See S.S.N., Nov., 1957, p. 4 (Maryland Attorney General rules that state funds donated to private colleges do not make them public).

[228] Pennsylvania v. Board of Directors of City Trusts of Philadelphia, 353 U.S. 922 (1957). See also Kerr v. Enoch Pratt Free Library, 149 F.2d 212 (4th Cir. 1945), *cert. denied*, 326 U.S. 721 (1945); *compare with* Norris v. Mayor and City Council of Baltimore, 78 F. Supp. 451 (D. Md. 1948) (private board; state funds; other aid; held, no state action).

[229] United States v. Buntin, 10 Fed. 730 (C.C.S.D. Ohio 1882). See the discussion of § 242 p. 136 *supra* and pp. 316–323 *infra*. For discussion of school segregation and the Civil Rights Acts see Note, *Implementation of Desegregation by the*

it applied to state action. Title 18 U.S.C. § 241, which also forbids deprivation of constitutional rights, but does not require "color of law," has not been extended beyond constitutional rights growing out of a citizen's direct relationship with the United States. According to this interpretation, it does not protect Fourteenth Amendment rights, which, it is said, arise in the first instance out of the relationship with one's state. Section 241 would, however, probably protect an individual's right to bring or pursue actions for desegregation in the federal courts,[230] for one who sought to block filing of such a suit would be interfering with access to the United States courts. Sections 241 and 242 are enforced criminally, which means that proof must be beyond a reasonable doubt and that the defendant is entitled to a jury. School officials, usually well respected in the community, would make poor subjects for such a prosecution.

Moreover, the requirement of specific intent of *Screws v. United States* [231] would raise novel questions in a school suit. Is a board violating the Constitution when it segregates, or only when it fails to desegregate with all deliberate speed? Put another way, is delay in desegregating, if justified under the deliberate speed formula, not violative of the civil rights laws? When we start applying concepts so elastic to a criminal wrong, do we have standards suitable for judicial administration? Criminal laws must meet certain constitutional standards of specificity. Would there not be constitutional questions which the intent requirement of *Screws* sought to meet, since "deliberate speed" is not a specific concept? An offender who clearly seems to be subject to the penal prohibitions, however, is one whose duty and desegregation timetable has already been defined in a civil desegregation action. In addition, school boards which have done nothing at all to conform with the Constitution appear to be vulnerable. In both cases there would seem to be no "intent" defense.

Title 42 U.S.C. § 1983 provides for civil action where rights secured by the Fourteenth Amendment have been denied under the color of law. Probably all school segregation suits by private parties have invoked it. Section 1985(3) further provides civil suit for damages against those who have conspired to deprive persons of the equal protection of the laws. But, as developed in more detail in chapter IX, section

---

Lower Courts, 71 HARV. L. REV. 486, 500 (1958); Note, *Legal Sanctions To Enforce Desegregation in the Public Schools*, 65 YALE L.J. 630, 648 (1956).

[230] See pp. 319–320 *infra* for discussion of § 241.

[231] 325 U.S. 91 (1945); discussed *infra* p. 317.

1985(3) has been construed not to apply to private persons except where their actions amount to taking over the government.[232] Civil suit is also available as a remedy to school boards which having desegregated are then harassed by dissident prosegregationists.[233] These civil statutes, however, suffer the limitation that *ad hoc* private enforcement by disadvantaged, often harassed Negroes is an ineffective manner of securing general adherence to a broad remedial constitutional provision of great public importance.

Because criminal and private civil remedies have these shortcomings, other approaches have been suggested. In chapter II we noted various authority for the participation of the Attorney General of the United States and several cases in which he appeared as a friend of the court. Going beyond this, it has been proposed that he be invested with power to bring civil suits in equity himself in order to secure Negroes' rights to school desegregation. The Civil Rights Act of 1957 gave him this authority in connection with the right to vote.[234] A general provision in the bill [235] which became that act, authorizing him to sue in equity to secure civil rights generally, was stricken out before passage. A proposed civil rights act of 1958 attempts once more to confer this power on the Attorney General.[236] But in addition, it seeks administrative implementation. The Secretary of Health, Education, and Welfare would be empowered to suggest desegregation plans for districts which have not desegregated their schools and, after appropriate hearings and opportunity to conform given the parties concerned, to refer the matter, if necessary, to the Attorney General, who then would be authorized to secure implementation of the proposed plan by suit in equity. The 1958 bill has sought to give affected districts the incentive toward desegregation of supplying federal funds to study and implement desegregation and of assuring them of federal monies to replace state aid which might be withheld for having desegregated.[237] Other proposed federal statutory approaches to this problem have been to grant federal aid for education only to schools which do not segregate,[238] or to furnish this aid only to districts which are

---

[232] See p. 323 *infra*.

[233] Brewer v. Hoxie School Dist., 238 F.2d 91 (8th Cir. 1956).

[234] 42 U.S.C.A. § 1971.   [235] H.R. 6127 § 121, 84th Cong., 2d Sess. (1955).

[236] S. 3257 § 601, 85th Cong., 1st Sess. (1958). See also the Celler-Douglas Bill, S. 810, H.R. 3147, 86th Cong., 1st Sess. (1959).

[237] S. 3257 §§ 201–501.

[238] *E.g.*, H.R. 3305, 84th Cong., 1st Sess. (1955); H.R. 11263, 84th Cong., 2d Sess. (1956); other such bills are discussed in N.Y. Times, April 24, 1958, p. 24

not defying a court decree to desegregate.[239] The latter proposal would, of course, on one hand, supply an additional reason for defendants to comply with a decree; on the other hand, it would provide no prod to districts where Negroes have not filed a lawsuit, and perhaps would put a premium on efforts to keep them from instituting action.

CONCLUSION

Now, approximately five years after the substantive decision in *Brown v. Board of Education* there is a sufficiently stable equilibrium to judge its effect and perhaps to make a guess about future evolution. Almost 400,000 children are in what *Southern School News* calls "integrated situations," that is, no official says they may not attend under at least some circumstances nonsegregated schools. These situations exist chiefly in border states and most thoroughly in their cities, including, for example, Baltimore, Kansas City, Louisville, St. Louis, Washington, D.C., and Wilmington, Delaware, an impressive list, and only part of the compliance picture. In smaller communities there has been considerable desegregation too, but here one more often encounters so-called "voluntary segregation." School officials continue to maintain Negro schools but permit some Negroes to transfer to "white" ones. Therefore, it is argued, no one is forced to be segregated; indeed, it is said, there is a democratic element of choice involved. Pupil assignment plans adopted by noncompliant states rest on this basis. Such systems enlist in support of segregation the hesitation and insecurity that many Negroes must overcome to shift from a segregated way of life to an integrated one, thus handing over to governmental and private intimidation a fruitful field for operation. The legal objection, that such arrangements involve state-operated Negro schools, *qua* Negro schools, and maintain public education in a manner assuring the continuance of segregation, has not yet been fully explored by the courts.

The really "hard-core" states have adopted not only pupil assignment plans but out-and-out prohibitions of desegregation to the point of closing down schools and possibly substituting "private" instruction.

(Roosevelt Amendment); for dispute over whether such proposal has helped to defeat federal aid bills see *inter alia* N.Y. Times, Feb. 1, 1958, p. 19, July 31, 1957, p. 22, July 27, 1957, p. 1, July 26, 1957, p. 1, July 6, 1956, p. 15.
   [239] H.R. 1213, 85th Cong., 1st Sess. § 104(c) (1957) (popularly known as one of the "Powell Amendments").

These gambits, as demonstrated by interposition of the National Guard at Little Rock and school shutdown in Virginia, hold no promise of nullifying the constitutional rule, but they have and will continue to delay its realization. By employing time-consuming legal action and governmental intimidation of Negroes (and whites who are sympathetic to them), all of these barriers will deter desegregation until overcome by lawsuits and changed social and economic conditions and attitudes—none of them factors that work uniformly or immediately. The passage of proposed bills to make implementation of the rule a federal responsibility, effected administratively and by the Attorney General's suit in equity, coupled with federal financial aid to desegregating districts, would be a strong procompliance force. These proposals, however, are deeply enmeshed in considerations of national politics, which, in turn, reflect questions of political action discussed in chapter V. If by legal action and other inducement a greater number of Negroes voted, the proposed federal stimuli to desegregation would be more likely to achieve reality. Until then the burden of making the legal effort will rest on private, usually organization-supported litigation, which has done almost all of the desegregation job so far.

Sometimes, where school desegregation has occurred officially, housing segregation tends to maintain the condition—North as well as South. This raises the questions about housing discussed in the next chapter. Some Northern communities already are seeking ways to integrate affirmatively without awaiting housing changes. There has been much discussion and some achievement with regard to relieving school segregation created by housing patterns, and the problem will draw increasing attention in the future. To the extent that the task is thrust upon the lawyer, his most likely forum will be legislative—*i.e.,* drafting laws, lobbying, counseling antisegregation groups—not judicial. The most powerful arguments are political force and persuasion, not judicial precedents.

Perhaps the experience of Northern, nondiscriminating colleges makes most clear the fact that a legal answer does not conclude the issue. As one expert, Richard L. Plaut, has written, "Negroes are not excluded from colleges or graduate and professional schools, either in theory or in practice, in the 31 Northern states. Attitudes towards their admission range from willing to eager." But only relatively small numbers of Negro students are prepared to take the opportunity offered. "The differences," Plaut states, "are . . . economic, cultural and preparational." [240] An organization like Plaut's NSSFNS can help in overcoming some of these deficiencies by identifying, motivating, and helping qualified Negroes. To the extent that education is a function of one's entire life-experience, however, fuller integration in schooling can only come with—at the same time it helps to create— similar changes in other aspects of society. Law has had, and continues to have, an important role not only in integrating schools but in promoting integration in other areas of life as well.

[240] Plaut, *Racial Integration in Higher Education in the North*, 23 J. NEGRO EDUCATION 310 (1954). Plaut is Executive Vice Chairman of the National Scholarship Service and Fund for Negro Students.

CHAPTER VIII

HOUSING AND REAL PROPERTY

The constraints imposed by law on minorities, and the customary discriminations of society as well, often can be inflicted through housing segregation alone. Where thorough and systematic it creates school segregation, notwithstanding the *School Segregation Cases*, and makes most segregation very difficult to alter. For example, school segregation is illegal in New York. Indeed, the Board of Education of New York City has approved a policy (within the limits discussed in chapter VII) of assigning pupils so that school populations will be racially mixed. This program, which is aimed at alleviating segregated school patterns to varying degrees, in scores of situations can do very little. Because of housing segregation many Negro children live so far from white neighborhoods that they can conveniently attend only all-Negro schools. Some Southern communities, hedging against the day when they may be required to desegregate, are building schools deep in Negro or white sections so that school segregation will flow from housing concentrations and not from law. Public accommodations generally—theaters, restaurants, parks, buses, trolleys, and so forth—also reflect to varying degrees the housing which surrounds them.

The Negro ghetto gives rise to or causes further deterioration of slums, forcing its residents to live like inferiors and helping to reinforce the image which purports to justify segregation. Yet not only do Negroes suffer, the community generally must bear the higher costs of slums, the additional fire and police protection required, the reduced tax revenues, impaired public health, and other evils. Nevertheless, Negroes continue to migrate to the cities, especially to the North, and ghettoes everywhere show no sign of dissolving.[1]

[1] See Grodzins, *Metropolitan Segregation*, Scientific American, Oct., 1957, p. 33, for detailed statistics; Chicago Defender, Nov. 2, 1957, p. 21; N.Y. Times, Nov. 19, 1956, p. 1 ("Non-Whites Up 41% in City, Whites Down 6% Since '50").

Some seek to justify separate housing by arguing that Negro entry into white areas depreciates property values, that Negroes are undesirable neighbors, and that white people do not want to live with them. These factors were stressed recently in New York City by opponents of the recently enacted ordinance to forbid segregation in private housing who at the same time avowed belief in equality in virtually all other activities.[2] Sometimes, however, opposition to integrated housing goes beyond advocacy and becomes violent, in the North as well as in the South. Despite the growth of opposition to housing segregation and the arguments which support it, it is, in fact, still quite difficult for Negroes to find dwellings in white areas in most places.

THE LEGAL FRAMEWORK

The statute books and judicial and administrative reports record repeated efforts and counterefforts to enlist law's aid in both housing segregation and desegregation. The chief implements for achieving residential segregation used to be the racial zoning ordinance and the restrictive covenant. Both have been outlawed under the Fourteenth Amendment but the concentrations and traditions they created linger on. Moreover, they are still sometimes surreptitiously used under the guise of nonracial regulations. We shall consider the legal remedies for such situations, and discuss also the various state and federal plans to build or stimulate housing, including public housing, urban renewal, and Federal Housing Administration (FHA) mortgage insurance. Here the area of indecision centers once more on how much governmental participation constitutes state action. Finally, we shall take up the growing number of statutes and ordinances designed to control housing bias.

RACIAL ZONING ORDINANCES

The most straightforward legal device for segregating housing was the racial zoning ordinance. As first reviewed by the Supreme Court in a case involving Louisville, Kentucky (*Buchanan v. Warley*, 1917),[3] the rule forbade occupancy by members of one race in areas where the majority of houses were occupied by members of the other. Other forms of the rule that later came under review provided that a member of one race might occupy property in areas zoned for another only if

[2] See N.Y. Times Magazine, July 21, 1957, p. 13.   [3] 245 U.S. 60 (1917).

most of the residents consented (*Harmon v. Tyler,* 1927, involving New Orleans) [4] or, in purported support of anti-intermarriage laws, that no one might purchase or lease in a block where most of the residents belonged to a race into which the would-be dweller could not legally marry (*City of Richmond v. Deans,* 1930).[5]

The *Buchanan* decision, which the others cited, and which was written while *Plessy v. Ferguson* was still deemed respectable law, held that racial zoning denied due process of law and that the separate-but-equal doctrine did not apply to rights in real property. *Buchanan* arose when a Negro attempted to escape a land purchase contract with a white seller on the ground that the sale violated the ordinance. The Court dwelt on the irrationality of the zoning: although the law was justified as being needed to preserve racial separation, it ignored the fact that Negroes did live next to white areas and it did not restrict the entry of Negro servants into the areas. While the ordinance was supposed to defend against "amalgamation," the case involved purely commercial considerations. The zoning also had been defended with the allegation that Negroes moving into white areas depreciate the real property values there, but, as the Court pointed out, certain whites could have the same effect.[6]

Buchanan's furthest-reaching aspect was its rejection of the argument that racial zoning was necessary to avert racial conflict. Said the Court:

It is urged that this proposed segregation will promote the public peace by preventing race conflicts. Desirable as this is, and important as is the preservation of the public peace, this aim cannot be accomplished by laws or ordinances which deny rights created or protected by the Federal Constitution.[7]

Judicial endorsement of a claimed right to use and sell land free of racial restraint relied on the still-developing interpretation of the Fourteenth Amendment, but was favored also by the common law's tradition of freedom in the alienation and use of land.[8] Paradoxically, perhaps, the defeat of the Louisville ordinance probably was aided by

[4] 273 U.S. 668 (1927), *per curiam.*   [5] 281 U.S. 704 (1930).
[6] 245 U.S. at 82.   [7] *Id.* at 81.
[8] See the discussion in 5 POWELL, REAL PROPERTY 537 *et seq.* (1956), and Annot., 3 A.L.R.2d 466, 488 (1949); see Bruce, *Racial Zoning by Private Contract, in the Light of the Constitutions and the Rule Against Restraints on Alienation,* 21 ILL. L. REV. 704 (1927). See also Stratton v. Conway, 301 S.W.2d 332 (Tenn. 1957) (owner has a right to make reasonable use of his property; sale to Negro was reasonable use; damage suit of neighbor dismissed).

the same pro-property rights attitude which colored the *Civil Rights Cases* (1883), providing momentum for that ruling which upheld the right of public accommodations proprietors to make private decisions to bar Negroes.

Despite the Supreme Court's consistency on racial zoning, a North Carolina ordinance had to go to the state Supreme Court in 1940 before it was conclusively defeated.[9] As late as 1949, Birmingham was enforcing such a rule because, as the president of the Birmingham City Commission stated, "I believe this matter goes beyond the written law, in the interest of peace and harmony and good will and racial happiness." [10] In *City of Birmingham v. Monk* (1950) [11] the Court of Appeals for the Fifth Circuit, affirming an injunction against the Birmingham zoning rule, held immaterial allegations that Negroes moving into white neighborhoods provoked violence; the Supreme Court denied certiorari. But even now a racial zoning law is on the books of Palm Beach, Florida, and is being observed.[12]

Although there is no other evidence that such blunt rules are being enforced today, the technique often finds expression in subtler requirements which on their surface have nothing to do with race.[13] Some zoning regulations have barred cooperatives—which might sell to minorities; others have imposed acreage, footage, or financial requirements—which, as administered, have been modified easily for whites but enforced strictly for Negroes; there has also been zoning of areas for industrial use in order to exclude residences which probably would be occupied by Negroes; similarly, land has been condemned for municipal use following the movement of Negroes into an area

[9] Clinard v. Winston-Salem, 217 N.C. 119, 6 S.E.2d 867 (1940). Other racial zoning cases, all with the same result, are Glover v. Atlanta, 148 Ga. 285, 96 S.E. 562 (1918); Jackson v. State, 132 Md. 311, 103 A. 910 (1918); Allen v. Oklahoma City, 175 Okla. 421, 52 P.2d 1054 (1935); Liberty Annex Corp. v. Dallas, 289 S.W. 1067 (Tex. Civ. App. 1926); Irvine v. City of Clifton Forge, 124 Va. 781, 97 S.E. 310 (1918).

[10] Record, City of Birmingham v. Monk, *infra* note 11, at 158-159.

[11] 185 F.2d 859 (5th Cir. 1950), *cert. denied*, 341 U.S. 940 (1951).

[12] Holland v. Board of Pub. Instruction, 258 F.2d 730, 731 (5th Cir. 1958).

[13] ABRAMS, FORBIDDEN NEIGHBORS 210-211 (1955). See Afro-American, April 10, 1956, p. 3 (proposed 400-home subdivision in Prince George County, Md.; minimum lot size raised from 5,500 to 6,500 square feet; minimum dwelling value set at $13,000; discrimination charged); *id.*, Nov. 24, 1956, p. 6 (Creve Coeur, Mo., to build baseball field where Negro physician commenced constructing home; discrimination charged). See Bolton v. Crane, 4 CIVIL LIBERTIES DOCKET 35 (Cook County Super. Ct., No. 57 S 6577, 1958) (defendants refuse to provide water, ordered to do so until final disposition). N.Y. Times, March 21, 1959, p. 43 (suit attacking condemnation of Negro's home in white suburb settled).

where they are not wanted. It is rarely easy to prove discrimination in such practices.

RESTRICTIVE COVENANTS

With the end of the frank racial zoning ordinance the most clear-cut legal device for segregating neighborhoods that remained was the restrictive covenant. A typical form of such a covenant might be an agreement among most or all of the property owners in an area providing that:

the said property is hereby restricted to the use and occupancy for the term of Fifty (50) years from this date, so that it shall be a condition all the time and whether recited and referred to or not in subsequent conveyances and shall attach to the land as a condition precedent to the sale of the same, that hereafter no part of said property or any portion thereof shall be, for said term of Fifty-years, occupied by any person not of the Caucasian race, it being intended hereby to restrict the use of said property for said period of time against the occupancy as owners or tenants of any portion of said property for resident or other purpose by people of the Negro or Mongolian Race.[14]

Negroes who took possession of such property became subject to suit to divest them of title and to revest it in the vendor or perhaps another member of the "Caucasian race."

The Supreme Court, as late as 1926, without ruling directly on the point, indicated that such covenants were enforceable.[15] Thereafter it declined a number of applications squarely to decide the issue. But in 1948 in a new civil rights climate and as the problem's importance became manifest, it agreed to review a number of covenant cases. In *Shelley v. Kraemer*,[16] Chief Justice Vinson held for a unanimous Court that judicial enforcement of a racially restrictive covenant is state action and thus forbidden by the Fourteenth Amendment. He wrote that although:

the restrictive agreements standing alone cannot be regarded as violative of any rights guaranteed to petitioners by the Fourteenth Amendment. . . .
. . . here there was more. These are cases in which the purposes of the agreements were secured only by judicial enforcement by state courts of the restrictive terms of the agreements.[17]

[14] This is an excerpt from the covenant treated in Shelley v. Kraemer, 334 U.S. 1, 4 (1948).
[15] Corrigan v. Buckley, 271 U.S. 323 (1926).
[16] *Supra* note 14.　　　　　　　　[17] 334 U.S. at 13-14.

And he added:

It is clear that but for the active intervention of the state courts, supported by the full panoply of state power, petitioners would have been free to occupy the properties in question without restraint.[18]

Replying to the argument that judicial action was impartial because covenants were enforceable whether they barred Negroes or whites, Vinson wrote that "equal protection of the laws is not achieved through indiscriminate imposition of inequalities." [19]

A companion case, *Hurd v. Hodge*,[20] reversed enforcement of a covenant by the District Court of the District of Columbia. The high Court did not address the question of due process under the Fifth Amendment, but instead cited one of the Civil Rights Acts (Title 8 U.S.C. § 42: "all citizens . . . shall have the same right . . . to inherit, purchase, lease, sell, hold and convey real . . . property) in support of its decision. Invoking the Supreme Court's supervisory power over lower federal courts, the decision rested also on the alternative ground that those courts should not enforce agreements contrary to the public policy of the United States. Mr. Justice Frankfurter concurred on similar grounds, pointing out that "equity is rooted in conscience" [21] and that federal equity courts should not enforce claims if to authorize such an injunction would violate rights so basic that, after the Civil War, their protection against invasion by the states was safeguarded by the Constitution.

Vinson's statement in *Shelley* that the restrictive agreements were valid but unenforceable conflicted with the only meaning that "legal right" can have in a judicial system. As Holmes wrote, "Just so far as the aid of the public force is given a man, he has a legal right." [22] In time, if *Shelley* were to stand, the courts had to come around to the view, in theory or at least in practical effect, that covenants were legal nullities. Actually, the Vinson contradiction has probably been overstressed as an attribute of the decision. It was only a dictum, perhaps a concession to gain unanimity of the Court (possibly including Vinson's own vote). Later events have shown the attempted reconciliation to be without force, although Vinson himself protested that it was meaningful.

Despite the fact that after *Shelley* violators could not be enjoined, some covenantors filed damage suits against them. State courts were

[18] *Id*. at 19.   [19] *Id*. at 22.   [20] 334 U.S. 24 (1948).
[21] *Id*. at 36.   [22] THE COMMON LAW 214 (1881).

divided on whether damages were a proper remedy [23] for violation until the Supreme Court in *Barrows v. Jackson* (1953) [24] held such suits impermissible as an indirect method of enforcement (Vinson, author of the *Shelley* opinion, was the sole dissenter). To uphold the defending white seller the majority ruled that he was protected by the right of the Negro purchaser not to be barred by judicial enforcement of the covenant. (His possession, plaintiff had acknowledged, could not be disturbed under *Shelley*).[25] If this transference of constitutional right had not been effected, *Shelley v. Kraemer* could have become meaningless.

But the essence of the covenant decisions remains that courts may not enforce private discriminatory agreements. Thus, one must inquire whether they can otherwise recognize race in adjudicating disputes over realty, or indeed, in any other conflicts. The Supreme Court faced the problem when an agreement to bury an American Indian was not honored by an Iowa cemetery because the contract provided for burial of Caucasians only.[26] Sued for damages (for mental suffering caused the plaintiff, his widow), the cemetery defended on the ground of the restrictive clause, while plaintiff argued that the clause was null under the covenant decisions. The Iowa Supreme Court upheld the cemetery. The United States Supreme Court affirmed by an evenly divided court, but on petition for rehearing dismissed the writ as improvidently granted after it realized that the Iowa legislature had earlier forbidden such discrimination.

The issue arose in another way in a Minnesota lower court case [27]

[23] Phillips v. Naff, 332 Mich. 389, 52 N.W.2d 158 (1952) (damages barred by *Shelley*); Correll v. Earley, 205 Okla. 366, 237 P.2d 1017 (1951) (damages recoverable on theory of conspiracy to violate the contract); Weiss v. Leaon, 359 Mo. 1054, 225 S.W.2d 127 (1949) (damages recoverable); Roberts v. Curtis, 93 F. Supp. 604 (D.D.C. 1950) (damages barred by *Shelley*).

[24] 346 U.S. 249 (1953).

[25] Assimilating the right of one person to another has been done occasionally. See, *e.g.*, NAACP v. Alabama, 356 U.S. 449, 458 (1958); Joint Anti-Fascist Refugee Comm. v. McGrath, 341 U.S. 123, 141 (1951); Pierce v. Society of Sisters, 268 U.S. 510, 534 (1925); Truax v. Raich, 239 U.S. 33 (1915).

[26] Rice v. Sioux City Memorial Park Cemetery, 349 U.S. 70 (1955), vacating the judgment in 348 U.S. 880 (1954), and dismissing certiorari. See pp. 55-56 *supra*.

[27] Paulson v. Keller, Hennepin County, Minn. Dist. Ct., Sept. 7, 1950. See also Harris v. Clinton, 142 Conn. 204, 112 A.2d 885 (1955) (action by assignees of a contract for specific performance to convey realty and for damages; vendors asserted breach of oral agreement not to assign without their consent; held, the contract is personal in character, therefore unassignable without consent, rejecting contention that that conveyance was refused because plaintiffs were Negroes). See Stratton v. Conway, *supra* note 8.

where a seller sought to rescind a deed alleging that he had not known previously that the vendee was colored, a case that could arise whenever Negroes, after having been rejected as purchasers, buy through dummies. The trial court denied rescission, holding, however, that damages would be granted if monetary loss could be shown; it could not. It is questionable whether in such cases damages, or at least reasonably forseeable damages, are capable of computation, for studies of the effect of Negroes moving into white neighborhoods show that values may rise, fall, or stay the same, reacting to unpredictable and subjective factors.[28]

The recently published Report of the Commission on Race and Housing, *Where Shall We Live?*, summarizes some of the salient aspects of the evidence concerning property values and race:

> More often than not, residential areas which nonwhites are permitted to enter are older neighborhoods where the housing is already obsolescent or deteriorating. Declining values in those districts, coinciding with nonwhite entry, have furnished much of the "evidence" for the thesis that nonwhites injure property values. . . .
>
> If the whites hasten to leave, the market may be glutted by an oversupply of houses offered for sale in a short period. Then, the expectation of a fall in property values becomes a "self-fulfilling prophecy." . . .
>
> On the other hand, if white residents of an area are in no hurry to leave, but nonwhites are eager to come in, the pressure of nonwhite demand may bid up the price of houses. . . .
>
> In a third type of situation, whites may not rush to leave an area but nonwhite demand may be weak, and the presence of nonwhites may discourage demand from whites. In these circumstances a decline of house prices is probable. In some cases which have been studied, however, the presence of a limited number of nonwhites in a good residential district or housing development seems not to have discouraged seriously white interest in the area. Interracial neighborhoods have come into existence, with both whites and nonwhites active as both buyers and sellers, and values have remained stable.[29]

Indeed, in a case like the Minnesota one, the very suit for fraud, if publicized, could create or crystallize anti-Negro attitudes, raising

[28] Morgan, *Values in Transition Areas*, Rev. of the Soc'y of Residential Appraisers, March, 1952, p. 9; Laurenti, *Effects of Nonwhite Purchases on Market Prices of Residences*, Appraisal J., July, 1952, p. 314. ABRAMS, *op. cit. supra* note 13, ch. XII. See also Grodzins, *supra* note 1, at 33; N.Y. Times, Aug. 4, 1957, § 8, p. 1 ("Rise in Value Found After Negro Influx"—Birmingham; but surrounding white areas diminish in value).

[29] COMM'N ON RACE & HOUSING, WHERE SHALL WE LIVE? (Report) 19-20 (1958).

an additional question as to the right to relief. It may be that damages in all such cases would be too speculative to be allowable,[30] evoking the constitutional query of whether a rule allowing damages on such elusive facts is not an open invitation to employ the courts for the enforcement of prejudice, and therefore invalid.

Ultimately, as we have noted, these cases reduce to the question of whether a court can recognize race at all as a ground for decision. If we acknowledge that a private property owner need not sell to Negroes, can the courts tell him that if he runs into racial problems in a transaction he should expect no judicial help with them? The covenant cases may reasonably extend to this point, but in the Iowa cemetery case and others the Supreme Court has shown a disinclination to decide this issue.[31]

Some deterrent effects of the pre-*Shelley* covenants linger on. There is the massive racial housing pattern which they helped to create. Then the notion persists that restrictive covenants still retain some validity. Recent suits [32] have cleared titles subject to covenants, which had caused uncertainty for owners holding contrary to their terms—demonstrating their utter invalidity but also showing that they retain enough psychological force to stimulate litigation. Recently, the American Red Cross, undoubtedly legally well advised, refused to perform a contract to purchase a District of Columbia home for its president because the property was encumbered by a racial covenant.[33] The covenant at least could serve as a public excuse for not completing the transaction, although public relations, or perhaps other reasons, no doubt weighed more in the decision than the restriction's legal effect.

Just as in the case of racial zoning ordinances and other invalid discriminatory rules, devices have cropped up to evade the covenant rulings. Charles Abrams writes that a number of judicially enforceable conditions on ownership or occupancy, usually silent about race, seek the same end. There is the "Van Sweringen" covenant, which prevents

[30] See, *e.g.,* McCoRMICK, DAMAGES § 26 (1935): "The certainty rule, in its most important aspect, is a standard requiring a reasonable degree of persuasiveness in the proof of the fact and of the amount of the damage. Through its use, the trial judge is enabled to insist that the jury must have factual data—something more than guesswork—to guide them in fixing the award."

[31] See pp. 55–56, 90, 185 *supra.*

[32] Robinson v. Mansfield, 2 R.R.L.R. 445 (Pima County, Ariz., Super. Ct. 1956); Smith v. Clark, 2 R.R.L.R. 200 (Denver City & County Dist. Ct. 1956).

[33] Chicago Defender, Feb. 16, 1957, p. 2. Despite the ruling in the covenant cases "such covenants continue to be written into deeds [in the District] and are on file in recorders' offices." N.Y. Times, Nov. 2, 1957, p. 38.

sale without consent of the original owner of the undeveloped tract; there are covenants requiring the joint concurrence of a stated number of adjoining owners before land can be sold for building; there are those requiring joint consent of adjoining owners for sale, lacking which the violator must forfeit agreed damages; plans requiring club membership before one may buy in the community; leasehold systems by which the occupant leases land for 99 years and may not convey his interest without consent of the community's overseers; cooperative plans whereby residents lease from a corporation in which they own stock; reversion clauses which provide that conveyance to certain classes revests the land in the original grantor; option agreements whereby the original owner retains the right to repurchase; and still other covenants phrased in terms of income, occupant density, health, and so on, which contain enough leeway to bar persons on racial grounds without explicit statement of the real reason.[34]

However, in a 1948 Texas case involving a racial reverter, property was sold to a person of Mexican descent, violating the restriction. The original grantor, considering the property his own because of the breach, sold to a different purchaser. The purchaser of Mexican descent brought a cross-action in trespass, to try title, against the original grantor and his vendee for title and possession. The Texas Court of Civil Appeals granted relief to the plaintiff, holding that denial would amount to enforcement of the covenant.[35]

On the other hand, invoking a different theory, a racial reverter clause has been approved by the Supreme Court of North Carolina.[36] Land had been conveyed to the Charlotte Park Commission on condition that "in the event that the said lands . . . shall not be kept, used and maintained for park, playground and/or recreational purposes, for use by the white race only . . . then . . . the lands hereby conveyed shall revert in fee simple to [the grantor], his heirs or assigns." [37] Negroes petitioned to use the park, and the commission sued for a declaratory judgment. The North Carolina Supreme Court rejected an argument that the reverter clause was invalid under the *Shelley*

---

[34] *Op. cit. supra* note 13, at 224–225.

[35] Clifton v. Puente, 218 S.W.2d 272 (Tex. Civ. App. 1948).

[36] Charlotte Park & Recreation Comm'n v. Barringer, 242 N.C. 311, 88 S.E.2d 114 (1955), *cert. denied*, 350 U.S. 983 (1956). The owners of the reversionary interest later sold it to the city which then admitted all. Leeper v. Charlotte Park & Recreation Comm'n, 2 R.R.L.R. 411 (N.C. Super. Ct. 1957).

[37] 242 N.C. at 313, 88 S.E.2d at 117.

rationale, holding that the land would revert not by state action, but "automatically . . . and . . . by its own limitation expressed in the deed." [38] The Supreme Court of the United States refused to review. But whatever may have been the metaphysical notion in the medieval English property law concerning shifting of title, it is unrealistic to hold that a reverter clause operates apart from the law of the state in which it exists or could be meaningful without it. It seems reasonable to assume that if the racial reverter became widespread, it will invite Supreme Court scrutiny in the light of modern notions of jurisprudence. Its general adoption seems unlikely, however, for it has been approved apparently only in North Carolina. Moreover, it appears that reverters are not looked upon with favor by title insurance companies. Less formal techniques are available which do not encumber property with doubtful limitations.

Newer types of racially restrictive agreements cast the question of discrimination into the realm of proof, the issue turning generally upon what a court will be inclined to believe. A party to such an agreement who desires to sell to a Negro (and knows the original purpose of the limitation) but who is denied permission by those with covenant-like control of his property possesses the knowledge to testify to the real reason.[39] Consistent rejection of Negro purchasers also may establish that race is the real standard. Yet this may be difficult to prove, for almost any purchaser has some characteristic which may support a claim that he is undesirable, or at least invite dispute, since human beings are not wholly faultless. To prove a case where evasion is attempted might require, as in the jury discrimination cases,[40] establishing a pattern of conduct by tracing all other rejected would-be purchasers, if any, and studying the possible reasons for their having been refused, an expensive and not necessarily fruitful inquiry.

We must also note, however, that sometimes these covenant-like schemes are not employed to restrict sales to Negroes. Arden, Delaware, which has the leasehold system, is nonsegregated; some cooperatives are among the better integrated communities in the nation; [41]

---

[38] 242 N.C. at 322, 88 S.E.2d at 123.

[39] See 6 WILLISTON, CONTRACTS § 1753 (rev. ed. 1938); 3 CORBIN, CONTRACTS § 580 (1951), concerning the parol evidence rule.

[40] See pp. 323–328 *infra*.

[41] See, *e.g.*, Trends in Housing, April–May, 1957, p. 3. A. E. Kazan, Executive Vice President of the United Housing Foundation, has written to the author: "One of the cardinal points of a genuine cooperative organization is the Rochdale

options are sometimes declined notwithstanding sales to Negroes.[42] There has been, and probably can be, no measurement of the extent to which the new limitations are used for racial purposes. But because these substitutes do not restrict resale as unambiguously as their predecessors and because their adoption must take place in a climate hostile to racism, their influence is unlikely to be as widespread as that of the old-fashioned covenant. While some real estate transactions involving the new-style agreements may be attractive for the restriction itself, or for other reasons, such as location, construction, or price, owners may well be reluctant to curtail their power to sell or build by submitting to the unpredictable consent of others founded on necessarily vaguely defined standards.

FEDERAL HOUSING PROGRAMS AND SEGREGATION

In 1934 the Federal Housing Administration (FHA) [43] was created and in 1937 the federal public housing program, administered by the Public Housing Administration (PHA) [44] was launched. Title I of the Housing Act of 1949, expanded in 1954,[45] provides for federal aid to and regulation of urban renewal or redevelopment by private interests. These laws have had important social consequences, among the most significant of which have been their dominant role in helping to create housing patterns of segregation and, less often, integration. FHA and Title I also present frontier legal questions of how much governmental aid and participation in a "private" undertaking transforms it into "state action" subject to the constitutional restraints of the Fifth and Fourteenth Amendments—issues posed by "private" schools, "private" political clubs, "private" parks, and so forth, treated generally in chapter II.

---

principle of open membership—no discrimination because of race, creed or color. True cooperative housing has always followed this policy, irrespective of the existence of any applicable legislation. In the cooperative developments sponsored by the Amalgamated Clothing Workers of America and the I.L.G.W.U. in New York, non-white families have been living peacefully with their neighbors and have also represented them on the tenants' committees working with management." Letter of November 3, 1958.

[42] ABRAMS, *op. cit. supra* note 13, at 225.

[43] The statutory provisions governing FHA are at 12 U.S.C.A. §§ 1702 *et seq.*

[44] Statutes governing federally aided public housing are at 42 U.S.C.A. §§ 1401 *et seq.* (United States Housing Act of 1937); 42 U.S.C.A. §§ 1501 *et seq.* (National Defense Housing Act).

[45] Statutes governing urban renewal are at 42 U.S.C.A. §§ 1441 *et seq.*

PUBLIC HOUSING

Usually public housing is owned by local housing authorities, even though it could not have been constructed without heavy federal assistance. Annual federal contributions (which in part secure original financing),[46] assured for periods of up to forty years, are one of the principal financial boons which permit public housing to operate at low rentals. Occasionally these projects are owned by the federal government, but it has conveyed most of its own properties to local authorities.[47] In any event, whatever projects are federally owned are managed by local authorities.

Federal control, however, even of locally owned projects, is thoroughgoing and significant. The need for the project must be demonstrated to the satisfaction of PHA; [48] federal funds must be reserved to cover the undertaking; [49] and PHA must approve the agreement between the local housing authority and the local governing body.[50] PHA makes a preliminary loan to the local authority for the purpose of getting the project underway; [51] reviews, approves, and submits to the President the contract providing for annual contributions; [52] and reviews and approves tenant income limits,[53] rentals,[54] size and cost of construction contracts,[55] sites,[56] personnel policies,[57] and budgets,[58] as well as other important factors. That body also has "final and conclusive" authority to determine whether there has been a substantial default in the "covenants, terms and conditions" with respect to federally imposed obligations.[59] Where such default exists the local au-

---

[46] 42 U.S.C.A. § 1410(f).

[47] Statutory bases for disposal of federal projects are 42 U.S.C.A. § 1412 and 42 U.S.C.A. § 1524.

[48] 42 U.S.C.A. § 1415(7)(a)(ii).

[49] Terms and Conditions of Annual Contributions Contract Between Local Authority and PHA Pt. Two (Sept. 1, 1951), § 401.

[50] 42 U.S.C.A. § 1415(7)(a)(b) (low-rent housing).

[51] 42 U.S.C.A. § 1415(7)(a) (low-rent housing); see also Terms and Conditions, *supra* note 49, § 408.

[52] 42 U.S.C.A. § 1406(d).

[53] 42 U.S.C.A. § 1415(8); Terms and Conditions, *supra* note 49, §§ 204 *et seq.*

[54] Terms and Conditions, *supra* note 49, §§ 205, 212.

[55] 42 U.S.C.A. § 1415(5)(6); Terms and Conditions, *supra* note 49, §§ 101, 110, 404.

[56] Terms and Conditions, § 103.

[57] Terms and Conditions, § 307; PHA Manual of Policy and Procedure § 3110:1 (Nov. 2, 1951); *id.* § 3112:14 (Dec.. 6, 1951).

[58] 42 U.S.C.A. §§ 1410, 1411; Terms and Conditions § 407.

[59] See Terms and Conditions §§ 501 *et seq.;* 42 U.S.C.A. § 1421a(1)(2).

thority at the option of PHA must convey title or possession of the defaulting project to PHA.[60]

The public housing statutes contain no explicit directive on the matter of segregation. The only tenant selection standards which they impose are that facilities should be made available:

First, to families which are to be displaced by any low-rent housing project or by any public slum-clearance, redevelopment or urban renewal project, or through action of a public body or court, . . . or which were so displaced within three years prior to making application to such public housing agency for admission [61] [there are also provisions for veterans' preference]. . . . in the selection of tenants (i) the public housing agency shall not discriminate against families, otherwise eligible for admission to such housing, because their incomes are derived in whole or in part from public assistance and (ii) in initially selecting families for admission to dwellings of given sizes and at specified rents the public housing agency shall (subject to the preferences prescribed in section 1410(g) of this title) give preference to families having the most urgent housing needs, and thereafter, in selecting families for admission to such dwellings, shall give due consideration to the urgency of the families' housing needs.[62]

If PHA required "open occupancy" (no racial restrictions) in public housing, it virtually would spell an end to locally compulsory segregated public housing, for few, if any, states could afford much of a public housing program without federal aid. Consequently there have been attempts, often in the courts, to require PHA to cease payments to segregating authorities.

PHA's reply to these suits has been twofold. First, it contends that suit against it is procedurally impossible. On the one hand, it cannot be sued in the District of Columbia, it maintains, for in any suit against it the segregating local authority should be joined. Except in the case of the Washington, D.C., housing authority (which does not segregate), jurisdiction cannot be obtained in the District of Columbia's courts over local housing authorities, for, because of federal rules governing venue, they must be sued in their own judicial districts. PHA has been supported to some degree in this stand by a 1954 decision of the Court of Appeals for the District of Columbia, which has held the respective local authority to be a "conditionally necessary" party in such cases.[63] However, the court has postponed deciding

---

[60] Terms and Conditions §§ 501 et seq.   [61] 42 U.S.C.A. § 1410(g).
[62] 42 U.S.C.A. § 1415(8)(c).
[63] Heyward v. Public Housing Administration, 214 F.2d 222, 224 (D.C. Cir. 1954).

whether the local body is indispensable until after suit has been brought in the district of the local body or there is a refiling of the case in the district court of the District of Columbia under Federal Rule of Civil Procedure 19(b), which permits, in the court's discretion, proceeding without a party who cannot be served. On the other hand, PHA also argues that neither can it be sued in the district of the local authority, but rather, only in the District of Columbia [64] (where, it has already urged, the absence of the local authority kills the suit). Nevertheless, by what may have been a tactical error, it submitted defenses on the merits in one segregation suit in a local authority's district, and the court of appeals held that it thereby submitted to jurisdiction, whatever the correctness of its argument about venue.[65] This case, however, was decided adversely for the plaintiff because, it was held, she was not genuinely an applicant for public housing.[66]

Second, PHA declares that it is without power on the segregation issue and that local authorities, so far as PHA is concerned, may do as they please.[67] But PHA has embodied a "racial equity" policy in its contracts, requiring local authorities without "open occupancy" rules to distribute apartments among Negro and white families in proportion to their housing needs. Where "equity" is accomplished through segregated projects within the same community, PHA approves the allocation in its contract with the local agency. A racial rather than an individualized system of evaluation creates thus the situation in which applicants are denied vacant apartments solely because the quota for their race has been filled.

The equity formula indicates that regulating the racial factor in the distribution of apartments is not beyond PHA's competence as it conceives it. By the same token there seems to be no reason why PHA could not require nonsegregation. Indeed, it has been argued—as yet without decision—that the underlying public housing statute, in enumerating standards of tenant selection, has precluded use of other criteria, including rejection on racial grounds of an applicant who meets the statutory standards. Because serious Fifth Amendment questions of due process are raised by PHA's participation in segregated housing, the theory has also been advanced that these public

[64] Heyward v. Public Housing Administration, 238 F.2d 689, 695 (5th Cir. 1956).
[65] *Ibid.*
[66] Cohen v. Public Housing Administration, 257 F.2d 73 (5th Cir. 1958), *cert. denied,* 358 U.S. 928 (1959).
[67] Heyward v. Public Housing Administration, *supra* note 64, at 694.

housing laws should be construed to avoid these questions, by holding
them implicitly to require that no racial standard may be imposed.
Finally, the argument has been made that if the statute itself does not
implicitly forbid segregation, then PHA's actions violate the Fifth
Amendment. The Fifth Circuit held that a suit against PHA alleging
these grounds should not be dismissed without a trial eliciting all the
facts.[68] On the trial, however, and on appeal, the issue was avoided by a
ruling which seems to hold that the plaintiff did not apply properly and
therefore was without standing to raise these substantial federal questions. The court of appeals opinion, moreover, seemed to endorse the
view that the issue should not be pressed, citing testimony to the
effect that "actual segregation is essential to the success of a program of
public housing in Savannah." [69] Presumably the term "actual segregation" was used in contrast to that of "legally enforced segregation."
Opponents of such litigation have argued that public housing would
be abandoned in the South (and perhaps entirely as a federal program)
if segregation were outlawed across the board.[70] (So far there are only
a few Southern instances of desegregation in public housing, although
the traditional Southern private housing pattern has not been as rigid
as that in the North.)

Lacking a conclusive adjudication of PHA's duty, suit after suit has
been filed against local authorities. Obviously, a local authority which
segregates is violating the Fourteenth Amendment, as almost a dozen
cases have held.[71] Many authorities have desegregated without the

[68] Heyward v. Public Housing Administration, *supra* note 64.
[69] Cohen v. Public Housing Administration, *supra* note 66, at 78.
[70] *E.g.,* House and Home, July, 1957, pp. 40 *et seq.*
[71] In addition to the *Heyward* case, *supra,* see Detroit Housing Comm'n v.
Lewis, 226 F.2d 180 (6th Cir. 1955); Jones v. City of Hamtramck, 121 F. Supp.
123 (E.D. Mich. 1954); Vann v. Toledo Metropolitan Housing Authority, 113
F. Supp. 210 (N.D. Ohio 1953) (Housing Authority adopted nonsegregation
policy subsequent to commencement of action; court gave reasonable time to
carry it out); Askew v. Benton Harbor Housing Comm'n (W.D. Mich., C.A.
No. 2512, Dec. 21, 1956); Davis v. St. Louis Housing Authority (E.D. Mo., C.A.
No. 8637, Dec. 27, 1955); Ward v. Columbus Metropolitan Housing Authority
(S.D. Ohio, C.A. No. 4299, Nov. 5, 1955); Woodbridge v. Housing Authority of
Evansville (S.D. Ind., Civ. No. 618, 1953); Banks v. Housing Authority of City
and County of San Francisco, 120 Cal. App. 2d 1, 260 P.2d 668 (1953), *cert.
denied,* 347 U.S. 974 (1954); Taylor v. Leonard, 30 N.J. Super. 116, 103 A.2d
632 (1954) (quota system and segregation violate Fourteenth Amendment);
Miller v. McComb, Camden County, N.J., Super. Ct., 1955 (consent decree);
cf. Seawell v. MacWithey, 2 N.J. Super. 255, 63 A.2d 542 (1949), *mod.* 2 N.J.
563, 67 A.2d 309 (1949). On Louisville and efforts of some white tenants there to
stop desegregation see Eleby v. City of Louisville Mun. Housing Comm'n, 3
R.R.L.R. 1199-1216 (W.D. Ky. 1958).

compulsion of litigation. As of March 31, 1956, about 30.7 percent of the Negro tenants in public housing lived in integrated projects.[72] Public housing provides some of the most instructive experiences in desegregated housing that the United States has had, an invaluable guide when any housing desegregation is considered.[73]

Some consent decrees and the practices of certain "open occupancy" authorities require deliberate assignment, or indirect encouragement, sometimes with quotas, to achieve integration. For example, one consent decree which registered agreement to the practice of nonsegregation has provided

that in assigning housing units in such projects said [authority] may limit the occupancy of said housing units by "nonwhites" to a percentage of the total housing units determined in accordance with the housing needs of the area served by such projects, as determined by the last United States census.

The overriding purpose of the decree was declared to be to

make a good faith effort to carry out a policy of racial integration [so that] no person would be segregated or discriminated against solely because of his race, or color, or creed or identification with any particular ethnic group.[74]

As with schools, the armed forces, and other activities, the question of quotas in housing is important. The chairman of the New York State Commission Against Discrimination has said that the state's housing program will head inevitably toward "ghettoization" if the problems of segregation and quotas are not solved. He has indicated that a public housing program could not prevent segregation if it rented solely on the basis of need and if at the same time "the need happens to be all Negro," for then the housing agency thereby would become "the real culprit in the creation of school segregation in the district." [75] Another reason advanced for selection designed to integrate affirmatively is that the presence of an extraordinarily large number of Negroes causes a unit to be known as "Negro housing," which tends

[72] Trends in Housing, Dec., 1956, p. 4.

[73] See generally PHA, Open Occupancy in Public Housing (1953) (based on experience in administration of federally aided low-cost projects occupied by more than one racial group). On desegregated public housing's effect on prejudice see Wilner, Walkley & Cook, Human Relations in Interracial Housing (1955); Deutsch & Collins, Interracial Housing (1951).

[74] Franklin v. Housing Authority of the City of Sacramento, Sacramento County, Cal., Super. Ct., March 28, 1952.

[75] N.Y. Times, March 3, 1957, p. 62.

to discourage other applicants. New Haven and other cities have to some extent followed an affirmative integration policy, based on a quota system, sometimes withholding vacant apartments from Negroes while waiting for white applicants. Pittsburgh has solicited white applicants through advertisements directed at university students and faculty, foreign language, and other groups whose members may be eligible on the basis of income.[76] But there is division on this issue: the executive director of the New York City Housing Authority has said that "we would have the law invoked against us if we followed the policy that Mr. Abrams' division has asked us to follow. . . . We would not have white apartments and black apartments and brown apartments set up in our projects." [77]

This suggests legal questions the converse of those usually heard in connection with housing segregation: May an authority recognize race to assign tenants in a manner designed to achieve balanced integration throughout a public housing system? It may be contended that such an effort is unconstitutional notwithstanding its motivation, pointing to jury selection analogies, which say that there may be neither inclusion nor exclusion on the basis of race;[78] or reference might be made to Justice Harlan's dissent in *Plessy v. Ferguson*: ". . . our Constitution is color-blind." [79] But, it could be asserted in return, a housing authority would merely be righting a situation created by conduct often long illegal or morally wrong in recognizing race as a basis for housing assignment. The Constitution does not require inflexible formalism, it looks to the substance of the issue. Besides, the jury decisions and the *Plessy* dissent were aimed against discrimination, while token representation, or separate-but-equal, were employed to evade constitutional mandates for equality, not to achieve a higher degree of equality, the goal here. How such arguments would fare in the case of an individual Negro denied an apartment because he was not within the quota has not been decided. Efforts toward integration like those described above apparently have been administered with a great deal of flexibility, and there is no report of an applicant's complaining that he had been forced to take housing he did not desire, or that he had been denied housing, which could give rise to a judicial test of the new scheme's validity.

[76] Trends in Housing, Dec. 1956, p. 4.   [77] N.Y. Times, May 14, 1956, p. 27.
[78] *E.g.*, Cassell v. Texas, 339 U.S. 282, 287 (1950) (proportional racial limitation forbidden).
[79] 163 U.S. 537, 552, 559 (1896).

Some problems of racial overconcentration in housing can probably be avoided by building on small, scattered sites, neither deep in white nor in colored areas. New York City is beginning to experiment with this method. But in cities such as Detroit, where 90 percent of the applicants for public housing are Negro, any solution in terms of a rule applicable to public housing alone would be difficult to achieve.[80] This, of course, increases the pressure to desegregate private housing. Yet even where there is some legal basis for desegregating private housing, it cannot be very successful in a social sense without a breach of existing employment and income patterns which would enable substantial numbers of Negroes to pay what most private housing costs.

URBAN RENEWAL

Urban redevelopment, or urban renewal, is chiefly a program sponsored by Title I of the United States Housing Act of 1949, although it may be wholly local, as in the case of Stuyvesant Town in New York City. Under Title I the federal government may make loans and grants to local governments for assembling land, clearing slums, and making the property available for private redevelopment in the interest of the entire community. Loans may be employed to acquire and prepare an area for reuse; grants are made to pay up to two thirds of the costs exclusive of construction. Municipal powers of condemnation are used extensively.

Urban renewal has had enormous consequences for housing segregation. In the greatest number of cases such projects have not been built on vacant land but on the sites of former slums populated largely by minority groups. The Urban Renewal Administration has reported that as of June 30, 1956, there was approval for more than 75,168 dwelling units replacing 112,420 units to be demolished. Sixty percent of the families to be displaced were nonwhite; nine out of ten of the displaced families that had already moved from these areas and into public housing were colored,[81] thus increasing the tendency of public housing to become heavily colored in occupancy.

[80] Trends in Housing, Dec., 1956, p. 4. In Chicago more than 80% of current applicants are Negro; New York City applications are 8-1; New Haven 6-4, *ibid.*

[81] *Id.* at 7; *id.,* Aug., 1956, p. 5. See Afro-American, June 18, 1957, p. 32 (about 700 families, most of them colored, evicted to make place for Baltimore urban renewal project to house some 360 families; no assurance that new housing will be open to Negroes; urban renewal officials intend to "favor those who erect housing without racial restrictions"; but is there such a builder in Baltimore?).

The redeveloper is obligated to relocate site dwellers in decent, safe, and sanitary facilities,[82] but in the case of Negroes this almost always means in Negro sections, already overcrowded and slum-like, or in public housing which thereby tends to become *de facto* segregated. While in December, 1954, 63 of 85 Title I projects were technically available without regard to color, perhaps 5 percent of the site dwellers ended up in the new housing [83] (the rentals are almost always too high for them, and there is in almost all places no authority to compel acceptance of Negro tenants in private housing). Thus, urban renewal has resulted in more segregation.

To some extent the displacement that occurs is a by-product of economic, social, or legal concepts of how renewal should proceed. Some believe that antiquated, unhealthy, and unsafe buildings (generally occupied by minorities) should be replaced by new housing immediately, or they insist that Title I requires this course. Others urge that Title I permits construction on vacant sites, a wiser social course, they claim, which adds new housing and does not further compress minority areas.[84] Although it seems that new building may be undertaken on vacant sites within the spirit and letter of the law, urban renewal, it has been charged, often is a deliberate method of uprooting long-established Negro or interracial communities to replace them with all-white dwellings or nonresidential buffers between colored and white sections. The housing resolution of the 1958 Convention of the NAACP asserted that the organization "is alarmed over the use of the urban renewal and redevelopment program to extend racial residential segregation." Thus, that which is forbidden by zoning ordinance and covenant cases may be achieved by even more direct governmental action.

Condemnation proceedings have been assailed—so far without success—as a method of clearing Negroes out of an area.[85] Victory in a condemnation case would stop renewal at the crucial point—when Negroes actually are uprooted. Such a case, however, is confronted

[82] 42 U.S.C.A. § 1455(c).

[83] ABRAMS, *op. cit. supra* note 13, p. 248. And see Trends in Housing, March–April, 1958, p. 1 ("the urban renewal program—operating within a pattern of segregated housing—is creating slums faster than it is clearing them").

[84] For the two opposing views, see ABRAMS, pp. 249–251.

[85] Kankakee Housing Authority v. Spurlock, 3 Ill. 2d 277, 120 N.E. 2d 561 (1954) (County Housing Authority complied with FHA request to submit estimate of distribution to achieve racial equity; but no showing that segregation will be enforced). And see the *Barnes* and *Tate* cases, note 92 *infra*.

with the argument that courts need not presume that illegality is going to take place in the future. But, like all presumptions, this one might be overcome by evidence which clearly shows that the contrary will in fact occur.

There has been no legal test of the right to exclude Negroes from federal urban renewal dwellings, but the New York State case of *Dorsey v. Stuyvesant Town* (1949) [86] involved similar factors. Eighteen square blocks on New York's East Side were cleared and redeveloped to house 25,000 families by Stuyvesant Town, a subsidiary of the Metropolitan Life Insurance Company. The city condemned the land for Stuyvesant Town, conveyed city streets to it, granted it substantial tax benefits, and required an agreement limiting rents and the return on the company's investment. The entire undertaking would not have been feasible without state and municipal legislation. Yet the court of appeals held (4-3) that Stuyvesant Town was under no constitutional obligation, state or federal, to abstain from racially discriminatory tenant selection.

Judge Bromley's majority opinion, recognizing the extent of government aid and regulation, focused first on the fact that the city and state legislating bodies considered and rejected policies of nondiscrimination for the Stuyvesant Town project or entities like it. And it concluded:

To say that the aid accorded respondents is nevertheless subject to these requirements, on the ground that helpful co-operation between the State and the respondents transforms the activities of the latter into State action, comes perilously close to asserting that any State assistance to an organization which discriminates necessarily violates the Fourteenth Amendment. Tax exemption and power of eminent domain are freely given to many organizations which necessarily limit their benefits to a restricted group. It has not yet been held that the recipients are subject to the restraints of the Fourteenth Amendment.[87]

Judge Fuld's dissent argued that this was not a case of some governmental aid and control, but one of sweeping and indispensable state and municipal involvement. He found in the City-Stuyvesant contract and in the municipality's acquiescence in Stuyvesant's discrimination an unconstitutional exercise of governmental power. Analyzing a long line of cases in which the Supreme Court found that there was a

---

[86] 299 N.Y. 512, 87 N.E.2d 541, 14 A.L.R.2d 133 (1949), *cert. denied*, 339 U.S. 981 (1950).
[87] 299 N.Y. at 535, 87 N.E.2d at 551.

sufficient nexus between public and private deeds for them to be deemed state action, he concluded that "even the conduct of private individuals offends against the constitutional provision if it appears in an activity of public importance and if the State has accorded the transaction either the panoply of its authority or the weight of its power, interest and support." [88] Moreover, he urged:

As a going community, Stuyvesant Town functions subject to supervision by governmental agencies. Upon dissolution, its surplus assets revert to the public. All in all, the resemblance between Stuyvesant Town and the company town of *Marsh v. Alabama* (326 U.S. 501) is strong, the analogy between this case and that one, clear.[89]

The United States Supreme Court denied certiorari. It has been suggested, however, that passage of New York City legislation forbidding discrimination in all similar future projects solved the problem for the city and obviated the need for far-reaching constitutional decision by the Court at that time.[90]

The question occurs as to the meaning of the *Stuyvesant Town* case for Title I urban renewal. The 4-3 opinion it received is hardly the unequivocal voice of the New York Court of Appeals and cannot claim the persuasiveness of most of its pronouncements. The majority opinion has been cited virtually not at all in subsequent cases despite its general implications and the vitality of the problem, which indicates its lack of persuasiveness. The egalitarian trend in judicial decisions since 1949, while not decisive of concrete cases, lends the Fuld opinion more power.

In addition, urban renewal differs from the Stuyvesant Town situation in significant respects, namely, that national participation in urban renewal is indispensable and generous: outright federal subsidy up to two thirds of the net cost incurred is the heart of the scheme.[91] Stuyvesant Town enjoyed no such direct subsidy; in fact, in terms of outright expenditure it paid its own way. But most important, Stuyvesant Town was a single situation. By the time it reached the Supreme Court local legislation had isolated its social effect. Urban renewal is designed to remake the cities of the nation. A grand national scheme invites constitutional control more compellingly than does *ad hoc* local discrimination. The probability is that urban renewal projects will be governed by the Fuld, not the Bromley view. But their middle- or

[88] 299 N.Y. at 536, 542, 87 N.E.2d at 551, 555.   [89] *Ibid.*
[90] See Rice v. Sioux City Memorial Park Cemetery, pp. 55–56, 281 *supra.*
[91] 42 U.S.C.A. § 1453(a).

high middle-income nature, for obvious reasons we have discussed elsewhere, works against there being much desegregation in these developments, at least for some time to come.[92]

FHA-AIDED HOUSING

The Federal Housing Administration has insured more than 33 billion dollars worth of mortgages involving millions of homes. Basically, FHA relieves lending institutions of the risk involved in placing mortgages on housing approved by it, for if a borrower defaults on an FHA-insured mortgage, FHA will make good the loss. FHA may insure a mortgage of up to 95 percent of the value of the property for up to thirty years.[93] (The Veteran's Administration performs a similar function for veterans; the principles discussed in this section which involve FHA generally also apply to the VA).[94] Premiums are paid for FHA insurance, but should there be deficiencies, losses are made good by the United States Government.[95] No builder, lender, or seller is required to engage FHA assistance, and some do not; but the economic advantages are usually so extensive that there is great incentive to qualify for its benefits. By exacting conditions for the enjoyment of its protection, FHA has exercised a tremendous influence on the nature and quality of housing in America, most markedly in the case of large builders who construct for a mass market and who could not merchandise their product without FHA assistance; FHA-aided Levittown, New York, and Levittown, Pennsylvania, have populations in excess of 50,000 each.

[92] Compare 64th St. Residences v. City of New York, 4 N.Y.2d 268, 150 N.E.2d 396 (1958), *cert. denied,* 357 U.S. 907 (held, Fordham University, a Roman Catholic institution, did not receive subsidy by buying land in Title I development, as purchase was subject to duty to improve land. The *Stuyvesant* case was not cited. Constitutional rights probably would have been denied if Fordham were excluded from bidding, the Court noted. But does this not suggest a paradox, for without state action there can be no denial of equal protection, which is probably the right that the court had in mind). See Barnes v. City of Gadsden, No. 17534, 5th Cir., June 30, 1959 (no threat of immediate injury; dismissed; but Judge Rives dissents, in part on the ground that the court should make a declaration that a redeveloper may not discriminate). See also Tate v. City of Eufala, 165 F. Supp. 303 (M.D. Ala. 1958) (it is only speculation that defendants will discriminate.

[93] 12 U.S.C.A. § 1709(b) (maximum principal obligation for one- or two-family residence, $20,000; three-family residence, $27,500; four-family residence, $35,000. FHA insurance may be granted to cover 75% to 95% of appraised value; maximum maturity of the mortgage may be 30 years). *Cf.* 12 U.S.C.A. § 1706c (supplementing other systems of mortgage insurance).

[94] As to VA mortgage insurance generally see, 38 U.S.C.A. §§ 694, 694a.

[95] 12 U.S.C.A. § 1710(d).

To assure an economically attractive product, large builders seek FHA approval before undertaking construction. This means that FHA is responsible in large part for the characteristics in general and in detail of the housing. Indeed, it may be said that FHA's minimum property requirements [96] have altered standards of construction and design for the whole industry. FHA inspects and approves the site to determine the best land development plan, street location, grades, drainage, sewage, and other factors. The lending institution, prior to construction, applies for an FHA commitment to insure and in support submits plans, specifications, and so forth. FHA sets a valuation on the property for the purpose of computing the size of the mortgage it will approve in terms of a loan to valuation ratio which it establishes. This, of course, determines in large measure how financially attractive an offer the seller can make.

FHA has even greater control over so-called "project" or multi-family housing, usually apartment houses.[97] It regulates rents, sales, charges, capital structure, rate and return, and methods of operation to provide reasonable rentals. The FHA commissioner holds sufficient stock in such projects (for which he pays only a nominal sum) to make his regulation effective. Where FHA's terms are violated, the commissioner may replace the directors with his own board.

Until 1949, FHA was a powerful proponent of racial segregation, indeed, probably the only branch of the federal government with such a program [98] (by that date the armed forces were abandoning this policy). While restrictive covenants proliferated in an *ad hoc* manner apart from FHA, under it they spread en masse under government compulsion, for FHA refused to aid construction for racially mixed occupancy. As of 1948 it had insured not a single nonsegregated project. Said the FHA underwriting manual: "If a neighborhood is to retain stability, it is necessary that properties shall continue to be occupied by the same social and racial classes." FHA drafted and urged adoption of a racial restrictive covenant. In numerous official pronouncements it advocated residential segregation. Its position was based upon the general, uncritically accepted assumption that the

[96] For the effect of minimum property standards on the building trades, evoking bitter opposition, see House and Home, Oct., 1957, p. 38.
[97] 28 U.S.C.A. § 1713.
[98] For a detailed description of FHA's role as a propagator of housing segregation see ABRAMS, *op. cit. supra* note 13, ch. XVII.

entry of Negroes into white neighborhoods diminishes property values.

After the *Restrictive Covenant* decisions, and much pressure, FHA retreated somewhat and has refused to insure properties under racially restrictive covenants recorded after February 15, 1950. It has stated, in addition, that it will operate properties which it repossesses without discrimination and has managed some in this manner. It also has insured some construction for mixed occupancy since 1950.[99] Moreover, it has recently announced a policy of refusal to issue insurance for builders who violate state and municipal laws forbidding segregation in housing.[100] But over strong objection from civil rights groups it has continued to insure housing from which Negroes are barred. This adamant stand probably will be the scene of a great forthcoming constitutional battle. The issues are whether a builder who could not operate as profitably without FHA may, notwithstanding its aid and control over his operations, discriminate as if he were a genuinely "private" operator, and whether FHA may aid him.

The issues invoke consideration of all the state action cases discussed in chapter II, but no appellate case yet has been concerned with a factual situation precisely like FHA's. The closest was the one in a suit against PHA's operation in Savannah,[101] in which it was argued that PHA could not give funds to local segregating authorities, whose activities it closely supervises. Were that true, there would be powerful argument that FHA cannot offer valuable insurance, not obtainable elsewhere, to segregating private builders, whom it regulates similarly. A constitutional rein on PHA could have been imposed, not only because it does business with state and local governments, but because it is an arm of the United States Government. But, this case ended inconclusively—dismissed because the plaintiff was held to be without standing to sue.

The responsibility of FHA and the recipients of its insurance has been litigated only a few times and then in lower courts. A 1955 federal district court case involving Levittown, Pennsylvania, held that "what the plaintiffs are saying in effect is that these agencies ought to be charged with [the] duty [of preventing discrimination in the

[99] See NATIONAL COMMUNITY RELATIONS ADVISORY COUNCIL, EQUALITY OF OP-PORTUNITY IN HOUSING 20 (pamphlet 1952); Trends in Housing, April–May, 1957, p. 8.
[100] N.Y. Times, Feb. 15, 1957, p. 1.
[101] Heyward v. Public Housing Administration, *supra* note 64.

sales of housing project properties]. . . . But that is something which can be done only by Congress." [102] As to Levitt, the developer, the court held that it lacked jurisdiction over him, writing that there was no claim that he had acted under Pennsylvania state law. The assertion that Levittown, like the company town in *Marsh v. Alabama*, was in essence a governmental entity was called "far fetched," [103] and, the court further held, there was neither pleading nor proof that to be able to purchase a home in Levittown would profit plaintiffs the $3,000 necessary for federal jurisdiction, the minimum amount which had to be at stake to sustain such jurisdiction. There was no appeal.

The federal jurisdictional questions were by-passed in *Ming v. Horgan*,[104] a California state court case against builders in Sacramento County. The trial judge first overruled a motion to dismiss, holding that if plaintiffs could prove the truth of their allegations, they would prevail. He then ruled for the plaintiffs on the evidence. FHA was not a party to this suit, but a number of builders were bound by the decree. They have not appealed. Possibly the builders believed that an affirmance by the state Supreme Court would create a far-reaching precedent more destructive of the racial practices of the housing industry than is the somewhat isolated trial court decision. Counsel for the plaintiffs has informed the author that as a result of the ruling a few Negroes have been able to purchase homes in the areas in question.

DISCRIMINATION BY PRIVATE PERSONS AND GROUPS

Elimination of segregated public housing and the end of government participation in segregated "private" housing would surely encourage ventures into private nonsegregated housing. Such a departure, however, would run counter not only to the pattern of past decades but to the prosegregation sentiment of most persons and institutions in the housing industry. FHA and other government housing agencies adopted their prosegregation bent from the real estate industry, which through these bureaus was able to transform its private antimixed occupancy policies into official dogma. In 1943 the National Association of Real Estate Boards (NAREB) advised its members as follows:

[102] Johnson v. Levitt & Sons, 131 F. Supp. 114, 116 (E.D. Pa. 1955); see also Novick v. Levitt & Sons, 200 Misc. 694, 108 N.Y.S.2d 615 (1951), *aff'd*, 279 App. Div. 617, 107 N.Y.S.2d 1016 (2d Dep't 1951) (lease allegedly not renewed because plaintiff allowed Negro children to play on lawn; dismissed).
[103] 131 F. Supp. at 117.
[104] 3 R.R.L.R. 693 (Sacramento County, Cal., Super. Ct. 1958).

The prospective buyer might be a bootlegger who would cause considerable annoyance to his neighbors, a madam who had a number of Call Girls on her string, a gangster, who wants a screen for his activities by living in a better neighborhood, *a colored man of means who was giving his children a college education and thought they were entitled to live among whites. . . .* No matter what the motive or character of the would be purchaser, if the deal would instigate a form of blight, then certainly the well-meaning broker must work against its consummation.

In 1947 the reference to the "colored man" was deleted, but until 1950 the code of ethics of the NAREB provided:

A Realtor should never be instrumental in introducing into a neighborhood a character of property or occupancy, members of any race or nationality, or any individuals whose presence will clearly be detrimental to property values in the neighborhood.[105]

In 1950 this provision was deleted, but evidence exists of its continued observance in many areas by many brokers. In a recent Utah case [106] a broker asserted that he could not participate in a sale to a Negro without first clearing the propriety of such a sale with the Salt Lake Real Estate Board. In Los Angeles two brokers were suspended by local real estate boards for having sold to members of minority groups.[107] Builders and mortgage lenders similarly once had open agreements not to sell to members of minority groups in certain areas,[108] but nowadays where such arrangements exist they are likely to be tacit. It is common knowledge that realtors and lending agencies in many areas will not participate in transactions destructive of neighborhood racial patterns, except perhaps when it has been decided to, as the phrase goes, "turn a neighborhood over to colored." [109]

Among the possible remedies against such private arrangements, the most effective legal tool would be a state or municipal law fashioned

[105] These quotations are from EQUALITY OF OPPORTUNITY IN HOUSING, *op. cit. supra* note 99, at 15–16 (italics added).

[106] Gaddis Inv. Co. v. Morrison, 3 Utah 2d 43, 278 P.2d 284 (1954).

[107] Trends in Housing, Aug., 1956, p. 4. See also *id.,* June–July, 1958, p. 6 (similar suspension). See MacGregor v. Florida Real Estate Bd., 99 So. 2d 709 (1958) (upholding real estate commission's right to suspend realtor for selling to Jew contrary to order of principal). The well-publicized refusal to sell to baseball star Willie Mays, later reversed, was based on the seller's fear that he would be boycotted—he was a builder. N.Y. Times, Nov. 15, 1957, p. 2.

[108] See text at note 117 *infra.* See N.Y. Times, Oct. 28, 1956, p. 1 (Negroes accuse New York lenders of bias; they reply that refusals are based on obsolescence of buildings).

[109] See the debate in N.Y. Times Magazine, July 21, 1957, p. 13; Grodzins, *supra* note 1, and his discussion of the "tipping point."

expressly for the purpose. Some jurisdictions have enacted legislation to cope with discrimination in state-owned or aided property. New York has been the first city to adopt such an ordinance for private housing.[110] We may also note the Federal Voluntary Home Mortgage Credit Program [111] through which members of minority groups who have unsuccessfully applied for FHA- insured or VA-guaranteed loans from at least two local or reasonably accessible mortgage lenders may be put in touch with willing lenders. But VHMCP has been of relatively little help in aiding Negro housing.[112]

In addition, there are legal theories, still largely untested, which might be applicable to the problem of housing discrimination. First, there are those that center in the federal antitrust laws. These condemn all combinations in restraint of trade in interstate commerce.[113] Refusal to sell to a certain class, or a boycott, is probably a restraint of trade when it reaches such proportions that it bars a large segment of the population from the bulk of a city's housing market. Indeed, boycott has been said to be a violation of the Sherman Act, even though it has not fixed prices, limited production, or deteriorated quality, and even though its motive has been to protect a trade from what it considers unethical practices.[114] Whether in a housing case there is sufficient interstate commerce to sustain federal jurisdiction would be a question of fact. But the Sherman Act extends to the full extent of the federal commerce power on which Justice Jackson wrote: "If it is interstate commerce that feels the pinch, it does not matter how local the operation which applies the squeeze." [115] A more difficult prob-

---

[110] N.Y.C. Administrative Code § X41-1.0 (discrimination in renting or sale of multiple dwellings or in one of ten or more contiguous one- or two-family houses controlled by one person forbidden; complaints may be filed with Commission on Intergroup Relations or it may act on own motion; if it finds discrimination it may refer to Fair Housing Practices Board; if it finds court action warranted it may refer to Corporation Counsel for equitable proceedings). See also the Pittsburgh ordinance, appendix A24; see appendix E (Colorado, Connecticut, Massachusetts, Oregon statutes regulating private housing).

[111] 12 U.S.C.A. §§ 1750aa et seq.

[112] Trends in Housing, April–May, 1957, p. 1.

[113] For a succinct, authoritative summary see U.S. Att'y Gen., Report of the National Committee To Study the Antitrust Laws (1955); Handler, Cases and Other Materials on Trade Regulation pt. I (2d ed. 1951). Antitrust and housing discrimination are considered specifically in Note, 63 Yale L.J. 1124 (1954).

[114] Fashion Originators Guild v. FTC, 312 U.S. 457 (1941). See 63 Yale L.J. supra note 113, at 1129 (concerted refusal of lending institutions to deal with open-occupancy builders and Negro home purchasers constitutes a boycott).

[115] United States v. Women's Sportswear Mfrs. Ass'n, 336 U.S. 460, 464 (1949). See also United States v. Employing Plasterers Ass'n of Chicago, 347 U.S. 186, 189 (1954).

lem might be to show that concert of action necessary to sustain a finding of conspiracy. Before 1950, when the NAREB canons of ethics were amended to remove the explicit ban on mixed occupancy, concert was patent, and in some places like Los Angeles and Salt Lake City a showing of concert still may not be difficult. But even the defunct pre-1950 canon may also be evidence of discrimination in the absence of a showing that its precepts have been abandoned, while a contemporary parallel course of action in refusing to deal with Negroes would be additional evidence. However, as the United States Attorney General's Committee to Study the Antitrust Laws has said, " 'Conscious parallelism' is not a blanket equivalent of conspiracy. Its probative value in establishing the ultimate fact of conspiracy will vary case by case. Proof of agreement, express or implied, is still indispensable to the establishment of a conspiracy under the antitrust laws." [116]

In 1946 the federal government in an antitrust action did obtain a consent decree against the Mortgage Conference of New York, enjoining an agreement among its members to refrain from making mortgage loans for Negro and Spanish-speaking occupancy in blocks other than those which it designated for such occupancy on a map prepared for the purpose.[117] As the decree involved other restraints, and was not litigated, it is a guide but not a controlling precedent to the law.

Another approach might be via antitrust actions in the state courts.[118] There are a few signs that state antitrust laws, long inactive, may be applied with increasing vigor.[119] Such suit would not require proof of interstate commerce. However, some state antitrust laws are uneven in coverage and perhaps may not regulate real estate transactions. New York's law [120] was recently amended to remove any ambiguity on this

---

[116] U.S. ATT'Y GEN., REPORT ON ANTITRUST LAWS, *op. cit. supra* note 113, at 39. See also 63 YALE L.J., *supra* note 113, at 1127.

[117] United States v. The Mortgage Conference of N.Y., FEDERAL ANTITRUST LAWS WITH SUMMARY OF CASES INSTITUTED BY THE U.S., Case No. 868 (1952); C.C.H. *Trade Cases* ¶ 62273 (1948–49).

[118] As to state antitrust generally see my study, *New York Antitrust Law and Its Role in the Federal System*, in N.Y. STATE BAR ASS'N, REPORT OF THE SPECIAL COMMITTEE TO STUDY THE NEW YORK ANTITRUST LAWS (1957). A state antitrust suit against the Southeast Realty Board (Cal.) for enforcing discrimination has been dismissed on the ground that defendant acted in good faith. Beddoe v. Southeast Realty Bd., 3 CIVIL LIBERTIES DOCKET 62 (Los Angeles, Cal., Super. Ct., No. 5GC 1050, 1958).

[119] New York has recently appropriated an additional $50,000 for state antitrust enforcement, L. 1957, ch. 895; California and Texas have indicated interest in intensified antitrust enforcement by the state. Greenberg, *supra* note 118, at 91a, and 112a.

[120] N.Y. GEN. BUSINESS LAW § 340 (1957).

point and now clearly governs real estate along with all other commercial transactions.[121]

The not yet fully charted law of state action, discussed in connection with FHA and detailed more fully in chapter II, may also come
into play in the case of certain important lenders, namely, the federally
chartered savings and loan associations, which also enjoy federal insurance of deposits.[122]

Finally, the "company town" theory of *Marsh v. Alabama* [123] should
be mentioned. The United States Supreme Court there held that a
distributor of religious literature in a company town was not a trespasser on private property, but enjoyed the mobility and religious
freedom available to those on municipal streets. The implication is
that when private persons appropriate so large an area that it partakes
of the character of a government unit, the restraints of government
may be placed upon it. The case stands alone and has had virtually no
application since its decision. Its pertinency after the developer has
sold all or most of his property is questionable, for then his control becomes less complete or nonexistent. But its rationale could in some circumstances apply to the Levittowns and Lakewoods, towns from
which Negroes were barred by the original developers in a manner
forbidden to *de jure* municipalities by *Buchanan v. Warley*. A few
attempts at courtroom application of the *Marsh* rule have so far produced no significant decision.[124]

LEGISLATION OPPOSING DISCRIMINATION IN HOUSING

Despite the unquestioned governmental character of public housing
and the varying degrees of state involvement in other housing, such
dwellings have been widely segregated, even in Northern areas. Despite
government aid, most of the housing industry—owners, builders, realtors, lenders—are ordinarily called private businessmen. Moreover,
many do business with little or no government assistance. Therefore,
legislation has been advocated and enacted to control more closely all
housing, both private and government-aided.[125] These laws have four

[121] N.Y. STATE BAR ASS'N, REPORT ON NEW YORK ANTITRUST LAWS, *op. cit. supra*
note 118, at 10.
[122] See 12 U.S.C.A. § 1464 (Federal Savings & Loan Associations).
[123] 326 U.S. 501 (1946), discussed pp. 51–55 *supra*.
[124] See Johnson v. Levitt & Sons, *supra* note 102 (rejecting the view); Ming v.
Horgan, *supra* note 104 (*Marsh* theory urged but relief awarded on other grounds).
[125] The legislation, ordinances, and housing authority resolutions discussed on
pp. 304–310 are cited in appendix A24, unless otherwise indicated. See N.Y. Times,
March 15, 1959, p. 1 ("13 States Weigh [Housing] Bias Legislation").

chief aims: (1) to restate the undebated duty of public housing and to arm local officials with explicit authority for insisting upon their obligation; (2) to educate the public; (3) to require nondiscrimination from those now not touched by commonly accepted rules or those whose coverage has been disputed; and, (4) to lift the burden of enforcement from the usually helpless would-be minority group dweller by empowering officials to proceed against discrimination.

Most of the new statutes, ordinances, or housing authority resolutions are aimed at elimination of discrimination in public housing, for here the governmental connection is plainest and the rules most readily enforceable. The largest number of such laws are couched in general terms of making public housing available without regard to race, color, creed, national origin, and so on. Some of these provisions cover public housing along with other types, but reflecting local needs, restraints, and pressures, others state their standards variously. Fresno's Authority requires assignment to the project nearest one's residence. The Pittsburgh Housing Authority has made it clear that it forbids segregated buildings as well as Housing Authority projects (some projects called nonsegregated have housed Negroes and whites in separate buildings). The San Francisco Board of Supervisors and the St. Louis Board of Aldermen, perhaps thinking of keeping buildings and projects from becoming segregated in fact, employ the terms "direct" and "indirect" discrimination in their statutes. But the Hartford Court of Common Council simply forbids discrimination and segregation. The Pontiac, Michigan, City Commission details the type of advertising and application forms to be employed (applications must be received without designation of specific building; all tenants must be made familiar with the nondiscriminatory policy). Minnesota, other states, and the underlying federal statute provide a preference for site dwellers and residents of the municipality. The Wilmington, Delaware, Housing Authority has applied its rule only to projects erected since accommodations in buildings completed about the beginning of 1954 have become available. Omaha's Housing Authority and that of Washington, D.C., have legislated that implementation shall proceed gradually. The Detroit Housing Commission and St. Louis's Board of Aldermen have phrased or viewed their requirements as apparently advisory only.

However, while in large measure there has been no question about the duty of obedience by local authorities to this legislation, in a number of places only litigation has secured compliance. Perhaps the reason has been that some authorities think as did the St. Louis Housing Authority, which opined that "the public would be more apt to accept any change of policy after a court ruling on the subject rather than an administrative decision." [126] Some, however, have just been opposed to desegregating.

The next-largest body of legislation requiring nonsegregated housing concerns dwellings other than public housing that have received substantial government aid. Probably the earliest was a 1939 New York law which encouraged the building of "limited-dividend" housing. A 1944 New York City ordinance, passed in response to the Stuyvesant Town dispute, provided that "no exemption from taxation, for any project, other than a project hitherto agreed upon . . . shall be granted to a housing company . . . which shall . . . refuse . . . accommodations . . . on account of . . . race." The largest part of government-aided housing, apart from beneficiaries of FHA, is that constructed as urban renewal. In a number of states and cities legislation forbids discrimination in occupancy of such construction. In some places housing receiving other types of government aid, such as tax exemption, condemnation of land, and insurance of loans, has been placed under the same requirement.

Connecticut has taken another legal approach. Its state commission against discrimination has held that real estate offices are places of public accommodation and must serve the public without discrimination.[127] So far as appears this declaration has not been enforced against an unwilling broker, but there may have been some voluntary acquiescence.

Connecticut, Massachusetts, New Jersey, New York, Oregon, and Washington have legislated to forbid discrimination in governmentally assisted housing, including FHA- and VA-aided dwellings. While one could hardly question a state's power to ban bias in the operation of state-subsidized projects, its competence recently has been challenged with respect to those receiving federal aid. Basically, the argument is that states are powerless to single out builders who enjoy federal mortgage insurance, as this is an unreasonable classification denying equal protection, and that a state may not legislate concerning a federal opera-

---

[126] See RACIAL RELATIONS SERVICE & DIV. OF LAW, HOUSING & HOME FINANCE AGENCY, NONDISCRIMINATION CLAUSES IN REGARD TO PUBLIC HOUSING, PRIVATE HOUSING, AND URBAN REDEVELOPMENT UNDERTAKINGS 19 (1956 ed.). The 1957 edition, on which appendix A24 relies in part, omits this quotation.

[127] Trends in Housing, Aug., 1956, p. 7.

tion—something like the burden-on-interstate-commerce-argument, which assails state and local interference and invokes federal supremacy. So far these objections have been unsuccessful: Oregon enacted its law over its Attorney General's objection; [128] New York courts have upheld its statute [129]—and it is unlikely that the opposition will prevail.

The classification of all government-aided housing in a category apart from other dwellings is not unreasonable. First, government-aided housing is more readily regulated than housing generally. Administrative measures, such as suspension of aid, are easily imposed sanctions. Moreover, FHA has pledged cooperation in enforcing state antidiscrimination laws, enhancing the effectiveness of implementation. Second, classification based on assistance from the taxes of all will commend itself to the sense of fairness of more persons than a rule covering operations deemed wholly private. The San Francisco Board of Supervisors expressed a thought like this in legislating to make its urban redevelopment bias-free with the phrase, "and for the further purpose of providing public participation." [130]

The question of whether these laws place a burden on the performance of a federal function also should be resolved in favor of the laws. The constitutional requirement is not hypothetical or abstract; real burden must be shown.[131] Even if a builder could show loss of sales or tenants, this would hardly constitute a burden imposed by the state or municipality on a function of the federal government, namely, the insuring of mortgages. Cooperation between FHA and states which have enacted these laws, considered in conjunction with the national policy against discrimination, indicates the contrary of burden. Rather, the state may be said to be enhancing federal policy; indeed, the Supreme Court has held that state-federal cooperation negates an argu-

[128] See Op. Att'y Gen. of Ore. No. 3640 (March 19, 1957), reported at 2 R.R.L.R. 746 (1957).

[129] Matter of N.Y. State Comm'n v. Pelham Hall Apartments, 10 Misc. 2d 334, 170 N.Y.S.2d 910 (1958); see also Matter of N.Y. State Comm'n v. Pelham Hall Apartments, 10 Misc. 2d 346, 171 N.Y.S.2d 558 (1958) (motion of white tenants to intervene denied). See Trends in Housing, June–July, 1958, p. 6 (first New Jersey hearings). Levitt sues to enjoin enforcement of New Jersey statute. Superior court holds that Division Against Discrimination has jurisdiction. *Id.*, Jan.–Feb., 1959, p. 8.

[130] See appendix A24.

[131] Rice v. Chicago Bd. of Trade, 331 U.S. 247, 256 (1947); Southern Pac. Ry. v. Arizona, 325 U.S. 761, 766 (1945); see also Frankfurter, J., dissenting in Hood & Sons v. DuMond, 336 U.S. 525, 564, 575 (1949).

ment of interference.[132] While in most preemption cases the court's first search is for the intent of Congress in enacting the legislation with which conflict is alleged,[133] Congress expressed no intent with respect to this preemption issue. Neither could conflict be found should the courts try to reconstruct congressional "intent" in terms of a balance of relevant national policies, as they sometimes do.[134] A strong argument can be made (see *Ming v. Horgan*) that Congress was constitutionally required to intend nondiscrimination.

Some of the other recent legislation against housing discrimination has restated the *Restrictive Covenant Cases*, and forbids such covenants or declares that they are without force.[135] Still other laws, usually in connection with urban renewal, have gone further and required that covenants requiring nondiscrimination be placed in deeds of redevelopment projects.[136] New Jersey and the state of Washington have legislated to forbid discrimination in the granting of mortgage loans,[137] while the New York City Council has passed a bill barring discrimination in private housing, with certain limitations as to size of apartment houses or private home projects. It is the first such law of its sort in the nation, but Pittsburgh has recently followed suit with a similar ordinance.[138] The Pittsburgh law also covers lenders and brokers. Colorado, Connecticut, Massachusetts, and Oregon have, as these pages go to press, just enacted private housing laws (described in Appendix E).

[132] Parker v. Brown, 317 U.S. 341, 358 (1943); California v. Zook, 336 U.S. 725, 735 (1949); United States v. South-Eastern Underwriters Ass'n, 322 U.S. 533, 562 (1944). Of course, where there is conflict the result may be otherwise. See Northern Secs. Co. v. United States, 193 U.S. 197, 344–345 (1904); Southern Pac. Ry. v. Arizona, *supra* note 131, at 781.

[133] See POWELL, VAGARIES AND VARIETIES IN CONSTITUTIONAL INTERPRETATION 165, 178 (1956); Southern Pac. Ry. v. Arizona, *supra* note 131, at 768; Charleston & W. Car. R.R. Co. v. Varnville Furniture Co., 237 U.S. 597, 604 (1915); California v. Zook, *supra* note 132, at 730; Rice v. Santa Fe Elevator Co., 331 U.S. 218, 236 (1947); Ill. Gas Co. v. Central Ill. Pub. Serv. Co., 314 U.S. 498, 508 (1942); Interstate Natural Gas Co. v. Federal Power Comm'n, 331 U.S. 682, 699 (1947).

[134] *Compare* Morgan v. Virginia, 328 U.S. 373 (1946) (state bus segregation law contributing to lack of uniformity in interstate travel unconstitutional), *with* Bob-Lo v. Michigan, 333 U.S. 28 (1948) (state antisegregation law bearing on foreign commerce constitutional).

[135] See appendix A24: statutes of Illinois, Minnesota, Wisconsin; ordinance of Denver; resolution of Los Angeles Board of Supervisors.

[136] See appendix A24: ordinances of Cleveland, Los Angeles, New York City, San Francisco; resolution of Minneapolis Housing and Redevelopment Authority.

[137] See appendix A24.

[138] *Ibid.* Those who administer the New York law have announced "tremendous progress," N.Y. Times, March 11, 1959, p. 27; *id.* March 12, 1959, p. 24. But Councilman Brown has called for more information. N.Y. Amsterdam News, April 11, 1959, p. 8.

Procedurally, these statutes cover a wide range. A few are merely hortatory; [139] some provide criminal sanctions;[140] and others empower administrative bodies to investigate, issue orders, and seek injunctions.[141] Presumably, all—except possibly the few, vague, general ones—prescribe a standard which would support a civil action for injunction or damages. Aside from civil suits against public housing, which could have been brought under the Federal Constitution without any local laws existing, there appears to have been little or no implementation apart from some administrative action,[142] excepting, of course, such voluntary compliance as may be inferred from evidence of nonsegregation in jurisdictions where there are laws.[143]

While there is not yet sufficient experience to assess the effect of this legislation, there is no evidence that its existence discourages construction. It appears that FHA- and VA-aided construction continues unabated in New York by the nondiscrimination requirement there.[144] A few moderately priced projects in New York City contain a substantial number of Negro families.[145] But they, perhaps, do not fairly reflect the law's efficacy, since they have been built, for the most part, by noncommercial organizations which approve of desegregation. At the same time it docs not appear that many Negro families have moved into "white" FHA dwellings in New York, although one hears of a few. Perhaps this is due, in part, to the fact that until very recently no real effort was made to enforce the law. Undoubtedly, however, the difficulty involved in finding moderately priced adequate housing for anyone is a factor working strongly against any real change of racial patterns. Even under the New York City requirement that private housing refrain from discrimination the fact that the vacancy rate there, as elsewhere, is only a few percent,[146] and that most three- and four-room apartments in privately constructed buildings in

---

[139] *Ibid.* (St. Louis and Detroit).

[140] *Ibid.* (Connecticut, Michigan, New York City).

[141] *Ibid.* (Connecticut, Massachusetts, New Jersey, New York, Oregon, Rhode Island, Washington).

[142] See note 129 *supra*.

[143] See LOTH & FLEMING, INTEGRATION NORTH AND SOUTH 21 *et seq.* (1956).

[144] See Letter to the Editor of the N.Y. Times by Stanley M. Isaacs, N.Y. Times, June 18, 1957, p. 32. Some builders, according to Charles Abrams, are beginning to move "cautiously, and in some cases, quietly" in the direction of selling to Negroes in otherwise "white" projects in Queens, the Bronx, Long Island, New Rochelle, and communities near Buffalo, N.Y. Times, Dec. 25, 1956, p. 1.

[145] Trends in Housing, Dec., 1956, pp. 1, 3, April–May, 1957, p. 3.

[146] See 26 THE REAL ESTATE ANALYST 331–333 (1957).

Manhattan rent for $130 to $200 a month [147] are moderating factors. Rent-controlled apartments need not be advertised; they often are obtained through the word of a friend, or the friend of a friend. Discrimination in new buildings for middle-income or high middle-income families which advertise and rent through agents can probably be discovered by law enforcement officials, but not many Negro families can afford such apartments. All in all, given the current lack of availability of housing, the new law can mean only a small, albeit significant—most significant perhaps in its effect as stating an ethical norm for the community—step toward generally desegregated housing.

CONCLUSION

Law has played a weighty role in determining racial patterns for housing. To take the most prominent example, the restrictive covenant made neighborhoods throughout the nation in the image of the covenantors. By securing court enforcement they could invoke the full force of government to preserve their racial schemes. When legal action destroyed the covenants' validity, Negroes in many cities spread beyond the confines in which they had been kept. An analysis of the nonwhite housing market as of 1950 by the Housing and Home Finance Agency reported:

The improved economic situation among non-whites enabled more of them to buy more houses of good quality and of higher values, some in the better class neighborhoods from which they were previously barred by various restrictions on the sale of properties to them. This movement to better neighborhoods has accelerated since May 1948 when the United States Supreme Court prohibited judicial enforcement of racial restrictive covenants.[148]

In Chicago alone it was estimated that as of 1952 "more than 21,000 colored families have purchased or rented homes in areas formerly restricted against them." [149]

The restrictive covenant has been replaced by evasionary agreements, but these are of only limited effectiveness. By and large they leave the housing market subject to other forces.

Law has segregated public housing in some places and integrated

[147] N.Y. Times, Aug. 26, 1957, p. 1.
[148] HOUSING & HOME FINANCE AGENCY, HOUSING OF THE NONWHITE POPULATION 15 (1952).
[149] CHICAGO COMM'N ON HUMAN RELATIONS, FOURTH CHICAGO CONFERENCE ON CIVIC UNITY 65 (1952).

it in others. Many state and municipal legislatures have started to move against bias in this type of project. But because of economic factors and the fact that private housing will usually never accept Negroes out of the ghetto, public housing is turning more and more colored in occupancy. The racial pattern of some urban renewal projects reflects a little the purpose of the new legislation, but it too is largely segregated. FHA, whose legal status so far as race is concerned has not yet been decisively adjudicated, has helped to propagate a vast amount of housing segregation. Court action has been aiming at exclusion of segregation in such dwellings, and some legislatures have banned it. But the results for FHA construction so far have been almost nil. The Commission on Race and Housing has called "for a complete program and time schedule looking toward the elimination of discrimination in the distribution of Federal housing benefits at the earliest time practicable." [150] This reform would include public housing, urban renewal, and FHA. But almost immediately, the administrator of the Housing and Home Finance Agency stated that neither the government nor the private real estate industry had caused segregation in housing, and that it was not up to the government to enforce integration.[151]

As with other aspects of race relations, law alone is far from the sole cause of racial patterns in housing and law alone cannot end them, although its contribution should not be minimized. Prejudice of those in the real estate industry, and of the public at large, sometimes even violence, keep Negroes out of neighborhoods into which they might otherwise move. The dogma that Negroes depreciate property values— now more frequently challenged and sometimes a prediction which causes the condition it foresees—is a powerful anti-integration force. The lower level of Negro income and the scarcity of housing also damp the effect of any legal rule designed to assure equal access to living accommodations. But the laws set a standard for the community which over the long run probably will be effective.

Pittsburgh's and New York City's ordinances, and the newly passed state statutes (like Colorado's), go just about as far as law can (certain aspects of procedure and implementation aside) to assure equality in housing—that is, if law is limited to a rule merely enforcing an egalitarian precept. Their long-run effect may be great, but for the time being not too much change can be expected because of them. Law

[150] WHERE SHALL WE LIVE? *op. cit. supra* note 29, at 64.
[151] Trends in Housing, Oct.–Nov., 1958, p. 1.

could, however, help to get more housing built at prices and in areas that would make it available to minorities; it could do something about locating this new housing in relation to ghettoes in such a manner as to eliminate them. As many legal rules designed to provide housing without regard to race tend to push the housing issue more into the realm of economic give and take, a large part of change from now on will come from providing housing generally and equipping minorities to participate in the struggle for it.

CHAPTER IX

THE CRIMINAL LAW

Quiet enjoyment of equal rights to housing, schooling, employment, and other aspects of living depends fundamentally on security of the person from lawless violence. Basic personal safety usually is assured by the peaceful habits of most of us and the armed protection of the criminal law which seeks to prevent or control the use of force. These rules of criminal law obviously are general and apply to situations involving racial factors as well as to other cases. The Emmett Till murder, for example, was subject to the same rules of criminal law in Mississippi as were other murders there. The law treating vandalism and violence directed against Negroes living in the once-white neighborhood of Trumbull Park, Chicago, would cover affrays against white persons as well. But some criminal laws may come into play more frequently in cases involving physical harm directed against Negroes— for example, rules about lynchings, police brutality, and other injury inflicted by governmental agents.

Sometimes, moreover, personal security against racial discrimination is protected by the reins which restrain the criminal law itself. For if prejudice were permitted freely to permeate such proceedings—as sometimes it has—the law could readily be used as a weapon of persecution. Such safeguards seek to keep out at least the more overt manifestations of prejudice and to take account of the fact that in some situations race may handicap a Negro defendant. These standards are found principally in the due process clause of the Fourteenth Amendment, in the Civil Rights Acts, and in the genius of the common law, which surrounds persons charged with crime with innumerable protections. Among these doctrines are special applications of age-old requirements: for example, a juror must be impartial; counsel may not appeal to prejudice; prisoners may not be subjected to the third degree. Other rules do not directly apply in prosecutions themselves but seek fairness by, for example, setting standards of conduct for the police.

Both types of precept help to set a moral tone and a level of fairness for society in general. Because they are so often dramatized in criminal suits where life or freedom is at stake, they bring home to many in unique fashion the egalitarian fundamentals of our society and our government.

We shall discuss these rules to the extent that they specially note a defendant's race or come into play with increased frequency when Negroes are involved, from the time an accused falls under suspicion, through trial, sentencing and, as sometimes occurs, escape from imprisonment. It may be noted at the outset, however, that although the law tries to filter racial factors out of criminal cases, and often succeeds at it, the effort is sometimes futile, for the fact that a defendant is a Negro so sets his life and the attitudes of those who try him that it may become impossible to tell whether race has played a part or to counteract the many subtle ways in which its influence works.

DEFENDANT'S RACE AND FAIRNESS UNDER
THE DUE PROCESS CLAUSE

Regard for the requirements of the Due Process Clause "inescapably imposes upon [the Supreme] Court an exercise of judgment upon the whole course of the proceedings [resulting in a conviction] in order to ascertain whether they offend those canons of decency and fairness which express the notions of justice of English-speaking peoples even towards those charged with the most heinous offenses." [1]

One of the factors to be taken into account is whether the defendant was prejudiced or handicapped because of his race.

In cases of coerced confession the Supreme Court has frequently stressed the defendant's race in determining whether an inculpatory statement was made voluntarily.[2] The fact that a suspect is Negro,

---

[1] Rochin v. California, 342 U.S. 165, 169 (1952). Supreme Court concern over due process rights asserted in coerced confession and right to counsel cases is demonstrated by the fact that although it generally confines review to cases of widespread public importance, its decision to hear a number of such cases can be explained only on the ground that it felt the judgment below was unjust on the facts. STERN & GRESSMAN, SUPREME COURT PRACTICE 129 (2d ed. 1954).

[2] Chambers v. Florida, 309 U.S. 227, 237, 238, 241 (1940); Ward v. Texas, 316 U.S. 547, 555 (1942); Harris v. South Carolina, 338 U.S. 68, 70 (1949); Gallegos v. Nebraska, 342 U.S. 55, 67 (1951) (defendant a Mexican); Ashcraft v. Tennessee, 322 U.S. 143, 156, 173 (1944) (Justice Jackson's dissent); Fikes v. Alabama, 352 U.S. 191, 196 (1957); Payne v. Arkansas, 356 U.S. 560 (1958).

confronted by armed, hostile white officers, and accused of a crime which has stirred racial prejudices is accorded weight along with his maturity, education, and mental stability.[3]

In cases involving the question of right to counsel the Court also has concatenated individual factors, except in capital punishment cases where the right has been deemed absolute.[4] Perhaps the only Supreme Court decisions on the counsel issue making a point of race are *Scottsboro* (a capital case) and *Moore v. Michigan*,[5] but such an important personal factor should always enter into the decision on right to counsel. Many Negroes—especially when charged with a crime stirring anti-Negro hostilities—could not ordinarily be expected to conduct an investigation and examination of adverse white witnesses with the same freedom and assuredness as a member of the bar, or indeed, a white suspect similarly situated.[6]

Although the due process criminal cases in which race has been considered as a prejudicial factor have chiefly involved confessions and to some extent, the right to counsel, the principle on which the consideration was based should be generally applicable. The fact that a man is colored should not rob him of fundamental judicial fairness.

[3] Haley v. Ohio, 332 U.S. 596, 599 (1948) (maturity); Ward v. Texas, *supra* note 2, at 555, and Harris v. South Carolina, *supra* note 2, at 70 (education); Fikes v. Alabama, *supra* note 2, at 196 (mental health); Payne v. Arkansas, *supra* note 2, at 567 (intelligence).

[4] THE CONSTITUTION OF THE UNITED STATES OF AMERICA (Corwin ed 1953), presents a fully detailed discussion of the advances and retreats made on this front at 1098–1109. Among the more important cases are Moore v. Michigan, 355 U.S. 155, 164 (1957); Gallegos v. Nebraska, *supra* note 2, at 64 (1951); Betts v. Brady, 316 U.S. 455, 472 (1942); Bute v. Illinois, 333 U.S. 640 (1948); Williams v. Kaiser, 323 U.S. 471 (1945); Gibbs v. Burke, 337 U.S. 773, 781 (1949); De Meerleer v. Michigan, 329 U.S. 663, 665 (1947); Palmer v. Ashe, 342 U.S. 134 (1951). Discussions of Supreme Court cases on the counsel issue appear in Annots.: 93 L. Ed. 137; 94 L. Ed. 1193; 96 L. Ed. 161.

[5] Powell v. Alabama, 287 U.S. 45, 57, 71 (1932) (the *Scottsboro* case); Moore v. Michigan, *supra* note 4. See also Haley v. Ohio, *supra* note 3 (capital case; fifteen-year-old Negro boy's confession illegal on ground, among others, that he was unassisted by counsel).

[6] See, *e.g.*, the following state decisions: State v. Simpson, 243 N.C. 436, 90 S.E.2d 708 (1956) (indictment for murder; impoverished, poorly educated colored woman unfamiliar with trial procedure, without counsel; due process denied; appointment of counsel mandatory by statute; reversed); Wilcoxon v. Aldredge, 192 Ga. 634, 15 S.E.2d 873 (1941) (capital offense—rape; defendant, a Negro, had court-appointed counsel; on habeas corpus alleged that counsel were ignorant, negligent to such a degree as to amount to virtually no counsel; reversed); Walker v. State, 194 Ga. 727, 22 S.E.2d 462 (1942) (capital offense—rape; counsel appointed but service to defendant was minimal; defendant stated he was not ready and wished counsel of choice; appointed counsel stated he was ready; postponement denied; reversed). See generally 5 ANDERSON, WHARTON'S CRIMINAL LAW AND PROCEDURE §§ 2012–2015 (1957).

THE RIGHT NOT TO BE "TRIED BY ORDEAL"

One risk an accused may face, especially if he belongs to an unpopular minority, is punishment by the police or third-degree pressure for the purpose of exacting a confession. Such acts obviously are illegal under state law,[7] but state law is not always enforced. One potent federal sanction against coerced confessions is the constitutional rule which reverses conviction where such confessions have been introduced into evidence. Another appears in the Civil Rights Acts enacted shortly after the Civil War partly in recognition of this danger and invoked by the Department of Justice where the state does not act first.[8] Although police brutality is by no means exclusively a racial problem, perhaps most of the police brutality cases reported under the Civil Rights Acts have involved assaults on Negroes.

The present principal effect of the Civil Rights Acts on police brutality is that of deterrence as an unrealized threat, for actual prosecutions have been few. But, because of their complexity and the difficult questions they raise in connection with their application to police violence, they require extended discussion. One of these statutes, 18 U.S.C.A. § 242, outlaws willful acts committed under color of law which deprive inhabitants of any state or territory of rights protected by the Constitution and the laws of the United States. "Under color of law" covers deeds performed by any governmental officer regardless of whether those deeds violate state law or not.[9] A sheriff who assaults a prisoner,[10] or "willfully" turns him over to a mob acts "under color of law"; [11] an officer who beats a prisoner cannot evade section 242 by first removing his badge; [12] a private detective who holds a special police officer's card also has been held to have acted

---

[7] See generally 2 WHARTON, CRIMINAL EVIDENCE ch. 7 (12th ed. 1955); 3 WIGMORE, EVIDENCE §§ 822 et seq. (3d ed. 1940); McCormick, Some Problems and Developments in the Admissibility of Confessions, 24 TEXAS L. REV. 239 (1946).

[8] Caldwell, The Civil Rights Section, Its Functions and Its Statutes (1957). This is an address by the chief of the Civil Rights Section, copies of which are distributed by the Department of Justice; it is also included in the Hearings on S. 83 Before the Senate Committee on the Judiciary, 85th Cong., 1st Sess. 222 (1957).

[9] This was made especially clear in United States v. Classic, 313 U.S. 299, 326 (1941): "Misuse of power, possessed by virtue of state law and made possible only because the wrongdoer is clothed with the authority of state law, is action taken 'under color of' state law."

[10] Screws v. United States, 325 U.S. 91 (1945).

[11] Lynch v. United States, 189 F.2d 476 (5th Cir. 1951), cert. denied, 342 U.S. 831 (1951).

[12] Crews v. United States, 160 F.2d 746 (5th Cir. 1947).

"under color of law." [13] A state officer's inaction sometimes is the equivalent of state action.[14] But a wholly private citizen does not fall into the governmental category.

Virtually unapplied since Reconstruction, section 242 came to life again in 1945 in *Screws v. United States*,[15] which has been discussed so thoroughly elsewhere that it would not repay further detailed analysis here. We may merely note in this context that although a Georgia sheriff had beaten a Negro prisoner to death the state took no steps to punish the murderer, whereupon the United States prosecuted him under section 242 for having deprived the victim of the constitutional right to be tried and punished according to due process of law and not by "ordeal." The defense argued that constitutional rights—especially due process of law—were concepts of such ineffable content that a defendant could never know whether he was committing a crime and therefore that section 242 was unconstitutionally vague. A Supreme Court majority held that the section could be constitutionally applied to a "willful" violator. In Mr. Justice Douglas's opinion "willful" was ascribed the special meaning of having "the purpose to deprive the prisoner of a constitutional right, e.g. the right to be tried by a court rather than by ordeal." [16] "Willfulness" in this sense overcame the charge of vagueness, for such a "willful" offender could not claim lack of notice as to which acts were prohibited.

Despite serious division of the Court in the *Screws* case and a persistent minority (Justices Frankfurter, Jackson, and Minton) which would have held section 242 unconstitutional, Douglas's opinion stands as the law today and more recently was applied by a majority in *Williams v. United States*.[17] It has developed, however, in *Williams* and in other cases that proof of "willfulness" may not be as forbidding as it originally seemed—although it still remains difficult. In *Williams* the trial judge had charged that "willfulness" could be inferred from all the circumstances of the assault and the relationship between the officers and the victim.[18] Elsewhere, a federal court of appeals has

[13] Williams v. United States, 341 U.S. 97 (1951).

[14] Lynch v. United States, *supra* note 11, at 480–481; Catlette v. United States, 132 F.2d 902, 906 (4th Cir. 1943); United States v. Konovsky, 202 F.2d 721, 729 (7th Cir. 1953); see HALE, FREEDOM THROUGH LAW ch. XI (1952); pp. 52, 242 *supra*.

[15] *Supra* note 10. For a thorough analysis of the *Screws* case and its background, as well as of § 242, see CARR, FEDERAL PROTECTION OF CIVIL RIGHTS 105–115 (1947).

[16] 325 U.S. at 107.   [17] *Supra* note 13.

[18] See also Koehler v. United States, 189 F.2d 711 (5th Cir. 1951), *cert. denied*,

held that a "willful" defendant need not have been thinking in terms of constitutional law; it is enough that he desired to deprive the prisoner of a courtroom trial.[19] But the need to prove "willfulness" does complicate trials before juries, which a priori are usually reluctant to convict. "Willfulness" might tend to be rebutted, for example, by showing that the officer beat the defendant solely from personal prejudice [20] or for personal vengeance.[21] Moreover, a conviction once attained will be reversed if the trial court does not point out the difference between "bad purpose in chastising a prisoner and willful intent in depriving such a prisoner of a constitutional right." [22] While "willfulness" is a substantive concept, it is, of course, also jurisdictional in the sense that federal power cannot come into play unless it can be proved. Much of the energy of the Civil Rights Section in the Department of Justice has been devoted to investigating federal jurisdictional facts,[23] of which "willfulness" is one of the most important.

"Willfulness" constitutionally could be omitted from 18 U.S.C.A. § 242 if it explicitly described the rights it protects, such as the right not to be punished without having been tried according to due process of law or the right not to be forced to confess. Then there would be no uncertainty over which acts are prohibited. Such an amendment has been proposed.[24]

A companion statute, section 241, may by some future decision be

---

342 U.S. 852 (1951). Justice Jackson dissented from the denial of certiorari on the ground that the willfulness requirement had been diluted so far as to impair the statute's constitutionality.

[19] Clark v. United States, 193 F.2d 294 (5th Cir. 1951).

[20] See CARR, op. cit. supra note 15, at 161–162.

[21] Crews v. United States, supra note 12, at 748, 749. See United States v. Henry, 4 CIVIL LIBERTIES DOCKET 38 (E.D.S.C. No. 21892 Crim. 1958), (directed verdict of not guilty; no proof of willfulness).

[22] Pullen v. United States, 164 F.2d 756, 761 (5th Cir. 1947).

[23] 1955 ATT'Y GEN. ANN. REP. 130–131. During fiscal 1954-55, 3,271 investigative matters were processed by the Civil Rights Section. It is unclear, however, just what this statistic means. The 1955 FBI REPORT states that it conducted 1,275 preliminary investigations in civil rights matters and that these are conducted upon the receipt of information alleging civil rights violations. REPORT OF JOHN EDGAR HOOVER, DIRECTOR 6 (1955). The FBI conducts special courses for training its agents to investigate civil rights charges and show local law enforcement officers how to avoid having such charges made against them. Afro-American, April 14, 1956, p. 5.

[24] As to proposals to amend the Civil Rights Acts see Putzel, Federal Civil Rights Enforcement, 99 U. PA. L. REV. 439 (1951); Gressman, The Unhappy History of Civil Rights Legislation, 50 MICH. L. REV. 1323 (1952); Maslow & Robison, Civil Rights Legislation and the Fight for Equality, 1862-1952, 20 CHI. L. REV. 363 (1953).

added to the sanctions against police brutality. This statute, unlike section 242, is not directed against acts committed under color of law. It also differs from section 242 in that it applies to conspiracies and does not condemn individual acts.[25] Its applicability might mean a substantial additional penalty, for while a conviction under section 242 is punishable by a $1,000 fine, a year in prison, or both, a sentence under section 241 may be a $5,000 fine and/or ten years in prison.

In *United States v. Williams*,[26] decided along with *Williams v. United States*, three Justices and the Chief Justice (Frankfurter, Jackson, Minton, and Vinson) held section 241 inapplicable to the same brutal police deeds which were held culpable in the latter case. But four others (Justices Burton, Clark, Douglas, and Reed) disagreed. The four opposed to the statute's application prevailed because Justice Black concurred with them but on a different ground. He believed that trial under this indictment was barred by the principle of *res judicata*, *i.e.*, that the suit previously had been conclusively adjudged. The only split on the Court was over statutory interpretation, not over whether the United States possesses the constitutional power to enact the interpretation contended for by the government. On that issue at least eight of the justices agreed that it does. It was the government's theory that section 241 applies to all federal rights, including the right not to be subjected to police brutality. However, Justice Frankfurter, expressing antipathy to the Civil Rights Acts of Reconstruction, wrote that 241 covers only federal rights involving the "relation of the victim and the Federal Government," not "rights which the Federal Government merely guarantees from abridgment by the States."[27] Examples of the former, he stated, are the right to vote in federal elections, the rights granted under the federal homestead acts, and the right not to be abducted from the custody of a federal marshal. These are the only kinds of cases to which section 241 had been applied in the past, indicating, he wrote, an understanding that it was so confined. The right not to be beaten by a state police officer is not among such "direct" rights; it stems from the Fourteenth Amendment.

[25] Another difference is that § 242 protects "inhabitants" and § 241 protects "citizens"; moreover, § 241 also applies if two or more persons go in disguise on the highway or onto the premises of another with intent to prevent or hinder his free exercise or enjoyment of any right or privilege secured by the Constitution or laws of the United States. The fact of conspiracy is often difficult to establish. See N.Y. Times, Oct. 20, 1957, § E, p. 7.
[26] 341 U.S. 70 (1951).   [27] *Id.* at 82.

If section 241 applied in the second *Williams* case, wrote Frankfurter, it would merely condemn a combination already forbidden by the general conspiracy law (18 U.S.C.A. § 371) which outlaws conspiracies to violate the laws of the United States including, of course, conspiracies to disobey section 242, which, as already mentioned, the defendants had violated. He thought it unlikely that Congress intended such redundancy.

Finally, he argued, section 241 does not contain the word "willfully" as does section 242. If section 241 were applicable to federal rights generally, the vagueness inherent in such widespread applicability would raise constitutional questions settled in the *Screws* case only because section 242 condemns "willful" violators.

Justice Douglas, for the dissenters, wrote that the statute's language—essentially similar to that of section 242—and legislative history indicate its applicability to all constitutional rights (including the right not to be given the third degree). As to "willfulness," he noted that the judge had charged that defendants could be found guilty only if they had intentionally deprived their victims of protected rights.

LYNCHING

Sections 241 and 242 of 18 U.S.C.A. are the principal federal sanctions available against lynchings, once a serious impediment to the orderly administration of criminal justice. These have decreased from a high of 130 in 1901 to 2 in 1950, 1 in 1951, and none thereafter until 1957, 1958, and 1959 [28] when there was by some definitions at least one in each of the years,[29] indicating that the legal problem is not entirely academic. Section 242 condemns participation in lynchings by state officers; in conjunction with the general conspiracy statute (18 U.S.C.A. § 371) it applies to private citizens acting in concert with officials; in combination with the prohibition against inducing or procuring the commission of a crime (18 U.S.C.A. § 2(a)) it out-

[28] Of course, there is the problem of the proper definition of "lynching"; but the figures indicate a clear decrease in mob violence. CUSHMAN, CIVIL LIBERTIES IN THE UNITED STATES 120 (1956); thorough studies of the lynching problem and proposed legislation appear in *Hearings on H.R. 41 Before Subcommittee No. 3 of the House Committee on the Judiciary,* 81st Cong., 1st & 2d Sess. (1949); *Hearings on H.R. 41 Before Subcommittee No. 4 of the House Committee on the Judiciary,* 80th Cong., 2d Sess. (1948).

[29] N.Y. Post, March 27, 1957, p. 5 (circuit judge denounces as lynching murder of Negro whose bound body was found submerged in creek near Hawkinsville, Georgia). On this crime see also N.Y. Post series March 26–29, 1957. See Afro-American, Jan. 18, 1958 (first lynching of 1958). On the Mack Parker lynching in Mississippi see, *inter alia,* N.Y. Times April 26, 1959, p. 1.

laws private attempts to secure willful police cooperation with lynchers. Section 241 has been held to cover a mob which seizes a prisoner from a federal marshal,[30] as this deprives the victim of federal protection.

In addition, it has been held that when a mob kills a prisoner in public custody, its members may be prosecuted even though the police are in no way implicated,[31] on the theory that there has been a conspiracy to deny the victim the federal right to be tried according to due process of law. It has also been said that failure (not only "willful" participation) of the police to give proper protection against mob violence is a federal offence.[32] Specific federal antilynching statutes have been proposed since the turn of the century, but as the problem has receded they have not been pushed actively.[33]

Although almost every state has had a lynching, most of them have taken place in the South with Negroes as victims.[34] It is therefore interesting to note that about a score of states, including almost half of those in the South, have statutes condemning lynchings or mob violence.[35] Some of these laws cover mob violence generally, others merely govern seizing a prisoner who is in jail. Sanctions vary and include automatic suspension of the sheriff, penalties against the county, long jail terms, heavy fines against the participants, and the death penalty. But state laws have resulted in few prosecutions and fewer convictions, and no convicted lyncher has ever been sentenced to death.[36]

Although the Civil Rights Acts have been strengthened in so far as the right to vote is concerned by empowering the federal government to sue for injunctions, it hardly seems appropriate to enjoin an officer from beating prisoners. The only effective federal deterrent would be criminal prosecution under a clear statute unencumbered by unnecessary issues. For while the record of prosecutions may not be a precise

[30] Logan v. United States, 144 U.S. 263 (1892).

[31] See, Coleman, *Freedom From Fear on the Home Front,* 29 Iowa L. Rev. 415, 427 (1944), citing unreported cases (Negro in prison awaiting sentencing seized in full public view and lynched; federal grand jury returned indictment against the jailer for, among other things, violating §§ 51 and 52 [now §§ 241 and 242]; defendant acquitted on the trial, but the legal basis of the indictment was sustained).

[32] *Id.* at 428. See cases cited note 14 *supra.*

[33] Maslow & Robison, *supra* note 24, at 380–385.

[34] Cushman, *op. cit. supra* note 28, at 120.

[35] See appendix A25. See Slaton v. City of Chicago, 8 Ill. App. 2d 47, 130 N.E.2d 205 (1955); Pennsylvania v. Williams, 3 R.R.L.R. 49 (1958) (Bucks Co., Pa., C.P. 1957) (injunction against mob).

[36] Maslow & Robison, *supra* note 24, at 383.

index of deterrence, a would-be offender who might weigh the likelihood and severity of punishment now administered under these acts could conclude that he would run small risk by violating them. The 1957 *Annual Report of the Attorney General of the United States* has this to say of police brutality proceedings under the Civil Rights Acts:

During the reported period indictments for this type of offense were returned by federal grand juries in Florida, Pennsylvania, and South Carolina.

In the month of June 1957 an extended inquiry into allegations of brutality in the Hinds County Jail located in Jackson, Mississippi, was conducted before the United States Grand Jury sitting in Jackson. A total of 56 witnesses were called to testify regarding allegations of the whipping of ten prisoners by the jail personnel. No indictments were returned. However, inasmuch as the Hinds County Jail has been approved by the United States Bureau of Prisons for the detention of federal prisoners, the evidence developed by the FBI in connection with these allegations has been turned over to the Bureau of Prisons.[37]

The 1956 *Report* is not clear, but it apparently indicates that no proceedings for such violations were commenced for the reported period.[38] The 1955 *Report* indicates only slight activity too in the application of these cumbersome laws.[39] The department has not fulfilled requests for more detailed information on complaints and their disposition.[40]

Earlier reference to the Emmett Till matter points up that often the sole available protection for minorities is vigorous enforcement of ordinary state laws forbidding violence against the person. It is probably redundant to note that where prosecutors will not prosecute or juries will not convict, there usually is no other remedy than the exercise of political power and general community awakening.

CIVIL SUITS FOR DAMAGES

The Civil Rights Acts allow civil suits for damages under 42 U.S.C.A. § 1983. In so far as police brutality is concerned, the courts have placed the same construction on this section as upon section 242.[41]

---

[37] 1957 ATT'Y GEN. ANN. REP. 109–110.   [38] 1956 ATT'Y GEN. ANN. REP. 122, 362.
[39] 1955 ATT'Y GEN. ANN. REP. 133.
[40] See letter from Deputy Attorney General Rogers to Senator Hennings, in *Hearings on S. 83, supra* note 8, at 221.
[41] Geach v. Moynahan, 207 F.2d 714 (7th Cir. 1953); Davis v. Turner, 197 F.2d 847 (5th Cir. 1952). An administrator may sue just as the victim might have.

Title 42 U.S.C.A. § 1985(3), which was discussed in connection with voting, also contains language which might appear to allow civil suit—it condemns conspiracies to deprive persons of the equal protection of the laws—but in *Collins v. Hardyman* [42] the Supreme Court held that only government can deny equal protection (private persons merely interfere with the enjoyment of such rights). For all practical purposes, therefore, section 1985(3) applies only to state action and adds nothing to section 1983.

Some states, such as New York, allow civil suits against municipalities for police brutality.[43] In recent years New York City has paid hundreds of thousands of dollars in judgments to persons who have been injured in this manner.[44] But liability of a municipality for assaults by its police varies with the law of the state and, under theories of sovereign immunity or municipal liability, most do not recognize the cause of action.[45]

JURY SELECTION

If a defendant has been indicted or tried by a jury from which members of his race have been excluded because of race, equal protection of the laws has been denied and the customary remedy is to reverse the conviction. In addition, Negroes qualified to serve may secure an

---

Davis v. Johnson, 138 F. Supp. 572 (E.D. Ill. 1955). See Note, 65 YALE L.J. 630, 652 (1956), on the issue of whether § 1983 secures equal protection as well as due process rights.

[42] 341 U.S. 651 (1951).

[43] See McCrink v. City of New York, 296 N.Y. 99, 71 N.E.2d 419 (1947); Burns v. City of New York, 141 N.Y.S.2d 279 (1955); Pacheco v. City of New York, 140 N.Y.S.2d 275, aff'd, 285 App. Div. 1031, 140 N.Y.S.2d 500 (1st Dep't 1954); app. denied, 309 N.Y. 1030, 129 N.E.2d 791 (1955). In both *Burns* and *Pacheco* judgment was for the city on questions of fact or weight of evidence. On police failure to protect adequately see Schuster v. City of New York, 5 N.Y.2d 75, 154 N.E.2d 534 (1958).

[44] A thorough description and analysis of police brutality in New York appears in a series published in the N.Y. World Telegram & Sun. See especially May 1, 1953, p. 22 (departmental investigations to take place immediately; prior mode had been to postpone action until completion of civil suit for damages, which took years); May 22, 1953, p. 3 (establishment of Civilian Complaint Review Board composed of high-ranking officers); March 10, 1953, p. 1 (Federal Civil Rights Act indictment of policeman).

[45] The cases are collected in McQUILLIN, THE LAW OF MUNICIPAL CORPORATIONS §§ 53.79-.80 (3d ed. 1950). A number of cities have been training policemen to deal with racial tensions. Afro-American, June 8, 1957, p. 11 (St. Louis); July 6, 1957, p. 8 (Baltimore); see LOHMAN, THE POLICE AND MINORITY GROUPS (1947); COMM. ON POLICE TRAINING, PRINCIPLES OF POLICE WORK WITH MINORITY GROUPS (Louisville 1950); CAL. DEP'T OF JUSTICE, GUIDE TO RACE RELATIONS FOR PEACE OFFICERS (1958).

injunction to compel jury commissioners to cease discrimination.[46] One of the Civil Rights Acts, 18 U.S.C.A. § 243, makes it a crime for jury selection officials to discriminate on grounds of race (section 242 also covers the same ground in more general terms).

The Civil Rights Act of 1957 eliminated from the federal jury selection statute the requirement that federal jurors possess the qualifications of state court jurors.[47] The amendment was an outgrowth of the debate over whether Civil Rights Act offenders should be tried by jury. Some had argued that exclusion of Negroes from juries because they could not vote in states where jurors must be voters would help to assure the acquittal of offending voting officials.

There is no affirmative right to have members of one's group on the jury, and their absence may be explained as having been caused by the fair application of objective standards.[48] Therefore, although the rule may have the effect of causing some Negro defendants to be tried by juries on which there are Negroes, an all-white jury may be entirely constitutional. Selection of Negro jurors in a fixed proportion set by their ratio in the population also is illegal as a method of inclusion and exclusion, for it is based upon race and sets upper and lower limits on Negro participation.[49] The rule's purpose is not so much to assure a balanced group of "peers" on the jury in a particular case, although it tends in that direction; rather, it seems to be directed at inculcating fairness into the system of justice. For a conviction will be reversed where there was discrimination in the composition of the grand jury which indicted although no claim of discrimination is made about the petit jury which passed on the merits.[50]

While this broader purpose is not mentioned today, it was advanced as a reason for reversal in the leading early case on the subject, *Strauder v. West Virginia*, in which the Supreme Court held that barring Negroes from juries

[46] Brown v. Rutter, 139 F. Supp. 679 (W.D. Ky. 1956); this remedy, however, is almost never employed. In Cassell v. Texas, 339 U.S. 282, 298, 303 (1950), Justice Jackson, dissenting from the reversal because Negroes were excluded from the grand jury, suggested that the proper remedy would have been suit for injunction by excluded would-be jurors.

[47] 28 U.S.C.A. § 1861.

[48] Brown v. Allen, 344 U.S. 443, 471 (1953); Neal v. Delaware, 103 U.S. 370, 394 (1880).

[49] Shepherd v. Florida, 341 U.S. 50 (1951); Cassell v. Texas, *supra* note 46.

[50] Cassell v. Texas, *supra* note 46; see especially Justice Jackson's dissent at 298. But the Court continues to adhere to its position. Eubanks v. Louisiana, 356 U.S. 584 (1958). See also Smith v. Texas, 311 U.S. 128 (1940); Pierre v. Louisiana, 306 U.S. 354 (1939).

is practically a brand upon them, affixed by the law, an assertion of their inferiority, and a stimulant to that race prejudice which is an impediment to securing to individuals of the race that equal justice which the law aims to secure to all others.[51]

One way of proving a prima facie case of exclusion is to show historically that no Negroes have served on panels or juries in the county in question, although in the particular case there may be no other demonstration that their absence is due to discrimination.[52] Moreover, persistent disproportionately low Negro representation on juries, or token representation, may be an indication of discrimination.[53] Some members of the Supreme Court have stated a belief that the source from which jurors are chosen may indicate whether selection procedure is biased, as where jurors are chosen only from among the jury commissioners' acquaintances, most of whom obviously will be white,[54] or where club membership lists requested from white clubs only are used. In *Hill v. Texas*, Chief Justice Stone wrote that "discrimination can arise from the action of commissioners who exclude all negroes whom they do not know to be qualified and who neither know nor seek to learn whether there are in fact any qualified to serve," [55] although in another case Justice Frankfurter, writing for Justices Burton and Minton, was not ready to condemn such a "rough and ready" method without evidence of discriminatory intent.[56] A selection limited to the tax rolls has been held valid where reasonable tax levies are used, even though these rolls contain proportionately fewer Negroes in relation to their ratio in the population.[57]

In a recent Supreme Court case, *Avery v. Georgia* (1953),[58] in which there was no evidence of discrimination in selection, but in which Negroes' names in the jury box were on yellow tickets and those of whites were on white tickets, the conviction was reversed because the system did afford the opportunity to discriminate. The decision parallels rulings in other areas designed to extirpate even the most veiled modes of discrimination. But as evasion becomes more difficult, more ingenious tactics are being developed.

[51] 100 U.S. 303, 308 (1879).

[52] Eubanks v. Louisiana, *supra* note 50; Hill v. Texas, 316 U.S. 400 (1942); Pierre v. Louisiana, *supra* note 50; Neal v. Delaware, *supra* note 48.

[53] Cassell v. Texas, *supra* note 46; Atkins v. Texas, 325 U.S. 398, 403 (1945); *cf.* Brown v. Allen, *supra* note 48, at 471.

[54] Cassell v. Texas, *supra* note 46, at 287; Hill v. Texas, *supra* note 52, at 404.

[55] *Supra* note 52.   [56] Concurring in Cassell v. Texas, *supra* note 46, at 292.

[57] Brown v. Allen, *supra* note 48, at 473.   [58] 345 U.S. 559 (1953).

In one case it was charged that the commissioners had announced a rule that persons who might claim exemption, *e.g.*, doctors, ministers, teachers, would not be called for jury service at all, but notwithstanding the rule, white persons in these categories were summoned.[59] As things stand in the South, where the Negro middle class is heavily represented by such professional persons, Negroes most qualified to sit would simply not be offered the personal option afforded whites of deciding whether to serve. Another more than occasional problem, treated in but few decisions, is posed by the practice of the state peremptorily to challenge all Negro jurors whom it cannot strike for some cause or other. Where their number is small enough to be disposed of within the allowable number of peremptory challenges, this creates all-white juries as invariably as the old-fashioned system. In some places counsel on both sides may agree to excuse Negro veniremen. It is well known that private litigants often take into account the racial, religious, and other backgrounds of prospective jurors. But such a practice usually does not permeate the entire system of criminal administration and is not directed at a single class; it is also not state action (at least not in the sense that a prosecutor's conduct is.) There is some authority which does not disapprove of such practice, although Judge Edgerton has written a vigorous dissent against it.[60]

As jury systems are reformed, or claim to have been reformed, the problem of the "transition case" arises.[61] This may, for example, involve a county where there has been discrimination in the past. Although at trial time now some Negroes will be on the panel, none will be allowed to serve on the jury in question. If time shows that the alleged reform is a ruse, that is, if it develops thereafter that Negroes never actually sit on a case without discrimination, and were on the panel only as token compliance, it would seem fair to permit postconviction attack on the judgment. Proof, of course, would have to be based upon evidence obtained from cases tried subsequent to the one under examina-

---

[59] See Fikes v. Alabama, 263 Ala. 89, 94, 96, 81 So. 2d 303, 307, 309 (1956), *rev'd on other grounds*, 352 U.S. 191 (1957); see Brief of Petitioner in the Supreme Court of the United States 18–21.

[60] See Hall v. United States, 168 F.2d 161 (D.C. Cir. 1948), *cert. denied*, 334 U.S. 853 (1948), and cases cited therein; Judge Edgerton's dissent is at 168 F.2d 165. See also Pennsylvania *ex rel.* Ashmon v. Banmiller, 391 Pa. 141, 137 A.2d 236 (1958) (three Negroes peremptorily challenged; affirmed); State v. Logan, 344 Mo. 351, 126 S.W.2d 256 (1939). See also United States *ex rel.* Goldsby v. Harpole, *infra* note 114.

[61] Brown v. Allen, *supra* note 48, at 479; Fikes v. Alabama, *supra* note 59, 263 Ala. at 95, 81 So. 2d at 309.

tion. As yet, there is no reported case in which it has been claimed that what looked like nondiscrimination has been proven by time to be but a mask.

In such novel cases, which present some of the real problems faced by defendants today, the proof problem may be formidable and require not only examination of the qualifications of hundreds or thousands of persons enrolled in a jury system, but of a larger number who have not been called. This may be most difficult, no matter how much money the defendant has, and usually he has little. There are few instances, too, in which counsel have undertaken such an exhaustive exploration.[62]

The United States Supreme Court has declined to pass upon the point, but the Texas Supreme Court has held that a white labor organizer who had opposed segregation was not wrongly convicted because Negroes were excluded from his jury.[63] The rule that only Negroes may raise the point of Negro exclusion—related to the general doctrine that one may not complain about acts which do not directly affect him—may be reasonable in terms of judicial administration, for if there were reversal whenever any group had been excluded, no conviction would be certain (there are countless ethnic and national groups in American society). But where there is a real connection between the defendant and the banned group, as in the Texas case, the administrative problem seemingly is outweighed by the greater chance that justice will be done when there is a nondiscriminatory panel, plus the overriding desirability of having a judicial system which in no way fixes a badge of inferiority on racial groups.

Apparently only one case has raised the issue of whether there may be racial discrimination in the selection of the jury commissioners—whose job it is to make up the panels. When these officials choose from among their acquaintances only, or predominantly, original discrimination in their appointment becomes amplified. The practice seems obviously to be unconstitutional; the main issue appears to be one of proof. But the only reported suit in which the point was raised made no decision on the question.[64]

[62] In Fikes v. Alabama, *supra* note 59, the printed record on motion to quash the venire was 180 pages and that was only part of the typewritten transcript.

[63] Alexander v. State, 160 Tex. Crim. 460, 274 S.W.2d 81 (1954), *cert. denied,* 348 U.S. 872 (1954); see also Barry v. State, 305 S.W.2d 580 (Tex. Crim. 1957), *cert. denied,* 355 U.S. 851 (1957), and the dissent of Judge Davidson, 305 S.W.2d at 585.

[64] Brief for petitioner in Payne v. Arkansas, *supra* note 2, at 22.

A SURVEY OF PRACTICES IN JURY SELECTION

About the end of 1957, Professor Jack B. Weinstein sent a questionnaire to Legal Aid societies throughout the United States making inquiry about actual practices in their purview related to the racial question in jury selection. The reliability of the information contained in these replies varies, of course, with the extent to which the writers were acquainted with the situation. Some respondents (a few were not Legal Aid attorneys but lawyers or officials to whom the questionnaires were, in turn, referred) candidly confessed that their familiarity with the question was not very extensive. Moreover, there has been no way of taking into account other factors which might impair the accuracy of the respondents' judgments. But from their positions, which in most cases were that of Legal Aid counsel, and from the supporting discussion in many of the letters it is probable that they sketch, although in broad and discontinuous outline, some of the prevailing practices today. The Legal Aid offices, however, exist chiefly in urban centers and this survey, therefore, tells nothing about more sparsely settled areas.

Some of the letters observe that few Negroes serve and offer as partial explanation the fact that peremptory challenges are used or that there are agreements among counsel to discharge a juror because of race. To some extent, apparently, these practices reflect the belief of some lawyers that Negroes will react differently to evidence than will whites. On one hand, it is thought that a Negro will lean over backwards to convict another Negro in an effort to display impartiality. On the other hand, it has been said that a Negro will favor a member of his race. Some feel that Negroes, coming usually from the poorer elements of the population, will be less apt to think in large financial sums in awarding verdicts. In certain places, however, such peremptory disqualification apparently does not exist. A number of writers explain a dearth of Negro jurors by other factors: the minority often does not have equal representation among voters; it is disproportionately represented among the poorer-educated classes; its proportion among property owners or taxpayers is smaller than for whites. Any or all of these indices may help to determine the make-up of the jury box. Moreover, Negroes are more likely to seek exemption, it is noted, because they can least afford losing their pay during periods of courtroom service.

A number of cities also report no discrimination at all and a significant number of Negroes serving on all kinds of juries. It is noteworthy, however, that there are Northern centers with substantial Negro populations—St. Paul and San Francisco—which have apparently never had a Negro on their grand juries.[65]

THE *Voir Dire*

In *State of Connecticut v. Higgs*, counsel for the defendant, a Negro charged with rape, attempted on the *voir dire*, or preliminary qualifying examination for jurors, to ask them:

Would it require any less evidence for you to find a Negro person guilty of such a crime [rape] than it would to find a white person? . . . would you have any reluctance in following any instruction the Court may give you as to the weight which may be given to the fact that the defendant or any witness in this case is a Negro? . . . would you have any prejudice against a defendant because of his color? [66]

The trial court refused to permit reply to these questions and forbade counsel to continue asking them. The Supreme Court of Connecticut reversed, writing,

it is almost uniformly held in other jurisdictions that it is reversible error in a criminal case in which a Negro is the defendant to exclude questions, propounded by him on the voir dire, designed to bring out that a prospective juror is so prejudiced against the Negro race that it would take less evidence to convince him that a Negro was guilty of the crime charged than to convince him that a white person had committed a similar crime.[67]

In fact, it does not matter that the trial takes place in a state where anti-Negro prejudice is rare. In reviewing a case from the District of Columbia the United States Supreme Court held that

the question is not as to the civil privileges of the negro, or as to the dominant sentiment of the community and the general absence of any disqualifying prejudice, but as to the bias of the particular jurors who are to try the accused. . . . if any one of them was shown to entertain a prejudice which would preclude his rendering a fair verdict, a gross injustice would be perpetrated in allowing him to sit. Despite the privileges accorded to the negro, we do not think that it can be said that

[65] See appendix D1 for abstracts of this correspondence. See Chicago Defender, March 6, 1957, p. 1 (New Orleans juries mixed to avoid suits).

[66] 143 Conn. 138, 140, 120 A.2d 152, 153 (1956). The *Higgs* opinion cites most of the cases in other jurisdictions. See also the annotations in 73 A.L.R. 1208 (1931); 54 A.L.R.2d 1204 (1957).

[67] 143 Conn. at 142, 120 A.2d at 154.

the possibility of such prejudice is so remote as to justify the risk in forbidding the inquiry.[68]

The Court reversed in the exercise of its supervisory power over the
lower federal courts. It has not, however, passed upon the question of
whether refusal to permit such inquiry constitutes denial of due process
of law.

SEPARATION OF JURORS

English common law opposed the separation of jurors from one another before decision for any reason; [69] later law permitted separation
only when necessary.[70] The purpose was apparently twofold: to shield
jurors from improper outside influences and to coerce their agreement.
But the general United States development has been away from a technical approach, and the courts now attempt to secure these ends by
other means.[71] Convictions are reversed, in general, only where it is
shown that the separation actually has been prejudicial to the defendant. The practice of segregating Negro jurors is not uncommon during
those times when state law would require that an all-white jury be kept
together, but the issue has not often arisen.[72] In such cases the courts
have generally looked only to the traditional considerations, but actually other factors are probably more important.

Segregation would seem to impress upon the juror that his position
is subservient, impairing his equality among the others. This possibility
has been recognized in a recent case [73] in which one Negro juror was
sent to a Negro restaurant while the eleven others ate lunch together
elsewhere. However, the court found no proof that the Negro juror

---

[68] Aldridge v. United States, 283 U.S. 308, 314 (1931).

[69] "By the law of England a jury after their evidence given upon the issue,
ought to be kept together in some convenient place, without meat or drinke, fire
or candle, which some bookes call an imprisonment, and without speech with
any, unless it be the bailife, and with him onely if they be agreed." COKE, FIRST
INSTITUTES 227-b.

[70] 24 How. St. Tr. 414 (1794).

[71] For a full discussion of separation of jurors, not limited to racial separation,
see 21 A.L.R.2d 1088 (1952); 53 AM. JUR. 626 et seq.; 15 LA. L. REV. 446 (1955).

[72] Harris v. State, 1 R.R.L.R. 401 (Tenn. 1955); see also Kee v. State, 28 Ark.
155 (1873) (Negro juror separated during refreshments; upheld); Lounder v.
State, 46 Tex. Crim. 121, 79 S.W. 552 (1904) (Negroes separated during dinner;
upheld); State v. Foster, 45 La. Ann. 1176, 14 So. 180 (1893) (Negro and white
jurors slept in separate rooms; no supervision; verdict set aside); Wright v.
State, 35 Ark. 639 (1880) (separate dining; upheld). In Barry v. State, supra note
63, the Negro juror was challenged because there were no facilities to house
and feed Negroes and whites.

[73] Harris v. State, supra note 72.

was actually embarrassed (and he testified that he was not). Probably it is unrealistic to expect that a single act of separation in a segregated community will alter lifetime attitudes, whether of independence or subservience, or that ordinary testimony could reveal segregation's effect. So far no court seems to have considered the problem in the light of the closely related *Strauder* rule, designed to purge the judicial system of "that race prejudice which is an impediment to securing . . . equal justice."

PREJUDICED ATMOSPHERE OF TRIAL

The most extreme example of a trial held in a prejudiced atmosphere was that dealt with by the courts in *Moore v. Dempsey* (1923) [74] which grew out of the Elaine, Arkansas, race riots. After brief trials held under mob surveillance five Negroes were sentenced to death for murder. Justice Holmes wrote:

If the case is that the whole proceeding is a mask,—that counsel, jury, and judge, were swept to the fatal end by an irresistible wave of public passion, and that the state courts failed to correct the wrong,—neither perfection in the machinery for correction nor the possibility that the trial court and counsel saw no other way of avoiding an immediate outbreak of the mob can prevent this court from securing to the petitioners their constitutional rights.[75]

In a recent Florida rape case, *Shepherd v. Florida* (1951),[76] mob violence had not physically reached inside the courtroom, but there had been extensive rioting and the press carried incessant scare headlines, vindictive stories, and cartoons. It was necessary for the judge to bar from the courtroom objects with which violence could be done. The Supreme Court reversed the conviction because there also had been proportional representation in jury selection, but Justice Jackson (joined by Justice Frankfurter), concurring in the reversal, stated that he could

not see, as a practical matter, how any Negro on the jury would have dared to cause a disagreement or acquittal. The only chance these Negroes had of acquittal would have been in the courage and decency of some sturdy and forthright white person of sufficient standing to face and live down the odium among his white neighbors that such a vote, if required, would have brought. To me, the technical question of discrimination in the jury selection has only theoretical importance.[77]

[74] 261 U.S. 86 (1923).　　　　[75] *Id.* at 91.
[76] 341 U.S. 50 (1951) (four Negroes accused of raping white girl).　　　[77] *Id.* at 55.

But bias may infect the jurors in other ways more difficult to discern. Among the carriers we sometimes find the prosecutors themselves.

PREJUDICED ARGUMENT OF PROSECUTOR

An unwitting or unscrupulous prosecutor may create a biased atmosphere by appealing to racial prejudice in the courtroom. This tactic, however, has been held erroneous in many cases, with some recognition of the fact that such argument is most harmful in cases where a Negro has been charged with assault on a white woman.[78] Similarly, where there has been a race riot, reference to it at the trial has been held wrong,[79] as has exhortation to the "Southern gentlemen" of the jury to do their duty.[80] But it has also been held that a cursory or hasty remark or reference to the defendant's race—especially where it is obvious—is not erroneous.[81] Thus, the intent underlying a remark about race may have some bearing on the treatment accorded it by an appellate court.[82] A few courts seem less likely to reverse if the defendant and his victim were both Negroes.[83] The rationale apparently is that equal antipathy was probably aroused toward the defendant and the victim; but at least the Tennessee courts consider this factor unimportant.[84]

Disparaging a witness's credibility by commenting on his race also may be deemed an error. To denounce a white character witness for having testified on behalf of a Negro [85] or to say that it is natural for

[78] Williams v. State, 25 Ala. App. 342, 146 So. 422 (1933) (racially prejudiced argument in miscegenation prosecution; reversed!); Garner v. State, 120 Miss. 744, 83 So. 83 (1919); Roland v. State, 137 Tenn. 663, 194 S.W. 1097 (1917). For an extensive annotation on counsel's appeal to prejudice see 45 A.L.R.2d 303 (1956); see also McLemore v. International Union, 264 Ala. 538, 88 So.2d 170 (1956) (defendant assailed as proponent of racial equality; new trial granted).

[79] State v. Jones, 127 La. 694, 53 So. 959 (1911).

[80] Blocker v. State, 112 Tex. Crim. 275, 278, 16 S.W.2d 253, 254 (1929).

[81] Davis v. State, 233 Ala. 202, 172 So. 344 (1936); Johnson v. State, 35 Ala. App. 645, 51 So.2d 901 (1951); D'Aquino v. United States, 192 F.2d 338 (9th Cir. 1951), cert. denied, 343 U.S. 935 (1952); Owens v. State, 215 Ala. 42, 109 So. 109 (1926).

[82] People v. Pacuicca, 134 N.Y.S.2d 381 (1954), aff'd, 286 App. Div. 996, 144 N.Y.S.2d 711 (1st Dep't 1955) (detective witness said to work with "Italian group"); Gordon v. State, 161 Tex Crim. 594, 280 S.W.2d 267 (1955) (reference to witness's race while praising him).

[83] Walker v. State, 94 Okla. Crim. 323, 235 P.2d 722 (1951); Dial v. State, 133 Tex. Crim. 610, 113 S.W.2d 905 (1938); cf. Hughey v. State, 106 So. 361 (Miss. 1926); Reed v. State, 99 So.2d 455 (Miss. 1958) ("they will next be robbing white people"; reversed).

[84] Manning v. State, 195 Tenn. 94, 257 S.W.2d 6 (1953) (prosecutor ridiculed white witnesses for Negro defendant; reversed).

[85] Ibid.

one Negro to testify for another has been held erroneous.[86] But—and the distinction often may be subtle, or even nonexistent—it has been held not improper to point out that members of the same race, nationality, church, and so forth, are likely to be influenced in favor of one another.[87] In one case in which the defendant raised the race issue himself to win sympathy, it was held that he could not complain that the state argued on a racial basis too.[88]

Courts differ as to how such improper commentary should be corrected. One holds that the conviction need not be reversed and that to have sustained an objection is enough; [89] others require a vigorous and prompt caution by the judge to the jury without which there will be reversal.[90] There is no Supreme Court decision holding whether this kind of comment denies Fourteenth Amendment due process, but in an evaluation of a whole record's fairness such an appeal to prejudice should weigh heavily.

RACE AS AN ELEMENT IN DETERMINING CRIME OR SENTENCE

Certain legislatures have made it a special offense, or imposed special sentences, for Negroes and whites to have sexual contacts. *Pace v. Alabama*,[91] decided by the United States Supreme Court in 1883, upheld under the equal protection clause Alabama laws which provided that two members of the same race guilty of fornication should be punished by six months' imprisonment (or more for repeated violation), but that where the offenders were of different races they should be imprisoned from two to seven years. The rationale of the decision was that both whites and Negroes who engage in such acts across racial lines are punished equally.

The *Pace* case has not been overruled, although it is incredible that the Supreme Court would reaffirm it in view of the extent to which racial considerations have been expunged from the law. Race as a

[86] Tannehill v. State, 159 Ala. 51, 48 So. 662 (1909).
[87] State v. Howard, 120 La. 311, 45 So. 260 (1907).
[88] Honda v. People, 111 Colo. 279, 141 P.2d 178 (1943).
[89] Herrin v. State, 201 Miss. 595, 29 So. 2d 452 (1947).
[90] Holland v. State, 247 Ala. 53, 22 So. 2d 519 (1945) (argument "eradicated by instructions"); Harris v. State, 22 Ala. App. 121, 113 So. 318 (1927) (insufficient admonition; reversed); Owens v. State, *supra* note 81 (adequate caution; affirmed); State v. Brown, 148 La. 357, 86 So. 912 (1921) (caution insufficient; reversed); State v. Washington, 136 La. 855, 67 So. 930 (1915) (improper caution; reversed); White v. State, 139 Tex. Crim. 660, 128 S.W.2d 51, *rev'd on other grounds*, 309 U.S. 631 (1940) (instruction negatived remark).
[91] 106 U.S. 583 (1883).

criminal factor, generally of the sort dealt with in *Pace,* does still exist, however, in Alabama, Arkansas, Florida, Louisiana, Nevada, and North Dakota.[92] (The legal status of these statutes and of the related miscegenation laws is discussed in chapter X.)

But far more pervasive than discrimination in defining crime is unequal sentencing at the discretion of judge or jury. Mr. Justice Stewart, while a circuit judge, wrote, although without reference to the racial question:

Justice is measured in many ways, but to a convicted criminal its surest measure lies in the fairness of the sentence he receives. Whether a sentence is fair cannot, of course, be gauged simply by comparing it with the punishment imposed upon others for similar offenses. But that test, though imperfect, is hardly irrelevant. It is an anomaly that a judicial system which has developed so scrupulous a concern for the protection of a criminal defendant throughout every other stage of the proceedings against him should have so neglected this most important dimension of fundamental justice.[93]

Guides for Sentencing, a publication of the National Probation and Parole Association, indicates that there is no basis upon which race can be justified as a factor in disposing of offenders.[94] But Gunnar Myrdal, in 1944, writing that there had been little change since 1908, recounted a survey made that year which concluded that a Negro is "far more severely punished than a white man for the same offense." [95] He also found that where crimes of Negro against Negro came to court, the offender was dismissed lightly, but that in Northern areas there was less differentiation on the basis of race.[96]

To ascertain whether the same conditions exist today the author has drawn upon two sources: (1) personal interviews with lawyers throughout the South and (2) replies to letters of inquiry to Legal Aid societies sent out by Professor Weinstein late in 1957 at about the same time that he sent them the questionnaires on jury selection. The replies were not of the sort that can be evaluated statistically; there is

[92] See appendix A26.

[93] Shepard v. United States, 257 F.2d 293, 294 (6th Cir. 1958); see also Bunce v. Williams, 159 F. Supp. 325 (E.D. Mich. 1958) (claim of discriminatory sentences in enforcement of narcotics statutes; suit brought against improper parties; dismissed).

[94] GUIDES FOR SENTENCING 37 (1957). For a bibliography in this field see INSTITUTE OF JUDICIAL ADMINISTRATION, DISPARITY IN SENTENCING OF CONVICTED DEFENDANTS (1954).

[95] MYRDAL, AN AMERICAN DILEMMA 547 (1944).   [96] *Id.* at 551.

also, as with replies to the jury questionnaire, the question of assessing the significance of the answers. But there is some meaningful correspondence between the information received from the two sources and from the different states. Altogether it indicates that in many Southern areas the pattern described by Myrdal's research survives, particularly with regard to sex crimes. Urban areas are apparently less likely to differentiate for racial reasons, and where the Negro vote is significant discrimination is likely to be less marked. The importance of voting was stressed by a number of those who were interviewed and is mentioned in a Legal Aid reply. Information concerning Atlanta, Columbia, and the Piedmont area of North Carolina indicates that they are fairer than other areas in the same states partly because of political factors. But voting is not the only item which can make a difference. In the District of Columbia where there is no vote at all those interviewed reported no perceptible difference in sentencing. The District has other characteristics which play a role: national policy emanates there; employment opportunities are greater; the population is national and cosmopolitan; universities, including Howard, are influential. In Arkansas disparate treatment was reported for most of the state, with urban areas somewhat better than others, but the fairest section was said to be around Fayetteville, apparently because it is under the influence of the state university. In Delaware the judges of courts of record ride circuit throughout the state and no race distinctions in their courts were reported. However, it is said that police court judges, or magistrates there, who often are not lawyers, not infrequently are unfair. But even where the respondents concluded that there was no discrimination, they pointed out that the generally lower socioeconomic level of the minority tends to create disparities in treatment.[97] Professor Weinstein has written of the impoverished defendant that:

[97] For excerpts from this correspondence see appendix D2. See N.Y. Post, April 29, 1959, pp. 3, 6 (in connection with Parker lynching Mississippi lawyer says: "We have four codes of justice here. One for white abusing white. One for Negro abusing Negro. One for white abusing Negro. One for Negro abusing white."). See also Turner, Dynamics of Criminal Law Administration in a Biracial Community of the Deep South (Ph.D. dissertation, Indiana Univ., 1956) (Mississippi community's sentencing practices becoming more uniform except in interracial offenses where Negro is victim; greatest change is that Negroes now receiving more protection from offenses committed by Negroes). See Newsom, Court Treatment of Intra- and Inter-Racial Homicide in St. Louis (Ph.D. dissertation, Washington Univ., 1956) (there is association between race of offender and of victim with respect to severity of punishment). See Rockefeller, *Are Army Courts-Martial Fair?* 4 FED. BAR NEWS 118 (1957) (Negroes usually receive longer sentences than white soldiers for same offense).

Watching the procession of defendants shuffling through Special Sessions in New York, one sometimes has the feeling that skilled and energetic legal aid lawyers might make a better impression on some judges, might accomplish more for some of their clients, if they supplied the client with a clean shirt instead of a sound legal or factual argument.[98]

Some of the correspondents attempted to offer justification for different treatment by reference to an alleged difference in sexual mores between Negroes and whites. But here too social level appears to be important. Kinsey has written that it is "already clear that Negro and white patterns for comparable social levels are close if not identical." [99] Concerning sentencing, we may note that in recent well-publicized cases of attack by a white person upon a Negro there have been occasional stiff penalties, with Southerners calling upon Northern critics to take notice.[100]

The most glaring disparities in punishment occur in sentences for rape. All of the Southern states provide a death penalty for this crime, typically at the discretion of the jury, and with one exception (Nevada) these are the only states in which rape is punishable by death.[101] Between 1930 and 1957, 361 Negroes were executed for rape in the South in contrast to 38 whites. During this period, although they executed no white person for rape, for this crime Florida executed 29 Negroes, Virginia 20, Louisiana 17, Mississippi 16, Oklahoma 4, the District of Columbia 2, and West Virginia 1. Statistics on executions for rape in the other Southern states during this period are: Texas, 12 white and 57 Negro; Georgia, 3 white and 54 Negro; North Carolina, 4 white and 40 Negro; South Carolina, 4 white and 35 Negro; Tennessee, 4 white, 21 Negro; Alabama, 2 white and 18 Negro; Maryland, 6 white and 18 Negro; Arkansas, 1 white and 17 Negro; Kentucky, 1 white and 9 Negro; and Delaware, 1 white and 3 Negro.[102]

In any of these cases had the judge or jury announced that the most

[98] Weinstein, Book Review of BEANEY, THE RIGHT TO COUNSEL IN AMERICAN COURTS, 56 COLUM. L. REV. 454, 457-58 (1956).

[99] KINSEY, POMEROY & MARTIN, SEXUAL BEHAVIOR IN THE HUMAN MALE 393 (1948).

[100] E.g., see N.Y. Times, June 23, 1959 ("4 White Youths Get Life Terms for Raping Florida Negro Co-ed"); see id. July 5, 1959, § E, p. 6 (Letter to Editor: verdict praised; commutation asked for four Negroes to be executed for rape of white women); see also id., April 26, 1956, p. 29 ("White Man Held in Negro's Death"); id., April 9, 1956, p. 1 ("Four Get 6 Months in King Cole Attack").

[101] See SHERWIN, SEX AND THE STATUTORY LAW 83 (1949). Delaware, however, recently has abolished capital punishment. DEL. CODE ANN. tit 11, § 107 (1958 Supp.).

[102] See FEDERAL PRISONS 99 (1957); FEDERAL BUREAU OF PRISONS, NATIONAL PRISONER STATISTICS, under caption "Executions" (1956).

severe penalty would be applied because of the defendant's race, the conviction surely would not be upheld. Since such a reason is hardly articulated publicly, motivation can be established only by the pattern of past cases, as in seeking out whether there has been discrimination in jury selection. There is the problem, however, that while a jury commission may hold office for years and build up a record of performance, a jury sits but once. It is the state, however, which owes equal protection of the laws, not a particular jury as such. It can be argued, therefore, that the verdicts of juries are those of the state and that its consistency, not that of particular tribunals, establishes a denial of equal protection. Yet proof of a consistent pattern also faces the further obstacle that no two cases are alike. In a Virginia case, popularly known as the *Martinsville Seven*,[103] the alleged circumstances of the rape were particularly aggravated, and it may have been difficult to find cases sufficiently like it upon which to base a comparison. The United States Supreme Court declined to review the case, although in view of Virginia's record one could question whether white defendants who had so raped a Negro woman would have been electrocuted. Allegations of a history of discriminatory sentencing in rape cases in Delaware have contributed there to commutation of the death sentence of a Negro for rape.[104]

When sentenced to jail or work camps Negro prisoners are required to be segregated by statute in almost all Southern states. However, these laws require or establish few institutions for Negro adult prisoners only; the general Southern rule apparently is one of segregation within a prison inhabited by members of both races.[105] Separate institutions for Negro and white youthful offenders are far more common.[106] A 1956 publication of the Children's Bureau of the Department of Health, Education, and Welfare, states:

[103] Hampton v. Commonwealth, 190 Va. 531, 58 S.E.2d 288 (1950), *cert. denied,* 339 U.S. 989 (1950); see also Florida *ex rel.* Copeland v. Mayo, 87 So. 2d 501 (Fla. 1956); Thomas v. State, 92 So. 2d 621 (Fla. 1957), *cert. denied,* 354 U.S. 925 (1957); Florida *ex rel.* Thomas v. Culver, 253 F.2d 507 (5th Cir. 1958).

[104] See Application of James Elbert Wilson to the Board of Pardons of the State of Delaware, May 26, 1955.

[105] See appendix A27.

[106] See AMERICAN PRISON ASS'N, STATE AND NATIONAL CORRECTIONAL INSTITUTIONS (July, 1953). See also MD. ANN. CODE art. 27, §§ 646 *et seq.* (1957). Maryland, however, is looking to end segregation at reformatories. The State Department for Welfare has proposed legislation for this purpose, Afro-American, Sept. 31, 1957, p. 1, March 23, 1957, p. 8, Jan. 26, 1957, p. 1. The Attorney General had ruled that under existing laws desegregation would be illegal, *id.,* March 23, 1957, p. 8. New Jersey recently closed its all-Negro reformatory at Bordentown, *id.,*

Sixty-seven of the 109 State training schools indicated that they admitted children of all races. Twenty-one schools admitted children of the white race only and 21 schools restricted their admissions to children of a non-white race. All but 9 of the schools serving children of one race only were in the Southern Region.[107]

The president of the American Correctional Association, now warden of the Westchester County prison, New York, has informed the writer that segregation in Northern institutions is virtually non-existent and that many Southern prisons, apparently notwithstanding the statutes mentioned above, do not always practice it. This he attributes to economic and administrative factors; for Northern jurisdictions there may be added the fact that the idea of segregation usually is repugnant to the dominant views in the state. Considerable self-segregation, however, does occur. Segregation in prisons has been attacked in apparently only one suit and without avail.[108]

EXTRADITION

In cases in which an escaped Negro prisoner's return is sought by a Southern state the defense often is made that the demanding state has treated the defendant in a discriminatory, cruel, or otherwise unconstitutional manner. In support of such claims evidence has been introduced of unconstitutional conviction, brutal institutional practices, and restrictions on commencement of postconviction proceedings in the demanding state. But, although such defenses as incorrect identification or that defendant was not in the demanding state when the crime occurred still exist,[109] the Supreme Court has virtually closed every

Aug. 23, 1957, p. 20. West Virginia has desegregated its training schools, *id.*, March 23, 1957, p. 8.

[107] HEW, SOME FACTS ABOUT PUBLIC STATE TRAINING SCHOOLS FOR JUVENILE DELINQUENTS (1956).

[108] Nichols v. McGee (N.D. Cal. No. 1089, 1957) (unreported) (on petition for habeas corpus, held, petition devoid of allegation that segregation caused inequality).

We may also note, in the correctional field, the use of race in employing and assigning probation officers. Hager, *Race, Nationality, and Religion, Their Relationship to Appointment Policies and Casework*, 3 NATIONAL PROBATION & PAROLE ASS'N J. 129 (1957).

[109] See, *e.g.*, Stenz v. Sandstrom, 143 Conn. 72, 118 A.2d 900 (1955) (to be a fugitive person must have been in demanding state when crime was committed); Audler v. Kriss, 197 Md. 362, 79 A.2d 391 (1951) (dictum); People v. Kennedy, 285 App. Div. 1166, 140 N.Y.S.2d 466 (4th Dep't 1955) (asylum state may inquire into issue of identity). These and other matters of proof and procedure leave room for legal maneuver within which tactics may defeat an extradition attempt when substantive considerations cannot.

avenue of judicial attack upon extradition by *Sweeney v. Woodall*, which held, *per curiam:*

Respondent makes no showing that relief is unavailable to him in the courts of Alabama. Had he never eluded the custody of his former jailers he certainly would be entitled to no privilege permitting him to attack Alabama's penal process by an action brought outside the territorial confines of Alabama in a forum where there would be no one to appear and answer for that state. . . .

By resort to a form of "self help," respondent has changed his status from that of a prisoner of Alabama to that of a fugitive from Alabama. But this should not affect the authority of the Alabama courts to determine the validity of his imprisonment in Alabama. The scheme of interstate rendition, as set forth in both the Constitution [Article 4, Section 2, Clause 2] and the statutes which Congress has enacted to implement the Constitution [18 U.S.C. § 3281], contemplates the prompt return of a fugitive from justice as soon as the state from which he fled demands him; these provisions do not contemplate an appearance by Alabama in respondent's asylum to defend against the claimed abuses of its prison system.[110]

It might appear from this quotation that exceptions to the rule of the *Sweeney* decision are cases in which the fugitive cannot obtain a hearing in the demanding state, or in which the demanding state has appeared in the asylum state's proceedings. The Supreme Court of Pennsylvania, however, ruled against the fugitive in *Commonwealth ex rel. Brown v. Baldi,* wherein the petitioner alleged unspeakable brutality, produced evidence that petitions were not permitted to be sent out of the Georgia work camp where he had been confined, and Georgia appeared in the Pennsylvania proceedings; the Supreme Court of the United States denied certiorari.[111]

The governor of the asylum state has discretion, however, to refuse to return the escapee. In *Kentucky v. Dennison* [112] the Supreme Court held that although a governor is under a "moral" duty to deliver a

[110] 344 U.S. 86, 89 (1952). In addition to the provisions cited in the quotation see 9 UNIFORM LAWS ANN. 263 (1957), the Uniform Criminal Extradition Act.

[111] 378 Pa. 504, 106 A.2d 777 (1954), *cert. denied,* 348 U.S. 939 (1955); see the dissent of Justice Musmanno, 378 Pa. at 513, 106 A.2d at 781. For earlier cases on extradition see Dye v. Johnson, 338 U.S. 864 (1949), *rev'g* 175 F.2d 250 (3d Cir. 1949), which had held that the actions of Georgia prison authorities constituted cruel and unusual punishment and had remanded the cause with direction to issue a writ of habeas corpus and discharge the petitioner. Johnson v. Matthews, 86 App. D.C. 376, 182 F.2d 677 (D.C. Cir. 1950), *cert. denied,* 340 U.S. 828 (1950); Ross v. Middlebrooks, 188 F.2d 308 (9th Cir. 1951), *cert. denied,* 342 U.S. 862 (1951); United States *ex rel.* Jackson v. Ruthazer, 181 F.2d 588 (2d Cir. 1950), *cert. denied,* 339 U.S. 980 (1950).

[112] 24 How. 66 (1861).

fugitive, the federal government could not compel his obedience. Exercising this discretion, the Governor of Pennsylvania denied extradition of the petitioner in the *Brown* case. Indeed, governors have refused extradition in a significant number of cases, often for equitable considerations like those involved in *Brown*. Pressure groups are frequently influential in securing the favorable exercise of such discretion.[113]

CONCLUSION

A recent opinion by Judge Rives in *United States ex rel. Goldsby v. Harpole* [114] demonstrates remarkably the close relationship between the rules considered in this chapter, those presented in other chapters, and conditions in society. Goldsby, a Negro, had been convicted of murder in Mississippi. His Mississippi lawyer, who was white, had not raised the issue of excluson of Negroes from the jury; none had served because jurors in that state must be voters and Negroes there are the victims of severe discrimination at the polls. In the course of his opinion Judge Rives noted the effect of jury discrimination on equality of punishment, writing that "systematic exclusion of Negroes from juries can result in inadequate protection of law-abiding Negroes against the criminal elements of their own race." [115] But the main point was made in holding that failure of local counsel to raise the jury issue had not waived it:

Conscientious southern lawyers often reason that the prejudicial effects on their client of raising the issue far outweigh any practical protection in the particular case. . . . Such courageous and unselfish lawyers as find it essential for their clients' protection to fight against the systematic exclusion of Negroes from juries sometimes do so at the risk of personal sacrifice which may extend to loss of practice and social ostracism.

[113] A recent, thorough extradition study appears in Note, 66 YALE L.J. 97 (1956), which analyzes numerous instances of governors' exercise of discretion and factors affecting it. Extradition cases posing racial issues continue to arise at a substantial rate. See, *e.g.*, Afro-American, June 30, 1956, p. 3 (North Carolina demands escapee in New York); Chicago Defender, Jan. 14, 1956, p. 1 (Mississippi "Fugitive Beats Extradition, Sues" [in East St. Louis, Ill.]); Afro-American, March 23, 1957, p. 15 ("New Haven governor refuses to return road gang escapee" [to North Carolina]); Afro-American, Jan. 19, 1957, p. 5 ("Governor of Ohio refuses to return man to Mississippi"); Afro-American, July 17, 1956, p. 2 ("Ala. Fugitive Wins Another Hearing" [in New York]); Afro-American, Jan. 14, 1956, p. 19 ("Willie Reid [in New York] wins month's stay from return to Fla."); Afro-American, Jan. 14, 1956, p. 16 ("S.C. backs down on De Laine extradition"); Afro-American, Jan. 21, 1956, p. 17 (Jones wins fight against extradition to Mississippi [from Belleville, Ill.]).

[114] 263 F.2d 71 (5th Cir. 1959).   [115] *Id.* at 79.

As Judges of a Circuit comprising six states of the deep South, we think it our duty to take judicial notice that lawyers residing in many southern jurisdictions rarely, almost to the point of never, raise the issue of systematic exclusion of Negroes from juries.[116]

The conviction was held unconstitutional. But from this it can be seen that except for the unusual case in which a defendant can afford to go through the lengthy proceedings in which Goldsby engaged the abstract principles governing sentencing, right to counsel, and jury selection may operate at a level well below the ideal.

Nevertheless, criminal law more than any other branch of law reflects society's concern for the individual. The legal doctrines which seek to nullify the influence of racial considerations in criminal cases are only some of the precepts of criminal law whose aim is objectivity and fairness. The aspiration of these rules of law reflects our highest ideals and their effect on justice and public opinion, though incapable of measurement, surely has been great.

There is, obviously, room for improvement in the rules of criminal law applicable to race. The Civil Rights Acts could do without the vexing requirement of "willfulness." They could be enforced more vigorously, notwithstanding the problem of unsympathetic juries. Refined techniques of proof might make it easier to uncover discrimination in jury selection and sentencing. Judicial attitudes toward racially prejudicial argument and segregation of jurors might well be stiffened.

Yet the real problem lies in areas where there must be discretion to deal with situations which fixed rules cannot foresee. Such flexibility or individuation is as necessary to justice as are fair and objective rules. Some elasticity is required in judicial adminstration, to take one instance, of jury selection systems. Whether to prosecute an offender is discretionary with the prosecutor. Sentencing is discretionary with judge or jury. Extradition, for somewhat different reasons, is discretionary with the governor of the asylum state. And, of course, the jury is the most unfettered of all judicial bodies in that it may acquit for any or no reason and completely nullify a statutory scheme, such as that of the Civil Rights Acts.

In these areas of discretion broader social forces and attitudes are most telling and fixed rules of law take second place. The role of environment is nowhere more apparent than in sentencing. In the North, in Southern or border urban areas, in a university community,

[116] *Id.* at 82.

or where the power of the federal government is strong (the District of Columbia), in short where the status of Negroes is above that in other parts of the nation, there has been a transformation in sentencing since 1944, although unfairness still exists. The year 1944, perhaps significantly, is the date of *Smith v. Allwright,* the case which broke the White Primary. These indices seem to point out further instances of the complex interrelationship of law and social forces as they affect race relations. The fairness of the criminal law is conditioned by community attitudes and the conduct of enforcement personnel; these positions are related, among other things, to political forces; Negro political force has been and can be further released by litigation (although in chapter V we observed that law has its limits in getting out the vote too).

Law can reform the criminal law, but it also can sometimes effect changes in other aspects of society which indirectly may reform the administration of criminal justice as much as may reform of the criminal law itself.

CHAPTER X

DOMESTIC RELATIONS LAW

Underlying opposition to the desegregation discussed in previous chapters is segregationist hostility to sexual relations between Negro men and white women and intermarriage. Indeed, some who could not be called strong supporters of segregation oppose such contacts. More states, including non-Southern ones, have antimiscegenation laws than any other kind of discriminatory statute. Much of the last-ditch opposition to school desegregation, and other desegregation, is based on the idea that it eventually will lead to intermarriage.[1] (But often opposition is based on the somewhat converse reasoning that the races are as biologically distinct as different species of animals and that as a matter of natural law members of a species associate with one another and not with members of other species.[2] It is, therefore, interesting to note that recent studies of animal behavior seem to indicate that one animal's affinity for another is environmentally conditioned and not innate).[3] The attitude also sometimes actually creates a legal issue in proceedings hardly directly concerned with relations between the sexes. A 1954 federal district court opinion (later reversed) frankly refused to desegregate the public pools and beaches in Maryland because, among other reasons, "the degree of racial feeling or prejudice in this State at this time is probably higher with respect to bathing, swimming and dancing than with any other interpersonal relations

---

[1] See generally MARTIN, THE DEEP SOUTH SAYS NEVER (1957), esp. pp. 19–20.

[2] See Florida *ex rel.* Hawkins v. Board of Control, 83 So. 2d 20, 27 (Fla. 1955) (Justice Terrell concurring); Hayes v. Crutcher, 108 F. Supp. 582 (D.C. Tenn. 1952).

[3] See, *e.g.*, LORENZ, KING SOLOMON'S RING, *e.g.*, 134 (1952) ("[a peacock] was the last survivor of an early-hatched brood which perished in a period of cold weather, and to save him, the keeper put him in the warmest room . . . [,] the reptile house with the giant tortises. For the rest of his life this unfortunate bird saw only in those huge reptiles the object of his desire").

except direct sexual relations."[4] Housing desegregation has been fought by the argued proposition that it will lead to intermarriage.[5] In a 1957 Georgia case, in which the NAACP was fined $25,000 because a branch president allegedly did not produce tax records upon demand, the trial judge felt constrained to announce that though he would be fair, he was opposed to "mongrelization"[6]—probably indicating his thought that the association's activities (which apparently never have included an antimiscegenation case or an active program for repeal of these laws) might tend to bring about such a result. But, as Myrdal has pointed out, Negroes view the problem differently. While many white people would use utmost vigor to preserve racial distinctions in matters involving or connoting sexual contact and view other discriminations in a descending order of importance, Negroes value change in an inverse ranking, in which miscegenation occupies last place.[7]

ANTIMISCEGENATION LAWS

Reflecting this concern among many whites, antimiscegenation laws still exist in twenty-two states.[8] (Curiously, perhaps, in most of these states these laws are on the books in the same sections as, or immediately next to, provisions forbidding incest.) The antimiscegenation provisions proscribe Negro-white marriages but often also forbid whites to marry Mongolians, Malays, Hindus, Koreans, and others. The laws cover a wider geographical area than those involving any other type of racial restriction: Nebraska, Utah, and Wyoming are hardly noted as states with legally required discrimination, yet they have antimiscegenation statutes.[9] Among the states which have had such laws and have repealed them [10] are Idaho (1959); Colorado and South Dakota (1957); North Dakota (1955); Montana (1953); and Oregon (1951). But North Dakota still provides a discriminatory penalty for interracial cohabitation.[11] The California Supreme Court held its anti-

[4] Lonesome v. Maxwell, 123 F. Supp. 193, 202 (D. Md. 1954), rev'd sub nom. Dawson v. Mayor, 220 F.2d 386 (4th Cir. 1955), aff'd, 350 U.S. 877 (1955).
[5] See City of Richmond v. Deans, 281 U.S. 704 (1930).
[6] Transcript of Proceedings, Williams v. NAACP (Fulton County, Ga., Super. Ct. 1957), p. 29.
[7] See p. 13 supra.   [8] See appendix A28.
[9] See Shokes, The Serbonian Bog of Miscegenation, 21 ROCKY MT. L. REV. 425 (1949) (concerning antimiscegenation statutes in the Far West).
[10] See appendix A28.   [11] See appendix A26.

miscegenation law unconstitutional in 1948.[12] But in 1957 a bill to repeal Nebraska's antimiscegenation law died in committee.[13]

The Supreme Court has never passed directly upon the validity of an antimiscegenation statute, and since 1883 (*Pace v. Alabama*) [14] has not reviewed special penalties for cohabitation or fornication by members of different races. During the past few years it has refused to review cases from two states which have presented the issue. One case came up from Alabama on certiorari.[15] Another recent case, from Virginia, came up on appeal,[16] which, unlike certiorari, the Court is obligated to hear if the federal questions are substantial and certain technical prerequisites are met. The Court sent the case back to secure clarification of questions concerning the parties' domicile. A fuller record on this point might have permitted a decision on some ground other than the controversial one of miscegenation's constitutionality, as, for example, if the parties were held to have been domiciled elsewhere, another state's law may have applied. But the Supreme Court of Virginia appeared to be determined to confront the United States Supreme Court with the bare issue of the statute's constitutionality, and ruled that no further clarification was possible. The United States Supreme Court was equally firm and then refused to hear the appeal for want of a sufficient record. In view of the consistency with which other forms of segregation are being deposed we may surmise that on the denial of certiorari to the Alabama court and the refusal to exercise appeal jurisdiction in the case of Virginia, the Court, or at least some of its Justices, did not believe that airing this inflammatory subject, of little practical significance, would be in the public interest while strident opposition is being voiced to less controversial desegregation because it allegedly leads to intermarriage.

There is no doubt that these statutes are unconstitutional. The ultimate ruling on miscegenation laws has been presaged by the

---

[12] Perez v. Lippold, 32 Cal. 2d 711, 198 P.2d 17 (1948). Roldan v. Los Angeles County, 129 Cal. App. 267, 18 P.2d 706 (1933), had held that the California statute did not bar a Malayan-white marriage; whereupon the legislature amended to include such unions.

[13] Chicago Defender, March 9, 1957, p. 1 (the vote was 5-2).

[14] 106 U.S. 583 (1883).

[15] Jackson v. State, 37 Ala. App. 519, 72 So. 2d 114 (1954), *cert. denied,* 260 Ala. 698, 72 So. 2d 116 (1954), *cert. denied,* 348 U.S. 888 (1954).

[16] Naim v. Naim, 197 Va. 80, 87 S.E.2d 749 (1955), *judg. vacated,* 350 U.S. 891 (1955), *judg. reinstated,* 197 Va. 734, 90 S.E.2d 849 (1956), *app. dism.,* 350 U.S. 985 (1956) ("devoid of a properly presented federal question").

Supreme Court of California in *Perez v. Lippold* (1948),[17] which held
that its statute violated the Fourteenth Amendment by unreasonably
restricting choice of one's mate. A Maryland court has recently held
unconstitutional that state's law making it a crime for a white woman
to bear a Negro's child.[18] A Nevada judge has ordered that a marriage
license be issued to a "caucasian"-nisei couple, overruling the state's
intermarriage statute.[19] The only legal support which might be cited
for antimiscegenation laws is *Pace v. Alabama,* which upheld a discriminatory penalty for fornication. Although the kind of thinking
that went into the *Pace* ruling might support a miscegenation law too
(forgetting for the moment the obvious distinction between marriage
and the conduct condemned in *Pace*), the reasoning in every segregation case in the Supreme Court of the past decade points the other
way.[20] Moreover, to other applicable constitutional protections we
might add the somewhat forgotten one of freedom of contract. But
until the Court feels that the time is appropriate to hear a miscegenation
case, or until state courts (like those of California, Maryland, and
Nevada) anticipate such a ruling, the obscure, complex law of miscegenation will remain important only to those few who live in antimiscegenation states and have not been deterred by the social difficulties which interracial marriage may present.[21] Therefore, we shall
consider some of the state law issues presented by such cases.

The legal consequences of antimiscegenation laws for the parties to
a mixed marriage may be diverse. There are, of course, criminal
penalties, often severe. So far as appears, in all but one of the antimiscegenation states the union is void *ab initio.*[22] In West Virginia it is

---

[17] *Supra* note 12.

[18] Maryland v. Howard, 2 R.R.L.R. 676 (Baltimore Crim. Ct. 1957).

[19] N.Y. Times, Dec. 11, 1958, p. 30.

[20] The trend appears in every chapter of this volume; for a detailed legal and
social scientific analysis see Weinberger, *A Reappraisal of the Constitutionality
of Miscegenation Statutes,* 42 CORNELL L.Q. 208 (1957).

[21] See Browning, *Anti-Miscegenation Laws in the United States,* 1 DUKE B.J.
26, 40 (1951) (test cases similar to *Perez* will be rare as plaintiffs are unlikely to
come forward).

[22] Hoover v. State, 59 Ala. 57 (1877) (void *ab initio;* parties guilty of fornication); Estate of Walker, 5 Ariz. 70, 46 Pac. 67 (1896) (void *ab initio;* child could
not inherit); State v. Pass, 59 Ariz. 16, 121 P.2d 882 (1942) (defendant convicted
of murder on wife's testimony; admissible because marriage void *ab initio*); IND.
STATS. ANN. § 44-105 (1952) ("absolutely void without any legal proceedings");
Mangrum v. Mangrum, 310 Ky. 226, 220 S.W.2d 406 (1949) (underage marriage
voidable only, but miscegenetic marriage void *ab initio*); *In re* Guthery's Estate,
205 Mo. App. 664, 226 S.W. 626 (1920) (incompetent's marriage voidable; miscegenetic marriage void); NEB. REV. STATS. § 42-328 (1943) (upon dissolution of

void from the time it is so declared by a decree of nullity.[23] (A void marriage can be attacked collaterally, as in an estate proceeding, by one who was not a party to the marriage;[24] a voidable marriage would have to be attacked by one of the parties.) Children of such marriages may be held illegitimate.[25] A spouse may not be able to claim the marital privilege against testimony by his mate in a criminal case.[26] The passage of property by will or in intestacy may turn on the question.[27] Even the right of a widow to workmen's compensation for her husband's death may be affected.[28] A minister who performs such a ceremony may be guilty of a crime.[29]

On some occasions such a couple has been ordered to leave the state under threat of prosecution.[30] This approach has had the ad-

---

miscegenetic marriage children illegitimate); *In re* Takahashi's Estate, 113 Mont. 490, 129 P.2d 217 (1942) (petitioner, a caucasian, denied letters of administration of Japanese husband's estate); State v. Miller, 224 N.C. 228, 29 S.E.2d 751 (1944) (void *ab initio;* parties guilty of fornication); Rodriquez v. Utilities Eng'r & Constr. Co., 281 P.2d 946 (Okla. 1955) (which states that it is proper to refuse compensation to worker's widow if of different race); Stevens v. United States, 146 F.2d 120 (10th Cir. 1944) (under Oklahoma law marriage of Negro to Indian a nullity, no property can devolve to the survivor); Eggers v. Olson, 104 Okla. 297, 231 Pac. 483 (1924) (void *ab initio;* Negro denied wife's property); Long v. Brown, 186 Okla. 407, 98 P.2d 28 (1939) (marriage of Negro and Indian void *ab initio;* no divorce needed); Grant v. Butt, 198 S.C. 298, 17 S.E.2d 689 (1941) (contract that Negro woman live with white man in return for one half his estate void as attempt to circumvent intermarriage laws); Sharp v. Seventh Judicial Dist. Court, 81 Utah 236, 17 P.2d 261 (1932) (marriage of epileptic void *ab initio;* this prohibition in same section as that against miscegenation); VA. CODE § 20-57 (1950) (marriages between white and Negro void without decree); Kinney v. Commonwealth, 71 Va. (30 Gratt.) 858 (1878) (marriage void *ab initio;* parties guilty of lewd and lascivious association); Greenhow v. James' Ex'r, 80 Va. 636 (1885) (plaintiff child of white man, Negro woman; children illegitimate and could not take remainder of father's estate).

[23] W. VA. CODE § 4701 (1955).

[24] See the following cases, all cited in note 22 *supra:* Estate of Walker, *In re* Guthery's Estate, Rodriquez v. Utilities Eng'r & Constr. Co., Eggers v. Olson, Grant v. Butt, *In re* Takahashi's Estate, Greenhow v. James' Ex'r; and Bennett v. Bennett, 195 S.C. 1, 10 S.E.2d 23 (1940); see also 55 C.J.S. *Marriage* 11.

[25] *E.g.,* NEB. REV. STATS. § 42-328 (1943); Greenhow v. James' Ex'r, *supra* note 22; *compare with* VA. CODE § 64-7 (1950) (issue of marriage deemed null in law shall nevertheless be legitimate).

[26] *E.g.,* State v. Pass, *supra* note 22.

[27] *In re* Takahashi's Estate, *supra* note 22; Stevens v. United States, *supra* note 22.

[28] Rodriquez v. Utilities Eng'r & Constr. Co., *supra* note 22.

[29] See, *e.g.,* ARK. STATS. ANN. § 55-105 (1947) (misdemeanor); GA. CODE ANN. § 53-9902 (1937) (similar); Mo. STATS. ANN. § 563.250 (1953) (similar).

[30] Afro-American, Sept. 15, 1956, p. 1 ("jury won't indict, but [San Antonio] D.A. banishes mixed pair"); *id.,* Dec. 1, 1956, p. 1 ("Va. Couple Banished. . . . ordered to leave the state by Police Court Justice"); see also Miller v. Lucks, *infra* note 37 (after indictment for unlawful cohabitation parties agreed to leave Mississippi; the case was *nol-prossed*).

vantage for the state of not exposing its law to judicial review. Similarly there have been attempts—sometimes successful—to influence military and immigration officials to keep mixed couples under their control out of the state.[31]

To be guilty of the offense, it has been held, there must be an intent to commit it. One who does not know that his or her spouse is a Negro has not violated the law.[32] Both parties could, in some circumstances, lack such knowledge and escape punishment. In these and other situations the definition of Negro, which varies from state to state, is important.[33]

Antimiscegenation states often have faced the issue of what to do when interracial couples go to other jurisdictions to marry. Because the general rule is that a marriage valid at the place of celebration is valid at the couple's domicile, and there is an exception that marriages which conflict with the domicile's public policy need not be recognized,[34] complex legal problems sometimes have arisen.

The rule of the Restatement of Conflict of Laws is:

§ 132. A marriage which is against the law of the state of domicil of either party, though the requirements of the law of the state of celebration have been complied with, will be invalid in the following cases: . . . (c) marriage between persons of different races where such marriages are at the domicil regarded as odious. . . .

§ 134. If any effect of a marriage created by the law of one state is deemed by the courts of another state sufficiently offensive to the policy of the latter state, the latter state will refuse to give that effect to the marriage.

In a number of states statutes expressly condemn as illegally married the couple which leaves its jurisdiction to avoid the antimiscegenation rule without changing domicile.[35] Professor Beale distinguishes between

[31] Afro-American, Oct. 20, 1956, p. 1 (Immigration Commissioner informs Virginia Congressman that white wife of Negro soldier stationed in Virginia cannot be deported); N.Y. Post, Sept. 8, 1957, p. 6 (Army allegedly advises Negro soldiers stationed in Germany not to bring their white wives to Texas); N.Y. Times, Feb. 7, 1958, p. 3 (Negro soldiers with white wives transfer before unit moves to Georgia).
[32] Bell v. State, 33 Tex. Crim. App. 163, 25 S.W. 769 (1894).
[33] See H. Cohen, *An Appraisal of the Legal Tests Used To Determine Who Is a Negro*, 34 CORNELL L.Q. 246 (1948); G. Cohen, *Who Is Legally a Negro*, 3 INTRA. L. REV. 91 (1948); *Legal Definition of Race*, 3 R.R.L.R. 571 (1958).
[34] See Annot. (recognition of foreign marriage as affected by local miscegenation law), 3 A.L.R.2d 240 (1949); RESTATEMENT, CONFLICT OF LAWS §§ 132, 133, 134 (1934); BEALE, CONFLICT OF LAWS §§ 121.1 *et seq.* (1935).
[35] *E.g.*, GA. CODE ANN. § 53-214 (1937) ("parties residing in this State may not evade any of . . . its laws as to marriage by going into another State for the solemnization of the marriage ceremony." Such a marriage is treated as if performed in Georgia). Similar provisions are: MISS. CODE ANN. § 459 (1942); W. VA. CODE § 4695 (1955); LA. REV. STATS. § 9:221 (1951) (this is the Uniform Marriage

Northern and Southern states in assessing the validity of such marriages. Where a couple leaves a Southern domicile to marry in a state which does not forbid miscegenation and then returns to the domicile, he says, the marriage will be held invalid. But if the couple does the same thing in the North the marriage will be validated.[36]

The rule also appears to be that a mixed marriage of domiciliaries of a state permitting such marriages, celebrated in a state where such marriages are valid, will be recognized in a forum which forbids such marriages. A leading Mississippi case has recognized the Illinois mixed marriage of Illinois domiciliaries (who previously had been domiciled and prosecuted for cohabitation in Mississippi), awarding property in an estate proceeding on the basis of such recognition. However, it perhaps indicated a different result had the parties lived in Mississippi:

The manifest and recognized purpose of this statute was to prevent persons of Negro and white blood from living together in this state in the relationship of husband and wife. Where, as here, this did not occur, to permit one of the parties to such a marriage to inherit property in this state from the other does no violence to the purpose.[37]

A Florida textwriter doubts whether the forum will recognize a marriage which is valid at the place of celebration between domiciliaries of a state which also recognizes such marriage if the parties at the time of the suit have become domiciled in the forum:

Whether such marriages between residents of a foreign jurisdiction . . . would be valid in case the parties came to Florida afterward, has not been decided by our court. However, the criminal statutes as to adultery and co-

---

Evasion Law). The Uniform Act, 9 U.L.A. XXI, was withdrawn from the active list of uniform laws in 1943. For critical commentary on its effectiveness see 23 TUL. L. REV. 584 (1949). For cases see 3 A.L.R.2d 240.

A clerk in the New York City Marriage License Bureau has estimated (the city compiles no such records) that about 500 licenses a year are issued to mixed couples, more than half of whom are residents of states which forbid interracial marriage. N.Y. Post, April 29, 1956, p. 10. The writer of the Post article, Ted Poston, has informed the author that the estimate was based on a complete count of two months' records and a sampling of two other months' records; the total number of licenses issued, Poston stated, was about 30,000. Upon consulting with the City Clerk's office the author learned that in many marriages of Puerto Ricans and Filipinos a fair-skinned party may reply "white" while a partner who is darker skinned may reply "colored" to the inquiry about race, thus accounting for a very large part of the "interracial" marriages in New York. See Afro-American, Oct. 12, 1957, p. 9 (the Rev. [Congressman] Adam Clayton Powell has performed over one hundred marriages per year for 27 years of which only four were interracial). On District of Columbia interracial marriages see Annella, *Some Aspects of Interracial Marriage in Washington, D.C.*, 25 J. NEGRO EDUCATION 360, 381 (1956).

[36] *Op cit. supra* note 34.

[37] Miller v. Lucks, 203 Miss. 824, 36 So. 2d 140, 2 A.L.R.2d 236 (1948).

habitation between whites and negroes leave the clear inference that such marriages might be recognized by our courts. . . . It must be made clear, however, that it would not be at all advisable from any standpoint for such persons to move to Florida. . . . our courts might follow the prevailing opinions and customs of the people of Florida and hold them . . . void. . . .[38]

We note also, consonant with this interpretation, that some Southern states have threatened to use antimiscegenation laws to keep out Negro soldiers with white wives transferred to bases in those states.[39] Apart from constitutional considerations of due process, equal protection, and full faith and credit, such assertions seem to conflict with the war power. The military should not have to alter its normal personnel policies to accommodate such states' laws. But the military's desire to avoid political conflict and the soldiers' choice to avoid personal and professional embarrassment have kept the issue from going to court.

COHABITATION LAWS

Most states have laws forbidding lewd and lascivious cohabitation or fornication.[40] Sometimes special penalties are imposed if the violators are of different races.[41] In antimiscegenation jurisdictions the parties to a mixed marriage may be prosecuted for cohabitation or fornication, for despite their "marriage" legally they are single.[42] While in some states persons guilty of fornication or cohabitation may escape penalty by marrying, in antimiscegenation states mixed couples do not have this opportunity.[43] *Pace v. Alabama*,[44] discussed in greater detail earlier in this chapter, specifically upheld such laws. But until such time as its constitutionality is reassessed the state courts will apparently continue to be concerned chiefly with two proof questions in such suits: Were the parties of different races? Did the acts occur? With the exception of the racial feature the constituent elements of the offense of unlawful cohabitation by an interracial couple are the same as in ordinary cases of this sort of crime.[45]

[38] CARSON, THE LAW OF THE FAMILY, MARRIAGE AND DIVORCE IN FLORIDA 49 (1950).
[39] See note 31 *supra* and p. 361 *infra*.
[40] See SHERWIN, SEX AND THE STATUTORY LAW 85 (1949).   [41] See appendix A28.
[42] See, *e.g.*, Hoover v. State, State v. Miller, Kinney v. Commonwealth, all *supra* note 22.
[43] *E.g.*, GA. CODE ANN. § 26-5801 (1953); VA. CODE ANN. § 18-82 (1950) (more severe penalty if parties cannot marry).
[44] *Supra* note 14.
[45] Metcalf v. State, 16 Ala. App. 389, 78 So. 305 (1918) (no proof that defendant, Negro woman, had lived with white man or that he was white); Gilbert v. State, 32 Ala. App. 200, 23 So. 2d 22 (1945) (intercourse on one occasion does

ADOPTION AND CUSTODY

Adoption was unknown to the common law and in all states is governed by statute.[46] A few states require that the racial background of the adopters and adoptee be the same; others provide that race be considered.[47] The balance make no mention of race and stress general considerations such as the child's "welfare" and the appropriateness of the adopters' home for the child's development.[48]

There are few reported cases dealing with interracial adoption, undoubtedly because it occurs infrequently.[49] The Court of Appeals for the District of Columbia has recently permitted the illegitimate child of two white parents to be adopted by a Negro who married the mother. The Court stated:

Nor can denial of the adoption rest on a distinction between the "social status" of whites and Negroes. There may be reasons why a difference in race, or religion, may have relevance in adoption proceedings. But that factor alone cannot be decisive in determining the child's welfare. It does not permit a court to ignore all other relevant considerations. Here we think those other considerations have controlling weight.

The child is living in the happy home of its natural mother and step-

---

not sustain conviction for fornication); Stewart v. State, 64 Miss. 626, 2 So. 73 (1887) (conviction upheld on proof that white defendant was often seen at Negro woman's house and there were mulatto children); Wildman v. State, 157 Fla. 334, 25 So. 2d 808 (1946) (intercourse, but no evidence of living together; reversed); Fields v. State, 24 Ala. App. 193, 132 So. 605 (1931) (defendants in house together but insufficient evidence); Wilson v. State, 178 Ark. 1200, 13 S.W.2d 24 (1929) (evidence of adultery, but insufficient evidence of living together; reversed); Parramore v. State, 81 Fla. 621, 88 So. 472 (1921); (continuing offense; affirmed); State v. Daniel, 141 La. 900, 75 So. 836, (1917) (defendant guilty whether relationship open or secret); Hovis v. State, 162 Ark. 31, 257 S.W. 363 (1924) (sexual relations alone insufficient to sustain conviction; defendant did not "live" with Negro woman employed as sleep-in domestic); State v. Brown, 108 So. 2d 233 (La. 1959) (statute constitutional; but no proof of intercourse; reversed).

[46] See Note, 59 YALE L.J. 715, 725–736 (1950).

[47] See appendix A29.

[48] All state statutes relating to adoption are digested in COUNCIL OF STATE GOVERNMENTS, SUMMARIES OF STATE LAWS PERTAINING TO ADOPTION OF CHILDREN (1954). Use of racial considerations, however, may be standard practice even in absence of statutory requirement. See, *e.g.*, Uhlenhopp, *Adoption in Iowa*, 40 IOWA L. REV. 228, 234 (1955) ("the adoption statute contains no restriction relative to race or religion, but these factors are considered by social workers and judges, in placements at least"). N.Y. Times, Dec. 6, 1958, p. 24 ("Mixed Racial Stock Decried as Barrier to State Adoptions").

[49] Note, 3 VAND. L. REV. 627, 642 (1950), summarizes the reasons that the Tennessee Welfare Department has refused to recommend some such adoptions; in none were racial differences the cause. See N.Y. Times, April 12, 1959, p. 58 (one in five placements by Louise Wise Services is interracial).

father, receiving the same loving care they give to the two children born of
their marriage. That it is in the best interests of the child to live in that
home with the natural mother is obvious. It is equally plain that the child
will continue to live there no matter what disposition is made of this case.
Hence denial of adoption could only serve the harsh and unjust end of
depriving the child of a legitimatized status in that home.[50]

Montana has denied an attempt to nullify an interracial (white-
Indian) adoption by a petitioner who would have taken in intestacy if
an adopted daughter were held not to have been legally adopted.[51] The
court held that the fact that the father and adopted daughter were of
different races "constituted no obstacle to adoption."

Custody cases generally turn upon statutes as do the adoption cases,
and present similar issues. But custody decrees may be modified as
circumstances warrant, whereas adoption decrees are rarely altered.

The New York courts have permitted a white mother who had a
child by her first husband (white), but who upon divorce married a
Negro, to have custody of her own child as against her mother, who
claimed custody for a variety of reasons (religion, quality of home,
quality of care), of which the underlying ground, though not articulated as such, was that the stepfather was a Negro.[52] Similarly, years
ago, when Virginia was confronted with a case in which a widowed
mother of a white child married a Negro (without sufficient Negro
"blood" to condemn the marriage as miscegenetic), the court held that
the child's care was good and that a state agency might not take it
from the mother. But, if the husband were a "statutory" Negro, the
opinion indicates the result might have been otherwise.[53]

A recent Connecticut case, in awarding custody to the white father
after his white wife had remarried to a Negro, gave as one ground that
the marriage had alienated the wife's parents and deprived the children
of their care and good influence; other grounds of the decision were
the wife's excommunication from the Catholic Church, that the father

[50] *In re* Adoption of a Minor, 228 F.2d 446, 448, (D.C. Cir. 1955).

[51] *In re* Pepin's Estate, 53 Mont. 240, 163 Pac. 104 (1917). *Cf.* Hodges' Heirs v.
Kell, 125 La. 87, 51 So. 77 (1910). C.J.S. *Adoption of Children* § 17 states that
the general rule is that racial differences are no bar to adoption. See Annot., 54
A.L.R.2d 909 (race as a factor in adoption); 23 A.L.R.2d 701 (religion as a
factor).

[52] People *ex rel.* Portnoy v. Strasser, 303 N.Y. 539, 104 N.E.2d 895 (1952) (the
opinion of the court does not stress the racial issue, but a reading of the record
reveals that it was perhaps the most important factor to the parties). Similarly,
the child's welfare governed in Cabassa v. Bravo, 27 P.R. 857 (1919), where the
mother who had remarried to a Negro was awarded custody.

[53] Moon v. Children's Home Soc'y of Va., 112 Va. 737, 72 S.E. 707 (1911).

already had custody of another child, and that both children should be together. The court specifically stated that the fact that the second husband was a Negro played no part in the decision.[54]

There has been no constitutional adjudication on the significance of race in adoption or custody cases. It seems that the Court of Appeals for the District of Columbia, quoted above, has employed a rule which may be assimilated to constitutional cases: race may be a personal factor in such cases which may be relevant in determining where a child's welfare lies, but "that factor alone cannot be decisive."

CONCLUSION

The issue that many believe expresses the anxiety underlying most race relations problems—fear concerning interracial sexual contact— is mirrored in more statutes covering a wider geographical area than any other type of racially restrictive law. Yet here is an area where law appears to be least appropriate as a means of social control. Those of different races who would brave social obloquy to marry will probably not be deterred by a statute. There are plenty of non-anti-miscegenation states to which they can move. The anti-intermarriage statute does, however, have this effect: it expressly announces that the state, and controlling forces in society, frown on such unions. Conformists—i.e., most people—thus are warned off.

Antimiscegenation laws are undoubtedly unconstitutional. But hostility to interracial marriage is so great, and the immediate social consequence of the statutes so small, that some courts apparently have been reluctant to declare the obvious and strike the laws down.

A remarkable fact about interracial sexual contacts, within and outside of marriage, is that while one hears much gossip and can find some antiquated studies, there is little evidence upon which a conclusion about the nature or extent of such relationships, or law's effect on them, can be based. The author directed an inquiry to the Institute for Sex Research at the University of Indiana (founded by Dr. Alfred C. Kinsey) to ascertain whether its research might shed any light on the subject. In reply Paul H. Gebhard, Executive Director, wrote:

[54] Murphy v. Murphy, 143 Conn. 600, 604, 124 A.2d 891 (1956); in Fountaine v. Fountaine, 9 Ill. App. 2d 482, 486, 133 N.E.2d 532, 535 (1956), the court held that it should take into account all relevant factors in ascertaining the child's best interest but that "the question of race alone [cannot] overweigh all other considerations and be decisive of the question. If this was the sole and decisive consideration on which the trial court based his decision, and it so appears from the record before us, we feel that his discretion was not properly exercised."

I fear that what data we have concerning miscegenation are not in a form which would be useful to you. When we interview a "white" person we do not inquire as to the racial traits of his or her sexual partners unless the person has had considerable number of partners. This decision was based on time-economy: a person with limited soci-sexual experience almost never has had miscegenation. We did question the more experienced "white" individuals *re* this matter and obtained a record of their sexual contacts with persons of other races. When interviewing Negroes, orientals, and others, we routinely questioned them as to sexual contact with other races, assuming (justifiably, I feel) that members of a racial minority are more exposed to the possibility of miscegenation. Unfortunately we cannot ordinarily specify the locality in which miscegenation took place. For example, let us say we have interviewed a man who has lived primarily in three states and who also saw foreign service during the last war; he may report having had coitus with 2 Negro females and 1 oriental, but we have no way of knowing whether this occurred in Brooklyn or in Paris.

Our miscegenation data exist at present only on the original case-histories, nothing has been transferred to punch-cards nor otherwise tabulated. My general impression is that miscegenation is quite rare where white females are involved, infrequent in white males who have not been abroad, and moderately common among males who have been stationed in lands occupied by persons of races other than their own. I do not think that any of us would hazard a guess concerning the number of Negro males and females with miscegenation experience; this must await tabulation.

I do not know when we shall concern ourselves with our miscegenation data. Perhaps it might fit in with our recently-begun analysis of sex-offenders since miscegenation is treated as a sex offense in some instances.

Our last impression may be of some interest to you: I feel that for the bulk of the population, Negro and white, miscegenation provides no special attraction. The prevailing attitude is more one of mild curiosity, almost an intellectual curiosity. A common answer to our query is, "No, but I've often wondered what it would be like." [55]

At any rate, pending final invalidation of antimiscegenation statutes, much of the recondite learning about out-of-state marriages, legitimacy, inheritance, concubinage, and so forth, remains meaningful, for without disposition on constitutional grounds litigants and others will continue to have their rights determined by the state laws on race and family relations.

[55] Letter from Paul H. Gebhard, Executive Director, Institute for Sex Research, Inc., Indiana University, Bloomington, Ind., Nov. 11, 1957.

CHAPTER XI

THE ARMED FORCES

The armed forces are in a sense out of the main stream of American life and often only remotely connected with the activities discussed in earlier chapters. Now that desegregation in them is no longer an active issue we fail to think of race and the military except in exceptional circumstances such as Little Rock, where state troops were used to frustrate desegregation and federal forces were used to achieve it. But today the national armed forces are the most thoroughly integrated major segment of American life. Great numbers of Americans, Negro and white, obtain their first contact with nonsegregation after they enter uniform, whether stationed North or South. What is more, after service they return to every corner of the country with some experience of how integration works and, often, a revised image of members of other groups. Over the long run this can have a critical effect on race relations throughout the nation. One tends to forget that not long ago the converse was true. Since Negroes as civilians sometimes had been able to avoid some of the discrimination described throughout this volume, many received their first total immersion in segregation when called to the colors. Arguing that the paradox was intolerable in a democracy, civil rights advocates incessantly campaigned against racial distinctions in military service, ultimately with success. Among the factors working for integration two were especially weighty: (1) segregation, it became recognized, wasted manpower; (2) military discipline could facilitate execution of the new policy. A prointegration policy was proclaimed by President Truman in 1948; by 1954, it was planned, no all-Negro units would remain. However, the Korean war accelerated the change. It was fought on a largely nonsegregated basis and established the military success of the program.

For Negroes, civilian jobs of rank and status comparable to those which they may earn in the armed forces are comparatively rare. Recently, the Civilian Assistant to the Assistant Secretary of Defense in charge of manpower and personnel wrote to the author concerning a Negro Army captain who had completed an advanced communications course at Fort Sill, ranking third in his class. He was then offered two identical positions teaching communications at the post, one as an officer, the other as a civilian employee. He chose the military, since

the military uniform affords protection, and status on and off the base. Various provisions assure against segregation and discrimination in providing equity of opportunity. Such advantages obtaining with greater certainty caused the captain and others to prefer the military career while awaiting the prospects of more equitable opportunity in civilian pursuits.[1]

Although as recently as 1940 there were only five Negro officers on active duty in the armed forces, there now is a Negro Air Force Brigadier General (the rank had been attained earlier by a Negro in the Army), and it is expected that others of the race will achieve that rank in the not distant future in the normal course of promotion. Negro colonels and majors are not uncommon, although we find few of comparable position in the Navy and Marines, where the prospect of their attaining such status is remote. In view of these generally better opportunities, it might be conjectured by some that the proportion of Negro servicemen has increased. This, however, has not been the case, as demonstrated by the following table.[2]

	July 1, 1949 (In percent)	July 1, 1954 (In percent)	July 1, 1956 (In percent)
Army officers	1.8	2.97	2.91
Army enlisted men	12.4	13.7	12.83
Navy officers	0.0	0.1	0.1
Navy enlisted men	4.7	3.6	6.3
Air Force officers	0.6	1.1	1.1
Air Force enlisted men	5.1	8.6	10.4
Marine Corps officers	0.0	0.1	0.1
Marine Corps enlisted men	2.1	6.5	6.5

Among Army reenlistment data for the first nine months of 1954, it was found that the immediate reenlistment rate for eligible Regular Army Negro personnel is almost identical with that for all personnel in

---

[1] Letter to author from James C. Evans, Civilian Assistant to the Assistant Secretary of Defense, May 16, 1957. See also Halberstam, *The Army Looks Good to Johnny Lawrence*, Reporter, Oct. 3, 1957.

[2] On positions held by Negroes in the armed forces see DEP'T OF DEFENSE, INTEGRATION IN THE ARMED SERVICES, *passim* (1955). Information for 1956 furnished by James C. Evans.

this category. In the Air Force, for the first six months of 1954, the last date apparently for which figures are available, the reenlistment rate was slightly lower than the proportion of Negro personnel shown in the tabulation. Within the same period the reenlistment rate of Navy stewards approximated one third of those eligible.[3]

THE BASIC DIRECTIVES

All discussions of racial distinctions, or their absence, in the armed forces involve law, for, perhaps apart from some unauthorized acts, military orders and practices are enforceable by the full force of government power. The basic documents controlling integration are actually few in number. The first was Executive Order No. 9981, July 26, 1948: [4] "It is hereby declared to be the policy of the President that there shall be equality of treatment and opportunity for all persons in the armed services without regard to race, color, religion or national origin." Somewhat amplifying this general directive was *Freedom to Serve* (1950), a report of the President's Committee on Equality of Treatment and Opportunity in the Armed Services, which reiterated and discussed the basic policy and the considerations underlying it. Beyond the generalities of the executive order and *Freedom to Serve*, no compilation of regulations or orders can be found. The Department of Defense took the position that greatest effectiveness would be achieved by not highlighting the program with a body of separate regulations and by, on the contrary, weaving the policy into the general body of materials bearing upon manpower and personnel. Authority for implementation has been kept in the regular chain of command. Over-all Defense Department supervision has been maintained by the Civilian Assistant to the Assistant Secretary of Defense in charge of manpower and personnel. For more than a decade this position has been held by James C. Evans, who has seen the services through the change-over from segregation to integration.[5]

The obvious question arises of whether, apart from Executive policy, the Fifth Amendment's due process clause does not forbid segregation in the armed forces. Does the government deny liberty without due process of law or equal protection of the laws when it

---

[3] INTEGRATION IN THE ARMED SERVICES, *op. cit. supra* note 2, at 4.

[4] 13 Fed. Reg. 4313 (1948).

[5] Because published materials do not present a meaningful picture, much of the information on which this chapter is based—in exclusive control of the military—has come from Mr. Evans.

segregates or discriminates against its soldiers? Or are the armed forces immune from this constitutional requirement? During the Second World War and thereafter at least two suits were filed charging that discrimination in the Armed forces was illegal, but they did not come to decision.[6] As there is no real possibility that segregation will be reintroduced, there almost surely will never be a court decision on this issue with regard to the federal military. Discrimination practiced by individual officers frequently is corrected by and within the service, although it sometimes is probably too elusive to form the basis for military or court action. But many National Guard units still segregate or even refuse to admit Negroes, and we shall consider the due process and equal protection questions in terms of closely related Fourteenth Amendment standards for the state National Guards.

FROM DRAFT THROUGH DISCHARGE

Draft boards have no racial quotas. But the discrimination of civilian life obtrudes into the military by affecting the competence of Negroes for service. When, as in 1957–58, the armed forces are being reduced in size and service standards are being raised, inferior education and other social handicaps become important factors in regulating the number of Negroes called to service and the tasks assigned them. It has been said that economic considerations occasionally play a part in areas where agricultural labor is colored—draft boards and enlistment offices tacitly refrain from calling or accepting Negroes to preserve the local labor supply during a cotton- or sugar-harvesting season. But such charges would be difficult to prove and are not unambiguously racial. In the long run they are of little importance; the draftee or enlistee probably will be taken later on.

However, there is an interim stage between draft or enlistment and actual service at which time segregation often is overt. The armed forces claim that they do not yet have jurisdiction; the draft boards claim that the draftee has passed beyond them. The responsibility is undoubtedly that of the United States, whatever the department. Yet in many places men on the threshhold of service are fed separately and otherwise segregated before they are transported to their first post.

[6] See 1940 NAACP ANNUAL REPORT 5 (Yancey Williams, whose application as a flying cadet was rejected, filed suit, Jan. 17, 1941; the suit apparently terminated as a result of establishment of a Negro flying unit at Tuskegee). See SPECIAL GROUPS, SPECIAL MONOGRAPH No. 10, SELECTIVE SERVICE SYSTEM ch. V (1953) (describing suits challenging armed forces segregation and relevant legal considerations).

In fact, the government has only recently advertised for contract bids to feed separately white and colored draftees.[7]

Perhaps the clearest symbol of racial subservience in the armed forces has been the almost all-Negro Navy stewards (or officers' servants) branch. Until 1954 there was separate recruitment of stewards, so that even after armed forces segregation had ended there was still a channel for bringing Negroes into the branch and keeping it all-Negro. It was difficult to keep some recruiting offices from urging Negro applicants to join the stewards branch. Today, there is no separate enlistment for stewards and a general training period is interposed between enlistment and assignment, after which the new properly qualified seaman may choose whatever work interests him.[8]

However, while some Negroes will still undertake stewards' service, white persons almost never will—the job is known as Negroes' work. A temporary influence which has helped to divert Negroes to other jobs is an arrangement made by the United States with the Philippines whereby several thousand Filipino volunteers for stewards' service in the United States Navy have been given a chance to acquire United States citizenship. The program is still in force and affords a measure of relief to the Philippines, as well as opportunity to those enlisting under the program. But it also tends to perpetuate the notion that stewards' work is for persons of darker complexion.

There have been complaints of refusal to assign Negro troops to certain areas in the world. Some local commanders apparently have employed quota systems, limiting the number of Negro troops they would accept in their command. Where found, these policies have been corrected.

A more current and open service-wide discrimination has been the failure until recently to appoint Negroes to military attaché posts in certain countries.[9] This treatment—the allegation was made specifically of Iceland and Ethiopia—has been based on the claim that the host

---

[7] Invitation to Bid No. 18-102-57-110; bid to be submitted by June 17, 1957, to Building No. T.-533 Fort Meade, Md.; signed by D. O. Robinette, Lt. Col. QMC; posted in United States Post Office, Baltimore, Md., June 11, 1957.

[8] Evans & Lane, *Integration in the Armed Forces*, 304 THE ANNALS 78, 82 (1956).

[9] On military-diplomatic posts see Chicago Defender, May 4, 1957, p. 11 ("U.S. Diplomacy Not Diplomatic Where Race Is Concerned"); Afro-American, April 7, 1956, p. 4 ("at the time the United States negotiated an agreement with Iceland to permit U.S. Air Force personnel to be stationed there, I was surprised to learn that no colored people were to be sent there"). *But see* the subsequent Chicago Defender, July 3, 1957, p. 2 ("observers . . . say they know of no countries which actually reject Negroes on embassy staffs except South Africa");

nation did not want Negroes (it has also been said that Liberia desired only Negroes). Investigation then revealed that no nations other than South Africa would actually ban Negroes (on the other side, Liberia has not yet changed its policy). But it is only recently that Negroes have been encouraged to apply for military attaché positions. Until their training and experience become adequate, there cannot be free representation of members of the race in these jobs. The close link between civilian and military discrimination is demonstrated by the fact that only a few years ago did such schools as George Washington, Georgetown, and American universities (all in Washington, D.C.), which give foreign service training, open their doors to Negroes. And, in the absence of an affirmative State and Defense Department employment policy, colored persons heretofore have been reluctant to take the training. As of mid-1957 no Negro marines served as U.S. embassy guards anywhere in the world.[10]

So far, most of the current distinctions we have discussed have been reflections of discrimination in civilian life or residues of segregation in the armed forces from the past. Today, official recognition of race in the active duty armed forces consists, for the greatest part, of "some monitoring to guard against racial concentrations. . . . The present effort is to prohibit any assignments solely by race and to keep an alert against concentrations and exclusions. This becomes a matter of administration rather than quota." [11] The policy resembles the public housing position proposed for New York by the chairman of the state Commission Against Discrimination, and once more does pose the quota issue.[12]

At the same time there are a good many complaints of discrimination by individual officers and "noncoms." The NAACP each week receives several complaints of bias relating to assignment, promotion, discipline, or the administration of military justice. Representations to the Defense Department often bring relief. However, so many subtle, impalpable factors enter into such cases that often perfectly valid charges may be impossible to prove. Moreover, there is danger that the officer complained of could retaliate against the complaint if his

---

id., Feb. 16, 1957, p. 1 (Ethiopia "called charges that it would not accept an American Negro soldier for duty with the military attaché at the Embassy in Addis Ababa, an 'out and out untruth' ").

[10] *Id.*, May 4, 1957, p. 11.
[11] Mr. Evans has supplied this statement of policy.
[12] See pp. 291–293, 250 *supra.*

identity became apparent. Therefore, at least some victims of discrimination must fear making complaints. It is impossible to tell, without extensive investigation, how many charges of discrimination reflect personal dissatisfaction with military life not directly related to racial factors.

Yet some officers have also made special allowance for racial prejudice off the post and permitted the transfer of Negroes from areas in which they personally could not stand community prejudice. Servicemen whose marriages violate intermarriage laws in the states where they are stationed may usually obtain transfers to other areas (and sometimes they are required to transfer against their wishes in such circumstances).[13]

The sporadic, unauthorized, but apparently not uncommon practice of discrimination by individuals is facilitated by the fact that racial designations are shown on orders. Thereby commanders who would discriminate can more readily select and assign on a racial basis. It was argued—a position apparently officially abandoned—that racial designations are necessary to forestall racial concentrations which reflect or possibly create bias.[14] Now a Defense Department policy, permissive, rather than mandatory, has urged the elimination of racial designations.[15] The Army, in 1953, barred racial designations in orders covering the reassignment of members in Army Reserve units.[16] In 1956 it forbade personnel announcements mentioning race.[17] In January, 1957, a message from the Department of the Army directed that on or after February 1, 1957, race was no longer to be indicated in reassignment orders [18] (no mention being made of other records). Two months after the policy had gone into effect orders in Europe still

[13] See p. 350 *supra*.

[14] Afro-American, Oct. 13, 1956, p. 13 (Letter from General J. E. Bastion, Jr., to Representative Henry S. Reuss stated, "Without this information, completely unintentional degrees of segregation might conceivably result requiring costly and time consuming administrative effort to accomplish redistribution").

[15] See SECRETARY OF DEFENSE WILSON REPORT (Jan. 1–June 30, 1954).

[16] INTEGRATION IN THE ARMED SERVICES, *op. cit. supra* note 2, at 3.

[17] In a memorandum of July 20, 1956, the Department of the Army ordered that "no notice posted or distributed, nor announcement made officially to troops, concerning levies or any other type of personnel action, except as directed by appropriate Department of the Army regulations, will specify race." But since then, complaints have been made of such announcements, Chicago Defender, March 2, 1957, p. 21.

[18] DA 488990 (Jan. 57), dated 15 January 1957. See N.Y. Times, Feb. 9, 1957, p. 8 (Army informs Congressman Powell of order and assures him that it supports "integration policies prescribed by the President").

carried racial designations. Servicemen still report that requests for men sometimes specify "Caucasian." Branches other than the Army have not implemented Defense Department policy on designations.

THE RESERVES

Reserve service may be offered in fulfillment of military obligations. The federally controlled Reserves are under the same mandate to integrate as are active duty groups, and some Southern ones contain Negroes. But there have been complaints, some well founded, of discrimination in the Reserves. A good many such groups are all white. With their reviews, dances, picnics, as well as military exercises, Reserve units often serve a club-like social purpose, and this is one reason why some whites, who would not welcome Negroes at their social functions, discourage Negro participation in their reserve units. Because military records are not public, it is difficult to tell whether an applicant for the reserves has been turned down or denied advancement because of race or for other reasons. The issue is compounded by the substantial autonomy given local commanders and a propensity of superiors to accept their explanations of apparently discriminatory situations. Again, the problem reflects civilian separation, much more so than does the active duty situation. The Civil Air Patrol is probably the only arm of the Reserves in which units have openly rejected Negro applicants on racial grounds, although some CAP outfits are mixed. The CAP is an official auxiliary of the Air Force which provides private citizens with aviation education and training to assist in meeting local and national emergencies. Its 1957 budget, paid by the United States, was estimated at about $6,000,000, and its units are located at Air Force bases.[19]

But while under official Reserve policy discrimination has been illegal and furtive (except in the case of CAP), or merely a reflection of the civilian milieu, bias is often official and overt in the National Guard in which one also may serve in fulfillment of federal military obligations. The Guard, too, often has a social function. Some Southern states that permit Negroes to serve in their National Guard allow segregated service only.[20] A 1959 survey made by the American

[19] On the CAP and segregation see Afro-American, April 20, 1957, p. 31, April 27, 1957, p. 8. The CAP says its application forms do not request information concerning race, Chicago Defender, June 15, 1957, p. 2.

[20] According to NAACP Press Release of July 15, 1955, these included Kentucky, North Carolina, Tennessee, Texas, and Virginia. See appendix A30 for state National Guard segregation laws.

Jewish Committee lists twelve states that bar segregation in the National Guard. In addition, Delaware, Oklahoma, and West Virginia have only recently abolished such segregation.[21] Some states practice total exclusion of Negroes.[22] However, we find some all-Negro units in most, if not all, of the antisegregation states, and often Negro participation in non-Negro outfits there is only nominal. It has been said that Negro officers of all-Negro organizations sometimes are reluctant to part with the authority which integration might bring. If state units were called into federal service all racial standards would have to be scrapped, but practical handicaps at such a time would undoubtedly impede the actual process of mixing.

The controlling cases dealing with judicial restraints on the National Guard appear to be *Sterling v. Constantin*[23] and *Aaron v. Cooper*.[24] In the former the United States Supreme Court upheld a federal court injunction based on constitutional grounds against the Texas Governor's use of the National Guard to restrict oil production. In the latter, one of the stages of the Little Rock litigation, the Arkansas National Guard was enjoined from interfering with school desegregation. Both indicate that the governor must conduct the Guard in consonance with the provisions of the Constitution. There has, however, been no direct judicial test of a state's power to make racial distinctions within its National Guard. Such a suit would raise questions of due process and equal protection like those which would have arisen in a suit challenging segregation in the armed forces of the United States. In addition, questions of national military policy are posed by the Guard problem, for Congress has declared the National

[21] See AMERICAN JEWISH COMMITTEE, THE PEOPLE TAKE THE LEAD, 1948–1959, at 5 (pamphlet 1959) (lists California, Connecticut, Illinois, Maryland, Massachusetts, Michigan, Minnesota, New Jersey, New York, Pennsylvania, Washington, Wisconsin). On Oklahoma see N.Y. Times, March 8, 1958, p. 17. See appendix A30 for state National Guard antisegregation laws.

[22] Mr. Clarence Mitchell in his testimony in *Hearings on H.R. 2967 Before Subcommittee No. 1 of the House Armed Services Committee*, 83d Cong., 2d Sess., pp. 2144–2146 (March 3, 1955), stated that the following states completely exclude: Arkansas, Georgia, Louisiana, Mississippi, and South Carolina. He proposed the following amendment: "All units of the State National Guard and the Air National Guard shall be open to qualified persons without regard to race," *id.* at 2146.

[23] Sterling v. Constantin, 287 U.S. 378 (1932). See also BECKWITH, LAWFUL ACTION OF STATE MILITARY FORCES 45 (1944); Wiener, *The Militia Clause of the Constitution*, 54 HARV. L. REV. 181 (1940); Wiener, *Courts-Martial and the Bill of Rights—The Original Practice*, 72 HARV. L. REV. 1, 266 (1958).

[24] The trial court injunction against Governor Faubus and the National Guard is reported at 2 R.R.L.R. 957 (1957); it was affirmed *sub nom.* Faubus v. United States, 254 F.2d 797 (8th Cir. 1958), *cert. denied*, 358 U.S. 829 (1958).

Guard "an integral part of the first line defenses of this Nation." [25]
Can a Guard unit meet its duty of preparing for ultimate federal service by training segregated units while the national military is integrated? The answer appears to be that it cannot.

The due process–equal protection standard need not be restated.
Gubernatorial acts are clearly subject to it. As early as the *Civil Rights
Cases* the Supreme Court held that the Fourteenth Amendment voids
"state action of every kind" inconsistent with its guarantees and
extends to manifestations of state authority in the shape of laws,
customs, or judicial or executive proceedings.[26] Moreover, constitutional standards other than those of the *Sterling* and Little Rock cases
have been placed upon the armed forces, chiefly but not always in
cases of courts-martial. Illegal sentences or trial of civilian dependents
accompanying the military will be nullified by the civilian judiciary.[27]
Indeed, civilian courts will look into court-martial proceedings, even
where there was military jurisdiction in a technical sense, to see
whether there was a gross departure from standards of fairness.[28] The
celebrated *Girard* [29] case proceeded on the assumption that the military
would obey the civilian courts and withhold Girard from Japanese
jurisdiction if there were no authority to turn him over. A military
discharge is subject to judicial review—at least within certain limits.[30]
These rulings demonstrate that claims of military autonomy completely
free of civilian standards are without foundation.

It could be urged that Article I, Section 8, Clause 16, of the Constitution, governing state militias, empowers Congress to regulate them,
but does not mention the courts, inferentially placing the governor's
conduct of the Guard beyond judicial control. To the same end it
might be argued that some militias antedate the Federal Constitution,
and therefore, that their commanders in chief retain control like that
of colonial times. But beyond the basis of the rulings in *Sterling* and
Aaron is the fact that the language introducing Clause 16 ("The
Congress shall have power") also precedes Clause 3 (the commerce
clause) of Article I, Section 8, and courts regularly decide issues under
that provision in the absence of congressional legislation. The com-

[25] Universal Military Training and Service Act, 50 U.S.C.A. app. § 451(d).
[26] Civil Rights Cases, 109 U.S. 3, 11 (1883).
[27] Reid v. Covert, 354 U.S. 1 (1957), overruling Reid v. Covert, 351 U.S. 487
(1956), and Kinsella v. Krueger, 351 U.S. 470 (1956).
[28] See Burns v. Wilson, 346 U.S. 137 (1953).
[29] Wilson v. Girard, 354 U.S. 524 (1957).
[30] Harmon v. Brucker, 355 U.S. 579 (1958).

merce clause parallel perhaps goes further. Lack of uniformity in the Guards, one may argue, is like divergent state practices affecting commerce: [31] if the diversity unduly burdens the national interest, it should be held unconstitutional even though Congress has been silent. Such a burden could readily be found to the extent that federal assimilation would be slowed in wartime by the need to merge integrated and segregated outfits, or to the extent that manpower is reduced because of exclusion of Negroes. Moreover, Article I, Section 8, Clause 16, has been described as having made congressional control "unlimited, except in the two particulars of officering and training," [32] a qualification of the governor's control so sweeping that it would be misleading to call his power "prerogative."

States with intransigent racist policies might argue that to desegregate would mean abolition of the Guard. It is questionable whether this argument draws much support from national military leaders, many of whom, apparently, do not look with favor on the Guards' continued existence.[33] At any rate, the abolition argument generally has not deterred judicial determination to desegregate elementary and high schools, colleges, parks, libraries, and so forth.

In 1955, following presentation of arguments for desegregation like those discussed above, Governor McKeldin of Maryland ordered that state's Guard desegregated, stating that he expected court action to follow if segregation were continued. At the time the Maryland Guard contained 177 Negroes out of a total membership of 5,710, and it had fought in Korea on an integrated basis. By 1957, following integration, at least 44 Negroes were serving in units that also contained white Guardsmen.[34]

James C. Evans, of the Defense Department, states that "the last remaining all-Negro units wearing Armed Forces uniforms are, paradoxically, to be found on the college campus in the student ROTCs." [35] However, when these students go to summer camp at military instal-

[31] See, e.g., Southern Pac. Ry. v. Arizona, 325 U.S. 761, 767 (1945).
[32] Houston v. Moore, 5 Wheat. 1, 16 (1820).
[33] See RIKER, SOLDIERS OF THE STATES ch. VI (1957).
[34] A copy of the Maryland petition may be found in the files of the NAACP Legal Defense Fund. See Afro-American, Jan. 21, 1956, p. 6 ("the governor said that in making the decision he took 'into consideration the sound points made in the petition' submitted by the 15 officers"). Id., May 4, 1957, p. 3 ("integration in Maryland's National Guard units has been proceeding slowly but satisfactorily, according to Maj. Gen. Milton A. Reckord, the adjutant general"). See S.S.N., Aug., 1958, p. 3 (166 Negroes in 8,032-man desegregated Oklahoma guard).
[35] Communication to the author.

lations, while undergraduates, or to officers' basic training after gradua-
tion and commissioning, they are integrated. For many this is their
first experience with nonsegregation. But so long as colleges segregate,
ROTC segregation will be practically beyond the reach of the armed
forces integration policy, unless ROTCs were to be removed from
segregated schools. There are also high school ROTCs which prepare
students either for college ROTC or for service in the armed forces.
Almost every large white high school in the South has such a unit.
Until recently there was no such training in Southern Negro public
high schools; it had been given only in a few border communities (the
District of Columbia, Indianapolis, Kansas City, and St. Joseph,
Missouri). Now there are ROTCs in three Negro high schools in
Texas, the only such public school groups in the South.

Once more, notwithstanding a clear policy of the federal military,
the civilian environment and the heavy hand of past discrimination
control the situation. The 1956 *Annual Report* of the Urban League of
Greater Boston gives a clear indication of this social drag in a statement concerning NROTC scholarships:

The results over the past five years have been exceedingly disappointing.
Each year the Navy has assigned Negro officers to cover all recruiting
districts across the nation in hopes that their appearances and personal
contacts might create a greater interest among minority youth. As you
doubtless know, Lt. A. P. Dean of the New York Recruiting office has
covered the New England states for the past two or three years. Having
checked with him since receiving your letter, he informs me that as far as
can be determined no Negro boys have shown up at the examining centers
to take the exams during that time and to his knowledge none have passed
the exams or were selected during that time.

The largest percentage of Negro boys taking the exams are usually in
the South.

It is doubtful if we have actually had more than half a dozen Negro boys
successfully qualify for NROTC through the annual competitive examinations and be selected for the college training program during the past five
years. None of these to my knowledge have been from the New England
states.

The Navy offers 2,000 such scholarships annually.

COLLATERAL ACTIVITIES

The military also furnishes some civilian-like facilities, such as
schools for dependents, higher education, dependent housing. Schools
for dependents on armed forces bases, North and South, even where

administered by local school boards, are nonsegregated.[36] But when the Department of Health, Education, and Welfare has made grants to federally impacted areas for schools to be operated by state officials for service personnel who have overburdened local facilities it has attached no nondiscriminatory conditions at all. As a consequence, a Pulaski County, Arkansas, school built with $650,000 of national money and attended only by the children of service personnel will not admit Negro children.[37] To avoid the on-base nonsegregation requirement, some local schools have moved off a base (*e.g.*, in Cecil County, Maryland);[38] then, Negro servicemen, like other Negroes, must send their children to segregated schools in the civilian community.

Off-duty courses conducted by American universities for the armed forces overseas are unsegregated. In the United States there must be no segregation on the base in either on-duty or off-duty classes, even if the courses are given by institutions which ordinarily exclude Negroes. Apparently to avoid this rule the University of Georgia withdrew from on-post activity June 1, 1956. While the University of North Carolina has openly given nonsegregated courses at Fort Bragg, state institutions of higher learning elsewhere have employed various fictions to satisfy the advocates of segregation. Alabama State Teachers College, at Troy, has given nonsegregated on-base courses, but Negro personnel taking this instruction have received credit at a colored institution, State Teachers College, at Montgomery. At Fort Campbell, Kentucky, Austin Peay State College (white) and the Industrial State University of Nashville (colored) have "jointly" conducted on-post courses; in fact, all classes were conducted by Austin Peay instructors.[39] For off-base training the Air Force has adopted a different approach. "When airmen are to be sent to schools in States having statutes requiring segregation, Negro airmen will be given the option of not going if they choose. In that event, the Negro airman will be sent to a school which can accept both white and Negro airmen."[40] But in at least one instance a University of Georgia course

[36] Secretary of Defense Wilson Report 18 (Jan. 1–June 30, 1956).

[37] See S.S.N., Nov., 1958, p. 8.

[38] Mitchell v. Connellee, 1 R.R.L.R. 645 (D. Md. 1956) (the school involved in this suit moved off base shortly after filing).

[39] Concerning training for servicemen given by civilian institutions see Afro-American, Nov. 10, 1956, p. 8 ("Army Integrates Off Duty Classes. . . . on southern military installations under contracts between the Army and private and public educational institutions").

[40] Evans & Lane, *supra* note 8, at 82.

off the base was apparently conducted without segregation in a Columbus high school building.[41]

Government-owned housing for the military may not be segregated, although the policy allegedly has been violated.[42] But civilians near military bases enforce segregation on their property. Owners of houses near guided missile bases in Maryland and Virginia which protect Washington have declined to lease to the Army without a provision barring Negroes, which the Army has refused to sign. However, the Army has informally accommodated to the civilian demands.[43] Other civilian facilities, such as rest rooms and water fountains, have been desegregated at all bases where they were previously separate.[44]

The armed forces employ a great many civilian workers, perhaps half of all government personnel. It has been observed that more than half of the Negroes in government civilian service work for the military. Here, as in all federal government service, discrimination is theoretically forbidden. But the Department of Defense itself states that there has hardly been full implementation of the policy, particularly in the case of women employees.[45] A congressman has said that in mid-1956 the Army had but one Negro woman civilian serving as a secretary in Europe. While the Army denied the charge, it did not assert that the number was any higher.[46]

COURTS-MARTIAL

It is worth noting that some of the issues discussed in connection with civilian criminal cases arise in courts-martial. Section 140(a) of the *Manual for Courts-Martial* states concerning charges of coercion

[41] Afro-American, Nov. 10, 1956, p. 8.

[42] *Id.*, June 29, 1957, p. 3 ("the U.S. Defense Department has been requested by the West Coast NAACP office to order housing segregation abandoned in the quarters provided here [Babbit, Nev.] for civilian and military personnel employed at the nearby naval ordnance depot").

[43] *Id.*, April 7, 1956, p. 5. ("the Army spokesman said that 'We aren't going into a neighborhood and force any of our men where they aren't wanted. In time the problem will resolve itself' ").

[44] Evans & Lane, *supra* note 8, at 83.

[45] INTEGRATION IN THE ARMED SERVICES, *op. cit. supra* note 2, at 7. See also DEP'T OF THE ARMY CIVILIAN PERSONNEL PAMPHLET No. 41-B-36, SUPERVISOR DEVELOPMENT PROGRAM, BASIC COURSE, NONDISCRIMINATION POLICY (1956).

[46] N.Y. Times, Aug. 25, 1956, p. 32 ("Powell Sees Bias By the Army Abroad"); *id.*, Sept. 20, 1956, p. 14 ("Army Replies on Negro; Tells Powell Secretary Was Treated Well in Europe"). See also Afro-American, March 23, 1957, p. 6 (racial discrimination alleged at naval gun factory; Negroes denied membership in union, a prerequisite for higher-paying positions).

of confession that "to be admissible, a confession or admission of the accused must be voluntary. A confession or admission which was obtained through the use of coercion, unlawful influence, or unlawful inducement is not voluntary." [47] In *United States v. Jones,* the Court of Military Appeals noted that it "has recognized . . . that there is even greater danger of involuntary confessions obtained from accused persons by military superiors than in the case of civilian interrogators." [48]

A question analagous to that of the jury discrimination issue has arisen in connection with the composition of courts-martial. The military courts have not held that proof of discrimination will not vitiate a conviction, but apparently no case has found such discrimination.[49] It has been held that an accused may examine members of the court on *voir dire* as to racial prejudice.[50]

CONCLUSION

Integration of the armed forces shows the potential of law for achieving changes in race relations. In a democracy no one is subject to greater legal control than those in the armed services, and no other aspect of American life is so subject to government management, no other control can be as swift and unequivocal. Rarely are people required to act in a social context in which they can refer so little to the folkways in which they were brought up. Integration has been rapid and largely successful. Not only have behavior patterns been changed, but apparently attitudes too have been influenced by the new policy.[51] Yet some implementation remains to be accomplished. The number of complaints concerning discrimination by individual officers or "non-coms" indicates that enforcement may not be as complete in some areas as in others. But the major problems of discrimination which trouble the military are now largely carry-overs or reflections of civilian life, namely, inferior education and other civilian-inflicted

[47] See Duke, *Aspects of the Military Law of Confessions,* 8 VAND. L. REV. 19 (1954). See Dep't of the Army order AGAM-P(M) 333.5 (8 Jan. 56) PMGO, forbidding practice of "lining up" all Negroes in unit if one is accused of crime.
[48] 7 U.S.C.M.A. 623, 626 (1957).
[49] United States v. Bryson, 10 C.M.R. 164 (1953).
[50] United States v. Parker, 6 U.S.C.M.A. 274 (1954).
[51] See NICHOLS, BREAKTHROUGH ON THE COLOR FRONT (1954), MANDELBAUM, SOLDIER GROUPS AND NEGRO SOLDIERS; Byers, A Study of the Negro in Military Service (mimeographed 1947; Schomburg Collection, N.Y. Public Library); PETERS, THE SOUTHERN TEMPER ch. 8 (1959).

inequalities, lack of information concerning military opportunity, lack of aspiration which derives from a history of segregation and discrimination, prejudice on the part of officers who cannot muster up the impartiality their positions require, and discrimination in surrounding civilian facilities which the military use.

THE PROSPECT

In the first chapter of this work we surveyed, largely in anticipation of the discussion which followed, the ways in which the law works to affect race relations, the social support it has, and the obstacles it faces. This, it is hoped, provided a perspective, which may have lent understanding to consideration of the more discrete issues which in subsequent chapters were sometimes necessarily discussed in legalistic detail. It is submitted that from all of the foregoing we may now conclude that the legal tide opposing racial distinctions is clear and strong and that it shows no sign of receding. It reflects other dominant trends, historical, political, social, economic, and moral. Although not generally and evenly applied, these pressures on legal development and enforcement are not transient. They may be expected to continue, accelerate, and spread. Thus the legal momentum against racial bias will accumulate and intensify. Law has demonstrated its capacity to change race relations, and in the future this ability will grow. A legal rule might falter or rebound if it ran counter to the other forces of life; the inherent frailties of legal procedure might stultify efforts to use law for social change in other circumstances; but in the nation and the world in which we live the application of legal rules governing race relations is bound to continue to bring social practices into line with the legal norm.

APPENDIX A

LEGISLATIVE MATERIALS

1. TRAVEL SEGREGATION STATUTES

ALA. CODE ANN. tit. 48, §§ 186, 196–198, 464 (1940); tit. 48, §§ 301(31a)–(31c) (1955 Supp.). ARK. STATS. ANN. tit. 73, §§ 1201, 1218–1221, 1747–1753 (1957). FLA. STATS. ANN. §§ 350.20–.21, 352.02–.18 (1958). GA. CODE ANN. §§ 18-205 to -210 (1935); §§ 18-223 to -224, 9918, 9919 (1958 Supp.). KY. REV. STATS. ANN. § 276.440 (1956). LA. REV. STATS. ANN. §§ 45:194–196 (repealed, Acts 1958, No. 261, § 1); §§ 45:521–34 (1950); §§ 45:1301–05 (1957 Supp.). MISS. CODE ANN. §§ 7784–7787, 7787.5 (1956). N.C. GEN. STATS. §§ 60-94 to -98, 135–137 (1950). OKLA. STATS. ANN. tit. 13, §§ 181–191; tit. 47, §§ 201–210 (1937). S.C. CODE ANN. tit. 58, §§ 714–720 (1952). TENN. CODE ANN. tit. 65, §§ 1313–1315 (1955). TEX. PEN. CODE arts. 1659–1661.1 (1953). TEX. REV. CIV. STATS. art. 6417 (1926). VA. CODE ANN. tit. 56, §§ 325–330, 390–404 (1950).

2. STATUTES FORBIDDING RACIAL DISCRIMINATION BY INSURANCE COMPANIES

MASS. ANN. LAWS ch. 151B, § 4(3A) (1957 Supp.) (unlawful for insurer or bonding company to inquire into applicant's race, etc., with respect to persons seeking bond or surety bond). MICH. STATS. ANN. § 24.12082 (1957) (no insurer to make distinction or discrimination between white or colored persons as to premiums or rates charged for life insurance policies; violation misdemeanor, imprisonment up to 1 year, fine $50 to $500, forfeiture to state $500). MINN. STATS. ANN. § 61.05 (1946) (discrimination in life insurance prohibited; $500 to $1,000 forfeiture; violation misdemeanor; revocation of license). N.J. STATS. ANN. § 17:34–44 (1939) (discrimination among persons because of race as to premiums or rates on life policies prohibited). N.Y. INS. LAW § 209(3) (1958 Supp.) (like the Michigan law). N.Y. PEN. LAW § 1191(4) (1944) (discrimination forbidden by N.Y. INS. LAW is a misdemeanor). OHIO REV. CODE §§ 3911.16–.17 (1954) (like the New Jersey law). WIS. STATS. ANN. § 942.04(c) (1958) (racial discrimination in sale of auto insurance forbidden; damages not less than $25; fine up to

$200, imprisonment 6 months, or both fine and imprisonment, but civil or criminal remedy exclusive).

The following provisions, typical of antidiscrimination clauses in the laws of most states, do not mention race. It does not appear that their applicability to racial discrimination has been adjudicated. ME. REV. STATS. ch. 60, § 149VII (1954) (it is an unfair method of competition to make unfair discrimination between individuals of same class and equal life expectancy in rates for life insurance; discrimination in premiums or policy fees charged for accident or sickness insurance prohibited); § 152 (Insurance Commissioner may issue cease and desist order). N.Y. INS. LAW §§ 209(1) and (2) (discrimination against individuals of same class by life, accident, or health companies prohibited); *compare with* § 209(3) *supra*. See N.Y. PEN. LAW § 1191(4) *supra* (penalty). S.D. CODE § 31.1515 (1939) (discrimination prohibited between policy holders of same class with respect to premiums, dividends, etc.; applies to life, health, accident insurers; violation misdemeanor, imprisonment 60 days to 6 months or $200 fine).

3. HOSPITAL SEGREGATION STATUTES

ALA. CODE tit. 45, § 4 (segregation in tubercular hospitals for prisoners); § 248 (1940) (segregation in hospitals for mental deficients). ARK. STATS. ANN. § 7-401 (tubercular hospital for Negroes); § 7-404 (1947) (county judge has discretion to admit Negroes who are without sufficient funds to this tubercular hospital). DEL. CODE ANN. tit. 16, § 155 (1953) (separate hospitals may be established for colored tubercular patients). GA. CODE ANN. § 35-225 (1935) (mental hospital segregated); § 35-308 (1957 Supp.) (training school for Negro mental defectives). KY. REV. STATS. § 215.078 (segregation in tubercular hospitals) and § 205.180 (1953) (segregation in mental hospitals) were both repealed in 1954. LA. REV. STATS. ANN. § 46:181 (1950) (separate facilities at homes for aged, infirm). MISS. CODE ANN. § 6883 (segregation at mental hospital); § 6927 (segregation at Mississippi State Charity Hospital); § 6973 (separate entrances at all state hospitals); § 6974 (1942) (colored nurses for colored patients). N.C. GEN. STATS. § 122-3 (1957 Supp.) (races segregated between two state hospitals for insane). OKLA. STATS. ANN. tit. 10, §§ 201–206.1 (1951) (Negro consolidated institute for blind, deaf, orphans, insane); tit. 63, §§ 531–532 (1949) (separate tubercular hospital). TENN. CODE ANN. § 33-602 (1955) (separate buildings for Negro and white patients in hospitals for insane). TEX. CIV. STATS. ANN. art. 3254a (1952) (Negro tubercular hospital). VA. CODE §§ 37-5 to -6 (1950) (hospitals for colored insane and epileptics). W. VA. CODE § 2632 (1955) (home for mentally deficient aged and infirm colored persons); § 2636 (1955) (TB hospitals for white persons); § 2638 (1957 Supp.) (tubercular hospital for Negroes discontinued; any person with chronic illness may be admitted).

4. RECREATION SEGREGATION STATUTES

ARK. STATS. ANN. §§ 84-2724 *et seq.* (1947) (all race tracks, other gaming establishments).* GA. CODE ANN. §§ 84-1603 to -1604 (1955) (poolrooms). KY. REV. STATS. ANN. § 97.470 (1955) (separate funds may be appropriated for white and colored parks), repealed by L. 1956, ch. 25. LA. REV. STATS. § 33:4558.1 (all public parks, recreation centers, playgrounds, community centers, swimming pools, dance halls, golf courses, skating rinks, and all other recreational facilities); §§ 4:451–454 (1958 Supp.) (all social and athletic functions must provide separate seating and sanitary facilities); § 4:5 (1951) (separate ticket booths and entrances at circuses). MISS. CODE ANN. § 4065.3 (1956 Supp.) (executive branch of government directed to prohibit the mixing of the races in, among other places, public parks, places of amusement, recreation, or assembly). MO. STATS. ANN. § 165.327 (1949) (board of education may establish separate libraries, public parks, and playgrounds notwithstanding repeal of § 163.130 which required separate school facilities). N.C. GEN. STATS. § 125-10 (1952) (had required separate library reading rooms; the 1955 library code, §§ 125-1 *et seq.* (1957 Supp.), omits mention of race). OKLA. STATS. ANN. tit. 17, § 135 (1953) (separate phone booths authorized); tit. 74, § 351j (1956) (state Planning and Resources Board may segregate recreational facilities); tit. 82, § 489 (1952) (separate boating). S.C. CODE §§ 51-1, 2.1–2.4 (1957 Supp.) (separate state parks); § 51-181 (separate public recreational facilities of city with population in excess of 60,000); § 5-19 (separate entrances at circus). TENN. CODE ANN. § 62-715 (1955) (policy of state not to interfere with "right" to provide separate facilities in public accommodations), § 48-824 (public parks). TEX. CIV. STATS. ANN. art. 1688 (separate libraries); art. 6070e (1957 Supp.) (separate park facilities). VA. CODE ANN. §§ 18-327 to -328 (1950) (any public entertainment or public assemblage).

5. STATUTES AUTHORIZING CLOSING OR SALE OF RECREATIONAL FACILITIES

ALA. CONST. amend. CXII (legislature may authorize alienation of public recreational facilities). ALA. CODE tit. 47, §§ 62(1)–(3) (1957 Supp.) (political subdivisions may alienate recreational facilities if approved by referendum). GA. CODE ANN. §§ 69-613 to -616 (1957) (political subdivision may alienate parks, etc.; provision for advertising, bidding, exceptions); § 26-3004 (misdemeanor to enter public property which has been closed). MISS. H.B. 1958, No. 1134 (authorizing governor to close parks). S.C.A. & J.R. 1956, No. 917 (closing park involved in *Clark v. Flory*, see note 60, ch. III).

* See appendix E.

6. PUBLIC ACCOMMODATIONS STATUTES

ALASKA COMP. LAWS § 20-1-3 (1949) (citizens entitled to full and equal public accommodations); § 20-1-4, as amended by L. 1949, ch. 21 (violation, aiding or inciting violation, displaying sign indicating racial discrimination are misdemeanors; $250, 30 days, or both). CAL. PEN. CODE § 365 (1955) (misdemeanor for innkeeper or common carrier to refuse service without just cause). CAL. CIV. CODE § 51 (all citizens given right to full and equal accommodations in enumerated and other places of public accommodation); § 52 (civil cause of action at law for violation of § 51; minimum damages $100); § 53 (unlawful to refuse admission to person over 21 who presents ticket or tenders admission price); § 54 (1954) (civil action for violation of § 53; actual damages plus $100). COLO. REV. STATS. § 25-1-1 (all persons allowed full and equal enjoyment of enumerated and other places of public accommodation and amusement); § 25-1-2 (civil action, damages $50 to $500, or misdemeanor, $100 to $300 and/or up to 1 year in jail; judgment in criminal or civil action bars other suit); § 25-2-1 (discriminatory advertising prohibited); § 25-2-5 (1953) (misdemeanor; fine $100 to $500 and/or 30 to 90 days); §§ 25-3-1 et seq. (1957 Supp.) (filing complaint with Colorado Antidiscrimination Commission; if this remedy is elected it is exclusive; procedures of §§ 80-24-5 et seq., i.e., employment, made applicable). CONN. REV. STATS. § 8375 (1949 Rev.) (no discrimination in enumerated places of public accommodation, resort, amusement; fine $25 to $100, 30 days, or both); § 3267d (any segregation or separation of races considered violation of act); § 3268d (1955 Supp.) (Commission on Civil Rights can receive complaints; may proceed as in case of refusal to employ under ch. 371, employment). D.C. CODE (1955 Supp.) §§ 33-604 to -607 (restaurants, ice cream parlors, etc., shall serve all well-behaved persons; $100 fine; forfeiture of license). Until John R. Thompson Co. v. Dist. of Columbia, 346 U.S. 100, 110 (1953), rev'g 203 F.2d 579 (D.C. Cir. 1953), there had been no prosecution under this statute since 1873; in Thompson it was argued that the legislation had been repealed and, alternatively, that the Legislative Assembly of the District had no power to enact it. The Supreme Court rejected both arguments. See the same case on remand, 214 F.2d 210 (D.C. Cir. 1954); by Act of June 10, 1869, amended March 7, 1870, and Order No. 56-874 of the District Commissioners licensees of enumerated places of amusement may make no racial distinctions; fine $50 to $300. ILL. STATS. ANN. ch. 14, § 9 (1951) (creates in Attorney General's office division for investigating and enforcing against civil rights violations); ch. 38, § 125 (enumerated places of public accommodation and amusement shall not discriminate); § 126 (misdemeanor, up to $500 and/or 1 year; suit for damages from $25 to $500); § 128a (violation of § 125 is public nuisance, may be enjoined); § 128b (action under § 128a may be brought in name of people); § 128c (violation of injunction is contempt); § 128d (duty of state and municipal officers to cooperate in enforcing act); § 128e (State's Attorney and Attorney General should diligently prosecute violators); § 128f (on failure to prosecute circuit judges may appoint special attorney); § 128k (no employee of state shall deny use of facility under his charge); § 128*l* (where employee violates § 128k, aggrieved may complain to his superior; if guilty, discharge follows; if not guilty, complainant must be notified); § 128m (if complainant not satisfied can sue to review superior's decision); § 128n (appointed head of department or agency who violates § 128k shall be removed by officer who appointed him); § 129 (1958 Supp.) (discriminatory advertising); ch. 43, § 133 (1944) (licensed sellers of intoxicating liquors must give full and equal accommodations); § 149 (1958 Supp.) (commission can revoke license of violators); ch. 105, § 468.1 (1952) (if state park concessionaire discriminates, lease terminated); ch. 127, §§ 214.1 *et seq.* (1953) (creates Commission on Human Relations). IND. STATS. ANN. § 10-901 (no discrimination in enumerated and other places of public accommodation); § 10-902 (1956) (civil action, damages up to $100; or in the alternative penalty of $100 and/or 30 days). IOWA CODE § 735.1 (all persons may use enumerated and other places of public accommodation); § 735.2 (1946) (misdemeanor; up to $100, up to 30 days). KAN. GEN. STATS. ANN. § 21-2424 (1949) (inns, hotels, common carriers, boarding houses, or any place of entertainment or amusement for which license required shall make no distinction of race or color; fine $10 to $1,000; liability for damages). ME. REV. STATS. ch. 137, § 50 (1954) (advertisements, etc., intended to discriminate in enumerated places of public accommodation unlawful; fine up to $100, up to 30 days).* MASS. ANN. LAWS ch. 140, § 5 (innholders and common victualers shall provide food and lodging for strangers and travelers); § 7 (innholder who refuses to give proper lodging to be fined not more than $50); § 8 (1957) (common victualer who refuses to supply food to traveler or stranger to be fined not more than $50); ch. 151B, §§ 5 *et seq.* (1957) (person aggrieved because of violation of public accommodation statutes or Attorney General may file complaint with Massachusetts Commission Against Discrimination, which after hearing may issue cease and desist order; review; enforcement); ch. 272, § 92A (places of public accommodation defined; advertising, displaying notice intended to discriminate prohibited; fine up to $100 and/or 30 days); § 98 (1956) (all persons must be accepted in enumerated and other places of public accommodation; fine up to $300 and/or 1 year in jail; forfeiture to aggrieved person of $100 to $500). MICH. STATS. ANN. § 28.343 (all persons entitled to full and equal accommodations in enumerated and other places of public accommodation, amusement, and recreation); § 28.344 (1957 Supp.) (minimum fine $100 and/or at least 15 days; civil suit for treble damages; license may be suspended or revoked). MINN. STATS. ANN. § 327.09 (1947) (no person shall be excluded from enumerated and other places of amusement, refreshment, entertainment, or accommodation; gross misdemeanor; civil damages up to $500). MONT. REV. CODE § 64-211 (1957 Supp.) (discrimination prohibited in any place of public accommodation or amuse-

* See appendix E.

ment). NEB. REV. STATS. § 20-101 (all persons entitled to full and equal enjoyment of enumerated and other places); § 20-102 (1943) (fine $25 to $100). N.H. REV. STATS. ANN. ch. 354:1-2 (prohibits publication, posting, or notice calculated to discriminate in places of public accommodation: hotel, restaurant, common carrier, theater, bathhouse, barbershop, or other public hall); ch. 354:4 (1955) (fine $10 to $100, 30 to 90 days). N.J. STATS. ANN. § 2A:170-11 (unlawful to refuse admittance in an air raid shelter because of race, creed, or color); § 2A:169-4 (1953) (fine not more than $1,000 and/or imprisonment for not more than 1 year); § 10:1-2 (all persons have equal rights in all places of public accommodation); § 10:1-3 (no exclusion because of race, color, or creed); § 10:1-4 (discriminatory ads are presumptive evidence of their authorization); § 10:1-5 (public accommodations enumerated); § 10:1-6 (forfeiture to state of $100 to $500 in action at law; misdemeanor, fine not more than $500 and/or 90 days); § 10:1-7 (1957 Supp.) (aggrieved may sue in name of state; out of judgment he receives costs and attorney fees, not less than $20, not more than $100); § 18:25-4 (all to obtain all accommodations, advantages, facilities, privileges of any place of public accommodation without discrimination); § 18:25-6 (creates Division Against Discrimination with power to prevent and eliminate discrimination); § 18:25-12 (defines unlawful discrimination); § 18:25-13 (aggrieved person or attorney may file complaint with commission); § 18:25-14 (commission investigates; tries to eliminate complaint by conference, conciliation, persuasion); § 18:25-17 (if commissioner finds discrimination can issue cease and desist order); § 18:25-19 (1957 Supp.) (circuit court will enforce, review decisions of commissioner). N.M. STATS. ANN. § 49-8-1 (state policy to prohibit discrimination in public accommodations); § 49-8-2 (right to full and equal advantages, facilities of any public accommodation a civil right); § 49-8-4 (discrimination in place of public accommodation unlawful); § 49-8-5 (public accommodations, etc., defined); § 49-8-6 (1957 Supp.) (employee and employer equally responsible). N.Y. CONST. art. I, § 11 (no person shall be discriminated against in civil rights). N.Y. CIV. RIGHTS LAW § 40 (all persons entitled to full and equal accommodations, etc., of enumerated and other places of public accommodation); § 40-b (no person over 21 who holds ticket may be refused admittance to or be ejected from any place of public entertainment); § 41 (1948) (civil actions for $100 to $500; misdemeanor, $100 to $500, 30 to 90 days or both). N.Y. EXEC. LAW § 290 (purpose is, *inter alia*, to eliminate and prevent discrimination in places of public accommodation); § 292 (defines places of public accommodation as those in CIV. RIGHTS LAW § 40, but some, *e.g.*, schools, are excepted); § 293 (creates commission); § 295 (power to investigate, conduct hearings, etc.); § 296 (defines unlawful discrimination in public accommodations substantially as does § 40 CIV. RIGHTS LAW); § 297 (any person or his attorney may file complaint with commission; commissioner will investigate, try to eliminate discrimination by conference, conciliation, and persuasion; if that fails, hearing follows; if commission finds violation, shall issue cease and desist order); § 298 (1957 Supp.) (State Supreme Court will issue order;

may review; appeals allowed). N.Y. Pen. Law § 513 (innkeeper who refuses accommodations guilty of misdemeanor); § 514 (exclusion from equal enjoyment of public accommodations is misdemeanor); § 515 (to discriminate in price of admission is misdemeanor); § 700 (discrimination in civil rights of another prohibited); § 701 (1957 Supp.) (violation of § 700 punishable by $100 to $500 fine and/or 30 to 90 days). Ohio Rev. Code § 2901.35 (no denial of full enjoyment of accommodations in enumerated places for sale of merchandise, public accommodation, or amusement; fine $50 to $500; 30 to 90 days; $50 to $500 to aggrieved); § 2901.36 (1953) (judgment in favor of aggrieved or punishment bars further prosecution). Ore. Rev. Stats. § 30.670, as amended by L. 1957, ch. 724 (all persons entitled to full and equal advantages of any public accommodation); § 30.675 (public accommodation means, *inter alia*, hotel, motel, motor court, any place offering to the public food or drink for consumption on the premises, or entertainment, recreation, or amusement, private clubs excepted); § 30.680, as amended by L. 1957, ch. 724 (violator civilly liable up to $500; operator, manager, employee liable jointly and severally); §§ 659.010–659.100 as amended by L. 1957, ch. 724 (person aggrieved by discrimination or Attorney General may file complaint with Commissioner of Bureau of Labor, who after hearing may issue cease and desist order; appeal to circuit court). Pa. Stats. Ann. tit. 18, § 4654 (1945) (all persons entitled to equal advantages of enumerated places of public accommodation; fine not more than $100 and/or up to 90 days). R.I. Gen. Laws §§ 11-24-1 to -3 (no person barred from full and equal enjoyment of accommodations in enumerated places of public accommodation, resort, or amusement); §§ 11-24-4 to -5 (1956) (creates Commission Against Discrimination; functions, generally, in same way as N.Y. and N.J. commissions). Vt. Act No. 109 (1957) (owner of public accommodation shall not discriminate; misdemeanor, fine up to $500, up to 30 days, or both). Wash. Rev. Code § 9.91.010 (1956) (those who deny, because of race, creed, or color, full enjoyment of any of enumerated accommodations, guilty of misdemeanor); § 49.60.010 (administrative agency created); § 49.60.020 (construction liberal); § 49.60.030 (right to enjoy fully public accommodations is civil right); § 49.60.040 (enumerates public accommodations); § 49.60.050 (creates state board); § 49.60.230 (aggrieved or board may file complaint); § 49.60.240 (conciliation, investigation); § 49.60.250 (hearing, order); § 49.60.260 (judicial enforcement); § 49.60.270 (1958) (judicial review). Wis. Stats. Ann. § 942.04 (1956) (whoever denies to another the full and equal advantages of enumerated and other facilities liable to aggrieved party in damages not less than $25; fine not more than $200 and/or 6 months; civil judgment bars criminal proceedings and vice versa); § 111.32 (administratively enforced statute; includes recreation); § 111.36 (commission may investigate, conciliate, issue orders); § 111.37 (1957 and 1958 Supps.) (judicial review). Wyo. Comp. Stats. §§ 9-836 to -837 (1957 Supp.) (no person of good deportment to be denied life, liberty, pursuit of happiness, or necessities of life because of race, color, creed, national origin; misdemeanor, fine up to $100, up to 6 months, or both; catchline reads: "Discrimination and Segregation Prohibited"). *Cf.* LA. REV. STATS. § 4:4 repealed by Acts 1954, No. 194, § 1 (all licenses to public resorts shall contain the following condition: open to accommodation of all persons without discrimination; forfeiture of license, closing business, civil suit for damages by the aggrieved).

7. *POLL TAX STATUTES*

ALA. CONST. (1901) art. 8, § 178, amend. XCVI (1953); amend. XLIX (1944) (exempts honorably discharged veterans from payment of poll tax); amend. CIX (exempts the blind and deaf); § 194 (sets a maximum age, 45, for payment of poll tax; legislature authorized to increase the maximum age to 60). ALA. CODE tit. 17, § 12 (1955 Supp.). ARK. STATS. ANN. § 3-104.2 (1947). MISS. CONST. art. 12, § 241. MISS. CODE ANN. §§ 3130, 3160, 3235 (1942). TEX. CONST. (1876) art. 6, § 2. 9 TEX. CIV. STATS. arts. 5.09 *et seq.* (1951). VA. CODE ANN. tit. 24, §§ 120–129.1 (1950).

POLL TAX REPEALERS

FLA. STATS. ANN. § 193.75 (1941). GA. CODE ANN. § 34–117 (1955 Supp.) (see editorial note). S.C. CODE § 65-151 (1952) (editor's note). TENN. CONST. art. IV, § 1, as amended (1953) (see compiler's notes).

8. *FEP STATUTES APPLICABLE TO STATE EMPLOYMENT* *

The following are expressly applicable and unless otherwise noted contain provisions like Colorado's: COLO. REV. STATS. § 80-24-2(5) (1957 Supp.) ("'Employer' shall mean the state . . . or any political subdivision"). CONN. GEN. STATS. § 7401 (1949). KAN. GEN. STATS. §§ 44-1001 *et seq.* (1955 Supp.) (applies to state and all subdivisions except school districts and educational institutions). MASS. ANN. LAWS ch. 151B, § 1 (1957). MICH. STATS. ANN. § 17.458(2) (1957 Supp.); see statement concerning the relationship of the Michigan FEPC and the Civil Service Commission *infra* appendix A10. MINN. STATS. ANN. § 363.01 (1957). N.M. STATS. ANN. § 59-4 (1953). PA. STATS. ANN. tit. 43, § 954 (1957 Supp.). WASH. REV. CODE § 49.60.040 (1951); but by § 49.60.300 the enforcement sections of the Washington law are not applicable to the state or its subdivisions.

The following FEP laws do not expressly cover state employment but may by implication. As indicated, in some instances authority validates this interpretation. They are similar to Alaska's: ALASKA LAWS ch. 114, § 2 (1957) (does not exclude state in setting forth exceptions). IND. STATS. ANN. § 40-2301 (1957 Supp.). N.J. STATS. ANN. § 18:25-5; the New York law, *infra*, on which New Jersey's was patterned (see Op. Att'y Gen. of N.J. No. 18, Sept. 2, 1954) has been interpreted to include the state. N.Y. EXEC. LAW § 292; see Op. Att'y Gen. of N.Y. (1946), p. 81 (includes state). ORE. REV. STATS. § 659.010 (1955). R.I. GEN. LAWS §§ 28-5-6 (1956). WIS. STATS. ANN. § 111.32 (1957).

* For California and Ohio see appendix E.

9. *STATUTES REGULATING GOVERNMENT EMPLOYMENT*
WHICH PROHIBIT RACIAL DISCRIMINATION

CAL. GOV'T CODE ANN. § 19702 (no discrimination because of sex, race, marital status); § 19704 (unlawful to require or permit notation of race, color, religion); § 18952 (1955) (any employee or citizen who feels aggrieved may petition the Personnel Board for a hearing to enforce observance of civil service laws). CONN. GEN. STATS. § 374 (1949) (no appointment, dismissal, demotion, favoritism because of political, religious affiliations, color; no question shall relate to these factors). Conn. Pub. Act No. 647, 1957 (grievance procedure). HAWAII REV. LAWS § 3-1(a) (1955) (equal opportunity regardless of race, etc.); § 3-22 (similar); § 3-26 (appeal to commission). ILL. STATS. ANN. ch. 24½, § 38b15 (1957 Supp.) (no applicant for employment in university system to be denied employment because of race). IND. STATS. ANN. § 36-163a (1957 Supp.) (professional employees of state Highway Commission to be employed, promoted, removed without racial or other specified discrimination). MASS. ANN. LAWS ch. 149, § 43 (1957) (application for employment by state, subdivision, or governmentally aided street railway shall not be affected by applicant's race). MICH. STATS. ANN. § 5.1191(9) (1957 Supp.) (applicant for county civil service not to be discriminated against because of race; submission of photograph not required). MINN. STATS. ANN. § 44.08 (1957 Supp.) (no permanent employee in classified service shall be dismissed or suspended without pay for more than 30 days, "except for just cause, which shall not be religious, racial, or political"). MO. STATS. ANN. § 36.150 (1951) (state merit system; "No appointment, promotion, demotion or dismissal shall be made because of favoritism, prejudice or discrimination"); § 43.050 (1957 Supp.) (racial discrimination with respect to applicants for highway patrol prohibited); § 226.080 (1957 Supp.) (only permissible discrimination in state Highway Department is to favor veterans). NEB. REV. STATS. § 19-660 (1954) (racial discrimination prohibited in appointments and removals in the civil service of cities adopting the city manager plan of government). NEV. REV. STATS. tit. 23, § 284.150(4) (classified service: "No person shall be discriminated against on account of his religious opinions or affiliations or race"); § 284.385(3) (no person in classified service may be dismissed for racial or religious reasons); § 284.390 (1957) (appeals to commission). N.H. REV. STATS. § 98:18 (1955) (no appointment, promotion, dismissal because of race). N.J. STATS. ANN. § 11:10-8 (1957 Supp.) (whenever appointment made from civil service list of person with lower instead of highest grade, appointee will not be placed on payroll until after appointing officer records reason and certifies that appointment was not made by reason of race, color, political faith, or creed). N.Y. CIV. SERV. LAW § 14-b (1946) (discrimination on account of race, creed, color, or national origin prohibited; administrative procedures established; repealed 1958; "there has been only one known racial appeal made under the provisions of § 14-b . . . subsequently withdrawn because of settlement," Letter from N.Y. State Department of Civil Service to Professor Jack B. Weinstein). ORE. REV. STATS. § 240.340 (1955) (no discrimination shall be exercised, threatened, or promised against or in favor of any applicant, eligible, or employee because of race, religious, or political opinions or affiliations).

10. *CIVIL SERVICE RULES OR PRACTICES PROHIBITING RACIAL DISCRIMINATION*

Maine—PERSONNEL RULES 6.6a (Competitive Examinations): "No test or question . . . shall . . . call for or lead to disclosure of any information concerning any political, religious, fraternal, or racial affiliations. . . . Any disclosure thereof shall be . . . disregarded." *Maryland*—Letter From Commissioner of Personnel: * "No provision in our Merit System law that strictly forbids racial discrimination. However, in recent years, we have deleted from our application blanks and all forms in this office anything that would denote the race, color, or creed of an individual so that we do not know the race or color of any applicants for positions in the State service. When we submit our eligible lists for vacancies, we submit the first five names on the list, and the appointive authority does not know the race or color of the individual." *Michigan*—CIV. SERV. COMM'N RULES (as amended March 28, 1956), Rule I: "All appointments and promotions . . . shall be based on merit. . . . A. No person shall be discriminated against in seeking employment, in being employed or promoted, in any conditions of his employment, in the state civil service, or any separation therefrom, because of race, color, religion, national origin, or ancestry, or because of partisan considerations." Statement of Michigan Civil Service Commission, March 3, 1957: "1. . . . Commission will continue to receive directly and to hear all appeals relating to alleged discrimination because of race. 2. Any employee or any applicant for employment in the state classified service may present a formal complaint to the Michigan Fair Employment Practices Commission. . . . Such decisions of the Fair Employment Practices Commission will be subject to review by the Civil Service Commission in accordance with its established procedures." *Minnesota*—Letter from Director, Civil Service Department: "Civil Service Rules based on the law go one step farther and provide that if the Civil Service Board finds that a dismissal action was taken by the appointing authority for any political, racial or religious reasons, the employee should be reinstated without loss of pay." *Missouri*—Letter from Director, Personnel Division: "There is no legal basis for discrimination in employment in those agencies operating within the Missouri Merit System Law. This agency accepts applications from all eligible individuals without regard to race, creed, etc." *Montana*—JOINT

* This letter and the others quoted in appendix A10 were written to Professor Jack B. Weinstein.

MERIT SYSTEM RULES art. 1, § II, ¶ 2:"No discrimination shall be made because of sex, nationality, political affiliation or religious belief"; art. 2, § X,
art. 3, § V (appeals and appeal procedures). *New Jersey*—CIV. SERV. LAW
& RULES (1949), Rule 27: "No question in any test or . . . application . . .
shall be so framed as to elicit information concerning . . . the political or
religious opinions . . . , race, color, national origin or ancestry of any applicant. Such disclosure . . . shall be discountenanced." *Oregon*—CIV. SERV.
RULES (1956), Rule VIII, § 3B: "The application form shall contain no
question so framed as to elicit any information concerning the political,
racial or religious affiliations of the applicant." *Vermont*—RULES & REGS.
FOR PERSONNEL ADM'N § 3.03 (discrimination in connection with any examination, appointment or promotion because of race or political or religious
opinions or affiliations is prohibited); §§ 15 and 16 (grievance and appeal
procedures). *Washington*—Merit System Rule of Personnel Adm'n (1956),
Preamble: "No person shall be disqualified from taking an examination for
appointment . . . nor from holding a position because of political or religious opinions or race"; art. VII, § 2 (no information solicited nor accepted
which reveals the religious or political affiliation of the applicant nor his
race or color); art. XVIII, § 2 (no examination question to elicit information concerning political or religious opinions; no discrimination because
of political or religious opinions or affiliations or race); art. XV (appeals;
if board finds that action complained of taken for political, religious, or
racial reason, employee shall be reinstated without loss of pay for period
of suspension).

11. REPLIES TO QUESTIONNAIRES INDICATING THAT THE RESPONDENT HAS NO RULES FORBIDDING DISCRIMINATION IN GOVERNMENT EMPLOYMENT

Georgia—Letter from Assistant Attorney General: * "No general laws
of the State on the subject. . . . We have no problem in this State regarding the matter"; *cf.* GA. CODE ANN. § 40-2207(b) (1957) (no discrimination
on political or religious grounds). *Idaho*—Letter from Secretary of State:
"We have no law on this subject." *Iowa*—Letter from Director of Personnel: "We have done some research relative to the question as to whether
or not the state of Iowa has any laws governing discrimination in government employment. I am unable to find any such statutes specifically applicable to said matter. It runs in my mind that, at one time, several sessions
past, such a law was introduced, but that it failed to become a law." *Kentucky*—Letter from Director of Research, Legislative Research Commission:
"While political, social and religious discrimination are prohibited by regulation, there is neither a regulation nor a statute covering racial discrimination." *Louisiana*—Letter from Director of Personnel: "Not found any legis-

---

* This letter and the others quoted in appendix A11 were written to Professor
Jack B. Weinstein.

lation or jurisprudence directly in point. . . . we have consulted with the Attorney General of Louisiana and he has reported that his staff has not rendered any opinions along these lines." *New Mexico*—Letter from Personnel Director: "No racial restrictions of employment in State Government. . . . no laws or regulations of discrimination in Governmental employment." *North Carolina*—Letter from Attorney General: "The state of North Carolina does not have in force any statutes or regulations which prohibit or forbid racial discrimination in governmental employment, and by the same token we do not have in force in this State any statutory regulations which require any racial discrimination in government employment." *Tennessee*—Letter from Acting Director, Department of Personnel: "There are no such laws or regulations forbidding racial discrimination neither are there laws encouraging racial discrimination in Governmental employment." *Utah*—Letter from Personnel Director: "Have not found anything forbidding racial discrimination in governmental employment . . . have never had to face that problem . . . our society seems to be well integrated. . . . Our constitution grants legal equality to all and up to this point this seems to have been adequate." *Virginia*—Letter from Personnel Director: "Nothing in the act either forbidding or inviting racial discrimination. . . . rules adopted in harmony with the act must conform."

12. *STATUTES REQUIRING RACIAL DISTINCTIONS ON THE JOB*

ARK. STATS. ANN. § 52-625 (1947) (separate washrooms in mines). LA. REV. STATS. §§ 23:971–975 (1957 Supp.) (employers to provide separate sanitary and eating facilities; violation a misdemeanor; fine $100 to $1,000, 60 days to 1 year). N.C. GEN. STATS. §§ 95-48 to -53 (1956) (all plants, other businesses required to maintain separate toilet facilities; violation a misdemeanor). OKLA. STATS. ANN. tit. 45, § 231 (1954) (separate bath houses in mines). S.C. CODE § 40-452 (1952) (unlawful for cotton textile manufacturer to permit different races to work together in same room, use same exits, bathrooms, etc.; $100 penalty and/or imprisonment at hard labor up to 30 days). TENN. CODE ANN. § 58-1021 (1955) (separate washrooms in mines). TEX. CIV. STATS. ANN. art. 5920 (1949) (coal mines required to have separate washing facilities).

13. *STATUTES, OTHER THAN FEP LAWS, WHICH FORBID DISCRIMINATION BY UNIONS*

CAL. LABOR CODE ANN. § 177.6 (1955) (unlawful for union to refuse to receive as apprentice on public works because of race). KAN. GEN. STATS. § 44-801 (1949) (union may not be representative if it discriminates because of race). NEB. REV. STATS. § 48-214 (1943) (policy of the state that no union shall discriminate against any person because of race in collective bargaining—but apparently no explicit right to membership). N.Y. CIV. RIGHTS LAW § 43 (no labor organization shall deny membership or equal treatment to members because of race); § 41 (1948) (violation of § 43 is misdemeanor, 30 to 90 days, $100 to $500, or both; defendant also liable to penalty, $100 to $500 in action by party aggrieved); the New York legislation was held constitutional in Railway Mail Ass'n v. Corsi, 326 U.S. 88 (1945). See also FEP legislation *infra* appendix A15.

14. STATE STATUTES REQUIRING NONDISCRIMINATION CLAUSES IN GOVERNMENT CONTRACTS

ARIZ. REV. STATS. §§ 23-371 to -375 (1956) (public contractors furnishing goods or services to the government; contract clause; misdemeanor penalty). CAL. LABOR CODE ANN. § 1735 (public works; violation a misdemeanor), § 1777.6 (1955) (unions on public works). ILL. STATS. ANN. ch. 29, §§ 17-24 (1935) (discrimination prohibited in employment in performance of work or service for government; violation a misdemeanor); §§ 24a-g (1958 Supp.) (unlawful for war defense contractors to discriminate, $100 to $500 fine). KAN. GEN. STATS. §§ 21-2461 to -2463 (1949) (no racial discrimination in connection with public works or service; act part of contracts; fine $50 to $1,000, imprisonment up to 6 months, or both). MASS. ANN. LAWS ch. 272, § 98B (1956) (discrimination in public works, $100 fine). MICH. STATS. ANN. § 17.458(4) (1957 Supp.) (contracts to which state is party must contain nondiscrimination clause; violation is material breach of contract). MINN. STATS. ANN. § 181.59 (1946) (contracts with state or subdivisions shall contain antidiscrimination clause; violation a misdemeanor and grounds for cancellation; second offense grounds for forfeiture of moneys due). NEB. REV. STATS. § 48-215 (1952) (manufacturers of military or naval supplies for state or federal governments may not discriminate). N.J. STATS. ANN. § 10:2-1 (1957 Supp.) (like Massachusetts). N.M. STATS. ANN. § 59-4-5 (1953) (breach may be regarded as material). N.Y. LABOR LAW § 220e (1958 Supp.) (like Massachusetts). OHIO REV. CODE § 153.59 (like Massachusetts); § 153.60 (1951) (forfeiture of $25 per person discriminated against; upon second violation contract may be canceled; money due forfeited). PA. STATS. ANN. tit. 43, § 153 (1952) (like Ohio).

15. STATE STATUTES CREATING COMMISSIONS AGAINST DISCRIMINATION *

The following citations relate not only to employment but to all of the commissions' areas of operation.

ALASKA LAWS (1953) ch. 18, as amended by L. 1957, ch. 114 (employment). COLO. REV. STATS. §§ 80-24-1 to -8 (employment); §§ 25-3-1 to -6

* For California and Ohio FEP laws see appendix E (which also contains housing amendments to the Colorado, Connecticut, Massachusetts, and Oregon FEP laws).

(1957 Supp.) (public accommodations). CONN. GEN. STATS. ch. 371, §§ 7400–7407 (1949), as amended by §§ 3034d, 3035d (1955 Supp.) (employment); ch. 417, §§ 8374 and 8375, as amended by §§ 3267d, 3268d (1955 Supp.) (public accommodations; publicly assisted housing). IND. STATS. ANN. §§ 40-2301-2306 (1957 Supp.) (employment). KAN. GEN. STATS. §§ 44-1001 to -1008 (1955 Supp.) (employment). MASS. ANN. LAWS ch. 151B, §§ 1–10 (employment, housing, public accommodations); ch. 151C, §§ 1–5 (1957 and 1957 Supp.) (education). MICH. STATS. ANN. §§ 17.458(1)–(11) (1957 Supp.) (employment). MINN. STATS. ANN. §§ 363.01–.13 (1957) (employment). N.J. STATS. ANN. §§ 18:25-1 to -28 (1957 Supp.) (employment, public accommodations, publicly assisted housing). N.M. STATS. ANN. §§ 59-4-1 to -14 (1953) (employment). N.Y. EXEC. LAW §§ 290-301 (1951 and 1957 Supp.) (employment, public accommodations, publicly aided housing). ORE. REV. STATS. §§ 659.010–.115, 659.990 (employment); §§ 30.670–.680 (public accommodations); §§ 345.240–.250 (education), as amended by L. 1957, ch. 724 (public accommodations, education, and mode of enforcement), and ch. 725 (publicly assisted housing). PA. STATS. ANN. tit. 43, §§ 951–963 (1957 Supp.) (employment). R.I. GEN. LAWS §§ 28-5-1 to -27 (employment); §§ 11-24-1 to -8 (1956) (public accommodations, public housing). WASH. REV. CODE §§ 49.60.010–.320 (1951) (employment, public accommodations, publicly assisted housing). WIS. STATS. ANN. §§ 111.31–.36 (1957 and 1958 Supp.) (employment, housing, education, welfare, recreation). Cf. Mo. L. 1957, p. 299 (establishing commission on human rights with no enforcement powers but authorized to "receive and investigate complaints of discrimination").

16. MUNICIPAL FAIR EMPLOYMENT ORDINANCES

The text or summaries of these ordinances may be found as cited.

Chicago: 17 L.R.R.M. 2257; Cleveland: 25 L.R.R.M. 3030; Duluth: 33 L.R.R.M. 3012; East Chicago, Ind: 31 L.R.R.M. 3030; Ecorse, Mich.: 35 L.R.R.M. 137; Erie: 33 L.R.R.M. 3013; Farrell, Mich.: 31 L.R.R.M.: 3032; Gary: 27 L.R.R.M. 3033; Hamtramck, Mich.: 35 L.R.R.M. 137; Milwaukee: 18 L.R.R.M. 3013; Minneapolis: 28 L.R.R.M. 3087; Monessen, Pa.: 31 L.R.R.M. 3019; Philadelphia: 27 L.R.R.M. 3036; Pittsburgh: 31 L.R.R.M. 3021; River Rouge: 31 L.R.R.M. 3035; St. Paul: 35 L.R.R.M. 137; Sharon, Pa.: 31 L.R.R.M. 3025; Toledo: 35 L.R.R.M. 137; Warren, Ohio: 31 L.R.R.M. 3015; Youngstown, Ohio: 27 L.R.R.M. 3039. For the recent San Francisco law see N.Y. Times July 7, 1957, p. 39, 2 R.R.L.R. 846 (1957). The Bakersfield, California, ordinance is described at Afro-American, Sept. 14, 1957, p. 8. On the Baltimore commission see ibid. and 1 R.R.L.R. 1113 (1956). For the St. Louis ordinance (No. 47957, 1956) restricted to public works supported in whole or in part by public funds see 2 R.R.L.R. 468 (1957). Similar ordinances are being enacted almost continuously, see R.R.L.R. passim.

17. STATUTES WHICH REFUSE TO PERMIT NONSEGREGATED SCHOOLS TO COME INTO BEING *

GA. CODE ANN. §§ 32-801 to -805 (provides that no public funds may be granted to support nonsegregated schools); § 32-9916 (1957 Supp.) (violator guilty of felony). LA. CONST. art. 12, § 1 (provides that all public schools shall be racially separate). LA. REV. STATS. §§ 17:331–333 (all public schools shall be segregated); § 17:334 (violation misdemeanor); see also §§ 17:341–344 (1957 Supp.) (method of designating schools for each race). MISS. CONST. art. 8, § 207 (separate schools shall be maintained). MISS. CODE ANN. § 4065.3 (all state executive officers required to prevent implementation of *School Segregation* decision by "lawful means"); § 6220.5 (1956 Supp.) (unlawful for white person to attend public school for Negroes; $1 to $25, up to 6 months, or both); other sections of Mississippi's education law are redundant of these segregation provisions. S.C. CODE § 21-2 (1957 Supp.) (appropriations inoperative for schools from and to which students transfer because of court order). VA. CODE §§ 22-188.5–6 (upon enrollment of members of both races, schools must close; control transferred to governor); §§ 22-188.30–.31 (1958 Supp.) (schools must be "efficient"; "efficient" means segregated). Va. Ass'y Acts, Extra Sess. 1956, ch. 71 (appropriations to "efficient" schools only); 1958, ch. 642 (similar).

18. STATUTES PROVIDING THAT NO CHILD SHALL BE FORCED TO ATTEND SCHOOL WITH CHILDREN OF ANOTHER RACE *

States in which the laws on their face forbid any desegregation are not included here.

ALA. CODE tit. 52, § 61(8) (1957 Supp.) (no child shall be compelled to attend school where races are commingled; child may receive aid for education). ARK. STATS. ANN. § 80-1525 (1957 Supp.) (no child required to enroll in mixed school). N.C. GEN. STATS. § 115-274 (1957 Supp.) (no child forced to attend school with children of another race). TEX. REV. CIV. STATS. art. 2901, § 8 (1958 Supp.) (similar to Alabama).

19. PUPIL ASSIGNMENT STATUTES *

ALA. CODE tit. 52, §§ 61(4) *et seq.* (1957 Supp.). ARK. STATS. ANN. §§ 80-1519 *et seq.* (1957 Supp.). FLA. STATS. ANN. § 230.232 (1957 Supp.). LA. REV. STATS. §§ 17:81.1 *et seq.*, 17:331 (1957 Supp.). MISS. CODE ANN. §§ 6334-01 *et seq.* (1956 Supp.). N.C. GEN. STATS. §§ 115-176 *et seq.* (1957 Supp.). S.C. CODE § 21-230(9) (1957 Supp.). TENN. CODE ANN. §§ 49-1741 *et seq.* (1958 Supp.). TEX. REV. CIV. STATS. art. 2901a(4) (1957 Supp.). VA. CODE §§ 22-232.1 *et seq.* (1958 Supp.).

* See also appendix E.

20. STATUTES AUTHORIZING OR REQUIRING THE ABOLITION OF SCHOOLING OR COMPULSORY EDUCATION *

ALA. CONST. amend. CXI of § 256 (state policy is to promote education, but legislature not limited in preserving peace or furnishing private schools). ALA. CODE tit. 52, § 56 (1957 Supp.) (compulsory school attendance law, repealed by Acts 1957, No. 367, § 11); but see tit. 52, § 297 (1957 Supp.) (compulsory attendance with right to choose whether or not shall attend school for members of own race); tit. 52, §§ 61(13)-(15) (closing by local boards after public hearings); § 61(16) (1957 Supp.) (local boards may sell or lease). Ark. Act No. 4, 2d Extraordinary Sess., 61st Gen. Ass'y, 1958 (governor may close schools and call election, ballot to read "For racial integration of all schools within the . . . school district," or "Against racial integration of all schools within the . . . school district"; unless majority of electors in district favor integration no school in district to be integrated; schools to remain closed until governor proclaims otherwise). Ark. Act No. 5, 2d Extraordinary Sess., 61st Gen. Ass'y, 1958 (pro rata share of state funds otherwise allocable to district to be withheld; these funds to be made available to private schools). FLA. STATS. ANN. § 230.23(f) (county boards may adopt regulations for closing schools during emergency; this provision antedates school controversy, its applicability to desegregation not clear); § 230.233 (1958 Supp.) (schools close automatically when federal troops used to prevent violence therein or in vicinity; absence during such period no violation of school attendance law). GA. CODE ANN. § 32-801 (expenditure of public funds for nonsegregated schools prohibited); § 32-801 (similar); see also the appropriation act, Ga. L. 1956, No. 454, § 7, which repeats this prohibition; § 32-805 (governor to close schools where integration occurs); § 32-809 (local boards may lease school property up to five years for private education); § 32-2117 (1957 Supp.) (governor may suspend operation of compulsory school attendance law). LA. REV. STATS. § 17:221 (compulsory attendance suspended in system where integration ordered); § 17:333 (1957 Supp.) (no state funds to nonsegregated school); § 17:336 (1958 Supp.) (governor may close nonsegregated school; board may sell). MISS. CONST. art. 8, § 213B (legislature may abolish public schools throughout state or authorize county or district to abolish public schools). Miss. compulsory school laws §§ 6509, 6510, 6512-6517 of Miss. CODE ANN. repealed by L. 1956, ch. 288; 1958, S.B. 2079 (governor may close any school if he determines closure to be in best interest of majority of children). N.C. GEN. STATS. §§ 115-26 et seq. (local boards may suspend operations; local option); § 115-166 (1957 Supp.) (no compulsory attendance where assignment is contrary to parents' wishes and it is not practicable to attend private school). S.C.A. & J.R. 1952 (47) 2223, A. & J.R. 1954 (48) 1695 repeal S.C. CONST. art. 11, § 5 (1895) which required legislature to maintain free public schools. S.C. CODE §§ 21-761 to -779 (regular school

* See also appendix E.

attendance) repealed by A. & J.R. 1955 (49) 85; § 21-2 (appropriations cut off to any school from which or to which any pupil transferred because of court order); § 21-230(7) (local trustees may or may not operate schools); § 21-238 (1957 Supp.) (school officials may sell or lease school property whenever they deem it expedient). TEX. REV. CIV. STATS. art. 2900a (no desegregation unless approved by election; violation forfeits accreditation and state funds); art. 2906-1 (1958 Supp.) (boards or governor may close schools where troops used on federal authority). VA. CODE § 22-188.6 (schools where members of both races assigned to close); §§ 22-188.41 et seq. and 22.488.46 et seq. (1958 Supp.) (schools close upon policing by federal authority). Va. Ass'y Acts of 1958, ch. 642 (appropriations for "efficient," i.e., segregated, schools only).

Cf. the statutes cited in Appendix A18 which excuse children from attending school with members of another race.

21. STATE SUPPORT OF PRIVATE SCHOOLING TO AVOID DESEGREGATION *

ALA. CONST. amend. CXI of § 256 (grants, loans, etc., for education; private schools may be established). ALA. CODE tit. 52, §§ 61(17)-(18) (1957 Supp.) (payments to children or private institutions from public funds where public schools unavailable). ARK. STATS. ANN. § 80-518 (1947) (private school may be taught in district school house; this law enacted long before desegregation issue but invoked in Little Rock dispute). Ark. Act. No. 5, 2d Extraordinary Sess., 61st Gen. Ass'y, 1958 (pro rata share of state funds ordinarily allocable to public schools payable to private schools when public schools closed to balk desegregation). GA. CODE ANN. §§ 32-805 to -808 (1958 Supp.) (educational grants from public funds). LA. CONST. art. XII, § 1 (authorizing financial assistance to private school students). LA. STATS. ANN. §§ 17:391.1 et seq. (educational expense grants); §§ 17:2801 et seq. (1958 Supp.) (authorizing establishment of private educational cooperatives). N.C. CONST. art. IX, § 12 (authorizing grants for private schooling). N.C. GEN. STATS. § 115-265 (payments for private education); §§ 115-274 et seq. (1957 Supp.) (comprehensive regulation of this program). VA. CODE §§ 22-115.10 to -.19 (grants for private education); § 22-188.9 (1957 Supp.) (governor may make grants available). Va. Ass'y Acts, Extra Sess. 1956, ch. 56 (grants; how computed).

22. STATE LAWS FORBIDDING DISCRIMINATION IN PUBLIC AND PRIVATE SCHOOLS

COLO. CONST. art. IX, § 8 (no racial distinctions in public education). CONN. GEN. STATS. § 1349 (1949 Rev.) (discrimination in public education prohibited). IDAHO CONST. art. IX, § 6 (no racial distinctions in public educa-

* See also appendix E.

tion). ILL. STATS. ANN. ch. 122, § 34-17(7) (boards of education in cities of over 500,000 not to exclude or segregate because of race); § 18-14 (districts must submit sworn statements that there is no segregation therein before filing claim for state aid); § 6-37 (no exclusion or segregation in districts of fewer than 1,000 persons); § 7-14 (similar rule for districts of 1,000 to 500,000 persons); § 15-15 (1957 Supp.) (school official who excludes child because of race may be fined from $5 to $100). IND. STATS. ANN. § 28-5156 (public policy is to furnish nonsegregated, nondiscriminatory education); § 28-5157 (no segregated schools to be maintained); § 28-5158 ("stair-step" scheme provided to abolish existing segregation); § 28-5159 (admission to schools without regard to race in district of residence); § 28-5160 (1957 Supp.) (no public school, college, or university supported in whole or in part by public funds to segregate or discriminate). MASS. ANN. LAWS ch. 151C, §§ 1-5 (Fair Educational Practices Act); § 2 (unfair educational practices defined); §§ 3-4 (1957) (cease and desist order after administrative proceedings; judicial review). MICH. STATS. ANN. § 15.3355 (1957 Supp.) (no segregated schools or departments). MINN. STATS. ANN. § 126.08 (no district to classify racially or separate pupils; violation forfeits public funds); § 126.07 (1946) (any member of board who votes for, or being present fails to vote against, exclusion, expulsion, suspension on account of race shall forfeit $50 to party aggrieved). N.J. CONST. art. I, § 5 (no segregation in public schools). N.J. STATS. ANN. §§ 18:25-1 *et seq.* (Law Against Discrimination; place of public accommodation includes schools on all levels; administrative enforcement); § 18:14-2 (1957 Supp.) (no exclusion for race; board member who votes to exclude may be fined $50 to $250, imprisoned 30 days to 6 months, or both). N.Y. EDUC. LAW § 3201 (no exclusion from public school on account of race); § 313 (1953) (Fair Educational Practices Act; post-secondary, business, and trade schools, subject to visitation; may not discriminate; administrative implementation by Commissioner of Education). N.Y. CIV. RIGHTS LAW § 40 (1948) (schools among places of public accommodation). N.Y. PEN. LAW § 514 (1944) (one who excludes guilty of misdemeanor). ORE. REV. STATS. §§ 345.240 and 345.250 (1955), as amended by L. 1957, ch. 724, § 11 (discrimination forbidden in trade, vocational, professional schools; fine $500, for corporation $1,000, 6 months, or both; suspension of license; administrative enforcement). PA. STATS. ANN. tit. 24, § 13-1310 (1950) (unlawful for school official to discriminate); tit. 18, § 4654(c) (1945) (public accommodations statute; place of public accommodation includes all educational institutions; fine up to $100, imprisonment up to 90 days, or both). R.I. GEN. LAWS § 16-38-1 (no exclusion from public school on account of race); § 16-38-12 (1956) (up to $50 or up to 30 days). WASH. CONST. art IX, § 1 (no racial distinction in education). WASH. REV. CODE §§ 9.91.010 *et seq.* (1951) (public accommodations statute); §§ 49.60.040 *et seq.* (1957 Supp.) (administrative regulation by state Board Against Discrimination). WIS. STATS. ANN. § 40.51 (exclusion for race unlawful; member of board who votes to exclude punishable by fine up to $100, imprisonment 30 days to 6 months, or both); § 111.32(5) (1957) (FEP law; discrimination in education included).

23. OUT-OF-STATE SCHOLARSHIP STATUTES

ALA. CODE tit. 52, § 40(1) (1955 Supp.) (travel, tuition, living expenses may be taken into account). ARK. STATS. ANN. § 13-522(F) (1957 Supp.) (fund for Negroes at A.M. & N. College and "out-of-state scholarships for Negroes"). KY. REV. STATS. ANN. § 166.160 (1955) (tuition and fees for those barred by constitution's separate school provision). La. Acts 1957, No. 2, Schedule 10(12) ($60,000 for Negro students enrolled outside state during 1956–57). MD. ANN. CODE art. 49B, §§ 2-7 (1957) (supplement amount it would cost to attend University of Maryland). MISS. CODE ANN. § 6726.5 (1953) (cost to students not to exceed estimated cost of instruction if it were available in Mississippi). MO. STATS. ANN. § 175.060 (1952) ("reasonable tuition fees"). N.C. GEN. STATS. § 116-100 (1952) (compensate for additional expense); repealed by N.C.L. 1957, ch. 1142. OKLA. STATS. ANN. tit. 70, §§ 1591–1592 (1950) (up to $250 per school year plus three cents a mile). TENN. CODE ANN. §§ 49-3207 to -3208 (1955) (without cost to recipient above cost at University of Tennessee; but *total* expenditure shall not exceed $2,500 per annum). VA. CODE §§ 23-10 to -13 (1949) (amount exceeding cost in Virginia institution considering tuition, living expenses, transportation). W. VA. CODE ANN. § 1894 (1955) (out-of-state tuition); repealed by W. Va. L. 1957, ch. 74.

24. STATUTES, ORDINANCES, AND RESOLUTIONS FORBIDDING DISCRIMINATION IN HOUSING *

Most of the legislation cited below is set forth in full in *Nondiscrimination Clauses in Regard to Public Housing, Private Housing and Urban Redevelopment Undertakings,* prepared by the Racial Relations Service and the Division of Law, Housing and Home Finance Agency (Oct., 1957).

STATUTES

CONN. GEN. STATS. §§ 3267d, 3268d (1955 Supp.) (public and publicly assisted housing in public accommodations law; enforceable by commission). ILL. STATS. ANN. tit. 67½, § 253-4 (neighborhood redevelopment corporation law; plan must provide for no discrimination); § 260(12) (no redevelopment corporation shall acquire title because of race, etc., of person claiming interest therein); tit. 67½, § 82 (1957 Supp.) (Land Clearance Commission's deeds not to contain racial covenants). IND. STATS. ANN. § 48-8503(b) (1950) (redevelopment act; this act does not authorize excluding citizen from zoned area because of race). MASS. ANN. LAWS ch. 121, § 26FF (1957) (low-rent housing; no racial discrimination); ch. 151B, § 1(10) (publicly assisted housing; enforceable by commission). MICH.

* See also appendix E.

STATS. ANN. § 28.343 (1957 Supp.) ("government housing" within public accommodations law). MINN. STATS. ANN. § 462.481 (housing redevelopment law; no discrimination; preference to site dwellers); § 462.525(8) (similar); § 462.641 (nonresidential uses in redevelopment project; no discrimination); § 507.18 (1957 Supp.) (no written instrument affecting real estate to contain racial covenants). Minn. L. 1957, ch. 953 (creating temporary commission to study discrimination in housing; opportunity to deal in property, obtain decent housing, is civil right). N.J. STATS. ANN. § 55:14A-39.1 (public housing; no discrimination); § 18:25-9.1 (Division Against Discrimination enforces laws of state against discrimination in housing built with public funds or public assistance; for compilation of New Jersey statutes for which § 25-9.1 provides enforcement see Preamble to N.J.L. 1954, ch. 198, p. 745); § 17:12A-78 (savings and loan associations; no discrimination in granting mortgage loans); § 17:9A-69 (1957 Supp.) (banks treated similarly). N.Y. CIV. RIGHTS LAW §§ 18a-c (1958 Supp.) (equal rights to publicly assisted housing accommodations). N.Y. EXEC. LAW § 296(3) (1957 Supp.) (enforcement by state Commission Against Discrimination). N.Y. PUB. HOUSING LAW § 223 (1955) (no discrimination in public housing). Ore. L. 1957, ch. 725, §§ 3, 4 (publicly assisted housing; administrative enforcement). PA. STATS. ANN. tit. 35, § 1664 (1957 Supp.) (public housing); tit. 35, §§ 1711(a)(1) and (8) (urban redevelopment); tit. 35, § 1590.12 (1949) (veterans' housing). R.I. GEN. LAWS § 11-24-3 (1957) (public housing in public accommodations law; administratively enforced). WASH. REV. CODE §§ 49.60.030 and 49.60, as amended by Wash. L. 1957, ch. 37 (publicly assisted housing; administrative enforcement; also bars discrimination by financial institutions making loans on such housing). WASH. L. 1957, ch. 42, § 17 (urban renewal; no discrimination). WIS. STATS. ANN. § 66.39(13) (veterans' projects; no discrimination); § 66.40(2m) (low-income housing; no discrimination); § 66.405(2m) (urban redevelopment; same); § 66.43(2m) (1957) (blighted areas law; same); § 75.14(14) (statutory note indicates that 1951 amendment failed to continue earlier provision that racially restrictive covenants survived issuance of tax deed).

ORDINANCES AND CITY COUNCIL RESOLUTIONS

California: Los Angeles Ordinance No. 97536, Jan. 12, 1951 (redevelopment plans should contain provision prohibiting discrimination; deeds, leases, contracts into which redevelopment agency enters shall forbid discrimination). Los Angeles Ordinance No. 109548, June 19, 1957 (similar). Los Angeles County Board of Supervisors Resolution, July 3, 1951 (no discrimination in use of county-owned land). Sacramento City Council Resolution No. 880, Oct. 28, 1954 (policy is that there shall be no discrimination in redevelopment projects; redevelopment plans shall forbid discrimination in sale, lease, transfer, occupancy, etc.; deeds, leases, contracts to contain such provision). San Francisco Board of Supervisors Resolution No. 8660, May 17, 1949 (policy of nondiscrimination in redevelopment projects; plans shall provide provisions precluding discrimination in sale, lease, transfer, etc.; deeds, leases, and contracts shall contain antidiscrimination provisions). San Francisco Board of Supervisors Resolution No. 9268, Nov. 21, 1949 (no discrimination or segregation in low-rent projects). San Francisco Board of Supervisors Resolution No. 10352, Sept. 27, 1950 (there shall be no discrimination in public housing turned over by Lanham Act). *Colorado:* DENVER CITY ORDINANCES § 652.6 (Aug. 15, 1953) ("no restrictive covenants shall appear on the face of the plat"). *Connecticut:* Hartford Court of Common Council Resolution, Jan. 24, 1949 (no applicant for quarters in housing constructed with aid of city funds, whether through tax waiver or abatement, land grant, or land development, or any other assistance from city shall be subjected to discrimination or segregation). *Illinois:* Chicago City Council Resolution, April 7, 1954 (city policy that public housing should be available to all without regard to race). *Massachusetts:* Boston City Council Resolution, June 28, 1948 (Boston Housing Authority is requested to include in applications for contracts with state Housing Board a covenant that there shall be no racial discrimination in operation of projects). *Michigan:* Pontiac City Commission Resolution No. 589, Dec. 14, 1943 (all public housing projects developed in city to be open without discrimination). *Missouri:* St. Louis Board of Aldermen Resolution No. 16, Sept. 25, 1953 (best interests of community served by administration of low-rent housing which results in nonsegregated occupancy). *New York:* N.Y.C. ADMINISTRATIVE CODE § W41-1.0 (1957) (no discrimination in dwellings erected with tax exemption, or on property sold by city below cost pursuant to Federal Housing Act of 1949, or on land assembled through city condemnation, or city funds supplied therefor, or if multiple dwelling financed by loan, repayment of which is insured by federal government, state, or city; religious or denominational organization's property operated as part of its activities exempt; violation misdemeanor; right of private action); § X41-1.0 (1958 Supp.) (discrimination in renting or sale of multiple dwellings or in one of ten or more contiguous one- or two-family houses controlled by one person forbidden; complaints may be filed with Commission on Intergroup Relations or it may act on own motion; if it finds discrimination it may refer to Fair Housing Practice Board, which, if it finds court action warranted, may refer to Corporation Counsel for injunctive proceedings); § 384.16.0 (1957) (all deeds, leases, instruments entered into by city for the purpose of specified housing construction to contain antidiscrimination provision); Ordinance No. 20, July 3, 1944 (no exemption from taxation for future construction unless there is no discrimination in dwellings). *Ohio:* Cincinnati City Council Declaration of Policy, Sept. 5, 1951 (urban redevelopment policy: in relocation of site dwellers no discrimination; in admission of occupants no discrimination). Cleveland Ordinance No. 2139-49 (no discrimination in public housing). Cleveland Ordinance No. 1422-A-52 (City Planning Commission may not enter into racially restrictive covenants; each redevelopment contract and conveyance shall provide that there shall be no discrimination in use of land; those claiming through redeveloper may not discriminate). Toledo Ordinance No. 738-51 (no discrimination in public housing). *Pennsylvania:* Philadelphia Ordinance, May 19, 1950 (no discrimination in public housing). Pittsburgh Ordinance, Dec. 8, 1958, supplementing Ordinance No. 237 (covers private housing in excess of five units, lending institutions, brokers; enforceable by commission; also criminal penalty). *Rhode Island:* Providence City Council Resolution, Oct. 10, 1950 (city council opposes racial discrimination or segregation in housing projects supported by federal, state, or city funds).

HOUSING AUTHORITY RESOLUTIONS

Arizona: Phoenix, Nov. 10, 1955 (no segregation in public housing; segregation to be abolished in existing projects). *California:* Fresno, Feb. 21, 1952 (applicants to be placed in projects nearest residence at time of application; in project on open land where few eligible tenants located near by, tenants to be selected on basis of need; no segregation). Richmond Housing Authority, Sept. 4, 1952 (in exercise of public powers or administration of any new program entailing public funds or powers, including tax exemption, public contribution, or cooperation, shall afford equal protection of the law). Sacramento Redevelopment Agency Resolution No. 70, May 19, 1954 (no discrimination or segregation in acquisition or disposition of property). *Delaware:* Wilmington Housing Authority Resolution, Dec. 10, 1953 (dwellings to be allocated on basis of need; resolution to take effect with availability of accommodations in specified projects under construction). *District of Columbia:* National Capital Housing Authority Resolution, June 4, 1953 (low-rent housing to be available without discrimination; timing of application of policy with regard to specific properties subject to formal action by Authority; policy may be deferred until there is evidence of public facilities to serve tenants without regard to race). *Illinois:* Chicago Public Housing Authority Resolution No. 50 CHA-17 (no segregation or discrimination; this is reaffirmation of long-established policy). *Maryland:* Baltimore Public Housing Authority Resolution, June 25, 1954 (local and national trend against segregation; existing policies impracticable to administer in conformity with law; proceeding to revise admission policies by eliminating factor of race). *Michigan:* Detroit Housing Commission Resolution, April, 1952 (commission will be guided by best interest of all people of city in accordance with laws of United States and Michigan). Pontiac Housing Commission Resolution No. 76 (advertising of vacancies shall not designate location; prospective tenants shall be made familiar with nondiscriminatory policy; statement of policy incorporated in application form and lease; no racial identifying information on official forms or information issued or kept by commission; tenant selection on basis of need; applicant who refuses to accept assignment made shall be placed at bottom of list). *Minnesota:* Minneapolis Housing and Redevelopment Authority Resolution No. 53-174 (re-use of Glenwood redevelopment area will be open to all persons responsible and financially able). Minneapolis Housing and Redevelopment Authority Resolution, Dec. 2, 1954 (conveyances and leases by the Authority shall contain covenant binding on successors that no discrimination shall be practiced; if breached Housing and Redevelopment Authority or any owner within confines of project may bring action to enforce). St. Paul Public Housing and Redevelopment Authority Resolution, April, 1950 (Authority is opposed to segregation and no segregation will be countenanced in certain named projects). St. Paul Housing and Redevelopment Authority Resolution, Aug. 14, 1953 (residential re-uses in redevelopment projects shall be open for occupancy to all families who are financially able to rent or acquire). *Nebraska:* Omaha Housing Authority Resolution, Nov. 9, 1951 (integration in public housing to be immediate in new projects, gradual in old project). *New Jersey:* Newark Housing Authority Resolution, Sept. 14, 1950 (dwelling accommodations shall be allocated on basis of need without regard to race). *Ohio:* Toledo Metropolitan Housing Authority Resolution No. 1838 (past policy was one of segregation which caused inefficiency in filling vacancies; henceforth families to be assigned without regard to race). *Pennsylvania:* Chester Housing Authority Resolution, Dec. 13, 1955 (accommodations to be allocated without regard to race). Philadelphia Housing Authority Resolution No. 3630 (public housing to be rented without discrimination). Pittsburgh (Allegheny County) Housing Authority Resolution No. 52-53-4 (public housing to be allocated without regard to race). Pittsburgh Housing Authority Resolution No. 115 (no discrimination or segregation either as to project, areas within project, or buildings located in project). *Washington:* Pasco Public Housing Authority Resolution No. 144 (selection of tenants without regard to race). *Wisconsin:* City of Superior Housing Authority Resolution No. 151 (no discrimination because of race; continuation of past policy).

25. STATUTES FORBIDDING LYNCHINGS

ALA. CODE tit. 14, §§ 354-356 (1940) (abusing any person to force him to confess to crime or to leave any part of state; up to 12 months, not less than $500 fine; where action results in death, crime constitutes lynching; 5 years to death; unlawful presence without active participation at a lynching, 1 to 21 years; police officer who through negligence or cowardice allows prisoner to be taken from custody and put to death or suffer injury, $500 to $2,000 and/or up to 2 years). CAL. PENAL CODE §§ 405a, 405b (1955) (lynching is the taking by means of a riot from lawful custody of officer; up to 20 years). GA. CODE ANN. §§ 26-5401 to -5404 (1953) (any person engaged in mobbing or lynching any citizen, 1 to 20 years; if death results the offense is murder; officer having knowledge of mob violence and failing to suppress same, misdemeanor; those summoned must aid officer). ILL. ANN. STATS. ch. 38, §§ 512-524 (1935 and 1958 Supp.) (mob defined as collection of persons assembled to harm one supposed guilty of violating law or to exercise correctional or regulative powers over him by violence; $100 to $1,000, 30 days to 12 months; where serious injury results, felony; up to 5 years, right of action for damages against local government; sheriff removed where person in his custody taken and lynched). IND. STATS. ANN. §§ 10-3301 to -3311 (1956) (similar to Illinois, but no action against local government; if death results active participant punishable by life imprisonment or death; inactive participant by 2 to 21 years). KAN. GEN. STATS. ch. 21, §§ 1001–1019 (1949) (act of violence by mob is lynching; where death results participant punishable by 5 years to life; if sheriff fails to do duty, office vacated). KY. REV. STATS. § 63.140 (peace officer losing custody of prisoner shall be removed); § 411.100 (liability of city); § 435.070 (lynching is injury to person in custody of peace officer by more than three persons; if death results penalty is life imprisonment or death; otherwise 2 to 21 years); § 437.110 (1955) (conspiracy to take from lawful custody is punishable in jury's discretion). MINN. STATS. ANN. § 613.67 (1947) (county where lynching occurs liable up to $7,500 to dependents of person lynched; officer having custody who fails to resist the taking removed from office). NEB. REV. STATS. §§ 23-1001 to -1008 (1954) (collection of people pretending to exercise correctional power, etc., is a mob; mob violence resulting in death is lynching; county liable up to $1,000; criminal penalties as for homicide or assault). N.J. STATS. ANN. §§ 2A:48-1 to -9 (1952) (mob-inflicted personal or property damage or death by lynching creates municipal or county liability up to $5,000). N.Y. PEN. LAW §§ 1391–1392 (1944) (mob violence on person in custody resulting in death is lynching, 20 years to life; if does not result in death, up to 10 years). N.C. GEN. STATS. § 14-221 (1953) (conspiracy or entering a jail to kill or injure any prisoner, felony; up to $500, 2 to 15 years). OHIO REV. CODE §§ 3761.01–.10 (1954) (lynching is act of violence by mob upon body of any person; damages from county up to $1,000; if permanent disability, $5,000). PA. STATS. ANN. tit. 18, § 3761-66 (1957 Supp.) (officers who neglect to prevent killing by mob guilty of crime; $5,000, 5 years, or both; officer having custody of prisoner who permits him to be taken by mob, $5,000 fine, 5 years, or both; county subject to forfeiture of $25,000). S.C. CONST. art. 6, § 6 (sheriff guilty of misdemeanor where prisoner taken by mob through negligence or connivance and suffers bodily harm or death; county liable up to $2,000). S.C. CODE § 10-1961 (1952) (similar to constitutional provision); §§ 16-57 to -59.4 (1952) (lynching first degree is where death results, death penalty unless jury recommends mercy, in which case 5 to 40 years; lynching second degree is where other than death results; 3 to 20 years). TENN. CODE ANN. § 8-820 (1955) (sheriff who allows prisoner to be taken and killed is guilty of high misdemeanor). TEX. PEN. CODE art. 1260a (1957 Supp.) (mob violence resulting in death is lynching first degree; death penalty or 5 years to life; where death does not result lynching second degree has been committed, 1 to 10 years). VA. CODE §§ 18-36 to -42 (1949) (lynching is act of violence upon body of person resulting in death; all persons composing the mob and every accessory thereto guilty of murder; lesser injuries punishable by up to 10 years). W. VA. CODE § 6038 (1955) (similar to Illinois; where serious injury results upon pretense of exercising correctional power, up to 5 years; where death results treated as murder; where injury occurs upon person charged with crime, 1 to 10 years; county liable up to $5,000). In addition, there are state laws forbidding riots, and, of course, violence generally.

26. STATUTES WHICH MAKE CRIMINAL INTERRACIAL SEXUAL CONTACTS OR WHICH IMPOSE SPECIAL PENALTIES THEREFOR

ALA. CODE tit. 14, § 360 (adultery, marriage, or fornication between white and Negro, 2 to 7 years); *compare with* § 16 (1940) (any man or woman living in adultery or fornication, first conviction punishable up to $100, up to 6 months; second conviction up to $300, up to 12 months; third and subsequent convictions, 2 years). ARK. STATS. ANN. § 41-806 (concubinage between white and Negro, 1 month to 1 year); §§ 41-807 to -810 (proof, enforcement); *compare with* § 41-805 (1947) (illegal cohabitation, first conviction $20 to $100; second, $100 minimum, up to 12 months; third and subsequent convictions, 1 to 3 years). FLA. STATS. ANN. § 798.04 (white and Negro living in adultery or fornication, up to $1,000 or 12 months); § 798.05 (habitual occupation of same room in nighttime by Negro and white couple, up to $500 or up to 12 months); *compare with* § 798.01 (living in open adultery, up to $500 or up to 2 years); § 798.02 (1944) (lewd, lascivious behavior, same punishment). LA. REV. STATS. § 14:79 (miscegenation statute includes habitual cohabitation of racially mixed couple; up to 5 years); *compare with* § 76 (bigamy, up to $1,000, or up to 5 years, or both); § 80 (1951) (carnal knowledge, up to 5 years). NEV. REV. STATS. ch. 201.240 (white and colored persons living and cohabiting in state of fornication, $100 to $500, 6 months to 1 year, or both); *compare with* ch. 201.200 (1955) (notorious cohabitation, 6 months to 1 year, $500 to $1,000, or both). N. DAK. REV. CODE ch. 12-2213 (unmarried racially mixed couple occupying same room; up to 1 year, $500 fine, or both); *compare with* ch. 12-2212 (1943) (unlawful cohabitation, 30 days to 1 year, or $100 to $500). TENN. CODE ANN. § 36-402 (1955) (marriage or living together as man and wife of racially mixed couple prohibited; 1 to 5 years or fine and imprisonment in county jail). *Cf.* MD. ANN. CODE art. 27, § 416 (1957) (crime for white woman to bear Negro's child; held unconstitutional in State v. Howard, 2 R.R.L.R. 676 (Baltimore Crim. Ct. 1957). See also appendix A28 *infra*, citing antimiscegenation statutes.

27. STATUTES REQUIRING RACIAL DISTINCTIONS IN IMPRISONMENT

ALA. CODE tit. 45, § 52 (no chaining or sleeping together; separate prisons at discretion of governor and director of prisons); §§ 121-23, 172, 183 (similar); tit. 12, § 188 (1940) (county jails, similar). ARK. STATS. ANN. § 46-122 (white convicts guarded by whites only); §§ 46-144 to -147 (separate apartments, furnishings, no handcuffing together); § 76-1119 (1947) (county system, separate eating and sleeping). FLA. STATS. ANN. §§ 950.05–.08 (1944) (counties; separate cells); § 945.08 (1958 Supp.) (state board may adopt regulations, including racial classifications; separation except where impracticable). GA. CODE ANN. § 77-310 (1958 Supp.) (Board of Correction may classify by race); § 77-9904 (1937) (misdemeanor to chain together). LA. REV. STATS. § 15:752 (separate apartments); § 854 (1951) (state penitentiary; separate as far as practicable). MISS. CODE ANN. §§ 4259, 7913 (county jails; separate rooms); § 7965 (penitentiary; similar); § 7971 (1957) (prison hospital; similar). N.C. GEN. STATS. § 153-51 (county; separate apartments); §§ 148-43 to -44 (1952) (state system; separate eating, sleeping and otherwise as far as practicable). S.C. CODE §§ 55-1 to -2 (1952) (segregation at all prisons and chain gangs except in state penitentiary and farms). TENN. CODE ANN. tit. 41, § 303 (1955) (female prisoners segregated by race). TEX. CIV. STATS. art. 6203c, § 2(E) (segregation at prison farm); art. 6166j (1949) (manager of state system may segregate by color). VA. CODE § 53-42 (1958) (penitentiary; races separate as far as possible).

28. ANTIMISCEGENATION STATUTES

ALA. CODE tit. 14, § 360 (1940) (marriage, adultery, fornication between white and Negro prohibited). ARIZ. REV. STATS. § 25-101 (1956) (marriage of person of Caucasian blood with Negro, Mongolian, Malay, or Hindu void; Indians originally included, deleted by 1942 amendment). ARK. STATS. ANN. § 55-104 (marriage between white and Negro or mulatto illegal); § 55-105 (1947) (misdemeanor, fine, and/or imprisonment). DEL. CODE ANN. tit. 13, § 101(a)(2) (marriage between white and Negro or mulatto void); § 102 (1953) ($100 fine, on default of payment, up to 30 days). FLA. STATS. ANN. § 741.12 (1944) (up to 10 years or fine up to $1,000). GA. CODE ANN. § 53-106 (declares it unlawful for a white to marry anyone but a white; marriage void); § 53-9903 (1935) (violation a felony, 1 to 2 years). IND. STATS. ANN. § 44-104 (1952) (marriage between white and Negro void). KY. REV. STATS. § 402.020 (marriage between white and Negro or mulatto void); § 402.990 (1955) ($500 to $5,000; if cohabitation continues, imprisonment 3 to 12 months). LA. CIV. CODE art. 94 (1952) (marriage between white and person of color void). LA. REV. STATS. § 14:79 (marriage or habitual cohabitation between white and Negro punishable by up to 5 years); § 9:201 (1951) (marriage between Indian and Negro prohibited). MD. ANN. CODE art. 27, § 398 (1957) (prohibits marriages between white and Negro, Negro and Malayan, white and Malayan; 18 months to 10 years). MISS. CONST. art. 14, § 263 (marriage between white and Negro unlawful and void). MISS. CODE ANN. § 459 (marriage between white and Negro or Mongolian void, punishable as if incestuous); § 2234 (punishes incestuous marriage, fine $500 and/or up to 10 years); § 2339 (1942) (anyone advocating or publishing matter advocating or suggesting equality of races or intermarriage subject to fine of $500 and/or 6 months). Mo. REV. STATS.

§ 451.020 (marriage between white and Negro or Mongolian void); § 563.240 (1949) (marriage between white and Negro void; 2 years in penitentiary or not less than 3 months in county jail, fine not less than $100, or both). NEB. REV. STATS. § 42-103 (1943) (marriages void when one party white, other Negro, Japanese, or Chinese). NEV. REV. STATS. § 122.180 (1957) gross misdemeanor for white to marry person of black, brown, yellow race).* N.C. CONST. art. XIV, § 8 (marriage between Negro and white prohibited). N.C. GEN. STATS. § 14-181 (marriage between white and Negro void; infamous crime 4 months to 10 years, fine, in discretion of court); § 51-3 (1953) (marriage between white and Negro or Indian void). OKLA. STATS. ANN. tit. 43, § 12 (marriage of anyone of African descent to one who is not prohibited); § 13 (1955) (up to $500 and 1 to 5 years). S.C. CONST. art. 3, § 33 (marriage of white and Negro or mulatto void). S.C. CODE §§ 20-7 to -8 (1952) (marriage of white with Negro, Indian, mulatto, or mestizo void; not less than $500 and/or not less than 12 months). TENN. CONST. art. 11, § 14 (intermarriage of white and Negro prohibited). TENN. CODE ANN. § 36-402 (same as constitution); § 36-403 (1955) (1 to 5 years; fine and imprisonment in county jail may be substituted on jury recommendation). TEX. CIV. STATS. ANN. art. 4607 (unlawful for person of Caucasian blood to marry person of African blood; marriage void). TEX. PEN. CODE art. 492 (1951) (2 to 5 years). UTAH CODE ANN. § 30-1-2 (1953) (marriage between white and Negro, Malayan, mulatto, quadroon, or octaroon void). VA. CODE § 20-54 (unlawful for white to marry anyone except white, or person with no other admixture of blood than white and American Indian); § 20-59 (1950) (1 to 5 years). W. VA. CODE § 4697 (1955) (white person prohibited from marrying Negro; up to $100, up to 1 year). WYO. COMP. STATS. § 50-108 (marriage of white to Negro, mulatto, Mongolian, Malayan void); § 50-109 (1945) ($100 to $1,000 and/or 1 to 5 years). See Browning, *Anti-Miscegenation Laws in the United States,* 1 DUKE B.J. 26 (1951). And see appendix A26 *supra* (penalties for interracial sexual relations).

STATES WHICH HAVE REPEALED ANTIMISCEGENATION LAWS *

Colorado: repealed, L. 1957, ch. 124. *Idaho:* statute repealed in early 1959; see 168 CIVIL LIBERTIES 4 (1959). *Iowa:* omitted from code in 1851. *Kansas:* omitted from code in 1857. *Massachusetts:* repealed, Acts 1840, ch. 5. *Michigan:* repealed and prior marriages legalized, MICH. STATS. ANN. § 25.6 (1957). *Montana:* repealed, L. 1953, ch. 4. *New Mexico:* repealed, L. 1886, p. 90. *North Dakota:* repealed, L. 1955, ch. 126. *Ohio:* repealed, L. 1887, p. 34. *Oregon:* repealed 1951, ORE. REV. STATS. § 106.210. *Rhode Island:* repealed, L. 1881, Jan. Sess., p. 108. *South Dakota:* repealed, L. 1957, ch. 38. *Washington:* repealed, L. 1887, pp. 47-48.

* According to Weinberger, *A Reappraisal of the Constitutionality of Miscegenation Statutes,* 51 J. NATIONAL MEDICAL ASS'N 215 (1959), California and Nevada repealed their statutes in early 1959.

29. *STATUTES ON INTERRACIAL ADOPTIONS*

Statutes Forbidding Interracial Adoptions

LA. Rev. Stats. § 9:422 (1951). Mo. Stats. Ann. § 453.130 (1952) (adoption can be set aside). S.C. Code § 16-553 (1952) (crime to give colored person custody of white child, but no racial distinctions in adoption procedures as such, §§ 10-2581 *et seq.* (1952)). Tex. Civ. Stats. Ann. art. 46a, § 8.

Statutes Requiring Race To Be Considered in Adoption

D.C. Code (Supp. IV) § 16-214 (1951) (race to be disclosed on petition). Md. Ann. Code art. 16, § 73 (1957) (similar to District of Columbia). Mass. Ann. Laws ch. 210, § 5A (1955) (due regard to race). Mich. Stats. Ann. § 27.3178(545) (1957 Supp.) (race shall be considered). N.H. Rev. Stats. Ann. § 461:2 (1955) (due regard to race). Ohio Rev. Code Ann. § 3107.05E (1953) (taking race into account). Oklahoma, see *infra.* Ore. Rev. Stats. § 109.310 (1953) (petition must state race or color of adopting parents). Pa. Stats. Ann. tit. 1, § 1 (1956 Supp.) (petition must set forth race of parties). S.D. Code § 14.0406 (1952 Supp.) (order to state race of petitioner and child). See the Uniform Adoption Act (9 U.L.A. 29), which makes no provision for racial factors either in the petition for adoption (§ 8) or in the investigation (§ 9). Oklahoma, the only state which has adopted the act, has added a racial factor to it, Okla. Stats. Ann. tit. 10, § 60.12(1)(c) (1957 Supp.).

30. *NATIONAL GUARD STATUTES*

Statutes Making Racial Distinctions

N.C. Gen. Stats. § 127-6 (1952) (separate enrollment; no colored troops to be permitted where white troops available; colored troops shall be under command of white officers). W.Va. Code § 1152 (1955) (governor may organize unit of Negro troops).

Statutes Prohibiting Discrimination

Calif. Mil. & Veterans Code § 130 (1955) (segregation and discrimination prohibited). Conn. Gen. Stats. § 27-59 (1958) (no discrimination; no units formed or duties assigned in manner as to result in segregation). Ill. Stats. Ann. ch. 129, § 220.07 (1958 Supp.) (no segregation or discrimination). Mass. Laws Ann. ch. 33, § 1A (1952) (no discrimination or segregation). Mich. Stats. Ann. § 28.631 (1954) (any association whose membership is confined to members of a particular race which discriminates against members of militia with respect to membership in said association is guilty of misdemeanor). Neb. Rev. Stats. § 55-108 (1957 Supp.) (no discrimination). N.H. Rev. Stats. § 110-A:75 (1957 Supp.) (equality of treatment without regard to race). N.J. CONST. art. 1, ¶ 5 (1954) (no segregation in, *inter alia*, militia). N.Y. MIL. LAW § 4 (1953) (equality of treatment without regard to race). WIS. STATS. ANN. § 21.35 (1957) (no denial of membership or segregation because of race).

NAACP LEGAL DEFENSE CASES
BEFORE THE SUPREME COURT

Presented by lawyers for the NAACP and the NAACP Legal Defense and Educational Fund in which there was a decision other than denial of certiorari from 1915 to 1958 (compiled largely from a mimeographed release of the NAACP Legal Defense and Educational Fund, March 13, 1958).

Voting and registration: Guinn v. United States, 238 U.S. 347 (1915) (brief *amicus curiae*); Lane v. Wilson, 307 U.S. 268 (1939). *Primaries:* Nixon v. Herndon, 273 U.S. 536 (1927); Nixon v. Condon, 286 U.S. 73 (1932); Smith v. Allwright, 321 U.S. 649 (1944). *Residential segregation ordinances:* Buchanan v. Warley, 245 U.S. 60 (1917); Harmon v. Tyler, 273 U.S. 668 (1927); City of Richmond v. Deans, 281 U.S. 704 (1930). *Restrictive covenants:* Corrigan v. Buckley, 271 U.S. 323 (1926); Hansberry v. Lee, 311 U.S. 32 (1940); Shelley v. Kraemer, 334 U.S. 1 (1948); Barrows v. Jackson, 346 U.S. 249 (1953). *Education:* Missouri *ex rel.* Gaines v. Canada, 305 U.S. 337 (1938); Sipuel v. University of Okla., 332 U.S. 631 (1948); Fisher v. Hurst, 333 U.S. 147 (1948); Sweatt v. Painter, 339 U.S. 629 (1950); McLaurin v. Oklahoma State Regents, 339 U.S. 637 (1950); Gray v. University of Tenn., 342 U.S. 517 (1952); Brown v. Board of Educ., 347 U.S. 483 (1954), 349 U.S. 294 (1955) (the caption of the four *School Segregation Cases*); Florida *ex rel.* Hawkins v. Board of Control, 347 U.S. 971 (1954), 350 U.S. 413 (1956), 355 U.S. 839 (1957); Lucy v. Adams, 350 U.S. 1 (1955); Tureaud v. Board of Supervisors, 347 U.S. 971 (1954); Frasier v. University of N.C., 350 U.S. 979 (1956); Cooper v. Aaron, 358 U.S. 1 (1958). *Interstate transportation:* Morgan v. Virginia, 328 U.S. 373 (1946). *Local transportation:* South Carolina Elec. & Gas Co. v. Flemming, 351 U.S. 901 (1956); Gayle v. Browder, 352 U.S. 903 (1956); Evers v. Dwyer, 358 U.S. 202 (1958). *Recreation:* Rice v. Arnold, 340 U.S. 848 (1950); Muir v. Louisville Park Theatrical Ass'n, 347 U.S. 971 (1954); Mayor & City Council of Baltimore v. Dawson, 350 U.S. 877 (1955); Holmes v. Atlanta, 350 U.S. 879 (1955). *Due process and equal protection in crimi-*

nal cases: Moore v. Dempsey, 261 U.S. 86 (1923); Hollins v. Oklahoma, 295 U.S. 394 (1935); Hale v. Kentucky, 303 U.S. 613 (1938); Hill v. Texas, 316 U.S. 400 (1942); Patton v. Mississippi, 332 U.S. 463 (1947); Taylor v. Alabama, 335 U.S. 252 (1948); Shepherd v. Florida, 341 U.S. 50 (1951); Brown v. Mississippi, 297 U.S. 278 (1936); Chambers v. Florida, 309 U.S. 227 (1940); Canty v. Alabama, 309 U.S. 629 (1940); White v. Texas, 309 U.S. 631 (1940); Ward v. Texas, 316 U.S. 547 (1942); Lyons v. Oklahoma, 322 U.S. 596 (1944); Lee v. Mississippi, 332 U.S. 742 (1948); Watts v. Indiana, 338 U.S. 49 (1949); Reeves v. Alabama, 348 U.S. 891 (1954); Fikes v. Alabama, 352 U.S. 191 (1957). *The power of courts-martial:* Burns v. Wilson, 346 U.S. 137 (1953). *Federal jurisdiction over crimes on federal lands:* United States v. Adams, 319 U.S. 312 (1943). *The right to associate for promotion of civil rights:* Bryan v. Austin, 354 U.S. 933 (1957); NAACP v. Alabama, 357 U.S. 449 (1958).

THE COURSE OF SOUTHERN SCHOOL DESEGREGATION

Communities not parties to the *School Cases,* which prior to the implementation decision acted to desegregate promptly or over a relatively short period of time, were the following. *Arkansas:* Fayetteville, S.S.N., Sept. 3, 1954, p. 2, and Charleston, S.S.N., Oct. 1, 1954, p. 3. *Delaware:* Arden, Newark, New Castle, and other small northern communities; summer schools in Wilmington and elementary schools for the forthcoming school year, S.S.N., Sept. 3, 1954, p. 3; Milford, S.S.N., Oct. 1, 1954, p. 4. *Kentucky:* Lafayette High School (1 Negro student); Griffin Elementary School (6 Negroes); perhaps two or three other schools, S.S.N., July 6, 1955, p. 8. *Maryland:* Baltimore, S.S.N., Sept. 3, 1954, p. 6. *Missouri:* by the beginning of the 1955 spring semester, of 177 districts with Negro pupils 110 had begun desegregation, S.S.N., March 3, 1955, p. 12; St. Louis (special schools); high schools there to be desegregated in second semester during 1955, S.S.N., Sept. 3, 1954, p. 9; by start of second semester 1955, 7 white and 2 Negro high schools had ended segregation, S.S.N., March 3, 1955, p. 12; Kansas City, some summer session and junior college classes; decision to desegregate high schools, Jan., 1955; schools in Clayton, Kirkwood, Mexico (three grades), Neosha, and other small communities, S.S.N., Sept. 3, 1954, p. 9; see also S.S.N., Oct. 1, 1954, p. 11. *West Virginia:* by fall of 1954, 12 counties completely desegregated, 13 partially, 18 awaiting further court action, S.S.N., Oct. 1, 1954, p. 14; see also S.S.N., Sept. 3, 1954, p. 14.

For the extent of desegregation in effect or in process at the beginning of the 1955 school year see S.S.N., Sept., 1955, p. 1. *Arkansas:* 4 districts. *Delaware:* 21 of 104 districts. *Kentucky:* limited desegregation in 10 counties, 4 larger cities. *Maryland:* some desegregation expected in 7 of state's 23 counties and Baltimore. *Missouri:* 114 districts including 80% of Negro children in state; most of those which did not act a year ago planned to continue segregation. *Oklahoma:* Oklahoma City and at least 88 districts out of 1,802. *Tennessee:* Oak Ridge. *Texas:* over 60 districts in southern and western sections have some desegregation. *West Virginia:* 44 of 55 counties start. Subsequent issues of *Southern School News* indicate that desegregation for 1955–56 was somewhat more extensive. See S.S.N., Oct., 1955, p. 1; Dec., 1955, p. 1; Nov., 1955, p. 2. Figures assembled in 1956, *infra*, indicate some discrepancies between 1955 estimates and 1956 realities.

For 1956 see S.S.N., Sept. 1956, p. 1. *Arkansas:* same as 1955. *Delaware:* 14 of 63 districts with mixed classes, 8 with policies of nondiscrimination; 4,100 of 11,000 Negro children in integrated situations. *Kentucky:* all but 15 of 120 counties have integrated situations. *Maryland:* 19 counties plus Baltimore with desegregation programs; 85% of Maryland's Negro pupils may attend desegregated schools. *Missouri:* 120 of 244 districts; 88% of state's Negro pupils in wholly or partly integrated systems. *Oklahoma:* "actual" integration in 161 districts; "policy" integration in 12 others; 26 still segregated, S.S.N., Sept., 1956, p. 7. *Tennessee:* Clinton. *Texas:* over 100 districts. *West Virginia:* 20 county systems fully desegregated, 21 partly, 3 segregated; 11 with no Negro pupils.

Southern School News published a summary as of Feb., 1958, showing the following ratio of desegregated districts to those with students of both races. Alabama: 0/111; Arkansas: 9/228; Delaware: 18/61; D.C.: 1/1; Florida: 0/67; Georgia: 0/196; Kentucky: 114/170; Louisiana: 0/67; Maryland: 21/23; Mississippi: 0/151; Missouri: 209/244; North Carolina: 3/172; Oklahoma: 215/271; South Carolina: 0/107; Tennessee: 3/141; Texas: 123/841; Virginia: 0/114; West Virginia: 47/43.* *A Statistical Summary, State-By-State, of Segregation-Desegregation Activity,* etc., Southern Education Reporting Service (1958).

As of Oct., 1958, the comparable statistics indicated almost a complete leveling off. Alabama: 0/113; Arkansas: 8/228; Delaware: 17/61; D.C.: 1/1; Florida: 0/67; Georgia: 0/196; Kentucky: 117/171; Louisiana: 0/67; Maryland: 21/23; Mississippi: 0/151; Missouri: 211/244; North Carolina: 3/172; Oklahoma: 238/271; South Carolina: 0/107; Tennessee: 3/141; Texas: 124/722; Virginia: 0/114; West Virginia: 47/43.*

"Desegregation," of course, is a word of several meanings and may indicate a policy which has been implemented little or not at all.

* The West Virginia fraction probably indicates that some districts where there are no Negro children have announced that such children would be admitted to desegregated schools if they resided there.

CORRESPONDENCE ON JURY SELECTION AND SENTENCING FOR CRIME

These inquiries originally were directed to Legal Aid Societies, but, as indicated, were occasionally referred elsewhere.

1. ABSTRACTS OF CORRESPONDENCE DISCUSSING JURY SELECTION PRACTICES

Atlanta: In our practice at the Legal Aid Society we do not handle defense of the accused in criminal cases, and do not actually observe the workings of the jury in such cases. About all that I could tell you about this is that a few Negroes are called up for jury duty and from time to time one will be left on a jury panel. I do not know of any particular practice or agreement on the part of counsel to excuse Negroes by agreement.

Baltimore: I have no statistics to back up the impression I have concerning negroes participating on juries. However, the impression I have is that negroes appear frequently on juries although I would say they represent a minority on any given jury. This may result from the method of choosing juries. I don't think there is any established practice concerning the challeneging of negroes but I feel that they are struck from the jury depending upon the particular facts of a case. Where a negro is a party to a case and the opposition represents a white person, I think that there may be a challenge. However this problem depends so much upon the factual situation that I do not think any rule could be drawn. Negroes will be found on juries in any type of case. I know nothing about the appearance of negroes in the grand jury, but I have the impression that they are represented there.

Boston: My answers are based on my personal experience in the eastern half of Massachusetts which takes in well over half the population of

Massachusetts. I have no reason to believe that they do not hold true throughout the state. Negroes serve on both grand juries and petit juries. Whether in *exact* proportion to the number of Negroes in the community I have no way of knowing, but the appearance of Negroes on juries is so common that it is not noticed. For instance, 3 or 4 cases may be tried before jurors composed entirely of white, and then the next jury will have 2 or 3 Negroes. Because we have a jury polling system, the same jurors are used for criminal and civil cases. The fact that the parties to a case, civil or criminal, are Negroes, has absolutely no bearing on the jurors sent to a particular courtroom. Actually, the fact is not known or gone into by anyone before the trial actually starts. There is no practice to challenge Negroes either by agreement or otherwise. Each attorney, of course, has his own idiosyncrasies when it comes to exercising peremptory challenges. For example; I prefer not to have a Negro on the jury if the defendant is Negro because I believe that it focuses too much attention on the Negro *juror* and puts him in a position that is unfair to both him and the defendant. I am always afraid that the Negro juror will subconsciously feel that if he should vote for acquittal, the white jurors might think that he is swayed because the defendant is a Negro and that to show his complete impartiality, he is more likely to vote for a conviction than a white man.

Charleston, South Carolina: The jury lists are made up from registered electors, males between 21 and 65, and two out of every three such electors must be on the jury lists. I mention this so you will realize the proportion of white to Negro on a jury is dependent on the proportion of the same among registered electors and the resultant jury lists. There has been a Negro on the recent grand jury of 18 men and there is one on the new grand jury. On every petit jury panel, for civil or criminal court, there is a large portion of Negroes. Our Solicitor . . . states he has had no evidence of agreement among lawyers to excuse them from jury duty nor is this accomplished by peremptory challenges; of course, where a case may involve a complicated factual situation demanding more than the ordinary degree of intelligence the lawyer would use his peremptory challenges to eliminate the less educated whether white or colored. Mr. _____ states Negroes often sit on civil and criminal cases where the litigants are all Caucasians. Unethical plaintiffs' lawyers perhaps often desire Negroes on their juries because of their possible venality, but this is nothing peculiar to their race, as persons of weak moral character of any race have doubtless always served the ends of such lawyers.

Chicago: As far as our experience shows, Negroes serve on juries in our community just as do white persons. We do not handle many jury cases and have no figures as to this. However, we daily see Negroes serving on juries.

Chicago (Office of the Public Defender): At this time there are many juries and grand juries that have negroes on them. There was a time however, and we would have to go back a number of years, that there would be an agreement between the State's Attorney and the Defense Counsel to excuse all negroes by agreement. However, that does not exist at this time and I believe it is correct in stating that they are accepted on juries as any other person might be if counsel felt that they would be helpful to their case in accordance with the facts as they know them during the selection of the jury.

Denver (Urban League): On the basis of our personal observations, plus information we have obtained from lawyers and judges there seems to be no unfair restriction against Negroes as jurors. Perhaps, the fact that Colorado has a Negro Attorney General, and Denver has a Negro municipal judge, and assistant District Attorney has helped promote visual acceptance of Negro jurors. We have no figures as to frequency but we know that Negro jurors are not confined to cases involving Negro parties.

Detroit: On my visits to the various court rooms where civil and criminal cases are tried, my observations are that in every case there are Negro members on the jury. I have noticed that in some cases, Negro jury members are in the majority. I have seen Negro Assisting Prosecuting Attorneys represent the People, where the defendant is white, and of course, vice versa. All criminal and civil jury panels have Negro membership. To my knowledge, I have not noticed any discrimination in our court for or against the service of Negroes on juries.

Durham, North Carolina: I have spoken to one or two of the members of our staff and while they have no statistics on the subject they assure me that negroes do serve on jury panels and juries. The only way I can answer your letter adequately would be to have somebody sit in a courtroom and make a study of the situation. I'm afraid we do not have the facilities to make this sort of inquiry.

Hartford: The grand jury is used very sparingly in this State. . . . The practical effect is that no petit juries are in use here and grand juries are used only when the offense is punishable by life imprisonment or death. It follows that the grand jury, because of its infrequency, would not provide a suitable forum to form an opinion as to Negroes on juries. Civil matters find the prevalent use of juries. Negroes are not barred from the jury panel but the number on a jury panel is infinitesimal as compared with their ratio to the total population. It is obvious that service on an actual jury, hearing a case, is almost non-existent. It has been noted that jury trials are almost wholly restricted to civil matters which usually involve money damages. If a Negro is on the panel, he will usually be challenged (not from the fact that he is a Negro–but because the average lawyer feels that he is not used to thinking in big figures; that his financial experience has usually dealt with a few dollars rather than thousands, and would, therefore, not help his claim for damages). When Negroes are on the panel, their economic status usually forces them to ask to be excused. They are usually daily wage earners and the loss of a day's pay creates an economic crisis at home. Negro participation is not confined to matters involving Negro parties and counsel never enters into an agreement to keep them out by peremptory challenge. Summarily, my observations are that there is no discrimination against the Negro in the selection of the jury panel. The Whites who live in the City have only a small representation on the panels and are in the same situation as the Negro. The economic factor seems to dictate that most of the panel come from suburbia; from among unoccupied housewives, retired business men, widows and persons who will not miss a day's pay. If there be discrimination in jury selection, it appears to be an economic discrimination rather than a racial one.

Lincoln, Nebraska: I am unable to state to what extent negroes serve on juries in this community or surrounding communities. Negroes do serve on both grand juries and petit juries and in both criminal and civil cases. I have not observed a practice of counsel to exercise peremptory challenges against negroes or excuse them by agreement.

New Orleans: It is my understanding that about 15% of the jury panel for the Parish of Orleans, which must have at least 750 names on it, are Negroes. However, the jury panel usually runs about 2000, and it serves the 8 sections of the Criminal District Court and the Grand Jury for the Parish of Orleans. I cannot recall ever being in Court and not seeing at least 5 or 6 Negroes on each petit jury panel. A grand jury of 12 persons is selected by each Judge in turn every six months out of a list of 75 names. Each of the 75 names are drawn by ballot from the wheel containing the 2000 names. Usually, the Judge has some Negroes in the 75 names. He has full discretion for whatever reason he sees fit to choose whomsoever he wants to serve on the Grand Jury. Up until 3 years ago no Negro had ever served on the Grand Jury in the Parish of Orleans with the exception of one instance about 30 years ago when a man was placed on the Grand Jury and it was thought he was a white man because of his color and the texture of his hair and skin. Since 3 years ago only two Grand Juries have had Negroes on them. The present Grand Jury does not. Most of the defense attorneys and the prosecuting attorneys by consent discharge a Negro if he is called to serve on a petit jury. If they could not reach an agreement by consent either the state or the defense will exercise a peremptory challenge. I, myself, will not take a Negro whether the defendant is white or black because I feel that he will not be fair in the sense that he will say to himself "I will show these over eleven men that we can do a good job and therefore I will convict this Negro" when in fact there may have been reasonable doubt on his part. I have also noticed that most of the Negroes on the petit jury panel are not as well educated as the average white man and that his employment is usually that of laborer, porter, etc., and therefore I will not take them. This is not based on prejudice but on my own ideas. The only time I was prepared to take a Negro because of his good mentality and appearance and prominent social and business standing in the community, he was peremptorily challenged by the State.

Philadelphia: There is hardly a jury in Philadelphia which is not composed of several Negroes. In this city Negroes serve on Grand Juries— petty juries, in criminal cases and in civil cases with the same frequency as white people do. There are fewer colored citizens than there are white citizens and therefore the actual number of Negroes serving on juries will be less than the number of white people who serve on juries. There is no practice of exercising peremptory challenges against Negroes or to excuse them by agreement. Exclusion rarely takes place, and only where the specific facts of the case induce counsel to see that he would get a better break if he excluded Negroes. On the other hand, there are cases in which counsel will strike off the white citizens in order to get as many colored persons on the jury as possible.

Phoenix: It is my opinion that there is no discrimination against colored people here in Arizona in so far as jury duty is concerned. Our jury panels are made up of drawing names of the voters roll with no consideration given to race, color or creed. There is no discrimination whatsoever regarding vote registration. There is no doubt that counsel in this vicinity exercise peremptory charges against negroes, however I doubt that it follows any wide spread pattern. I personally have tried cases here in the state with negroes on the jury and have seen many juries in this state with negroes on them. However . . . I am not attempting to speak as an authority on the subject.

Phoenix (Office of the County Attorney): Your questions were referred to the entire staff. The answers I am about to give you are, of course, our opinion based upon our collective experience in this field. Negroes appear on jury panels in our community in proportion to their appearance in the population of the community. They serve on the juries to the same extent as anyone else does on jury duty. They appear with the same frequency on petit juries in criminal and civil cases. We do not use a grand jury, even though it is provided for by statutes, for the reason that we file complaints before a justice of the peace; then have a preliminary hearing and the defendant may be held for trial by a petit jury. There is no practice of exercising peremptory challenges against negroes by agreement. In elaborating on that, however, some attorneys have reasons best known to themselves, and will strike a negro juror if a negro is going to be a witness or a defendant. That practice is not prevalent however.

Portland, Oregon (retired attorney active in B'nai B'rith): My answer is the jury commissioners draw the names for juries from the list of registered voters. There is nothing in this list to indicate the race, religion, or national origin of the voters. Hence, Negroes are subpoenaed, as well as Whites, in the proportion they appear on the registration list. You must keep in mind that many Negroes, particularly from the South, do not take advantage of their right to vote here and hence do not bother to get on the registration lists and hence they would never be drawn for jury duty. When it comes to actual serving on juries, this involves survival of examination for cause and peremptory challenging. Hence, there are prejudices of counsel and principles involved. It is my opinion and, this is only a guess, which may be affected by own antagonism towards racial prejudice that whether the Negro is retained or rejected from the jury is controlled by the opinion of counsel, as to whether or not the Negro would be susceptible to arguments or prejudice invoked by the other side. Courthouse scuttlebutt is that generally a Negro juror would be biased in favor of a litigant who is a Negro or even to the side which produces Negro witnesses. Conversely, I remember in my younger trial days, we were advised never to keep an Irishman on the jury, if we were representing an Irishman. My guess is that Negroes do not appear on grand juries with the same frequency that they do on trial juries. I am not able to answer your question as to whether there is a practice of counsel to exercise peremptory challenges against Negroes or to excuse them by agreement. The exclusion of Negroes from jury duty by agreement of counsel, merely because they are Negroes, would not be approved by the court. There is another factor which you must not overlook in evaluating prejudice in relation to Negro jury service. The fees paid jurors in this jurisdiction are very small. It does involve a financial sacrifice for an employed person to accept jury service. A man or his wife, white or colored, can earn much more at their regular employment than by doing jury duty. This rule certainly applies to Negroes and I daresay, many requests to be excused for jury duty come from Negro men and women who do not wish to experience loss in earnings. One other factor which you should consider. Before World War II, Portland Negro population was very small—not over 2,000 and these people were primarily engaged in railroad work, porters, waiters, etc. During the war immense shipyards and other defense industries were established here. To man these enterprises trainloads of Negroes from the deep South were brought into Portland. About half of these folks still remain. To a great extent, much more so than our native Negro population, they gave evidence of the under-privileged status and environment from which they came. In my opinion, many of these folks would not be good jury material and this has nothing to do with their being Negroes, and their lack of qualifications soon become evident by interrogation in a courtroom.

St. Paul: I submitted the questions in your December 20th letter to the Chief Deputy Clerk of the District Court. . . . The practice in this county is for each of the 8 District Court Judges to pick 450 names each year from the City Directory. Race does not appear in the directory so a goodly number of persons chosen are Negroes. Of this list 250 are called in for jury duty each two weeks. The same rules for excusing jurors apply to Negroes as well as other races, so Negroes are on the jury panel in approximately the same proportion as they appear in this county. The next question is— do they actually serve as jurors on specific cases. The Deputy Clerk states that Negroes do actually serve. He could not state whether attorneys were prone to exercise peremptory challenges against Negroes. There does not seem to be any agreement between counsel to excuse Negroes. There is no practice to accept Negroes as jurors only in certain types of cases or only when the parties are Negroes. I asked if Negroes ever served on criminal cases and was informed that they did. There was one case the deputy recalled where a Negro juror served on a criminal case involving a Negro. The defendant was found guilty. . . . The situation is somewhat different concerning grand juries. Grand juries are not selected on quite such a random basis. The Judges generally select persons better known and of greater standing in the community than Negroes customarily enjoy. The deputy did not recall any Negroes being on grand juries during his experience.

Salt Lake City: Under our statutes colored people are permitted to serve on juries. However, there are very few who serve on juries, but the explanation is that we have a very small colored population. Another requirement for serving on juries is that the person must be a tax payer. While there are few colored people in our community, likewise there are very few colored property owners among them. This, of necessity, limits the number on juries. After receiving your letter I discussed its contents with our jury clerk, who has been serving in his present capacity for 17 years. I also discussed it with two of our judges, one of whom for 24 years has been on the bench, the other is starting his 18th year on the bench. All of these men express the view that I have stated above. However, they all inform me that at no time during their term in office have colored people been excluded from the jury—petty or grand. I know of no practice among attorneys to exclude colored people by peremptory challenges. The Judges and the jury clerk also stated that they were aware of no such agreement among attorneys, and said that they were sure that this was not a practice in our community, as during that time these people have served on juries and have been accepted by both counsel.

San Francisco (Office of the Public Defender): We have many negroes serving on juries in our criminal courts. I am not aware of how they are selected. However, I know that there is not a jury panel called in that does not have some negroes on it. We never excuse a negro or exercise challenge against a negro when he is on the jury unless for specific reason or cause. There are no negroes serving on the Grand Jury in San Francisco, and, to my knowledge, there has been no instance where a negro has served on the Grand Jury. We have found that even the District Attorney very seldom exercises peremptory challenges against negroes on juries, and there is never any agreement entered into between the District Attorney's office and ourselves to excuse a negro person by agreement from serving on a jury. In answer to your last statement, as to whether we have any observations which would account for the nature and degree of negro participation on juries, I might state that the people of the City and County of San Francisco are fairly tolerant towards all nationalities and races, as this is quite a cosmopolitan city.

Seattle (Office of the Prosecuting Attorney): The frequency of appearances of Negroes on juries in King County, Washington, is affected only by a population ratio which might result in fewer Negroes on a given panel than persons of another racial group.

Washington, D.C.: I am glad to answer . . . based upon personal observation and my experience in general over a period of 25 years. 1. Negroes appear on jury panels quite regularly. 2. They also serve on juries to the same extent. 3. I am unable to tell you what the situation is as to criminal cases because of my lack of experience in that connection. I think I know the situation as to civil cases, however. 4. Negro participation is not confined to cases involving members of their own race. There is little or no effort to challenge or excuse negroes because of race alone. Always there are other considerations present. 5. As I have suggested, I know of no particular kind of cases in which the practice of excusing or challenging negroes prevails on the ground of race alone. 6. Of course, in this District there is a large population of negroes; consequently, they are called upon for jury duty to a larger extent than might otherwise be the case. Also, despite the population aspect, there appears to be no serious discrimination against their serving on jury panels. Furthermore, a substantial number of them have had experience in Government service and, consequently, they are fairly intelligent members of prospective jury panels.

2. ABSTRACTS FROM CORRESPONDENCE CONCERNING DISPARITIES IN SENTENCING FOR CRIME

Arlington, Virginia (Office of the Commonwealth Attorney): With the exception of "lover's quarrels" the punishment for crime is fairly equal between colored and white on the normal run of criminal cases. In the more serious crimes of murder and rape, the sentence imposed upon a convicted colored criminal appears to be somewhat lighter in our jurisdiction than on a similar convicted criminal who is white. . . . no particular increase in punishment results from a crime by a negro against a white person other than the more serious felonies and usually in those cases, the guilty person exhibits a personality in Court that I believe results more in the heavy penalties by the jury than the fact that the crime committed was one involving a white person.

Atlanta: Just from observation, it is probably correct that in some areas in our State a negro found guilty of a crime against a white person might receive a more severe sentence than a white person found guilty of a similar crime against a negro. It may also be true that where a negro has been found guilty of a crime against another negro, the penalty might be minimal. In a metropolitan center like the Atlanta area, I doubt that you would find as much of this as you would in the rural areas. . . . I have the impression that the statement that Mr. Myrdal made would apply in [a rural] county.

Atlantic City: Absence of discrimination. . . . The factors of presentence investigation and a heavy negro population [vocal and active in political matters] would seem to preclude differentiation.

Boston: I have never felt that the fact that a defendant was a Negro had too much bearing on the sentence. On the other hand the fact can not be ignored that if a particular judge for some reason or the other dislikes Negroes that fact is, consciously or unconsciously, going to show up in the sentence. I think in isolated cases there can be no question that a Negro might receive a more severe sentence than a white man charged with the same crime. On the other hand I can think of many cases where he would get a lesser sentence. I think that in fornication and adultery cases judges are more apt to impose lesser sentences than they would against white people because they feel that the Negro, many of them coming from states which recognize common law marriages, is naturally going to ignore many of the sex laws. . . . After handling criminal cases for over twenty years I do not feel that, *in this area*, the Negro gets any better or worse treatment than the white man.

Charleston, South Carolina: There is no difference in sentencing where the criminal and victim are of different races, except in sex crimes, of which we have very few. In instances of white against white, the sentence is usually much more severe than in cases of Negro against Negro, as in the latter the Court usually sentences in accordance with the Negroes' own standards of conduct. Mr. _____ calls attention to two rather parallel recent cases in which Negro against Negro drew a sentence of $250 or 60 days, while in the white against white the sentence was thirty-five years.

Chicago (Office of the Public Defender): All [of ten assistants in this office] seem to concur in the answer and opinion that at this time race does not enter into sentencing, and that is my opinion also. All that have been in this Office for at least ten years did state that approximately ten years ago this fact had some bearing in the sentence but at this time it certainly does not.

Des Moines: No discrimination.

Durham, North Carolina: Guess is that racial distinctions seldom, if ever, make a difference.

Gary, Indiana (city court judge): At no time do we consider a person's color.

Hartford: No apparent racial distinctions.

Jacksonville (Office of the County Solicitor): We can only attempt to answer based on general experience in the prosecution of violations of the Criminal Law of Florida as no racial distinction is made by this office and therefore no racial statistics are kept by this office. In answer to your question as to whether the conditions described exist in this community today, the answer is no; in that a Negro, as such, is held to the same degree of responsibility and accountability as any other person or member of the community. However, it is well recognized by every law enforcement agency that persons with little education and low I.Q.'s which result in little feeling of community responsibility and a different set of mores and taboos than their neighbor are dealt with less severely than their more fortunate neighbor. I feel safe in saying that this is true not only in the United States but throughout the world. If an individual Negro happens to be a part of this group, he is accordingly dealt with less severely, not because he is a Negro but merely because he falls within that classification be he Negro or White. Needless to say, a white person who falls within this classification is held to the same lesser degree of responsibility. In all fairness, I think it is safe to say that in the South the majority of this group is made up of Negroes, while at the same time, pointing out that a large part of the Negro race in the South are intelligent, educated and active in community affairs and held to the same degree of responsibility as white persons of a similar situation. It is difficult to answer your second question as to whether racial distinctions are made in sentencing other than to say that each case must stand by itself and the sentence will and should reflect a realistic understanding of the problems and persons involved. Naturally, community considerations will also enter in the imposition of the sentence no matter where the jurisdiction.

Kansas City, Missouri: Criminal court judges in Kansas City, on the whole, are equitable and fair in such cases. . . . they would give the same sentences to both white and Negro defendants convicted of the same crime and other circumstances being equal. There is, however another factor. . . . The tactics of the lawyer . . . could be divided into two categories. 1. When the crime is committed against another Negro. In such cases, the lawyer will offer a plea of "not guilty," and attempt to get an all white jury. His argumentation would then consist of a sociological and psychological appeal to the white jury in the sense that the Negro defendant is a victim of circumstance, discriminated against most of his life, and is a poor unfortunate who should be set free. Generally, this technique works and regardless of the severity of the crime against another Negro, the defendant is often freed or given a light sentence. . . . 2. When a Negro commits a crime against a white person. In this case, the lawyer often persuades the defendant to plead "guilty" on the basis that he, the lawyer, will make a "deal" with the court and get the defendant a light sentence. More often than not, there is no "deal" made and instead of a light sentence, the defendant receives a heavy sentence.

New Orleans: In Louisiana the most heinous crime in the eyes of the public is a rape of a white woman by a negro man. In these cases as a rule the jury convicts. If it is the rape of white against white or black against black I would say that the jury comes back in 99% of the cases with a not guilty verdict, unless it happens to be what we colloquially refer to as "a cabbage patch job." * Under the felony-murder doctrine whether the victim be white or black and the assailant white or black there is usually a conviction. The rest of the cases—theft, carnal knowledge, simple burglary, etc., the defendants are treated equally. As you can see from the above, it is only when there is violence to the person involved that both the juries and the Judges, without admitting it, take into consideration the color of the defendant.

Philadelphia: Where a Negro has been found guilty of a crime against a white person, he is not likely to receive a more severe sentence than a white person found guilty of a similar crime against a Negro, all things

* Defined in a subsequent letter "as one where force and violence is used in obtaining the sexual pleasure desired by the male, as differentiated from the 'why don't you come up to my place and see the paintings' type of rape case."

being equal. But they never are. . . . the Judge is apt to study the defendant's family background and work record, consider the possibility of future misconduct, and then will often conclude that the uncertain family background and irregular work record of the Negro defendant call for a heavier sentence than would otherwise be the case. Where a Negro has been found guilty of a crime against a Negro, the penalty may sometimes be light, but, . . . it too would not be based on any considerations of race. In the run-of-the-mill case, both the prosecutor and the accused are shown to be less than substantial citizens. Assaults are usually committed in tap rooms or on the street, in the early hours of the morning, where neither the prosecutor nor the defendant apparently have understandable reasons for being. In many of these cases the conduct of the prosecutor leaves much to be desired, with the result that the aversion of the court to the prosecutor is reflected in a light sentence of the defendant.

Phoenix (Office of the County Attorney): Your questions were referred to the entire staff. The answers . . . [reflect] . . . our collective experience in this field. Where a negro has been found guilty of a crime against a white person, *he will not* receive a more severe sentence than a white person found guilty of a similar crime against a negro. Where a negro has been found guilty of a crime against another negro, the penalty will be the same as if it were a white man against a white man. The courts do not dismiss the matter as being of no real consequence. The courts in this area state, and rightfully so, that the crime is against the state and not against the individual.

Portland, Oregon (retired attorney active in B'nai B'rith): Limiting myself to conditions in the Portland area, as they presently exist, I am happy to report that the differences between the races as they are manifested in court procedure is much less than formerly. If I should ask public officials, I am sure that they, whether judges or prosecuting attorneys, would insist that there is no difference. _____ is presently a Deputy District Attorney here in Portland. A couple of weeks ago, he prosecuted vigorously a Negro who had stabbed to death another Negro. The defendant was convicted of the charge for which he was indicted, to wit, second-degree murder for which life imprisonment is mandatory. The fact that the deceased was a Negro in no wise lessened the seriousness of the case.

St. Paul: The person in this county in the best position to comment . . . is the Deputy Clerk of the District Court who handles the criminal calendar, files and the making up of the decrees, etc. This particular deputy has served in that capacity many years. He sees every sentence made by all of the judges. His opinion is that he can see no difference in the sentences imposed on Negroes as compared with sentences imposed on white persons. The only difference he has noted is that a Negro may be allowed more latitude in telling his story if he chooses to take the stand than a white person. This latitude doesn't apply to the race necessarily but may be more related to the defendant's apparent ignorance, lack of education, or lack of ability to express himself.

Salt Lake City: Has been no difference.

San Francisco (Office of the Public Defender): As far as our office is concerned, we handle approximately 60% of criminal cases in the City and County of San Francisco. We have found that race plays no part whatever in sentencing following criminal conviction. Whether a defendant is colored, white, or any other race is not considered by the judge in passing sentence or determining whether probation should be granted. To my knowledge, over the last four years, I cannot remember one instance in which a negro person who had been found guilty of a crime against a white person received any different sentence than a white person might receive who had been found guilty of a similar crime against a negro. Again in this respect there has been no thought given by the judge to the question of whether the accused is negro and the person injured white, or vice versa. There has been no distinction in the imposition of sentences when a colored person is found guilty of a crime against another colored person. He is given the same sentence as if the crime were perpetrated by one white person against another white person.

Savannah: Certain crimes which negroes do not regard as seriously as whites do. Rape and various sex offenses being some of them. . . . several years ago two young negroes were charged in Superior court with raping two fifteen year old girls (also negro). The evidence was overwhelming in that they had committed a violent act of rape. Everyone in the court room expected a sentence of fifteen years, however, the verdict was two years. . . . It is very difficult to generalize about inter-racial crimes as the punishment depends on the individual involved but, I would say the white criminal receives substantially same punishment as the comparable negro.

RECENT LEGISLATION

As the foregoing pages went to press fresh legislation, some favoring, some opposing racial distinctions, was enacted in a number of states. The more significant of these statutes are summarized here. Where feasible, reference has been made to this legislation in the text. In other instances the preceding appendixes have been cross referenced to this one.

1. *STATUTES DESIGNED TO DEFEAT OR MINIMIZE DESEGREGATION*

EDUCATION

Arkansas: SJR No. 5 (1959) (§ 1. proposed constitutional amendment: public policy of state to provide financial aid for education to be administered in manner determined at local level; § 3. electors of each district may provide either for free public schools or for student-education financial aid, to be available for equal benefit of all; § 8. manner of applying financial aid for education shall be changed whenever approved by majority of qualified electors of district; § 13. effective date: after approval at November, 1960, General Election). Act No. 207 (1959) (§ 1. if school district director is incarcerated, his office shall not be declared vacant; action taken in his absence void *ab initio;* § 2. sheriff having custody of such director shall make arrangements for school board meetings to be conducted at place of incarceration). Act No. 236 (1959) (whereas *School Segregation Cases* were based on psychological effect of segregation on Negroes but ignored psychological impact of integration on certain white children and whereas legislation is needed to protect health, etc., of white children, the following is enacted: § 1. no person shall be required to attend school with students of different race; § 2. whenever school which anyone would normally attend becomes racially integrated, parent may apply to State Board for tuition grants for nonintegrated public or accredited nonprofit, nonsectarian private education; § 6. amounts paid as tuition grants

deducted from state funds otherwise allocable to district). Act No. 461
(1959) (§ 1. legislative finding of need for more flexible and selective procedure for establishment of units, facilities, curricula, and qualification and
assignment of pupils; § 2. any general or arbitrary reallocation of pupils
according to rigid rule of proximity of residence or according solely to
request of pupil would be disruptive; § 3. local boards not required to make
general reallocation and shall have no authority to administer general order
from any source whatsoever without finding that placement of each individual pupil is consistent with tests of this act; § 4. criteria; these are
adapted from Alabama statute, see p. 233 *supra;* § 7. parent may file objections; hearing; investigation; § 8. no child compelled to attend any school
where races commingled; entitlement to aid for education; § 9. appeals to
state courts; board members' immunity from suit). *Georgia:* Act No. 7
(1959) (§ 1. whenever Governor determines that continued operation of a
public school is likely to cause public disorder such school shall be closed;
§ 2. he may close school from which and to which pupil would transfer; § 3.
thereafter it shall be unlawful for public authorities to operate such school;
expenditure of public funds for such school shall also be unlawful; § 5.
authorities shall arrange for transfer of pupils to other public schools; § 6.
if such transfer cannot be arranged, Governor shall provide for educational
grants; § 8. operation of closed school is misdemeanor). Act No. 8 (1959)
(§ 1. Governor may close any school, institution, or any branch under
control of Board of Regents of University System of Georgia whenever he
shall find that continued operation is likely to result in or cause violence,
etc.). Act No. 9 (1959) (§ 1. state to designate counsel to defend certain
suits; § 2. fees, expenses, to be paid by state). Act No. 10 (1959) (§ 1. no
person to be admitted to undergraduate school of University of Georgia
after age 21; no admission to graduate or professional school after 25;
teachers may be admitted notwithstanding age, subject to regulations of
Board of Regents; person of unusual ability and fitness may be admitted
notwithstanding age). Act No. 212 (1959) (§ 1. municipalities with independent school systems may levy taxes for support of segregated public
schools; § 2. if court holds that such municipality cannot maintain separate
schools power conferred by this act terminates; at suit of taxpayer superior
court of county shall have jurisdiction to enjoin attempt to exercise such
power). *Virginia:* Ch. 32 (1959) (§ 2. school boards authorized to close
schools whenever military or civilian personnel are employed under federal
authority to police public schools for purpose of preventing violence). Ch.
49 (1959) (§ 1. school boards may provide transportation for children enrolled in nonsectarian private schools; may be reimbursed out of state funds;
§ 2. funds for transportation may be allotted for same). Ch. 53 (1959) (§ 2.
governing body of counties, cities, towns shall appropriate amounts necessary to provide scholarships for children attending nonsectarian private
schools outside locality; § 4. State Board may promulgate rules for such
schools but shall not deal with eligibility for admission; § 5. amount of grant,
how computed). Ch. 68 (1959) (§ 1. election to determine whether school

properties are needed for public purposes; sale according to applicable law). Ch. 80 (1959) (§ 1. notwithstanding any provision of law any existing building may be used for operating any private elementary or high school). Ch. 71 (1959) (§ 1. State Board shall make rules for use by local boards in making placements to provide for orderly administration, health, safety, best interest, and general welfare; § 2. placements shall be made by local boards; § 3. children first attending school or those recently moved into district must apply; § 4. appeals to local boards; § 6. procedure on appeal to State Board; § 9. appeals to state courts; § 11. appeals by five interested heads of families who are residents of governmental unit involved in placement).

Public Accommodations

Arkansas: Act No. 226 (1959) (§ 1. any person who shall enter public place of business and create disturbance or breach of peace in any way whatsoever shall be fined not more than $500, imprisoned not more than six months, or both).

2. STATUTES OPPOSED TO DISCRIMINATION

Employment

California: Assembly Bill No. 91 (1959) (added to Labor Code commencing with § 1410) (Fair Employment Practices Act). *Ohio:* Am. S.B. No. 10 (1959) (§§ 4112.01 to .08 inclusive and § 4112.99 Rev. Code) (Ohio Fair Employment Practices Act).

Housing

Colorado: House Bill No. 259 (1959) (Fair Housing Act) (§ 1. administered by State Antidiscrimination Commission; § 2. persons covered include one or more individuals, partnerships, associations, corporations, legal representatives, trustees, receivers; owners, lessees, proprietors, managers, agents, employees, the state and political subdivisions; housing covered includes all dwellings except premises maintained by the owner or lessee as household of family and not more than four boarders or lodgers; § 4. commission may pass upon complaints alleging unfair housing practice in transfer, rental, lease, hire, occupancy; § 5. it is unfair housing practice to refuse to transfer, rent, lease, or otherwise deny housing because of race, etc.; discrimination in financial assistance for acquisition, construction, repair, maintenance forbidden; § 6. commission procedure as in FEP act). *Connecticut:* §§ 53-35 & 53-36, *1958 Revision as Amended Effective Oct. 1, 1959* (public accommodations statute now includes housing accommodations offered for sale or rent which are one of five or more housing accommodations all of which are located on a single parcel of land or parcels of land that are contiguous without regard to highways or streets, and all of which any person owns or otherwise controls the sale or rental of). *Massachusetts:*

House Bill 1209 (1959) (§ 1 of ch. 151B amended as follows: "contiguously located housing" is housing offered for sale, lease, or rental by a person who owns or at any time has owned or otherwise controlled sale of ten or more housing accommodations located on land that is contiguous, exclusive of streets, or housing which is offered for sale, lease, or rental and which at any time was one of such ten or more lots; § 4 of ch. 151B is amended to cover the owner, lessee, sublessee, assignee, or managing agent of multiple dwelling or contiguously located housing accommodations who refuses to rent or lease or otherwise denies housing accommodations because of race, creed, color, or national origin; to so discriminate in contiguously located housing). *Oregon:* Senate Bill No. 249 (1959) (amending ORS 659.033 and repealing ORS 659.032 and 659.034) (no person engaged in the business of selling real property shall solely because of race, etc., refuse to sell, lease, or rent, expel a purchaser, make any distinction in price, terms, etc., relating to sale, rental, lease, or occupancy of real property, attempt to discourage sale, rental, lease; no real estate broker or salesman shall accept or retain listings with understanding that purchaser may be discriminated against because of race). Senate Bill No. 250 (amending ORS 696.300) (broker may be disciplined, including revocation of license for violating ORS 659.033).

PUBLIC ACCOMMODATIONS

Maine: (§ 50 of ch. 137 of revised statutes repealed and replaced by following: no discrimination in public accommodations; no discriminatory advertising concerning such accommodations).

SELECT BIBLIOGRAPHY

The topical bibliographical discussion which follows is designed to aid in pursuing further the concepts treated in chapter I and to supplement the documentation in other chapters. Numerous other references are placed throughout the book in connection with specific matters. A selective alphabetical list of the principal ones follows this essay.

An extensive bibliography on race relations is not presented here since several good ones already exist. See VIET, SELECTED DOCUMENTATION FOR THE STUDY OF RACE RELATIONS (International Committee for Social Sciences Documentation 1958); an older list appears in WAXMAN, RACE RELATIONS (Rosenwald Fund 1945). A number of issues of *Race Relations Law Reporter* also contain bibliographies; 1 R.R.L.R. 501 (1956), 1 R.R.L.R. 835 (1956), 2 R.R.L.R. 287 (1957), 2 R.R.L.R. 913 (1957), 3 R.R.L.R. 589 (1958), 3 R.R.L.R. 1279 (1958); these are helpful particularly to those who are interested in law and race relations.

On law's capacity to affect society see the following writings of POUND, concerned with, in terms of the title of one of his articles, *Effective Limits of Legal Action*, 3 A.B.A.J. 55 (1917): SOCIAL CONTROL THROUGH LAW (1942); THE TASK OF LAW (1944), esp. ch. 3 ("What May Be Done Through Law"). The subject is treated exhaustively in STONE, THE PROVINCE AND FUNCTION OF LAW (1946), esp. pt. III ("Law and Society"), ch. XX ("Law as Adjustment of Conflicting Interests") and ch. XXVII ("Law and Social Control"). And see SIMPSON & STONE, LAW AND SOCIETY ch. IV (1949).

On the question of racial change see MacIVER, THE MORE PERFECT UNION (1948) (setting forth a number of coordinated approaches, including the legal, to intergroup relations); ALLPORT, THE NATURE OF PREJUDICE (1954), esp. ch. 29 ("Ought There To Be a Law?"); Clark, *Desegregation—An Appraisal of the Evidence*, 9 J. SOCIAL ISSUES No. 4 (1953) (probably the most thorough catalogue of desegregation experiences, including those brought about by law); Maslow, *The Uses of Law in the Struggle for Equality*, in NATIONAL COMMUNITY RELATIONS ADVISORY COUNCIL, THE USES OF LAW FOR THE ADVANCEMENT OF COMMUNITY RELATIONS (1955); Maslow, *Prejudice, Discrimination, and the Law*, 275 THE ANNALS 9 (1951) (assessing the efficacy of law with particular regard to how the workings of the legal system affect the outcome); MYRDAL, AN AMERICAN DILEMMA pt. VI (1944) (bringing out, among other things, the relationship between politics and law enforcement); SUCHMAN, DEAN, & WILLIAMS, DESEGREGATION—SOME PROPOSITIONS AND RESEARCH SUGGESTIONS (1958) (the most up-to-date compendium of social science conclusions in the race relations field; see esp. ch. 2, "Power in the Community"); DEAN & ROSEN, A MANUAL OF INTERGROUP RELATIONS (1955) (directed primarily to community workers); BERGER, RACIAL EQUALITY AND THE LAW (UNESCO 1954) (emphasizes the matter of employment discrimination; see esp. "Law and Human Behaviour," p. 66 *et seq.*). See also SIMPSON & YINGER, RACIAL AND CULTURAL MINORITIES chs. 14 and 15 (rev. ed. 1958) (a thorough discussion of minorities and the American political and legal process). And see Llewellyn, *What Law Cannot Do for Inter-Racial Peace*, 3 VILL. L. REV. 30 (1957).

On education see Black, *Paths to Desegregation*, New Republic, Oct. 21, 1957, p. 10 (if confronted by firmness, recalcitrant communities will desegregate rather than commit themselves to perpetual turmoil); *The Courts and Racial Integration in Education*, 21 J. NEGRO EDUCATION (1952) (the Yearbook issue, containing a number of valuable articles); WITH ALL DELIBERATE SPEED (Shoemaker ed. 1957) (a description and analysis of border and Southern school desegregation by writers for *Southern School News*); WEY & COREY, ACTION PATTERNS IN SCHOOL DESEGREGATION (1959) (an analysis by educators for Phi Delta Kappa, the educators' fraternity, on how to desegregate, based upon the experiences of communities which did); WILLIAMS & RYAN, SCHOOLS IN TRANSITION (1954) (analyzing numerous instances of Northern and border school desegregation).

Concerning employment see BERGER, RACIAL EQUALITY AND THE LAW, *supra,* and BERGER, EQUALITY BY STATUTE (1952) (a painstakingly thorough analysis of the New York State Commission Against Discrimination and its role in creating social change); Davis, *Negro Employment—A Progress Report,* Fortune, July, 1952, pp. 102, 158 (setting forth successful instances of employment desegregation); SEIDENBERG, NEGROES IN THE WORK GROUP (N.Y. State School of Industrial & Labor Relations Research Bull. No. 6, 1950) (experiences with desegregation on the job and techniques for effecting transition); FLEISCHMAN & RORTY, WE OPEN THE GATES (1958) (labor union action to effect desegregation).

On housing see DEUTSCH & COLLINS, INTERRACIAL HOUSING (1951), and WILNER, WALKLEY & COOK, HUMAN RELATIONS IN INTERRACIAL HOUSING (1955) (intensive analyses of desegregated public housing).

On the armed forces see MANDELBAUM, SOLDIER GROUPS AND NEGRO SOLDIERS (1952) (a sociopsychological view of race relations in the armed forces); NICHOLS, BREAKTHROUGH ON THE COLOR FRONT (1954) (desegregation during the Korean war); Byers, A Study of the Negro in Military Service (mimeographed 1947) (an excellent study of the preintegration military, which is available at the Schomburg Collection, New York Public Library).

For a description of polls conducted for the *Catholic Digest* about the beginning of 1956, for the American Institute of Public Opinion between 1951 and 1956, and a survey of the National Opinion Research Center covering attitude shifts between 1942 and 1956, all related to desegregation, see TUMIN, SEGREGATION AND DESEGREGATION 94–112 (1957); Tumin's own intensive study of a North Carolina county's views on desegregation issues appear in his book, DESEGREGATION—READINESS AND RESISTANCE (1958). See also The Wage Earner Forum, Vol. 58, No. 2, July 15, 1958 (sponsored by Macfadden Publications, Inc.) (a poll of wage earners on civil rights and prejudices). See also Hyman & Sheatsley, *Attitudes Towards Desegregation*, Scientific American, Dec., 1956, p. 35.

On prejudice generally see ALLPORT, *op. cit. supra*, and SAENGER, THE SOCIAL PSYCHOLOGY OF PREJUDICE (1953). For valuable observations concerning discrimination and prejudice in other lands see MASON, AN ESSAY ON RACIAL TENSION (1954); RICHMOND, THE COLOUR PROBLEM (1955).

Concerning the changing South: ASHMORE, AN EPITAPH FOR DIXIE (1957) (stressing the social and economic inevitability of change); DABBS, THE SOUTHERN HERITAGE (1958) (emphasizing the moral pressures for change); GINZBERG, THE NEGRO POTENTIAL (1956) (on the economic necessity of abandoning discrimination, particularly in employment); KING, STRIDE TOWARD FREEDOM (1958) (story of the Montgomery bus boycott); PETERS, THE SOUTHERN TEMPER (1959).

On group activity see 319 THE ANNALS (1958), an issue entitled UNOFFICIAL GOVERNMENT—PRESSURE GROUPS AND LOBBIES; among the articles in this issue Vose, *Litigation as a Form of Pressure Group Activity*, discusses or cites most of the earlier materials. See also HORN, GROUPS AND THE CONSTITUTION (1956); Robison, *Organizations Promoting Civil Rights and Liberties*, 275 THE ANNALS 18 (1951); for the best concise description of the NAACP's program and goals see the statement of Roy Wilkins in *Editorial Comment—Mr. Huntley's Astounding Proposal*, 28 J. NEGRO EDUCATION 85 (1959); an excellent article on Negro leadership is Morsell, *Comment on Frank F. Lee's "Changing Structure of Negro Leadership,"* Crisis, May, 1958, p. 261.

On group activity to enforce the law outside the civil rights field see, *e.g.*, HALL, THEFT, LAW AND SOCIETY 171, 172, 199–204, 276–277, 340–345 (2d ed. 1952) (role of insurance companies and private investigators); Handler, *False and Misleading Advertising*, 39 YALE L.J. 22, 45 (1929) (activities of Better Business Bureaus and advertising agency associations).

Throughout this work R.R.L.R. signifies *Race Relations Law Reporter* and S.S.N. *Southern School News*.

ABRAMS, FORBIDDEN NEIGHBORS (1955), 278 n. 13, 282 n. 28, 283, 284 n. 34, 286 n. 42, 294 nn. 83 and 84, 298 n. 98
ACLU, DEMOCRACY IN LABOR UNIONS (pamphlet 1952), 185 n. 120
Albright, *What Are "Standards"?* S.S.N., June, 1958, pp. 1, 2, at 210 n. 11
A.L.I. RESTATEMENT OF AGENCY (1933), 103 n. 88
A.L.I. RESTATEMENT, CONFLICT OF LAWS (1934), 348

ALLPORT, THE NATURE OF PREJUDICE (1954), 26, 27

AMERICAN JEWISH COMMITTEE, THE PEOPLE TAKE THE LEAD, 1948–1959 (pamphlet 1959), 362, 363 n. 21

AMERICAN JEWISH CONGRESS, CHILDREN, TOGETHER (pamphlet 1957), 249 n. 153

AMERICAN POLITICAL SCIENCE ASS'N, REPORT OF THE COMMITTEE ON AMERICAN STATE LEGISLATURES (Zeller ed. 1954), 147 nn. 73 and 74

AMERICAN PRISON ASS'N, STATE AND NATIONAL CORRECTIONAL INSTITUTIONS (July, 1953), 337 n. 106

5 ANDERSON, WHARTON'S CRIMINAL LAW AND PROCEDURE (1957), 315 n. 6

Annella, *Some Aspects of Interracial Marriage in Washington, D.C.*, 25 J. NEGRO EDUCATION 360 (1956), 349 n. 35

Anti-Defamation League pamphlets, "Field Reports on Desegregation in the South," 245 n. 141

ASHMORE, AN EPITAPH FOR DIXIE (1958), 88 n. 23, 155, 212 n. 16

—— THE NEGRO AND THE SCHOOLS (2d ed. 1954), 134 n. 6, 209 n. 5

Bacote, *The Negro Voter in Georgia Politics Today*, 26 J. NEGRO EDUCATION 307 (1957), 147 n. 76, 153 n. 101

Ballard, *Federal Regulation of Aviation*, 60 HARV. L. REV. 1235 (1947), 129 n. 46

1 BASU, COMMENTARY ON THE CONSTITUTION OF INDIA (3d ed. 1955), 47 n. 60

BEACH & WILL, THE STATE AND NONPUBLIC SCHOOLS (1958), 268 n. 227

BEALE, CONFLICT OF LAWS (1935), 348, 349

—— INNKEEPERS (1906), 96 n. 63, 98

BECKWITH, LAWFUL ACTION OF STATE MILITARY FORCES (1944), 363 n. 23

Bendiner, *Could You Stand a Four-Day Week*, Reporter, Aug. 8, 1957, pp. 10, 11, at 80 n. 3

BERGER, EQUALITY BY STATUTE (1952), 199, 200 n. 168

Berle, *The Changing Role of the Corporation and Its Counsel*, 10 THE RECORD 266 (1955), 50

—— ECONOMIC POWER AND THE FREE SOCIETY (Fund for the Republic pamphlet 1957), 50 n. 66

BERLE & MEANS, THE MODERN CORPORATION AND PRIVATE PROPERTY (1932), 46 n. 58

Bickel, *Integration, the Second Year in Perspective*, New Republic, Oct. 8, 1956, pp. 12, 14, at 216 n. 27

—— *The Original Understanding and the Segregation Decision*, 69 HARV. L. REV. 1 (1955), 216 n. 27

BIENSTOCK & COXE, PROGRESS TOWARD EQUALITY OF OPPORTUNITY IN THE NEW YORK STATE COLLEGES (The University of the State of New York 1950), 266 n. 213, 268 n. 225

Bond, *Cat on a Hot Tin Roof*, 27 J. NEGRO EDUCATION 519 (1958), 210 n. 10

BOWIE & FRIEDRICH eds., STUDIES IN FEDERALISM (1954), 47 n. 57

Browning, *Anti-Miscegenation Laws in the United States*, 1 DUKE B.J. 26 (1951), 346 n. 21

Bruce, *Racial Zoning by Private Contract, in the Light of the Constitutions and the Rule Against Restraints on Alienation*, 21 ILL. L. REV. 704 (1927), 277 n. 8

1 BRYCE, THE AMERICAN COMMONWEALTH (3d ed. 1909), 10 n. 5

Byers, A Study of the Negro in Military Service (mimeographed 1947; Schomburg Collection, N.Y. Public Library), 369 n. 51

CAHN, *Jurisprudence*, 1954 ANNUAL SURVEY OF AMERICAN LAW, 30 N.Y.U.L. REV. 150 (1955), 44 n. 51, 45

—— *Jurisprudence*, 1955 ANNUAL SURVEY OF AMERICAN LAW, 31 N.Y.U.L. REV. 182 (1956), 44 n. 51

CAL. DEP'T OF JUSTICE, GUIDE TO RACE RELATIONS FOR PEACE OFFICERS (1958), 323 n. 45

Caldwell, The Civil Rights Section, Its Functions and Its Statutes (address 1957), 316 n. 8

CARDOZO, THE NATURE OF THE JUDICIAL PROCESS (1921), 3 n. 4

CARMICHAEL & JAMES, THE LOUISVILLE STORY (1957), 69 n. 151, 217 n. 31, 220 n. 51, 221 n. 54, 237 n. 107

CARR, FEDERAL PROTECTION OF CIVIL RIGHTS (1947), 317 n. 15

Carter, *New York Law Against Discrimination*, 40 CORNELL L.Q. 40 (1954), 193 n. 143

CASH, THE MIND OF THE SOUTH, (Anchor ed. 1941), 12 n. 6

CAYTON & MITCHELL, BLACK WORKERS AND THE NEW UNIONS (1939), 185 n. 120

CHICAGO COMM'N ON HUMAN RELATIONS, FOURTH CHICAGO CONFERENCE ON CIVIC UNITY (1952), 166 n. 41, 310 n. 149

—— MERIT EMPLOYMENT IN CHICAGO (1956), 202 n. 174

Christensen, *The Constitutionality of National Anti-Poll Tax Bills*, 33 MINN. L. REV. 217 (1949), 146 nn. 66, 67, and 70

Civil and Criminal Contempt in the Federal Courts, 17 F.R.D. 167 (1955), 73 n. 166

Clark, Elias, *Charitable Trusts, the Fourteenth Amendment, and the Will of Stephen Girard*, 66 YALE L.J. 979 (1957), 50, 51 n. 68

Clark, Kenneth, *Desegregation—An Appraisal of the Evidence*, 9 J. SOCIAL ISSUES 17 (1953), 267 n. 219

Cohen, G., *Who Is Legally a Negro*, 3 INTRA. L. REV. 91 (1948), 348 n. 33

Cohen, H., *An Appraisal of the Legal Tests Used To Determine Who Is a Negro*, 34 CORNELL L.Q. 246 (1948), 348 n. 33

COKE, FIRST INSTITUTES, 330 n. 69

Coleman, *Freedom From Fear on the Home Front*, 29 IOWA L. REV. 415 (1944), 321 nn. 31 and 32

Comment, *The Impact of* Shelley v. Kraemer, *on the State Action Concept*, 44 CALIF. L. REV. 718 (1956), 48 n. 61

Comment, *Judicial Regulation of the Railway Brotherhoods' Discriminatory Practices*, 1953 WIS. L. REV. 416, at 176 n. 82

Comment, *Legality of Plans for Maintaining School Segregation*, 54 MICH. L. REV. 1142 (1956), 240 n. 123

COMM'N ON RACE & HOUSING, WHERE SHALL WE LIVE? (report 1958), 282 n. 29, 311 n. 150

CONN. COMM'N ON CIVIL RIGHTS BULL., vol. 1, no. 12, at 110 n. 122

1953–54 CONN. COMM'N ON CIVIL RIGHTS REPORT, 110 nn. 120 and 121, 111 n. 125

1954–55 CONN. COMM'N ON CIVIL RIGHTS REPORT, 110 n. 123, 111 n. 124

1955–56 CONN. COMM'N ON CIVIL RIGHTS REPORT, 111 n. 126

1956–57 CONN. COMM'N ON CIVIL RIGHTS REPORT, 111 n. 126, 200

CORBIN, CONTRACTS (1951), 285 n. 39

CORWIN, THE PRESIDENT, OFFICE, AND POWERS (3d ed. 1948), 78 n. 191

CORWIN ed., THE CONSTITUTION OF THE UNITED STATES OF AMERICA (1953), 34 n. 11, 71 n. 159, 119 n. 15, 315 n. 4

Cothran & Phillips, *Expansion of Negro Suffrage in Arkansas*, 26 J. NEGRO EDUCATION 287 (1957), 145 n. 60, 146 n. 65, 153 n. 101

COUNCIL OF STATE GOVERNMENTS, SUMMARIES OF STATE LAWS PERTAINING TO ADOPTION OF CHILDREN (1954), 351 n. 48

Cox, *The Role of Law in Preserving Union Democracy*, 72 HARV. L. REV. 609 (1959), 58 n. 102

CUSHMAN, CIVIL LIBERTIES IN THE UNITED STATES (1956), 320 n. 28, 321 n. 34

DABBS, THE SOUTHERN HERITAGE (1958), 155

Dauer & Kelsay, *Unrepresentative States*, 44 NAT'L MUNIC. REV. 571 (1955), 147 n. 71

Davis, John A., *Negro Employment—A Progress Report*, Fortune, July, 1952, pp. 102, 158, at 26 n. 13

Davis, Kenneth Culp, *Administrative Remedies Often Need Not Be Exhausted*, 19 F.R.D. 437 (1957), 64 nn. 120 and 125

DEUTSCH & COLLINS, INTERRACIAL HOUSING (1951), 26 n. 13, 291 n. 73

Douglas, *United States v. Peters*, 19 F.R.D. 185 (1957), 71 n. 160

DOWLING, CASES ON CONSTITUTIONAL LAW (5th ed. 1954), 62 n. 108

Duke, *Aspects of the Military Law of Confessions*, 8 VAND. L. REV. 19 (1954), 369 n. 47

DULUTH FEPC REPORT (June, 1957), 202 n. 174

1955 EAST CHICAGO, IND. FEPC REPORT, 202

1957 ERIE COMMUNITY RELATIONS THIRD ANNUAL REPORT, 197 n. 157, 202 n. 174

Evans & Lane, *Integration in the Armed Forces*, 304 THE ANNALS 78 (1956), 359 n. 8, 367 n. 40, 368 n. 44

FBI REPORT OF JOHN EDGAR HOOVER, Director (1955), 318 n. 213

FEDERAL BUREAU OF PRISONS, FEDERAL PRISONS (1957), 336 n. 102

—— NATIONAL PRISONER STATISTICS (1956), 336 n. 102

Fenton, *The Negro Voter in Louisiana*, 26 J. Negro Education 319, 322 (1957), 153 n. 101

Field, Civil Service Law (1939), 164 n. 35

Fleischman & Rorty, We Open the Gates (1958), 26 n. 13, 174 n. 71

Franklin, The Militant South (1956), 12 n. 6

Frazier, Black Bourgeoisie (1957), 155 n. 3

Freund, *Storm Over the American Supreme Court*, 21 Modern L. Rev. 345 (1958), 216 n. 27

Friedmann, *Corporate Power, Government by Private Groups and the Law*, 57 Colum. L. Rev. 155, 176 (1957), 50 n. 66

—— Legal Theory (3d ed. 1953), 117 n. 7

Galarza, Strangers in Our Fields (1956), 157 n. 11

Gellhorn, Individual Freedom and Governmental Restraints (1956), 167 n. 50

Ginzberg, The Negro Potential (1956), 155, 207, 212 n. 16

Ginzberg & Bray, The Uneducated (1955), 155 n. 5, 209 n. 5

Ginzberg & Others, The Ineffective Soldier (3 vols. 1959), 155 n. 5

Gomillion, *The Negro Voter in Alabama*, 26 J. Negro Education 281, (1957), 153 n. 101

Goostree, *The Iowa Civil Rights Statute—A Problem of Enforcement*, 37 Iowa L. Rev. 242 (1952), 109 n. 117

Governors of Civil Rights States Conference, Report on Fair Employment Practices at Work in Twelve States (1958), 193 n. 144, 195 n. 149, 196 nn. 153 and 155, 197 nn. 160 and 161, 198 nn. 162, 163, and 164, 199 n. 167, 202 n. 176, 205 nn. 180 and 181, 206 n. 183

Gray, The Nature and Sources of the Law (2d ed. 1927), 49

Green, Lectures on the Principles of Political Obligation (1941 ed.), 49 n. 63

Greenberg, *New York Antitrust Law and Its Role in the Federal Systems*, in N.Y. State Bar Ass'n, Report of the Special Committee To Study the New York Antitrust Laws (1957), 303 nn. 118 and 119

—— *Social Scientists Take the Stand—A Review and Appraisal of Their Testimony in Litigation*, 54 Mich. L. Rev. 953 (1956), 44 n. 51

Gressman, *The Unhappy History of Civil Rights Legislation*, 50 Mich. L. Rev. 1323 (1952), 318 n. 24

Griffin & Freedman, Mansfield, Texas—A Field Report on Desegregation in the South (Anti-Defamation League pamphlet), 234 n. 96

Grodzins, *Metropolitan Segregation*, Scientific American, Oct., 1957, p. 33, at 275 n. 1, 282 n. 28, 301 n. 109

Hager, *Race, Nationality and Religion, Their Relationship to Appointment Policies and Casework*, 2 National Probation & Parole Ass'n J. 129 (1957), 338 n. 108

Halberstam, *The Army Looks Good to Johnny Lawrence*, Reporter, Oct. 3, 1957, 356 n. 1

HALE, FREEDOM THROUGH LAW (1952), 48 n. 61, 317 n. 14

HANDLER, CASES AND OTHER MATERIALS ON TRADE REGULATION (2d ed. 1951), 302 n. 113

HART & WECHSLER, THE FEDERAL COURTS AND THE FEDERAL SYSTEM (1953), 48 n. 61, 52 n. 73, 61 n. 106, 63 n. 120

Hartmann, *Racial and Religious Discrimination by Innkeepers in U.S.A.*, 12 MODERN L. REV. 449 (1949), 97 n. 66

HAYT, HAYT & GROESCHEL, LAW OF HOSPITAL PHYSICIAN AND PATIENT (2d ed. 1952), 89 n. 36

Hearings on H.R. 29 Before the Subcommittee on Elections of the Committee on House Administration, 80th Cong., 1st Sess. (1947), 146 n. 66

Hearings on H.R. 41 Before Subcommittee No. 4 of the House Committee on the Judiciary, 80th Cong., 2d Sess. (1948), 320 n. 28

Hearings on H.R. 41 Before Subcommittee No. 3 of the House Committee on the Judiciary, 81st Cong., 1st & 2d Sess. (1949), 320 n. 28

Hearings on H.R. 2967 Before Subcommittee No. 1 of the House Armed Services Committee, 83d Cong., 2d Sess. (March 3, 1955), 363 n. 22

Hearings on H.R. 140 Before Subcommittee No. 5 of the House Committee on the Judiciary, 85th Cong., 1st Sess. (1957), 141 n. 37

Hearings on Migratory Labor Before the Senate Subcommittee on Labor and Labor-Management Relations, 82d Cong., 2d Sess. (1952), 158 n. 12

Hearings on S. 83 Before the Senate Committee on the Judiciary, 85th Cong., 1st Sess. (1957), 316 n. 8, 322 n. 40

Hearings on S. 83 Before the Subcommittee on Constitutional Rights of the Senate Committee on the Judiciary, 85th Cong., 1st Sess. (1957), 137 n. 20, 139 n. 27, 141 n. 37, 142 nn. 40 and 42

Hearings on S.J. Res. 25 Before the Senate Judiciary Committee, 83d Cong., 1st Sess. (1954), 146 n. 70

HEW, SOME FACTS ABOUT PUBLIC STATE TRAINING SCHOOLS FOR JUVENILE DELINQUENTS (1956), 337, 338 n. 107

Hewitt, *The Right to Membership in a Labor Union,* 99 U. PA. L. REV. 919 (1951), 171 n. 59

Hill, *The Negro College Faces Desegregation,* College and University, April, 1956, p. 291, at 263 n. 198

1 & 2 HINDS, PRECEDENTS OF THE HOUSE OF REPRESENTATIVES (1907), 151 n. 95

Holcombe, *The Coercion of States in a Federal System,* in FEDERALISM MATURE AND EMERGENT 137, 150 (MacMahon ed. 1955), 47 n. 59

HOLMES, THE COMMON LAW (1881), 3 n. 4, 280

—— *Law and Social Reform,* in LERNER, THE MIND AND FAITH OF JUSTICE HOLMES 399 (1943), 3 n. 4

HOOVER, JOHN EDGAR, *see* FBI REPORT

Horowitz, *Discriminatory Fraternities at State Universities—A Violation of the Fourteenth Amendment?,* 25 SO. CALIF. L. REV. 289 (1952), 267 n. 215

—— *The Misleading Search for "State Action" Under the Fourteenth Amendment,* 30 SO. CALIF. L. REV. 208 (1957), 48 n. 61

HOUSING & HOME FINANCE AGENCY, HOUSING OF THE NONWHITE POPULATION (1952), 310

Howe, *Political Theory and the Nature of Liberty* (Foreword), 67 HARV. L. REV. 91 (1953), 50 n. 66

24 HOW. ST. TR. 414 (1794), 330 n. 70

INSTITUTE OF JUDICIAL ADMINISTRATION, *see* JUDICIAL ADMINISTRATION, INSTITUTE OF

Irving, *The Future of the Negro Voter in the South*, 26 J. NEGRO EDUCATION 390 (1957), 153 n. 101

JELLINEK, ALLEGEMEINE STAATSLEHRE (3d ed. 1914) (reprinted and translated in 2 SIMPSON & STONE, LAW AND SOCIETY 1559–1560 [1949]), 3 n. 3

1935 J. NEGRO EDUCATION YEARBOOK, 209 n. 5

1945 J. NEGRO EDUCATION YEARBOOK, 209 n. 5

1947 J. NEGRO EDUCATION YEARBOOK, 209 n. 5

JOHNSON, PATTERNS OF NEGRO SEGREGATION (1943), 115 n. 1

Jones, Edgar L., *City Limits*, in WITH ALL DELIBERATE SPEED 82 (Shoemaker ed. 1957), 218 n. 45, 220 n. 51

Jones, J. W., LAW AND LEGAL THEORY OF THE GREEKS (1956), 26 n. 15

JUDICIAL ADMINISTRATION, INSTITUTE OF, DISPARITY IN SENTENCING OF CONVICTED DEFENDANTS (1954), 334 n. 94

Kallenbach, *Constitutional Aspects of Federal Anti-Poll Tax Legislation*, 45 MICH. L. REV. 717 (1947), 146 n. 66

Kempton, *The Conscience of Our Servants*, N.Y. Post Magazine, June 28, 1958, at 191 n. 139

Kesselman, *Negro Voting in a Border Community—Louisville, Kentucky*, 26 J. NEGRO EDUCATION 273 (1957), 157 n. 102

Kiehl, *Preparation of the Negro for His Professional Engineering Opportunities*, Negro History Bull., Nov., 1957, p. 40 at 207 n. 184

—— Preparation of the Negro for His Professional Engineering Opportunities (Ph.D. dissertation, Rutgers University School of Education, 1957; mimeographed), 207 n. 184

KINSEY, POMEROY & MARTIN, SEXUAL BEHAVIOR IN THE HUMAN MALE (1948), 336

KLINEBERG, RACE AND PSYCHOLOGY (UNESCO publication 1951), 210 n. 10

Kovner, *The Legal Protection of Civil Liberties Within Unions*, 1948 WIS. L. REV. 18, at 172 n. 62

Krislov, *Union Decertification*, 9 IND. & LAB. REL. REV. 580 (1956), 180 n. 99

Lasch, *Along the Border*, in WITH ALL DELIBERATE SPEED 60 (Shoemaker ed. 1957), 12

Laurenti, *Effects of Nonwhite Purchases on Market Prices of Residences*, Appraisal J., July, 1952, p. 314, at 282 n. 28

LeBreton, *The Michigan Fair Employment Practices Act*, 34 U. Det. L.J. 337 (1957), 193 n. 143

Lee, Fraternities Without Brotherhood (1955), 267 n. 214

Leflar, *"Law of the Land,"* in With All Deliberate Speed 1 (Shoemaker ed. 1957), 43 n. 47

Leflar & Davis, *Segregation in the Public Schools—1953*, 67 Harv. L. Rev. 377 (1954), 208 n. 3

Leland, *"We Believe in Employment on Merit, But . . . ,"* 37 Minn. L. Rev. 246 (1953), 193 n. 143

Lewis, Anthony, *An Appreciation of Justice Frankfurter*, N.Y. Times Magazine, Nov. 10, 1957, p. 25, at 216 n. 26

—— *Legislative Apportionment and the Federal Courts*, 71 Harv. L. Rev. 1057 (1957), 147 n. 71, 149, 150 n. 90

Lewis, Earl M., *The Negro Voter in Mississippi*, 26 J. Negro Education 329 (1957), 153 n. 101

Lipset, Trow & Coleman, Union Democracy (1956), 183 n. 120

Llewellyn, *Remarks on the Theory of Appellate Decision*, 3 Vand. L. Rev. 395 (1950), 104 n. 96

Lohman, The Police and Minority Groups (1947), 323 n. 45

Long, *The Relative Learning Capacities of Negroes and Whites*, 26 J. Negro Education 121 (1957), 210 n. 10

—— Segregation in Interstate Railway Coach Travel (mimeographed), 121 n. 25

Lorenz, King Solomon's Ring (1952), 343 n. 3

Loth & Fleming, Integration North and South (1956), 88 nn. 23, 24, and 31, 89 n. 34, 92 n. 45, 109 n. 118, 246 n. 149, 247 n. 150, 267 n. 219, 309 n. 143

Louisville Comm. on Police Training, Principles of Police Work With Minority Groups (1950), 323 n. 45

Lubell, *The Future of the Negro Voter in the United States*, 26 J. Negro Education 408 (1957), 134

McCain, *The Negro Voter in South Carolina*, 26 J. Negro Education 359 (1957), 153 n. 101

McCall, *History of Texas Elections Laws*, 9 Tex. Rev. Civ. Stats. XVII (1951), 143 n. 49

McCormick, Damages (1935), 283 n. 30

—— *Some Problems and Developments in the Admissibility of Confessions*, 24 Texas L. Rev. 239 (1946), 316 n. 7

McGuinn & Spraggins, *Negro in Politics in Virginia*, 26 J. Negro Education 378 (1957), 153 n. 101

McGurk, U.S. News and World Report, Sept. 21, 1956, pp. 92–96, at 210 n. 10

McKay, *Segregation and Public Recreation*, 40 Va. L. Rev. 697 (1954), 80 n. 2, 94 n. 50

—— *"With All Deliberate Speed"—A Study of School Desegregation,* 31 N.Y.U.L. REV. 991 (1956), 214 n. 20, 244 n. 135

—— *"With All Deliberate Speed"—Legislative Reaction and Judicial Development 1956–1957,* 43 VA. L. REV. 1205 (1957), 240 n. 123, 244 n. 140

McQUILLIN, THE LAW OF MUNICIPAL CORPORATIONS (3d ed. 1950), 323 n. 45

MANDELBAUM, SOLDIER GROUPS AND NEGRO SOLDIERS (1952), 26 n. 13, 369 n. 5

Marshall, *Concrete Curtain—The East Palo Alto Story,* Crisis, Nov., 1957, p. 543, at 246 n. 149, 247 n. 150, 249 n. 154

MARTIN, THE DEEP SOUTH SAYS NEVER (1957), 343 n. 1

Maslow, The Enforcement of Northern Civil Rights Laws, Address at Fisk Institute on Race Relations, June 28, 1950, at 108

Maslow & Robison, *Civil Rights Legislation and the Fight for Equality, 1862–1952,* 20 U. CHI. L. REV. 363 (1953), 193 n. 143, 318 n. 24, 321 nn. 33 and 36

MASON, AN ESSAY ON RACIAL TENSION (1954), 27 n. 16

1954–55 MASS. COMM'N AGAINST DISCRIMINATION ANNUAL REPORT, 111 n. 132

Meiners, *Fair Employment Practices Legislation,* 62 DICK. L. REV. 31 (1957), 193 n. 143

MICH. FEPC INFORMATION BULL. (April–May, 1957), 201

MILL, JOHN S. AUTOBIOGRAPHY (Harvard Classics ed. 1909), 49 n. 63

MILLER, RACIAL DISCRIMINATION AND PRIVATE EDUCATION, 48 n. 61, 51, 58, 267 nn. 216 and 218, 268 nn. 221 and 223

Ming, *The Elimination of Segregation in the Public Schools of the North and West,* 21 J. NEGRO EDUCATION 265 (1952), 245 n. 143

1956 MINNEAPOLIS FEPC ANNUAL REPORT, 197 n. 157, 202 n. 171

1957 MINNEAPOLIS FEPC ANNUAL REPORT, 198 n. 165

Moon, *The Negro Vote in the Presidential Election of 1956,* 26 J. NEGRO EDUCATION 219 (1957), 133 n. 2

—— *The Southern Scene,* 16 PHYLON 351 (1955), 134 nn. 3 and 4

Morgan, *An Analysis of State FEPC Legislation,* 8 LAB. L.J. 469 (1957), 193 n. 143

—— *Values in Transition Areas,* Rev. of the Soc'y of Residential Appraisers, March, 1952, p. 9, at 282 n. 28

Moskovitz, *Contempt of Injunctions, Civil and Criminal,* 43 COLUM. L. REV. 780 (1943), 73 n. 166

Murphy, *Can Public Schools Be Private?* 7 ALA. L. REV. 48 (1954), 240 n. 123

MURRAY, STATES' LAWS ON RACE AND COLOR (1950), 82 n. 7, 91 n. 42

MYRDAL, AN AMERICAN DILEMMA (1944), 13, 115, 334, 335, 344

NAACP 49th Annual Convention Resolutions (1958), 57 n. 101

1934 NAACP ANNUAL REPORT, 35

1936 NAACP ANNUAL REPORT, 159 n. 14

1937 NAACP ANNUAL REPORT, 159 n. 14

1938 NAACP ANNUAL REPORT, 151 n. 14

1939 NAACP ANNUAL REPORT, 151 n. 14

1940 NAACP ANNUAL REPORT, 151 n. 14, 358 n. 6

1941 NAACP ANNUAL REPORT, 151 n. 14

NAACP LEGAL DEFENSE & EDUCATIONAL FUND REPORT (Summer, 1954), 246 n. 149, 248 n. 150

NAACP LEGAL DEFENSE & EDUCATIONAL FUND REPORT (Sept., 1954), 246 n. 149, 247 n. 150

NAACP LEGAL DEFENSE & EDUCATIONAL FUND REPORT (Jan., 1957), 248 n. 152

Nabrit, *The Future of the Negro Voter in the South*, 26 J. NEGRO EDUCATION 418 (1957), 134

NATIONAL BAR ASS'N, COMM. ON HUMAN RIGHTS FOR THE WESTERN STATES, ANOTHER LOOK AT HUMAN RIGHTS FOR THE WESTERN STATES (pamphlet), 102 n. 83

NATIONAL COMMUNITY RELATIONS ADVISORY COUNCIL, EQUALITY OF OPPORTUNITY IN HOUSING (pamphlet, 1952), 299 n. 99, 301 n. 105

—— THE USES OF LAW FOR THE ADVANCEMENT OF COMMUNITY RELATIONS (1955), 28 n. 18

NATIONAL PROBATION AND PAROLE ASSOCIATION, GUIDES FOR SENTENCING (1957), 334

Newsom, Court Treatment of Intra- and Inter-Racial Homicide in St. Louis (Ph.D. dissertation, Washington Univ., 1956), 335 n. 97

Newton, *Expansion of Negro Suffrage in North Carolina*, 26 J. NEGRO EDUCATION 351 (1957), 153 n. 101

N.J. DEP'T OF EDUCATION, DIV. AGAINST DISCRIMINATION, ANNUAL REPORT (July 1, 1954–June 30, 1955), 199 n. 165

—— 1955 ANNUAL REPORT, 197 n. 158

—— ANNUAL REPORT (July 1, 1955–June 30, 1956), 195 n. 150

1953 N.Y. SCAD REPORT, 110

1954 N.Y. SCAD REPORT, 111 n. 127

1955 N.Y. SCAD REPORT, 111 nn. 128, 129, and 131

1956 N.Y. SCAD REPORT, 196 n. 156, 203 n. 177

N.Y. STATE BAR ASS'N, REPORT ON NEW YORK ANTITRUST LAWS, 304 n. 121

N.Y. STATE JOINT LEGISLATIVE COMM. ON MIGRANT LABOR, REPORT (Leg. Doc. No. 51, 1955), 158 n. 12

NICHOLS, BREAKTHROUGH ON THE COLOR FRONT (1954), 26 n. 13, 369 n. 51

Nicholson, *The Legal Standing of the South's School Resistance Proposals*, 7 S.C.L.Q. 1 (1954), 240 n. 123

NLRB TENTH ANNUAL REPORT, 180

Note, *Availability of Injunctive Relief Under State Civil Rights Acts*, 24 U. CHI. L. REV. 174, 175 (1956), 107 n. 111

Note, *Civil Rights—Extent of California Statute and Remedies Available for Its Enforcement*, 30 CALIF. L. REV. 563 (1942), 108 n. 113

Note, *The Constitutionality of Racial Classifications in Mortality Tables* 11 RUTGERS L. REV. 757 (1956), 87 n. 21

Note, *Contempt by Strangers to a Federal Court Decree*, 43 VA. L. REV. 1294 (1957), 73 n. 166

Note, *De Facto Segregation in the Chicago Public Schools*, Crisis, Feb., 1958, p. 87, at 255 n. 172

Note, *The Disintegration of a Concept—State Action Under the Fourteenth and Fifteenth Amendments*, 96 U. PA. L. REV. 402 (1948), 48 n. 61

Note, *Effect of Desegregation on Public School Bonds in the Southern States*, 10 VAND. L. REV. 580 (1957), 214 n. 20, 228 n. 78

Note, *The Exhaustion of Administrative Remedies*, 2 R.R.L.R. 561 (1957), 64 n. 120

Note, *Fair Educational Practices Acts—A Solution to Discrimination?* 64 HARV. L. REV. 307 (1950), 266 n. 212

Note, *Implementation of Desegregation by the Lower Courts*, 71 HARV. L. REV. 486 (1958), 73 n. 166, 269 n. 229

Note, *Interposition vs. Judicial Power*, 1 R.R.L.R. 465 (1956), 244 n. 135

Note, *Legal Definition of Race*, 3 R.R.L.R. 571 (1958), 348 n. 33

Note, *Legal Sanctions To Enforce Desegregation in the Public Schools—The Contempt Power and the Civil Rights Acts*, 65 YALE L.J. 630 (1956), 73 n. 166, 269 n. 229, 322 n. 41

Note, *Obstacles to Federal Jurisdiction—New Barriers to Non-Segregated Public Education in Old Forms*, 104 U. PA. L. REV. 974 (1956), 64 n. 120

Note, *Private Attorneys-General—Group Action in the Fight for Civil Liberties*, 58 YALE L.J. 574 (1949), 36 n. 18

Note, *State Action—A Study of Requirements Under the Fourteenth Amendment*, 1 R.R.L.R. 613 (1956), 48 n. 61, 52 n. 73

1954 NSSFNS REPORT, 211

1958 NSSFNS REPORT, 211 n. 14

PA. FEPC ANNUAL REPORT, 197 n. 157

Pasley, *The Non-Discrimination Clause in Government Contracts*, 43 VA. L. REV. 837 (1957), 187 n. 123, 188 n. 128

PEA, THE STATUS OF THE PUBLIC SCHOOL EDUCATION OF NEGRO AND PUERTO RICAN CHILDREN IN NEW YORK CITY (pamphlet 1955), 255, 256, 259

PETERS, THE SOUTHERN TEMPER (1959), 369 n. 51

PHA, OPEN OCCUPANCY IN PUBLIC HOUSING (1953), 291 n. 73

1956 PHILADELPHIA COMM'N ON HUMAN RELATIONS ANNUAL REPORT, 201 n. 170, 202

PIERCE & OTHERS, WHITE AND NEGRO SCHOOLS IN THE SOUTH (1955), 209 n. 5

PLATO, LAWS, 26 n. 15

Plaut, *Racial Integration in Higher Education in the North*, 23 J. NEGRO EDUCATION 310 (1954), 211 n. 14, 273, 274

4 POMEROY, EQUITY JURISPRUDENCE (5th ed. 1941), 101 n. 80

Popham, *Report on Bus Desegregation*, N.Y. Times, Feb. 3, 1957, § E, p. 8, at 80 n. 1

Pound, *Equitable Relief Against Defamation and Injuries to Personality*, 29 HARV. L. REV. 640 (1916), 101 n. 80

5 POWELL, RICHARD, REAL PROPERTY (1956), 277 n. 8

Powell, T. R., Vagaries and Varieties in Constitutional Interpretation (1956), 308 n. 133

President's Comm. on Civil Rights, To Secure These Rights 29–30 (1947), 157 n. 9

President's Comm. on Equality of Treatment & Opportunity in the Armed Services, Freedom To Serve (1950), 357

President's Comm. on Government Contract Compliance, Report on Equal Economic Opportunity (1953), 187 n. 124, 189 nn. 129, 130, 132, and 133, 190 nn. 134 and 135, 191 n. 137, 193 n. 144

President's Comm. on Government Contracts, Equal Job Opportunity Program (1956), 189 n. 123

—— Third Annual Report on Equal Job Opportunity (1955–56), 191 n. 140

—— Fourth Annual Report on Equal Job Opportunity (1957), 189, 192

President's Comm. on Government Employment Policy, First Report, 162 n. 26

—— Second Report (1958), 162 n. 26

President's Comm. on Migratory Labor, 1956 Report, 158 n. 12

Putzel, *Federal Civil Rights Enforcement*, 99 U. Pa. L. Rev. 439 (1951), 318 n. 24

Racial Relations Service & Div. of Law, Housing & Home Finance Agency, Nondiscrimination Clauses in Regard to Public Housing, Private Housing, and Urban Redevelopment Undertakings (1956 ed., 1957 ed.), 306 n. 126

Redding, *Desegregation in Higher Education in Delaware*, 27 J. Negro Education 253 (1958), 263 n. 196

Reitzes, Negroes and Medicine (1958), 88 nn. 24, 30 and 31, 169, 207 n. 184

Renner, The Institutions of Private Law and Their Social Functions (1949 ed.), 46 n. 58

1954 R.I. Comm'n Against Discrimination Annual Report, 111 n. 132

1955 R.I. Comm'n Against Discrimination Annual Report, 111 n. 132

1956 R.I. Comm'n Against Discrimination Report 5, 111 n. 132, 199 n. 165, 200

Riker, Soldiers of the States (1957), 365 n. 33

Robison, *Protection of Associations From Compulsory Disclosure of Membership*, 58 Colum. L. Rev. 614 (1958), 244 n. 140

Rockefeller, *Are Army Courts-Martial Fair?* 4 Fed. Bar News 118 (1957), 335 n. 97

Ruchames, Race, Jobs and Politics (1953), 193 n. 143

Ruggiero, *Liberalism*, in 9 Encyc. Soc. Sci. 435 (1933), 48 n. 63

Sabine, A History of Political Theory (1950), 48 n. 63

Saenger, The Social Psychology of Prejudice (1953), 26 n. 14

St. Paul FEPC Interim Report (July, 1956–July, 1957), 202 n. 172

SEAGLE, LAW—THE SCIENCE OF INEFFICIENCY (1952), 17, 18

SECRETARY OF DEFENSE WILSON REPORT (Jan. 1–June 30, 1954), 361 n. 15

SECRETARY OF DEFENSE WILSON REPORT (Jan. 1–June 30, 1956), 367 n. 36

SEIDENBERG, NEGROES IN THE WORK GROUP 45 (N.Y. State School of Industrial & Labor Relations Research Bull. No. 6, 1950), 26 n. 13

SELECTIVE SERVICE SYSTEM, SPECIAL GROUPS, SPECIAL MONOGRAPH No. 10 (1953), 155 n. 5, 212 n. 15, 358 n. 6

Shagaloff, Desegregation of Public Schools in Delaware, 24 J. NEGRO EDUCATION 188 (1955), 217 n. 34, 218 n. 46, 237 n. 107

—— A Study of Community Acceptance of Desegregation in Two Selected Areas, 23 J. NEGRO EDUCATION 330 (1954), 246 nn. 148 and 149, 247 n. 150

SHERWIN, SEX AND THE STATUTORY LAW (1949), 336 n. 101, 350 n. 40

SHOEMAKER ed., WITH ALL DELIBERATE SPEED (1957), 261, 262 n. 192, 263 nn. 197 and 199, 267 n. 219

Shokes, The Serbonian Bog of Miscegenation, 21 ROCKY MT. L. REV. 425 (1949), 344 n. 9

SHUEY, THE TESTING OF NEGRO INTELLIGENCE (1958), 210 n. 10

SIMPSON & STONE, LAW & SOCIETY (1949), 3 n. 3

SOUTHERN SCHOOL NEWS, SOUTHERN EDUCATION REPORTING SERVICE, A STATISTICAL SUMMARY, STATE-BY-STATE, OF SEGREGATION-DESEGREGATION ACTIVITY (1958), 245 n. 142, 404

1957 STATISTICAL ABSTRACT OF THE UNITED STATES, 154 n. 2

STERN & GRESSMAN, SUPREME COURT PRACTICE (2d ed. 1954), 314 n. 1

STORY, BAILMENTS (9th ed. 1878), 96 nn. 63 and 64, 97 n. 66, 98 n. 71

Stephan, Population Ratios, Racial Attitudes, and Desegregation, 26 J. NEGRO EDUCATION 22, 27 (1957), 12 n. 7

Summers, Legal Limitations on Union Discipline, 64 HARV. L. REV. 1049 (1951), 171 n. 60

—— The Right To Join a Union, 47 COLUM. L. REV. 33 (1947), 171 n. 59

TAFT, ECONOMICS AND PROBLEMS OF LABOR (1948), 185 n. 120

1 & 2 TARN, ALEXANDER THE GREAT (1951), 1 n. 1

TELLER, A LABOR POLICY FOR AMERICA (1945), 185 n. 120

Teple, A Closer Look at "Right To Work" Legislation, 9 W. RES. L. REV. 5 (1957), 179 n. 96

Turner, Dynamics of Criminal Law Administration in a Biracial Community of the Deep South (Ph.D. dissertation, Indiana Univ., 1956), 335 n. 97

Uhlenhopp, Adoption in Iowa, 40 IOWA L. REV. 228 (1955), 351 n. 48

URBAN LEAGUE OF GREATER BOSTON, 1956 ANNUAL REPORT, 366

1955 U.S. ATT'Y GEN. ANN. REP., 318 n. 23, 322 n. 39

1956 U.S. ATT'Y GEN. ANN. REP., 157 n. 10, 322 n. 38

1957 U.S. ATT'Y GEN. ANN. REP., 322 n. 37

U.S. ATT'Y GEN., REPORT OF THE NATIONAL COMMITTEE TO STUDY THE ANTITRUST LAWS (1955), 302 n. 113, 303

U.S. BUREAU OF THE CENSUS, DEP'T OF COMMERCE, SER. P-50, No. 66, CURRENT POPULATION REPORTS (March, 1956), 154 n. 1

1956 U.S. BUREAU OF THE CENSUS POPULATION REPORTS, 165 n. 38

U.S. DEP'T OF THE ARMY, CIVILIAN PERSONNEL PAMPHLET No. 41-B-36, SUPERVISOR DEVELOPMENT PROGRAM, BASIC COURSE, NONDISCRIMINATION POLICY (1956), 368 n. 45

U.S. DEP'T OF COMMERCE, PERSONAL INCOME BY STATES (1956), 155 n. 3

U.S. DEP'T OF DEFENSE, INTEGRATION IN THE ARMED SERVICES (1955), 356 n. 2, 257 n. 3, 361 n. 16, 368 n. 45

—— MANUAL FOR COURTS-MARTIAL, 368

Valien, *Expansion of Negro Suffrage in Tennessee*, 26 J. NEGRO EDUCATION 362 (1957), 148 nn. 82 and 83, 153 n. 101

—— *Racial Desegregation of the Public Schools in Southern Illinois*, 23 J. NEGRO EDUCATION 303 (1954), 246 n. 149, 247 n. 150

—— THE ST. LOUIS STORY (Anti-Defamation League pamphlet 1956), 217 n. 32, 220 n. 52, 237 n. 107

Vose, *NAACP Strategy in the Covenant Cases*, 1955 W. RES. L. REV. 101 (1955), 36 n. 18

Watt & Orlikoff, *The Coming Vindication of Mr. Justice Harlan*, 44 ILL. L. REV. 13 (1949), 48 n. 61

WEAVER, NEGRO LABOR (1946), 155 n. 3

Wechsler, *Reflections on the Conference*, 3 COLUMBIA LAW ALUMNI BULL., No. 2 (1958), 28

Weinberger, *A Reappraisal of the Constitutionality of Miscegenation Statutes*, 42 CORNELL L.Q. 208 (1957), 346 n. 20; *id.*, 51 J. NATIONAL MEDICAL ASS'N 215 (1959), 398

Weinstein, Book Review of BEANEY, THE RIGHT TO COUNSEL IN AMERICAN COURTS, 56 COLUM. L. REV. 454 (1956), 336 n. 98

Wellington, *Union Democracy and Fair Representation*, 67 YALE L.J. 1327 (1958), 58 n. 102, 171 n. 59

WEY & COREY, ACTION PATTERNS IN SCHOOL DESEGREGATION (1959), 217 n. 30

2 WHARTON, CRIMINAL EVIDENCE (12th ed. 1955), 316 n. 7

Wiener, *Courts-Martial and the Bill of Rights—The Original Practice*, 72 HARV. L. REV. 1 (1958), 363 n. 23

—— *The Militia Clause of the Constitution*, 54 HARV. L. REV. 181 (1940), 363 n. 23

3 WIGMORE, EVIDENCE (3d ed. 1940), 316 n. 7

WILLIAMS & RYAN, SCHOOLS IN TRANSITION (1954), 246 nn. 147 and 149, 247 n. 150

6 WILLISTON, CONTRACTS (rev. ed. 1938), 285 n. 39

WILNER, WALKLEY & COOK, HUMAN RELATIONS IN INTERRACIAL HOUSING (1955), 26 n. 13, 291 n. 73

Winter, *Recent Legislation in Mississippi on the School Segregation Problems*, 28 MISS. L.J. 148 (1957), 244 n. 140

WOODWARD, THE STRANGE CAREER OF JIM CROW (1957), 5, 115 n. 1
Wright, *Racial Integration in the Public Schools of New Jersey*, 23 J. NEGRO EDUCATION 282 (1954), 246 n. 149, 247 n. 150

1954 YOUNGSTOWN FEPC REPORT, 202
1957 YOUNGSTOWN FEPC REPORT, 202 n. 174

TABLE OF CASES

INDEX

Abrams, Charles: administration of SCAD, 203, 204; housing desegregation problems, 283, 309*n*

Administrative implementation: as means of enforcement of civil rights laws, 15, 16, 17, 69; participation by federal and state governments in civil rights suits through, 76; in public accommodations, 106, 110-12, 114; in school segregation and integration, 253-54; of laws prohibiting segregation in private schools, 268; in proposed civil rights act of *1958*, 271; in housing litigation, 307, 309

Administrative remedies: remand to state jurisdiction for exhaustion of, 63-66; pupil assignment and review systems, 65-66, 232-36; as procedural defense in violation of voting rights, 138; resistance laws in school desegregation and, 231

Adoption, 351-54, 399

AFL-CIO constitution, 173-74

Agricultural workers: migratory labor, 157-58; exemption from FEP laws, 194

Agriculture, Department of, 187

Air Force, U.S.: data on Negro officers and personnel, 356, 357; off-base training, 367

Airports, variation of segregation practices, 115, 129-30

Air travel, 115, 129-31

Alabama: attitude of state courts in race relations cases, 10-11; travel segregation laws, 117, 126; discriminatory practices against Negro lawyers, 168; miscegenation case, 345

— *criminal law:* and sexual contacts between negroes and whites, 333; laws considering race as criminal factor,

334; execution of Negroes for rape, 336

— *education:* pupil assignment, 65, 233-34, 235-36; resistance laws, 232; abolition of public and establishment of "private" education, 240; interposition resolution, 244; segregation in institutions of higher learning, 266; course of school desegration, 404

— *elections:* Negro vote in 1956 presidential election, 133; Boswell Amendment, 140; discrimination in voting rulings, 141, 142; poll tax, 145; apportionment and political power of rural areas, 148; "single shot voting," 152

Alabama, University of, 14, 168, 229-30

Alabama Public Service Commission, 128

Alabama State Teachers College, 367

Alabama Supreme Court, attitude on race relations, 10-11

Alaska: public accommodations laws, 101; FEP statutes, 193, 196

Aliens, employment discrimination against, 167

Allport, Gordon, cited on psychology of prejudice, 26, 27

Amalgamated Clothing Workers of America, cooperative housing developments, 286*n*

American Civil Liberties Union, 23

American Federation of Labor: AFL-CIO constitution, 173-74; change in discrimination policy, 183*n*

American Fund for Public Service, 34; *see also* Garland Fund

American Jewish Committee, surveys, 249, 362-63

American Jewish Congress, 204

American Medical Association, 89

321-22; against violators of antimiscegenation laws, 346, 347-48
Custom, segregation in recreation facilities by, 80, 91-92

Dabbs, James, cited, 155
DAD, see New Jersey Division Against Discrimination
Dallas, Texas, school desegregation, 226, 231
Damages: liquidated damages provisions in government contracts, 190; see also under Civil suits
Dance halls: discrimination in, 111n; segregation statutes, 374
Davis, John W., 219n
Death sentences, for rape, statistics in Southern states, 336
Decertification of labor unions, 179-83
Declaration of Independence, equality ideal in, 1
De facto segregation, 249-55
Defense, Department of: compliance with antidiscrimination clauses in government contracts, 187; directives on racial distinctions, 357, 361; complaints of discrimination addressed to, 360
De jure segregation, 249
Delaware: school desegregation, 6, 214, 226, 403, 404; innkeeper rule, 98; discriminatory sentencing question, 335, 337; execution of Negroes for rape, 336; abolition of segregation in National Guard, 363
Delaware State College for Negroes, 262-63
Delay, devices of, 17-20; appeals as, 20; antidiscrimination commissions' efforts to overcome, 20-21; reference to state courts, 61-63; exhaustion of administrative remedies, 63-67; passage of new legislation, 66; denial of stay of execution and, 68; opposition of district and appellate tribunals to, in school desegregation, 222-24; see also Administrative remedies
"Deliberate speed" formula, 215-17; in Supreme Court ruling, 212; in higher education, 264; delay and, 270
Democratic Party, and White Primaries, 143-45
Denver, Colo., jury selection practices, 407
Desegregation, law's effect upon, 4-5; study on attitudes toward, 9; Negro-white population ratio's effect on, 12-

13; Myrdal's hierarchy of resistance to, 13
Des Moines, Iowa, no disparities in sentencing, 413
Detroit, Mich.: percentage of public schools with nonwhite majority of pupils, 249; Negro concentration in public housing, 293; jury selection practices, 407
Detroit Housing Commission, 305
Dining cars, desegregation in, 7, 121; separate-but-equal space issue, 41, 121
Dining rooms, segregation in hotel, 97-98
Diplomatic service, Negroes as military attachés, 359-60
Discretionary powers, in prosecuting and sentencing, 341
Disfranchisement, political, see under Elections
Disorderly conduct, 120
District of Columbia: public accommodations laws, 5, 101, 109-10; civil rights statute, 5, 109-10; biased referrals of employment agencies, 166; restrictive covenants on housing, 280, 283; local housing authority, 288-89; no discrimination in sentencing on basis of race, 335; executions of Negroes for rape, 336
— education: rapid progress of desegregation, 5; School Segregation decision, 6, 214; option plans, 220-21; attacks on desegregation, 228; study on desegregated schools of higher education, 261; segregation in high school ROTC units, 366
Domestic relations law, 343-54; antimiscegenation laws, 344-50; cohabitation laws, 350; adoption and custody, 351-54
Domestic workers, exemption from FEP laws, 194
Domicile, validity of mixed marriages in place of, 348-49
Douglas, William O.: attitude toward Alabama county unit system, 149; opinion in Screws v. United States, 317; dissent in United States v. Williams case, 319, 320
Draft boards, 358
Due process clause: racial classification and, 34; application in School Segregation Cases, 43, 212, 214; FHA's subjection to, 54; state segregation statutes on intrastate travel and, 82-

Hyman, Herbert, study on attitudes in race relations, 9

ICC, *see* Interstate Commerce Commission
Idaho: public accommodations laws, 102; provisions forbidding school segregation, 245; repeal of antimiscegenation laws, 344; absence of rules forbidding discrimination in state employment, 382
Illegitimate children, of mixed marriages, 347
Illinois: law's effect on school desegregation, 5; public accommodations laws, 101, 104, 108-9; provisions forbidding school segregation, 245, 246; schools segregated by rule, 247-48
Illinois Central Railroad, reaction to ICC rulings, 125-26
Illinois State Employment Service, 166
Implementation: law's inefficiency and, 17-20; of antidiscrimination statutes in public accommodations, 106-10; Supreme Court school opinion of *1955*, 215-17; proposed bills to make implementation of schools decision a federal responsibility, 273; *see also* Administrative implementation
Imprisonment: segregation in, 337-38; statutes requiring racial distinctions, 396-97
Income, proportion between white and Negro, 154
India, Constitution of, 47
Indiana: public accommodations laws, 101; fair employment laws, 193; budget of FEPC, 203*n*; provisions forbidding school segregation, 245
Indiana, University of, Institute for Sex Research, 353
Indianapolis, Ind., segregation in high school ROTC units, 366
Industrialization, effect on South and racial relations, 8, 9
Industrial relations, union-employer-employee relationship, 170-75
Industrial State University of Nashville, on-post courses at Fort Campbell, 367
Injunction, 71-72; by aggrieved person or public official, as technique of enforcement, 15, 17; to enforce school desegregation, 71-72; use of, by federal and state governments in civil rights suits, 76, 77; right of attorneys general to seek, 77; against violation

of antidiscrimination laws in public accommodations, 107-8; in violation of voting rights, 137-38; for non-compliance with antidiscrimination clauses in government contracts, 189; for enforcement of FEP city ordinances, 197; possible use of, to prevent school closing, 243; to compel jury commissioners to cease discrimination, 324
Inn, defined, 96
Innkeeper's rule, obligations under common law, 82, 96; exceptions used against Negroes, 98; difference between public accommodations laws and, 105-6; in interstate automobile travel, 131; statutes regarding, 375
Institute for Sex Research (University of Indiana), 353
Insurance, mortgages insured by FHA, 297
Insurance companies: rates and discrimination, 87; impact of SCAD statute on employment practices, 198-99; statutes forbidding racial discrimination by, 372-73
Intermarriage: hostility to, 13, 343, 353; proscription in antimiscegenation laws and legal consequences, 344, 346-50; inheritance difficulties in, 347; validity of out-of-state marriages in place of couple's domicile, 348-49; out-of-state couples in New York City, 349*n*; prosecution for fornication or cohabitation of mixed married couples, 350; statutes regarding, 396
International Ladies Garment Workers Union, cooperative housing developments, 286*n*
Interposition, 243-45
Interracial custody of children, 353
Interstate commerce, in housing cases, question of, 302
Interstate Commerce Act, 120-22; lawsuits involving, 41; equal treatment of travelers requirement, 118
Interstate Commerce Commission: travel segregation laws held void by, 117; decisions of November 7, *1955*, 122-25; reactions of rail carriers to rulings by, 125-27; discrimination in stations, quoted, 239
Interstate travel, 115-32; desegregation in, 13; civil rights suits supported by NAACP, 37; outlawing of state travel segregation laws, 41; segregation his-